D0336191

"TO THE BEST OF MY ABILITY"

THE AMERICAN PRESIDENTS

GENERAL EDITOR

JAMES M. McPHERSON

EDITOR

DAVID RUBEL

AN AGINCOURT PRESS PRODUCTION

THE SOCIETY OF AMERICAN HISTORIANS
To encourage literary distinction in the writing of history and biography

DK Publishing, Inc.

An Agincourt Press Production
President: David Rubel

Copy Editor: Ron Boudreau
Proofreader: Laura Jorstad

Art Direction and Production: Oxygen Design
Interior Design: Tilman Reitzle, Sherry Williams
Image Research: Deborah Goodsite, Lani Labay, Julia Rubel

LONDON, NEW YORK, MELBOURNE,
MUNICH, and DELHI

REVISED US EDITION 2004
Project Editor: Anja Schmidt
Senior Art Editor: Susan St. Louis
Jacket Designer: Tai Blanche
Art Director: Dirk Kaufman
DTP Coordinator: Milos Orlovic
Production Manager: Chris Avgherinos
Project Director: Sharon Lucas
Creative Diretcor: Tina Vaughan
Publisher: Chuck Lang

FIRST US EDITION 2000
Art Director: Dirk Kaufman
Production Controller: Sara Gordon
Editorial Director: LaVonne Carlson
Creative Diretcor: Tina Vaughan
Publisher: Sean Moore

CITY AND COUNTY OF
SWANSEA LIBRARIES

Cypher	10.09.04
973.099 MCP	£12.99
	SR

For photo credits, see pp. 485–486.

First American edition, 2000

4 6 8 10 9 7 5 3

Published in the United States by DK Publishing, Inc.
375 Hudson Street New York, NY 10014

Published in the United Kingdom by Dorling Kindersley Limited
80 Strand, London, England WCR ORL

© 2000, 2002, 2004 by Dorling Kindersley Limited

All rights reserved under the International and Pan-American Copyright Conventions. No
part of this publication may be reproduced, stored in a retrieval system, or transmitted in
any form or by any means, electronic, mechanical, photocopying, recording, or otherwise,
without the prior written permission of the copyright owner.

Color reproduction by Colourscan, Singapore

Printed and bound by L. Rex Printing Company Limited, China

A CIP catalog record for this book is available from the British Library

Library of Congress Cataloging-in-Publication Data

To the best of my ability: the American presidents / James M. McPherson, editor.—1st
American ed.
    p. cm.
Includes index.
ISBN 0-7894-5073-9 (alk. paper)
1. Presidents—United States—History. 2. Presidents—United States—Biography. 3.
United States—Politics and government. I. McPherson,
James M. II. Title.

E176.1 T59 2000
973'.09'9—dc 21
                                                                00-021569

CONTENTS

INTRODUCTION
by James M. McPherson 7

THE PRESIDENTS 11

GEORGE WASHINGTON
by Gordon S. Wood 12

JOHN ADAMS
by James M. Banner, Jr. 22

THOMAS JEFFERSON
by Joseph J. Ellis 28

JAMES MADISON
by Jack N. Rakove 36

JAMES MONROE
by Jack N. Rakove 44

JOHN QUINCY ADAMS
by John Patrick Diggins 50

ANDREW JACKSON
by Robert V. Remini 56

MARTIN VAN BUREN
by Richard M. Pious 66

WILLIAM HENRY HARRISON
by Daniel Walker Howe 72

JOHN TYLER
by Richard M. Pious 78

JAMES K. POLK
by Thomas Fleming 84

ZACHARY TAYLOR
by Catherine Clinton 92

MILLARD FILLMORE
by Jean Harvey Baker 98

FRANKLIN PIERCE
by James A. Rawley 104

JAMES BUCHANAN
by Jean Harvey Baker 110

ABRAHAM LINCOLN
by James M. McPherson 118

ANDREW JOHNSON
by Hans L. Trefousse 126

ULYSSES S. GRANT
by Michael Les Benedict 132

RUTHERFORD B. HAYES
by James A. Rawley 140

JAMES A. GARFIELD
by Ari Hoogenboom 146

CHESTER A. ARTHUR
by Bernard A. Weisberger 154

GROVER CLEVELAND
by Vincent P. De Santis 160

BENJAMIN HARRISON
by Catherine Clinton 168

WILLIAM McKINLEY
by Morton Keller 174

THEODORE ROOSEVELT
by Allen Weinstein 180

WILLIAM HOWARD TAFT
by Mark C. Carnes 188

WOODROW WILSON
by James Chace 196

WARREN G. HARDING
by Morton Keller 206

CALVIN COOLIDGE
by Robert Cowley 212

HERBERT HOOVER
by Robert Dallek 218

FRANKLIN D. ROOSEVELT
by Susan Ware 224

HARRY S. TRUMAN
by Allen Weinstein 234

DWIGHT D. EISENHOWER
by Herbert S. Parmet 242

JOHN F. KENNEDY
by Richard Reeves 250

LYNDON B. JOHNSON
by Robert Dallek 258

RICHARD M. NIXON
by Tom Wicker 266

GERALD R. FORD
by Laura Kalman 274

JIMMY CARTER
by Douglas Brinkley 282

RONALD REAGAN
by James T. Patterson 288

GEORGE BUSH
by Herbert S. Parmet 296

BILL CLINTON
by Evan Thomas 302

GEORGE W. BUSH
by William H. Chafe 308

THE CAMPAIGNS AND
INAUGURAL ADDRESSES 315

About the Contributors 464
Index 467
Photo Credits 485

INTRODUCTION

James M. McPherson

ORE THAN A CENTURY AGO, British historian Sir John
Robert Seeley expressed an aphorism that governed the
writing of history for a long time thereafter: "History is past
politics; and politics, present history." Seeley's *The Expansion of England*
told the story of kings and queens—and, from the seventeenth century
on, of prime ministers and foreign ministers—with a few generals and
admirals thrown in where appropriate.

Historians in the United States inherited this tradition of historical
writing, and our national (as distinguished from our colonial) history
became a story of political acts and their military consequences: the
Louisiana Purchase, "Mr. Madison's War" (1812–15), the annexation
of Texas, "Mr. Polk's War" (1846–48), and so on. During the twentieth
century, however, the history of historical writing in this country
reflected a steady movement away from what detractors have called
"presidential synthesis." First came the "new history" of James Harvey
Robinson and Charles Beard, which focused on nonpolitical circumstances affecting the lives of ordinary people: economic growth,
inventions and technology, labor unions, immigration, urbanization,
and the like. This approach merged with "Progressive history," which
emphasized the struggle between the "people" and the "robber barons"
for control of American destiny. Class struggle became an even more
central theme for Marxist historians, who were particularly active during
the 1930s and 1940s.

Although presidential synthesis never disappeared entirely from
Progressive and Marxist reconstructions of the past, the writers associated with these schools retold American history essentially as a political
and economic contest between the Jeffersonian vision of America as a
nation of sturdy yeomen and artisans and the Hamiltonian view of the

country as an urban-industrial society dominated by corporate capital-ism. Along the way, certain presidents came to be associated with the cause of the masses: Thomas Jefferson, Andrew Jackson, Abraham Lincoln and Theodore Roosevelt (equivocally), Woodrow Wilson, Franklin D. Roosevelt, and Harry Truman.

Most of the American historians who wrote a generation ago about these men and their times were politically to the left of center. They sympathized with the Jacksonian Democrats against the "elitist" Whigs, with the reformers against the standpatters, with the New Dealers against the economic royalists. Most were also white males writing about other white males. They focused on issues of political and economic power, whether that power was wielded on the shop floor, in the corporate boardroom, at the factory gate, in the halls of Congress, or in the

"MEN MAKE HISTORY AND NOT THE OTHER WAY AROUND."

—Harry S. Truman—

executive mansion. Yet this version of the past left out the great majority of people who didn't hold office, belong to a labor union, own stocks or bonds, or (before 1920) vote. It was a history that largely ignored the common people whose lives revolved around home and family, the workplace, and the school—people who struggled to make a living and a life away from the public arena. It was a history that pushed women and children and racial and ethnic minorities to the margins of visibility.

In the 1960s, the pendulum of historiography began swinging far in the other direction. The invisible became highly visible. A new generation of historians defined a new discipline of "social history" with numerous related fields of research: African-American history, Latino history, women's history, gender history, family history, ethnic history, working-class history, and so on. "History from the bottom up" became fashionable; "elitist" history went out of style. Presidential synthesis was tossed on the scrap heap. Writing the history of DWM (dead white males) became almost as discreditable as being arrested for DWI. Seeley's aphorism was inverted, and history became the story of the past with the politics left out. Meanwhile, traditional American heroes became goats: Jefferson was a hypocritical slaveholder, Jackson a slaveholder and an Indian killer, Lincoln a white supremacist who did *not* free the slaves (they freed themselves), and Theodore Roosevelt not a reformer but a warmonger.

The vogue of social history has vastly enriched our understanding of the past. It has given a voice to ordinary people whose experiences are as much a part of history as the actions of presidents and generals. Never again can historians conceive of their discipline as "past politics" alone. During the 1980s, though, some social historians began to question whether they'd swung the pendulum too far. The kinds of issues they wrote about were, after all, profoundly affected by political power. The historical fate of Indians, slaves, married women, immigrants, the unemployed, children, the unborn, the mentally ill, and a host of other groups all depended on the actions and decisions of presidents, governors, legislators, judges—most of them dead white males. As commanders in chief, wartime presidents made decisions that literally determined whether millions would live or die. Some slaves freed themselves, but most would have remained in slavery were it not for the Union victory in the Civil War, a victory shaped by the actions of President Lincoln and General Grant. Similarly, Wilson, FDR, and Truman all made decisions that determined the fates not only of Americans but also of people around the world. Laws passed by Congress and enforced by the executive branch expanded or contracted the rights, opportunities, and welfare of virtually every American, whether of high or low estate.

A S AWARENESS OF THESE TRUTHS spread among historians during the 1990s, the movement to put politics back into social history became a prominent historiographical theme. Presidential synthesis even made a comeback in the form of an effort to fashion a new "narrative synthesis" that might integrate the diverse subfields of social history. Its goal was to produce a pattern that, if not precisely following presidential administrations, was at least shaped by political history.

Thus, as Americans enter a new millennium, historians are newly conscious of the broad impact at home and abroad of U.S. presidential elections and the people such elections place in power. That consciousness is the rationale for this volume, containing forty-two essays on the forty-two men who have thus far served as presidents of the United States. This project is sponsored by the Society of American Historians, whose members are elected because of their proven capacity to write lucid, significant, challenging, and readable history. These essays, written by society members, aren't capsule biographies, though they do contain essential biographical information. Rather, they focus on the dominant themes and achievements of each presidency, particularly as these were shaped by the personality and ideology of the president and the political context of his administration. The essays are supplemented by brief histories of the presidential election campaigns, statistics concerning the voting in each election, and the complete texts of all the inaugural addresses. The result—in addition to being an attractive and valuable handbook of the American presidents—is an incisive interpretive history of their records in office, written by some of America's leading historians.

Of the forty-two presidents, ten by definition must be ranked in the lowest quartile in the periodic polls taken among historians of the presidency. Textbooks and other genres of political history are often negative, even scathing, in their treatments of these low-ranking presidents, who usually include William Henry Harrison and his grandson Benjamin Harrison, John Tyler, Millard Fillmore, Franklin Pierce, James Buchanan, Andrew Johnson, Ulysses S. Grant, Warren G. Harding, Calvin Coolidge, and sometimes Herbert Hoover or Richard M. Nixon. In the essays that follow, Pierce and Buchanan get low marks for their roles in making worse the problems that led to the Civil War, Andrew Johnson for his role in making worse the problems of Reconstruction, and Benjamin Harrison for his general mediocrity.

Perhaps surprisingly, however, the essays on the other traditional also-rans reveal a number of redeeming features; in the cases of Grant and Coolidge particularly, they offer an eye-opening reappraisal of these presidents' positive achievements. In these two cases, the essays reflect more favorable reappraisals contained in recent scholarship; in the others, the authors attain such a high degree of empathy with their subjects that readers are better able to appreciate the difficult political constraints and problems faced by these men. None of the essays is wholly uncritical; none is a whitewash. Yet the balance on the whole tends toward the positive. This tendency may help explain why the United States has been the most democratic polity and one of the most stable countries in the world during the past two centuries.

★ ★ ★

THE PRESIDENTS

George Washington

1ˢᵗ President · 1789–1797

Gordon S. Wood

Even in his maturity, George Washington (shown here in a Gilbert Stuart portrait) had an imposing physical presence. At six feet two inches tall with broad, muscular shoulders and large hands, he stood out particularly because Americans were rather smaller in the eighteenth century than they are today.

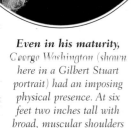

Washington was sixteen *when he learned the basics of surveying, a profession that appealed to his practical, meticulous nature. This compass was among the equipment he used.*

ALTHOUGH LIGHT-HORSE HARRY LEE famously eulogized George Washington as "first in war, first in peace, and first in the hearts of his countrymen," it is most important that Washington was the first president of the United States. As the first president, he faced circumstances that no other American leader would ever face, and he was probably the only person in the country who could have met the challenge they posed. Reared in monarchy, the American people had never known a chief executive who was not a king, and Washington somehow had to satisfy their deeply rooted yearnings for patriarchal leadership while creating a new republican presidency.

Because the United States had never had an elected chief executive like the one created by the Constitution of 1787, Washington had virtually no precedents to follow. Not only did he have to justify and flesh out the new office, he also had to bind the new nation together and prove to a skeptical world that America's grand experiment in self-government would succeed. That he accomplished all this in the midst of a world at war—and did it without sacrificing the country's republican character—is an astonishing achievement, one that the successes of no other president can match.

The delegates to the Constitutional Convention that met in Philadelphia in 1787 would never have created such a powerful executive office had they not been certain that Washington would become its first holder. Not that he sought the office; no one could have expressed more reluctance. Yet he felt an obligation to serve because no one had been more responsible than he for getting the Constitution ratified. "Be assured," James Monroe, an opponent of the Constitution, told Thomas Jefferson, "his influence carried this government." In 1789, Washington received every electoral vote, the only president in history so honored.

Daniel Huntington's The Republican Court *portrays a levee hosted by the Washingtons in February 1790, four days after the president's birthday. Such receptions generally ended at nine o'clock, the Washingtons' bedtime.*

H E WAS THE ONLY AMERICAN in 1789 who possessed the dignity, patience, restraint, and reputation for republican virtue that the untried but potentially powerful office required. With his imposing tall figure, Roman nose, and thin-lipped stern face, the former general was already, at age fifty-seven, an internationally famous hero, less for his military exploits during the Revolutionary War than for his moral character. At times during the war, he could probably have become a dictator, as some wanted him to be, but he resisted these

"THERE WERE FEATURES IN HIS FACE TOTALLY DIFFERENT FROM WHAT I HAD OBSERVED IN ANY OTHER HUMAN BEING."

—*Gilbert Stuart*—

blandishments. Washington always respected civilian authority over the army, and at the moment of his victory in 1783, he had unconditionally surrendered his sword to Congress. He promised not to take "any share in public business hereafter" and returned to his farm at Mount Vernon. This self-conscious retirement from public life, a virtually unprecedented refusal to accept political rewards commensurate with his military achievements, had electrified the world and immediately established his international reputation.

BORN
February 22, 1732

BIRTHPLACE
Pope's Creek, Virginia

DIED
December 14, 1799

PARTY AFFILIATION
Federalist

CHILDREN
none

MAJOR EVENTS

MARCH 4, 1789

The First Congress convenes in the temporary federal capital of New York City. However, with only eight senators and thirteen representatives present, neither house is able to muster a quorum.

SEPTEMBER 25, 1789

Congress submits to the states twelve proposed amendments to the Constitution. Of these, only the first ten will be approved. When they are ratified in December 1791, they become the Bill of Rights.

JULY 10, 1790

The first part of a deal worked out between Alexander Hamilton and Thomas Jefferson is enacted when the House of Representatives votes to locate the permanent federal capital on the Potomac River. The deal is completed on July 26, when the House agrees to assume Revolutionary War debt held by the states.

Because eighteenth-century Virginia society was somewhat confined, Washington probably knew Martha Dandridge from the time of her first marriage to Daniel Parke Custis. When Custis died in 1757, he left his entire estate to his wife (shown here in a miniature by Charles Willson Peale), making her one of the richest widows in the colony. Washington apparently visited her twice in March 1758, leaving the second time with a promise of marriage. The union greatly increased Washington's holdings, adding seventeen thousand acres to his five thousand as well as three hundred more slaves.

If Thomas Jefferson had had his way, the nation's capital would have been the size of a college campus. Instead, Washington (shown here surveying the District of Columbia with Pierre L'Enfant) backed the French architect's plan for a magnificent federal city that Washington hoped might one day rival, if not surpass, the powerful capitals of Europe.

Having previously promised the nation that he would seek no political office, Washington entered the presidency with everything to lose and little to gain. Only his virtuous concern for the nation's welfare overcame his hesitation—a wariness appreciated by the American people, who were aware that he was risking his fame in taking on the presidency. In 1792, when his initial term in office was up, only the most earnest entreaties kept him from returning home. This sincere willingness to surrender power is what gave Washington his remarkable moral authority.

Although some Americans in 1789 wanted to turn the presidency into an elective monarchy, Washington resisted these efforts and was relieved when senatorial attempts to give him a royal-sounding title failed. Nevertheless, like other high-toned Federalists, he believed in a social hierarchy and consequently often acted as though he were an elected king. He initially favored "His High Mightiness" as an appropriate title and in public pronouncements referred to himself in the third person. He accepted the presence of kingly iconography everywhere and made public appearances in an elaborately ornamented coach drawn by six horses and attended by four servants in livery. He established excruciatingly formal levees in emulation of European royal courts; and, like the English kings, he went on progresses throughout the country, welcomed by triumphal arches and ceremonies befitting royalty. In fact, Washington was the only part of the new government that really caught the imagination of the American people.

NO ONE DID MORE than Washington to make the presidency the powerful national office it became. Having led an army, he well understood how to exercise authority. Indeed, he had more people working for him at Mount Vernon than initially in the new federal government. A systematic and energetic administrator, he kept careful records and communicated regularly with his department heads, to whom he delegated considerable authority. Yet he always made it clear that they were merely his assistants and responsible to him. Many of them, including Treasury Secretary Alexander Hamilton and Secretary of State Thomas Jefferson, were brilliant men, yet Washington was always his own man and insisted that the government speak with a single voice. Lacking the genius and the intellectual confidence of his advisers, he consulted with them often, typically moving slowly and cautiously to judgment; but when ready to act, he acted decisively and, in the case of controversial decisions such as his acceptance of Hamilton's Bank of the United States and his 1793 Proclamation of Neutrality, never second-guessed himself.

Washington especially knew that whatever he did would set precedents. "We are a young Nation," he said, "and have a character to establish. It behooves us therefore to set out right, for first impressions will be lasting." He was particularly concerned with the relationship

> ## "HIS MIND...WAS SLOW IN OPERATION, BEING LITTLE AIDED BY INVENTION OR IMAGINATION, BUT SURE IN CONCLUSION."
>
> —*Thomas Jefferson*—

between the president and the Senate, which he believed should advise and consent to appointments and treaties in the manner of a council. Expecting an arrangement similar to that he enjoyed as commander in chief, he assumed that much of the Senate's advice and consent, if not concerning appointments then at least with regard to treaty making, would be delivered orally.

In August 1789, President Washington went to the Senate to obtain its advice and consent regarding a treaty he was negotiating with the Creeks. However, rather than offering their opinions as Washington's senior officers had during the Revolutionary War, the senators began debating each section of the treaty—despite the president's impatient glares. When one senator finally moved that the treaty be submitted to a committee for study, Washington jumped to his feet in exasperation and cried, "This defeats every purpose of my coming here!" He calmed down, but when he finally left the Senate chamber, he was overheard to say that he would "be damned" if he ever went there

FEBRUARY 25, 1791

President Washington signs a bill chartering the Bank of the United States. Jefferson has opposed the bank, arguing that it falls outside the constitutional powers specifically granted to Congress. According to Hamilton's doctrine of "implied powers," however, Congress's power to collect taxes and regulate trade implies the power to charter a national bank.

AUGUST 3, 1795

In the Northwest Territory, Gen. Anthony Wayne signs the Treaty of Greenville with the twelve Ohio tribes he defeated at the August 1794 Battle of Fallen Timbers. The Indians cede much of their land, after which a boundary is set between the remaining Indian land and that belonging to white settlers.

This portrait, *painted by Charles Willson Peale in 1779, shows Washington at the January 1777 battle of Princeton. "I have a constitution hardy enough to encounter and undergo the most severe trials and, I flatter myself, the resolution to face what any man durst," the general once wrote.*

George Washington delivers
his first inaugural address
in New York City.

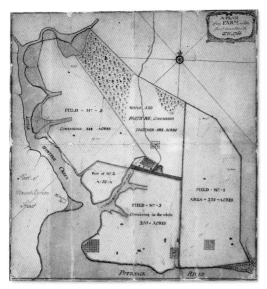

This 1766 map, *drawn by Washington with characteristic exactitude, shows the layout of his plantation on the banks of the Potomac River near Alexandria.*

again. The advice part of the Senate's role in treaty making was thus more or less permanently forgotten. When the president issued his Proclamation of Neutrality regarding the war between England and revolutionary France, he didn't even bother to ask for the Senate's consent, thus establishing the executive's nearly sole authority over the conduct of foreign affairs.

In the great struggle over Jay's Treaty with Great Britain (negotiated by John Jay in 1794 and ratified by the Senate a year later), Washington made a series of courageous decisions. With the United States and Britain on the verge of war because of British seizures of neutral American ships, sending Jay to England in the first place was one, signing the treaty amid an outcry of popular opposition was another, and standing up to a March 1796 attempt by the House of Representatives to scuttle the ratified treaty (by refusing to vote funds for its implementation) was a third. Washington thus refused to recognize for the House a role in the treaty process. To do so, he said, not only "would be to establish a dangerous precedent" but also would violate the Constitution, which allowed only the president and the Senate to make treaties.

Realizing only too keenly the fragility of the new nation, Washington devised a number of schemes to foster a stronger sense of nationhood. Because he understood the power of symbols, he was willing to sit for long hours having his portrait painted. With American nationalism not yet developed, popular celebrations of Washington during the 1790s

This 1852 lithograph *by Nathaniel Currier depicts George Washington (albeit speculatively) superintending Mount Vernon. Left to himself, Washington would most likely have avoided politics and instead pursued his great passion: the breeding of mules.*

often became a substitute for patriotism; indeed, commemorations of his birthday rivaled those of the Fourth of July. It's not too much to say that for many Americans he embodied the Union.

As president, he was particularly sensitive to the diverse interests of the new country and fervent in his efforts to prevent its fragmentation. He undertook his two extended tours of the country, in 1789 and in 1791, so that he might personally bring the government to the farthest reaches of the land and reinforce the loyalty of people who had never seen him. He promoted roads, canals, the post office—anything and everything that would bind the different states and regions together. He spent an enormous amount of time considering appointments because he wanted not only to choose the best men available but also to build broad local support for the new federal government. He thought constantly about the future of the nation and those he called the "millions unborn." Never taking the unity of the country for granted, he remained preoccupied throughout his presidency with creating the sinews of nationhood. Even in the social life of the "republican court" in New York City and (after 1790) in Phila-delphia, he and his wife, Martha, acted as matchmakers, consciously bringing together couples from different parts of the United States. In these and other ways, Washington, more than anyone, promoted the sense of Union that Lincoln and others would later uphold.

In 1790, Vice President John *Adams commissioned Edward Savage to paint these portraits of the president and first lady (depicted in one of the elaborate head-dresses she favored). When Adams left office in 1801, he took the paintings home with him, displaying them at his Quincy residence, where they remain.*

THE DECADE OF THE 1790S was not a time of ordinary politics. The parties that emerged during this period, the Federalists and the Democratic-Republicans, were not modern parties. The Federalists never even considered themselves a party but rather the beleaguered legitimate government beset by those seeking to destroy the Union. Although the Jeffersonian Republicans did reluctantly describe themselves as a party, they believed that their own organization was a temporary one, designed to prevent the establishment of a Federalist-led monarchy. Because neither the Federalists nor the Democratic-Republicans accepted the legitimacy of the other, partisan feelings ran very high and made the period one of the most passionate and divisive in American history.

With the leaders of these two hostile factions—Hamilton and Jefferson—both in his cabinet, Washington was able to use his immense prestige and good judgment to restrain fears, limit intrigues, and stymie opposition that otherwise might have escalated into vio-lence. In 1794, he delicately combined coercion and conciliation and avoided bloodshed in putting down the Whiskey Rebellion, an antitax uprising of hundreds of farmers in western Pennsylvania. Despite the intensely partisan feelings, Washington never entirely lost the respect of the party leaders—a circumstance that enabled him to reconcile, resolve, and balance their clashing interests. Jefferson scarcely foresaw the half of it when he remarked as early as 1784 that "the moderation and virtue of a single character...probably prevented this revolution

These fishhooks
*often accompanied
Washington on
surveying expeditions.
The experience that
he gained of the land
in Western Virginia
during those
expeditions made him
an especially valuable
militia major during
the French and
Indian War.*

O P P O S I T E :

With their own union
*(and those of other
Virginia families) in mind,
the Washingtons tended to
think of marriage in
dynastic terms—that is, as
a way to build alliances
and consolidate a ruling
aristocracy. Although
Washington fathered no
children himself, he did
adopt John and Martha
Custis, his wife's children
by her first husband.*

from being closed, as most others have been, by a subversion of that liberty it was intended to establish."

Although many thought that Washington could serve as president for life, he retired to Mount Vernon in 1797 at the conclusion of his second term, thus establishing a precedent unbroken until 1940. His hortatory Farewell Address became a sacred part of the American faith until well into the twentieth century. In it, he stressed above all the value of the Union, warning against extreme partisanship within the nation and passionate attachments or antagonisms to any foreign nation.

IN 1799, SIX MONTHS BEFORE his death, some frightened Federalists urged the former president to come out of retirement and stand once again for the presidency. He refused, declaring that new political conditions in the country made his candidacy irrelevant. Democracy and party politics had taken over, and personal influence and distinctions of character no longer mattered. The parties could now "set up a broomstick" and get it elected, he ruefully observed.

"IF I SHOULD CONCEIVE MYSELF IN A MANNER CONSTRAINED TO ACCEPT [THE PRESIDENCY]... THIS VERY ACT WOULD BE THE GREATEST SACRIFICE OF MY PERSONAL FEELINGS AND WISHES THAT EVER I HAVE BEEN CALLED UPON TO MAKE."

—Letter, 1788—

Although Washington wrote this out of anger and despair, he was essentially correct. The political world had changed, and parties, not great men, would soon become the objects of contention. To be sure, the American people have continued to long for great heroes, and right up through Dwight Eisenhower they have periodically elected Washingtons manqué to the presidency. But democracy has made great heroes no longer essential. Although Washington had aristocratic predilections and never meant to popularize politics, he nonetheless performed a crucial role in creating that democracy. He was an extraordinary man who made it possible for ordinary men to rule.

★ ★ ★

John Adams was smart, he knew it, and he couldn't resist letting others know it as well. "Vanity is my cardinal vice and cardinal folly," he wrote in his diary.

These buttons adorned *the coat that Adams wore in 1785 when he was presented to King George III as the first minister plenipotentiary (what we would now term ambassador) of the United States.*

John Adams

2ⁿᵈ President · 1797–1801

John Adams

James M. Banner, Jr.

NO MAN WAS LESS SUITED by temperament to be president when he occupied the office than the abrasive John Adams of Massachusetts. Yet no man's character better suited the nation's particular needs at the time. Such is the great paradox of Adams's presidency.

Adams had the deepest and most far-ranging intelligence of all his extraordinary contemporaries. And at a time when experience and proven capacity for statecraft were considered essential qualifications for executive office, no one north of the Potomac had a better résumé than this diminutive New Englander, Washington's vice president for two terms. By ability and experience, if not because of popularity, he was also Washington's most fit successor; none, except the first president, had served longer or with more distinction through decades of revolution and constitution making. When he became president in 1797, a time of severe danger from foreign powers, Adams was, along with Thomas Jefferson, the nation's foremost expert on foreign policy.

HE WAS, HOWEVER, insecure, volatile, impulsive, irritable, suspicious, self-pitying, self-righteous, and filled with often combustible rage. He knew, as he wrote, that he was considered "the most vain, conceited, impudent, arrogant Creature in the World," yet others could describe him as having "the clearest head and finest heart." Of all the Founders, he was the wittiest, most loving, most passionate, and, because of his robust sense of humor, among the most companionable. Adams is often thought of as a latter-day Puritan for his ceaseless self-scrutiny, but he was just as much a Martin Luther–like figure, bawdy and given to scourging contemporaries for their failings while mercilessly flagellating himself for his most modest deficiencies.

Adams assumed office as two major crises, the first since the adoption of the Constitution in 1787, simultaneously broke upon the nation. One was a matter of foreign policy, specifically the war between Britain and France that threatened to engulf America; the other, the nation's first outbreak of bitterly partisan politics. These crises intersected at a time when the nation's independence was not yet secure—as it would not finally be until 1815—and when political parties, then in their infancy, were considered illegitimate, dangerous, and contrary to the public good. Had either crisis befallen another president, each might have been resolved differently. But it was Adams's fate, and the nation's advantage, that of all values he held dear, the two that most reflected deep needs within him were those of balance and independence, both his nation's and his own. For Adams as president, the question of the nation's independence came down to how he might keep it free of European entanglements. Balance, on the other hand, meant not allowing any political party, even his own, to become too powerful or extreme. Like Washington, Adams sought to be above parties.

Paul Revere's sensationalized *engraving of* The Bloody Massacre *created such a furor in 1770 Boston that the royal governor was forced to arrest the soldiers involved and charge them with murder. Of all the lawyers in town, only John Adams and Josiah Quincy were willing to argue the soldiers' defense. Adams feared that, for political reasons, innocent men might be railroaded to the gallows.*

Even so, Adams was unmistakably a Federalist, although many party members had little use for him. They claimed Washington as their figurehead and for guidance looked to former treasury secretary Alexander Hamilton rather than to the president. Furthermore, Adams's cabinet was stocked with holdovers from Washington's, for it wasn't yet conventional to appoint new department heads with each new administration. These cabinet members, loyal to Hamilton, constantly betrayed Adams's confidence and undercut him. They induced him, for example, to appoint Washington and Hamilton to lead a military force to overawe a minor civil disturbance in Pennsylvania. They also opposed

BORN
October 30, 1735

BIRTHPLACE
Braintree, Massachusetts

DIED
July 4, 1826

PARTY AFFILIATION
Federalist

CHILDREN
Abigail, John Quincy, Susanna, Charles, Thomas

MAJOR EVENTS

AUGUST 28, 1797

In order to end costly pirate attacks on American merchant shipping in the Mediterranean Sea, the United States signs a treaty with the Barbary Coast state of Tunis. The agreement, ratified by the Senate in January 1800, requires the United States to pay tribute to Tunis.

JANUARY 8, 1798

The Eleventh Amendment, ratified today, prohibits suits against states filed by citizens of other states or citizens of foreign countries.

APRIL 24, 1800

Vice President Thomas Jefferson persuades Congress to establish a library for itself. The Library of Congress will spend its first five-thousand-dollar appropriation primarily on law books.

Abigail Adams was considered sharper than a woman ought to be; she also read more than a woman was supposed to and spoke out even when the custom of her time and gender called for silence. In a famous March 1776 letter, she beseeched her husband to "remember the ladies" when making laws for the new republic: "Do not put unlimited power in the hands of husbands," she wrote. "Remember, all men would be tyrants if they could."

Adams's dispatch of a mission to France to seek resolution of several outstanding issues with that revolutionary nation. When Adams's mission resulted in the infamous XYZ Affair, with the French seeking bribes from the American envoys, an undeclared naval war ensued—the so-called Quasi-War. The Hamilton loyalists gloated, while Adams, characteristically indecisive, fumed but did nothing.

Because he was uncomfortable exercising firm leadership, Adams often went along with the policies pushed on him by the Federalist-controlled Congress. It helped, of course, that he agreed in principle with many of them: For instance, while determined to avoid war with both England and France, he concurred with other Federalists that U.S. interests lay more with the island than with the Continental nation. He also signed the most infamous Federalist-sponsored legislation of his administration: the Alien and Sedition Acts of 1798, which gave the president special powers to deport dangerous foreigners and suppress critical speech.

NOTHING DID MORE TO DIVIDE American politics during the late 1790s than those laws. Their passage and the criminal prosecutions brought under them provoked bitter denunciations from Adams's political opponents, the Democratic-Republicans, led by Jefferson and James Madison, the former being Adams's vice president and erstwhile close friend. In response to the hated acts, and with an eye to their own political fortunes, these two future presidents penned the fateful Virginia and Kentucky Resolutions, which loosed upon the land the argument that states could legitimately interpose their authority between their citizens and the federal government, parent principle to the future concepts of nullification and secession. By 1799, the political atmosphere had become poisoned with the worst bitterness and invective in the nation's history—just the situation Adams had wished to avoid.

In the midst of this domestic turmoil arrived intimations that France was again ready to treat with the United States. Like Washington before him, Adams was so determined to keep the nation free of involvement in European affairs that he appointed envoys to Paris without first consulting his cabinet. The High Federalists, pro-English Hamiltonians always hoping for a conflict with France, were outraged at the move, which they feared might anger Britain. But Adams, possessing a grander strategic vision and correctly sensing the public

These watches belonged to John and Abigail Adams, the larger being John's.

mood for peace, stuck to his guns. The resulting Convention of 1800 with France ended the conflict at sea and resolved many other outstanding issues between the two nations. Peace returned, and the foundation for the epoch-making 1803 purchase of Louisiana was laid.

But Adams's party was irreparably split. Enraged by the assaults upon him, he summarily fired three of his cabinet secretaries. At last, but too late, he was coming into his own. In retaliation for Adams's action, and with the intention of denying him renomination, Hamilton published a scathing public attack on him. Although Adams's triumphant diplomacy had gone far to restore the party's fortunes, nothing

Adams *(shown here in a 1798 portrait by William Winstanley) often worried that Washington and Franklin were overshadowing him. "The history of our Revolution," he wrote Benjamin Rush, "… will be that Dr. Franklin's electrical rod smote the Earth and out sprang General Washington. That Franklin electrified him with his rod—and thence forward these two conducted all the policy, negotiations, legislations, and war."*

could save him from the chaos in Federalist ranks. His impulsive, but warranted, decision to break with the High Federalists had preserved national security, redeemed his reputation, and given him control of his office. Yet when the balloting for president ended in the fall of 1800, Adams had lost to Jefferson by eight electoral votes. Embittered, he slipped out of the unfinished White House in the early hours of Jefferson's inauguration day rather than attend his successor's swearing-in.

Adams's undignified leave-taking symbolized the passing of Federalist rule and the ideological triumph of Jeffersonian democracy. Yet Adams's search for national security through neutrality and his deep, if tortured, moralism never disappeared from American politics. Instead, they went into remission, reemerging in such later guises as the Monroe Doctrine and the antislavery politics of New England and the Midwest.

NOVEMBER 17, 1800

Congress meets for the first time in Washington, D.C.. Since the site for the permanent federal capital was chosen in 1790, the city has been planned but only partially built.

FEBRUARY 13, 1801

The outgoing Federalist Congress passes the Judiciary Act of 1801, which creates a large number of federal judgeships that President Adams will fill with fellow members of the Federalist party. They are known as the Midnight Judges because Adams works until midnight on March 3, his last day in office, completing the necessary paperwork.

"HE IS VAIN, IRRITABLE, AND A BAD CALCULATOR OF…THE MOTIVES WHICH GOVERN MEN. THIS IS ALL THE ILL WHICH CAN POSSIBLY BE SAID OF HIM."

—*Thomas Jefferson*—

OPPOSITE:

John Singleton Copley painted this portrait in late 1783 when he and Adams were both in London. The scroll in Adams's right hand is believed to be a reference to the recently signed Treaty of Paris ending the Revolutionary War and acknowledging the independence of the United States. Copley's work is the only known life-size portrait of the future president.

Analysts and "pundits" two hundred years later might be tempted to see Adams's presidency as the first historical confirmation of their cynical axiom: Let no president show his true colors. After all, Adams's refusal to bear further insubordination in his cabinet for the sake of party unity (and against the interests of the nation) cost him reelection. Yet this conclusion would be as wrong as the axiom itself.

More valid would be the verdict that, concerning the Alien and Sedition Acts, Adams's sensitivity to criticism led him to confuse uniformity with unity and to seek consensus through legal force—errors committed by later presidents and politicians as well. Yet even this verdict would unjustly blame Adams for seeking what nearly everyone else at the time, Jefferson included, also sought to achieve: an end to partisan strife and the creation of a serene national consensus on all matters. Such harmony wasn't possible or realistic then, nor has it become so since.

"NO MAN WHO EVER HELD THE OFFICE OF PRESIDENT WOULD CONGRATULATE A FRIEND ON OBTAINING IT."

—*Letter following the election of his son, 1825*—

Therefore, one must draw other lessons from Adams's presidency. His compass set on what he sought to achieve (peace with all nations) rather than, like other Federalists, on what they sought to avoid (robust debate in the court of public opinion), Adams had the firmer character and the larger perspective. He also left an impressive legacy. Besides maintaining neutrality and regaining peace, his administration created a separate Department of the Navy, put the army on a surer footing, and left a solvent treasury. In addition, one of his shrewdest acts was surely the appointment of moderate Federalist John Marshall as chief justice of the Supreme Court.

Those who succeeded Adams also drew a useful lesson from his presidency: It is difficult, perhaps impossible, to govern independent of a party. Having to fight fellow Federalists as well as Democratic-Republicans did his career no good. Still, as Adams once wrote, he always sought "to preserve my Independence, at the Expense of my Ambition." As president, he was true to this demanding principle.

By the time he became president, John Adams needed these spectacles to correct his vision, weak from his youth. He also wore a set of ill-fitting dentures, which gave him a lisp.

★ ★ ★

Thomas Jefferson

3rd President · 1801–1809

Joseph J. Ellis

Thomas Jefferson (shown here in an 1805 portrait by Rembrandt Peale) was tall, even taller than Washington, but he lacked the general's posture. "He sits in a lounging manner on one hip, commonly, and with one of his shoulders elevated much above the other," one senator observed.

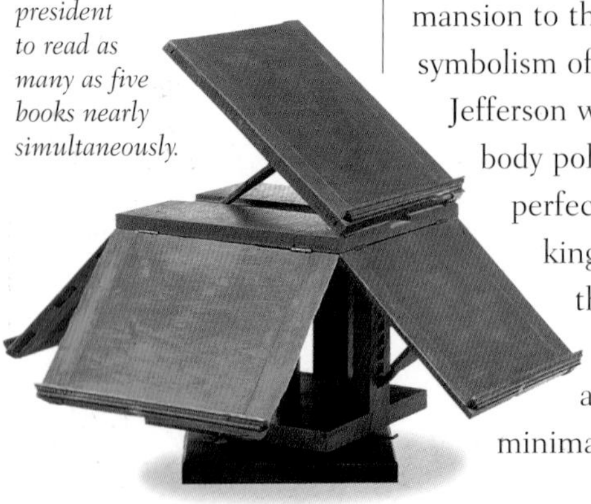

This handy revolving bookstand, of Jefferson's own design, allowed the president to read as many as five books nearly simultaneously.

AS THOMAS JEFFERSON took the oath of office as the third president on March 4, 1801, several important precedents were being set. For the first time, the press had played a major role in electing the president, transforming what had been polite electoral competition into a bitterly partisan affair. Also for the first time, power was changing hands—from the incumbent party, the Federalists, to Jefferson's opposition party, the Democratic-Republicans—and this was occurring peacefully, almost routinely. Finally, the man who had spent his entire public career opposing all forms of centralized political authority, whether it be the arbitrary policies of George III or the consolidated national government of Alexander Hamilton, was himself inheriting the very executive powers that he had so vehemently denounced as excessive. Jefferson was the first, but hardly the last, president to assume office promising to dismantle the same federal government he had been elected to head.

It helped that Jefferson was also the first president to take office in the new capital city—for Washington, D.C., wasn't really a city at all but a mosquito-infested swamp where the main street, Pennsylvania Avenue, still had stumps protruding all the way from the unfinished presidential mansion to the unfinished legislative chamber on Capitol Hill. The symbolism of the scene was positively Jeffersonian, not just because Jefferson was on record as believing that cities were "sores on the body politic," but also because the new American capital contrasted perfectly with European capitals like London and Paris, where kings and courtiers gathered in conspicuous splendor. It was the perfect setting for an unimperial presidency.

In several respects, Jefferson's subsequent two terms as president represented a successful implementation of his minimalist ideal. His leadership style, for example, put a premium

This symbolic painting by John Trumbull, which decorates the Capitol Rotunda, suggests that Jefferson presented the Continental Congress with a fait accompli. Actually, the Declaration of Independence, presented June 28, endured a week of debate before an edited version finally passed on July 4.

on silent and nearly invisible decision making. Unlike George Washington and John Adams, Jefferson presented all his legislative proposals to Congress in writing rather than in person. Even within the cabinet, he required his department heads to submit recommendations in written form, which he then revised and returned in the same fashion. The making of policy throughout Jefferson's presidency was essentially an editorial process. This approach played to his acknowledged brilliance as a prose stylist yet also sidestepped his notorious weakness as an orator and his inveterate shyness in public forums. As far as we can tell, Jefferson made only two public speeches during his eight years in office—his first and second inaugural addresses. Instead of displaying executive authority, he made a point of concealing it.

INDEED, THE ONLY OCCASIONS Jefferson ever appeared, apart from his daily horseback rides in the woods of Rock Creek Park, were the weekly dinners he scheduled when Congress was in session. These were decidedly informal affairs that made a point of dispensing with the ornate codes of etiquette that governed European courts. Seating arrangements were "pell-mell," meaning that diplomatic rank was not observed, and Jefferson himself often showed up fresh from his horseback ride, attired in corduroy pants and riding boots. When ambassadors came to call on him at the presidential mansion, he frequently greeted them in

BORN
April 13, 1743

BIRTHPLACE
Goochland County, Virginia

DIED
July 4, 1826

PARTY AFFILIATION
Democratic-Republican

CHILDREN
Martha, Jane, (unnamed son), Mary, Lucy, Lucy, Thomas Woodson (unconfirmed), Beverly Hemings, Madison Hemings, Eston Hemings

MAJOR EVENTS

FEBRUARY 24, 1803

The Supreme Court, acting in the case of Marbury v. Madison, strikes down an act of Congress for the first time. William Marbury, one of John Adams's Midnight Judges, had asked the Court to compel Secretary of State James Madison to turn over his judicial commission, which had been left undelivered in Adams's haste to vacate the presidency.

SEPTEMBER 25, 1804

The ratification of the Twelfth Amendment corrects a defect in the Constitution that nearly made Vice President Aaron Burr president. (In the election of 1800, Burr received the same number of electoral votes as Jefferson.)

By the time Jefferson became president, he had been a widower nearly twenty years. No portrait survives of Martha Jefferson, but contemporary accounts describe her as pretty, though frail. She died in 1782 of complications following the birth of a daughter who died at age three. In fact, only two of Jefferson's white children lived to adulthood. His oldest daughter, Martha (shown here in a 1789 miniature), was called Patsy by the family. She served for a time as her father's White House hostess but became destitute in 1828 following the death of her husband, Thomas Mann Randolph, a former governor of Virginia.

This is the key to Monticello, the house that Jefferson designed for himself. Monticello's unique contrivances include beds that fold up into the walls and a weather vane linked to an indoor gauge that allowed Jefferson to determine the wind direction without stepping outside.

his slippers and shirtsleeves. No one could possibly have confused him with a king.

Jefferson made the elimination of the national debt, which then stood at $112 million, his major policy priority. He instructed Albert Gallatin, his extremely competent treasury secretary, to prepare a federal budget that retired the debt at the rate of $7 million annually. Because federal revenues each year amounted to $9 million, Jefferson was proposing to operate the entire federal government on $2 million a year. Soon the embryonic federal bureaucracy—in 1801, there were 130 federal employees in Washington—was reduced by nearly half. This allowed Jefferson to remove lingering Federalist officeholders from the payroll while also delivering on his promise to make the American republic that rarest of things, a nation-state that functioned without the customary mechanisms of the state.

ALL THIS WAS PERFECTLY in keeping with the promise Jefferson had made in his first inaugural. He had described his vision in lyrical terms: "a wise and frugal Government, which shall restrain men from injuring one another, shall leave them otherwise free to regulate their own pursuits of industry and improvement, and shall not take from the mouth of labor the bread it has earned. This is the sum of good government, and this is necessary to close the circle of our felicities." Implicit in this message was Jefferson's judgment that the consolidated and coercive government created by the Federalists had been a dangerous aberration, indeed a hostile takeover of the revolutionary legacy. This was why, years later, he described his election as "the revolution of 1800," meaning that "the true republican principles" of 1776 had been restored after a decade of Federalist corruption.

The Hamiltonian money changers had at last been driven from the temple, which was once again in the hands of "the people" rather than those who claimed to speak for them. His ascendance to the presidency represented the recovery of America's original liberal ethos. American society wasn't something that needed to be managed from above or afar; it needed only to be liberated.

The first cloud to darken this uncluttered horizon actually presented itself as a heaven-sent opportunity. In 1803, Napoleon Bonaparte made a sudden if strategic decision to sell the vast region stretching from the Mississippi Valley to the Rocky Mountains. France had only recently acquired this huge tract from Spain, but with the resumption of the Anglo-French war, Napoleon recognized the need to consolidate his resources.

Jefferson immediately recognized the truly providential opportunity offered by Napoleon's decision. Not only would the purchase of the Louisiana Territory nearly double the national domain, not only would it remove from the western borders the lingering threat of mischief by a major European power, it would also extend the duration of the agrarian way of life in America for several generations, thereby prolonging the open-ended, uncrowded conditions that permitted republican principles

"THE NATURAL PROGRESS OF THINGS IS FOR LIBERTY TO YIELD AND GOVERNMENT TO GAIN GROUND."

—Letter, 1788—

to flourish. Jefferson had always regarded the West as America's fountain of youth, the place where social problems went to find solutions. Now, in one dramatic moment, he was being granted the chance to extend the youthful phase of national development. Already dispatched to Paris, James Monroe was instructed to meet Napoleon's terms and handle all negotiations with the urgent sense that success or failure would determine "the future destinies of the republic."

It quickly became apparent, however, that the seizure of an empire required an imperial president. Jefferson took personal charge of the diplomatic preparations in Washington, gently elbowing Secretary of State James Madison off to the side. When Albert Gallatin protested that the fifteen-million-dollar cost of the new territory would wreck all plans for eliminating the national debt, Jefferson told him to look up from his accountant's ledgers long enough to see the boundless western skies this purchase made possible. And then there were the constitutional

JUNE 4, 1805

The Tripolitan War ends when the Barbary state of Tripoli agrees to a peace treaty ending U.S. tribute payments. However, the United States will continue to pay tribute to Algiers, Tunis, and Morocco until 1816.

NOVEMBER 7, 1805

After crossing the Rockies and canoeing down the Salmon, Snake, and Columbia Rivers, Lewis and Clark reach the Pacific Ocean. They are aided on this final leg of their journey west by Sacajawea, the Shoshone wife of their French-Canadian interpreter.

MARCH 29, 1806

Congress authorizes the construction of a public road (variously known as the National Road and the Cumberland Road) from Cumberland, Maryland, to Wheeling on the Ohio River.

MARCH 2, 1807

At Jefferson's request, Congress bans the importation of slaves after January 1, 1808. This is the earliest date permitted by Article I, Section 9, of the Constitution.

Jefferson was serving
as Washington's secretary of state when Charles Willson Peale painted this portrait of him in 1791.

Jefferson glued into the pages of this scrapbook an odd assortment of materials that, for one reason or another, captured his interest. Most are clippings—from newspapers, speeches, even some original poetry he wrote—but the scrapbook also contains such unlikely objects as an oak leaf pressed between two pages. The president, in a surprisingly sentimental gesture, apparently kept this leaf as a remembrance of a friend.

"I LIKE THE DREAMS OF THE FUTURE BETTER THAN THE HISTORY OF THE PAST— SO, GOOD NIGHT!"

—

Letter to John Adams, 1816

questions raised by the acquisition of territory not included within the original borders of the American nation. Jefferson acknowledged that the Constitution made no provision for such a massive enlargement of the Union. Strictly speaking, and according to his own narrow definition of federal authority, the Louisiana Purchase could occur only after a constitutional amendment was passed by Congress and ratified by the states. But this clumsy and time-consuming procedure would have placed the entire purchase at risk. So Jefferson simply abandoned his own long-standing constitutional scruples: "The less that is said about my constitutional difficulty, the better," he declared, adding that "it will be desirable for Congress to do what is necessary *in silence.*"

Indeed, every aspect of the Louisiana Purchase defied Jefferson's heartfelt convictions about limited federal government and a weak chief executive. Even before news that the deal had gone through reached Washington, Jefferson had instructed Meriwether Lewis, his private secretary, to mount an expedition to explore the prospective new land and to keep going beyond even its borders, into Spanish possessions all the way to the Pacific, in order to discover the best water route across the continent. (As it turned out, there was none.) According to his own principles, as well as the principles of international law then in effect, what came to be known as the Lewis and Clark expedition was an illegal venture. In order to disguise its questionable character, Jefferson obtained authorization from Congress under the pretense that it was merely a scientific exploration and, as he also described it, "a literary pursuit."

ONCE NEWS OF THE TREATY reached the United States in July 1803, Jefferson took personal charge of interpreting the ill-defined borders of the Louisiana Territory in the most expansive fashion possible. The French foreign minister, Talleyrand, had acknowledged that no one in France could tell the Rio Grande from the Mississippi (or, he might have added, the Rocky Mountains from the Alps). "You have made a noble bargain for yourselves," Talleyrand observed, "and I suppose you will make the most of it." Jefferson required no urging along these lines. His reading of the maps yielded the conclusion that the purchase included the entire Gulf Coast of modern Florida and all of present-day Texas. Spanish authorities protested vehemently, but Jefferson responded by observing that "to lose our country by a scrupulous adherence to written laws would be to lose the law itself."

Finally, Jefferson requested and received from Congress nearly autocratic power over the provisional government to be established in the Louisiana Territory. He proposed a governor appointed by the president, which is to say himself, and a council or senate called the Assembly of Notables appointed by the governor and approved by the president. This quasi-monarchical scheme defied all his most cherished republican principles. In the Senate debate over the authorization of this government structure, John Quincy Adams observed that Jefferson would possess "an assumption of implied powers greater than all the assumptions of implied powers in the years of the Washington and Adams administrations put together." Adams might well have added that Jefferson would wield more arbitrary power over the residents of Louisiana than George III had wielded over the American colonists.

This map of North America, drawn by Aaron Arrowsmith in 1802, was considered the best of its day. Its detail persuaded Jefferson, Lewis, and Clark that the Missouri River would provide the best route to the Columbia.

THE ENABLING LEGISLATION granting Jefferson imperial power over the Louisiana Territory served as a fitting capstone to what, in the full sweep of American history, must take its place as the most dramatic and far-reaching executive decision ever made by an American president. All the major decisions Jefferson reached—to override his constitutional scruples, to insist on a boldly expansive interpretation of the territorial borders, to explore the region with a covert reconnaissance team, to install an arbitrary provisional government—can be justified in retrospect as eminently practical improvisations that assured the successful seizure of a serendipitous opportunity. And, again in retrospect, there is every reason to concur with the historical verdict that the Louisiana Purchase was the crowning achievement of Jefferson's presidency.

But the ironies abound. First and foremost is the glaring contradiction between Jefferson's long-standing commitment to limiting federal power and his flamboyantly imperial style throughout the Louisiana matter. It would be both unfair and misguided to regard this contradiction as an example of his hypocrisy or as an early illustration of the subsequent presidential custom of promising one thing and practicing another. Jefferson's inconsistencies in fact exposed the inherently rhetorical character of his sincere but wholly theoretical convictions about consolidated political power in the Federalist mode. All his convictions had developed as the leader of the opposition. Once

In a journal entry dated February 25, 1806, William Clark, attending to his scientific duties, drew this sketch of a eulachon, a food fish of the Pacific not previously known.

Jefferson left specific instructions (shown here) for his tombstone. The epitaph he wanted (and received) read: "Here was buried Thomas Jefferson, author of the Declaration of American Independence, of the statute of Virginia for religious freedom, and father of the University of Virginia."

OPPOSITE:

This Caleb Boyle portrait of Jefferson dates to his first term in office. In a well-known episode of that term, British diplomat Anthony Merry, calling on Jefferson at the White House, was appalled to find the informal chief executive "not merely in undress, but standing in slippers down at the heels...in a state of negligence actually studied."

he was in office himself, the political imperatives that come with the actual exercise of power required practical adjustments to accommodate the patently obvious reality that executive leadership was essential if the American republic was to fulfill its national destiny.

THE FINAL IRONY BECAME VISIBLE only over the next fifty years, when the newly acquired Louisiana Territory became the chief battleground in the political war over slavery. Jefferson wanted desperately to keep the combustible question of slavery off the national agenda, but it emerged whenever each territory applied for admission as a state. The West became, then, not a place where American problems went for solutions, but the breeding ground for the most ominous problem of all. Moreover, the imperial precedent he set in acquiring and governing the Louisiana Territory became the rallying cry for those leaders of the antislavery cause, like Abraham Lincoln, who argued that the federal government possessed sovereign jurisdiction over the eventual resolution of this national contradiction. To put it mildly, that was not what Jefferson had in mind.

"I THINK THIS IS THE MOST EXTRAORDINARY COLLECTION OF HUMAN TALENT [EVER] GATHERED AT THE WHITE HOUSE— WITH THE POSSIBLE EXCEPTION OF WHEN THOMAS JEFFERSON DINED ALONE."

—*John F. Kennedy, speech at a dinner honoring Nobel Prize winners*—

Meanwhile, history was preparing for him a number of surprises in the international arena that were destined to make his second term a headlong fall from grace. The resumption of the Anglo-French war produced in the Atlantic and Caribbean naval blockades that stymied American shipping, reduced revenues from foreign commerce, and reignited the old hostilities toward English naval supremacy, most especially the impressment of American sailors on the high seas. Jefferson's solution, the Embargo Act of 1807, was an unadulterated calamity that ruined the U.S. economy by closing all ports to foreign trade and forced Jefferson, once again, to expand his definition of executive power in order to enforce the embargo. Both his greatest achievement as president, the Louisiana Purchase, and his greatest failure, the Embargo Act, were violations of his own professed principles.

★ ★ ★

James Madison

4ᵗʰ President · 1809–1817

Jam Madison

Jack N. Rakove

James Madison often
gave *the impression of
being weak, nervous, and
young for his age. In part,
this was because he was
modest, soft spoken, and
somewhat shy.*

These buckles once
decorated *a pair of
Madison's shoes. The
shortest president, he
stood barely five feet four
inches tall and weighed
just one hundred
pounds. He was careful
in his appearance and
usually dressed entirely
in black.*

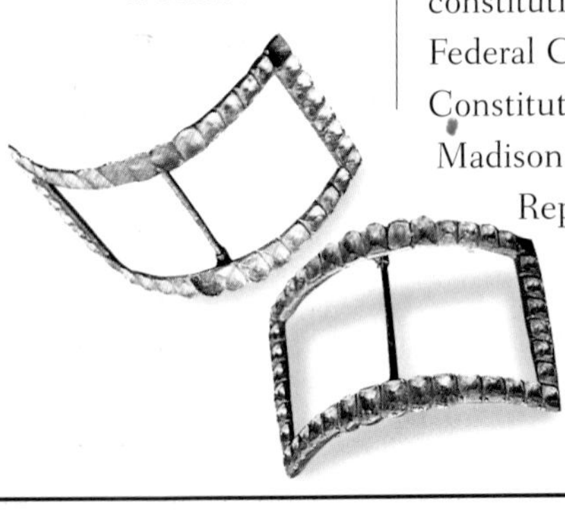

FEW AMERICAN STATESMEN have earned so admired a place in the nation's history as the acutely intelligent Virginian remembered as the Father of the Constitution. James Madison's two terms as president, however, are commonly regarded as the one serious blot on his otherwise distinguished career. His first term was dominated by the diplomatic buffeting that led him to seek a declaration of war against Great Britain in June 1812, and his second was marked by the disastrous conduct of that war. In all, Madison's decidedly mixed record during this period suggests that his talents as a constitutional lawgiver weren't those required for vigorous wartime leadership. Yet he left office convinced that the Constitution and the system of government it created had been vindicated, not impeached, by the war—and most of his countrymen seemed to agree.

At the time of his first inauguration in March 1809, the fifty-seven-year-old Madison was ending his third decade of active involvement in national politics. Two extended terms of service in the Continental Congress, beginning in March 1780, had been punctuated by three years' attendance in the Virginia assembly. Throughout the 1780s, too, Madison was preoccupied with the problems of national constitutional reform. He played leading roles in promoting the Federal Convention that met at Philadelphia in 1787, in drafting the Constitution, and finally in obtaining its ratification by the states. Madison then served four consecutive terms in the new House of Representatives before briefly retiring in 1797 to his family's estate in Orange County, Virginia, with his bride of three years, the widow Dolley Payne Todd. By 1799, however, he was back in the Virginia assembly, and then, following the bitterly contested election of 1800, he took up his first executive post as secretary of state in the newly formed administration of his close friend and Virginia neighbor, Thomas Jefferson.

Unlike Alexander Hamilton, his political ally in the 1780s and opponent in the 1790s, Madison never believed that vigorous executive leadership was an essential element of sound republican government. Rather, he shared with Jefferson a healthy respect for the dangers of unchecked executive power—a position informed by his familiarity with the contentious rise of ministerial government in eighteenth-century Britain. True, he went to the Federal Convention of 1787 believing in the importance of protecting the executive from the "encroachments" likely to arise from the "impetuous vortex" of the legislature. But executive independence, in Madison's view, meant only that the president should be empowered to administer the government with a due measure of energy and a high degree of responsibility. It didn't mean the president was entitled to usurp the deliberative powers of the legislature.

THE EVENTS OF THE 1790s made Madison even more aware of the dangers posed by a strong executive—so much so, in fact, that he came to believe that, under certain circumstances, the executive could be as prone to "encroachments" as the legislature. Some of this concern can be traced to Madison's early opposition to the financial policies of Secretary of the Treasury Hamilton, but it owed much more to the succession of foreign policy crises that first erupted in 1793.

With Secretary of State Jefferson, Madison believed that U.S. foreign policy should favor France, its Revolutionary War ally, while remaining wary of the ulterior designs of Britain, which was at that time leading the

When the departure of the British *from Washington allowed the Madisons to return on August 27, 1814, they visited the ruins of the Capitol and the presidential mansion (shown here in a contemporary engraving). For this national humiliation, the press made Madison its whipping boy.*

BORN
March 16, 1751

BIRTHPLACE
Port Conway, Virginia

DIED
June 28, 1836

PARTY AFFILIATION
Democratic-Republican

CHILDREN
none

MAJOR EVENTS

JULY 2, 1809

Alarmed by treaties ceding more and more land to whites, the Shawnee chief Tecumseh begins organizing a confederacy among the tribes of the Mississippi Valley to resist further incursions.

MARCH 16, 1810

Chief Justice John Marshall delivers the Supreme Court's decision in Fletcher v. Peck, *a case involving the corrupt sale of state land in Georgia. The ruling, which strikes down a Georgia law reversing the sale, sets an important precedent concerning federal authority.*

NOVEMBER 4, 1811

The Twelfth Congress convenes with many new Democratic-Republican members from the South and West who are impatient with Madison's temporizing on British impressment. Henry Clay and John C. Calhoun are among the leaders of these young War Hawks.

This illustration from the 1815 Stationer's Almanack shows British forces under Maj. Gen. Robert Ross and Rear Adm. George Cockburn capturing the city of Washington on August 24, 1814.

Madison was already well known in 1794 when he met the fashionable widow Dolley Payne Todd *(shown here in a portrait by Gilbert Stuart). Most people presumed that Madison, then forty-three, was a confirmed bachelor, yet "the wooing that followed was swift and ardent," according to one Madison biographer. As first lady, Dolley Madison exhibited a vivaciousness that made up for many of her husband's social inadequacies. She ate heartily, gambled some at cards, and (unlike many first ladies) enjoyed the custom of calling on those who had recently called on her.*

Thomas Jefferson *so treasured this campeachy, or siesta, chair that he gave one just like it to his friend Madison. The name comes from the Mexican state of Campeche, where mahogany used to make this style of chair was grown.*

European coalition seeking to blunt the revolutionary challenge from France. When Hamilton invoked a broad definition of executive power to defend George Washington's 1793 decision to declare American neutrality in the escalating European war (a decision taken without congressional consultation), Madison felt compelled to make the case for congressional participation. This and later controversies (notably the Alien and Sedition Acts of 1798) persuaded Madison that crises, particularly those of foreign relations, gave the executive crucial political advantages that enabled the president to ignore the constitutional rules that precluded him from exercising unilateral authority.

> "THE GREAT DIFFICULTY LIES IN THIS: YOU MUST FIRST ENABLE THE GOVERNMENT TO CONTROL THE GOVERNED AND IN THE NEXT PLACE OBLIGE IT TO CONTROL ITSELF."
>
> —The Federalist *No. 51, 1788*—

As secretary of state from 1801 to 1809, Madison naturally moderated these views. After war between Britain and the new imperial regime of Napoleon Bonaparte resumed in 1803, Madison accepted the burdensome responsibility of managing the nation's diplomacy as he and Jefferson attempted, with mixed results, to protect U.S. neutrality against the pressures of the two belligerents. Though stripped of their illusions about France, the two leaders still believed Britain posed the greater threat to American interests. In their view, Britain was a predatory economic power that remained resentful of the loss of its former colonies.

President Jefferson's response to the disruption of the Atlantic trade and the impressment of American sailors was the ruinous Embargo Act of 1807, which closed U.S. ports to foreign shipping in the belief that such an action would compel Britain and France to respect U.S. neutrality. When it became clear that the victims of the embargo were disproportionately American, Congress replaced it with the

Non-Intercourse Act of 1809, which limited the trade restriction to Britain and France. As president, Madison enforced the new policy, enacted in the final days of the Jefferson administration, but it too had little effect. In May 1810, this act was itself replaced with Macon's Bill No. 2, which provided that if *either* Britain or France agreed to respect U.S. neutrality, the United States would suspend trade with the other.

THREE FACTORS SEVERELY HAMPERED Madison's ability to conduct an effective foreign policy. First, the Democratic-Republican party he led was far less unified in power than it had been in opposition. Madison had his detractors in Congress and even within his own cabinet, and as a result he couldn't simply propose the policies he deemed expedient and trust they would be promptly endorsed and implemented. Second, consistent with his constitutional principles, he felt that he shouldn't preempt congressional deliberations. Third, and most important, Madison fundamentally miscalculated that American commerce was so valuable that one or both of the belligerents would have to recognize the rights the United States claimed as a neutral power. In reality, of course, the struggle for control of Europe was far too deadly to allow the claims of a puny power like the United States to trump the deepest interests of Britain or France.

In the spring of 1812, vague statements of goodwill from Napoleon persuaded Madison to use the power granted him under Macon's Bill No. 2 to reimpose nonintercourse with Britain. Coincidentally, in early June the British government revised the orders-in-council that permitted seizure of U.S. ships. But Madison's war message was already working its way through Congress, and the decision for war was taken before news of the shift in British policy reached American shores. Even then, once the news arrived, sounder voices might have counseled a suspension of hostilities, but the hope that preemptive assaults on Canada might gain a lasting strategic advantage enabled the southern and western War Hawks to prevail.

This hope proved terribly naive. The outbreak of war found U.S. troops poorly armed, poorly led, and poorly provisioned, and all the early expeditions to Canada failed. With Napoleon's power collapsing after his Russian disaster, British reinforcements soon became available in numbers sufficient to invade the United States. Madison meanwhile faced enormous difficulties: his usual problems securing the cooperation of Congress; the fact that pro-British, Federalist New

SEPTEMBER 10, 1813

Flying a banner that reads "Don't Give Up the Ship," twenty-eight-year-old Oliver Hazard Perry defeats a British fleet in the battle of Lake Erie. Perry's victory forces the British to abandon Detroit and makes possible an invasion of Canada led by Gen. William Henry Harrison.

DECEMBER 15, 1814

Federalist delegates from all over New England meet at Hartford to protest the War of 1812, which has been ruining the region's shipping-dependent economy. The Hartford Convention will consider breaking up the Union but disbands after issuing a report that only hints at secession.

Charles Willson Peale
painted this watercolor-on-ivory miniature in 1783. The portrait of Madison, then thirty-two, is set within a gold case that also contains a braided lock of Madison's hair.

While the presidential mansion *was being rebuilt, the Madisons lived in the rented Octagon House. Because all the official china had been destroyed in the fire set by the British, the Madisons used their personal service for state functions. This plate is part of that set, purchased in France for the Madisons in 1806.*

OPPOSITE:

This stipple engraving, *from a Thomas Sully portrait, shows Madison as he appeared during his presidency. The Father of the Constitution would live another twenty years—long enough to witness the 1832 nullification crisis and hear the argument for disunion made on the basis of his own Virginia Resolutions. Written in response to the Alien and Sedition Acts of 1798, these resolutions argued that states could properly oppose federal laws if those laws were unjust.*

England had essentially chosen to sit out the war; and the inclusion in his own cabinet of an incompetent secretary of the navy and an insubordinate secretary of war. In August 1814, moreover, Madison became the only president to see serious combat in the field when he witnessed the battle of Bladensburg, an American defeat that gave the British unimpeded access to Washington, D.C.

HAD THE BRITISH CHOSEN TO DO SO, they might well have undone the American Revolution. However, exhausted from their struggle against the French, they chose to accept the peace concluded at Ghent in late December 1814. The decision was likely a wise one, as Andrew Jackson's January 1815 defeat of a British expedition to New Orleans demonstrated. The War of 1812 was a near thing for the Americans, but it ended with independence confirmed and a rebirth of nationalist feeling that might easily have been another casualty of war.

James Madison benefited personally from the relief that war's end brought, but he found deeper consolation in the principles that he believed had been vindicated. Like most intellectuals—and Madison was certainly the most penetrating political thinker of his generation—he took pride in his consistency; and since the 1790s, he had been convinced that unbridled executive power, especially in time of war, posed a great threat to the cause of republican government. The War of 1812 could doubtless have been better fought, and a more vigorous executive (of the Hamilton sort) would likely have made that better war possible. Yet Madison, with his profoundly philosophical temperament, could finally conclude that his actions had preserved the Union and the Constitution, as well as the political values these institutions embodied.

Most Americans agreed. The conduct of the war didn't become the object of partisan recriminations; instead, Americans (and President Madison along with them) happily returned their attention to domestic affairs. The final two years of Madison's presidency saw his popularity rise, and when he left office in March 1817 for his home, Montpelier, he retired as a respected statesman.

During his lengthy retirement of nearly two decades, Madison's active correspondence rarely touched on his conduct as president. His letters instead dwelled on the constitutional achievements on which his deeper legacy rests—and increasingly on the dangers to the Union posed by the peculiar institution of slavery, which was promoting a new and disturbing form of sectionalism in the years before his death.

★ ★ ★

James Monroe

5th President · 1817–1825

James Monroe

Rembrandt Peale painted this portrait near the end of James Monroe's second term in office. Standing just over six feet tall, the president had broad shoulders and a large frame.

Jack N. Rakove

JAMES MONROE WAS THE LAST member of the revolutionary generation to occupy the presidency and the last of the four Virginians who held that office for eight of its first nine terms. When Monroe moved into the White House in March 1817, the Democratic-Republican party he had served faithfully reigned supreme. His reelection in 1820, by a nearly unanimous vote in the electoral college, ushered in the Era of Good Feelings, so called because the rancorous partisanship that had roiled American politics since the mid-1790s had finally abated. Yet Monroe's reelection came amid the Missouri statehood debate that first exposed how deeply the question of slavery threatened to divide the republic along sectional lines. Divisions of another kind soon became evident in the sharply contested election of 1824. The idea that Monroe presided over an era of nonpartisan reconciliation is thus at best a half truth. New forces, new issues, and new personalities were already swirling through national politics, and the perturbations they released would be felt for years, indeed decades, to come.

Like his predecessors, Monroe brought a rich and varied experience to the presidency. At seventeen, he left the College of William and Mary to fight under Gen. George Washington in the military campaign of 1776, suffering a nearly fatal wound during Washington's Christmas Night assault on Trenton. Promoted from lieutenant to captain for his heroism, he recovered sufficiently to spend the winter of 1777–78 with the troops at Valley Forge. In December 1778, he resigned his commission and returned to Virginia, where he was appointed the state's military commissioner in 1780. Two years later—after reading law under the tutelage of his mentor, Thomas Jefferson—Monroe won election to the Virginia assembly and then,

These holster pistols are among Monroe's few surviving personal effects.

a year after that, to the Continental Congress. While Jefferson was abroad serving as minister to France, Monroe and James Madison became correspondents, allies, friends, and joint investors, purchasing a tract of land in central New York. Yet Monroe opposed adoption of the Constitution that Madison had labored so hard to produce, and the two men ran against each other for election to a House seat in the First Congress—a race Monroe lost.

NEVERTHELESS, AFTER MONROE'S 1790 election to the Senate, he joined the opposition faction that Madison and Secretary of State Jefferson soon formed. Despite this affiliation, he was able to secure in 1794 a diplomatic appointment to revolutionary France. President Washington's esteem for him slowly dwindled, however, when it became clear that Monroe's fondness for France made it uncomfortable for him to defend the administration's policy of strict neutrality. The mission ended with Monroe's recall in 1796 and his permanent estrangement from the Federalist administrations of Washington and John Adams.

Three terms as the Democratic-Republican governor of Virginia (from 1799 to 1802) were then followed by new European missions under President Jefferson (including the sensitive negotiation of the Louisiana Purchase in 1803). In 1808, Monroe and Madison again became rivals for their party's nomination to succeed Jefferson. Madison's victory produced a brief period of cool relations between the two men, ending with a strong mediating boost from Jefferson. In 1811, Madison made Monroe his secretary of state and, three years later during the War of 1812, he additionally asked Monroe to take on the duties of secretary of war from the discredited John Armstrong. In 1816, Monroe's turn finally came for the Democratic-Republican presidential nomination, bestowed on him by the party's congressional caucus by a margin of eleven votes, 65–54. Monroe handily defeated Federalist Rufus King in the ensuing general election.

This map shows the Western Hemisphere as it was known to cartographers during the early nineteenth century.

BORN
April 28, 1758

BIRTHPLACE
Westmoreland County, Virginia

DIED
July 4, 1831

PARTY AFFILIATION
Democratic-Republican

CHILDREN
Eliza, (unnamed son), Maria

MAJOR EVENTS

MARCH 15, 1817

Prodded by Gov. DeWitt Clinton, the New York state legislature approves funds for the construction of a canal between Buffalo and the Hudson River near Albany.

DECEMBER 26, 1817

President Monroe gives Gen. Andrew Jackson command of U.S. forces fighting the First Seminole War in Spanish Florida. Monroe feels justified in allowing Jackson to operate beyond the Georgia border because the Spanish have been unable or unwilling to control Seminole raiding.

FEBRUARY 2, 1819

The Supreme Court rules in Dartmouth College v. Woodward *that the state of New Hampshire has no right to change Dartmouth College's charter. The decision establishes the principle that states may not interfere with private contracts.*

As first lady, Elizabeth Monroe introduced to Washington social life a number of French customs. The most controversial of these involved the making and returning of social calls. The American custom was to call on visiting strangers— a practice that kept previous first ladies very busy. Mrs. Monroe, however, announced that, following the French custom, she would neither make nor return these calls. Her decision brought much grumbling, but Louisa Adams, John Quincy's wife, applauded the change, pointing out that the first lady shouldn't be "doomed to run after every stranger."

Monroe wore this formal suit while attending diplomatic functions as the U.S. minister to France.

The War of 1812 had led to a rebirth of American nationalism. Yet beneath this resurgent patriotism, serious disagreement remained over the nature of the American federal union and the role the national government should play in American life. Should it actively promote "internal improvements," such as turnpikes and canals, that would foster a national economy and thereby knit the Union more closely together? Should it use its regulatory authority over western territories, and its power to admit new states to the Union, to slow or halt the expansion of slavery?

On these issues, Monroe generally upheld the viewpoint of those Jeffersonians who voiced the deepest constitutional scruples and political doubts about the legitimacy and propriety of federal action. On the issue of internal improvements, Monroe denied that the government possessed a general authority to legislate, and he followed his predecessor, James Madison, in insisting that a constitutional amendment was required before such a policy could be pursued. Monroe worked hard to draft an earnest, if rather labored, defense of this interpretation, which he submitted to Congress along with his veto of a modest internal improvements bill. As one might have expected, Congress showed no interest in pursuing the required amendment.

THUS, IN THE DOMESTIC SPHERE, Monroe held to his belief in limited government; in foreign relations, however, he supported Secretary of State John Quincy Adams's assertion of a strong presence in international affairs. The landmark doctrine bearing Monroe's name—a declaration that the United States would not accept future colonization of the Americas by any European power—was announced in his annual message to Congress in December 1823. Its occasion was a suggestion from the British that the two nations issue a joint declaration against the transfer to any foreign power of the Latin American colonies that had recently revolted against Spanish rule. Preferring to avoid the implication that the United States needed British support for such a statement, Secretary of State Adams recommended to Monroe a unilateral declaration of policy, and the president agreed. The resulting doctrine far outlasted Monroe's tenure and indeed became more significant in the twentieth century than it was in the nineteenth.

More important (and ominous) at the time was the protracted crisis over statehood for Missouri, the single most troubling issue of Monroe's two terms in office. At the heart of this struggle lay a simple constitutional question: Could Congress use the seemingly routine occasion of admitting a new state to the Union to prohibit the existence of slavery in that state? In the House, where a majority of the representatives sat for northern states, newly vocal opponents of slavery had enough votes to win approval of motions linking Missouri's admission to such a prohibition on slavery. In the Senate, where sectional representation was essentially equal, these efforts were doomed. But while the impasse lasted,

"HE HAD A WONDERFUL INTELLECTUAL PATIENCE AND COULD...HOLD [A] SUBJECT IMMOVABLY FIXED UNDER HIS ATTENTION UNTIL HE HAD MASTERED... ALL OF ITS RELATIONS."

—*John C. Calhoun*—

congressmen debated heatedly the lawfulness and morality of slavery, the rights of states to regulate their own institutions, and the exact meaning of relevant language in the Constitution. And by no means were these debates, and the passions they vented, confined to Congress.

As president, Monroe neither controlled nor sharply influenced the course of debate in Congress—although his veto power certainly gave him an important role in its final resolution. He was convinced that Congress couldn't restrict the right of Missouri, once it became a state on equal footing with the rest, to choose its own institutions—just as Congress had no right to choose for South Carolina or New York. If slavery was lawful elsewhere, Monroe believed, it could be made so in Missouri. Yet, at the same time, he actively participated in the 1820 compromise, whereby Missouri and the free state of Maine were admitted simultaneously (thus preserving sectional equilibrium in the Senate) and a line was drawn in the remaining territory of the Louisiana Purchase indicating where slavery could exist and where it would be banned.

FEBRUARY 22, 1819

In a treaty negotiated by Secretary of State Adams, Spain cedes Florida. In exchange, the United States abandons its claim to Texas and assumes five million dollars' worth of Spanish debt.

MARCH 6, 1819

In another precedent-setting decision, the Supreme Court rules in McCulloch v. Maryland that states cannot tax the Bank of the United States (or limit any other power granted to the federal government by the Constitution).

Jean François Sené *painted this miniature of Monroe in Paris sometime during 1794.*

Most people in 1820 believed that Gov. William Plumer of New Hampshire cast his electoral vote for John Quincy Adams because he wanted to preserve George Washington's place as the only unanimously elected president. However, Plumer's son later suggested that his father simply didn't like Monroe (shown here in silhouette).

OPPOSITE:

Despite earning twenty-five thousand dollars a year as president, Monroe (shown here in an 1817 Gilbert Stuart portrait) left the White House seventy-five thousand dollars in debt. "Mr. Monroe...has received more pecuniary reward from the public than any other man since the existence of the nation, and is now dying, at the age of seventy-two, in wretchedness and beggary," John Quincy Adams wrote in 1831.

Monroe's support of the Missouri Compromise illustrates the inherent ambiguity in his legacy as president. On the one hand, the ability of Congress and the executive to fashion the Missouri Compromise suggested that men of good will could find solutions to the most difficult questions. Notwithstanding the passions this controversy roused, Monroe gained the easiest possible victory in his subsequent bid for a second term. Only a single presidential elector, isolated in the mountain fastness of New Hampshire, withheld his vote from the incumbent. For all practical purposes, the Federalist party had disappeared, and Monroe's great ambition, to bury the rancorous partisanship of the previous decades, had seemingly been attained. Like his predecessors, Monroe viewed the organized political competition of Democratic-Republicans and Federalists as a necessary evil at best; now that the necessity for competition had evaporated, the evils of party politics could also disappear.

> ## "I HAVE ALWAYS CONSIDERED [THE EXISTENCE OF POLITICAL PARTIES] THE CURSE OF THE COUNTRY."
>
> —Letter, 1822—

THE DEEPER REALITY WAS that the ideal of nonpartisan politics—indeed, the Era of Good Feelings itself—was a passing illusion. The debate over Missouri had exposed in the nation's politics an ulcerating wound that could be occasionally treated but never healed. As Monroe aged during his second term, the emerging leaders of the post-Revolutionary generation—John Quincy Adams, Henry Clay, John C. Calhoun, William Crawford, Andrew Jackson—began jockeying to become his successor. The ensuing presidential election of 1824 was bitterly fought and even more bitterly remembered. When Jackson received a plurality in both the popular and the electoral vote only to see John Quincy Adams emerge victorious in the House of Representatives, party politics was reborn. The Monroe presidency was thus but an interlude in the transition of power from one generation to the next and from one duality of political parties to another.

★ ★ ★

John Quincy Adams

6th President · 1825–1829

J. Q. Adams

John Patrick Diggins

Although his enemies accused him of rewarding supporters, punishing opponents, and otherwise playing the game of politics, John Quincy Adams was probably the most apolitical president in American history.

Adams used this microscope to pursue his lifelong interest in natural history. Among his hobbies was the domestication of wild plants.

OUR PERCEPTION OF American presidents is marked by irony. Although we desire from politics peace and prosperity, we tend to discount those politicians who preside over good times. Eras of stability and comfort are intrinsically the wrong times for producing great presidents because, without a war or an economic depression or the urgency of a moral cause, politics continue as usual and history remains inert, uneventful, prosaic.

Such was the setting of the administration of John Quincy Adams, the sixth president of the United States and the son of the second president, John Adams. Under less bland circumstances, this great man might well have made a great president, yet the reality of his career was such that he accomplished far more before and after he became president than when he actually occupied the White House. Before his administration, he served in many diplomatic positions in Europe, including ministries to Prussia and Russia, and he authored the Monroe Doctrine, declaring the Caribbean and South America off-limits to European imperial expansion. After his presidency, Adams played an even greater role in history, fighting as a congressman for the right to bring unpopular subjects (including slavery) to the floor of the House. He also defended a group of Africans who had seized control in July 1839 of the slave ship *Amistad*, winning their freedom in trials that went all the way to the Supreme Court.

JQA's presidency, however, could boast of few domestic accomplishments. It wasn't that he lacked driving ambition. On the contrary: What he had in mind for the country was a vigorous national government that would sponsor the building of roads, canals, universities, and other internal improvements as well as equip a strong army and navy. As president, he subscribed to an

active theory of states-
manship and went before
Congress often to present
his vision of America's
future. Yet, as Richard
Hofstadter wrote: "His
first annual message to
Congress was one of the
most wholly impolitic
documents in the history
of government," for it
went far beyond what
the polity was willing to
support. Not a single
section of the country
rallied to Adams's agenda,
and his administration
confronted a wall of
massive indifference.

The White House ball that Secretary of
State Adams gave for Sen. Andrew Jackson
was the social highlight of the Monroe
administration. Adams's flair for entertaining,
inspired by his foreign service, continued
during his own term.

Y ET IF ADAMS'S
message was impolitic,
it was also prophetic.
Many of the projects he called for were soon undertaken: canals
connecting the Chesapeake Bay to the Ohio and Delaware Rivers,
national roads binding regions of the country together, military
academies that trained the brightest youths in the service of the
nation. More significant, the prescience of Adams's overall project
was underscored by his awareness that the future of America depended
on the development of the nation's intellect. "Among the first, perhaps
the very first, instrument for the improvement of the condition of men
is knowledge," Adams told Congress in a message that called for the
establishment of astronomical observatories ("light-houses of the sky"),
research centers, and other educational institutions that would make
America an enlightened republic inspired by technological innovation—
such as the United States has become at the turn of the twenty-first
century. But Adams was facing a complacent country and feared its
stagnation: "Were we to slumber in indolence or fold up our arms and
proclaim to the world that we are palsied by the will of our constituents,
would it not be to cast away the bounties of Providence and doom
ourselves to perpetual inferiority?"

BORN
July 11, 1767

BIRTHPLACE
Braintree, Massachusetts

DIED
February 23, 1848

PARTY AFFILIATION
Democratic-Republican

CHILDREN
*George, John, Charles,
Louisa*

MAJOR EVENTS

OCTOBER 26, 1825

*After eight years
of construction, the
363-mile-long Erie
Canal opens for use.
Immediately, freight rates
between Buffalo and New
York City drop from one
hundred dollars to ten
dollars a ton. Canal tolls
will earn back its cost in
less than ten years.*

MAY 19, 1828

*Adams signs a tariff bill
originally introduced to
protect nascent New
England industry but later
amended by Jacksonians
in Congress to embarrass
the president and ensure
its defeat. The amended
rates on imports are so
high that both southern
planters and New
England shipping interests
call the new law the Tariff
of Abominations. The
tariff passed, however,
because New England
legislators decided that the
protection it offered was
worth the higher cost of
imported raw materials.*

Adams's marriage did little to change his solitary habits. He was twenty-nine years old and on a diplomatic errand to London when he began courting twenty-one-year-old Louisa Johnson, the English-born daughter of the American consul. "Though a social creature," White House historian William Seale has written, the first lady "brooded behind the scenes, often troubled by anxieties." According to Seale, the Adamses' marriage had its difficulties and they were "never happy together."

Adams was going against a Jeffersonian grain that distrusted the power of the state and believed that anything worthwhile could emanate only from the people. Adams's political cohorts had yet to see the virtue of increasing the authority of the president; meanwhile, the opposition Democrats disliked debts, monopolies, and centralized control, believing that government planning could lead only to political favoritism (which the Jacksonians ironically brought about with the spoils system).

John Quincy Adams came to the presidency as well prepared as a person could be. He was seven years old when the American Revolution broke out, and he would later remember watching with his mother the British assault upon Bunker Hill. At age ten, he accompanied his father on a diplomatic mission to France. Except for a brief return home in 1779, young Adams spent the next seven years in Europe, assisting his father and studying at universities in Germany, Russia, Sweden, England, Holland, and France. Returning again to Massachusetts in 1785, he attended Harvard, then studied law and was admitted to the bar before serving as U.S. minister to the Netherlands under George Washington and to Prussia under his father. He was

> # "IT IS SAID THAT HE IS... STIFF AND ABSTRACTED IN HIS OPINIONS, WHICH ARE DRAWN FROM BOOKS EXCLUSIVELY."
>
> —*William Henry Harrison*—

John Singleton Copley painted this portrait of the precocious U.S. minister to the Netherlands in 1796, the year that his father was elected to succeed George Washington as president.

elected to the Massachusetts State Senate in 1802 and the U.S. Senate (by his colleagues in the Massachusetts state legislature) the following year. While in Washington, he became disgusted with a Federalist party, now out of power, that had forsaken the nationalism his father had espoused and succumbed to factionalism and sectionalism. With tensions between the United States and England building during the years of the Napoleonic Wars, and with Federalist New England threatening to secede over Jefferson's embargo, Adams considered the Federalists unpatriotic, and he grew to dislike all political parties for putting their interests ahead of those of the nation. In 1814, he served as chief negotiator of the Treaty of Ghent, which ended the War of 1812, and the following year President James Madison named him U.S. minister to Great Britain.

In 1817, Adams became secretary of state in the Monroe administration. In that capacity he wrote masterful, if not always popular, state papers explaining how America should conduct itself in the area of international relations. He stood, for example, almost alone in his support for Gen. Andrew Jackson's attacks on Spanish Florida. Yet during his own presidency, Jackson would be his nemesis.

BY THE ELECTION OF 1824, the Era of Good Feelings that had characterized Monroe's years as president was over, and the Democratic-Republican party had splintered into factions. This was a period when no public figure openly "ran" for office but instead quietly maneuvered to attain his goal by one means or another. Having served brilliantly as secretary of state, Adams seemed the most qualified and most likely choice for president, but he had to prevail in a five-way race. Treasury Secretary William Crawford of Georgia thought he should be nominated after winning a caucus vote, Speaker of the House Henry Clay of Kentucky represented the rising West, and Secretary of War John C. Calhoun of South Carolina stood for the Deep South. Towering over the field, however, was the popular military hero Sen. Andrew Jackson of Tennessee.

For the first and only time in American history, no candidate obtained a majority of the electoral votes, so the election was sent to the House of Representatives. In January 1825, as the House prepared to vote, tension swept up and down Pennsylvania Avenue while large crowds followed the reports of wheeling and dealing by the backers of Adams and Jackson. When Adams emerged victorious on February 9 and announced that he would appoint Clay as his secretary of state, the cry of "corrupt bargain" went up from the Jackson supporters, who charged that Adams had "bought" the presidency by promising positions to Clay and others. Thus was the Democratic party born, as a vehicle to ensure the defeat of President Adams and the election of Jackson in 1828.

Had Adams been a partisan politician, he would have cleaned house on entering office. Instead, he allowed all Monroe's appointees to remain. Even worse, he refused to defend himself against the Democrats (for this would have

JULY 4, 1828

Ninety-year-old Charles Carroll, the richest American, breaks ground for the Baltimore & Ohio Railroad on the same day that President Adams turns over the first spadeful of dirt for the Chesapeake & Ohio Canal. The two projects are competing to haul freight across the Allegheny Mountains. In 1830, the B&O will become the first U.S. railroad to begin operation; the C&O canal, however, will never be completed.

__Charles Francis Adams__ purchased this desk, used by his father in the House of Representatives, at auction sometime around 1870. It was seated at this desk that John Quincy Adams suffered his fatal stroke in February 1848.

OPPOSITE:

Mathew Brady created this daguerreotype of Adams during the mid-1840s. Adams's nickname at the time was Old Man Eloquent, earned during his postpresidential career in the House.

This is the original manuscript of a poem that John Quincy Adams composed for his father on the occasion of John Adams's eighty-eighth birthday in 1823.

In conducting his extensive studies of the heavens and the earth, Adams used two matching globes: one terrestrial (shown here), and the other celestial. The globes were made c. 1800.

meant descending to the level of party politics). And he didn't see the need to build a coalition loyal to himself. He assumed that his unswerving integrity would suffice in place of popularity. Stern, short, and stocky, with a massive bald head and rheumy eyes, Adams was the last of a generation of gentry-class leaders who wouldn't stoop to cater to the masses in order to retain power. So he lost it. Blocked by the

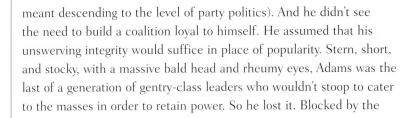

"MAY OUR COUNTRY BE ALWAYS SUCCESSFUL, BUT WHETHER SUCCESSFUL OR OTHERWISE, ALWAYS RIGHT."

—Letter to John Adams, 1816—

steadfast opposition of the Jacksonians in Congress, Adams had few substantial accomplishments as president. These primarily involved relations with South America and Mexico, where trade agreements were signed and new regimes encouraged to live by republican principles.

During the 1828 election, American politics sank into the sewers. The two candidates, the scholar Adams and the hero Jackson, seemed to offer the country a choice between, as the quip went, "one who can write and one who can fight." Adams's supporters accused Jackson of adultery, and the Jacksonians charged Adams with being a monarchist and an aristocrat, with having procured a servant woman for the emperor of Russia, and with having installed a billiard table in the White House at public expense. Jackson easily won the election, carrying the South and West as well as most working-class artisans and backwoods farmers. Jackson's was a class victory for democracy and a defeat of the intellectual in politics.

John Quincy Adams, America's most learned president, knew seven languages. He impressed Alexis de Tocqueville with his fluent French, read the classics in Latin and Greek, and stayed abreast of the latest developments in science. He saw himself as an educator as well as a philosopher, one who would lead public opinion rather than follow it. He favored conviction over compromise and preferred discipline to convenience. A rare president.

★ ★ ★

Andrew Jackson

7th President · 1829–1837

Andrew Jackson

Robert V. Remini

FOR MOST OF HIS LIFE, Andrew Jackson was an extremely controversial figure—yet ordinary Americans loved him, trusted him, and honored him "before all other living men," according to biographer James Parton. Jackson's credentials as a presidential candidate couldn't begin to match those of his predecessors, but because of his great victory over the British at the battle of New Orleans, he was elected in 1828 to the highest office in the land. Although many people loathed his presidential style and actions and others feared he might become an American Napoleon, they soon discovered that Jackson was a passionate spokesman for democracy. "The people are sovereign," he repeatedly insisted throughout his administration. "Their will is absolute." He even urged the direct election of all federal officers, including members of the judiciary. The term *Jacksonian Democracy* was later coined to describe the evolution of this country during the antebellum period from a republic to a popular democracy.

This extraordinary man was born on March 15, 1767, in the Waxhaw Settlement of South Carolina, the third son of Andrew and Elizabeth Hutchinson Jackson, farmers who had recently arrived in America from Carrickfergus, Ireland. Whatever prospects young Andrew might have had in the New World were dimmed by his father's death shortly before the future president's birth. Nevertheless, he attended local schools in the Waxhaws and at age thirteen joined the Continental Army. After serving as a messenger at the Battle of Hanging Rock, he was captured in April 1781 at the home of his cousin and taken prisoner. When he refused to clean a British officer's boots, he was slashed on the hand and forehead, the latter sword blow leaving a permanent scar. Jackson was then imprisoned at Camden, where he contracted smallpox, but was later released in a prisoner exchange. His mother, who had

Most portraits of Andrew Jackson omit the scar on his forehead, the result of a sword slash during the Revolutionary War. For Jackson, however, that scar was a permanent reminder of his hatred for the British.

Even these glasses couldn't obscure the steely blue of Jackson's eyes, which contemporaries described as "penetrating."

nursed him through his case of smallpox, died that same year of cholera while treating other American prisoners-of-war at Charleston. Jackson's two brothers also died during the Revolution.

IN 1784, HAVING DECIDED to become a lawyer, he moved to Salisbury, North Carolina, where he studied first with Spruce McCay and then with Col. John Stokes. He meanwhile gained a reputation for being, as James Parton has written, "the most roaring, rollicking, game-cocking, horse-racing, card-playing mischievous fellow, that ever lived in Salisbury." Despite this reputation, Jackson eventually received his license to practice law and, in 1788, migrated to Nashville in what was then the western district of North Carolina (later the state of Tennessee). There he fell in love with Rachel Donelson Robards, the estranged wife of Lewis Robards. The lovers fled to Spanish-held Natchez, where—believing that Robards had already obtained a divorce—they supposedly married sometime during 1791. Actually, Rachel's divorce wasn't finalized until 1793, when it was granted on the grounds that she had deserted her lawful husband and "hath, and doth, still live in adultery with another man." Andrew and Rachel were then legally married on January 17, 1794. They later adopted one of Rachel's nephews, naming him Andrew Jackson Jr.

The first attempt on a president's life took place at the Capitol on January 30, 1835, when house painter Richard Lawrence fired two pistols directly at Jackson. Both misfired. Lawrence was later declared insane and committed to an asylum.

BORN
March 15, 1767

BIRTHPLACE
Waxhaw, South Carolina

DIED
June 8, 1845

PARTY AFFILIATION
Democrat

CHILDREN
none

MAJOR EVENTS

SEPTEMBER 15, 1829

The abolition of slavery in Mexico so angers American settlers in the Mexican province of Texas that Mexican president Vicente Guerrero will later exempt them from the ban. Even so, the settlers are not appeased.

JANUARY 19–27, 1830

Daniel Webster of New Hampshire and Robert Y. Hayne of South Carolina engage in a famous Senate debate over the Tariff of Abominations. Hayne argues that states have the right to nullify federal laws, while Webster insists that all such laws must be obeyed.

AUGUST 21, 1831

In Southampton County, Virginia, Nat Turner leads the first (and only) sustained slave revolt in U.S. history. About sixty whites are killed before federal, state, and local militia use overwhelming force to put down the revolt two days later.

The charge that Andrew Jackson committed adultery with Rachel Donelson (shown here in a posthumous 1830 portrait) while she was still married to Lewis Robards became an important point of character assassination during the 1828 campaign. Although Jackson tried to shield his wife, she soon learned that her reputation had become the scuttlebutt of the political press corps. This may or may not have worsened her chronic heart condition. In any event, she died in December 1828. At her funeral, the president-elect declared, "Those vile wretches who have slandered her must look to God for mercy."

Jackson's marriage into one of the first families of Tennessee, his ability as a lawyer, and his close relationship with territorial governor William Blount advanced his political career rapidly. He served in 1796 as a delegate to the convention that drafted Tennessee's first constitution and was elected the state's first U.S. representative later that year. In 1797, the state legislature sent him to the U.S. Senate, but Jackson resigned the office after only five months to assume the duties of judge of the Superior Court of Tennessee. He served in that capacity for the next six years.

During his early career, Jackson engaged in several notable duels. In 1806, he quarreled with Nashville lawyer Charles Dickinson over a horse-race wager and killed him, but only after Dickinson had fired a bullet deep into Jackson's chest. Too close to his heart to be removed safely, the bullet remained lodged in Jackson's body for the remainder of his days. Another memorable gunfight, against brothers Jesse and Thomas Hart Benton, took place in 1813. This time, Jackson was shot in the shoulder, and again the bullet stayed with him until it was surgically removed in the White House in 1832.

> ## "I CANNOT BE INTIMIDATED FROM DOING THAT WHICH MY JUDGMENT AND CONSCIENCE TELLS ME IS RIGHT BY ANY EARTHLY POWER."
>
> —Letter, 1824—

This black felt hat, now faded to a greenish brown, was made for Jackson by Washington haberdasher S. W. Handy. Its wide black mourning band honored the memory of his late wife, Rachel.

Jackson also fought Indians successfully during his early years in Tennessee, and in 1802 he was elected major general of the state militia. Following the outbreak of war in 1812 and the Creek massacre of white settlers at Fort Mims, Jackson won a series of battles against the Creeks that brought him national acclaim. His most notable victory came on March 27, 1814, at Horseshoe Bend, where he crushed the remaining Creek forces. He then went on to defeat an invading army of eight thousand highly disciplined British regulars at New Orleans on January 8, 1815. Jackson's ragtag army of approximately four thousand soldiers consisted of a few regulars, some militiamen from Tennessee and Kentucky, townspeople, free blacks, pirates, and Indians. Casualties were more than two thousand for the British, fewer than two dozen for the Americans. This magnificent victory assured that, for the remainder of his life, Jackson would be a national hero—indeed, the most popular man in the United States. His soldiers called him Old Hickory in recognition of his strength and because of his devotion to their care and well-being. The nickname proved very useful in the political campaigns to come.

In 1817, President Monroe ordered General Jackson to the Georgia frontier to stop raids by Seminoles and runaway slaves operating out of Spanish-held Florida. Jackson exceeded his orders, however, when he invaded Florida in 1818 and turned out the Spanish governor. With the support of Secretary of State John Quincy Adams, he managed to avoid censure, and as a result of his boldness, Spain agreed to sell Florida to the United States. Jackson was appointed its first territorial governor in 1821 but served only a few months.

COMPARED TO SOMEONE LIKE John Quincy Adams, Jackson was poorly educated, with rather limited experience as a public servant. Yet his popularity among voters had reached such heights by 1824 that he inevitably became a contender for the presidency. In fact, the general won a plurality of both the popular and the electoral votes but fell short of the majority of electoral votes he needed for victory. The election instead went to the House of Representatives, where John Quincy Adams was chosen president on the first ballot. Jackson's supporters immediately charged Adams and Speaker of the House Henry Clay with having made a "corrupt

bargain" to deny Jackson his "rightful" election. That charge became the leading issue four years later when Jackson soundly defeated Adams.

At the outset of his presidency, Jackson promised strict economy in governmental expenditures so that he could eliminate the national debt, a goal he achieved by 1835 and one never repeated by any administration. To make government accessible to all— and to reward those who had assisted him in his election,

DECEMBER 12, 1831

The National Republicans, organized after 1824 to support President John Quincy Adams and oppose Jackson's Democrats, become the first major political party to hold a nominating convention, choosing Henry Clay to run for president. Previously, congressional leaders chose candidates in private caucuses.

APRIL 6, 1832

The Sauk Indian chief Black Hawk leads his people back to their Illinois homeland, from which they were evicted by government troops a year earlier. In response, the governor of Illinois calls out the state militia, and the Black Hawk War begins. In August, militiamen will corner Black Hawk's band in southern Wisconsin and massacre the Sauks.

APRIL 14, 1834

Encouraged by Henry Clay, Jackson's political opponents form the Whig party. Its members include National Republicans, anti-Jackson Democrats, and southerners who favor states' rights.

The artist who created *this poor likeness of General Jackson evidently believed that, because he acted like Napoleon, he must also look like the French emperor.*

President-elect Andrew Jackson greets well-wishers on his way to the capital.

Ralph E. W. Earl painted this portrait of Jackson during his first presidential term. Although most Americans thought of Old Hickory as a backwoodsman, he actually dressed quite fashionably.

Thousands of ordinary Americans traveled to Washington in March 1829 to see their hero take his oath of office. Afterward, most followed Jackson back to the White House, where merrymakers mobbed the mansion, breaking dishes, ripping draperies, and trampling the furniture. Jackson himself felt it necessary to escape the jubilant crowd through a back door.

particularly friendly journalists—Jackson also initiated what he called a "policy of rotation." Its avowed purpose was to end elitism and privilege in the operation of government, but critics called it the "spoils system" after the remark by Sen. William L. Marcy of New York, a Jackson ally, that "to the victors belong the spoils." Jackson was sincere in his desire to curtail elitism, yet, like many other presidents, he saw the advantages of using patronage as a political weapon to favor friends and punish enemies.

HIS FIRST MAJOR ACTION, which brought intense criticism then and later, was his enforcement of the Indian Removal Act of 1830. This act, which Jackson enthusiastically supported, authorized the coerced transfer of Native Americans to the newly created Indian Territory west of the Mississippi River (later the state of Oklahoma). The Cherokees sued in the Supreme Court to prevent their removal, but they were ultimately forced westward along the infamous Trail of Tears. The Seminoles in Florida fought a second war, lasting seven years, rather than submit to removal, but they too were finally defeated and transported west. The horror of the removal beggars the imagination and constitutes one of the most disgraceful and dishonorable actions in American history. Yet Jackson took comfort in his belief that removal, in addition to strengthening the security of the southern frontier, would prevent the inevitable annihilation of the Indians should they remain in the Southeast.

Meanwhile, South Carolina created an even more difficult problem for Jackson in 1832 when it passed an Ordinance of Nullification, declaring a recently enacted federal tariff null and void and threatening to secede if force be used against her. The state felt that continuing high tariffs on imported goods disproportionately benefited New England; however, its claim of the right to nullify unjust laws was most probably triggered by fear of future federal action against slavery. Jackson's response—his Proclamation of December 10, 1832—rejected nullification and secession as legitimate powers of a state. He thus became the first president to take this position publicly. "Disunion by armed force is treason," he stormed. "Are you ready to incur its guilt?" He insisted that

> "I HAVE GREAT CONFIDENCE IN THE VIRTUE OF THE GREAT MAJORITY OF THE PEOPLE, AND I CANNOT FEAR THE RESULT."
>
> —*Letter, 1828*—

"the Constitution and the laws are supreme, and the *Union indissoluble.*" Fortunately, passage of a compromise tariff in 1833, acceptable to both sides, ended the controversy and the immediate threat of civil war.

Even more controversial at the time, however, was Jackson's demand that Congress alter the operations of the Second Bank of the United States, believing the bank wrongly involved itself in political matters and provided the wealthy with unfair financial advantages. Ignoring the president's demands, Congress passed a bill in 1832 renewing the bank's charter, which Jackson promptly vetoed. The issue dominated the presidential election campaign of 1832, alienating eastern financial interests but helping Jackson with his core constituency of farmers and artisans. In the end, along with running mate Martin Van Buren, the president was reelected overwhelmingly.

"The Bank, Mr. Van Buren, is trying to kill me," Jackson said during the election, "*but I will kill it.*" And he did, instructing Secretary of the Treasury William Duane in September 1833 to withdraw all government deposits from the Second Bank. Duane refused because the law required him to notify Congress beforehand and Congress wasn't in session— whereupon the president sacked him and appointed Roger B. Taney in his place. Although Taney had not yet been confirmed by the recessed Senate, he carried out Jackson's orders, spending the fall and winter of 1833 placing federal funds in selected state banks, called the "pet banks."

MARCH 6, 1836

After a twelve-day siege, a large Mexican army under Gen. Antonio López de Santa Anna storms the San Antonio mission where 187 Texans under Col. William Barret Travis have been holding out. Only women, children, and a slave are spared. However, Travis's men, including frontier legends Jim Bowie and Davy Crockett, manage to slay 1,600 Mexicans (during the siege and the battle) before perishing themselves.

This cartoon first appeared *during the fall of 1833 soon after Jackson's order that no federal deposits be kept in the Second Bank. It illustrates the charge that, in acting without congressional approval, he had despotically exceeded his constitutional authority.*

OPPOSITE:

By 1845, the seventy-eight-year-old Jackson was in such poor health that few believed he could live out the year. Eager to capture the dying president's image while they still could, photographers such as Mathew Brady hurried to Nashville. Brady took this daguerreotype (still a new process) just seven weeks before Jackson's death.

When the Senate finally came back into session in December, Henry Clay persuaded his colleagues to censure both the president and Taney. Jackson fired back a "Protest" message in which he asserted his right, as head of the government, to determine and direct national policy. He claimed this power because, he said, he was the sole representative of all the people and responsible to them. The censure was expunged from the Senate's journal just prior to the end of Jackson's final term.

NEVER INTIMIDATED by Congress, Jackson vetoed more legislation than all his predecessors combined. In fact, by the skillful use of his veto power, Jackson gained enormous advantages over Congress and won for himself a significant role in the legislative process. In practice, unless a bill met with his approval prior to its passage, he promised a veto, something that Congress has often found difficult to override. One such veto struck down a bill funding a sixty-mile road in Kentucky from Maysville to Lexington, and this action seemed to block any further federal attempts at internal improvements.

"IF GENERAL JACKSON WANTS TO GO TO HEAVEN, WHO'S TO STOP HIM?"

—Anonymous—

In yet another controversial action taken while Congress was out of session, Jackson issued in July 1836 the Specie Circular, prohibiting the use of paper money in the purchase of federal lands. The enormous inflation that had followed Jackson's destruction of the Second Bank, an inflation Jackson himself had precipitated by not providing a substitute national banking system, demanded action. Totally committed to a policy of hard money (gold and silver), Jackson believed that requiring payment in specie for the purchase of public land would help end the land speculation craze then gripping the nation. Congress repealed this requirement almost immediately after the financial panic of 1837 swept over the country.

At the conclusion of his second term in office, Jackson retired to the Hermitage, his home outside Nashville, from which he kept up an active involvement in national politics until his death on June 8, 1845. He is buried beside his wife in the garden next to the mansion.

Jackson's pocket watch is among the personal items preserved at the Hermitage, once his Tennessee home and now a museum.

★ ★ ★

Martin Van Buren

8th President · 1837–1841

Richard M. Pious

Although Martin Van Buren certainly didn't cause the depression that dominated his term, he failed to take swift and effective measures to alleviate the suffering. This seemingly cold and callous attitude made him the Herbert Hoover of his day.

This hat case traveled with the president, who was considered in his time something of a dandy. Certainly, his fashion sense went well beyond what was typical for a Democratic politician of the Jacksonian age.

AS A FOUNDING MEMBER of the Albany Regency, Martin Van Buren created in New York State a political machine that came to dominate politics there after 1817. His early support for Andrew Jackson was instrumental in creating the new Democratic party during the 1820s, and he did more than most to elect Jackson president in 1828. For these reasons, among others, Jackson considered Van Buren his chief political heir and in 1836 smoothed the way for Van Buren to succeed him in the White House.

SHORT AND PORTLY and dandified in dress and manner, Martin Van Buren was no Andy Jackson. Political opponents ridiculed his foppish appearance and charged that he was a backstairs intriguer. Thurlow Weed, Whig boss of New York, liked to disparage Van Buren's "non-commitalism," while John Quincy Adams condemned his "fawning civility" to those in power. Van Buren, for his part, thought of himself as a man of prudence who preferred "to move step by step."

Personality aside, Van Buren was certainly one of the sharpest and most experienced politicians ever to become president. His impeccable credentials included service as both secretary of state and vice president under Jackson. Yet by 1840, one of the largest voter mobilizations in American history resulted in his defeat by a Whig candidate pledged to the concept and practice of a weak presidency. What had happened?

In March 1837, Van Buren took the oath of office from Chief Justice Roger B. Taney, a fellow Democrat. While Van Buren had only once been rejected by the Senate (after Jackson appointed him minister to Great Britain in

1831), Taney had been rejected twice, first as treasury secretary in 1833 and then as an associate justice two years later. To those who attended, the swearing-in ceremony appeared to signal the final triumph of the Democrats over the anti-Jacksonians who had previously dominated the Senate. However, the reality was that Van Buren entered office with the slimmest of margins, taking just 51 percent of the popular vote against William Henry Harrison and two other regional Whig candidates. Although the Democrats did have control of the Senate, Van Buren was

CAUCUS on the SURPLUS BILL.

This 1836 cartoon lampooned Jackson's reluctant endorsement of the Distribution Act, a Whig measure distributing surplus federal funds to the states. Knowing that Congress would override a veto, Jackson signed the popular "surplus bill" to abet Van Buren's campaign for the presidency that year.

without a working majority in the House. Even after the 1838 midterm elections, the Democrats had but a six-seat edge. Retaining the bulk of Jackson's loyal and experienced cabinet, Van Buren kept a firm hand on the executive branch, but his influence in the legislature, despite the high degree of party-line voting, was minimal.

To hold the Democrats together, Van Buren took a prosouthern position on slavery—which he never viewed as a moral issue, having been raised in a household with six domestic slaves. In his inaugural address, he identified himself—not for the first time—as "the inflexible and uncompromising opponent of every attempt on the part of Congress to abolish slavery in the District of Columbia." He further pledged to "resist the slightest interference with it in the States where it exists," threatening to veto any legislation that would do so. As proof of his good faith, he ordered returned to Cuba the fugitive slaves who had mutinied aboard

BORN
December 5, 1782

BIRTHPLACE
Kinderhook, New York

DIED
July 24, 1862

PARTY AFFILIATION
Democrat

CHILDREN
*Abraham, John,
Martin Jr., Smith*

MAJOR EVENTS

DECEMBER 29, 1837

In the Niagara River, Canadian troops burn the U.S. steamer Caroline, which has been ferrying supplies to Canadian rebels on Navy Island. The death of an American in the attack fuels anti-British sentiment.

MARCH 31, 1840

President Van Buren orders a ten-hour workday for laborers employed in federal public works projects. The ten-hour workday is among the chief goals of the nascent U.S. labor movement.

JUNE 1840

In London, William Lloyd Garrison leaves the World Anti-Slavery Convention when he learns that no female delegates will be seated. Among those turned away are Lucretia Mott and Elizabeth Cady Stanton, who begin to consider how other rights have been denied them.

Van Buren married his childhood sweet-heart, Hannah Hoes, whose family had also been living in Kinderhook for many generations. As one might expect, the Hoeses and the Van Burens were substantially intermarried, and by their closest relationship Hannah was Martin's first cousin once removed. The couple had four children before Mrs. Van Buren's death in 1819 from tuberculosis. Historians know very little about her because Van Buren mentioned her rarely in his correspondence and not at all in the eight hundred pages of his autobiography.

the Spanish ship *Amistad* in July 1839. (The order was later reversed by the Supreme Court.)

To appease the South even further, Van Buren continued Jackson's hard-line Indian policy. Under the terms of a treaty fraudulently obtained, the Cherokees were scheduled to be removed from Georgia during the spring of 1838. Van Buren wanted time to study the circumstances surrounding the treaty negotiations, but the governor of Georgia warned him of violence should federal troops delay in the removal. Thus, in Van Buren's mind, the only alternative to a massacre of the Cherokees was their inhumane and illegal relocation to the Indian Territory. For similar reasons, Van Buren continued fighting the Second Seminole War in Florida. It remains unclear whether the Seminoles, who resisted removal until 1842, or the Cherokees, who lost one-quarter of their number along the Trail of Tears, ended up better off. Certainly, both experiences gainsaid Van Buren's claims to Congress that the removals had been accomplished with "energy and humanity" and that government inter-action with the tribes had been "just and friendly throughout." With these remarks and also in his handling of the slave issue, Van Buren established the practice of northern Democratic leaders abetting southern interests. By the 1850s, such men would be disparagingly called "doughfaces."

Southern support, however, could do little to help Van Buren with the economic problems that beset the country just two months after his inauguration. On May 10, 1837, facing a shortage of hard currency, New York banks began refusing to convert paper money into gold or silver. The result was a panic. Five days later, Van Buren called for a special session of Congress to deal with the crisis. But the House refused to pass the president's proposed sub-treasury bill, and as the situation worsened, Van Buren's legislative maneuvers and countermaneuvers produced only stalemate and defeat. His subtreasury plan envi-sioned a system of depositories to hold government funds, replacing the network of "pet banks" favored by Jackson. It was the centerpiece of his presidency and of the post-Jackson Democratic anti–Second Bank crusade; therefore, the Whigs in Congress would have none of it, blocking Van Buren's program as best they could until the Independent Treasury Act was finally forced on them in 1840. Meanwhile, Van Buren had to rely solely on his executive prerogatives,

This wood engraving, which decorated an 1836 election ticket, depicts the diminutive Van Buren as the Little Magician, a nickname he acquired because of his reputation for political adroitness.

ordering collecting officers to hold public funds rather than deposit them in state banks—so many of which had failed, taking federal money with them. As a result, four-fifths of the treasury expenditures in 1838 were made by drafts drawn on collecting officers, in effect creating the subtreasury system by fiat.

The depression that followed the Panic of 1837 was in some ways a tonic for a president whose policies emphasized discipline, austerity, and sacrifice rather than an unearned distribution of national wealth. Believing the economy would improve only "by retrenchment and reform," Van Buren cut public expenditures by 20 percent and opposed internal improvements (and naval construction) that would have greatly reduced unemployment. (Individual states, meanwhile, borrowed more money to pay for such projects, particularly roads and canals to the West.)

The president unwisely chose this period of national suffering to redecorate the White House. Although he spent only the usual amount,

" HE ROWED TO HIS OBJECTIVE WITH MUFFLED OARS. "

—Rep. John Randolph—

about the same as John Quincy Adams had a decade earlier, the armies of painters, paperhangers, and upholsterers who marched in and out of the mansion each day made a poor impression and left him vulnerable to criticism. Nor did the posting of guards to prevent gate crashing at formal levees enhance his reputation. The president's enemies called him "Martin Van Ruin," blamed him for the depression, and generally derided his aristocratic manners and tastes—a put-on, in any case, because his father had been not a Dutch patroon but an upstate New York taverner.

ALTHOUGH FOXY in his acquisition of power, an overly cautious Van Buren was generally outfoxed while in possession of it. His prosouthern policies antagonized voters in his only real base of support (New York); consequently, as soon as he got into trouble, he had no reservoir of goodwill on which to fall back. As Jackson's protégé, he'd been forced on the party by Old Hickory in 1835, and those who had been bypassed relished the opportunity for some payback.

With regard to foreign policy, most antebellum presidents schemed to prevent the encirclement of the Union by acquiring as much additional territory as possible. Not Van Buren. Against the advice of most of his cabinet, he refused to move on either Texas or Canada. In August 1837, he refused Texas's offer to join the Union, fearing a renewed controversy

The scuttlebutt around Washington in 1828 was that Mrs. Peggy Timberlake was having an affair with Andrew Jackson's close friend John Eaton. Within several months, Mrs. Timberlake's husband died, she married Eaton, and Eaton became Jackson's secretary of war. Most of Washington society, particularly the wife of Vice President John C. Calhoun, ostracized Peggy Eaton (shown here in a Mathew Brady portrait); but Van Buren (with no wife to stop him) saw an opportunity to outflank his rival Calhoun. Van Buren's willingness to socialize with the Eatons pleased President Jackson immensely and was a significant factor in Jackson's choice of Van Buren for his running mate in 1832.

Although not a very good likeness, this commemorative clock graces a mantelpiece at Lindenwald, Van Buren's home in Kinderhook, New York. Lexicographers have speculated that the expression OK comes from Old Kinderhook, one of the president's many nicknames.

OPPOSITE:

When this daguerreotype was taken during the late 1840s, Van Buren was retired from government service but not from politics. His 1848 Free Soil candidacy, for example, was another illustration of the Red Fox compulsively playing the angles (and not getting anything lasting out of it). With both major parties drawing from the North and South—and therefore unable to act decisively on the issue of slavery—all Van Buren did was swing the election from the Democrats, who had repudiated his policies, to the Whigs, who had always opposed them.

over slavery, and instead negotiated an agreement with Mexico for claims arbitration. Two years later, he tamped down the bloodless Aroostook War over the unsettled boundary between Maine and New Brunswick. Van Buren's diplomatic maneuvers regarding Canada did isolate Great Britain from Mexico, making President James K. Polk's bold territorial coup of 1846 a viable policy—but this wasn't an advantage for which Van Buren was credited in 1840. During the presidential campaign that year, the Whigs sang "Van, Van's a used-up man" as they steamrollered over him, carrying even New York. One might say that Harrison's victory repudiated all that Van Buren had stood for—unless, as his critics have contended, the first professional party politician in the White House stood for nothing other than office.

> ## "IT WOULD BE DIFFICULT TO SAY FROM HIS PERSONAL APPEARANCE WHETHER HE WAS MAN OR WOMAN BUT FOR HIS LARGE...WHISKERS."
> *—Davy Crockett—*

IN 1844, VAN BUREN tried for another Democratic presidential nomination. He led on the first ballot with a majority of the votes, but his opposition to the annexation of Texas made him unpopular with the southern delegates, who denied him the two-thirds majority he needed to win. The first dark-horse nominee, Polk, was eventually chosen on the ninth ballot. Four years later, Van Buren ran yet again, this time resurrecting himself as the candidate of the Free Soilers. A Democratic splinter group with some support among "conscience" Whigs, the Free Soil party wasn't abolitionist but did oppose the extension of slavery to the territories, an issue Van Buren had consistently sidestepped as president in deference to his former party's southern regulars. Although he failed to win a single electoral vote, Van Buren did attract enough Democratic votes, especially in New York, to tip the election to Zachary Taylor and the Whigs. It was Van Buren's last hurrah (of sorts). Subsequently returning to the Democratic fold, he died in 1862, but not before witnessing the terrible consequences of the divisions between North and South that his presidency had tried to paper over.

★ ★ ★

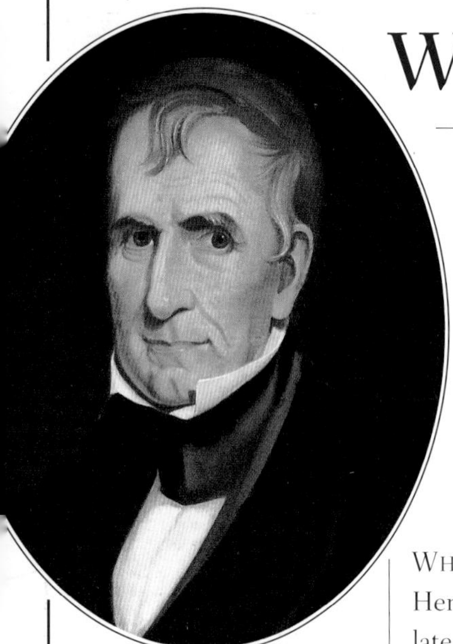

William Henry Harrison

9th President · 1841

Daniel Walker Howe

Unlike Whig leaders *Henry Clay and Daniel Webster, William Henry Harrison had no well-known views that might make him controversial.*

WHILE THE CAPITAL CITY was preparing for the inauguration of William Henry Harrison as president, Daniel Webster made excuses for his own late arrival at a dinner party. "I've just killed seventeen Roman pro-consuls," he explained in jest. Webster had been editing Harrison's lengthy inaugural address, and he felt that the new president was too eager to show off his classical learning. Even after Webster's pruning, Harrison's speech remained much longer and more learned than most inaugural addresses. The new president was trying to overcome the impression created by his campaign supporters that he was a back-woodsman who drank a lot. The campaign had been perhaps too successful, and Harrison needed a different image now. He wanted to be presidential, to show that he was really a Virginia gentleman in the manner of Washington, Jefferson, and Madison.

This desire would never be fulfilled. Instead, Harrison, nicknamed Old Tippecanoe, is best remembered for his military exploits, for winning the election of 1840 with the innovative "log cabin and hard cider" campaign, and for being the first president to die in office.

Like most successful politicians, Harrison knew how to cultivate a public image. His actual circumstances were far removed from the simplicity of the log cabin. He was born in 1773 to a wealthy and prominent family in the Tidewater section of Virginia. His father, Benjamin Harrison, served in the Continental Congress, signed the Declaration of Independence, and became governor of Virginia. William grew up a typical member of the Virginia gentry: sociable, hospitable, generous. He respected high culture and tolerated slavery.

In 1791, Harrison enrolled at the University of Pennsylvania Medical School, only to learn shortly after his arrival that his father had died. Obeying the late

The general would stand on this bootjack with one foot in front of the other, then wedge the heel of his front foot into the V-shaped notch. The notch held his boot in place as he pulled out his foot.

man's wishes, he continued his medical education until money became a problem later that year. In August, with the help of political connections, he obtained a commission in the army and, assigned to the Northwest Territory, saw action in 1794 at the Battle of Fallen Timbers as aide-de-camp to Gen. "Mad" Anthony Wayne. Wayne's victory over the Indians led in 1795 to the Treaty of Greenville, which opened up southeastern Ohio to white settlement.

I N 1798, HARRISON turned to politics, securing a position as secretary of the Northwest Territory. A year later, the territory chose him as its nonvoting congressional delegate. Surprisingly, he became chairman of the House committee on public lands, responsible for the Land Act of 1800, which made federal lands in the Northwest more available and easier to purchase. After the division of the Northwest Territory that same year, President John Adams appointed the twenty-seven-year-old Harrison governor of the Indiana Territory. Reappointed by Jefferson, he served twelve years.

The hoopla associated with the 1840 campaign mobilized voters, but there were also real issues at stake, especially those arising out of the ongoing depression.

A year before leaving office, Governor Harrison led the territorial militia against an Indian tribal confederacy organized by two Shawnee brothers, Tecumseh and Tenskwatawa (known as the Prophet). On November 7, 1811, Harrison's sleeping force was surprised near Tippecanoe Creek, a tributary of the Wabash, by a predawn raid. Harrison's men fought off the Indian attackers and destroyed their village, but Tecumseh's alliance remained strong and sided with the British during the War of 1812. Commanding U.S. forces in the Northwest, Harrison couldn't prevent a British invasion, but he did pursue the British and their Indian allies into Ontario as they withdrew, and his victory at the Thames River on October 5, 1813, secured the region. Notably, Tecumseh was among those killed.

BORN
February 9, 1773

BIRTHPLACE
Charles City County, Virginia

DIED
April 4, 1841

PARTY AFFILIATION
Whig

CHILDREN
Elizabeth, John Cleves, Lucy, William Henry Jr., John Scott, Benjamin, Mary, Carter, Anna, James

MAJOR EVENTS

MARCH 9, 1841

The Supreme Court rules in the case of the 1839 Amistad mutiny, freeing the mutineers and permitting them to return to Africa because they have been enslaved illegally. Former president John Quincy Adams argued the case on the Africans' behalf.

APRIL 1, 1841

George Ripley and twenty other Transcendentalists found Brook Farm, a utopian community in West Roxbury, Massachusetts, outside the bustling city of Boston. Especially praised for its innovative educational theories and practices, Brook Farm will become one of the most influential American experiments in communal living before it is disbanded in March 1846.

Harrison's inaugural address, the longest ever, lasted an hour and forty minutes. At sixty-eight, Harrison was also the oldest president ever inaugurated until sixty-nine-year-old Ronald Reagan took the oath of office in 1981.

Privately, Anna Symmes Harrison regretted her husband's decision to run for president in 1840. "I wish," she said after hearing the election results, "that my husband's friends had left him where he is, happy and contented in retirement."

After the war, Harrison, now a national hero, shifted his political base from Indiana to Ohio. As a congressman from Ohio, he joined with the followers of Henry Clay during the debates on Missouri statehood and helped Clay gain Ohio's electoral votes in the 1824 presidential election, eventually won by John Quincy Adams. Late in the Adams administration, Harrison was appointed minister to Colombia in accordance with Secretary of State Clay's pursuit of good relations with South America. It couldn't have pleased Clay that Harrison soon fell out with Colombian president Simon Bolívar, yet Andrew Jackson's election rendered the matter trivial. After Jackson's inauguration, the president recalled Harrison as part of his wholesale removal of Adams's appointees to make room for his own.

IN 1836, HARRISON made his first bid for the presidency, working with the new Whig party that had coalesced in opposition to Jackson and Van Buren. The Whigs, however, were not yet ready to unite behind a single standard-bearer, so the party ran several candidates. Harrison was the most impressive, winning seven states and coming close in Pennsylvania. These encouraging results persuaded Harrison and his supporters to devote themselves to securing the Whig nomination for 1840. At the party's national convention (held in December 1839), Harrison enjoyed the support of most northern Whigs, while the southerners generally favored Henry Clay. However, the adoption of a unit rule, by which all the votes of a state delegation were cast for the candidate with the majority of that state's votes, favored Harrison and gave him the nomination. Although the Harrison managers offered to let Clay choose the vice-presidential nominee, the defeated Kentuckian was too angry to respond. Attempting nevertheless to placate the southern wing of the party, the Harrisonians picked John Tyler of Virginia. Tyler had supported Clay for the nomination, but—as became apparent later—he lacked any commitment to the Whig party program.

The presidential campaign of 1840 is remembered for being the first of the modern sort, waged between two well-organized national parties, each employing speeches and demonstrations as well as printed media to attract attention and mobilize voters. The efforts were successful: 80.2 percent of legally qualified voters cast ballots, the third highest level of participation for any presidential election. When a visiting political speaker came to town, his supporters would typically organize a parade and pitch a huge tent to accommodate the anticipated crowd. Outside the tent, a barker would urge the curious to enter. (Techniques such as these—pioneered by itinerant revival preachers, for the clergy were the public relations experts of the time—were later adopted by traveling circuses.) Inside the tent, in addition to the speeches, there would be demonstrations and music. The most famous song of the campaign trumpeted the Whig slogan "Tippecanoe and Tyler, Too."

UNLIKE MODERN CANDIDATES, however, neither Harrison nor Martin Van Buren made public speeches or attended party rallies; this was left to their supporters. In fact, except for Stephen A. Douglas in 1860, no presidential nominee campaigned actively until William Jennings Bryan won the Democratic nomination in 1896. The first incumbent president to campaign personally for his own reelection was Theodore Roosevelt in 1904.

The most famous Whig symbols of 1840, the log cabin and the barrel of hard cider, came from a Democratic blunder. A party newspaper in Baltimore, intending to caricature Harrison's advanced age and lack of intellectual depth, wrote, "Give him a barrel of hard cider, and settle a pension of two thousand a year on him, and he will sit the remainder of his days in his log cabin." The Whigs seized upon the remark to demonstrate that their Virginia aristocrat shared the tastes of the common man.

Yet along with all the campaign hoopla, some serious issues were discussed. The campaign of 1840 took place during a depression brought on by the Panic of 1837. The Whig party's solution was a rechartered national bank that would issue more currency and thereby stimulate a recovery. The Whigs also argued for higher tariffs to protect domestic manufacturing and federal aid to interstate transportation projects (commonly called internal improvements). In its goals, this program was strikingly similar to that developed by John Quincy Adams and Henry Clay a decade earlier, called by Clay the American System. (Later, Harrison's death and Tyler's vetoes again frustrated Clay's efforts to enact the plan.) The incumbent Democrats countered that such massive government intervention would favor special interests and invite corruption.

> "IT WAS NOT THE ELECTION OF GENERAL HARRISON THAT WAS EXPECTED TO PRODUCE HAPPY EFFECTS, BUT THE MEASURES TO BE ADOPTED BY HIS ADMINISTRATION."
> —*Abraham Lincoln*—

Harrison's nickname *derived from his 1811 victory at Tippecanoe Creek, depicted here in a period image. "No military man in the United States commands more general confidence in the West," Henry Clay reported in 1812.*

OPPOSITE:

This mezzotint of Harrison was published in 1841. The people who knew him best thought him considerate, genial, and generous, perhaps overly so.

The Whigs drew support from manufacturers and commercial farmers hoping to benefit from the new tariffs and improved transportation. Many social reformers and evangelical Christians also backed the Whigs, seeing in a stronger government the means to promote public education, obtain justice for the Indians, discourage alcohol abuse, and perhaps even take steps against slavery. Unlike the Democrats, the

"HE COULD NOT STAND THE EXCITEMENT OF SEVENTEEN MILLION PEOPLE BUT DIED OF THE PRESIDENCY IN ONE MONTH."

—*Ralph Waldo Emerson*—

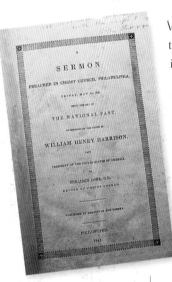

Special sermons were delivered all over the country on May 14, 1841, a national day of mourning for the late president. Being president, Harrison had received the best medical care available, which included bleeding and blistering—and unfortunately did more harm than good.

Whigs allowed women to participate in their campaign, an innovation that may have encouraged a few women to begin suffrage agitation later in the decade.

When the votes were counted, they revealed a landslide for the Whigs. In addition to ousting Martin Van Buren, the party won both houses of Congress and control of many state legislatures. On a cold March 4, 1841, Harrison delivered his long inaugural address designed to dispel any doubts about his qualifications. In it, he promised to implement faithfully the program of his party's congressional majorities. To demonstrate his vigor, he chose to brave the icy wind without a hat or an overcoat—a mistake, because he caught a cold that weakened him, making him vulnerable to the pneumonia that subsequently killed him.

In the one month his administration lasted, Harrison appointed a strong cabinet, led by Secretary of State Daniel Webster, and summoned a special session of Congress to remedy the economy. His tragic death robbed the American people of their chosen leader and the Whig party of the fruits of its triumph. Harrison was succeeded by his vice president, John Tyler, who quickly alienated the party that had elected him. Unlike his predecessor, Tyler had no intention of letting Daniel Webster (or Henry Clay) decide which Romans he could invoke or what programs he should support.

★ ★ ★

John Tyler

10th President · 1841–1845

John Tyler [signature]

Richard M. Pious

JOHN TYLER WAS BORN to wealth, privilege, and public service. He was raised on a Virginia plantation overlooking the James River and attended William and Mary College before joining a prestigious Richmond law firm headed by former U.S. attorney general Edmund Randolph. Tall and slender, with a patrician's Roman profile, the young Tyler enjoyed a conventional career in politics: member of the Virginia House of Delegates (from 1811 to 1816), four years in the House of Representatives, another two in the Virginia legislature, and then (like his father before him) governor of Virginia from 1825 until 1827, the year that he entered the U.S. Senate. Tyler was a consummate Washington insider who used his father's familiarity with leaders such as Thomas Jefferson (and his own friendship with Dolley Madison) to acquaint himself with all the people in the capital worth knowing.

Yet Tyler was more than just a well-connected planter's son. He had strong ideas and convictions: He opposed a standing army and high tariffs, thought the Missouri Compromise such an abuse of federal power that he resigned from Congress in protest, and later abandoned the governorship of Virginia because that office had too little power. Tyler reluctantly supported Andrew Jackson's elections in 1828 and 1832 because he shared with Jackson the same position on tariffs. However, when Jackson threatened to use federal force against South Carolina during the 1832 nullification crisis, Tyler twice condemned the president on the floor of the Senate for what he considered Jackson's abuse of executive power. Tyler felt so strongly, in fact, that he cast the only vote in the Senate against the compromise that defused the crisis. He ended his Senate career in 1836, when he resigned rather than vote to expunge a resolution of censure passed earlier against Jackson.

John Tyler showed, importantly, that a president without a shred of popular, party, or cabinet support could defy Congress and determine the course of the nation. Moreover, he demonstrated this during a period in which the Jacksonian version of a strong executive had been repudiated.

This sketch of Tyler was drawn (not very well) by artist Samuel F. B. Morse, whose development of the telegraph was encouraged by the president.

This 1844 cartoon shows Tyler quitting the presidential race to follow his new wife, Julia, down the road to Texas.

BORN
March 29, 1790

BIRTHPLACE
*Charles City County,
Virginia*

DIED
January 18, 1862

PARTY AFFILIATION
Whig

CHILDREN
*Mary, Robert, John Jr.,
Letitia, Elizabeth, Anne,
Alice, Tazewell, David,
John Alexander, Julia,
Lachlan, Lyon, Robert
Fitzwalter, Pearl*

MAJOR EVENTS

DECEMBER 3, 1844

After years of effort, former president John Quincy Adams (now a Massachusetts congress-man) finally persuades his colleagues in the House to lift the gag rule regarding antislavery petitions.

JANUARY 23, 1845

Congress creates a national election day, specifying that presidential elections in every state will henceforth be held on the first Tuesday following the first Monday in November.

MARCH 3, 1845

On the last day of Tyler's term (and for the first time in U.S. history), Congress overrides a presidential veto. The bill in question prevented the treasury from paying for new ships commissioned by Tyler.

Tyler then joined the Whig party being organized by Henry Clay and Daniel Webster and in the 1836 election ran as the vice-presidential candidate on two of the four regional anti-Jackson tickets. As a states' rights advocate, he was useful to the Whigs, who thought his position might entice southern Democrats to abandon New Yorker Martin Van Buren. Although the Whigs lost that election, Tyler emerged untarnished—except that, by defecting from the Democrats, he ended any conventional career he might have pursued in Virginia politics.

THE WHIG PARTY'S presidential nominee for 1840, William Henry Harrison, had been born in the same Virginia county as Tyler, and both their fathers had served as Virginia governors; yet Harrison had long since become associated with Ohio, where he now resided, and the Whigs still needed a southerner to balance their 1840 ticket. After 1837, Tyler had a following in neither major party. He disagreed with the Democrats on constitutional issues and with the Whigs on financial and tariff programs. Yet the Whig convention unanimously chose Tyler for its vice-presidential nominee because he came from the right state and was fiercely anti-Jackson. For his part, Tyler accepted the Whig nomination primarily to undercut Van Buren, who was running for reelection. It didn't seem to matter that Tyler's own ideas were more Democratic than Whiggish, particularly his financial policies.

When Harrison died exactly one month into his four-year term, he left Tyler in a somewhat precarious position, both politically and constitutionally. In the case of a president's death (something that had never

Contemporaries often described Tyler's first wife, Letitia, as quiet and introverted. However, the wealth and political prominence of her family, the Christians, made her an advantageous match for Tyler. Their marriage was apparently happy, but an 1839 stroke left her partially paralyzed, and she died in September 1842 during Tyler's second year as president.

Tyler sincerely mourned his first wife, but the fifty-two-year-old president was determined to remarry. After a socially acceptable interval, he began discreetly courting Julia Gardiner, the twenty-two-year-old daughter of a New York state senator. Their marriage—held in New York City on June 26, 1844—was kept secret until the newlyweds returned to Washington.

happened before), the Constitution says "the same" shall devolve upon the vice president, but the antecedent of this phrase is unclear: "The same" may refer to "the powers and duties of the office" (in which case Tyler would remain vice president) or to the office itself (in which case Tyler would become president). Riding into Washington from his plantation the day after Harrison's death, Tyler was addressed by Whigs as the "Vice President, Acting as President." Tyler, however, insisted on being called "President Tyler," and he later made his point by refusing to open mail addressed to "Acting President Tyler."

H IS PENCHANT FOR STRONG unilateral action quickly established the pattern for his presidency. At his first cabinet meeting, the Harrison appointees who made up the Whig cabinet pressed the idea that Tyler should obtain their consensus before acting. It was a throwback to the "conciliar government" favored by Madison, Monroe, and John Quincy Adams. "I am very glad to have in my Cabinet such able statesmen as you," Tyler replied. "But I can never consent to being dictated to as to what I shall or shall not do....I am the President....When you think otherwise, your resignations will be accepted."

> "HE LOOKED SOMEWHAT WORN AND ANXIOUS, AND WELL HE MIGHT, BEING AT WAR WITH EVERYBODY."
>
> —*Charles Dickens*—

At Whig urging, he called a special session of Congress (the regular session not being due to convene until December). Henry Clay pressed the Whig banking bill, which was designed to overturn Jacksonian banking policies by abolishing Van Buren's subtreasuries and resurrecting the Bank of the United States, killed a decade earlier by Jackson's veto. Near the end of the session, Tyler himself vetoed a compromise measure drafted by Daniel Webster with cabinet approval. Two days after this veto, all the cabinet secretaries (except for Secretary of State Webster, who was engaged in sensitive negotiations with Great Britain) resigned, claiming that Tyler had deceived them. Once Congress adjourned, the

Whigs issued a statement disassociating themselves from the president. He was now truly a man without a party. Whigs called for his resignation so that the Whig president pro tempore of the Senate might succeed him, followed by a special election (under existing law) to fill the remainder of Harrison's term.

Tyler refused to buckle. "My back is to the wall," he wrote a friend, adding that he would "beat back the assailants." Using recess appointments to avoid confirmation votes that he knew he would lose, Tyler formed a cabinet of Democrats and blocked Whig bills that would have distributed among the states the receipts from the sale of public lands to pay for public works and other internal improvements. When Tyler failed to get his own financial program enacted, the stalemate resulted in reinstatement of the ineffective Jacksonian system of depositing federal funds in unstable state banks.

Like Andrew Jackson, Tyler played for high stakes, and hostile congressional majorities were just as unable to bring him down. This daguerreotype shows the little-scarred Tyler in his postpresidential years.

Frustrated Whigs replayed the censure politics used against Jackson and got the same result. Led by John Quincy Adams, a Whig-dominated Select Committee of Thirteen charged in its report to the House that Tyler had so misused his veto power that the misuse constituted an impeachable offense. As Jackson had, Tyler responded with a "Protest" in which he defended his conduct. Taunting the Whigs, the president declared that if he had really committed an impeachable offense, Congress should be able to remove him from office; any lesser sanction, Tyler said, such as a vote of censure or an adverse committee report, had no constitutional standing.

When Webster finally resigned in 1842 following completion of the Webster-Ashburton Canadian border treaty, Tyler eagerly took control

of foreign policy. So beleaguered in other respects, he could freely, in foreign affairs, use the prerogative powers of the presidency to make national policy. His agents at the Texas Convention promoted the new republic's second application to join the Union, and after the Senate

This is a view of the parlor at Tyler's Charles City, Virginia, plantation, which he named Sherwood Forest.

In 1840, four years before marrying Tyler, Julia Gardiner appeared in this unusual ad for a New York City department store. "I'll purchase at Bogert & Mecamly's," says the sign she's carrying. "Their goods are beautiful and astonishingly cheap." The advertisement is noteworthy because it was one of the first in the country to feature a testimonial.

OPPOSITE:

A month before he left office, Tyler (shown here in a G. P. A. Healy painting) threw a huge ball at the White House. As the crowds mobbed the East Room, he remarked, "They cannot say now that I am a president without a party." It was one of the few times Tyler cracked a joke in public; he much preferred to share his humor and zest for life with his lovely young wife and eight children from his previous marriage. (He would later have seven more with Julia.) "Wit I prefer to youth!" she wrote him on his sixty-second birthday.

defeated the treaty of annexation he had submitted, the president developed a roundabout strategy to accomplish his goal. He got congressional supporters to introduce a joint resolution of annexation that required only majority votes in the House and Senate, thus completing the annexation through legislative rather than treaty means.

THE ANNEXATION OF TEXAS was particularly controversial because it couldn't be separated from the question of expanding slavery westward. Tyler pushed for annexation for three reasons: He was an expansionist at heart, he was sympathetic to the slaveholders, and he hoped also to gain support for a third-party candidacy of his own in 1844. On the other hand, by opposing Tyler's annexation policy, Henry Clay ingratiated himself with northern antislavery Whigs and cemented his own strength within the party. Denied the Democratic nomination in 1844, Tyler did briefly run as a third-party candidate, but he withdrew before the election so that Democrat James K. Polk could defeat the Whigs. Exhausted from his battles, Tyler was happy to leave Washington in 1845 and return to plantation life.

But he didn't leave politics altogether. In 1852, he rejoined the Democratic party, and in February 1861, Tyler presided over the Richmond Peace Convention, during which he tried to arrange a compromise between the regions. Shortly before Abraham Lincoln's inauguration in March, Tyler met with the president-elect at Willard's Hotel in Washington, where he delivered to Lincoln resolutions passed by the convention. (These included a proposal to extend slavery along the Missouri Compromise line all the way to the Pacific.) When Lincoln chose not to support Tyler's initiative (because he didn't believe that the Peace Convention delegates had much support among southern Democrats), the former president joined other prominent Virginians in accepting the inevitability of secession. In November 1861, Tyler was elected to the newly formed Confederate House of Representatives, but he died before taking his seat.

Until the Peace Convention, Tyler had always been a maverick and a loner, and it's ironic that, near the very end of his career, he tried to forge a national consensus—especially given his expansionist policies, which had done so much during the 1840s to exacerbate tensions between the regions.

★ ★ ★

James K. Polk

11ᵗʰ President · 1845–1849

Thomas Fleming

James K. Polk, shown here in his official portrait (painted in 1846), represented well the will of the majority. "If he had ever tried to control or dominate the people," one historian has noted, "his colorlessness would have been fatal, but as a mirror he was adequate to his task."

This inkwell of Polk's was made from volcanic ash.

THE DEFINING MOMENT in James Knox Polk's life occurred in 1823, when he asked Gen. Andrew Jackson for advice on how to further his political career. "Stop this philandering!" Jackson said. "You must settle down as a sober married man."

The handsome twenty-seven-year-old Polk was secretary of the Tennessee state senate—a job that had ignited in him a passion for politics. But he had been giving the ladies of Tennessee equal time in his off-hours.

"Which lady shall I choose?" Polk asked. One suspects a wry evasion in the question. The austere fifty-six-year-old warrior was an unlikely source of matrimonial advice.

"The one who will never give you no trouble," Jackson said. "Her wealth, family, education, and health are all superior. You know her well."

"You mean Sarah Childress?" Polk asked, amazed by the general's perspicacity. The young lady in question had already made an impact on his psyche. "I shall go at once and ask her."

Tall, dark, and intelligent, nineteen-year-old Sarah Childress revealed that she too had a passion for politics. She told Polk she would accept his proposal if he ran for a seat in the state legislature—and won. He did exactly that, and they were married on January 1, 1824.

A year later, Polk was in Congress, where he was soon recognized as a steadfast backer of Andrew Jackson and an ardent member of the Democratic party. For eight tumultuous years, Polk politicked for Jackson in the House of Representatives, backing his controversial veto of the Bank of the United States and his negotiations to acquire Texas from Mexico. Polk was undoubtedly privy to Old Hickory's continuing desire to bring this immense territory into the Union after the revolt led by Tennesseans such as Sam Houston and Davy Crockett had set up the Texas Republic in 1836.

From 1835 to 1839, Polk was speaker of the House, a tribute both to his leadership abilities and to Sarah's talents as a Washington hostess. His second term as speaker coincided with turmoil in the Democratic party and in the nation. The Panic of 1837 rocked the economy, and Martin Van Buren was a weak president. The resurgent Whig party, led

The Mexican War *was the first covered by large number of U.S. correspondents, which contributed to its popularity. Publishers had difficulty keeping up with the demand for lithographs, such as this one commemorating the battle of Monterrey.*

by Henry Clay, began winning state and congressional elections. Polk decided to leave Washington and run for governor of Tennessee in order to reclaim for the Democrats Jackson's home state. He and Sarah hoped that a victory would make him the Democratic party's vice-presidential candidate in 1840.

Polk won the election, and Old Hickory did everything in his power to get him the vice-presidential nomination. But Martin Van Buren decided not to select a vice president in his run for a second term, so Polk was relegated to seeking reelection as governor of Tennessee in 1841. He collided with a backwoods Whig buzz saw named Slim Jimmy Jones, who used witticisms and sarcasm, and the momentum of the Whigs' 1840 presidential victory, to defeat the earnest Polk. In 1843, Slim Jimmy repeated the performance, seemingly putting an end to Polk's political career.

BORN
November 2, 1795

BIRTHPLACE
Mecklenburg County, North Carolina

DIED
June 15, 1849

PARTY AFFILIATION
Democrat

CHILDREN
none

MAJOR EVENTS

DECEMBER 29, 1845

The United States annexes Texas, which becomes the twenty-eighth state. The formalities come nine months after Mexico's severance of formal diplomatic relations with the United States in response to President Polk's support for annexation.

JUNE 14, 1846

American settlers in California declare their independence from Mexico. The insurrection becomes known as the Bear Flag Revolt because the flag the settlers raise above Sonoma features a large grizzly bear.

JULY 1, 1847

The first U.S. adhesive postage stamps go on sale. People desiring to send mail can purchase either five-cent Ben Franklin or ten-cent George Washington stamps.

In 1848, when the first gaslights were installed in the White House, Sarah Childress Polk (who preferred candlelight) refused to allow workers to convert the chandelier in the Blue Room. On the night of the first gaslit reception, all the burners went out around nine because no one had thought to ask the Capital's gas plant to stay open late. The White House went dark, except for the spot beneath the Blue Room chandelier where Sarah Polk stood bathed in candlelight.

Polk (pictured here with his cabinet) *personally planned the overall strategy for the Mexican War and supervised the details of the campaign all the way down to the purchase of mules.*

The next year, Andrew Jackson discovered that Van Buren, the front-runner for the 1844 Democratic nomination, was waffling on the admission of Texas to the Union. Old Hickory, who had remained the real leader of the Democratic party, decreed that it was time for a new candidate, and he settled on James Knox Polk. With the British meddling in the politics of the bankrupt Texas Republic as well as disputing American claims to Oregon, Polk hardly needed marching orders from the Hermitage. He made annexation of Texas the cutting edge of his campaign and said he wanted Oregon all the way up to latitude 54°40', then the boundary of Russian Alaska. For Polk it was "Fifty-four Forty or Fight!" The slogan stirred every Jacksonian Democrat in America.

YOUNG HICKORY, as some Democrats called Polk, won the election by a whisker-thin margin. A shift of just five thousand votes in New York, for example, would have given the White House to Henry Clay. Some presidents in his position, feeling that they lacked a mandate to govern, might have begun seeking compromise solutions with the opposing party in Congress. Instead, in the style of his mentor, Polk told a fellow Tennessean: "I intend to be myself President of the United States." One observer was soon telling Andrew Jackson, "Our friend… came here to be THE PRESIDENT, which at this date is as undisputed as that you was THE GENL. at New Orleans."

In the spring of 1845, Andrew Jackson died, and Polk confronted a Democratic party split into antagonistic factions. In the North, Martin Van Buren and his followers sulked and criticized. In the South, slavery was already disturbing the Democrats' solidarity with their northern brethren. Other leaders, such as Thomas Hart Benton of Missouri, put their own egos and presidential ambitions far ahead of loyalty to the party or Polk.

The new president was undaunted. He told friends that he had four goals: (1)

to pass a tariff that would be acceptable to both the North and the South; (2) to bring order out of the country's financial system by establishing an independent treasury, an idea he had pushed through as speaker of the House only to see it repealed by the Whigs; (3) to settle the Oregon boundary; and (4) to acquire California. He might have added a fifth goal: to keep Texas, which had been annexed in the closing days of the Tyler administration with the covert help of President-elect Polk. Meanwhile, the Mexicans were making ominous noises about reconquering the Lone Star State.

When Congress met in the fall of 1845, Polk had a tariff reduction measure and an independent treasury bill waiting. Using personal cajolery as well as relentless pressure applied by members of his cabinet, Polk

> # "THOUGH I OCCUPY A VERY HIGH POSITION, I AM THE HARDEST WORKING MAN IN THE COUNTRY."
>
> —*Diary entry, 1847*—

spent the next six months working on recalcitrant congressmen and getting the bills passed. Soon after, he settled the Oregon boundary by skillfully isolating the extremist westerners in his party and accepting a British offer to make the Forty-ninth Parallel the border. Texas and California, however, proved to be more difficult to settle politically.

The Mexican government, having broken relations with the United States after the annexation of Texas, spurned Polk's attempts to negotiate. Twice the Mexicans refused to talk with envoys Polk dispatched to Mexico City. Meanwhile, both diplomats warned the president of the "clamor for war" that had broken out in Mexico. By the spring of 1846, both countries had armies on the Rio Grande, and when the Mexicans ambushed an American cavalry patrol, killing sixteen men, Polk declared war.

Polk was taking a huge gamble. The Mexicans had a well-equipped army of thirty-two thousand veterans, hardened by years of civil war. The U.S. regular army numbered just seven thousand and had fought no one but a few restless Indians for the previous three decades. But Polk swiftly proved himself a masterful commander in chief:

JANUARY 24, 1848

While building a sawmill for John Sutter on the American River about forty miles from Sacramento, James Marshall discovers gold. When news of the find appears in the August 19 New York Herald, gold seekers rush to California, swelling the population there from fifteen thousand to three hundred thousand.

JULY 19–20, 1848

About three hundred women and forty men attend the women's rights convention in Seneca Falls, New York, the hometown of Elizabeth Cady Stanton. In addition to organizers Stanton and Lucretia Mott, attendees include Frederick Douglass, who delivers an impassioned speech on behalf of women's right to vote.

Sarah Polk *wore this cameo brooch, featuring a likeness of the president, during her years in the White House.*

George P. A. Healy,
who painted Polk's
official White House
portrait in 1846,
captured a substantially
more aged president
in 1848.

Andrew Jackson
appeared frequently
in satires of the 1844
campaign. In this one,
he is shown leading
Polk and running mate
George M. Dallas toward
Salt River, a figure of
speech meaning
political disaster.

He blended enthusiastic volunteer regiments with the regulars, avoiding the disastrous reliance on raw militia that had made such a fiasco of the War of 1812.

Polk also displayed an audacity worthy of Andrew Jackson in his prime. While the main American army invaded Mexico to "conquer a peace," he dispatched smaller armies to New Mexico and California, which they captured with ease. The American army, officered in the lower ranks by hundreds of recent graduates of West Point, never lost a battle.

On the home front, however, the war turned into a political nightmare. Gen. Zachary Taylor started running for president after winning a series of battles on the Rio Grande and in northern Mexico. He smeared Polk with vicious letters to friends, who leaked them to the press. A divided Congress refused to let Polk create a new rank of lieutenant general so that he could appoint a commander loyal to him.

I N AUGUST 1846, Rep. David Wilmot—a Democrat but from Pennsylvania, a state that hated Polk's lowered tariff—stabbed the president in the back by proposing an amendment to an appropriations bill banning slavery in any territory acquired from Mexico. Whig newspapers, scenting victory in 1848, belabored Polk for fighting a war for territory rather than principle. In New England, the Mexican War was denounced as a proslavery conspiracy.

Polk grimly hunkered down in this political firestorm. He was determined to pursue the war until Mexico agreed to negotiate the surrender of California and New Mexico. This final goal of his presidency he achieved in the fall of 1847, when an American army led by Gen. Winfield Scott battered its way into the Mexican capital. Polk shrewdly sweetened the ensuing peace treaty when he agreed to pay Mexico fifteen million dollars for its lost provinces.

Polk's victorious war and his peaceful settlement of the Oregon boundary dispute made the United States the continental power we know

PILGRIMS' PROGRESS.

today. Yet Polk left office an unpopular and very tired man. He had achieved his goals by making himself a strong president in the Jacksonian tradition. Unfortunately, Polk had neither the military reputation nor the overpowering personality to manage this role easily. Scarcely a voice in the Democratic party rose to defend him when Whig newspapers sneeringly called him Jim Thumb, after P. T. Barnum's famous midget.

President Polk instead had to rely on unremitting toil: endless negotiations with influential congressmen; countless conferences with cabinet members; and backbreaking labors at his desk, preparing instructions to generals and diplomats and special messages to Congress. On March 3, 1848, Polk noted in his diary: "This day closes my third year in the presidential office. They have been years of incessant labor [and] anxiety."

James and Sarah Polk posed by themselves for the camera only once. This daguerreotype was taken in the White House during 1847 or perhaps a year later.

President Polk wore this smoking jacket during his very few hours of relaxation in the White House.

"A GREAT PRESIDENT. SAID WHAT HE INTENDED TO DO AND DID IT."

—Harry S. Truman—

Sarah Childress Polk was the president's chief confidante and adviser during his four-year marathon, and she watched with growing concern as Polk's health began to deteriorate. As a congressman, when under political stress, he had suffered severe bowel and stomach complaints. Now these ailments began to recur with alarming frequency, especially during his last year in the White House.

Polk's lack of personal popularity didn't help his condition. During an 1847 trip to North Carolina, one of his few brief vacations from the White House grind, he drew no crowds; it seemed to observers that no one had the slightest interest in meeting him. When he left office in 1849, Polk traveled home to Tennessee by a circuitous southern route through New Orleans in order to spare himself the abuse he feared he would receive if he took a more direct overland route.

Sarah Polk carried this gift from her husband on his inauguration day. The fan is decorated with the portraits of Polk and his ten presidential predecessors.

COMPOUNDING POLK'S sense of failure was the election of his treacherous enemy, Gen. Zachary Taylor. The vengeful Martin Van Buren had split the Democratic vote in 1848 by running as the candidate of the antislavery Free Soil party. An appalled Polk, who believed (as Andrew Jackson had) that the Democratic party's ability to transcend the issue of slavery was vital to the survival of the Union, could only say, "Mr. Van Buren is the most fallen man I have ever known."

A few weeks after he returned to Tennessee, the exhausted Polk felt well enough to begin lining the shelves of his library with books. This mild effort brought on another intestinal attack. On June 15, 1849, three months after he left the White House, Polk was dead.

"THOUGH IN NO SENSE A MAN OF BRILLIANT PARTS, HE MAY BE SAID TO HAVE BEEN A THOROUGHLY REPRESENTATIVE MAN OF HIS CLASS, A STURDY, UPRIGHT, STRAIGHTFORWARD PARTY MAN."

—*Woodrow Wilson*—

OPPOSITE:

The Whig campaign slogan for 1844—"Who Is James K. Polk?"—was not very catchy, but quite a reasonable question. Except for some politicians, few people outside Tennessee had ever heard of him.

If there is a Valhalla where great presidents gather, it's not hard to imagine Andrew Jackson standing at the gates, welcoming James Knox Polk to the select company. Young Hickory surely demonstrated the bold determination and unillusioned view of men and events that would have entitled him to walk arm in arm with the best of them.

★ ★ ★

Zachary Taylor

12ᵗʰ President · 1849–1850

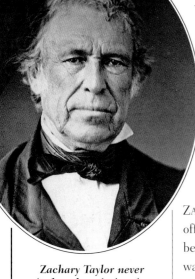

Zachary Taylor never bothered much about his appearance. His hair and clothes were frequently unkempt, and even as an army officer, he typically wore a jumble of military and civilian clothing.

Catherine Clinton

ZACHARY TAYLOR WAS NO POLITICIAN. His election to the highest office in the land was the result of his first (and last) campaign. In fact, before 1848, he'd never even voted in a presidential election. His reason was that, as a career soldier, he preferred not to be put in the position of casting a ballot against a future commander in chief.

Taylor won the presidency in 1848 for the simple reason that he was the nation's most famous Mexican War hero. Yet the popular general did have some strong views on the vexing questions of the day, even if he kept them to himself. At the time of Taylor's election, the prospect of secession over the extension of slavery to the western territories was quite real, and most people expected him, being a slaveholder, to sympathize with the southern point of view. Nevertheless, during his brief sixteen months in office (he died in July 1850), Taylor publicly blossomed into a fervent nationalist, outraging the southerners who had supported him.

Like six other presidents before him, Taylor was Virginia born, the son of a Revolutionary War officer. He was raised, though, not in Tidewater gentility but on the rough-and-tumble Kentucky frontier, where his family had a tobacco plantation outside Louisville. When he did decide to leave the plantation in 1808, his family's connections smoothed the way. With the help of his second cousin James Madison, then secretary of state, Taylor obtained a commission as a first lieutenant in the army.

Taylor was fond of this decorative pipe, richly carved to resemble an eagle's claw.

In the years leading up to the War of 1812, Taylor distinguished himself fighting Indians on the western frontier, earning plaudits from the acting territorial governor of Indiana, who reported that Taylor was the "one bright ray amid the gloom of incompetency" that plagued military leadership on the frontier. Except for one yearlong interlude, when he resumed the life of a planter, Taylor's army career progressed steadily upward. Successful commands during the Black Hawk War of 1832 and the Second Seminole War, in which Taylor fought from 1837 until 1840, garnered him favor in Washington, and he was breveted brigadier general in 1837. His men called him Old Rough and Ready (in contrast to Winfield Scott's Old Fuss and Feathers nickname) because Taylor was willing to do whatever it took to get the job done, even if that meant wading through mud beside lowly privates. A taciturn man, Taylor neither smoked nor drank, and he was devoted to his wife, Margaret.

I N THE SPRING OF 1846, Taylor had command of the First Department of the West, headquartered at Fort Jesup, Louisiana. The general and his troops, however, were in Texas, where they had been ordered into the disputed territory between the Nueces River and the Rio Grande. When the Mexican War began in earnest in May, triggered by this provocative "reconnaissance," Taylor was again provided with ample opportunity to distinguish himself, particularly as Americans sharply focused their attention on the army's subsequent forays into Mexico.

Victories at Palo Alto on May 8 and Resaca de la Palma on May 9 won Taylor a commendation from President James K. Polk and the brevet rank of major general. Taylor's next target was the heavily fortified Mexican stronghold of Monterrey, located high on a riverbank and therefore difficult to approach. Following a four-day siege, Taylor's troops reduced the fortress and routed its defenders. Yet in exchange for a

This 1847 Nathaniel Currier lithograph shows a mounted Taylor directing artillery fire during the February 23 battle of Buena Vista. "A little more grape, Captain Bragg," the general calmly orders (in Currier's bowdlerized version, that is).

BORN
November 24, 1784

BIRTHPLACE
Orange County, Virginia

DIED
July 9, 1850

PARTY AFFILIATION
Whig

CHILDREN
Anne, Sarah Knox, Octavia, Margaret, Mary Elizabeth, Richard

MAJOR EVENTS

JULY 1849

After hearing rumors that she will be sold farther south, twenty-nine-year-old Maryland slave Harriet Tubman escapes to the North along the Underground Railroad. In December 1850, she will return to Maryland to lead her sister and two children to freedom. Thereafter, Tubman will become one of the Underground Railroad's most active "conductors."

APRIL 19, 1850

The United States and Great Britain sign the Clayton-Bulwer Treaty, which states that the two countries will jointly control and safeguard any canal constructed across Central America. This agreement mistakenly anticipates that a canal between the Atlantic and Pacific Oceans will be built there sometime soon.

Lt. Zachary Taylor married Margaret Mackall Smith in Kentucky on June 21, 1810, shortly before he was promoted to captain and assigned to Fort Knox, Indiana Territory. Peggy Taylor (of whom no image survives) spent the next fourteen years following her husband from post to post before Taylor finally settled his family down at Cypress Grove, a two-thousand-acre, eighty-slave plantation near Baton Rouge. Because the first lady, then chronically ill, didn't have the strength to manage formal state dinners, she turned over the duties of White House hostess to her daughter Betty Taylor Bliss (pictured here).

Mexican surrender on September 25, Taylor agreed to generous terms that included his promise not to pursue the retreating Mexicans for eight weeks. When news of the arrangement reached Washington, a furious President Polk immediately canceled the armistice and transferred most of Taylor's command to the army of Gen. Winfield Scott, Taylor's superior, who was preparing a campaign against Mexico City. Polk, it was widely believed, simply wanted Taylor to resign, but the general hung on, stoically insisting that he'd "remain and do my duty, no matter under what circumstances."

Whether or not Taylor saw his command as a pathway to a political career, his February 1847 performance at the battle of Buena Vista certainly grabbed the attention of the opposition Whigs. In that battle, which can justifiably be called legendary, Taylor's remaining troops used superior artillery to defeat a force under Mexican general Antonio López de Santa Anna nearly three times larger. Taylor himself narrowly escaped injury when one bullet tore a button from his uniform and another grazed his arm.

The fame that followed his victory at Buena Vista made Taylor obvious presidential material, and although he had initially expressed some reluctance, in November 1846 he awkwardly confessed, "I will not say I would not serve if the good people were imprudent enough to elect me." Taylor was an exceedingly attractive potential candidate because he appeared to be able to transcend the increasingly bitter sectional rivalry, particularly regarding the issue of slavery. He was so attractive, in fact, that the Whigs chose the general as their candidate for 1848, even though most Whigs had vigorously opposed the war that made him famous.

Taylor died at 10:35 P.M. on July 9, 1850. According to the caption printed on this contemporary Currier lithograph, his last words were: "I am prepared. I have endeavored to do my duty." The Boston Cultivator reported news of Taylor's death in a short story buried inside its July 13 edition.

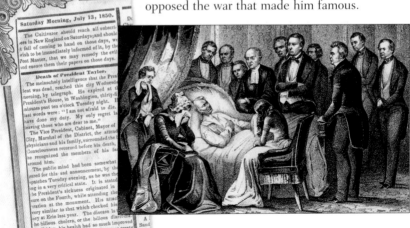

As the first president never to have served as a legislator, Taylor was a political unknown, which worked to his advantage during the campaign. In the absence of a strong platform, Americans inclined to vote for Taylor because of his heroism had nothing to hold them back. While Peggy Taylor prayed for her husband's defeat (so he might remain permanently at home in Louisiana), Taylor's candidacy was actively supported by his former son-in-law, Democratic senator Jefferson Davis, who influenced many southerners to vote for Taylor.

D AVIS HAD GOTTEN TO KNOW TAYLOR—and Taylor's second daughter, Knox—after he was appointed to Taylor's staff in 1832. Having already seen his oldest daughter married to an army surgeon, Taylor opposed the match, declaring, "I'll be damned if another daughter of mine will marry into the army." Nevertheless, Knox Taylor defied her parents' will and married Davis in 1835. Her death later that year provided the opportunity for a reconciliation between Taylor and Davis, who had resigned his commission following the marriage. Although Davis briefly rejoined the army during the Mexican War (serving again with Taylor at Buena Vista), his new career was politics. Elected senator from Mississippi in 1847, he championed the extension of slavery into the West (something Taylor condemned) and dabbled in secession movements (to which Taylor had violent objections). For the election of 1848, however, Davis crossed party lines to campaign for Taylor, claiming that the general had always been a "Jeffersonian Democrat" and pointing out that Taylor kept more than eighty slaves on his Louisiana plantation.

During the campaign, Taylor pledged not to veto congressional legislation concerning slavery in the territories, thereby mollifying proslavery and antislavery elements. Sidestepping the issue in this way enabled him to defeat both Democrat Lewis Cass and Martin Van Buren, running as the nominee of the antislavery Free Soil party.

Peggy Taylor dutifully accompanied her victorious husband to Washington, but she rarely socialized, leaving the White House only to attend St. John's Episcopal Church. Meanwhile, President Taylor enjoyed frequent walks, strolling by himself the streets of the District and then returning to the White House to watch his favorite mount, Whitey, graze on the lawn.

In the nation at large, however, the discovery of gold in California had changed the political climate. The proslavery and Free Soil forces in Congress remained deadlocked on the issue of expanding slavery, but with forty-niners flooding west, the issue of California's admission to the

The news of Taylor's nomination was telegraphed from Philadelphia to Memphis and thence carried on to Baton Rouge by side-wheeler. At the same time, Whig party chairman John M. Morehead sent a formal notification by mail…to which Taylor didn't reply. It turned out that the letter, sent without postage, never reached him. Stamps had been introduced only recently, and it was still common to send letters without postage. In fact, Taylor had been receiving so many postage-due letters from admirers that he'd instructed the local post office not to deliver them anymore. Morehead's message sat in the Baton Rouge dead letter office for nearly six weeks before being rescued and acknowledged by the general.

This flask commemorates *Taylor's four-decade-long military career. At the time of his enlistment in 1808, the army provided one of the few opportunities for a young man of modest birth to acquire financial and social status.*

OPPOSITE:

Taylor had no formal education *(and no desire for one), but he did have frontier common sense and a healthy contempt for both political tricksters and "their obvious forms of nonsense." This is the last daguerreotype ever taken of the president.*

Union demanded resolution. Although disturbed by the aggressive and potentially violent nature of the political debate, Taylor surprisingly weighed in with a definite policy of his own: He wanted to admit the recently acquired territories of California and New Mexico (which then included Utah and other future states) immediately as states, thereby bypassing the inflammatory issue of slavery in federal territories.

> "GENERAL TAYLOR'S BATTLES WERE NOT DISTINGUISHED FOR BRILLIANT MILITARY MANEUVERS; BUT IN ALL HE SEEMS RATHER TO HAVE CONQUERED BY THE EXERCISE OF A SOBER AND STEADY JUDGMENT."
>
> —*Abraham Lincoln*—

IN THE EARLY MONTHS OF 1850, Henry Clay proposed an omnibus bill linking California's admission to the Union with several other measures, including abolition of the slave trade in the District of Columbia (a sop to abolitionists) and a strong fugitive slave law (to appease the South). Clay's plan would also establish new territories in New Mexico and Utah and leave up to the citizens of these territories the question of whether to permit or ban slavery. The chambers of Congress soon resounded with impassioned speeches by the likes of Daniel Webster, William H. Seward, and John C. Calhoun. Less than a month from his death, Calhoun was so ill that a colleague had to deliver his speech.

Alienated by secessionist fire-eaters (including Jefferson Davis)—whom, in a choleric mood, he once threatened to hang if they chose to carry out their threats—Taylor blocked passage of the compromise. The way suddenly cleared, however, when Taylor was struck down by terrible stomach cramps on Independence Day, 1850. After a full afternoon in the broiling heat, he had sated himself with a bowl of cherries and a pitcher of milk. Because sanitary conditions in 1850 Washington left much to be desired, it's likely he contracted a form of cholera, which killed him five days later. Conspiracy theorists later suggested that the president might have been poisoned, but a 1991 exhumation of Taylor's remains debunked this speculation. Even so, proslavery forces in Congress must have been relieved at his passing, which allowed the more pliable Millard Fillmore to become president.

★ ★ ★

Millard Fillmore

13th President · 1850–1853

Jean Harvey Baker

As a young man, Millard Fillmore was considered eye-catchingly handsome. Age, however, added weight to his face and frame, and he became somewhat doughy.

MILLARD FILLMORE HAS FADED from the memories of Americans, his anonymity such a joke to members of the Millard Fillmore Society that they meet annually on his birthday to celebrate his invisibility. Along with Zachary Taylor, Franklin Pierce, and James Buchanan, Fillmore has taken his place among those inept pre–Civil War presidents who failed to stanch the growing sectionalism of the United States. For those who consider the war an avoidable conflict, and therefore the result of failed policies and bungling leaders, the last presidential representative of the Whig party deserves to be forgotten, just as his party has been.

PERHAPS, HOWEVER, it is time now to reassess Fillmore's abbreviated presidency, viewing it not so much from the perspective of its outcome as from its contemporary context and the ways in which the president met various domestic challenges. As an accidental president raised to chief executive when Zachary Taylor died after only sixteen months in office, Fillmore lacked the authenticity and power that elected presidents carry with them to the White House. Nor did he have any mentor or cadre of supporters like those enjoyed by William H. Seward, his chief rival for control of the Whig party in New York.

Practical friction matches weren't developed until 1831, but their use spread quickly. Fillmore kept his matches dry in this match safe, a common piece of personal equipment during the nineteenth century.

By nature modest and unassuming—*amiable* was the word contemporaries often used to describe him—Fillmore acknowledged in his first message to Congress the suddenness that "by a painful dispensation of Divine Providence" had called him "to the responsible station I now hold." He promised that the Constitution would be his guide and that "all its provisions would be equally binding." In an age when Congress held primacy, he acknowledged the authority of the national legislature. "With you is the power, the honor, and the responsibility of the legislation of the country," he told the lawmakers. "My only desire is to discharge my duty and…to act for the good of the whole country."

Fillmore had reason to be uncertain about his ability to handle the presidency. Unlike most American presidents, he had been raised in humble circumstances, being one of the few who could authentically lay claim to birth in a log cabin. The economic trajectory of most American farmers moved them toward prosperity, yet Fillmore's father had lost his land, reducing the family to tenancy in Cayuga County, New York, part of the Finger Lakes region. After being apprenticed to a tailor who abused him, Millard returned to his father's farm, where he caught the eye of a local judge and later became a self-taught, successful lawyer in Buffalo. Like many other young and ambitious lawyers of this period, he was attracted to politics, serving first in the New York legislature and then four terms (from 1833 to 1835 and again from 1837 to 1843) as a Whig congressman from Buffalo. He was defeated in 1844 in his bid for the governorship of New York, but in 1848 the Whig national convention chose him, something of a dark horse, as the running mate for Zachary Taylor. A rousing nomination speech by a New York delegate and more controversial competitors were mostly responsible for Fillmore's selection.

The public policy that defined Fillmore's presidency was the Compromise of 1850, a complex piece of legislation that many Americans of the period celebrated as the solution to the intensifying hostility between the North and the South. This cluster of five bills supposedly balanced northern and southern interests: On the one hand, Congress

In November 1852, Fillmore sent Commo. Mathew C. Perry to persuade the Japanese to open their ports. (Japanese ports had been closed to foreign trade for more than two centuries.) The result of Perry's mission of intimidation can be seen in this 1861 Japanese woodcut showing an American ship being loaded at Yokohama.

BORN
January 7, 1800

BIRTHPLACE
Cayuga County, New York

DIED
March 8, 1874

PARTY AFFILIATION
Whig

CHILDREN
Millard, Mary

MAJOR EVENTS

SEPTEMBER 20, 1850

Congress makes the first land grant to a railroad. The bill, backed by Illinois senator Stephen A. Douglas, transfers federal land to the Illinois Central, which will sell it to raise funds for the construction of track between Cairo and Galena.

FEBRUARY 15, 1851

A mob breaks into a Boston jail to free an escaped slave before he can be returned to the South. Although not all northerners opposed to the Fugitive Slave Law act so boldly, many others have chosen more discreet ways to disobey the law.

MAY 29, 1851

In Akron, Ohio, at the second Women's Rights Convention, fifty-four-year-old Sojourner Truth delivers her famous "Ain't I a Woman?" speech, in which she compares her experiences as a slave to those of typical middle-class women.

Nineteen-year-old Millard Fillmore met *twenty-one-year-old Abigail Powers while pursuing what today would be called adult education. As the sister of a local judge, Abigail had a social standing well above poor Millard's, but the two nevertheless kept company during the winter of 1819–20 and fell in love. Millard insisted on postponing their marriage until he had established himself as a lawyer, so Abigail waited. Nearly six years passed, during which time she rarely saw Millard, but they sustained their relationship through letters and occasional visits.*

agreed to the draconian Fugitive Slave Law, which made it easier for southerners to reclaim escaped slaves. On the other hand, the compromise permitted California to enter the Union as a free state, not split into two states with one allowing slavery. Congress also passed legislation ending the slave trade in the District of Columbia. A fourth bill granted the territories of Utah and New Mexico the right to decide for themselves the issue of slavery, and in a neglected part of the compromise, Texas abandoned its claims to one hundred thousand square miles of territory in New Mexico in return for ten million dollars.

Led by some of the most formidable legislators in American history—including Henry Clay, Stephen A. Douglas, Jefferson Davis, John C. Calhoun, and Daniel Webster—Congress had been debating the various parts of the Compromise of 1850 for nearly five months when Fillmore took office. Lacking the forcefulness of presidents who have advanced their policies through judicious patronage and alliances with powerful congressmen, Fillmore also seemed to lack the personality to forward the policies he supported.

However, there was more to the crisis of 1850 than just an angry debate in Congress. Texas, supported by other slaveholding states, was threatening to invade New Mexico and take by force the land it claimed across the Pecos River. This territorial conflict, a legacy of the Mexican War, has been overlooked as a precursor to the trouble in Kansas that was handled so indecisively by Fillmore's successors, Pierce and Buchanan. If the Texas militia had indeed moved across the border into New Mexico and encountered federal troops, the Civil War might have begun right then. South Carolina was already preparing for war.

To his credit, Fillmore acted promptly and decisively. To discourage an invasion, he sent 750 more federal troops to New Mexico and reminded the governor of Texas that the boundary between New Mexico and Texas had been established by treaty and that the New Mexico territory belonged to the United States. A few months later, with federal officials in South Carolina resigning, he learned that South Carolinians were preparing to seize the federal forts in Charleston as a first step

This ornamental inkstand was owned and used by Fillmore.*

toward secession. Acting quickly, Fillmore strengthened the Charleston forts, posted more troops in North and South Carolina, and urged Gen. Winfield Scott to develop a contingency plan in case an armed insurrection should occur.

Using language similar to that voiced by Lincoln in 1861, Fillmore bluntly told Congress that "if the laws of the United States are opposed and obstructed in any state or territory by combinations too powerful to be suppressed by the judicial or civil authorities...it is the duty of the President either to call out the militia or to employ the military and naval force of the United States or to do both if in his judgment the exigency of the occasion shall so require." In the face of such a resolute president, the Texas congressional delegation backed down and accepted the compromise. The crisis subsided for a time.

> " FILLMORE LACKS PLUCK....HE MEANS WELL, BUT HE IS TIMID, IRRESOLUTE, UNCERTAIN, AND LOVES TO LEAN."
>
> —*Horace Greeley*—

FILLMORE PRAISED the Compromise of 1850, calling it "a means of healing sectional differences" and noting that "all mutual concession in the nature of a compromise must necessarily be unwelcome to men of extreme opinions." Locating himself as a man "with an American heart," Fillmore was prepared to resist those whom he believed to be northern extremists.

These included northerners—and there were many of them—not entirely satisfied with the Fugitive Slave Law. The new law made it so easy for southerners to reclaim escaped slaves that it seemed to grant open season to kidnappers of free blacks, thousands of whom fled to Canada in the early 1850s. On many grounds, particularly its failure to permit jury trials and its removal of protections for northern free blacks, the law was a travesty. It was also an insult to growing antislavery opinion in the North. Tepidly antislavery—he opposed it but would not touch it in states where it existed—Fillmore didn't like

JUNE 2, 1851

Maine passes the first statewide temperance law, banning the manufacture and sale of alcoholic beverages. The Maine law reflects a growing national sentiment, encouraged by religious revivalists, that liquor is sinful.

This image of Fillmore *was circulated widely on a cabinet card.*

Fillmore's decision to run as the nominee of the American (Know-Nothing) party in 1856 did little to promote his reputation. This contemporary cartoon suggests the combativeness of the Know-Nothings' and immigrant, anti-Catholic platform.

OPPOSITE:

In 1855, Fillmore sailed to England and visited Oxford, where he was offered an honorary degree. When he learned that the citation would be in Latin, he modestly declined: "I had not the advantage of a classical education, and no man should, in my judgment, accept a degree he cannot read." Perhaps he had in mind the jokes still being told about Andrew Jackson's acceptance of an honorary degree at Harvard. On that occasion, Jackson concluded his remarks by shouting the few Latin phrases he knew: "E pluribus unum! Sine qua non! Quid pro quo! Ne plus ultra!"

the bill and delayed signing it. Still, he correctly considered it a contingent part of a sectional contract that he believed might bring harmony to the United States. Therefore, he concluded that, as president of the Union, he must sign it and enforce the law.

Yet even after Fillmore signed the bill into law, many northerners denied its legitimacy and refused to uphold its provisions. Ironically, some northern states passed so-called personal liberty laws that attempted to nullify the federal legislation. Resisting these challenges to federal authority, Fillmore consistently authorized the use of federal force to assist local marshals and commissioners in carrying out the return of slaves. Northerners were so outraged that they began calling him the "perfidious Fillmore."

> " HOWEVER MUCH I MAY BE OPPRESSED BY…THE DISCHARGE OF THE DUTIES [OF THE PRESIDENCY]…I DARE NOT SHRINK [FROM THEM]. "
>
> —*Letter, 1850*—

DURING THESE CRISES, Millard Fillmore, a man with limited pretensions who always seemed surprised to be where he ended up, served the Union well. While many Americans at the time recognized that the Fugitive Slave Law was morally vicious, within the context of his presidency Fillmore thought he was doing the right thing. The law had been accepted as constitutional, and Fillmore was as stalwart a defender of the Constitution as anyone.

His final words to Congress expressed his credo and personal sense of accomplishment. "Called by an unexpected dispensation to a position of highest trust at a season of embarrassment and alarm," Fillmore said, "I entered upon its arduous duties with extreme diffidence. I claim only to have discharged them to the best of a humble ability, with a single eye to the public good, and it is with a single eye to the public good…that I leave the country in a state of peace and prosperity." Neither Pierce nor Buchanan would so determinedly adhere to the Constitution, the separation of powers, or the necessity for impartiality.

★ ★ ★

Franklin Pierce

14th President · 1853–1857

Franklin Pierce [signature]

James A. Rawley

Franklin Pierce,
perhaps the most
handsome president,
suffered from a variety
of respiratory ailments.
A chronic bronchitis, for
example, left him with a
disturbing cough that
persisted throughout
his presidency.

FRANKLIN PIERCE WAS an affable man, an effective orator, and a boon barroom companion, possessing both personal magnetism and a desire to please others. With strong features and opaque gray eyes, the well-dressed Pierce, erect in bearing, contributed greatly to the gaiety of Washington society. Aware of personal weaknesses and given to melancholy, he sought to accommodate all. Yet this temperament, though useful in the pursuit of party unity, proved unequal to the extraordinary stresses of his presidency.

Born in Hillsborough, New Hampshire, Pierce was the grandson of a militia brigadier and the son of a governor. He was graduated from Bowdoin College in 1824 and admitted to the bar in 1827. Well born and well launched in New Hampshire society, Pierce, a Democrat, was sent to Congress in 1833, serving two terms in the House and most of a term in the Senate. In 1834, he married Jane Appleton, daughter of a former Bowdoin College president. They had three sons, each dying before he attained maturity.

His service in the Mexican War, during which he rose from private to brigadier general, may not have been heroic, but it enhanced his availability for high office. Party loyalty, his support for prosouthern measures, his northern residence, his bland spirit, and divisive factionalism combined to bring Pierce, on the forty-ninth convention ballot, the Democratic nomination for president in 1852. In the ensuing election, running against the Whig Winfield Scott and the Free Soiler John P. Hale, Pierce carried all but four states yet enjoyed a majority of fewer than sixty thousand votes. In the North, he stood as a minority candidate.

Pierce owed his office largely to southern Democrats. Seeking party unity, he folded into his cabinet members from New York,

This sword
accompanied
Pierce to Mexico.
His wife, Jane,
didn't want
him to go,
but Pierce's
revered father
had fought
with great
distinction in
the Revolutionary
War, and Pierce
himself was determined
to fight as his father had.

This 1852 Currier cartoon satirizes Pierce's alleged ineptness as an officer during the Mexican War. In August 1847 at Contreras, poorly aimed artillery fire had caused Pierce's horse to jump, driving his groin sharply against the pommel of his saddle. The excruciating pain made him pass out. Whigs later unearthed this story and accused Pierce of "fainting" under fire.

Massachusetts, Michigan, Pennsylvania, Kentucky, North Carolina, and Mississippi. Party leaders such as Lewis Cass, Stephen A. Douglas, and James Buchanan were absent.

IN HIS INAUGURAL ADDRESS, the president announced his intentions: an aggressive foreign policy, including expansion of territory; strict regard to "the limits imposed by the Constitution"; and support for the Compromise of 1850. Slavery, he pointed out, was recognized by the Constitution and an "admitted right...I fervently hope that the question [of slavery] is at rest." Months later, he amplified his positions: As chief executive, he would adhere strictly to the past rather than attempt creative statesmanship. In domestic affairs, he favored a policy of laissez-faire, and as to federal support for a proposed transcontinental railroad, the government's role should be "incidental rather than primary." As his administration unfolded, Pierce opposed a homestead bill and vetoed another that would have provided government aid to establish institutions for the indigent mentally ill.

Pierce's ambition to conduct an aggressive foreign policy had a mixed outcome. A Young America movement, backed by Stephen A. Douglas, favored expansion, especially southward. Early success came in 1854 with the Gadsden Purchase, by which the United States for ten million dollars bought from Mexico the land that now makes up southern New Mexico and southern Arizona. The acquisition of this strip of territory particularly

BORN
November 23, 1804

BIRTHPLACE
Hillsborough,
New Hampshire

DIED
October 8, 1869

PARTY AFFILIATION
Democrat

CHILDREN
Franklin Jr., Frank
Robert, Benjamin

MAJOR EVENTS

MARCH 31, 1854

On his second trip to Japan, the first having come a year earlier, Commo. Mathew C. Perry signs the Treaty of Kanagawa, Japan's first diplomatic understanding with a Western nation. The agreement allows American ships to take on food and supplies at two designated Japanese ports and anticipates more extensive trade in the future.

APRIL 22, 1856

Henry Farnam rides the first train to cross the Mississippi River. It uses the 1,535-foot-long bridge he has built between Rock Island, Illinois, and Davenport, Iowa. Steamboat operators have opposed construction of the bridge, which they claim is a navigation hazard, because they don't want the railroads competing for their freight business.

The word most commonly used to describe Jane Means Appleton Pierce is delicate. She was petite, shy with strangers, and apparently somewhat frail. But she had been raised as a New England aristocrat, and there was nothing at all delicate about her mind. At the time of their marriage in 1834, Frank was buoyant and sociable, qualities that must have attracted the melancholy Jane. Gradually, however, Pierce's affability began to grate on his wife, who hated public life and regularly implored her husband to give up politics.

When Pierce won the Democratic nomination in 1852, Nathaniel Hawthorne, a Bowdoin College friend, volunteered to write the candidate's campaign biography.

pleased southerners because it straddled the most likely route for a transcontinental railroad linking the South to the Pacific.

For years, some Americans had also favored acquiring Cuba—valuable for security, commerce, and slavery expansion. After Spanish authorities in Havana seized a U.S. vessel, the *Black Warrior,* the Pierce administration instructed its ministers in Spain, France, and England to devise a policy for Cuba. The misguided product of this troika (which included James Buchanan) was the Ostend Manifesto, a blunt statement that if Spain refused to sell the island, and if the United States believed Spain's possession endangered "our internal peace and the existence of our cherished Union," the United States would be "justified in wresting it from Spain." Intended to be secret, this notorious document nevertheless became public and aroused a stormy protest, particularly in the North, thus defeating its purpose.

LONG-STANDING PROBLEMS with Great Britain were eased by a reciprocity treaty that improved trade relations and fishing privileges for Americans. Soon after, however, the British minister to the United States, charged with illegally recruiting American mercenaries for the British army, was handed his passport at Pierce's insistence, over his secretary of state's objections. At the same time, Pierce unwisely recognized the Nicaraguan regime of William Walker, an American adventurer who had set himself up as dictator, to the further annoyance of Great Britain with its substantial interests in Central America.

The central feature of Pierce's administration, however, was the so-called Kansas Question. The Kansas area had been made free soil by the Missouri Compromise of 1820, which prohibited slavery in Louisiana Purchase lands north of latitude 36°30'. Then, early in 1854, Sen. Stephen A. Douglas sponsored a bill to organize formally the territories Kansas and Nebraska, opening them to settlers and potential railroad builders. In doing so, Douglas's bill repealed the Missouri Compromise ban on slavery extension and substituted for it a doctrine of local choice that he called popular sovereignty. Needing support from an executive who had pointedly expressed his hope that the question of slavery be at rest, party leaders hastily arranged a Sunday conference in the executive mansion, where they extracted sanction from the beleaguered president.

A storm of outrage swept through the North and Congress. Pierce demanded party loyalty to what was now an administration measure. Antislavery Democrats, Free Soilers, and northern Whigs united to form what became the Republican party, a drastic realignment that produced a northern antislavery party and an increasingly solid Democratic South. Pierce had unwittingly propelled the nation into sectional and party division that boded ill for tranquility and national unity. When congressional elections were held in the autumn, Democrats lost all but two northern states.

Had Pierce exercised as firm a hand in administering the law as he had in passing it, he might have enjoyed a higher stature than historians have since accorded him. Under his watch, however, freedom wasn't given a fair field in the Kansas Territory. A proslavery man, John W. Whitfield, became Kansas's territorial delegate to Congress as the result of a fraudulent election, and even more serious damage to freedom and popular sovereignty occurred in March 1855, when thousands of Missourians, branded Border Ruffians, streamed into Kansas to elect a proslavery legislature.

Pierce's earliest appointees as territorial governors were also unfortunate. The first, Andrew Reeder, was a Pennsylvanian who sympathized with the South and anticipated filling his pockets through land speculation. Nevertheless, in his first speech in Kansas, he pledged to protect the integrity of the ballot box. It was only in the presence of armed men, his life threatened, that Reeder accepted the dishonest March 1855 election returns that established the proslavery legislature.

A fundamentally honest Reeder subsequently repaired to Washington to beseech the president to proclaim his disapproval of the lawless measures and pledge administration opposition, including troops, to prevent outside interference. Pierce supinely refused. The illegitimate legislature meanwhile established slavery in the territory, and Pierce soon after replaced Reeder with Wilson Shannon, an Ohioan with "no antislavery prejudices."

Meanwhile, antislavery settlers in Kansas organized a rival government and requested admission to the Union. Meeting in Topeka, the Free Staters drafted a constitution that prohibited slavery and also the

> " INVOLUNTARY SERVITUDE...IS RECOGNIZED BY THE CONSTITUTION [AND] STANDS LIKE ANY OTHER ADMITTED RIGHT."
>
> —*Inaugural address, 1853*—

MAY 21, 1856

Border Ruffians sack Lawrence, the center of antislavery activism in Kansas. The town's hotel and newspaper offices are burned, and at least one man dies.

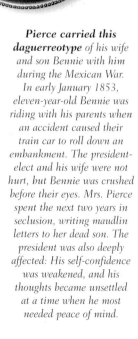

Pierce carried this daguerreotype *of his wife and son Bennie with him during the Mexican War. In early January 1853, eleven-year-old Bennie was riding with his parents when an accident caused their train car to roll down an embankment. The president-elect and his wife were not hurt, but Bennie was crushed before their eyes. Mrs. Pierce spent the next two years in seclusion, writing maudlin letters to her dead son. The president was also deeply affected: His self-confidence was weakened, and his thoughts became unsettled at a time when he most needed peace of mind.*

OPPOSITE:

Of the presidents who preceded him, Pierce had a special admiration for James K. Polk, who once offered to make Pierce his attorney general. (After Pierce chose instead to enlist as a private in his local company of Mexican War volunteers, Polk intervened to make Pierce a colonel in the regular army.) Pierce particularly appreciated Polk's attention to detail and his belief in the virtues of comprehensive paperwork. Pierce's own devotion to writing reports may well have exceeded that of Polk.

"WE HAVE FALLEN ON GREAT TIMES FOR LITTLE MEN."

—

New York Tribune
editorial, 1852

Carpetbags—suitcases actually made of carpet— were widely used by travelers during the nineteenth century. Pierce used this one.

entry of blacks into the territory. As 1856 opened, the Free Staters elected a rival government; violence flared, participated in by Border Ruffians; and the Republican party swelled to great proportions in the northern states. Yet in his annual message to Congress, Pierce blandly asserted that nothing had happened in Kansas "to justify the interposition of the Federal executive."

FINALLY, IN LATE JANUARY 1856, Pierce sent a special message to Congress about Kansas. He reviewed the territory's history, characterized the work of the Free Staters as revolutionary, and declared, "It is not the duty of the President of the United States to volunteer interposition by force to preserve the purity of elections either in a state or territory." Days later, by proclamation, he ordered the Free Staters and Border Ruffians to disperse under threat of the local militia and federal troops.

In March, Congress was confronted with rival measures: the Free State element's request for statehood and an administration bill permitting Kansas to hold a constitutional convention. Congressmen raged over the rival plans, failed to approve a middle way proposed by a Georgia member, and meanwhile gathered evidence of fraud in Kansas. On May 22, Sen. Charles Sumner of Massachusetts, an antislavery advocate, was brutally beaten by Rep. Preston Brooks of South Carolina on the floor of the Senate, and two days later fanatical abolitionist John Brown and his band murdered five proslavery settlers near Pottawatomie Creek.

Pierce aspired to a second term, but Bleeding Kansas, the Ostend Manifesto, and his sorry record militated against him. The Democratic party, proclaiming its unqualified approbation of his measures, nevertheless repudiated him and nominated another prosouthern northerner, James Buchanan. The Kansas Question remained unresolved at his term's end.

Pierce's ideology of limited government together with his personal traits of accommodation and deference to the powerful southern wing of his party made for an inept president who piloted the ship of state to the shoals of secession and civil war. His remaining years Pierce passed in relative obscurity—traveling, taking time to denounce Abraham Lincoln's Emancipation Proclamation, and drinking. Virtually unmourned, he was buried beside his wife, who had preceded him in death.

★ ★ ★

*James Buchanan's **apparent** weakness as president was all the more pitiful because, personally, he was a highly decent man. Quietly but persistently, he bought slaves in Washington, D.C., then set them free in Pennsylvania.*

In May 1860, as the Democratic party was literally breaking apart, a large delegation of Japanese visited Washington to sign the first commercial treaty between the two nations. This is the Japanese dictionary that Buchanan owned and might have consulted, had he the time and inclination.

James Buchanan

15ᵗʰ President · 1857–1861

James Buchanan

Jean Harvey Baker

FEW PRESIDENTS HAVE entered the White House with more impressive credentials and extensive training in public life than James Buchanan. Even fewer have left office with such a tarnished reputation. The Civil War that began just six weeks after Buchanan's departure from Washington was not of his making; perhaps it was in no president's power to prevent. Yet Buchanan's administration certainly made it more probable. Granting that he faced many challenges brought on by the intensifying division between the North and the South, reasonable Americans of all parties still had cause to expect that if anyone could quiet the passions of sectionalism, it would be the Sage of Wheatland. Instead, Buchanan's presidency demonstrated the harm that can result when great talent and experience are shackled to a personality ill suited to the pressures of the office.

James Buchanan was born in 1791 near Mercersburg, Pennsylvania, to prosperous Scotch-Irish parents. By the time of his presidential nomination in 1856, he had already spent nearly half a century in diverse and significant public offices. A college graduate and member of the Pennsylvania state legislature at age twenty-three, he was elected to the first of five terms in Congress before he turned thirty. In recognition of his talents (and after his change of party from the expiring Federalists to the Democrats), congressional leaders named him chairman of the House Judiciary Committee. Soon he caught President Jackson's eye and was appointed minister to Russia. From 1834 until 1845, he served as a U.S. senator; in 1845, President Polk appointed him secretary of state, thereby bestowing upon him what was then a common launching pad for the presidency. In 1852, Buchanan was for a time the front-runner at the

Democratic national convention, leading from the twentieth to twenty-ninth ballots. The victor on the forty-ninth ballot, little-known Franklin Pierce, subsequently acknowledged Buchanan's support, appointing him to yet another prized office: minister to the Court of St. James's.

Buchanan would rather have been president; yet, stationed in faraway London, he avoided the need to take positions on the vexing sectional issues that bedeviled Pierce, especially the Kansas-Nebraska Act. (By overturning the Missouri Compromise and establishing the principle that Americans could decide at some local level whether they wanted slavery, the Kansas-Nebraska Act carried the volatile possibility of slavery becoming nationalized.)

O N THE OTHER HAND, while in London Buchanan confronted many of the international issues in which he considered himself, and indeed was, so well schooled. In the Ostend Manifesto of 1854, Buchanan called for the purchase of Cuba—and if that couldn't be accomplished, its annexation by force. A well-known supporter of Manifest Destiny, Buchanan had always been an expansionist. What was notable about the Ostend Manifesto, however, was the target of Buchanan's expansionism: the island of Cuba, long associated with the southern dream of expanding that region's cotton slaveocracy.

SOUTH CAROLINA'S "ULTIMATUM."

This cartoon, published early in 1861, mocks Buchanan, for waffling on the issue of Fort Sumter, and South Carolina governor F. W. Pickens, for imperiously insisting that Sumter be evacuated.

As the 1856 election neared, Buchanan's dossier of public service lacked only the presidency, and with Pierce discredited, he was the logical Democratic nominee. In an unusual race against American party candidate Millard Fillmore and John C. Frémont, nominee of the new Republican party, Buchanan easily won the electoral vote. However, his opponents together polled nearly four hundred thousand votes more than he did, and the three northern states that gave Buchanan his victory were even then moving away from his party into the Republican camp.

BORN
April 23, 1791

BIRTHPLACE
Cove Gap, Pennsylvania

DIED
June 1, 1868

PARTY AFFILIATION
Democrat

CHILDREN
none

MAJOR EVENTS

AUGUST 24, 1857

The failure of the Ohio Life Insurance Company triggers the Panic of 1857. Five thousand businesses will go bankrupt this year, with another eight thousand failing during 1858 and 1859.

AUGUST 21, 1858

Abraham Lincoln, the Republican candidate for senator from Illinois, and Stephen Douglas, the Democratic incumbent, meet in the first of seven debates. Each lasts about three hours, with one speaker taking the first hour and last half hour and his opponent the ninety minutes in between.

OCTOBER 16, 1859

A band of sixteen whites and five blacks led by John Brown captures the federal armory at Harpers Ferry, Virginia. Brown plans to use the captured arms to start a slave revolt, but Col. Robert E. Lee blocks Brown's escape and arrests him.

Buchanan poses with his cabinet in mid-1859. To his right are Secretary of State Lewis Cass (standing) and Secretary of War John B. Floyd (seated).

Buchanan was the only president who remained a bachelor his entire life. During his presidency, his orphaned niece Harriet Lane, then in her middle twenties, served as the official White House hostess. Harriet had been placed in her uncle's care during the 1840s following the death of her mother, Buchanan's sister Jane, in 1839 and that of her father two years later.

This mezzotint, after an 1834 painting by Jacob Eichholtz, shows a still-youthful Buchanan as he appeared at the beginning of his first Senate term.

In his inaugural address, Buchanan signaled his desire to serve as a peacemaker at a time when "the whole Territorial question" over slavery could be "settled upon the principle of popular sovereignty—a principle as ancient as free government itself." Earlier he had warned that "disunion is a word which ought not to be breathed amongst us even in a whisper." Yet he undermined his pledge to seek union by appointing a cabinet that did not include representatives from major factions of his own party. Few Americans expected him to appoint Republicans or Know-Nothings, but northern Democrats associated with the Stephen Douglas wing of the party expected some representation and received none. Any administration hoping to end sectional problems required, at the very least, a coalition cabinet made up of diverse elements of the governing party. Yet Buchanan remained stubbornly oblivious to the need for different views, relying mainly on the advice of friends and cronies, most of whom were southerners. Grateful as well to southerners for his election and opposed to antislaveryism, which he considered extremism, the self-defined moderate Buchanan lost any sectional balance and increasingly favored southern positions. In a cabinet of seven, four were slaveholding southerners, and of the three northerners, one was a doughface, the derogatory label given northerners with southern views.

Soon Buchanan himself earned that label as he railed against the abolitionists whom he believed had created the sectional controversy. Attacking the North, Buchanan argued that the South might have endured northern support for an unfair prohibition of slavery in the territories and for its refusal to return escaped slaves. What the South couldn't tolerate, however, was the "incessant and violent agitation of the slavery question [that] produced its malign influence on the slaves and inspired them with vague notions of freedom. Hence a sense of security no longer exists….Many a matron throughout the South retires at night in dread of what may befall herself and her children." At a time when many northerners were shifting their allegiances to oppose the immorality of slavery and, at the least, its expansion into new states, no southerner could have taken a more inflammatory position.

Buchanan's proslavery actions spoke as loudly as his words. He improperly intervened in the 1857 *Dred Scott* case, encouraging Associate Justice Robert Grier, a fellow Pennsylvanian, to provide a northern vote for the Supreme Court decision that nationalized slavery. Then, as the North erupted in anger, Buchanan endorsed a Kansas constitution written by proslavery settlers, again infuriating many northerners and inspiring southerners to expect even more from a president they had reason to consider their special advocate.

As the controversy between North and South spun out of control, Buchanan (who depended on collaborative decision making) increasingly limited himself to the narrow range of opinion presented by his advisers. He was passed over for renomination, as Pierce had been, but continued to proclaim fervently his loyalty to the party. More important, he recognized the need for the Democrats to remain united if they were to defeat the Republicans. Yet he never overcame his hostility to Stephen Douglas, and their antagonism helped split the party in two. Thus, Buchanan's legacy to the Democrats was schism in the party. By nominating two candidates—Douglas and John C. Breckinridge of Kentucky, who had been Buchanan's vice president—the Democrats assured the election of Abraham Lincoln in November 1860.

A S STATES BEGAN TO LEAVE THE UNION—first South Carolina on December 20, 1860, followed by six others by the time Buchanan left office in March—cabinet officers from the soon-to-be Confederacy resigned, but not before Secretary of War John B. Floyd of Virginia had sent federal arms to Texas. Meanwhile, a president who, on paper, had superior schooling in diplomacy and public affairs seemed immobilized. Buchanan denied the legality of secession but also the power of the federal government to coerce any state. All he could tell Congress in his December 1860 annual message was that the cause of secession rested in "the long-continued and intemperate interference of the northern people with the question of slavery."

Then—fortified by new, less pro-southern cabinet officers (men such as Edwin M. Stanton and John A. Dix) and by a swell of Unionist opinion in the North—the vacillating Buchanan astonished southerners by rejecting their demands that he surrender Fort Sumter in Charleston Harbor. One of the last garrisons in southern territory still in federal hands, Sumter quickly emerged as a symbol of national sovereignty infuriating to the future Confederates. However, when Gen. Winfield Scott asked Buchanan's permission to resupply Sumter, the rudderless president gave orders that led to a bungled operation. Buchanan thus delivered to his successor, Abraham Lincoln, the unresolved issue that would ignite the war.

JANUARY 9, 1861

South Carolina shore batteries fire on a civilian ship sent by President Buchanan to resupply Fort Sumter. The shelling causes the Star of the West *to withdraw without fulfilling her mission.*

FEBRUARY 4, 1861

Delegates from the six seceded states meet in Montgomery, Alabama, to form the Confederate States of America. Five days later, they will choose former Mississippi senator Jefferson Davis to be the first (and only) president of the Confederacy.

George Caleb Bingham's 1853–54 *painting* Stump Speaking *depicts campaigning as it was practiced during the 1850s (as well as throughout much of the nineteenth century).*

OPPOSITE:

Buchanan believed that man's duty on earth was to submit to God's will with humble resignation. "In all calamitous events," he told Harriet Lane following the unexpected death of a young cousin, "we ought to say, emphatically, 'Thy will be done.'" This passive philosophy may explain, in part, why Buchanan did so little to forestall the Civil War.

When the time came to go home to Pennsylvania in March 1861, James Buchanan was ready. As he and Lincoln rode together to the inauguration ceremony, Buchanan commented that if Lincoln was as happy to be entering the presidency as he was to be leaving it, then Lincoln was indeed a happy man. During the remaining seven years of his life, Buchanan spent much of the time justifying his administration, whose policies would surely have allowed the seven seceded states to maintain their independence.

WHAT THEN IS THE EXPLANATION for this presidential failure, especially given the background of James Buchanan and his roots in southern Pennsylvania, a vantage point from which he could well appreciate different sectional views? The answer lies not so much in the obvious intractability of the national issues, though they were that, as in the personality and character of the holder of the office. Despite his caution and prudence, James Buchanan was an erratic trimmer who twisted this way and that, and once he made up his mind, he stubbornly adhered to his positions. Having filled his administration with southerners, he was hardly the kind of impartial leader the country needed in the 1850s.

> "IF YOU ARE AS HAPPY, MY DEAR SIR, ON ENTERING THIS HOUSE AS I AM IN LEAVING IT AND RETURNING HOME, YOU ARE THE HAPPIEST MAN IN THIS COUNTRY."
>
> —*Remark to Abraham Lincoln, March 4, 1861*—

Buchanan's strength as a lawyer (and somewhat as a politician) wasn't his intellect— he wasn't remarkably bright. Rather, it was his painstaking preparation.

A sixty-five-year-old bachelor overly dependent on his friends, Buchanan fussed and fumed from the start of his administration and turned a deaf ear to the shifting opinion in the North that ultimately elected Lincoln. When at the end of his term in office, his advisers changed and northern support for the Union became obvious, he finally denied the right of secession and fitted out a feckless expedition that only shored up the aggressiveness of the South. Needing self-assurance, he ultimately found it during his retirement when, with exculpatory vehemence, he asserted that he had warned the nation about northern abolitionists. The war was their fault.

★ ★ ★

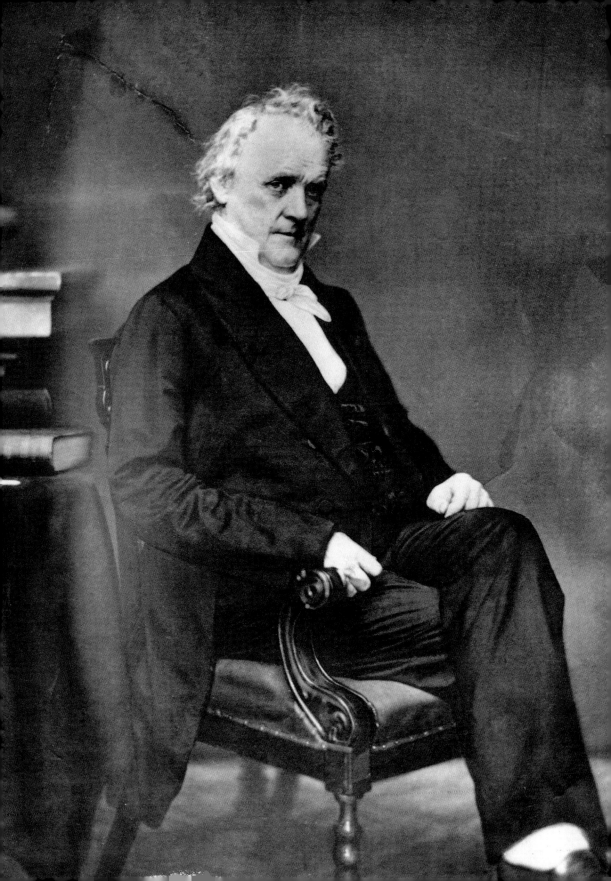

Abraham Lincoln

16th President · 1861–1865

Abraham Lincoln

James M. McPherson

Abraham Lincoln was the first extensively photographed president, posing for portraits on at least sixty-one separate occasions. Images taken before his election (such as this one from 1860) show Lincoln clean shaven. Those taken during and after 1861 show his familiar beard.

ON THE WET MORNING OF February 11, 1861, one day before his fifty-second birthday, President-elect Abraham Lincoln stood on the rear platform of a special train ready to leave Springfield, Illinois, for Washington. As he prepared to say good-bye to the crowd of friends and neighbors, his thoughts drifted back over the quarter century he'd lived in Springfield and forward to his inauguration three weeks later. "My friends," Lincoln said, "no one, not in my situation, can appreciate my feeling of sadness at this parting. To this place, and the kindness of these people, I owe everything....Here my children have been born, and one is buried. I now leave, not knowing when, or whether ever, I may return, with a task before me greater than that which rested on Washington."

The crisis awaiting the sixteenth (and, many feared, the last) president of the United States may indeed have been greater than that faced by the first. George Washington had steered the young republic through the buffetings of internal divisions and foreign menace; Lincoln confronted a vast civil war that threatened to end the existence of the *United* States. Washington's legacy was one nation, perhaps divisible, with liberty for some; Lincoln's was one nation, indivisible, with liberty for all.

Lincoln's origins gave little promise of greatness. He was born of illiterate parents on the hardscrabble Kentucky frontier. Soon after he came of age in 1830, he struck out on his own and moved to the Illinois village of New Salem, where he spent six formative years and made many friends. For a time, he drifted from one job to another: store clerk, mill hand, partner in a general store that failed, postmaster, surveyor. But he also acquired purpose and direction as a local schoolmaster, appropriately named Mentor Graham, guided his self-study of mathematics and literature.

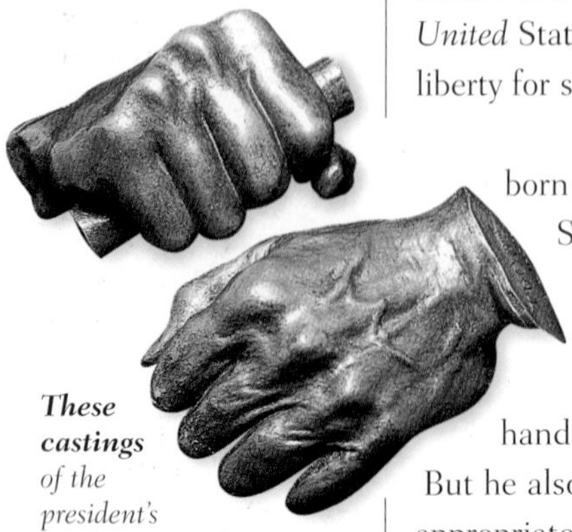

These castings of the president's hands were made during his lifetime.

In New Salem, Lincoln also began his lifelong love affair with politics—running unsuccessfully for the Illinois legislature in 1832, then winning in 1834 and serving four consecutive terms. He was a Whig, a follower of Henry Clay, whom Lincoln described as "my beau ideal of a statesman." Clay's American System—emphasizing government support for education, internal improvements, banking, and economic development—attracted Lincoln with its promise of upward mobility for those who seized the opportunities. Lincoln also began to study law, then as now a ticket to economic success and a political career. In 1837, he moved to nearby Springfield, the state capital, to begin practicing law.

BECOMING ONE OF THE LEADING Whigs in Illinois, Lincoln won election to Congress in 1846. In the House, he criticized Democratic president James K. Polk for having provoked war with Mexico. However, Whig opposition to the Mexican War was unpopular in Illinois, and Lincoln chose not to run for reelection in 1848. Six years later, a seismic political upheaval propelled him back into politics. The Kansas-Nebraska Act, rammed through Congress by Illinois senator Stephen A. Douglas, revoked the ban on slavery (imposed by the Missouri Compromise of 1820) in territories north of 36°30'. Although a longtime opponent of slavery, Lincoln had said little in public about the issue before 1854. But the Kansas-Nebraska Act, he later recalled in the third person, "aroused him as he had never been before." Over the next six years, Lincoln made 175 public

Two weeks after Antietam, *the president visited the Maryland battlefield. Flanking Lincoln are detective Allan Pinkerton, the Union army's intelligence chief, and Gen. John A. McClernand.*

speeches whose central theme was the necessity to exclude slavery from the territories as a step toward its eventual end everywhere.

Lincoln joined an "anti-Nebraska" coalition that fell just short of electing him to the U.S. Senate in 1855. A year later, he helped found the Illinois Republican party, which nominated him to run against Douglas for the Senate in 1858. Lincoln accepted the nomination and set the tone for his campaign with the famous "House Divided" speech.

BORN
February 12, 1809

BIRTHPLACE
Hardin County, Kentucky

DIED
April 15, 1865

PARTY AFFILIATION
Republican

CHILDREN
Robert, Edward, William, Thomas

MAJOR EVENTS

JULY 21, 1861

At the first battle of Bull Run, Confederate troops halt a Union advance and counterattack, routing Lincoln's "three-month men." The chaotic Union withdrawal is complicated by the presence of congressmen and other civilians who have ridden out from Washington with picnic baskets to watch what they imagine will be an easy Union victory.

APRIL 4, 1862

Gen. George McClellan begins his long-awaited Peninsular Campaign when navy transports begin landing one hundred thousand Union soldiers on the Virginia peninsula formed by the York and James Rivers. The Union commander will shortly move within striking distance of Richmond, the Confederate capital, but his extreme caution will eventually lead to withdrawal rather than a victory.

One of Lincoln's *Springfield acquaintances described him as unable to hold a lengthy conversation with a lady because he was "not sufficiently educated and intelligent in the female line." Mary Todd, however, was apparently gracious enough for the both of them. They met at a dance in 1839, seven years before this photograph was taken, and after a hesitant courtship married in 1842. Their first several years together were pleasant and peaceful, but the Todds had a history of mental illness, and Mary gradually began to show signs of instability herself. While he was alive, Lincoln was able to calm her, but after his death her mental health deteriorated rapidly.*

"'A house divided against itself cannot stand,'" he said. "I believe this government cannot endure, permanently, half *slave* and half *free*." When Republicans gained control of the government, he continued, they would reimpose the ban on slavery in the territories, thus stifling its growth and placing it "where the public mind shall rest in the belief that it is in course of ultimate extinction."

During the campaign, Lincoln and Douglas held seven debates in all parts of the state. Douglas insisted that the country *could* continue to flourish half slave and half free, as it had done since 1789. Such an assertion, responded Lincoln, made a mockery of the ideals of liberty on which the nation had been founded.

D EMOCRATS RETAINED a narrow majority in the state legislature (which then chose U.S. senators) and reelected Douglas. But Lincoln's performance in the debates gave him national visibility, which he increased by well-received speeches in the Northeast in early 1860. By the time the Republican national convention met in May, circumstances had elevated Lincoln from an Illinois favorite son to a serious contender for the presidential nomination. Republicans were certain to carry all but a handful of northern states, as they had in 1856. But they had no support in the South or the border states, so they needed the swing votes of Pennsylvania, Indiana, and Illinois to win the presidency. Lincoln seemed stronger in these states than the preconvention favorite, New York senator William H. Seward, who led on the first ballot. Lincoln caught up on the second and won on the third.

The ensuing four-party campaign was the most fateful in American history. The Democrats had split into northern and southern parties, while a remnant of the old Whigs formed the Constitutional Union party. Lincoln carried every free state except New Jersey and thereby won the election despite garnering only 40 percent of the popular vote—and no popular votes at all in nine slave states. Believing Lincoln's election a harbinger of the "ultimate extinction" of slavery, seven of these states seceded. By the time of Lincoln's inauguration on March 4, 1861, they had formed the Confederate States of America, elected Jefferson Davis president, and begun to organize an army.

Despite Lincoln's pledge to prevent the further expansion of slavery, he tried to reassure southerners that he had no constitutional

Six feet four inches tall *with a lanky rawboned look and unruly coarse black hair, the youthful Lincoln had a gregarious personality and a penchant for telling humorous stories. This 1846 daguerreotype is the earliest known likeness of him.*

power to act against slavery in states where it already existed. Lincoln repeated this point in a December 1860 letter to Alexander H. Stephens of Georgia (who soon became vice president of the Confederacy), but added: "I suppose, however, this does not meet the case. You think slavery is *right* and ought to be extended; while we think it is *wrong* and ought to be restricted. That I suppose is the rub."

"THE MONSTROUS INJUSTICE OF SLAVERY...DEPRIVES OUR REPUBLICAN EXAMPLE OF ITS JUST INFLUENCE IN THE WORLD—ENABLES THE ENEMIES OF FREE INSTITUTIONS, WITH PLAUSIBILITY, TO TAUNT US AS HYPOCRITES."

—Speech, 1854—

It was indeed the rub. Moreover, Lincoln's election without a single southern vote was a sign that the slave states had lost control of the national government and probably could never regain it. In his inaugural address, Lincoln invoked the common national heritage of North and South: "Though passion may have strained it must not break our bonds of affection. The mystic chords of memory, stretching from every battlefield and patriot grave to every living heart and hearthstone all over this broad land, will yet swell the chorus of the Union, when again touched, as surely they will be, by the better angels of our nature." For most secessionists, however, there was no turning back, and they ignored Lincoln's appeal.

The passion that broke those bonds of affection flared at Fort Sumter, the most significant piece of property in the Confederacy still held by the United States. The installation in Charleston Harbor was a flash point. As Confederates demanded its evacuation, Lincoln came under enormous pressure to yield

This photograph was taken at the Gettysburg cemetery just before the dedication ceremonies began. Lincoln is almost completely obscured by the crowd of notables (and bodyguards) surrounding him on the platform.

JULY 3, 1863

The failure of Pickett's Charge ends the three-day battle of Gettysburg and any expectation that the Confederacy might win the war.

JULY 4, 1863

Confederate commander John C. Pemberton surrenders Vicksburg to Gen. Ulysses S. Grant after a six-week siege. The capture of this Mississippi port—and with it, control of the Mississippi River— splits the Confederacy.

JULY 13–16, 1863

Inspired by the Copperhead slogan "Rich Man's War, Poor Man's Fight," laborers in New York City riot against the nation's first conscription law, passed in March. The rioters want no part of a war that will free slaves to compete with them in the job market.

NOVEMBER 16, 1864

After capturing Atlanta on September 2, Gen. William T. Sherman regroups his army for a march across Georgia that destroys nearly everything of economic value in its path. Sherman's March to the Sea will end with the occupation of Savannah on December 22.

APRIL 9, 1865

Following the fall of Richmond on April 3, Robert E. Lee surrenders to Grant at Appomattox Court House, Virginia.

> ### "I CLAIM NOT TO HAVE CONTROLLED EVENTS, BUT CONFESS PLAINLY THAT EVENTS HAVE CONTROLLED ME."
>
> —*Letter, 1864*—

the fort to preserve peace. After several sleepless nights, he made his decision. To give up the fort would constitute de facto recognition of the Confederacy. Even at the risk of war, he must preserve this symbol of Union. He decided to resupply the fort but in such a way as to put the onus of starting a war on the other side. Instead of sending reinforcements, he'd merely send provisions—"food for hungry men"—and notify southern authorities of his peaceful intentions. He did so, and Jefferson Davis ordered Confederate artillery to reduce the fort before the supply ships arrived. On April 12, 1861, Confederate batteries opened fire; after thirty-three hours of bombardment, Sumter's tiny garrison lowered the American flag in surrender.

These events united the North, which poured forth thousands of volunteers in response to Lincoln's call for troops; this call in turn caused four more states to secede and turned the South into an armed camp. As Lincoln put it four years later in his second inaugural address: "Both parties deprecated war; but one of them would make war rather than let the nation survive; and the other would accept war rather than let it perish. And the war came."

Lincoln was the only president whose entire tenure was bounded by the parameters of war. The latest news of the supply crisis at Fort Sumter was waiting on his desk the day he took office, and he was assassinated before the last of the Confederate armies had surrendered. Because of the war, Lincoln's constitutional duties as commander in chief superseded normal presidential activities. He devoted most of his efforts to shaping Union war aims, mobilizing armies, devising strategy, goading commanders, and holding together a fractious coalition of Radical Republicans, moderates, War Democrats, and border-state Unionists who supported the war.

Lincoln poses with his youngest son, *Thomas, known to the family as Tad. Tad was a particular comfort to his father after the death in 1862 of eleven-year-old Willie Lincoln, the only presidential child to die in the White House. Tad himself died young, passing away in 1871 at the age of eighteen.*

In his dedicatory address at the cemetery for Union soldiers killed at Gettysburg, Lincoln defined the purpose for which those men had given "the last full measure of devotion." It was the preservation of a nation "conceived in liberty, and dedicated to the proposition that all men are created equal." This Civil War was the great test of "whether that nation, or any nation so conceived and dedicated, can long endure." Only victory could assure that "government of the people, by the people, for the people, shall not perish from the earth."

Lincoln's conception of the strategy necessary to win that victory evolved through several stages as the war escalated to a level of destruction undreamed of by those who'd fired the first shots at Sumter. Union strategy in 1861 was designed to "suppress…combinations too powerful to be suppressed by the ordinary course of judicial proceedings," as Lincoln put it in his initial call for seventy-five thousand militia to serve three months. Those southern "combinations," however, refused to be "suppressed," and by 1862 Lincoln had called for a million soldiers to serve three years. Their mission was to invade, conquer, and occupy the rebellious states. These efforts achieved considerable success in 1862, as Union armies captured fifty thousand square miles of enemy territory in the lower Mississippi and Tennessee River Valleys and thousands more around the coastal perimeter of the Confederacy.

Y ET THIS ALSO FAILED to suppress the rebellion; indeed, Confederate armies mounted counteroffensives that recaptured much territory and even invaded the North. Lincoln learned that as long as these enemy armies remained intact, so would the Confederacy. "Destroy the rebel army," Lincoln wired Gen. George B. McClellan during the campaign climaxed by the September 1862 battle of Antietam. When McClellan proved unable or unwilling to do so, Lincoln got rid of him and continued to seek commanders who shared his emerging total-war strategy. By 1864, he finally had such generals in top commands: Ulysses S. Grant, William T. Sherman, Philip Sheridan, and George Thomas. They took the battle to the enemy, destroying or capturing enemy armies and demolishing the southern infrastructure that sustained the Confederate war effort.

The most important part of that infrastructure was slavery, which provided the bulk of the labor for the southern war economy. From the outset of the war, abolitionists and Radical Republicans had urged Lincoln to strike at slavery in order to weaken the Confederate economy and cripple the planter class that had taken the South out of the Union. Despite his own antislavery convictions, Lincoln initially resisted this pressure

A ticket to the April 14, 1865, performance of Our American Cousin at Ford's Theatre.

On April 11, 1865, two days after Lee's surrender at Appomattox, Lincoln spoke to celebrants on the White House lawn, hinting that his Reconstruction policy would enfranchise some freed slaves. "That means nigger citizenship," muttered Confederate sympathizer John Wilkes Booth. "Now, by God, I'll put him through. That is the last speech he will ever make." Three nights later, Booth entered the president's box at Ford's Theatre and shot him in the head. The contents of Lincoln's pockets that night (shown here) have since been deposited in the Library of Congress.

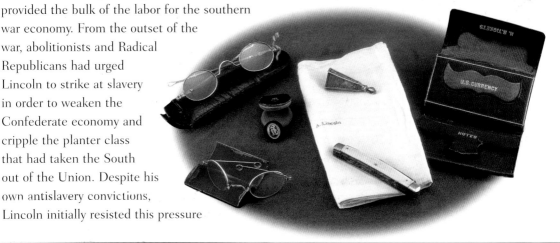

OPPOSITE:

Among the constituent elements of Lincoln's complex character was a reflective, almost brooding quality that sometimes descended into serious depression. During one of these bouts with "the hypo," as Lincoln called it, he wrote to a friend: "I am now the most miserable man living. If what I feel were equally distributed to the whole human family, there would not be one cheerful face on earth."

In Kentucky, where he was born (in the log cabin shown here), and in Indiana, where his family moved in 1816, Lincoln picked up a smattering of education in one-room schoolhouses. Determined to rise above his father's station in life, the teenage Lincoln developed a passion for self-improvement, devouring every book he could borrow from the meager libraries of his neighbors.

because he believed that an early declaration of emancipation would weaken the North (by alienating Democrats and border-state Unionists) more than it would weaken the South.

By the latter half of 1862, however, the logic of total war had convinced Lincoln that he must smite the "heart of the rebellion"—slavery. As president in peacetime, he would have no constitutional power of emancipation. But as commander in chief in wartime, he did have the constitutional right to seize enemy property being used to wage war. Slaves were such property. On September 22, 1862, he issued a preliminary proclamation warning that in states still in rebellion on January 1, 1863, he would use his war powers to declare their slaves "then, thenceforward, and forever free." January 1 came, and Lincoln fulfilled his promise. As he signed the Emancipation Proclamation, he told colleagues who witnessed the act: "I never, in my life, felt more certain that I was doing right than I do in signing this paper. If my name ever goes into history, it will be for this act, and my whole soul is in it."

> ## "HE IS A BARBARIAN, SCYTHIAN, YAHOO, A GORILLA IN RESPECT OF OUTWARD POLISH, BUT A MOST SENSIBLE, STRAIGHT-FORWARD OLD CODGER."
>
> —Lawyer George Templeton Strong—

For the slaves to become "forever free," the abolition of slavery would have to be made part of the Constitution. Lincoln won reelection in 1864 on a platform pledging this. Three months later, Congress passed the Thirteenth Amendment, though the president didn't live to see it ratified.

Without Lincoln's determined and skillful leadership, the North might have lost the war, and the United States as we know it today might not exist. Instead, Union victory resolved two festering problems left unresolved by the Revolution of 1776 and the Constitution of 1789: whether the republic would "long endure" or "perish from the earth" and whether the "monstrous injustice" of slavery would continue to mock a nation "conceived in liberty." The republic endured, and slavery perished. That is Lincoln's legacy.

★ ★ ★

Andrew Johnson

17th President · 1865–1869

Hans L. Trefousse

From adolescence,
Andrew Johnson was galled by the power that the South's planter aristocracy exercised over the common yeoman. He loved the South but not as much as he hated the plantation owners.

ANDREW JOHNSON HELD three strong prejudices: a bias favoring yeoman farmers over the planter elite, the certainty that blacks were inferior to whites "in point of intellect," and a reverence for the Constitution, which he believed should be strictly interpreted. These convictions influenced his actions in profound ways during much of his career.

During the secession crisis that followed Abraham Lincoln's election, Johnson, then a U.S. senator, took a firm stand for the Union, reflecting the preferences of his East Tennessee constituency as well as his own predilections. His stand against secession, however, didn't mean he was unsympathetic to the cause of preserving the South's "peculiar institution." On the contrary: A slaveholder himself, he declared on the floor of the Senate that the maintenance of the Union was essential for slavery's perpetuation, because the South couldn't manage as well on its own. During the 1860 election, he even supported prosouthern presidential candidate John C. Breckinridge, but he remained loyal to the national government throughout, even after the formation of the Confederacy.

In line with his strict constructionist principles and in order to reassure border states and northern Democrats that the Civil War wasn't an abolitionist crusade, he cosponsored the Johnson-Crittenden Resolutions, which declared that the war was being fought merely to maintain the supremacy of the Constitution and not to interfere with established institutions among the several states. The only senator from a seceding state to have remained in Congress, Johnson was appointed military governor of Tennessee in March 1862. While governor, he saw to it that his home state remained exempt from the Emancipation Proclamation, and not until the summer of 1863 did he finally begin to champion emancipation as a

Johnson used this iron *(also called a goose)* *and these shears at his tailor shop in Greenville, Tennessee.*

These seven Republican congressmen acted as prosecutors during Johnson's Senate trial. *Thaddeus Stevens is seated on the left with a cane in his right hand.*

BORN
December 29, 1808

BIRTHPLACE
Raleigh, North Carolina

DIED
July 31, 1875

PARTY AFFILIATION
Democrat-Union

CHILDREN
Martha, Charles, Mary,
Robert, Andrew Jr.

necessary war measure. Later, after the Republican Lincoln chose the War Democrat Johnson as his 1864 Union party running mate (in order to attract border-state unionists and northern Democrats), Johnson made speeches promising to lead blacks, as Moses had led the Jews, to their freedom. Even so, his racist views never diminished, as confirmed by his actions as president, which evidenced little concern for the fate of the freed people.

"SHOW ME THE MAN WHO MAKES WAR ON THE GOVERNMENT, AND FIRES ON ITS VESSELS, AND I WILL SHOW YOU A TRAITOR."

—*Public statement, 1861*—

Johnson's vice presidency proved to be of short duration. Having taken too many drinks of whiskey to fortify himself (he'd been ill), Johnson delivered an inaugural speech so rambling that it horrified his audience. Lincoln defended Johnson—declaring, "Andy ain't a drunkard"—but hardly a month later, Lincoln was dead and Johnson president.

The most difficult problem facing the new administration was Reconstruction. How were the southern states to be restored? And what was to be done with the newly freed blacks? Given the shock of total defeat and the fear of retaliation from angry northerners in the wake of Lincoln's assassination, the South would have acquiesced, if not gracefully, in Reconstruction measures that enfranchised some blacks

MAJOR EVENTS

MAY 13, 1865

Gen. Kirby Smith, commanding rebel troops west of the Mississippi River, orders his men to surrender. Smith's action ends the last organized Confederate resistance to the Union.

DECEMBER 24, 1865

In Pulaski, Tennessee, former Confederate soldiers organize the Ku Klux Klan, which begins as a social club for veterans but quickly becomes a focus for violent southern resistance to Radical Reconstruction.

JULY 30, 1866

The attempt to give black men the right to vote provokes a race riot in New Orleans. The murder of forty-eight radicals of both races fills newspaper headlines in the North and turns many moderates against Johnson's lenient Reconstruction policy.

This cartoon, drawn during Johnson's presidency, suggests not only his fixation on the Constitution but also his orneriness, reminiscent of Andrew Jackson's and in many ways admirable.

Eighteen-year-old Andrew Johnson married sixteen-year-old Eliza McCardle in May 1827, just eight months after his arrival in Greenville, Eliza's hometown. Over the next ten years, she taught him how to read and write more effectively and how to spell fairly well. Of course, spelling was not yet a respected art. As Andrew Jackson once told his secretary (upon being informed that he had misspelled his own name), "It is a man of small imagination who cannot spell his name more than one way."

and disenfranchised some leading Confederates. Thus the president had a splendid opportunity to assuage the difficult problems of Reconstruction and race relations. But because of his firm prejudices, especially his desire to maintain white supremacy in the South, he mishandled this opportunity.

Although Johnson thundered against the Confederate leaders and called for their personal punishment, he believed the states they represented were, in fact, still part of the Union and therefore guaranteed representation in Congress. Thus he desired their immediate restoration—not readmission, because in his view they'd never left. He preferred that this restoration take place after each state had ratified the Thirteenth Amendment abolishing slavery, but he wasn't inclined to insist on even this condition. Nor did he seek any safeguards for the freed people.

T HE THIRTY-NINTH CONGRESS wasn't scheduled to convene until December 1865. In the meantime, Johnson's Reconstruction policy unfolded through his own unilateral action. On May 29, six weeks after becoming president, he issued two proclamations: One offered amnesty to all but fourteen excluded classes of Confederates, among them wealthy southerners whose property exceeded twenty thousand dollars in value; the other named W. W. Holden provisional governor of North Carolina so that he might call a convention, its delegates chosen by the voters of 1861, to amend that state's constitution in preparation for restoration. Similar proclamations for the other seceded states followed, resulting in the election of legislative bodies so conservative that some even refused to repeal their secession ordinances, much less abolish slavery or repudiate the Confederate debt, as Johnson had requested. Instead, they passed black codes virtually remanding the freed people to a position not far removed from slavery and elected leading former Confederates—including Alexander H. Stephens, Jefferson Davis's vice president—to Congress.

When Congress finally convened in December, Johnson suffered his first setback. At the behest of the Radical Republicans, particularly Thaddeus Stevens, the clerk of the House refused to call the names of any southern representatives, even the most loyal. Instead, Congress established a Joint Committee of Fifteen on Reconstruction, to which all matters pertaining to the South were referred. As the radicals were still a minority faction, Johnson might well have cooperated with the numerous moderates who preferred accommodation. Yet his conviction that the white race was superior to the black made him unwilling to compromise, and his strict constructionist views led him to veto the Freedmen's Bureau and civil rights bills, thereby alienating the moderates who had framed them. When Congress proposed the Fourteenth Amendment in June 1866, Johnson might easily have accepted it, but he decided to oppose the amendment on the grounds that no constitutional changes could be made so long as the southern states were without representation.

T HE WIDENING BREACH between the president and Congress became the focal point of the 1866 midterm elections. To rally his Union party followers (a coalition of conservative Republicans and unionist Democrats), Johnson undertook a journey to the West, called the "swing around the circle," during which he delivered a series of ill-considered speeches blaming the radicals for a race riot in New Orleans. Johnson's blunders contributed to the defeat of congressional candidates who would have supported him, greatly strengthening the radicals.

In the final days of the Thirty-ninth Congress, the radicals were thus able to begin passing measures designed to shackle the president and give them control of Reconstruction. The most notable of these, the Tenure of Office Act, required the president to obtain Senate approval before dismissing any officeholder whose appointment had been made with the Senate's consent. In addition, the Fortieth Congress, which wouldn't ordinarily have met until December 1867, was called into immediate session. This unusual action allowed the radicals not only to oversee implementation of the First Reconstruction Act, which remanded southern states to military rule, but also to keep an eye on Johnson, who would otherwise have been left alone in Washington for the better part of the year.

After most of Johnson's vetoes were overridden, he tried to strike back in another way. Unlike other Lincoln appointees who'd resigned because of their differences with the president, Secretary of War Edwin M. Stanton had stayed on because his position within the cabinet made him quite useful to Johnson's opponents. In August 1867, Johnson suspended Stanton and appointed Gen. Ulysses S. Grant secretary ad interim.

> ## "HIS FAITH IN THE PEOPLE NEVER WAVERED."
>
> —*Epitaph on Johnson's grave in Greenville*—

MARCH 30, 1867

Secretary of State William H. Seward negotiates the $7.2 million purchase of Russian-held Alaska. Those who question the wisdom of buying this "large lump of ice" dub the purchase Seward's Folly.

NOVEMBER 6, 1868

Sioux chief Red Cloud ends two years of war when he agrees to the Treaty of Fort Laramie. In exchange for an end o Indian raiding, the government promises the Sioux control of their Dakota homeland, including the sacred Black Hills, in perpetuity.

DECEMBER 25, 1868

In one of his final official acts as president, Johnson proclaims a general amnesty for all those who took part in the rebellion.

By this 1818 document, *Andrew Johnson, an impoverished nine-year-old without a day of schooling in his life, was indentured to James J. Selby of Raleigh to learn the tailor's trade. Johnson ran away six years later.*

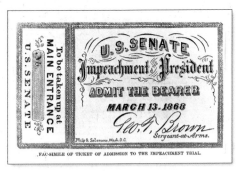

FAC-SIMILE OF TICKET OF ADMISSION TO THE IMPEACHMENT TRIAL.

This ticket admitted the bearer to the opening day of Johnson's impeachment trial. The market for gallery seats was brisk, and scalpers received exaggerated sums.

Having come to the conclusion that Reconstruction was impossible so long as Johnson remained in the White House, able to frustrate their measures by interpreting them loosely, the radicals now sought to impeach him. The House Judiciary Committee, searching for appropriate charges since January, finally brought a resolution in December, but the bill of particulars was so weak that the full House refused to impeach. Then, in January 1868, when the Senate sought to reinstate Stanton, Johnson quarreled with Grant over Grant's surrender of the War Department to Stanton. This controversy led to another impeachment effort, but it was only when the president dismissed Stanton in open defiance of the Tenure of Office Act that the sitting House voted to impeach.

A LENGTHY TRIAL followed. Most of the eleven counts concerned the Tenure of Office Act, but the president was also accused of bringing Congress into disrepute and failing to carry out the Reconstruction Acts. Because the facts were acknowledged, the trial—a great event in Washington—came down to whether the charges amounted to violations of the Constitution. On May 16, 1868, on the eleventh article, the catchall, the Senate voted 35–19 in favor of conviction, thus falling one vote short of the two-thirds necessary to remove the president. Johnson had made deals with some senators, promising not to continue his interfere with Reconstruction and to appoint Gen. John M. Schofield secretary of war. Others who backed Johnson, despite tremendous party pressure to convict, feared that doing so would undermine the government's tripartite division of power—and still others preferred Johnson to his putative successor, Benjamin F. Wade of Ohio, the ultraradical president pro tempore of the Senate.

One result of Johnson's acquittal was that, for the next 130 years, no president was impeached on merely token grounds. Another outcome was the strengthening of those in the South who would eventually overthrow Reconstruction. Although the trial ended Johnson's national political career, he remained popular in Tennessee, which returned him to the Senate in 1875. Johnson died in office a few months later, having contributed to keeping the South a "white man's country" for several more generations. For this reason, from his point of view and considering his prejudices, his administration wasn't wholly unsuccessful.

OPPOSITE:

This portrait was taken by Mathew Brady in his Washington, D.C., studio. Johnson's scowl typically masked a sincere populism. He championed the cause of homesteading, for instance, so that working families could afford their own farms.

★ ★ ★

Ulysses S. Grant

18ᵗʰ President · 1869–1877

Michael Les Benedict

Despite his tough public image, *Ulysses S. Grant was squeamish, soft spoken, and shy. For example, he always bathed in a closed tent so that others wouldn't see him naked. "There was a broad streak of the feminine in his personality," one Grant biographer has written. "He was almost half-woman, but this strain was buried in the depths of his soul."*

ULYSSES S. GRANT IS COMMONLY considered a great general who made a terrible president. He has been consistently ranked near the bottom of the list of chief executives (although a few historians have recently been more sympathetic), and it's likely that many of Grant's contemporaries would have agreed with this assessment. Political reformers of the 1870s, for example, blasted Grant for his partisanship and for winking at the corruption all around him. The charge has largely stuck.

Few at Grant's March 1869 inauguration would have predicted this particular criticism. Even those who'd voted against the man respected him. He wasn't the first choice of many members of his party, yet Grant had the reputation of being a no-nonsense administrator whose single criterion for selecting and keeping subordinates was whether or not they did the job. Reformers expected him to run his administration with little or no regard to partisan politics. "The office has come to me unsought," Grant declared in his inaugural address; "I commence its duties untrammeled." Yet slowly, as he became the real (and not merely titular) leader of the Republican party, Grant threw his support behind the means and goals of disciplined party politics.

At the time Grant entered the White House, it appeared the great issues of the Civil War had all been resolved. Most of the Confederate states had been restored to the Union and were being governed by Republican regimes sustained largely by black voters. The Fourteenth Amendment had already been ratified, and Congress had just sent the Fifteenth Amendment to the states. It seemed just the time for a capable administrator such as Grant to remedy the economic problems that had long been neglected.

Outside the cash-starved states of the South and West, most Americans believed the government needed to begin redeeming war-era

During the war, *General Grant often smoked twenty cigars a day. This is one of his cigar cases.*

paper currency (known as "greenbacks") and thus return to a specie standard. The funds necessary to pay off the devalued greenbacks would have to come from tariff revenues, and those in turn depended on stable and prosperous trade. The protective tariffs designed to shelter particular industries were hampering the economy, reformers argued, whereas free trade with the rest of the world would promote prosperity by reducing prices. The new challenges were financial and economic, they continued, requiring a government staffed by experts, not party hacks. Yet, despite reformers' hopes that President Grant might become their champion, Republican senators refused to surrender control over patronage appointments, and Grant, bowing to reality, filled his cabinet with Republican regulars as well as some reformers.

GRANT FURTHER DISAPPOINTED the reformers when he refused to exercise positive leadership on major public issues—an approach that had worked well for him during his years as a military commander, when he'd been content to leave policy making to President Lincoln and Congress. In the meantime, he'd found the best men to serve under him, established the general tactics they were to follow, and left them to work out the details.

General Grant usually gave advice only when asked, and President Grant similarly promised to impose no policies of his own. Congress would set policy, and his administration would carry it out, each cabinet

The president poses with a Chinese diplomat. Grant's years in office were marked by anti-Chinese rioting, particularly in California.

BORN
April 27, 1822

BIRTHPLACE
Point Pleasant, Ohio

DIED
July 23, 1885

PARTY AFFILIATION
Republican

CHILDREN
Frederick, Ulysses Jr., Ellen, Jesse

MAJOR EVENTS

FEBRUARY 25, 1870

Hiram R. Revels of Mississippi, the first black congressman, takes his seat in the Senate.

MARCH 30, 1870

Ratification of the Fifteenth Amendment makes it illegal to deny U.S. citizens the right to vote "on account of race, color, or previous condition of servitude." However, economic pressures and political violence still keep many freedmen from the polls.

JULY 8, 1871

The New York Times begins a series of articles exposing the corrupt Tweed Ring, which has dominated New York City politics since 1866. Instrumental in William M. Tweed's downfall have been the Harper's Weekly cartoons drawn by Thomas Nast, which have turned public opinion against the Democratic political boss.

For relaxation, Grant liked to drive around Washington in a gig (a light two-wheeled carriage). Once he was ticketed for speeding on M Street by a police officer who somehow didn't recognize the president.

Grant fell in love with Julia Dent, the sister of his West Point roommate, shortly before the outbreak of war with Mexico. During their four-year engagement, the couple saw each other only once but kept their relationship lively with a correspondence that included its share of sexual innuendo. Although never considered attractive, Mrs. Grant had the self-image of a southern belle and entertained in a lavish manner. Her greatest triumph was the May 1874 White House wedding of her daughter, Nellie. As late as 1902, the wedding was still being hailed as one of the most brilliant ever given in the United States.

secretary managing his own department without presidential meddling. The trouble was that Congress set no overall public policies, and Grant offered little advice. His most significant early action was to speed Reconstruction in the three states (Mississippi, Texas, and Virginia) not yet restored. That accomplished, Grant had no war to fight, no comprehensive program to implement. Because Congress traditionally set tariff policy, Grant said nothing about it. Nor did he encourage Treasury Secretary George Boutwell to take action in this regard. Instead, with Grant's approval, the Treasury Department promoted financial stability, reduction of the national debt, and the gradual resumption of a specie currency.

" I AM MORE OF A FARMER THAN A SOLDIER."

—Remark to Otto von Bismarck, 1879—

Grant's hands-off approach blew up in September 1869, when his passivity encouraged speculators James Fisk and Jay Gould to believe they could corner the gold market. Their plan relied on the ability of Grant's brother-in-law to prevent the president from ordering the sale of government gold. On September 24—Black Friday—the price of gold soared, threatening financial institutions with ruin. Only at the last minute did Grant avoid catastrophe by ordering Boutwell to sell government reserves. The market recovered, but the episode badly undermined confidence in Grant's administrative ability.

With regard to civil service reform, Grant was similarly passive, allowing each cabinet member to set his own rules. Some experimented with merit examinations; others followed more traditional partisan customs. As the reform-oriented *Nation* observed dryly, Grant "certainly has redeemed his promise to have no policy of his own." Party leaders benefited personally from Grant's laissez-faire attitude, but the party as a whole needed the president to set an agenda. Without a specific policy around which to rally, the party of Lincoln began to drift and break apart. In northern states, disgruntled Republicans echoed reformers' complaints about patronage-driven machines, and they were joined by leading newspaper editors whose influence in the party was waning.

In the South and the border states, matters were even worse. Grant and most northerners craved peace, but ex-Confederates weren't willing to accept Republican state governments beholden to black voters. Their determination was reinforced by the activist policies of these governments, which increased taxes on white property holders (rather than on impoverished former slaves) in order to boost state spending. Most southerners denounced the expensive new programs as the work of demagogic Republicans bidding for black support, while dissident, reform-minded Republicans, complaining about the party's dependence on black voters,

This 1845 photograph shows a youthful U. S. Grant (left) with fellow lieutenant Alexander Hays, probably at an army camp in Louisiana. During the Civil War, Hays would command a division under Grant before losing his life at the May 1864 Battle of the Wilderness.

urged greater liberality toward ex-Confederates. Ignoring the racism and violence encouraged by white southern politicians, the reformers made alliances with Democrats to oust Republican regulars from power. Successes in Virginia, West Virginia, and Tennessee in 1869 encouraged similar "liberal Republican" movements elsewhere.

DURING ALL THIS, Grant's cabinet remained divided. Some sympathized with the reformers, urging neutrality in the fight between party factions and opposing any action to restrain violence against blacks in the South. Others strongly backed the party leaders, distributing jobs in their departments to reward loyal Republicans and punish bolters. However, as southern Republicans began losing to Democratic–liberal Republican coalitions in elections often marred by violence, party regulars in Congress demanded that Grant do something. The Civil War issues weren't dead after all.

Although Grant's earlier refusal to set policy had disappointed reformers, the same reluctance now outraged the regulars, who punished Grant by rejecting his nomination of Attorney General Ebenezer R. Hoar (a reformer) to the Supreme Court. Reformers again urged Grant to repudiate the machine politicians, and they redoubled their pressure for civil service reform and free trade. "My whole argument," one reformer

JUNE 2, 1874

Treasury Secretary William A. Richardson is forced to resign after it is revealed that he made a deal with tax collector John D. Sanborn allowing Sanborn to keep half of the money he collected. Few believe that Grant knew of Richardson's arrangement, yet many question his judgment in appointing such a man to high government office.

NOVEMBER 18, 1874

Meeting at a church in Cleveland, 135 women from seventeen states form the Woman's Christian Temperance Union. The WCTU will publish pamphlets, sponsor debates, and stage demonstrations to further its goal of banning the sale and consumption of alcohol.

JULY 1875

"Let no guilty man escape," Grant tells prosecutors in the Whiskey Ring case. However, when his personal secretary Orville E. Babcock is charged, Grant meddles to win Babcock's freedom.

JUNE 25, 1876

On the Little Bighorn River, Col. George A. Custer discovers a large encampment of Sioux and Cheyenne "hostiles" who have ignored a government order to return to their reservations. Unaware or unconcerned that he is greatly outnumbered, Custer attacks.

After leaving office, Grant lent his name to a brokerage firm run by Ferdinand Ward, a scoundrel who fleeced both Grant and their clients. Forced to declare bankruptcy in 1884, Grant began writing his memoirs in the hope that their publication would provide his family with financial security. This photograph shows a terminally ill Grant in June 1885, less than a month before his death, finishing the book that would ultimately earn more than a half million dollars (1880s dollars, that is) in royalties.

This 1873 cartoon illustrates the horror with which the press reacted to news that Grant had appointed Alexander R. Shepherd to govern the District of Columbia. "Boss" Shepherd was already notorious among reformers for his alleged extravagance and corruption as head of the district's board of public works.

wrote after lobbying Grant, "is that he must be the head of the party; and give it a policy." But the reformers' plans went awry when reform congressmen (and even some cabinet members) opposed a treaty that would have annexed the island nation of Santo Domingo (now the Dominican Republic), which Grant wanted for a naval base.

From this repudiation, Grant learned the virtues of party discipline and the consequences of party disorganization. He subsequently secured the resignations of the cabinet secretaries who had sympathized with the reformers and openly associated himself with the party regulars who ran the Senate, replacing federal officeholders who had backed liberal Republicans and appointing partisans to key federal offices around the country. In March 1871, he urged Congress to pass legislation to combat the Ku Klux Klan, confirming his complete break with liberal Republicans, who strongly opposed such action. Regular Republicans, once cool to Grant, now backed his 1872 renomination; reformers, once his enthusiastic backers, organized to nominate their own candidate in cooperation with the Democrats.

FROM 1871 ONWARD, Grant consistently pushed for party discipline and supported Republican governments in the South. At the same time, his reform opponents, many of whom were influential opinion makers in the press and intellectual circles, made only slow headway. In the 1872 election, Grant routed liberal Republican Horace Greeley, editor of the *New York Tribune,* even though the Democrats backed Greeley as well.

Grant's new course made the suppression of southern violence a central test of his administration's ability to enforce its will. At first, he seemed to be succeeding: The anti-Klan legislation of 1871 authorized him to declare martial law. Although he could do so only temporarily,

this was enough to scatter the Klan and allow Republican regulars to carry most southern states, losing ground only in those states with significantly larger white than black populations.

But then, after the 1872 election, Grant dismayed the Republicans he'd helped elect by reaching out to southern Democrats, hoping for some measure of reconciliation to the changes wrought by Reconstruction. He failed, though, because the differences were too fundamental: Not only were most of the white southerners deeply racist, they also objected to state services for blacks, which inevitably came at the expense of the mostly white taxpayers. In addition, activist state government created an environment that encouraged both peculation and bribery—the blame for which, most white southerners firmly believed, fell squarely on blacks who had no business voting.

The situation was so bad that the white southerners felt violence was justified. Emboldened by Grant's postelection vacillation, in state after state they formed White Leagues and other paramilitary organizations to keep blacks from the polls, often by violent means. Meanwhile, offended by reports of southern Republican corruption, reformers absolved ex-Confederates of responsibility for their actions and condemned Grant whenever he tried to stop the bloodshed or counteract its effects. Likewise, most northern Republican leaders chose to overlook the peculation that did exist among their southern colleagues, arguing that no amount of corruption could justify the electoral violence.

But northern resolve was weakening. Criticism of the use of federal troops to protect black voters grew, as did distaste for southern Republican politicians. By 1875, it was clear that Grant could no longer forestall the Democratic takeover of southern state governments. During 1875 and 1876, in elections marked by intimidation and bloodshed, the remaining Republican regimes were roughly ousted.

At the same time, Grant's alliance with the machine politicians came under increasingly bitter attack. The Crédit Mobilier scandal implicated leading Republican congressmen in a railroad bribery scheme, the public reacted angrily to legislation that retroactively increased congressional pay (the so-called Salary Grab), and evidence grew of corruption among politically active Treasury Department employees. In New York, Boston, Chicago, and other cities, government officials traded bribes for tax breaks (most notoriously in St. Louis, where the Whiskey Ring operated). More and more people blamed Grant.

For nearly a century, generation upon generation of Democratic presidential candidates counted on the electoral votes of the Solid South. As this 1880 cartoon attests, the origins of the Solid South can be found in the policies of carpetbag government and bayonet rule endorsed by the Republican Grant.

During a fall 1879 tour of the West, the former president visited a Nevada silver mine.

When Grant declared
*bankruptcy in 1884,
showman P. T. Barnum
offered him a hundred
thousand dollars for the
right to display his Civil
War memorabilia. Grant
declined. Most of the
equipment later ended
up in the West Point
Museum. Grant's army
lantern (shown here) is
part of that collection.*

OPPOSITE:

This Mathew Brady
*photograph shows Grant in
June 1864 during the siege
of Petersburg. Lincoln's
advisers regularly urged
him to dismiss the general
because of Grant's high
casualty figures. In one
month, for example,
Grant's 118,000-man
army lost nearly 45,000
men. Lincoln refused.
"I cannot spare this man,"
the president said.
"He fights."*

The president never really understood the criticism. Believing the reformers simply wanted to substitute themselves for the existing Republican leadership, he refused to credit their allegations of corruption (which he considered exaggerated) and took charges against his subordinates as attacks on his administration. His animosity blinded him to the corruption that did exist, and his resentment undermined what had been his greatest asset—his ability to identify able subordinates who could be trusted to carry out his wishes.

GRANT WAS MOST SUCCESSFUL in the area of financial policy. He quietly backed the Treasury Department's slow reduction of the paper currency, and when economic depression hit in 1874, he resisted the strong pressure to increase the money supply. Grant's veto of the resulting legislation earned him the plaudits of even his most severe critics, and the following year Congress endorsed his stand by voting to make all paper money convertible to specie as of January 1, 1879.

Despite all the corruption and the failure of his southern policy, Grant remained a hero to Republican regulars—the stalwart defender of the party's principles and organization. His reputation in the nation at large also rebounded strongly as he remained calm and resolute

"THE GODS, THE DESTINIES, SEEM TO HAVE CONCENTRATED UPON HIM."

—Walt Whitman—

during the crisis brought on by the disputed presidential election of 1876. He made clear that he wouldn't tolerate violence, nor would he use force to install Republican candidate Rutherford B. Hayes. The eventual compromise led to Hayes's peaceful inauguration.

Grant's hold on Republicans remained so strong that they nearly nominated him for president again at the 1880 convention. Delegates had remembered his strengths and forgiven him his shortcomings. Not so, however, the intellectual elites who would later write the history of the Grant era, and it has been their view that has so far determined Grant's historical reputation.

★ ★ ★

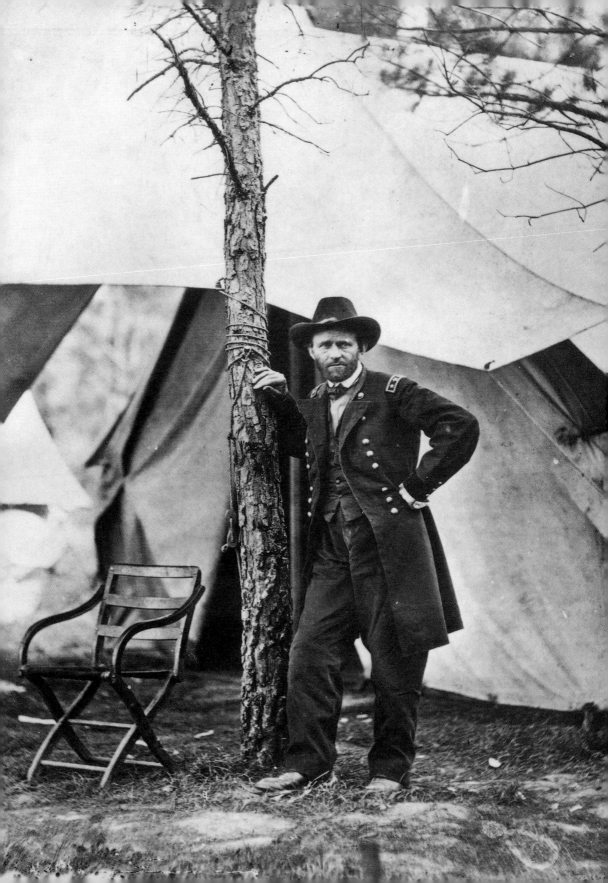

Rutherford B. Hayes

19th President · 1877–1881

James A. Rawley

THE NINETEENTH PRESIDENT stood out from many of his predecessors in his humanitarian outlook, particularly regarding ethnic minorities. In his first annual message to Congress, Rutherford Hayes acknowledged that "many, if not most, of our Indian wars have had their origin in broken promises and acts of injustice upon our part"—a remarkable admission for a U.S. president to make just one year removed from the battle of Little Bighorn. Hayes reinforced his words with proposals for the industrial and general education of young Indians, land allotments in place of reservations, and citizenship. Yet none of these aims was fulfilled, reflecting a pattern of Hayes's presidency: the setting of exemplary Christian goals, followed by the achievement of less-than-exemplary results, particularly when Congress was concerned.

Rutherford Birchard Hayes was born in Delaware, Ohio, where he spent his early years under the influence of his moralistic mother and a benevolent bachelor uncle who lent him financial support. Hayes was graduated first in his Class of 1842 from Kenyon College in Gambier, Ohio, and three years later he completed his studies at the Harvard Law School. Beginning a law practice, he displayed tendencies toward political reform, social justice, and humanitarian causes. His 1852 marriage to Lucy Webb, a vigorous opponent of slavery and the first college-educated first lady, further influenced his views on temperance, slavery, and good works.

During the 1850s, he practiced law in Cincinnati and became more deeply involved in Whig (and then Republican) politics, making speeches for Abraham Lincoln in 1860. With the reduction of Fort Sumter and Lincoln's recourse to arms, Hayes volunteered for military service, becoming in June 1861 a major in the Twenty-third Ohio

The presidency of Rutherford B. Hayes, Mark Twain predicted, would "in its quiet and unostentatious but real and substantial greatness…steadily rise into higher and higher prominence." Instead, even Hayes's friends began to criticize him for not being active enough.

Like John Quincy Adams, Hayes kept an extensive diary of his life and presidency. The volume shown here covers most of 1862, including the September day on which Hayes was nearly killed at the Civil War battle of South Mountain.

Volunteer Infantry. He served four years, was wounded five times, and in 1865 was breveted major general. That same year, he won election to the House of Representatives, where he largely adhered to party policy. Hayes generally supported Radical Republican efforts to enforce Reconstruction policy in the South, and he voted for Andrew Johnson's impeachment. Yet, at the same time, he disapproved of the means by which party leaders railroaded bills through the House, once rejoicing "that the despotism of the committees and the older members was rebuked." Hayes's political career advanced in 1867, when he was elected governor of Ohio.

This "snapshot" commemorates the president's October 21, 1880, visit to Yosemite. Among those accompanying him were his wife, his son Rutherford Platt Hayes, and Secretary of War Alexander Ramsey.

T WICE REELECTED, Hayes was serving as governor when the Republican party met in Cincinnati in 1876 to choose its presidential nominee. Knowing that the Democrats would make Grant-era corruption a major campaign issue, the Republicans on the seventh ballot settled on Hayes. His heroism as a Civil War general, his record as a reform governor, and Ohio's position as a pivotal state contributed to make him an attractive candidate.

Even so, most northern voters were tired of Reconstruction controversies, and it appeared that Samuel J. Tilden and the Democrats would win the White House for the first time since 1856. The man credited with breaking up the notorious Tweed Ring, Tilden took the popular vote and led in the electoral college, 184–166, but 19 votes remained uncertain. The returns of three Republican-controlled states—Louisiana, Florida, and South Carolina—were in dispute, and one of Oregon's votes was also being challenged. A special electoral commission, composed of fifteen congressmen and Supreme Court justices, was appointed to make a determination. The extraordinary denouement came only two days before the inauguration when, voting 8–7 along party lines, the commission gave all 19 disputed votes—and the presidency—to Hayes.

BORN
October 4, 1822

BIRTHPLACE
Delaware, Ohio

DIED
January 17, 1893

PARTY AFFILIATION
Republican

CHILDREN
Sardis, James, Rutherford, Joseph, George, Fanny, Scott, Manning

---

MAJOR EVENTS

MAY 6, 1877

Worn down by the army's relentless pursuit, the Sioux warrior Crazy Horse surrenders in exchange for the promise (which the government will never honor) of a reservation in Montana's Powder River country. Following its humiliating June 1876 defeat at the battle of the Little Bighorn, the army has redoubled its efforts to force dissident Sioux onto government reservations.

JANUARY 10, 1878

Sen. A. A. Sargent of California introduces a constitutional amendment granting women the right to vote. The women's suffrage amendment, also know as the Susan B. Anthony Amendment, is defeated in committee, but it will be introduced again and again until it finally passes Congress in 1919 and is sent to the states for ratification.

In his diary, Hayes described nineteen-year-old Lucy Webb with abundant admiration: "Her low sweet voice is very winning, her soft rich eye not often equaled; a heart as true as steel....Intellect she has, too, a quick sprightly one.... By George! I am in love with her!" Unlike most Victorian women, the young Mrs. Hayes had definite political views, especially when it came to slavery and alcohol. As first lady, she was known as Lemonade Lucy because she banned liquor in the White House and often served lemonade instead. Her notoriety made her the first celebrity first lady since Dolley Madison.

When some southern Democrats threatened rebellion over what they considered the obvious theft of an election, a deal was struck that committed Hayes to ending the military occupation of the South, rebuilding the southern economic infrastructure, and including a southern Democrat in his cabinet. The deal also ensured that Hayes would enter the White House with less than the usual complement of presidential authority.

Hayes assumed office during the economic depression that followed the Panic of 1873. The railroads, having recently engaged in a rate war, were among the worst sufferers. Soon after Hayes took office, however, in an era before antitrust laws, the nation's four largest lines agreed to raise rates and simultaneously lower wages by 10 percent. This pay cut, the second major reduction since the depression began, led to the July 1877 Great Uprising, during which striking workers shut down most U.S. railroad service. As fighting between strikers and state

> ## "HIS AMIABLE CHARACTER, HIS LACK OF PARTY HEAT, HIS CONCILIATORY ATTITUDE TOWARDS THE SOUTH ALIENATED RATHER THAN ATTRACTED THE MEMBERS OF HIS PARTY."
>
> —Woodrow Wilson—

militiamen intensified, Hayes sent federal troops to restore order in West Virginia, where the trouble had begun at a Baltimore & Ohio yard in Martinsburg, and then to Pittsburgh, where local militiamen had sided with the strikers. Although Hayes pursued these deployments cautiously, they nevertheless made him the first president since Andrew Jackson to use federal troops in a labor dispute. The mere presence of the troops quelled the violence.

Among other groups, such as farmers, the labor unions had been pressing Hayes to inflate the currency, primarily through the unlimited coinage of silver. But Hayes held fast to his belief in hard money. According to the Specie Resumption Act of 1875, the government would begin redeeming devalued Civil War–era paper greenbacks for gold beginning on January 1, 1879—a policy that Hayes favored. Complicating matters was the Bland-Allison Act of 1878, passed over Hayes's veto, which required the federal government to purchase and

Hayes posed for this daguerreotype while a law student at Harvard in 1845.

coin at least two (but not more than four) million dollars' worth of silver each month. Believing the coinage of silver would stain the nation's credit, Hayes ordered Treasury Secretary John Sherman to purchase the minimum amount. The depression lifted, greenbacks rose to par, and specie payments were smoothly resumed.

H AYES AGAIN EXPERIENCED the antagonism of Congress when he tried to further civil service reform, one of his top domestic priorities. Using his executive power, he issued an order in June 1877 prohibiting federal employees from taking part in political activity. This directive exacerbated the already troublesome factionalization of the Republican party, particularly alienating the conservative Stalwarts. This wing of the party was led by Sen. Roscoe Conkling of New York, whose power emanated largely from his control of lucrative patronage appointments in the Port of New York.

When vast corruption was discovered among Conkling's men (including future president Chester Arthur) at the New York Custom House, Hayes sent the Senate fresh nominations. Following the custom of member courtesy, however, the Senate deferred to Conkling. Hayes wrote in his diary, "I am now in a contest on the question of the right of Senators to control nominations....But I am right, and will not give up the contest." Once the congressional session ended, Hayes suspended the incumbents and used recess appointments to replace them with men of merit. When the lawmakers returned, thirteen Republicans joined twenty Democrats in sustaining Hayes's actions. The president thus took a long stride toward increased executive independence, weakened during the Johnson and Grant administrations.

Hayes took a second step following the election of 1878, in which the Democrats won control of the Senate (they already controlled the House). Southern members soon placed at the top of the majority's agenda the repeal of Reconstruction legislation authorizing the president to employ federal troops to protect the rights of black voters. The tactic favored by the Democrats was that of attaching riders to unrelated appropriations bills. On April 29, 1879, an outraged Hayes vetoed an army appropriations measure carrying such a rider. A month later, the Democrats passed a bill prohibiting federal troops from serving as peacekeepers at polls unless requested to do so by a state. Hayes

FEBRUARY 18, 1878

The murder of rancher John Tunstall sparks the Lincoln County War, in which rival ranchers fight for control of government beef contracts in New Mexico. The most notorious combatant will be former Tunstall ward William H. Bonney, better known as Billy the Kid.

FEBRUARY 22, 1881

President Hayes bans the sale of alcohol on military posts. Most soldiers blame the first lady for this unpopular policy, her views on temperance being quite well known.

The aging former president enjoys a March 1892 meal in the dining room of his Fremont, Ohio, home. His daughter, Fanny, is seated at the head of the table, facing the camera.

OPPOSITE:

Of medium height and sunny
countenance, with
broad shoulders, a high
forehead, and a full
sandy beard, Hayes
(shown here in a Brady
portrait) enjoyed a fine
presence and made
friends readily. He
liked to travel, for
example, in the
smoking cars of trains
so that he could meet
and converse with the
other passengers.

During the September
1862 battle of South
Mountain, a prelude to
Antietam, Hayes's regi-
ment was advancing
under heavy fire when
a musket ball hit the
colonel just above the
elbow, fracturing his arm
and leaving a gaping hole.
When his men fell back,
Hayes was left barely
conscious between his
own line and the enemy's.
He nearly died from loss of
blood before rescuers were
able to reach him.

hurled back another successful veto. In all, Congress passed seven such bills, five saddled with riders repealing the election laws and two designed to circumvent them. With his seven vetoes, Hayes fulfilled his oath to enforce the nation's laws and moreover increased unity within the Republican party as members rallied to his support.

MEANWHILE, ANTI-CHINESE SENTIMENT in the West caused Congress to pass a bill, in violation of the 1868 Burlingame Treaty, restricting Chinese immigration. Hayes forthrightly vetoed the bill, recalling that "our experience in dealing with the weaker races—the negroes and indians for example is not encouraging." Then, to ease tensions on the West Coast, he had Secretary of State William M. Evarts negotiate with China a new treaty that restricted (but did not ban) future immigration. (This treaty was superseded by the Chinese Exclusion Act of 1882, passed over President Arthur's veto, which banned Chinese immigration for ten years.)

Yet Hayes remained unable to pursue his program affirmatively. To black suffrage, for example, he linked education, which he believed was necessary for informed voting, reform, and equality. In various forums, he broadcast his ideas, though little came of them. To his disappointment, the Blair bill extending national aid for education never reached his desk.

As the election of 1880 neared, Hayes rebuffed entreaties to stand for a second term and instead became an exemplary retired president. He served on the boards of philanthropic organizations seeking to improve education for blacks and whites, as a trustee of several colleges and universities in Ohio, and as a reform president of the National Prison Association. He also found satisfaction in his record, perhaps more than another might have. He mused that he had successfully dealt with "the Southern question; the money question; the hard times and riots; the Indian question; the Chinese question; the reform of the civil service; the partisan bitterness growing out of a disputed election; a hostile Congress; and a party long in power on the verge of defeat."

Hayes served during an era characterized by unexampled complexity as well as rapid economic and social change. Inheriting a weakened presidency, sectional bitterness, and widespread corruption, he dexterously handled the emergence of an industrial America divided by class, ethnicity, and extreme partisanship.

★ ★ ★

James A. Garfield

20th President · 1881

Ari Hoogenboom

"ONE THING THOU LACKEST YET," John Hay wrote James Garfield on his election to the presidency, "and that is a slight ossification of the heart. I woefully fear that you will try too hard to make everybody happy—an office which is outside of your constitutional powers." What Hay, who'd been Lincoln's private secretary, perceived as a potential liability in his friend had, in fact, been an asset during Garfield's long career in the House of Representatives. It had also enhanced his appeal at the 1880 Republican national convention, where he was nominated after the followers of former president Ulysses S. Grant, Sen. James G. Blaine, and Treasury Secretary John Sherman deadlocked.

Like Hay, Garfield's congressional colleagues found him intelligent and likable, but they also regarded him as inconsistent and weak. "Garfield is a grand, noble fellow, but fickle, unstable, more brains but no such will as Sherman, brilliant like Blaine but timid and hesitating," concluded Sen. Henry L. Dawes, who spent a dozen years with Garfield in the House.

Despite similar reservations, President Rutherford B. Hayes, recognizing Garfield's appeal as a vote getter, called him the "ideal candidate." Garfield had risen from poverty and obscurity (from the boy on the canal towpath) to scholar, major general, and statesman. Carried away by his enthusiasm, Hayes exclaimed, "The truth is no man ever started so low that accomplished so much in all our history. Not Franklin or Lincoln even."

Hayes exaggerated, but not excessively. Born in 1831 in a log cabin near Cleveland, Ohio, James Garfield was left destitute when his father died two years later. His mother worked in the fields and took in washing. Meanwhile, a precocious and "rather lazy" Garfield escaped his poverty by reading novels and living a fantasy

When guests at an 1877 dinner party were stumped by the question, "In a republic, what political motive is an adequate substitute for patronage?" James A. Garfield declared, "This is the central difficulty that underlies the civil service."

This calendar, which sat on Garfield's White House desk, hasn't been reset since the day he was shot.

life so vivid that he became accident prone. To pursue his dream of a sailor's life, he left home at sixteen and worked on a canal boat for six weeks, falling overboard fourteen times before taking seriously ill with chills and a fever. While nursing him back to health, his mother persuaded him that he needed an education—and in March 1849 she scraped together seventeen dollars and packed him off to Geauga Academy, where he discovered his lifelong love of learning. When the seventeen dollars ran out, he worked as a carpenter and taught classes to meet expenses. Despite the political advantages of being born to poverty, Garfield later lamented that "seventeen years passed before I caught up any inspiration which was worthy of my manhood." (And even then, those early disadvantages marked him with a lifelong insecurity that made him susceptible to get-rich-quick schemes.)

OVER THE NEXT DOZEN YEARS, Garfield remained in the classroom as a student and teacher. He also became in March 1850 an ardent Disciple of Christ (Campbellite) and in time a lay preacher. He attended the Western Reserve Eclectic Institute at Hiram, Ohio, and graduated from Williams College in 1856 before returning to Western Reserve as a teacher and soon its president.

Studying under Mark Hopkins, the renowned Williams president, had broadened Garfield's religious views and awakened him to the evils of slavery, which in turn led him to consider careers in the law and politics. Elected as a Republican to the Ohio state senate in 1859, he campaigned vigorously for Lincoln in 1860 and, abandoning his pacifism, welcomed the Civil War as a struggle between "Slavery and Freedom." Prior to secession, Garfield had been dissatisfied, restless, and irresolute about his future, but war ended that vacillation. Being a prominent politician, he was commissioned a lieutenant colonel; merit, luck, and well-placed friends left him, by late 1863, a major general. He served effectively in eastern Kentucky and gallantly at Chickamauga.

In this photograph, the first ever taken of a national party convention, Garfield delivers his famous speech nominating John Sherman. It was this speech that made Garfield the obvious choice when the front-runners deadlocked.

BORN
November 19, 1831

BIRTHPLACE
Orange, Ohio

DIED
September 19, 1881

PARTY AFFILIATION
Republican

CHILDREN
Eliza, Harry, James, Mary, Irvin, Abram, Edward

MAJOR EVENTS

MAY 21, 1881

Civil War nurse Clara Barton, a pioneer of battlefield medicine, founds the American Red Cross, using the international Red Cross (founded in 1864) as her model. Once known to wounded Union soldiers as the Angel of the Battlefield, Barton will soon write an amendment to the constitution of the international Red Cross offering its aid during natural disasters as well as during wartime.

JULY 4, 1881

African-American educator Booker T. Washington founds the Tuskegee Normal and Industrial Institute in Tuskegee, Alabama. The curriculum of the all-black school will emphasize vocational skills, in keeping with Washington's belief that whites will accept blacks only when blacks have gained economic clout.

This contemporary illustration depicts the scene at the Baltimore & Potomac railroad station on July 2, 1881.

On June 18, 1881, the president and first lady rode from the White House to the Baltimore & Potomac railroad station, where they boarded a train for the Jersey Shore. Charles J. Guiteau, the man who would shoot Garfield in that same station two weeks later, was waiting with a loaded pistol. When he saw the first lady, however, he decided not to shoot the president—at least not yet. "Mrs. Garfield looked so thin, and she clung so tenderly to the president's arm, that I did not have the heart to fire upon him," Guiteau recalled at his trial. Garfield had married Lucretia Rudolph (shown here in 1881) in November 1858 after years of hesitation and second thoughts. Their relationship was troubled for several years, but it endured and in time love flourished, with Garfield enjoying a rewarding domestic life.

A hero to the home folks, Garfield was elected to the House in 1862 and served there until he became president. Although the youngest member when he took his seat in December 1863 (after resigning his commission), he was a conspicuous Radical Republican and proved himself intelligent, informed, and eloquent. Having little use for Lincoln's caution or magnanimity, Garfield wished to free the slaves, confiscate their masters' estates, and execute or banish rebel leaders. With peace, he moderated his radicalism, calling himself "a poor hater." At the same time, colleagues noted his failure to be a dependable partisan. Hayes, for instance, dismissed Garfield as "a smooth, ready, pleasant man, not very strong."

Garfield's tendency to doubt himself was heightened by his ability to appreciate the complexities of public issues. Envying the assuredness of extremists, he often remarked on the pain of seeing "too many sides of a subject." By the early 1870s, he'd become the House's leading expert on government finance and generally sympathized with the liberal reformers who advocated hard money, free trade, civil service reform, and amnesty for ex-Confederates (yet he never joined their 1872 revolt against Republican party regulars).

Just as emancipation had been a moral issue for Garfield before the war, so hard money became one after it. (Like most "honest" money advocates, he regarded inflated currency as legalized theft and urged a return to the gold standard.) However, these were the only important public issues on which his views remained consistent. Garfield's

"PAPER MONEY MUST REPRESENT WHAT IT PROFESSES ON ITS FACE. I DO NOT WISH TO HOLD IN MY HANDS THE PRINTED LIES OF THE GOVERNMENT."

—Speech, 1866—

commitment to free trade, for example, never extended to products made by his constituents, and his support for civil service reform was neither dependable nor what ardent reformers had in mind. Garfield had doubts, for instance, about the wisdom of establishing merit examinations with no regard for political considerations. And though he did speak out against political assessments (the practice of extracting from civil servants a percentage of their salaries to finance campaigns), he didn't consider the practice corrupt. Government employees (and those who wanted government jobs) were virtually the only contributors to campaigns, and Garfield recognized that political parties necessarily depended on the spoils system for workers and money.

This engraving from the September 24, 1881, issue of Frank Leslie's Illustrated Newspaper shows Garfield's September 6 arrival at Elberon, New Jersey. Railroad tracks were laid nearly to the door of his oceanside cottage to make the ailing president's trip as comfortable as possible.

Though he flirted with reform, Garfield was also a powerful politician burdened with five children and a low income. Occasionally, he yielded to those who would purchase his influence. For example, having invested nothing, he received from the Crédit Mobilier either a $329 dividend or, as he claimed, a $300 loan, which he repaid. Even more questionable was a $5,000 fee from the DeGolyer McClelland Company, which received a contract for paving the nation's capital that Garfield, then chairman of the House Committee on Appropriations, had helped secure. These revelations damaged Garfield's reputation—but not enough to preclude his nomination for president.

To win the 1880 general election, Garfield had to carry New York—not likely without the active support of the spoils-minded Stalwarts who ran the state and answered to Sen. Roscoe Conkling. Ambiguously agreeable, Garfield activated Conkling's lieutenants (and other spoilsmen around the nation) with vague promises of patronage. (He also quietly urged the assessment of civil servants to meet campaign expenses.) Although most reformers agreed with George William Curtis that Garfield's "fiber" wasn't "steel," they stuck with him because he was more of a reformer than his Democratic opponent, Gen. Winfield Scott Hancock.

GARFIELD'S STRATEGY—which President Hayes characterized as talking "so equivocally as to have the benefit of opposing nobody"—won him the election but paralyzed his presidency. His superb understanding of the federal government and the issues before it—the tariff, for example—went for naught because he'd aroused expectations of patronage (especially in Conkling) greater than he wished to fulfill. Three weeks into his administration, a wavering Garfield allowed Secretary of State James G. Blaine to persuade him to nominate a Blaine lieutenant as collector of the Port of New York, the chief patronage plum in the country. Feeling betrayed, Conkling "raged and roared," according to Senator Dawes. Charging that the nomination violated senatorial courtesy, the practice that permitted members to

In the army, Garfield became a man of war and the world. Escaping the restraints of church and campus, he played cards, drank, and even had an affair with a young widow. He poses here in the uniform of a Union brigadier.

The most newsworthy *story of Garfield's brief presidency was his patronage battle with Roscoe Conkling. This* Puck *cover from May 1881 shows Conkling quixotically tilting at a Garfield-shaped windmill. The illustrator might have also been making reference to Garfield's reputation for responding to the prevailing breeze.*

OPPOSITE:

This photograph *of Garfield with his only surviving daughter, Molly, was taken during the early 1870s, when Garfield was already a congressional (and Union) veteran. Educated at private schools in Cleveland and Connecticut after the death of her father, Molly (christened Mary) later married the much older Joseph Stanley-Brown, a presidential secretary during Garfield's brief term.*

control key appointments in their states, Conkling urged his colleagues to reject Garfield's choice.

Although conscious that he'd blundered, Garfield refused to withdraw the nomination. Dawes tried to heal the breach but soon threw up his hands: "For a great man I think our President has some of the weakest, and Conkling some of the ugliest streaks I have ever seen…. The one wants to be watched like a child, the other like an assassin." After a struggle of nearly two months, Conkling, facing defeat, resigned from the Senate, believing that his New York machine would return him to that body with a renewed mandate. In fact, his followers deserted him, and Conkling retired to private life.

Garfield had prevailed, but he never got the opportunity to put his administration on track. On July 2, a deranged office seeker, shouting that he was a Stalwart, shot Garfield in the back. At times in agonizing pain, he lingered more than two months while doctors probed his wound, never finding the bullet. Meanwhile, blood poisoning set in.

For reformers, it turned out, a dead Garfield proved much more valuable than a living one. With what Henry Adams called "cynical impudence," they transformed their previous opinion of him as a weak, spineless tool of Blaine into reverence for a fearless reformer, murdered by the spoils system. Capitalizing on the public outrage, reformers

"HIS WILLPOWER WAS NOT EQUAL TO HIS PERSONAL MAGNETISM."

—*Sen. John Sherman*—

secured as a memorial to the fallen president the 1883 Pendleton Civil Service Reform Act, which established permanent merit exams and outlawed political assessments. Ironically, the president had little sympathy for the law's principles.

A complex and contradictory man, Garfield defies easy characterization. The strict morality of his early years conflicted with the lax materialism of the Gilded Age, and the proverbial ego of the politician remained at odds with his insecure personality. Part reformer and part spoilsman, part moralist and part corruptionist, Garfield was both maligned as a shady politician and deified as a noble martyr—with some justification.

★ ★ ★

Chester A. Arthur

21ˢᵗ President · 1881–1885

Bernard A. Weisberger

Chester A. Arthur's
*gracious manner and skill
as a raconteur contributed
to his reputation as a
man of dignity and wit.
According to biographer
Thomas C. Reeves,
however, Arthur was also
"a deeply emotional, even
romantic person, capable
of great loyalties and easily
brought to tears."*

**Throughout his political
career,** *Arthur feared and
despised the press, avoiding
reporters and granting few
interviews. Not
surprisingly, these
practices often led
to harsh coverage.
This* Puck *cover
from 1882 derides
Arthur (somewhat
unfairly) for
allegedly agreeing
to Chinese exclu-
sion in exchange
for western electoral
support.*

JUNE 1880 FOUND Chester Alan Arthur, a longtime insider in the corrupt New York State machine of Sen. Roscoe Conkling, temporarily out of office. Two years earlier, he'd been removed from his lucrative patronage job in the New York Custom House by President Hayes on suspicion of corruption. When the Republicans, meeting that month in Chicago, chose Arthur as their vice-presidential nominee, reformer Edward L. Godkin had at least one consoling thought: "There is no place in which [Arthur's] powers of mischief will be so small as in the Vice Presidency." After all, the prospect of a healthy James Garfield, two years Arthur's junior, dying in office was plainly "too unlikely a contingency" to contemplate.

Thirteen months later, however, with Garfield slowly dying from an assassin's bullet, Godkin—who once described Arthur's past associations as a "mess of filth"—had reason to regret his casualness. Like other would-be purifiers of the Grand Old Party, he thought, "Arthur for President! Conkling the power behind the throne!" It was a recipe for disaster.

And yet, surprise! Though succeeding generations have more or less forgotten Arthur, at least two friendly biographies remind posterity that Arthur didn't, as reformers feared, pack his cabinet with Conkling henchmen. On the contrary, he signed the Pendleton Act of 1883, which curtailed the spoils-manship that had sustained the "boss" system and established a modern civil service system based on competitive exams. Overall, Arthur conducted a responsible, if undistinguished (and unimportant), presidency: He pursued grafters from previous admin-istrations, proposed modest reforms in the swollen tariff, spurred modernization of the aging Civil War navy, and supported foreign policy initiatives (rejected

The president enjoys *some bass fishing in the St. Lawrence River near Alexandria Bay. The time is late September 1882.*

BORN
October 5, 1829

BIRTHPLACE
Fairfield, Vermont

DIED
November 18, 1886

PARTY AFFILIATION
Republican

CHILDREN
William, Chester Alan Jr., Ellen

MAJOR EVENTS

JANUARY 2, 1882

At the suggestion of lawyer Samuel C. T. Dodd, the owners of thirty-nine oil companies turn their stock over to a board of trustees headed by John D. Rockefeller, creating the Standard Oil trust. Dodd's legal device allows Rockefeller to run the nation's oil industry as though it were his own private business.

SEPTEMBER 4, 1882

Thomas A. Edison's steam-powered generating plant, located on Pearl Street, begins supplying electric power to New York City, which now glows with the warmth of Edison's incandescent light.

MARCH 3, 1883

Congress approves construction of three cruisers, the first ships in the new Steel Navy being advocated by President Arthur. Previously, all navy ships had been made of wood.

by Congress) to expand U.S. hemispheric and world trade. He vetoed pork-barrel spending bills, such as the Rivers and Harbors Act of 1882, and an immigration restriction act that would have undercut the Treaty of 1880 with China. One might even say that he began to reassert prerogatives of the presidency that had withered during Reconstruction, except that Congress typically overrode his vetoes. Even so, Arthur probably did deserve the bronze statue erected to him in New York City's Madison Square Park and the eulogies that accompanied its 1899 unveiling.

THIS SAGA OF REDEMPTION, long pooh-poohed by muckraking historians, is now (more or less) the accepted academic wisdom, and Arthur's reputation may yet be transformed, much as he transformed himself as president. Nonetheless, this revisionism can't remake Arthur into a dominating figure of his time, nor can it provide a more stimulating narrative for his life.

Arthur was the fourth vice president to succeed a dead president. The examples of his three predecessors well illustrated the ridiculous gamble at the core of the system by which candidates were nominated for this essentially useless office. The vice president's job, it seemed, was simply to wait for the possible lightning strike that might make him president—an occurrence only slightly less ordinary than a tie vote in the Senate, which he was also empowered to break. Because no politician of stature and prospects wanted to waste four years in semiparalysis, the nomination generally went to second-string party regulars with a regional following—men who largely lacked the leadership skills necessary should they suddenly be thrust into command. In Arthur's case, the nomination was a conciliatory second prize to a losing faction, a sop to Conkling's

Ellen Herndon, called Nell, spent most of her youth in Washington, D.C., but she was born in Virginia and considered herself a southerner. When the Arthurs were married in 1859, this didn't pose much of a problem—until the Civil War began, when most of the Herndons took up arms against the Union. With jokes about his "little rebel wife," Arthur did his best to laugh off the consequent stiffness in his marriage, but the friction persisted even after the war when Mrs. Arthur took objection to her husband's habit of feasting with his cronies until late in the evening. Nell Arthur enjoyed her husband's money and status, but she didn't like feeling abandoned. According to their son, the Arthurs were preparing to separate in January 1880 when Mrs. Arthur died suddenly of pneumonia.

conservative Stalwarts from James G. Blaine's moderate Half-Breeds, who had put over Garfield at the 1880 convention.

Such philosophical ticket balancing posed the steady threat that an accidental president might repudiate, or at least refashion, the agenda of his late predecessor, thus igniting bitter intraparty warfare. Such had been the case with John Tyler and to some extent with Millard Fillmore. Andrew Johnson, of course, disastrously went to war with the Republican leadership in Congress, with which Lincoln had so painfully learned to work. Arthur, in contrast, stayed the course, retreating from both Stalwart corruption and staunch Stalwart principles. Nor did Arthur conduct a purge of Half-Breed appointees or make any major new enemies among Republicans. His administration stands out therefore as the first of the accidental variety to be tranquil. Arthur's capable performance may even have postponed serious reconsideration of the vice presidency, because another century (and five more successions) passed before political forecasters began thinking seriously about the stature and qualifications of presidential running mates and presidents themselves began preparing vice presidents to succeed them.

A RTHUR WAS FORTUNATE that he inherited the White House at a time when not much was expected or desired of its occupant. The president's power in relation to Congress was at an all-time low, and any strong initiatives put forth by Arthur would surely have died on Capitol Hill. This imbalance kept him from receiving much credit for the state of the nation, but it also spared him very much blame.

During a tour of the poorly maintained White House several weeks after Garfield's death, Arthur announced, "I will not live in a house like this." For the next three months, Arthur lived elsewhere while supervising on a daily basis the mansion's redecoration. A year later, he hired Louis Comfort Tiffany to carry out more ambitious plans, which included the installation of this stained-glass screen in the main entrance hall.

The reenergized, potent, and dynamic presidencies of Theodore Roosevelt and Woodrow Wilson were still decades away. In fact, the country and its far smaller federal government hardly needed a president—or so it seemed during the two and a half months that a dying Garfield was unable to attend to business.

This undemanding role precisely suited the style of Chester Arthur, who was undoubtedly a man of his era. He was a nonideologue at a time when Americans were still recoiling from the ideological clashes of the Civil War. A New Englander by birth, he joined a New York City law firm

> ## "IF HIS CONDUCT OF AFFAIRS BE CRITICIZED AS LACKING AGGRESSIVENESS, IT MAY CONFIDENTLY BE REPLIED THAT AGGRESSIVENESS WOULD HAVE BEEN UNFORTUNATE, IF NOT DISASTROUS."
>
> —*Secretary of the Navy William Chandler*—

in 1854 and by the summer of 1861 had become an antislavery Republican, a politically safe choice for an ambitious thirty-one-year-old lawyer in that locality. Arthur was anything but impassioned about the subject of Negro rights in general. His own part in the Civil War was businesslike: As quartermaster general for the state, he competently fed, uniformed, armed, and supplied New York's hastily formed regiments, for which he received two politically useful rewards—status as a veteran and familiarity with contractors. As an orthodox Republican, he supported the party line on Reconstruction, but later as president he did little to interrupt the dismantling of its last remnants.

Even when it came to partisanship, Arthur was less than zealous. Politics was for him a profession, not a calling. As collector of customs for the Port of New York from 1871 until 1878 (an appointment he owed to Conkling), Arthur enjoyed an income from fees and "perks" amounting in some years to fifty thousand dollars, or what the president was making at the time. Not bad for the son of a poor clergyman, who knew perfectly well that shakedowns, kickbacks, and bribes were part of the business of staying in office. In 1881, he confessed that if he should "get going about the secrets of the campaign, there is no saying what I might say to make

MAY 24, 1883

With great fanfare, President Arthur and New York governor Grover Cleveland open the new Brooklyn Bridge, under construction since 1869. Its span of nearly sixteen hundred feet is half again longer than that of any existing suspension bridge.

NOVEMBER 18, 1883

Frustrated U.S. and Canadian railroads establish (for scheduling purposes) a system of standardized time zones, each zone being separated from adjacent zones by exactly one hour. These time zones replace the railroads' erstwhile reliance on unsystematic local times. Local time in Baltimore, for example, is currently an awkward ten minutes and twenty-seven seconds behind local time in New York City.

This is Chester Arthur *as he appeared in 1859, untouched by the future effects of prosperous wining and dining.*

Besides interior design work, President Arthur also gave Tiffany (then the country's most fashionable designer) the White House's china business. This plate is one of several dozen purchased by Arthur from Tiffany & Co. in May 1882. "History remembers only a few things about [Arthur]," White House historian William Seale has written, but "one is that he had taste."

OPPOSITE:

In New York City, the stylish Arthur was known as a "gentleman boss." His preferences in food, clothing, and furnishings were patrician, and they gave him the very sort of presidential image cherished by reformers who were, at the same time, denouncing his tainted political past.

trouble." He prudently had his personal papers burned, but it's unlikely that he felt morally compromised by his associations. The world was the world, and like many businessmen and officials of the day, he took it as he found it, warts and all.

Even so, on three issues Arthur did make a certain amount of noise. With regard to Chinese immigration, his veto of the Chinese Exclusion Act did force Congress to reduce its ban from twenty to ten years (in order to win enough votes for the override). On the tariff, Arthur created a special commission in 1882 to reduce rates sharply, but Congress subverted his intentions, producing a bill so laden with special exemptions that it became known as the Mongrel Tariff. Regarding civil service reform, however, Congress was unable to dodge the will of an electorate irate over the assassination of a president by a man portrayed in the media as a "disappointed office-seeker." Nonetheless, Arthur's commitment to the Pendleton Act shocked regulars and reformers alike.

ONE ADVANTAGE ARTHUR enjoyed was looking the part of a statesman. Tall and dignified, he dressed his 225-pound frame impeccably and expensively. No workaholic, he limited his presidential office hours to six a day, from ten to four, after which he pursued the life of a bon vivant. He savored fine food and drink, could hold his liquor, and was "the last man to go to bed in any company," according to an old friend of Custom House days. It was also his nature to keep such enjoyments private—and likewise his personal sorrows. Few knew of his deep grief at the passing of his wife, Ellen, in January 1880 or that as president he suffered from Bright's disease, a then-fatal kidney ailment that killed him in 1886. This reserve, so unexpected in a graduate of machine politics, restored to the presidency some dignity lost during the tenures of Johnson and Grant.

During the early 1880s, the country was in a transition period, with the parties almost equally balanced in strength. Times were generally prosperous, Civil War animosities were waning, and the hour was not yet ripe for excitement and innovation. Much preferred was low-keyed accommodation to the status quo—and so the waters of presidential history closed behind Arthur with hardly a ripple. Not seriously considered for renomination, he died less than two years after leaving office and was generally forgotten by the time of the Great War. Yet Arthur's very lack of memorable qualities and actions may have been precisely the soothing and conciliatory tonic his ailing country needed at that moment.

★ ★ ★

Grover Cleveland

22nd & 24th President
1885–1889 · 1893–1897

Vincent P. De Santis

At a brawny 250 pounds, Grover Cleveland was the heaviest president yet. He had a bull neck, a thick torso, and enormous hamlike fists. This portrait was taken in 1892.

Although John Tyler preceded him as the first president to marry while in office, Grover Cleveland became the first president wed at the White House itself. After the ceremony, he and the first lady sent absent friends pieces of their wedding cake (such as this one).

GROVER CLEVELAND IS GENERALLY considered the ablest and most important president between Abraham Lincoln and Theodore Roosevelt. He's a curiosity, however, because he obtained this reputation not by virtue of his positive achievements but with two terms of rancor and obstructionism. A largely negative president, he firmly believed it was his duty to prevent hurtful things from happening, rather than to make beneficial things take place.

Yet, as historian Thomas Bailey has perceptively contended, not all effective leadership is of a positive nature, even though the constructive leader is generally more praised than the obstructive one. William Leuchtenburg has reinforced Bailey's point with his own observation that if Cleveland's achievements were largely negative, "even that was something of a virtue when too many politicians were saying 'yes' to the wrong things." Cleveland is therefore remembered less for his accomplishments (or his personal brilliance) than for his character—specifically, for his courage, firmness, uprightness, and sense of duty.

Cleveland was born in Caldwell, New Jersey, the fifth of nine children. His family, which moved to upstate New York before he turned five, was governed by strict rules set down by his father, a Yale- and Princeton-educated Presbyterian minister. After his father's death in 1853, it became necessary for the sixteen-year-old Cleveland to end his formal education and begin work. In 1855, he moved to his uncle's cattle farm near Buffalo, where he received ten dollars a month plus room and board to edit the *American Shorthorn Handbook.* Cleveland's uncle also arranged for him to study law at a Buffalo firm. In 1859, at age twenty-two, he was admitted to the bar.

As a young lawyer, Cleveland became active in the Democratic party and in 1870 was elected sheriff of Erie County.

President Cleveland *poses in early 1893 with the members of his second cabinet, none of whom served in his first administration.*

BORN
March 18, 1837

BIRTHPLACE
Caldwell, New Jersey

DIED
June 24, 1908

PARTY AFFILIATION
Democrat

CHILDREN
Ruth, Esther, Marion, Richard, Francis

MAJOR EVENTS

MAY 4, 1886

A day after police gunfire kills four strikers, thirteen hundred more gather at a protest rally in Chicago's Haymarket Square. When the local police move in, someone throws a bomb, killing seven officers.

JUNE 19, 1886

The Haymarket trial of eight labor leaders, all immigrant anarchists, opens in Chicago. Although the prosecution presents no evidence linking the defendants to the bomber, they are still convicted of conspiracy to commit murder.

FEBRUARY 4, 1887

Congress passes the Interstate Commerce Act to fill the void left by a recent Supreme Court decision precluding states from regulating interstate railroads. The new Interstate Commerce Commission will be the nation's first independent regulatory agency.

During his two years in office, he eliminated routine graft and earned a reputation for incorruptibility that would follow him throughout his political career. He also personally sprang the trap on two convicted murderers because he didn't want to ask his deputies to do something he wouldn't do himself. While Cleveland was serving as the recently elected mayor of Buffalo in 1882, the *Buffalo Sunday Times* suggested that he run for governor, an office he won handily. During the two years he spent in Albany prior to his 1884 election as president, Cleveland supported modest reforms to improve the political process and vetoed what he considered to be legislative wastefulness and improper public assistance programs.

AT THIS TIME, one of the strongest assets a politician could have was an exemplary Civil War military record. Most presidents of the era enjoyed one (inflated or not), but for Cleveland, this was a liability: He had sat out the Civil War, staying at home to support two of his sisters and his widowed mother while two of his brothers (the third being a minister) entered the military. When drafted, he made use of a provision in the Conscription Act of 1863 that allowed him to hire a substitute (for $150) to serve in his place—a Polish immigrant who, in fact, survived the war. Republicans had difficulty exploiting Cleveland's war liability in the 1884 campaign, however, because their own candidate, James G. Blaine, had also engaged a substitute.

Cleveland appealed to many Gilded Age Americans because he seemed a plain man who acted consistently in accordance with what he believed to be right. Many voters also admired him for what they called his "you-be-damnedness" and for the political enemies that he made.

In 1897, after a good day's duck hunting,
former president Grover Cleveland relaxes
at his camp near the mouth of the
Santee River in South Carolina.

***Grover Cleveland
first*** *met Frances
Folsom shortly after
her 1864 birth.
When her father,
Cleveland law
partner Oscar
Folsom, died in
1875, Cleveland
administered
Folsom's estate
and thereafter
kept watch over his
family. It's not clear
when Cleveland's
regard for Frances turned
romantic, but the forty-
eight-year-old president
proposed to her by letter
in August 1885, and she
readily accepted. They
were married at the
White House on June 2,
1886. Cleveland worked
as usual until the 7 P.M.
ceremony, then took the
rest of the evening off.*

Cleveland was often
*the target of Republican
dirty tricks. This 1884*
Judge *cover illustrates
the charge that he had
fathered an illegitimate
child. Cleveland wasn't
sure himself whether he
was the father, but he
freely admitted his past
relationship with the
boy's mother and his
subsequent assumption
of financial responsi-
bility for the child.*

He became president at a time when the prestige of
the office was low and political power vested mainly with
Congress. Gilded Age presidents largely accepted the
Whig-Republican view that the president should confine
himself to implementing the laws enacted by Congress.
They didn't believe that vigorous executive leadership
in economic and social matters was either necessary or
desirable; and though Cleveland was a Democrat, he
shared this view with regard to domestic matters. In
Cleveland's opinion, for example, Americans were entitled
to economy, purity, and justice in their government and nothing
more. He considered his role as president to be that of a righteous
watchdog, ensuring a fair field for all and favors to none. Thus he
opposed special benefits for industry, for war veterans, and for railroads
at a time when special treatment was considered routine and proper.

> ## "EVERY THOUGHTFUL AND PATRIOTIC MAN HAS AT TIMES BEEN DISAPPOINTED BY THE APPARENT INDIFFERENCE AND DEMORALIZATION OF THE PEOPLE."
>
> *—Speech, 1890—*

The key to Cleveland's presidency was his intense dislike of
paternalism in government. He strongly resisted the idea of government
providing aid to citizens in distress, a view best illustrated by his veto of
an 1887 Texas seed bill that would have relieved farmers suffering from an
acute drought. The ten thousand dollars being appropriated was a trivial
amount, yet Cleveland declared coldly that he could "find no warrant for
such an appropriation in the Constitution." In other oft-cited phrases of
this memorable veto message, he pointed out that "the lesson should be
constantly enforced that though the people should support the government, the government should not support the people" and "federal aid
in such cases weakens the sturdiness of our national character."

This attitude also made Cleveland less than sympathetic to the
plight of workers. His two nonconsecutive terms straddled some of the
most serious labor strife in the country's history, including the 1886 general strike (for an eight-hour workday) that produced the brutal Haymarket
Riot in Chicago and the violent Pullman strike of 1894. In the case of the

Pullman strike, which was provoked by a 30 percent pay reduction, Cleveland used federal troops to end a nationwide boycott of trains carrying Pullman cars organized by Eugene V. Debs, then president of the American Railway Union. Using as a pretext the fact that the strike had stopped mail traffic in and out of Chicago, Cleveland obtained a court order restoring service and enforced it with the use of the U.S. Army over the objections of Illinois governor John P. Altgeld. "If it takes the entire army and navy…to deliver a postal card in Chicago," Cleveland declared, "that card will be delivered."

NOR DID CLEVELAND SYMPATHIZE with the problems of others beaten down by the depression that followed the Panic of 1893—the most severe economic crisis the country had yet seen—probably because he'd never considered the role that government should properly have in an expanding industrial society. The depression, which dominated his second term, began in February 1893, when the Philadelphia & Reading became the first of seventy-four railroads to fail that year, along with six hundred banks. The subsequent rush to redeem devalued silver certificates for gold started a run on the U.S. Treasury that Cleveland tried to halt by calling a special session of Congress to repeal the 1890 Sherman Silver Purchase Act. The president got his way but succeeded mainly in splitting his party between conservative "goldbugs" and populist "silverites," paving the way for the nomination of William Jennings Bryan in 1896.

By 1895, treasury reserves had fallen so low (to $41.3 million) that Cleveland found himself forced to borrow $62 million in gold from a consortium put together by J. P. Morgan. Although necessary, the deal made it seem to average Americans that the president had sold out to the bankers.

This wasn't the first time that an economic issue had gotten Cleveland in trouble. In his December 1887 annual message to Congress, he had argued strongly for a steep tariff reduction, calling the current rates "indefensible extortion and a culpable betrayal of American

MARCH 25, 1894

An "army" of unemployed workers led by Jacob S. Coxey leaves Ohio for Washington, D.C. Coxey hopes that the march will persuade Congress to fund public works programs. Coxey's Army is greeted with applause, but Coxey is arrested for trespassing on the Capitol lawn.

JANUARY 21, 1895

The Supreme Court rules in U.S. v. E. C. Knight that the Sherman Anti-Trust Act cannot be applied to the sugar trust, even though it controls 98 percent of the market. This decision guts the Sherman Act, which the Court says applies only to sellers, not manufacturers.

MAY 18, 1896

In Plessy v. Ferguson, the Supreme Court rules that segregation is constitutional so long as blacks are provided with comparable facilities. This "separate but equal" doctrine will remain law until 1954, when Brown v. Board of Education overturns it.

Cleveland (shown here in 1905) *spent his retirement lecturing at Princeton. His thinner appearance reflects surgery, performed secretly in 1893, to remove cancerous tissue from his jaw. The press reported rumors that he was seriously ill, but the White House quashed them with an emphatic denial.*

In March 1889,
a departing yet defiant
Frances Cleveland
told a White House
butler, "We'll be back!"
Her prediction
proved accurate.
Had you possessed
this ticket in March
1893, it would have
admitted you to
the inauguration
of Cleveland's
encore term.

OPPOSITE:

One of the many
principled stands that
Cleveland (shown here in
1888) took while in office
concerned the annexation
of the Hawaiian Islands.
In January 1893, with
the help of U.S. marines,
American planters led by
Sanford B. Dole overthrew
Queen Liliuokalani and
negotiated a treaty of
annexation with the
Harrison administration.
Five days after taking
office, Cleveland with-
drew the treaty and
ordered the queen
restored—an order that
Dole, of course, ignored.

fairness." He later ran for reelection on this issue and was defeated by the Republicans, who responded that the high tariffs on imported goods protected U.S. businesses from foreign competition.

Despite his ups and downs, Cleveland had an impact on the presidency that can be seen in several important ways: He was the first president to use the veto freely, going well beyond its sparing employment by his predecessors. Taken together, they vetoed 205 bills, while Cleveland rejected 414 bills in his first term alone. It should be noted, however, that most of these were private Civil War pension bills, handed out by congressmen as favors to cronies, more than a few of whom had never served in the war. Previous presidents routinely authorized this mild form of graft, not wanting to bother with it, but Cleveland read each and every one of these bills, refusing those he deemed without merit.

> "HE FOLLOWED THE RIGHT
> AS HE SAW IT. BUT HE SAW IT
> THROUGH A CONSERVATIVE AND
> CONVENTIONAL CAST OF MIND."
>
> *—Dean Acheson—*

CLEVELAND ALSO RESTORED many of the powers and prerogatives of the presidency lost by Andrew Johnson during his battles with Congress. He succeeded in terminating the notorious Tenure of Office Act, which had served as the basis for Johnson's impeachment and harassed presidents ever since. He likewise strengthened the presidency during the 1895 border dispute between Venezuela and the British colony of Guiana, when he personally supervised negotiations with Great Britain. Cleveland later told a friend that his "aim was at one sharp stroke to compel England to yield to arbitration, and put Congress in a position where it could not interfere."

It's significant to note that, having observed the administrations of Johnson, Grant, Hayes, Garfield, and Arthur, future president Woodrow Wilson concluded that there was no hope for the office, that congressional supremacy would have to be recognized. Yet after living through Cleveland's two terms in office, Wilson changed his opinion, noting the strength of Cleveland's albeit negative leadership. Wilson praised Cleveland as the only president between 1865 and 1898 who "played a leading and decisive part in the quiet drama of our national life."

★ ★ ★

Benjamin Harrison

23rd President · 1889–1893

Catherine Clinton

Benjamin Harrison *was five feet six inches tall and stocky. He was also among the last of the nineteenth-century statesmen to wear a full beard.*

During the 1888 campaign, *the Republican propaganda machine also dragooned Lew Wallace, best-selling author of Ben Hur (and the brother of Harrison's former law partner), into writing Harrison's campaign biography.*

BENJAMIN HARRISON WAS JUST SEVEN years old in 1841 when his grandfather, war hero William Henry Harrison, became the ninth president of the United States. Forty-eight years later, Harrison the Younger became the nation's twenty-third president—but Adamses, the Harrisons were not. Benjamin's election was less a date with destiny than a turn of fate, albeit one skillfully engineered by the well-oiled Republican machine. Even Harrison realized that he was the lucky benefactor of an enormous windfall.

Benjamin was one of thirteen children born to John Scott Harrison, eight of whom lived to maturity. He spent his childhood years at The Point, a six-hundred-acre farm in North Bend, Ohio—a gift from the first President Harrison. Because declining family fortunes prevented him from attending college in the East, as his father had hoped, Benjamin remained at The Point until the death of his mother, Elizabeth, in August 1850. A month later, he enrolled as a junior at Miami University in Oxford, Ohio, from which he was graduated in 1852 near the top of his class.

At college, Harrison distinguished himself in the debating society as he honed his talent for public speaking. Although he came to be known as a rather cold fish in person (one political opponent dubbed him "an iceberg"), Harrison could hold an audience spellbound, a talent that moved him toward a legal career. This was a reasonable choice as well because, with little help expected from his family, his financial prospects were poor.

After his admission to the bar in 1854, Harrison moved to Indianapolis with his new wife, the former Caroline Scott, and hung out a shingle. Persuasive closing arguments and successful verdicts soon caught the attention of the governor's son, William Wallace, who invited Harrison to become his partner and share in his burgeoning caseload. The struggling young attorney didn't have to be asked twice, and it wasn't long before Harrison also began lending his talents to the Republican party. A popular and effective stump speaker, he ran for city attorney of Indianapolis in 1857 and won.

WHEN THE CIVIL WAR BROKE OUT in April 1861, Harrison, then the father of two young children, decided not to join the army. However, after the governor approached him directly, he did enlist, raising the Seventieth Indiana Volunteer Infantry Regiment and serving with that unit from July 1862 until June 1865. He entered the army as a second lieutenant but within three weeks made colonel. Harrison's troops weren't tested by combat until May 15, 1864, but at the battle of Resaca in central Georgia they fought well enough to earn Harrison a brevet promotion to the rank of brigadier. His military service was frequently interrupted, however, as party bosses often summoned him home to campaign for local candidates, a widespread Republican practice.

Like other "war heroes," Harrison was wooed by Republican kingmakers, though he'd already promised his wife he wouldn't run for Congress because "it would take me away from home so much." Instead, he focused on his law practice in order to support not only his immediate

This photograph shows *Harrison making a rare campaign appearance away from Indianapolis. His instructions in general were to stay at home and deliver prepared speeches from his front porch.*

family but also three of his brothers. One, a veteran, had contracted tuberculosis; another was simply a hapless farmer; and his youngest sibling, John Scott Jr., reportedly "couldn't make a dime."

In 1871, Harrison became a national symbol of Republican loyalism when, at the request of President Ulysses S. Grant, he defended Union generals in a civil action arising out of the Supreme Court's 1866 decision in *Ex Parte Milligan*. As that decision established, Lambdin P. Milligan, a civilian, had been illegally tried and imprisoned by a military court, and

BORN
August 20, 1833

BIRTHPLACE
North Bend, Ohio

DIED
March 13, 1901

PARTY AFFILIATION
Republican

CHILDREN
Russell, Mary, Elizabeth

MAJOR EVENTS

APRIL 22, 1889

At noon, a gunshot signals the opening of the Indian Territory to white settlement. Fifty thousand people join the rush to claim two million acres in what will become the state of Oklahoma. Those who have made their claims illegally early are called "sooners."

NOVEMBER 2, 1889

North Dakota and South Dakota join the Union. They are the first of six western states admitted during Harrison's term. The president, who signs the required documents in private, never reveals which of the two states he admitted first.

JANUARY 31, 1890

James "Buck" Duke creates the American Tobacco Company to end a cigarette price war. The new trust controls so much of the market that it can set the price at which farmers sell their crop.

Harrison usually quit working at noon so that he could spend time with his grandchildren. Here, the president's son poses with the children and their pet goat. Once, Old Whiskers escaped and ran down Pennsylvania Avenue with the top-hatted president, waving his cane, in hot, panting pursuit.

At Miami University, Harrison met and fell in love with Caroline Scott. The match was an odd one: Harrison was somber and socially clumsy, while Scott was vivacious and irreverent. A pious Presbyterian, Harrison refused to commit the sin of dancing, yet Scott lured him to dances regardless, and while he sat, she flirted with other boys. During the fall of 1892, while campaigning for her husband, Carrie Harrison contracted tuberculosis and died just two weeks before the election.

now Milligan was suing for damages. Harrison's job was to limit the amount to a token sum. When the jury came back with a five-dollar award, Harrison became an instant favorite of the Republican faithful, stepping into the national limelight and making well-received speeches on the veterans' circuit. At these events, Harrison typically called for the disenfranchisement of "every man who had fought against the flag" and championed Radical Republican governments in the South.

Meanwhile, the financial success of his law practice finally permitted him to risk public service. After declining invitations to run for more than a decade, he entered the 1876 race for governor of Indiana—and lost. He was completely unprepared for the rough-and-tumble of a political campaign, and his Democratic opponent, a populist known as "Blue Jeans" Williams, taunted him: "Give Harrison a kid glove client and a two-thousand-dollar fee...." It's not clear why Williams would make such obvious reference to a campaign slur against Harrison's grandfather that backfired so badly on the Democrats in 1840, but this time it worked. The nickname stuck, and "Kid Gloves" Harrison suffered the fate that befalls most stiff, cheerless candidates.

HARRISON'S NEXT OFFICE he won by appointment, the Republican-controlled Indiana legislature making him a U.S. senator in 1881. Once again, Harrison proved surprisingly unprepared for the rigors of the political process, and he was rarely admitted to the Senate back rooms where deals were made and alliances formed. He served Republican interests mainly by staying out of trouble and wooing veterans, personally introducing over a hundred petitions for pensions—including some for former Union soldiers discovered later to have been deserters.

Yet by 1888, Harrison was looking for another job after the Indiana legislature, now controlled by Democrats, denied him a second term. At the same time, the Republicans needed someone to run against incumbent president Grover Cleveland—who had proven himself a crusading reformer by, among other actions, vetoing the sort of pension bills that Harrison had been so fond of introducing. Nevertheless, Harrison had kept his nose remarkably clean in the Senate at a time when most Republican politicians were tarred by graft and other forms of corruption. The fact that Harrison had managed to serve a full term in the Senate without taking any public positions on the major issues also suited Republican power brokers, who backed Harrison because he seemed unlikely to do the party any harm—hardly a ringing endorsement.

The influential Republican press churned out profiles designed to soften and improve Harrison's stuffed-shirt image, while at the same time employing smear tactics and disinformation to undermine Cleveland's support. The Republicans made much of Cleveland's never having served in the Union army, his efforts to return captured Confederate battle flags, and the fact that he allegedly went fishing on Memorial Day 1888. But the most notorious scheme involved an elaborate con, in which the British ambassador was tricked into giving his views on the upcoming election. A Republican trickster, pretending to be British born, wrote to Lord Sackville-West asking his advice on how to vote. Sackville-West replied that England would prefer the election of Cleveland. As a result, Cleveland (despite winning the 1888 popular vote) lost the Irish vote in New York and by that margin his home state and the election.

A TTRIBUTING HIS VICTORY TO "divine intervention," Harrison told his campaign manager, the shady political boss Matt Quay, "Providence has given us victory." Later, Quay chortled privately that Harrison "would never know how close a number of men were compelled to approach the penitentiary to make him President."

Harrison's inaugural address, delivered in a drenching rain as his grandfather's had been, was about as memorable. Nor did Harrison grow into the office; he simply followed the lead of the party bosses who'd manufactured his election. He signed the highly protective McKinley Tariff of 1890, which sent consumer prices skyrocketing (and resulted in the reelection of Cleveland two years later). Harrison also supported the 1890 Sherman Silver Purchase Act, requiring the government to buy nearly all the silver then being produced by U.S. mines. During the Panic of 1893, Cleveland called a special session of Congress to have this act repealed because the redemption of silver notes for gold

DECEMBER 28, 1890

Custer's old regiment, the Seventh Cavalry, intercepts 350 Sioux scared off their reservation by news of Sitting Bull's murder. The next day, after disarming the Indians, the soldiers massacre as many as three hundred near Wounded Knee Creek.

MAY 19, 1891

Farmers and factory workers meet in Cincinnati to launch the Populist party (also known as the People's party). Built around an existing network of Farmers' Alliances, the new party opposes the high tariffs imposed on behalf of its enemy, big business.

JULY 6, 1892

The strike at Andrew Carnegie's Homestead steel works turns violent when three hundred armed Pinkertons attempt to regain control of the plant. Sixteen people are killed before the Pinkertons surrender. Six days later, however, eight thousand Pennsylvania militiamen arrive to get the factory running again.

The 1888 Republican campaign song "Grandfather's Hat Fits Ben!" gave Democrats an opportunity to lampoon the short, stocky Harrison. Cartoons such as this one, however, didn't stop Harrison from becoming the first and only grandson of a president to win the presidency himself.

VIEW FROM THE NORTH
PENN AVE

In 1891, the first lady persuaded Sen. Leland Stanford of California to introduce a bill that would have funded a major reconstruction and expansion of the White House. The plan (shown here), personally developed by the first lady, would have added new east and west wings and joined them to the original structure with semicircular colonnades. The measure failed, but Mrs. Harrison soon took charge of an extensive redecoration required by the recent installation of electricity.

OPPOSITE:

Harrison's comfort with crowds *but discomfort with people confounded his friends. According to one, "He possessed a fine sense of humor but kept it a carefully guarded secret." Another colleague pointed out that "he can make a speech to ten thousand men and every man will go away his friend [but] let him meet the same ten thousand men in private and every one will go away his enemy."*

was dangerously draining U.S. reserves. The other major law Harrison signed, the Sherman Anti-Trust Act of 1890, would a decade later become Theodore Roosevelt's most important trustbusting tool, yet Harrison's own Justice Department failed to enforce it.

During his White House years, Harrison never quite shed his stodgy public image: Like most well-to-do men of his generation, he wore a beard and sideburns, smoked cigars, played billiards, and went duck hunting. He was also the regular object of public jesting, in much the same way Gerald Ford was a century later. Harrison's December 1889 raccoon-hunting trip made national news, for example, when the president shot a pig by mistake.

"HE IS A COLD-BLOODED, NARROW-MINDED, PREJUDICED, OBSTINATE, TIMID OLD PSALM-SINGING INDIANAPOLIS POLITICIAN."

—Theodore Roosevelt—

TURNED OUT OF THE WHITE HOUSE after a single term, Benjamin Harrison headed back to his beloved Indianapolis; he went back, however, without his wife, who'd died of tuberculosis just two weeks before the 1892 election. He might have wished for some comfort from his children during his retirement, but they objected to his relationship with (and eventual marriage to) their mother's first cousin, Mary Dimmick, a widow twenty-five years his junior who'd lived with the Harrisons in the White House. In any case, his new wife apparently brought him great happiness—as well as another child, born in 1897, when the former president was sixty-three years old.

Harrison spent his final years writing the political memoir *Views of an Ex-President*, which he published in 1901, the year he died. Although he entered the White House hoping to burnish the heroic glory once associated with his grandfather's name, Harrison instead (and ironically) proceeded much as his grandfather might have done (had he lived), doing the bidding of party leaders and trying to stay out of trouble. Sadly, Benjamin Harrison might well be remembered more fondly today had his administration also ended prematurely.

★ ★ ★

William McKinley

25th President · 1897–1901

Morton Keller

According to Secretary of State *John Hay, William McKinley had "a genuine Italian ecclesiastical face of the fifteenth century." Whether Hay meant to invoke Niccolò Machiavelli is unclear, but he certainly thought that McKinley was equally cunning.*

THE LEADING (THOUGH UNFINISHED) BIOGRAPHY of Franklin D. Roosevelt is called *The Age of Roosevelt;* the major biography of William McKinley, *In the Days of McKinley.* This is as it should be: FDR bestrode his epoch; McKinley mirrored his time.

McKinley's presidency was a significant one, but not primarily because of what he did or thought or said. Rather, its importance lies in the degree to which the major events of the 1890s—industrial depression, agrarian revolt, and the acquisition of an American empire—made the McKinley administration a transition from the politics of the Gilded Age to the politics of the Progressive Era.

McKinley's native state of Ohio was home to six of the seven Republicans elected president between 1876 and 1920. It had a substantial number of electoral votes; a population that blended the cultures of the East, South, and Midwest; and a rich mix of agriculture, mining, manufacturing, and retail businesses. McKinley quickly rose in this political forcing house, first as a congressman and then as

This Puck cartoon, *which appeared during the 1900 campaign, shows William Jennings Bryan using a blow-pipe labeled "speeches" to inflate a McKinley-shaped "imperialism" balloon.*

governor of the state. It helped that he had a distinguished Civil War record, all but obligatory for politicians at the time. Just eighteen when he enlisted as a private in June 1861, he fought with such distinction at Antietam that he was promoted to second lieutenant and assigned to the staff of Col. Rutherford B. Hayes. In March 1865, at age twenty-two, he was breveted a major.

As regards the personal qualities that contributed to McKinley's political success, both friends and foes agreed: He had a notable sweetness of disposition, a devout (Methodist) faith not conspicuously cloaked in hypocrisy, and a moral sense that most notably expressed itself in his lifelong devotion to his epileptic, seriously neurotic wife. Small in stature, formal in dress and manner, he was, as one contemporary said, a "Christian gentleman."

Political enemies accused McKinley of passivity and lack of purpose—of being the puppet of his political Warwick, Ohio businessman Marcus A. Hanna—but those who knew him best thought his impassive demeanor concealed a rich store of political cunning. John Hay, Lincoln's private secretary and no fool when it came to judging people, observed with surprise that "there are those who think Mark Hanna will run him!"

I T WAS WITH SURE INSTINCT that McKinley became the leading exponent of the most powerful theme of the late-nineteenth-century Republican party: American nationalism. Many Republicans defined themselves by waving the "bloody shirt" of the Civil War or inveighing against Catholics and immigrants or consumers of alcohol, but McKinley would have none of it. Instead, he made the issue of tariff protection the core of his party's creed. High tariffs, he argued, would assure prosperity for workingmen, lucrative domestic markets for farmers, and a united and prosperous people. When hard times came in the early 1890s, he suffered politically for his close identification with protectionism. (The McKinley Tariff of 1890 was widely blamed for the Panic of 1893 and the depression that followed.) But over the long term, his approach bound farmers, the rising urban middle class, and (non-Catholic) industrial workingmen to the Republican party.

President McKinley delivers *a speech on one of his favorite topics: the need for higher tariffs.*

BORN
January 29, 1843

BIRTHPLACE
Niles, Ohio

DIED
September 14, 1901

PARTY AFFILIATION
Republican

CHILDREN
Katherine, Ida

MAJOR EVENTS

JULY 7, 1897

Congress enacts the Dingley Tariff, whose rates are even higher than those set by the McKinley Tariff of 1890. They reflect the consensus among Republican businessmen that American prosperity depends on keeping foreign goods out of U.S. markets.

APRIL 30, 1898

At the outbreak of the Spanish-American War, Commo. George Dewey sails into Manila Bay. The next day, he destroys Spain's ten-ship Pacific fleet and captures the Philippines.

DECEMBER 10, 1898

The Treaty of Paris, dictated by the United States, formally ends the Spanish-American War. Spain grants Cuba independence, cedes Guam and Puerto Rico to the United States, and sells the Philippines to the United States for twenty million dollars.

At the time of her marriage to McKinley in 1873, Ida Saxton was beautiful, vivacious, and charming. However, within a few years, she lost her health and her spirit. It's difficult to know what caused this decline, but at some point she developed epilepsy. Only people very close to McKinley knew what a burden his wife's condition placed on him, yet he adapted well. Although protocol dictated otherwise, Ida McKinley was always seated next to her husband in case she had a seizure. When she did, McKinley calmly placed a napkin over her head and kept it there until the seizure passed.

This photograph shows McKinley arriving at the Pan-American Exposition's Temple of Music on September 6, 1901. It was taken about fifteen minutes before he was shot.

The election of 1896 challenged this Republican ideology as no other had since the Civil War and no other would until the Great Depression. The hard times of the 1890s had spurred an agrarian discontent that, in turn, had sparked the populist movement of the early 1890s and enabled William Jennings Bryan and the free silver cause to capture the Democratic party. At the 1896 Democratic convention in Chicago, Bryan delivered the most memorable of American party convention speeches, in which he assaulted Republican support of the gold standard: "You shall not press down upon the brow of labor this crown of thorns," he thundered. "You shall not crucify mankind upon a cross of gold." His call for unlimited coinage of silver carried with it the promise of monetary inflation that would ease farmer indebtedness.

The McKinley-Hanna response was a political masterstroke. Before the campaign, McKinley had been indifferent to the currency issue. He had no objection to bimetallism; tariff protection was his forte. But Hanna, who managed the campaign, and McKinley decided to merge the gold standard and protectionism into a platform that promised to restore prosperity and guarantee social order and morality. Free coinage of silver, the Republicans argued, would create a "57-cent dollar" that robbed workingmen of their just wages.

McKinley's sober bearing strongly reinforced this message. While Bryan stumped the country as no candidate had before, McKinley conducted a "front-porch campaign," receiving hundreds of thousands of visitors at his home in Canton. "I might just as well put up a trapeze on my front lawn and compete with some professional athlete as go out speaking against Bryan," McKinley observed. "I have to *think* when I speak."

Meanwhile, Hanna extracted large sums from a frightened American plutocracy and used the money—estimates range from $3.5 million to $16 million, compared to about $500,000 raised by Bryan—to educate (or propagandize) voters on a scale never seen before. Theodore Roosevelt said of Hanna's tactics: "He has advertised McKinley as if he were a patent medicine!" In its intensity, substance, and magnitude, the 1896 contest was the first modern presidential election.

The result was the largest Republican presidential victory since Grant's in 1872, with Bryan winning no state north of the Mason-Dixon line and east of the Mississippi. Once in office, McKinley did what was expected of him. He oversaw the passage of a new protective tariff and moved cautiously toward a gold-backed currency. However, in 1898, business as usual was upset by a foreign policy crisis unlike any since the early days of the republic.

Cuban revolutionaries had for many years been engaged in grim struggle with Spain for control of their island. Now, with a sensationalist U.S. press battening on front-page stories of Spanish atrocities, earlier American indifference gave way to a rising demand for intervention. Immigrants and former Confederates seeking closer identification with

"THE MISSION OF THE UNITED STATES IS ONE OF BENEVOLENT ASSIMILATION."

—Letter, December 1898—

their country, populists soothed by an improving farm economy, and geostrategists desiring a more powerful American navy (and a Panamanian canal) backed the cause of Cuban independence. McKinley was no jingo—"I have been through one war. I have seen the dead pile up, and I do not want to see another," he declared—but the February 1898 sinking of the battleship *Maine* in Havana Harbor forced his hand. Stampeded by the public and the press, he sent a war message to Congress on April 11, even though Spain had already agreed to most U.S. demands.

McKINLEY'S RELIGIOUS MORALISM and Republican nationalism made it easy for him, once committed, to define the war as both a righteous crusade and a commercial opportunity. His missionary desire to uplift the lesser breeds later provided a comforting rationale for the new American empire the war would bring about. "While we are conducting war and until its conclusion, we must keep all we get," McKinley proclaimed. "When the war is over, we must keep what we want." Trade, he knew, followed the flag.

The Spanish-American War did much to alter the nature of the presidency. The White House clerical staff ballooned from six to eighty people to keep up with the enormous increase in paperwork. McKinley's private secretary, George B. Cortelyou, became the first (unofficial) presidential press secretary, the exigencies of war having turned the White House into a primary source of news.

SEPTEMBER 6, 1899

Secretary of State John Hay sends diplomatic notes to several interested nations proposing an open door policy toward China. Rather than continue carving up China into "spheres of influence," Hay suggests opening all Chinese markets to everyone.

JUNE 20, 1900

Chinese nationalists known as Boxers surge into Peking, where they besiege foreign diplomats and Chinese Christians. The Boxers' goal is to drive all the "foreign devils" from their country. The arrival of an international army in August, however, ends the siege and, for all practical purposes, the Boxer Rebellion.

***Mark Hanna** was repeatedly caricatured as a plutocrat determined to buy McKinley the presidency.*

Whether to maintain the gold standard or coin silver freely was the great controversy of the 1896 campaign. Those who, like McKinley, supported the gold standard were called goldbugs. Many advertised their views with pins such as this one.

The tone and character of domestic policy shifted as well. The growing importance of foreign markets eroded support for McKinley's protectionism, and the president himself backed off. "Isolation is no longer possible or desirable," he declared. "The expansion of our trade and commerce is the pressing problem."

PROSPERITY AND EMPIRE were the themes of McKinley's 1900 campaign. A weakened Bryan, more Hanna money, and McKinley's very real popularity won him easy reelection. He went on a triumphal tour of the West and in September 1901 visited the Pan-American Exposition in Buffalo, where he became the third president to be assassinated.

In every presidential assassination, the mental derangement of the killer exists within a larger political context. John Wilkes Booth rationalized his murder of Abraham Lincoln by calling it an act of revenge for the defeated Confederacy. Charles Guiteau considered himself a member of a Republican faction whose patronage claims had

"HE KEEPS HIS EAR SO CLOSE TO THE GROUND IT'S FULL OF GRASSHOPPERS."

—Rep. Joseph Cannon—

been unfairly rebuffed by James A. Garfield. McKinley's assassin, anarchist Leon Czolgosz, reflected the anomie and class hatred suffusing the urban-industrial world of the late nineteenth century. An unemployed millworker in his late twenties, Czolgosz drifted through the industrial cities of the upper Midwest, reading anarchist newspapers and adopting the revealing name of Fred Nieman—literally, "nobody." He learned that McKinley would be visiting the Buffalo exposition, joined the reception line (McKinley was one of the great handshakers of his day), and shot twice at point-blank range the man he had come to regard as the embodiment of privilege.

McKinley was a transitional man, straddling the Americas of the late nineteenth and early twentieth centuries. He was felled by a product of the social anomie that came with mass, industrialized, urban society: the world of the century to come.

★ ★ ★

OPPOSITE:

This photograph of McKinley was taken in 1899. The pink carnation in his lapel was considered the president's personal trademark. It symbolized both his warm disposition and his relaxed manner. Often, he would pluck the flower from his coat and present it to a guest— a gesture that usually made a lasting positive impression.

Theodore Roosevelt

26th President · 1901–1909

Theodore Roosevelt (signature)

Allen Weinstein

Theodore Roosevelt
(shown here in 1904) had the broadest range of personal interests of any American president, with the possible exception of Thomas Jefferson.

These spurs, *which belonged to Roosevelt, are part of the permanent collection at Sagamore Hill, TR's summer home on Long Island, now a national historic site.*

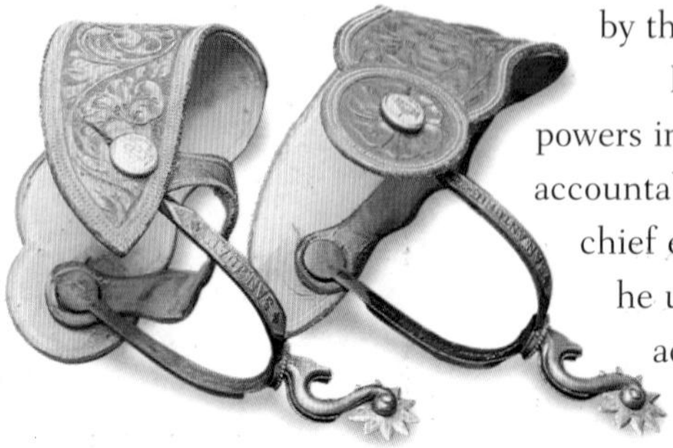

WITH THE DEATH OF PRESIDENT William McKinley on September 14, 1901, Theodore Roosevelt became the third vice president in less than forty years to attain the presidency because of an assassin's bullet. At forty-two, he was the nation's youngest chief executive, although one who already had a wider range of professional experience than most before or since. By the time he reached the White House, TR (the first president commonly known by his initials) had already been a rancher, a scholar, a writer, a naturalist, a state legislator, a civil service commissioner, a New York City police commissioner, an assistant secretary of the navy, an army colonel, a war hero, and a governor of New York. Famously energetic and impulsive, he reacted to McKinley's murder with customary candor, telling a friend, "It is a dreadful thing to come into the presidency this way; but it would be a far worse thing to be morbid about it."

IN JULY 1908, after nearly seven years in office, Roosevelt wrote to another friend that he had "a very definite philosophy about the Presidency. I think it should be a very powerful office, and I think the President should be a very strong man who uses without hesitation every power that the position yields; but…he should be sharply watched by the people [and] held to a strict accountability by them."

Extraordinary energy and unabashed exercise of the office's powers indeed mark the presidency of Theodore Roosevelt. As for accountability, however, TR had other ideas. More than any previous chief executive (with the possible exception of Abraham Lincoln), he used what he called the president's "bully pulpit" to hold accountable not himself but powerful corporations, belligerent unions, and disrespectful foreign governments.

"Roosevelt more than any man living," historian Henry Adams observed, "showed the singular primitive quality that belongs to ultimate matter—the quality that medieval theology ascribed to God—he was pure act." Before TR moved in, the White House had been a sedate refuge and its occupants men of polite rectitude. But Roosevelt brought to Washington youthful exuberance in ways that echoed both his personal lifestyle and his approach to national governance.

Woodrow Wilson once called Roosevelt (shown here in full oratorical exuberance) "the most dangerous man of the age."

At the time of McKinley's death, TR piously promised "to continue absolutely unbroken" his predecessor's policies, including McKinley's cautious approach to executive authority. Yet from almost his first day in office, the irrepressible Roosevelt designed and pursued a much more activist conception of presidential leadership. In his first message to Congress, delivered in December 1901, he contrasted the hostile behavior of industrial conglomerates, indifferent to public accountability, with an innovative

> ## "I TOOK THE CANAL ZONE AND LET CONGRESS DEBATE, AND WHILE THE DEBATE GOES ON, THE CANAL DOES ALSO."
>
> *—Speech, 1911—*

presentation of national economic interest: "There is a widespread conviction in the minds of the American people that the great corporations known as trusts are in certain of their features and tendencies hurtful to the general welfare….Corporations engaged in interstate commerce should be regulated if they are found to exercise a license working to the public injury."

Roosevelt called for the establishment of a new cabinet position to monitor the trusts, leading to the creation of the Department of Commerce and Labor in 1903. He also demanded for the national government previously unimagined authority to inspect the records of

---

BORN
October 27, 1858

BIRTHPLACE
New York, New York

DIED
January 6, 1919

PARTY AFFILIATION
Republican

CHILDREN
Alice, Theodore Jr., Kermit, Ethel, Archibald, Quentin

MAJOR EVENTS

OCTOBER 16, 1901

In his first controversial move as president, Roosevelt invites Booker T. Washington to join him for dinner at the White House. White supremacists in the South respond to the gesture with violent attacks against blacks.

JANUARY 21, 1905

When the Dominican Republic defaults on its debt to European banks, Roosevelt takes control of the Dominican treasury. This first application of the Roosevelt Corollary shifts loan oversight to U.S. banks.

JANUARY 22, 1905

On Bloody Sunday, Russian tsar Nicholas II orders his troops to fire on demonstrators outside the Winter Palace in St. Petersburg. The unarmed factory workers had intended to present a petition of grievances to the tsar. Hundreds are killed or wounded.

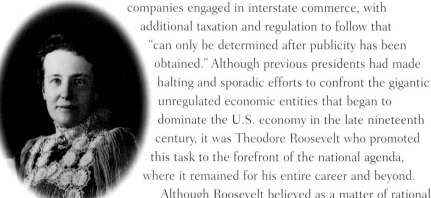

Edith Carow was Roosevelt's second wife. Although Teddy and Edith grew up next door to each other on East Twentieth Street in New York City (and even developed a romantic attraction as adolescents), they drifted apart when TR went off to Harvard, where he met his first wife, Alice Lee. After the first Mrs. Roosevelt died in 1884 giving birth to a daughter, TR left the infant in the care of his sisters and moved to the Dakota Territory for a year. Upon his return, after meeting Edith again, they resumed their relationship and were married in 1886.

Americans loved the rambunctious Roosevelt family. The president's oldest daughter, Alice, caused a particular stir when it became public knowledge that she smoked and bet on horses. "I can do one of two things," her father said. "I can be president of the United States, or I can control Alice. I cannot do both."

companies engaged in interstate commerce, with additional taxation and regulation to follow that "can only be determined after publicity has been obtained." Although previous presidents had made halting and sporadic efforts to confront the gigantic unregulated economic entities that began to dominate the U.S. economy in the late nineteenth century, it was Theodore Roosevelt who promoted this task to the forefront of the national agenda, where it remained for his entire career and beyond.

Although Roosevelt believed as a matter of rational economic policy that trusts and other anticompetitive entities should be regulated rather than broken up, he felt a critical first step needed to be taken to establish their subordination to federal authority. A congressional investigation in 1900 had already identified 185 industrial conglomerates with an astounding (for the time) total capitalization of more than three billion dollars. All but one of these megacompanies had been incorporated during the previous three years, attesting to the rapidity with which the industrial, financial, and transportation sectors of the economy were consolidating. Most of the trusts had been created by a few powerful banking houses, notably that led by J. P. Morgan.

Carefully but audaciously, Roosevelt chose the ground for his confrontation with Morgan. In 1902, he instructed his attorney general, Philander C. Knox, to bring suit against the Northern Securities Company, a consolidation of three major railroad systems put together by (among others) Morgan and Edward H. Harriman. Its purpose had been to end the ruinous competition among the Northern Pacific, Great Northern, and Chicago, Burlington & Quincy Railroads. Bringing suit under the Sherman Anti-Trust Act of 1890 was risky, however, because the Supreme Court had previously questioned the statute's constitutionality. Hoping to avoid a costly struggle, Morgan rushed to Washington, but his meeting with the president merely reinforced Roosevelt's determination to rein in the trusts. "Mr. Morgan could not help regarding me as a big rival operator, who either intended to ruin all his interests, or else could be induced to come to an agreement to ruin none," he afterward told Knox.

In March 1904, by a five-to-four vote, the Supreme Court judged the Northern Securities merger illegal and ordered the company dissolved. This decision, directly affirming the constitutionality of the

Sherman Act, provided the legal basis for all future antitrust regulation and greatly increased Roosevelt's popularity among voters, if not among tycoons. His margin of victory in the 1904 election was the largest of any Republican president to that point. Subsequently, he brought similar antitrust actions against other giant corporations, including Standard Oil, the American Tobacco Company, and Du Pont. Although Roosevelt preferred government regulation to such "trustbusting," his public image was periodically enhanced by these legal actions, which asserted the supremacy of the government over private economic interests, no matter how powerful those interests were. "The great development of industrialism," he observed in 1905, "means that there must be an increase in the supervision exercised by the Government over business enterprise."

I N LABOR RELATIONS AS WELL, TR found compelling reasons to bridle corporate power. During the anthracite coal strike of 1902, for example, his threat to nationalize the mines forced a settlement more acceptable to labor than to management (although the president's primary concern was the impending coal shortage). Roosevelt also urged Congress to enact labor-friendly statutes (another presidential first), including child labor laws and a workmen's compensation bill covering all federal employees.

At other times, though, Roosevelt used troops to break up legitimate strikes, and similar inconsistencies marked his actions with regard to the regulation of big business. Private agreements he reached with U.S. Steel and other powerful corporations suggested that his targets for antitrust action were chosen as much for their unpopularity as for their abusive behavior. Moreover, although TR initiated a number of additional reform proposals for congressional action during his final years in office, he wasted little time or political capital trying to forge legislative coalitions between "progressive"

JUNE 27, 1905

In Chicago, charismatic labor leader William "Big Bill" Haywood helps found the Industrial Workers of the World. Unlike more conservative trade unions, the militant Wobblies will welcome all workers regardless of their skills, race, or gender.

JULY 11–13, 1905

W. E. B. Du Bois and other civil rights leaders gather in Niagara Falls to launch the Niagara Movement, whose goals include equal opportunity for blacks in political and economic life as well as an end to segregation. The group meets on the Canadian side of the river because no hotels on the U.S. side will allow them to register.

APRIL 18, 1906

A hugely destructive earthquake shakes San Francisco. The fires that it causes will last three days and raze two-thirds of the city, leaving half a million people homeless.

TR's lifestyle was *remarkably physical. He sparred with boxing champion John L. Sullivan in the White House gym and regularly went on "obstacle walks," leaving namby-pamby congressmen and overweight ambassadors panting in his wake. He is shown here with naturalist John Muir atop Yosemite's Glacier Point in 1906.*

Colonel Roosevelt poses with his Rough Riders on San Juan Hill. The regiment saw very little action in Cuba, but one day's hard fighting was enough to glorify Roosevelt. He later remembered the day as the greatest of his life. "I killed a Spaniard with my own hand, like a jackrabbit," he wrote home. "Oh, but we had a bully fight!"

This New Year's Day 1902 cover of Puck illustrates the confidence that Americans already had in Roosevelt, even though he'd been guiding the ship of state just three months.

Republicans and Democrats in Congress to enact these measures. Rhetoric aside, Roosevelt proved far less an implacable adversary than the tycoons imagined, and he was far less dedicated to reform than many of his supporters among Progressives believed.

Turn-of-the-century Progressivism embraced a variety of economic and social programs that promised to make the United States a more decent society. Because many of Roosevelt's own policies (notably antitrust enforcement) similarly advanced this goal, he was often associated with the Progressives, whose ranks included members of the Socialist and Prohibition parties as well as Democrats and Republicans. When muckraking journalist Upton Sinclair published *The Jungle* in 1906, the country recoiled at the novel's horrifying account of conditions in Chicago meatpacking plants. Responding to the widespread outrage, Roosevelt proposed government regulation of the nation's food supply, quickly enacted in the Meat Inspection and Pure Food and Drug Acts of 1906. Yet TR never intended to reject capitalism; born to wealth, he was himself a capitalist. He wished mainly to curb capitalism's excesses and thus protect big business from its own abuses so that socialism wouldn't obtain a foothold in America.

Roosevelt's energy also spurred his emphatic involvement of the United States in foreign affairs—not only within the Western Hemisphere, America's traditional realm of engagement, but in Europe and Asia as well. Close to home, he dealt in a crisp, dramatic fashion with Colombia when that nation balked at U.S. plans for a transoceanic canal across the Isthmus of Panama, then a province of Colombia. After the Colombian Senate rejected in August 1903 a treaty granting the United States a hundred-year lease on a canal zone, the Roosevelt administration backed a revolutionary movement in Panama. When the anticipated uprising occurred in early November, TR quickly recognized Panamanian "independence" and sent a warship to prevent Colombian troops from reclaiming the province. Two weeks later, the new Panamanian regime signed essentially the same lease rejected by Colombia, and construction on the waterway began.

> "NOW, LOOK! THAT DAMNED COWBOY IS PRESIDENT OF THE UNITED STATES!"
>
> ———
>
> *McKinley campaign manager Mark Hanna*

Various disputes between European powers and Latin American nations over the collection of debts soon led TR to announce in December 1904 that the United States would henceforth play the role of "international police power" in the Western Hemisphere, especially in the Caribbean. This so-called Roosevelt Corollary to the Monroe Doctrine went well beyond what any president had previously asserted.

Elsewhere, Roosevelt's aggressive projection of U.S. involvement in global affairs further expanded the reach of American (that is, presidential) leadership. In September 1905, he mediated (at Portsmouth, New Hampshire) an end to the Russo-Japanese War, for which he was awarded a Nobel Peace Prize. The following year, he helped bring about the Algeciras Conference, at which European heads of state negotiated conflicting claims to Morocco. He also sent an armada of ships, the so-called Great White Fleet, on a "goodwill" tour of the world, which had the intended effect of demonstrating America's growing military might.

WHILE THUS WRESTLING WITH the trusts and wresting from the world recognition of U.S. leadership, Roosevelt additionally managed to focus greater attention than any of his predecessors on the preservation of America's natural resources. His two years as a rancher in the Dakota Territory and his lifelong passion for exploration were among the factors that gave TR a special interest in conservation issues, reflected in his appointment of dedicated conservationists Gifford Pinchot (as chief of the Forest Service) and presidential son James R. Garfield (as secretary of the interior). Moreover, Roosevelt devoted much of his own time and attention to educating Americans about the need for environmental protection. Using the authority granted him under the 1891 Forest Reserve Act, he withdrew from development more than two hundred million acres of forestland, an amount greater than that withdrawn by his three predecessors combined. In 1908, he sponsored the first-ever White House National Conservation Congress, at which plans were made for protecting natural resources in the future. Bolstered by Roosevelt's persistent publicity, the issue of conservation eventually entered mainstream national politics.

Despite having broken with tradition on several policy fronts, TR determined in 1908, after having served nearly two full terms, that he wouldn't seek another one. He chose instead to support the candidacy of his close friend and secretary of war, William Howard Taft. After Taft's

Roosevelt stands on the steps of City Hall in New York City, where he spoke at a September 1918 Lafayette Day ceremony. His mourning band honors the memory of his son Quentin, an army pilot killed two months earlier over France. Quentin's death overwhelmed Roosevelt's boyishness, and by January 1919 a cheerless TR was himself dead.

In 1902, Roosevelt *went bear hunting in Mississippi, but the only bear he found was a small cub, which he refused to shoot. Hearing this story, Clifford Berryman drew a cartoon of the incident for the* Washington Post, *which Brooklyn toy store owner Morris Michtom placed in his window next to a stuffed animal he called Teddy's Bear. The name was later shortened to "teddy bear" (an early example is shown here).*

OPPOSITE:

Roosevelt salutes *the Great White Fleet on its December 1907 departure from Hampton Roads. The fleet's around-the-world, flag-waving jaunt lasted two years, covered forty-six thousand miles, and occupied all sixteen battleships of the U.S. Navy. When it was over, few could doubt the presence of the United States among the world's military powers.*

victory, Roosevelt turned his attention briefly to travel (including a yearlong African safari) and writing, only to reenter politics following a series of personal and political disagreements with his designated successor. An unfortunate battle for the 1912 Republican nomination ensued, won by Taft. But Roosevelt didn't quit, carrying his challenge into the general election as the candidate of a newly organized coalition of reformers calling itself the Progressive party. In the end, Taft and Roosevelt split the Republican vote, electing Democrat Woodrow Wilson with merely a plurality of the popular vote.

> "WHEN THEODORE ATTENDS A WEDDING, HE WANTS TO BE THE BRIDE, AND WHEN HE ATTENDS A FUNERAL, HE WANTS TO BE THE CORPSE."
>
> —*Attributed to a Roosevelt relative*—

IN APRIL 1917, AS THE UNITED STATES entered World War I, the fifty-eight-year-old former Rough Rider appealed to Wilson for a wartime commission to lead a division to France. Two hundred thousand men enthusiastically volunteered to go with him, but Wilson (whom TR had previously called a coward for keeping America out of the war) curtly rejected the plan. Roosevelt died in January 1919, six months after the death of his son Quentin, an army pilot killed when he was shot down behind German lines.

Asked at one point about his White House legacy, TR provided this capsule response: "While President I have *been* President, emphatically; I have used every ounce of power there was in the office and I have not cared a rap for the criticisms of those who spoke of my 'usurpation of power'; for I knew that the talk was all nonsense and that there was no usurpation." Whether dealing with J. P. Morgan or the Colombian government, expanding American power or negotiating regional peace, throughout his years in office Theodore Roosevelt tested and extended the limits of the American presidency—emphatically.

★ ★ ★

William Howard Taft

27ᵗʰ President · 1909–1913

Mark C. Carnes

Teddy Roosevelt was but one of many to link William Howard Taft's "most lovable personality" to his breadth of belt: "One loves him at first sight," TR declared.

WILLIAM HOWARD TAFT'S PRESIDENCY was not a success, as he readily acknowledged. Taft is remembered, if at all, for being the fattest president. His obesity has become a staple of quiz shows and trivia games, a humorous sweetener that generations of historians have sprinkled through bland lectures on the tariff and monetary policy. A favorite joke concerns Taft's tenure as governor-general of the Philippines, back when the United States brought civilization to the Filipinos by crushing them. Taft had gone on a trip to take stock of America's first colony, and on his return he cabled Secretary of War Elihu Root: "Stood trip well. Rode horseback twenty-five miles." To which Root famously replied, "How is the horse?"

T AFT TOOK IT ALL, or at least much of it, in fun. That too is part of his legacy. Victorian Americans commonly regarded a big body, at least in a man, as an expression of physical well-being and pecuniary clout. The character of a "man of substance" was often mirrored in his physique. Thus Taft's girth was something of a political asset. Journalist Mark Sullivan observed that Taft was "too big a man" to engage in petty politics. "In all three hundred thirty pounds of him," Sullivan added, "not a pound nor an ounce nor a gram was deceit."

With unusual unanimity, friends, critics, and biographers have all described Taft as "good-natured." In fact, his joviality sometimes masked his intelligence. (He graduated second in his class at Yale and was admitted to the Ohio bar even before his 1880 graduation from the University of Cincinnati Law School.) Taft advanced briskly in Ohio politics and was serving as a federal judge when President William McKinley, another Ohio Republican, sent him in 1900 to

Taft was given this watch by a New York City jewelers association in 1912.

establish a civil government in the newly acquired Philippines. Taft proved a fair, effective administrator, and in 1904 President Theodore Roosevelt named him secretary of war.

Taft's admiration for Roosevelt was boundless, and Roosevelt basked in the big man's adulation. Taft soon became TR's right-hand man, an able lieutenant who cheerfully and unquestioningly carried out the president's decisions. In 1907, when Roosevelt decided not to run for reelection, it came as no surprise that he chose Taft as his successor— and TR's good word was enough to give Taft the Republican nomination.

Breaking with precedent, *the president and first lady ride together in an open carriage from the grounds of the Capitol to the White House following Taft's inauguration. In the past, the new president had typically been accompanied by the outgoing chief executive.*

The decision was unfortunate. Roosevelt mistook Taft's amiable deference for philosophical agreement (in fact, Taft was less activist than TR); and Taft, who longed for the contemplative life of a Supreme Court justice, dreaded the political spotlight. He accepted the nomination only because he could find no way to resist Roosevelt's exhortations.

After the Republican convention, as his misgivings mounted, Taft fled to Hot Springs, Virginia, where he took up golf as a means of escape. The beauty of the sport, he noted, was that "you cannot permit yourself to think of anything else." While others urged him to commence campaigning, he procrastinated. A worried Roosevelt prodded Taft to be more energetic. TR counseled him to forget the golf (a sport considered effete by voters in the West) and accentuate the more manly aspects of his personality. "For all your gentleness and kindliness and generous good

BORN
September 15, 1857

BIRTHPLACE
Cincinnati, Ohio

DIED
March 8, 1930

PARTY AFFILIATION
Republican

CHILDREN
Robert, Helen, Charles

MAJOR EVENTS

MARCH 25, 1911

A fire at the Triangle Shirtwaist Company in New York City kills 146, mostly immigrant women, who are trapped inside the sweatshop by locked doors (to keep them at their machines). The tragedy inspires unions to demand improved worker safety.

MAY 15, 1911

Ruling in a suit brought by the Justice Department, the Supreme Court orders the breakup of Standard Oil. The size and wealth of this trust have allowed John D. Rockefeller to drive smaller oil companies out of business.

NOVEMBER 10, 1911

Andrew Carnegie donates $125 million to found the Carnegie Corporation, dedicated to the "advancement and diffusion of knowledge." Following the steel magnate's example, John D. Rockefeller will establish a similar foundation in 1913.

Taft was the third president to ride in an automobile but the first buried in Arlington National Cemetery.

Besides that which came from TR, Taft often received prodding from his wife, Nellie. The daughter of a U.S. attorney, she had attracted Taft with her intelligence and pluck, and one might even say that she came to dominate him. "Quick-witted and energetic," according to White House historian William Seale, "she was less a charmer than her husband, and more of a pusher when it came to having her way." Suffering a stroke in May 1909, she spent most of Taft's term recovering. By 1911, however, she was apparently "quite disposed to sit as a pope and direct me as of yore," a relieved Taft wrote.

nature," TR pleaded, "there never existed a man who was a better fighter when the need arose." Increasingly, Roosevelt took to the hustings to praise Taft and denounce Democratic candidate William Jennings Bryan as a demagogue, a hypocrite, and, withal, "what a small man!"

With Roosevelt at the controls, the Republican machine hoisted Taft to victory. Yet Taft's foreboding lingered, and his inaugural address was remarkable for its leaden tone: "Anyone who has taken the oath I have just taken must feel a heavy weight of responsibility," he began grimly. Though an effective lieutenant under Roosevelt, Taft had little sense of what he wanted to accomplish as president. Insofar as his administration had any direction, it came from the cabinet members, most of whom were undistinguished, and from a handful of powerful Republican senators, notably Nelson W. Aldrich of Rhode Island, whose vision was clear but fixed far to the right.

TAFT FOLLOWED THEIR LEAD and endorsed, albeit reluctantly, a protective tariff. Aldrich was euphoric and Roosevelt, who had skirted the tariff issue, alarmed. Then TR intimate Gifford Pinchot, the nation's chief forester, charged Interior Secretary Richard Ballinger with improperly disposing of some Alaskan coal fields. Taft responded to Pinchot's insubordination (Ballinger was his superior) by dismissing Pinchot. Roosevelt returned from an extended African safari bristling with indignation. Taft, it seemed, was abandoning the liberal wing of the Republican party, which Roosevelt increasingly associated with the will of the people. Roosevelt's belief that Taft had misjudged the national mood was underscored in 1910, when Democrats regained control of the House in midterm elections.

In foreign affairs, Taft was somewhat more successful. His foreign policy, known as Dollar Diplomacy, sought to substitute, in the president's words, "dollars for bullets." Of course, like every other twentieth-century president, Taft routinely used U.S. troops to secure American interests abroad, but he also encouraged the use of economic power to stabilize and control foreign governments, particularly in Asia and Latin America. Taft's policy was an extension of Roosevelt's own corollary to the Monroe Doctrine, but it did little to appease TR.

The final break between Taft and Roosevelt occurred in 1911, when Attorney

During four years in the Philippines, in addition to suppressing the insurrection led by Emilio Aguinaldo, Taft worked to reform a corrupt judiciary, open public schools, upgrade health care, and improve harbors and roads.

General George W. Wickersham filed an antitrust suit against U.S. Steel. The Taft administration had already filed successful suits against American Tobacco and Standard Oil, but the suit against U.S. Steel was different because Roosevelt had personally consented (in 1907) to the trust's formation. Therefore, the suit implied that TR had approved an illegal monopoly.

> ## "IT IS NOT THE HEIGHT OF MY AMBITION TO BE POPULAR. I HAVE EVEN BECOME QUITE PHILOSOPHICAL WITH RESPECT TO THE DISLIKE THE PEOPLE MAY FEEL FOR ME."
>
> —*Letter to his wife, 1912*—

The celebrated trustbuster was furious, even after Taft explained that he'd never meant to embarrass Roosevelt. According to Taft, Wickersham had filed the suit without apprising the president of the particulars. But this explanation was problematic: Either it was untrue, and Taft had indeed belittled his mentor, or it was true, and Taft had been woefully inattentive to the conduct of his administration. Roosevelt meanwhile denounced his protégé as a "flubdub with a streak of the second rate and the common in him." In truth, TR's chief complaint wasn't that Taft occupied the White House, but that he didn't. Soon enough, Roosevelt announced he would run again for president.

During the primaries, Roosevelt lashed out at Taft, calling him, among other epithets, a "fathead" and a "puzzlewit." Initially stunned, Taft attempted to ignore TR's invective. He was "big enough," he explained, to resist the taunts of his foes. But in the end, Taft was obliged to fight.

AUGUST 14, 1912

President Taft sends marines to put down a rebellion against the Nicaraguan government, which has been particularly friendly to U.S. business. In response, Democratic presidential candidate Woodrow Wilson promises to replace Dollar Diplomacy with a foreign policy rooted in morality, not economics.

FEBRUARY 25, 1913

The Sixteenth Amendment is ratified, making income taxes legal. In October, as part of the Underwood-Simmons Tariff, Congress will enact a graduated income tax, which Progressives argue is the fairest way for the government to raise money.

Because Taft had once *become stuck in an ordinary bathtub, a special tub (shown here) was installed in the White House. It measured seven feet long and nearly four feet wide and easily held three of the workers who installed it.*

When reporters complained in 1908 that his campaign trail seldom strayed from the fairways, Taft explained that he was exercising to lose weight: "It's not easy to be a presidential candidate, not much easier than it is to keep down one's flesh."

OPPOSITE:

Throughout his term in office, Taft was miserable, and as his troubles grew, so did he. Food became his principal solace, and he regularly circumvented the diets imposed by his strict wife. He hid food, sneaked out of the White House for snacks, and scheduled trips that he knew would include lavish banquets. He gained 50 pounds in two years, reaching a zenith of 355 pounds just in time for the 1912 presidential election.

"I was a man of straw," he declared, "but I have been a man of straw long enough." Then he unwisely added: "Even a rat in a corner will fight."

Roosevelt won the key primaries—taking even Ohio, Taft's home state—but Taft held the party regulars and prevailed at the convention. While Taft exulted, an indignant TR formed the Progressive party (nicknamed the Bull Moose party) and accepted its nomination. With the Republicans divided, it became a foregone conclusion that Democrat Woodrow Wilson would take the general election. Taft professed hope yet confessed that "in my heart I have long been making plans for my future."

AFTER HIS PRESIDENCY, Taft returned to Yale, where he taught constitutional law until Republican Warren Harding succeeded Wilson in 1921. That June, Taft achieved his lifelong goal when Harding named him chief justice of the Supreme Court. In all, Taft's decisions as chief justice were far more conservative than his record as president would have suggested. In *Bailey v. Drexel Furniture* (1922), he wrote that Congress couldn't use its taxing power to discourage child labor because such a use would "wipe out the sovereignty of the States." The same year, he ruled in *United Mine Workers v. Coronado Coal* that the Sherman Anti-Trust Act could be used against unions that employed illegal strikebreaking tactics. His main contributions, however, were administrative: Taft streamlined the court's deliberative procedures and improved the manner in which it supervised the federal judiciary.

Taft's historical reputation, though, remains fixed by his 1912 struggle with Roosevelt. The traditional narrative pits Taft, the bumbling conservative, against Roosevelt, the vigorous progressive. But this ideological template emerged only after the fact. On the one issue of enduring significance—the regulation of monopolies—Taft's record is far more progressive than TR's.

Ultimately, the dispute between the two men had more to do with personality than with political ideology. Roosevelt endorsed an activist presidential style, while Taft increasingly cloaked his own passivity in constitutional garb. At the time, critics derided Taft for worrying too much about rampant executive power. Yet the subsequent rise of the "imperial presidency" has shown Taft's apprehension to be, if not prescient, at least not preposterous. He'll never be regarded as a great president or even a good one, but perhaps someday his obesity may cease to be his legacy.

★ ★ ★

Woodrow Wilson

28ᵗʰ President · 1913–1921

James Chace

Thomas Woodrow Wilson was named after his maternal grandfather, the Reverend Thomas Woodrow. After his graduation from Princeton, he went by the name T. Woodrow Wilson and soon enough dropped the first initial.

The president often used this portable typewriter while traveling. He took it with him in September 1919, for example, when he left Washington to rally support around the country for ratification of the Versailles Treaty.

"IT WOULD BE AN IRONY OF FATE if my administration had to deal chiefly with foreign affairs," Woodrow Wilson remarked as he left New Jersey for his first inauguration in 1913. That, however, was precisely the irony fate had in store for the century's first Democratic president. Wilson sent troops on frequent forays into Latin America; led the United States into a European war; and destroyed his health in an effort, noble but marked by a fatal rigidity, to shape the war's aftermath. Behind all these actions was his belief in America's historical mission: to make the world safe for democracy.

From his earliest days, Thomas Woodrow Wilson was trained in the art of performance. His father, a Presbyterian minister, had a stunning gift for oratory and an equally stunning ego. Young Tommy Wilson, the eldest son, doted on his father obsessively; in return, the father demanded a perfection that Tommy couldn't possibly fulfill. Yet in one aspect of his father, Wilson excelled. As a boy, he spent hours perfecting the oratorical delivery his father had mastered and learning not so much what to say as how to say it. His supreme gift was style.

Wilson might have had a peaceful life had he followed his father into the clergy; instead, while still a teenager, he made the momentous decision to enter politics. As a young man, he idolized British prime minister William Gladstone, a figure who combined the crusading zeal of a missionary with the celebrity of a national leader. After his graduation from Princeton in 1879, Wilson began the obvious legal path toward what he liked to call "statesmanship." But the law bored him, and when he opened his first practice, he was seized by an overpowering melancholy, which periodically marked his life.

Leaving the law and entering the academic world, Wilson hoped he might get into politics through the back door. But the long years teaching at Bryn Mawr, Wesleyan, and later at Princeton made him nearly despair of his goal. He married Ellen Axson, a compassionate woman who tirelessly ministered to her husband's maladies: his depressions, his digestive disorders, his blinding headaches.

Wilson is blindfolded as he prepares on September 30, 1918, to draw the first number in the Selective Service Act draft lottery.

D ESPITE THESE FRUSTRATIONS, Wilson kept abreast of national politics, and by the end of the nineteenth century he'd formulated a system of beliefs that would determine his behavior throughout the rest of his career. The terms *liberal* and *conservative* have a peculiar connotation when applied to Woodrow Wilson because he shied away from violence and radical action on both ends of the political spectrum (the strikes and riots of the 1890s having disturbed him deeply). He distrusted the labor movement while also demonstrating antipathy toward big business. Although he wished to reform the abuses of capitalism, he advocated one goal above all others—social order—and one means of attaining it—representative government. Anyone who threatened that goal, whether from the left or the right, was anathema to this introverted, strangely driven man.

Wilson's chance to address a national audience finally came after his election as president of Princeton in 1902. Quickly he engaged the dean of Princeton's graduate school in a bitter debate over the social and

BORN
December 28, 1856

BIRTHPLACE
Staunton, Virginia

DIED
February 3, 1924

PARTY AFFILIATION
Democrat

CHILDREN
Margaret, Jessie, Eleanor

MAJOR EVENTS

MAY 31, 1913

Ratification of the Seventeenth Amendment means that henceforth U.S. senators will be elected directly by the voters of each state rather than by state legislatures.

MAY 7, 1915

A German U-boat sinks the Lusitania, drowning nearly 1,200 people (including 128 Americans). Although the Germans point out correctly that the passenger liner was carrying munitions, the attack without warning turns U.S. public opinion against the Central Powers.

NOVEMBER 25, 1915

At a meeting outside Atlanta, William J. Simmons revives the disbanded Ku Klux Klan. Under Simmons's leadership, membership will swell to one hundred thousand over the next six years.

Socializing rarely and having few male friends, Wilson quickly became emotionally dependent on his first wife, Savannah-born Ellen Axson. They met in April 1883 at the Rome, Georgia, home of a Wilson cousin and became engaged five months later. A meditative woman, Ellen Wilson preferred gardening to socializing (the White House Rose Garden was her idea) and cared little for the celebrity of being first lady. When she died of Bright's disease in August 1914, her crushed husband spent the entire train ride back to Georgia sitting beside her coffin.

About seven months after the death of his first wife, Wilson met Edith Bolling Galt, a Washington widow who captivated him. Less than two months after their first meeting, the president proposed. "Oh, you can't love me, for you don't really know me," Mrs. Galt responded. Nevertheless, they announced their engagement in October 1915 and were married two months later. Edith Wilson lacked the shrewdness and intellectuality of the president's first wife, but following his 1919 stroke she assumed substantial decision-making responsibility.

educational stratification of student life—a quarrel less important for its details than for Wilson's ability to portray himself as a champion of egalitarianism. Having watched with the closest interest the advances made by the Progressive movement during the domestic upheavals of the 1890s, Wilson began to clothe his opinions in language that betrayed less his distrust of labor than his antipathy for capital.

He didn't win the Princeton battle but did attract the attention of New Jersey's Democratic political bosses, who made him their candidate for governor in 1910 and helped secure his election. Once in office, Wilson turned on his sponsors in the state machine, a betrayal that netted him praise from liberal Democrats and Progressives throughout the country. By 1911, he was a candidate for president. His victory over incumbent William Howard Taft and Theodore Roosevelt, who broke with the Republicans to become the Progressive party candidate, was largely due to the split in the Republican ranks. Had TR gained that party's nomination, he almost certainly would have won.

DURING THE 1912 CAMPAIGN and his first term in office, Wilson embraced many Progressive programs. In fact, he was desperate to instill a new dynamism into his conception of liberal democracy. The Socialist party had garnered nearly a million votes in 1912, and Wilson felt pressured by the rising tides of radicalism on the right and left.

Proclaiming his allegiance to what he trumpeted as the New Freedom, Wilson fought off the bitter attacks of special-interest groups and made progress toward dismantling Republican protectionism. He bought the support of the southern bourbons by offering them patronage and filling half his cabinet with resident or expatriate southerners. With consummate skill, he pursued four great reforms: the Underwood-Simmons Tariff, which lowered rates and included the first graduated income tax (made possible by the recently ratified Sixteenth Amendment); the creation of the Federal Trade Commission, which intensified government regulation of business; the Clayton Anti-Trust Act, which strengthened the Sherman Act of 1890; and, above all, the Federal Reserve Act, which reformed the banking system by creating a European-style central bank that could monitor the nation's money supply and smooth dangerous fluctuations. All this he accomplished in the first two years of his administration.

The prominence of southern Democrats in the administration took its toll in race relations, leading to the imposition of formal segregation in federal facilities and other indignities sanctioned by Wilson. Born and raised in the nineteenth-century South, Wilson was certainly a white supremacist (though hardly militant about it); after a private White House screening of D. W. Griffith's *Birth of a Nation*, which extolled the activities of the Ku Klux Klan, Wilson praised the film as "history written with lightning."

> ## "OUR GREATNESS IS BUILT UPON OUR FREEDOM— IS MORAL, NOT MATERIAL."
>
> —*Speech, 1911*—

To distinguish himself further from the preceding Republican administration, Wilson proclaimed his commitment to anti-imperialism and promised that the United States would "never again seek one additional foot of territory by conquest." Nonetheless, he demanded "orderly processes" in Latin America and stability in "the markets which we must supply." Believing that the American way had prospered because it had shunned revolutionary change, he became what historian Walter LaFeber has called "the greatest military interventionist in U.S. history."

Political instability in Central America and the Caribbean often meant that governments in that region refused or were unable to pay their debts to American bankers. To ensure proper financial supervision, the Wilson administration intervened in Haiti, the Dominican Republic, and Nicaragua, which the United States occupied off and on until 1933. Meddling in Mexico, however, cost Wilson dearly. Since the late 1870s, U.S. citizens had owned over 40 percent of Mexico's real estate. In 1911, when aged dictator Porfirio Díaz was toppled, chaos threatened American lives and property, and continued turmoil over the next few years led Wilson to fear meddling by foreign powers. In April 1914, he used

SEPTEMBER 14, 1918

A federal judge sentences Socialist party leader Eugene V. Debs to ten years in jail for violating the Espionage Act. This 1917 law made it illegal to oppose U.S. involvement in World War I, which Debs did.

OCTOBER 28, 1919

Over President Wilson's veto, Congress passes the Volstead Act, which enforces the Eighteenth Amendment, ratified in January 1919. The new law bans nonmedicinal alcohol beginning January 16, 1920.

JANUARY 2, 1920

Attorney General A. Mitchell Palmer orders nationwide raids on the homes and meeting places of suspected radicals. Six thousand people, most foreign born, are arrested in the Palmer Raids.

AUGUST 26, 1920

Ratification of the Nineteenth Amendment, which Congress only narrowly approved, finally grants women the right to vote. In the presidential election this fall, new women voters will strongly support Harding.

Though Wilson sought to rid Princeton of its eating clubs and other forms of class bias, he refused to support the admission of blacks to the university.

President Wilson poses at his White House desk in 1913.

This 1915 caricature of the president seems to evoke Grant Wood's American Gothic—but Wood wouldn't paint American Gothic until fifteen years later.

news of a German-owned steamer transporting arms to Mexico as an excuse to send in eight hundred troops with orders to seize the customs house at Veracruz.

By November 1914, Wilson had withdrawn the American forces from Veracruz; but two years later, rebel general Francisco "Pancho" Villa led a raid across the U.S. border into New Mexico, provoking a battle that left dead seventeen Americans along with more than one hundred Mexicans. In response, Wilson dispatched Gen. John J. "Black Jack" Pershing to command a punitive expedition of almost seven thousand men. Pershing pushed south 350 miles into Mexico in a vain search for Villa that Wilson didn't call off until February 1917, two months before the United States entered World War I.

The outbreak of war in Europe in August 1914 had heightened Wilson's sense of urgency about America's world mission. Throughout his first term, Wilson struggled to maintain America's neutrality and, at the same time, present himself as a mediator of the conflict. In early 1917, however, Germany announced that it would attack

"HE THINKS HE IS ANOTHER JESUS CHRIST COME UPON THE EARTH TO REFORM MEN."

—*French president Georges Clemenceau*—

This microphone was used by Wilson for the first live remote radio broadcast ever made (and Wilson's only radio address). The program originated from the library of Wilson's Washington home on November 10, 1923, the eve of the fifth anniversary of Armistice Day.

without warning all ships, enemy and neutral, found near British waters. With this declaration of unrestricted submarine warfare, it was all but inevitable that America would enter the war on the Allied side.

Behind this threat to American economic interests was an implied German threat to U.S. security. In late February 1917, the British passed on an intercepted telegram from German foreign minister Arthur Zimmermann to the Mexican foreign office proposing a military alliance. Should war between Germany and the United States break out, the Zimmermann Telegram advised, Germany would help Mexico "gain back by conquest" territories lost to the United States in the Mexican War of 1846–48.

By this time, Wilson saw himself as a savior of the world. As he envisioned America's role in the war, it went well beyond preventing the collapse of Britain and the elimination of the British fleet that protected America from Germany. In his April 2, 1917, address to Congress asking for a declaration of war, he stated: "We shall fight for the things we have always carried nearest our hearts—for democracy, for the right of those who submit to authority to have a voice in their own governments, for the rights and liberties of small nations, for a universal dominion of right by such a concert of free peoples as shall bring peace and safety to all nations and make the world itself at last free….The world must be made safe for democracy." What Wilson wanted was not an equilibrium based on a balance of power but a universalistic peace rooted in American moral values.

This pass from 1919—albeit rarely used—entitled the president to attend baseball games as the guest of the American League.

WILSON'S GOALS BECAME more specific in a January 8, 1918, speech setting forth the Fourteen Points that he designated as America's war aims. These included open diplomacy, national self-determination, and the establishment of a League of Nations to mediate international disputes. His remedy of collective security, supported by the weight of public opinion and the principles of international law, assumed that the nations of the world would unite against aggression. But if they chose not to, there was no means of enforcement.

During the peace treaty deliberations at Versailles, Wilson had to yield time and again on the issue of self-determination—when, for example, it was revealed that the British and French had secretly promised to compensate lesser allies with territory seized from the Central Powers (Germany, Austria-Hungary, and Turkey). Wilson accepted these setbacks by persuading himself that all such questions would ultimately be resolved within the framework of the League of Nations.

With the Treaty of Versailles in hand, he returned to America in July 1919; his enthusiasm was tempered, however, when it became clear that key members of the Republican-controlled Senate opposed its ratification. Two questions loomed large: Were members of the League of Nations obligated to use force to uphold the Versailles settlement? And did this mean that existing borders and governments were sacrosanct? Henry Cabot Lodge, chairman of the Senate Foreign Relations Committee, proposed reservations to the league's

Wilson continued the presidential tradition, begun in 1910 by William Howard Taft, of throwing out the first baseball of the season.

President Wilson *took these top hat and gloves with him to the peace conference at Versailles.*

covenant. In essence, they asserted Congress's constitutional role in making foreign policy; specifically, they ensured that America would assume no obligation to preserve the territorial integrity or political independence of any country unless authorized to do so by Congress. Asked by the French ambassador whether he would accept these reservations, Wilson retorted, "I shall consent to nothing. The Senate must take its medicine."

To UNDERMINE LODGE, the president decided to mobilize public opinion in support of the treaty. He would take his case to the people on a ten-thousand-mile trip across the United States. On September 26, 1919, however, the day after he gave an impassioned speech in Pueblo, Colorado, Wilson awoke to nausea and uncontrollable facial twitching. His doctor ordered an immediate return to Washington, where a massive stroke paralyzed Wilson's left side. The president lay in bed for six weeks, seeing virtually no one but his physician and his second wife, Edith.

"SOMETIMES PEOPLE CALL ME AN IDEALIST. WELL, THAT IS THE WAY I KNOW I AM AN AMERICAN."

—Speech, September 8, 1919—

Because he refused to resign, it was left to Edith Wilson to run her husband's political affairs. Although he recovered partially—enough to remain in office until the end of his term—Wilson never lessened his intransigent opposition to any modification of the Versailles agreement. Twice the Senate rejected it. The United States, therefore, never joined the League of Nations, and Germany remained saddled with a treaty neither draconian enough to eliminate its power nor generous enough to strengthen its fledgling democracy.

Had Wilson been willing to compromise with Lodge, the treaty would have been ratified, and the United States would have tied its fate to that of Europe. Perhaps the next world war might then have been avoided, in which case the twentieth century would have had a far less tragic history.

★ ★ ★

OPPOSITE:

Wilson (shown here at Versailles in January 1919) *arrived at the conference determined to produce a lasting peace. His great creative achievement, the League of Nations, persuaded the Nobel committee to award him a Peace Prize in December 1920, but Wilson was never able to persuade the Senate of the League's value.*

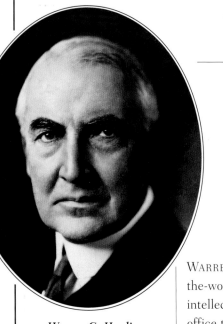

Warren G. Harding
posed for this portrait in June 1920, the month that he became the Republican nominee for president. Although he achieved little in office, it's unlikely that any other viable candidate would have accomplished much more.

Harding had expensive tastes *and enjoyed fine things, such as these silk pajamas. He was also vain about his appearance and had so many clothes that new closets had to be built in the White House to hold his extensive wardrobe.*

Warren G. Harding

29ᵗʰ President · 1921–1923

Morton Keller

WARREN GAMALIEL HARDING has a secure place on everyone's who-is-the-worst-president list. The reasons are obvious enough: his limited intellect and minimal leadership capacity; an unimpressive term in office truncated by sudden death; a swirl of corruption charges leading to the imprisonment of a cabinet officer; and the posthumous revelation of a sensational love affair, complete with an illegitimate child.

As we know today, corruption and personal scandal do not necessarily impeach a president (in the broad, not the technical, sense). More important is how he responded to the major public issues of his time. The low standings of James Buchanan, Andrew Johnson, Ulysses S. Grant, and Herbert Hoover derive not from their lack of character or morals but from their inability to deal with national crises. While Harding certainly had *substantial* personal failings, his low repute can also be traced ultimately to his poor performance as president, specifically his failure to give post–World War I America the leadership it required. The consensus among historians is that he was not intellectually up to the job.

How did so unlikely a prospect make it to the White House? Harding grew up in the archetypal small midwestern town of Marion, Ohio, in a middling family tainted by the stigma of possible black ancestry. After desultory stabs at teaching and law, he settled down to editing and publishing the *Marion Star*, a typical small-town weekly of the 1880s. It was an ideal milieu for Harding to display his talent for making friends, his mild and kindly personality, and his taste for ornate prose.

As the success of his newspaper grew, so too did his involvement in the complex politics of his state. He made no claims to intellectual prowess or independent political thinking, but he played the game of Ohio politics shrewdly and well. Harding's greatest strength, his easygoing manner, embodied both the attitudes and the style of small-town America, and it made his persona ideal for electoral politics. A regular among Republican regulars, he won a state senate seat in 1899, ran (unsuccessfully) for governor in 1910, and nominated William Howard Taft at the Republican national convention in 1912. In 1914, he won a seat in the U.S. Senate.

H ARDING'S SENATE YEARS were as uneventful and undistinguished as one might expect. During his first and only term, he was considered a second-tier senator, a standpat Republican who was amiable and popular with his fellows. Theodore Roosevelt, contemplating a run for the 1920 presidential nomination, thought of Harding as a possible running mate. The most prominent contenders for the nomination after Roosevelt's January 1919 death were self-proclaimed TR heir Gen. Leonard Wood, Illinois governor Frank Lowden, and Sen. Hiram Johnson, a Progressive from California. None of them could muster enough support at the party's June 1920 convention, so the delegates adjourned after nine ballots, deadlocked. The next day, an exhausted convention readily accepted the available, affable Harding as a compromise choice. As journalist William Allen White concluded, "He was nominated because there was nothing against him, and the delegates wanted to go home."

Legend has it that Harding was the choice of a cabal of party leaders who met all night in a "smoke-filled" suite on the thirteenth floor of Chicago's Blackstone Hotel. Most of these men, while not objecting to

Proving that influence peddling is not of recent origin, this curious photograph records a "camping party" held in 1921. Among those accompanying President Harding were industrialists Henry Ford and Thomas Alva Edison.

BORN
November 2, 1865

BIRTHPLACE
Corsica, Ohio

DIED
August 2, 1923

PARTY AFFILIATION
Republican

CHILDREN
none

MAJOR EVENTS

MAY 19, 1921

Responding to public anxiety about the flood of immigrants from central and southern Europe, Congress passes the Emergency Quota Act. This law establishes the first general restrictions on immigration into the United States, limiting the number of people who can enter the country each year according to their country of origin.

JULY 14, 1921

A Massachusetts jury finds immigrants Nicola Sacco and Bartolomeo Vanzetti guilty of murdering two men in the course of a shoe factory robbery in South Braintree. The case has attracted national attention because so little evidence linked Sacco and Vanzetti to the crime. Their conviction, it is suspected, has more to do with their accents and their radical politics than their guilt.

Florence Kling DeWolfe was the daughter of the richest man in town. She was also, by the time Harding met her, the divorced mother of a young son. Within a year, she had cornered and married Harding. The two were never close—her haughty manner kept an emotional distance between them— but Harding admired his wife's toughness, ambition, and appetite for hard work. She helped him make a success of the Marion Star and encouraged his political career. She was also keenly aware of his limitations. "I can see but one word written over the head of my husband if he is elected," she warned in 1920 (about the time this photograph was taken), "and the word is 'Tragedy.'"

Harding, in fact continued to support other candidates. It was rather Harding's status as the second choice of most delegates (and the lack of a compelling alternative) that made him the nominee.

Harding was well situated for the general election that followed. Because of Woodrow Wilson's September 1919 stroke, the nation was essentially leaderless during the crucial months following the end of World War I. By the 1920 election, inflation and rising joblessness, the ugliness of the Palmer Raids (which targeted foreign-born political radicals), and the corrosive fight over the League of Nations had thoroughly tarnished Wilson's political legacy and made his high-minded wartime rhetoric seem empty and hypocritical.

The avuncular, semischooled, bloviating (the word he used to describe his own oratory) Harding was as unlike Wilson as could be imagined—and this was precisely the source of his popular appeal. His May 1920 declaration that "America's present need is not heroics but healing, not nostrums but normalcy" spoke to the dominant strain of public opinion in postwar America. In November, he won by what was then the largest popular majority in American presidential history.

It isn't rare for presidents to bemoan the cares and burdens of office. But Harding's complaints were noteworthy, both for their frequency and for their insight. Even before his election, he wrote to a friend, "The only thing I really worry about is that I might be nominated and elected. That's an awful thing to contemplate." To another he later declared: "I am not fit for this office and should never have been here."

Yet to the limit of his abilities, Harding appears to have taken the job seriously. Those in a position to know considered him a hardworking president. He filled his cabinet with some of the best minds of the day: Charles Evans Hughes at State, Herbert Hoover at Commerce, Henry C. Wallace (father of FDR vice president Henry A. Wallace) at Agriculture, and, more questionably, Andrew Mellon at Treasury. But—as with other presidents—the trust he placed in old friends of doubtful reputation made for trouble. He named poker buddy (and former Senate colleague) Albert B. Fall secretary of the interior and appointed Ohio political fixer Harry M. Daugherty attorney general.

Harding poses during the 1920 campaign for a photo op in the print shop of the Marion Star.

While such appointments were not unusual, they had disastrous consequences for Harding's personal and political reputations.

While he was president, given the prevailing standards, Harding's performance seemed adequate. He ducked the League of Nations controversy but gave qualified support to U.S. entry into the World Court. More important, he backed Hughes's plan for international naval disarmament, accepted by Great Britain, France, Italy, and Japan at the Washington Conference of 1921–22 (a conference widely, if mistakenly, believed to have promised an end to the arms race). On domestic matters, in addition to economy in government, he endorsed Mellon's tax reduction plan, which incorporated accepted conservative Republican policy. He even persuaded Congress to adopt unified federal budget making. Yet he did little to help farmers battered by falling crop prices or workers facing unemployment and wage cuts, and he generally went along with majority sentiment favoring immigration restriction and Prohibition.

On a (typically) more personal and humane note, he pardoned Eugene V. Debs, the Socialist party leader who'd been imprisoned under the 1917 Espionage Act for opposing American involvement in World War I. Although most people (even his political opponents) felt Debs shouldn't have been jailed for simply speaking his mind, freeing him was something Wilson had obdurately refused to do.

G IVEN THE INCREASINGLY conservative tone of Wilson's last months in office—and the fact that Harding's successor, Calvin Coolidge, reversed few of Harding's policies—one might wonder why his performance in office has consigned him to such obloquy. His renomination in 1924 seemed certain, and when he died unexpectedly in August 1923, he was widely commended for having pacified a divided and crisis-ridden government.

It was what emerged after Harding's death that destroyed his reputation. A series of congressional investigations uncovered corruption in the Veterans Bureau and Harry Daugherty's Justice Department. Meanwhile, it was discovered that Interior Secretary Fall had apparently been taking payoffs in return for valuable leasing rights at the

Harding, a compulsive joiner, wanted to join the Masons most of all, but his hometown lodge wouldn't have him until August 1920, when he was about to become president. The red fez that Harding wears in this photo symbolized membership in the Aladdin Temple, Ancient Arabic Order of Nobles of the Mystic Shrine. Harding was also a member of the Concatenated Order of the Hoo Hoo (a fraternal order for lumbermen).

This Masonic ring was cherished by the president.

"WE DREW TO A PAIR OF DEUCES AND FILLED."

—

Remark on learning of his presidential nomination, June 12, 1920

Harding kept his cigarettes in this diamond-studded case. Although he was careful never to be photographed holding a cigarette, it was well known that he smoked. In fact, Sunday school teachers wrote to him regularly urging him to give up the habit because it set such a bad example.

OPPOSITE:

Harding's health declined during the spring of 1923, and the usually jovial president began to seem tired and worried. His schedule that summer included a trip to Alaska, which his doctors thought was a good idea so long as he got some rest. Instead, the Republican party used the trip to lay groundwork for the 1924 campaign. On July 27, aboard a train from Seattle to San Francisco, Harding complained of nausea and pains in his chest. He died in a San Francisco hotel room one week later.

government's Teapot Dome and Elk Hills oil reserves. Sordid subthemes—the suicides of several of the accused, tales of orgies in a "little green house on K Street"—added to the pervasive sense of scandal. Then in 1927, Nan Britton published *The President's Daughter*, a lurid tale of her trysts with Harding in hotels and later the White House. *The Strange Death of President Harding*, published three years later, presented a farrago of accusations by Gaston Means, one of the shadier figures on the fringes of the Harding administration. Means's principal charge was that Harding had been poisoned by his wife and doctor.

"HIS SPEECHES LEFT THE IMPRESSION OF AN ARMY OF POMPOUS PHRASES MOVING OVER THE LANDSCAPE IN SEARCH OF AN IDEA."

—Sen. William G. McAdoo—

THE GREAT DEPRESSION, widely blamed on the policy mistakes of the 1920s, only reinforced the readiness of Americans to believe the worst of Harding. Influential books by prominent journalists—William Allen White's *Masks in a Pageant* (1928), Frederick Lewis Allen's *Only Yesterday* (1931), and Samuel Hopkins Adams's *Incredible Era* (1939)—encouraged the belief that Harding and his times were uniquely corrupt. A more balanced view became possible after 1964, when Harding's presidential papers were opened to scholars. But by then such a deeply entrenched public perception was unlikely to be changed.

According to one of his biographers, Harding was "neither a tool nor a fool." And it can be said that, to some degree, he restored a presidency badly abused by Wilson's long invalidism. Yet the fact remains that he did little to meet the economic and social needs of postwar America. He was, at best, a mediocre president, a man in over his head (if not noticeably more so than Millard Fillmore or Calvin Coolidge). It seems unlikely that the cruel judgment of Alice Roosevelt Longworth, TR's trenchant daughter, will ever be replaced: "Harding was not a bad man," she said. "He was just a slob."

★ ★ ★

Calvin Coolidge

30th President · 1923–1929

Robert Cowley

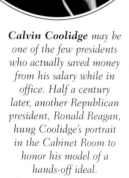

Calvin Coolidge may be
one of the few presidents
who actually saved money
from his salary while in
office. Half a century
later, another Republican
president, Ronald Reagan,
hung Coolidge's portrait
in the Cabinet Room to
honor his model of a
hands-off ideal.

**This
electrically
operated**
horse became an
embarrassment
to Coolidge
when it was
revealed
that he
liked to whoop
and holler
while riding it.

HISTORIANS HAVE NOT TREATED Calvin Coolidge kindly. The thirtieth president has been portrayed as a man who practically slept through his five and a half years in the White House. His failure to rein in stock market speculation has been blamed for the Crash of 1929 and the Great Depression that followed. Frederick Lewis Allen has called Coolidge "one of the most negative characters ever to attain high office," and it's hard to identify him with a lasting piece of legislation. In an often-quoted 1962 ranking of the presidents, his name appears near the bottom—as his contemporary H. L. Mencken put it, "among the vacuums."

Coolidge's public record does not make the case for his defense easy. He cut a drab and uncharismatic figure, with a scrawny frame that seemed even smaller than his height of five feet nine inches. In photographs today, one sees hardly a trace of warmth in that hatchet face. The blue eyes are hard, the thin lips rarely smiling, the hair firmly set in place with Vaseline. His speech and his writings were famously laconic: Someone once calculated the length of the average Coolidge sentence to be 18 words, compared to 26.6 words for Lincoln and 51.5 for Washington. When his death was announced, humorist Dorothy Parker supposedly commented, "How could they tell?"

And yet the very austereness of the man remains curiously refreshing. What you saw was what you got. If he had depths, he managed to keep them hidden, as much from his generally approving public as from posterity: He destroyed all his private papers. In an era of furious change, Coolidge seemed a throwback to a simpler time when change was hardly noticeable. (He was the last president without a telephone on his desk.) He countered the excess surrounding him with a stinginess that was proverbial. He was rigidly honest at the very moment when honesty in public life was most called for. Coolidge belonged to the he-who-governs-best-governs-least school of political action (or nonaction), and for better or worse he never wavered in that stand. His luck, too, was proverbial, and the luckiest stroke of all was that he left the presidency just in time.

President Coolidge autographs a sap bucket for the collection of Henry Ford. Other tycoons present at this gathering include Harvey Firestone (left), Thomas A. Edison, and Russell Firestone (standing). The president's wife and father are seated at the right.

ALTHOUGH THREE PRESIDENTS have died on the Fourth of July, Calvin Coolidge was the only one born on the national holiday, in 1872. His father, John, ran the general store in Plymouth Notch, Vermont, and was a figure of local political prominence. After his graduation from Amherst College, Class of 1895, Coolidge settled in nearby Northampton, Massachusetts, reading for the law and becoming involved in Republican politics. (The mythmakers of the 1920s made much of Coolidge's rural background, but he actually spent most of his life in this small city.) He relentlessly climbed the ladder of local and then state politics, rising from the Northampton city council to become its mayor, president of the Massachusetts state senate, and finally governor. In twenty elections, he lost only once, running for the school board. The cause may have been the unaccustomed weeklong vacation he took during the election—his honeymoon. Someone once asked him, "Mr. Coolidge, what is your hobby?" "Holding public office," he replied.

Little distinguished Coolidge's political career until the Boston police strike of September 1919. An underpaid police force had joined the American Federation of Labor. The police commissioner dismissed the union leaders, and most of the force walked out in protest. There

BORN
July 4, 1872

BIRTHPLACE
Plymouth, Vermont

DIED
January 5, 1933

PARTY AFFILIATION
Republican

CHILDREN
John, Calvin Jr.

MAJOR EVENTS

MARCH 10, 1924

J. Edgar Hoover takes over the Federal Bureau of Investigation. Eager to clean up a bureau tarnished by Harding administration scandal, the zealous Hoover begins requiring that all agents be college graduates.

MAY 26, 1924

Moving beyond the Emergency Quota Act of 1921, Congress passes the Johnson-Reed Act, which drastically reduces the immigration quotas on southern and eastern Europeans and bars Asian immigrants altogether.

JULY 10–21, 1925

Tennessee prosecutes John T. Scopes for teaching Darwin's theory of evolution. Scopes has violated a state law, passed in March, banning from the schools any theory denying God's creation of man. Losing the verdict, Scopes is fined one hundred dollars.

Calvin Coolidge and
*Grace Goodhue lived on the
same street in Northampton,
Massachusetts. The first time
she saw him was through
an open window. He was
standing in his underwear,
wearing a hat and shaving.
She laughed, causing him to
look up. Later, he asked to
be introduced to her. On
their first date, he explained
that he regularly used the
hat to keep an unruly lock
of hair out of his eyes.
Socially, Grace Coolidge
(shown here with her pet
raccoon) provided an
important buffer between
her husband and the world.
She was extremely outgoing
with a genuine interest in
people, while Coolidge
was…Coolidge.*

Henry Standing Bear
*makes the president a
Sioux chief during his
1927 summer vacation
in the Black Hills.
Although a publicly
dour man, Coolidge had
an unusual propensity
for being photographed
in comical (on
him) costumes.*

were two nights of rioting and looting during which three men died.
On September 10, Boston's mayor called out the local National Guard.
The next day, Governor Coolidge called out the entire Massachusetts
militia—by which time the worst violence was already under control—
and sent a telegram to AFL president Samuel Gompers. "There is no
right," it read, "to strike against public safety by anybody, anywhere,
any time." He apparently felt he was committing political suicide, yet
that single sentence made him a national figure. He got the credit
for putting down the strike and was reelected two months later in a
landslide. Even so, his nomination the following summer as Warren
Harding's running mate came as a fatigued afterthought at the end of a
long Republican convention in Chicago. It was Coolidge's luck again,
and in November voters swept the pair into office.

Coolidge, the secret workaholic, found himself doomed to the
least-interesting years of his life. His relations with the Senate, over
which he presided, were chilly, and he contributed little to the Harding
administration, except to make the obligatory public appearances. In the
Senate restaurant, he became a familiar yet forlorn figure, eating alone
in a corner with his face to the wall. The scuttlebutt was that Harding,
who referred to Coolidge as "the little fellow," would drop him before
the election of 1924.

WHEN HARDING'S HEART stopped beating in a San Francisco
hotel room on the night of August 2, 1923, the man about
to be dumped was visiting his father in Plymouth Notch.
The news, relayed through Washington, took hours to reach the Coolidge
homestead—which still had no electricity, no indoor plumbing, and no
telephone. Members of the vice president's entourage roused John
Coolidge, who appeared at the door in his nightshirt. He called upstairs
to wake the new president. In a
front parlor lit only by a kerosene
lamp, the senior Coolidge, who was
a notary, held the family Bible and
swore in his fifty-one-year-old son.

That Lincolnesque scene in a
remote Vermont farmhouse couldn't
have come at a better moment.
Harding cronies had already been
implicated in illegal schemes, and
congressional investigations were
seeking bigger targets. Coolidge-

sponsored legislation was hardly considered, much less passed, as the hunt consumed both the Senate and the House. The president dismissed one target, Attorney General Harry M. Daugherty, a holdover from the Harding administration. Another, former interior secretary Albert B. Fall, was accused of taking bribes from oilmen in return for leasing rights to a pair of government reserves, Teapot Dome in Wyoming and Elk Hills in California. Fall later went to prison, the first cabinet member in history sentenced for misconduct in office. Coolidge's efforts at damage control were sure-handed. One can argue that his greatest achievement as president was to restore respect for the office—and, in the process, assure Republican ascendancy for the next eight years. His own reelection in 1924 was not just a landslide but an avalanche. (The triumph was tarnished by the death that summer of his younger son from an infection.)

Y ET, FOR THE MOST PART, Coolidge failed to translate his mountainous victory into legislative victories; perhaps he wanted it that way. The next four years were notable more for what he refused to do than for what he accomplished. He regarded government, unlike business or industry, as being nonproductive: His task, therefore, was not to innovate but to improve on what already worked. His goal, which amounted to an obsession, was to hold down costs. He rarely hesitated to wield the veto, and popular pieces of legislation went down before his pen—including raises for postal workers, bonuses for veterans of the Great War (which, passed over his veto, would come back to haunt his successor, Herbert Hoover), and the McNary-Haugen bill two years running. This last measure, designed to relieve an already burgeoning agricultural depression, would have established farm price supports. Coolidge wouldn't stand for it: "Government price fixing, once started," he said, "has alike no justice and no end." He believed that governments, like people, should live within their means. When he left office in 1929, the budget he'd inherited in 1923 had risen by only four million dollars.

Yet the politics of deliberate inaction had its liabilities. The "Coolidge boom," which hardly affected the six out of ten Americans who didn't have extra money, was more a speculation madness sucking in those who did. Rather than take action to arrest the speculation, Coolidge clearly felt that even suggesting brakes be applied might hurt an apparently healthy economy. The president, who did not really understand economics except when it came to saving, left

MAY 10, 1927

President Coolidge sends five thousand marines to Nicaragua to put down a rebellion against the U.S.-backed government. The insurgents, led by Gen. Augusto César Sandino, retreat to the mountains, where they regroup and launch a guerrilla campaign.

"THE CHIEF BUSINESS OF THE AMERICAN PEOPLE IS BUSINESS."

—*Speech, 1925*—

Vice President Coolidge *works out with Speaker Frederick Gillett in the House gymnasium in late January 1923. As Harding's number two, Coolidge had plenty of time on his hands.*

On the night Harding died, *Coolidge's father, a notary public, used this Bible to swear in his son. Writers who enjoy noting the worst of Coolidge point out that he immediately returned to bed. But he was up a bare three hours later and heading to Washington. As he left the house, he put his foot on a loose stone step and told his father, "Better have that fixed," before driving away.*

OPPOSITE:

Coolidge was a **creature** *of routine: He rose every morning at 6:30 A.M. and was at his desk by 8:00. Promptly at 12:30 P.M., he would pause (though he detested the ritual) to shake hands with an average of four hundred callers per day. After lunch, he would take a two-hour nap, then work into the evening (as well as on weekends and during what passed for vacations). He wrote his own speeches and was the first president to hold regular press conferences, twice a week and 520 in all.*

the driving to his secretary of the treasury, Andrew Mellon, the third richest man in America. Mellon mostly kept his hands off the wheel.

In the field of foreign relations, two Coolidge-approved initiatives did seem bright with calming promise for the world—although no one in the administration foresaw the possibility of international collapse, either. The Dawes Plan of 1924 temporarily solved an international crisis by reducing German reparations payments and stabilizing the shaky German economy. It also earned Charles G. Dawes a vice-presidential nomination and a Nobel Peace Prize for his efforts. A second Nobel Peace Prize went to Coolidge's secretary of state, Frank B. Kellogg, for negotiating one of the great chimeras of the 1920s, the Kellogg-Briand Pact of 1928, which purported to outlaw war "as an instrument of national policy."

> "NOBODY HAS EVER WORKED HARDER AT INACTIVITY, WITH SUCH FORCE OF CHARACTER, WITH SUCH UNREMITTING ATTENTION TO DETAIL, WITH SUCH CONSCIENTIOUS DEVOTION TO THE TASK."
>
> —*Columnist Walter Lippmann*—

D URING A BLACK HILLS VACATION in the summer of 1927, Coolidge announced abruptly, "I do not choose to run for president in 1928." He never went back on what became his most famous words. "Isn't that just like the man!" his wife said. "I had no idea." Instead, Commerce Secretary Herbert Hoover won the Republican nomination for president and the election of 1928.

Coolidge returned to the two-family house in Northampton that he'd rented since his marriage in 1905. But the unrelenting stream of sightseers soon drove him to buy a larger, more secluded home. He completed his autobiography, 247 pages of spare sentiment and large type, and also wrote a nationally syndicated newspaper column. It earned him $203,045 in one year, but he gave it up. He had little to say about the stock market crash or the fast-developing economic crisis. On January 5, 1933, Grace Coolidge came back from shopping to find her husband dead on the floor of his room, the victim of a heart attack: He was sixty. At this, the low point of the Great Depression, the man who hadn't seen it coming was mourned but not missed.

★ ★ ★

Herbert Hoover

31st President · 1929–1933

Robert Dallek

Herbert Hoover embraced public service with a moralistic passion, but he was never much of a public personality. Journalist William Allen White once described Hoover's disposition as decidedly "low voltage."

HERBERT HOOVER WAS ONE OF THE least-successful presidents in American history. His failure in the White House was the result of circumstances beyond his control as well as an inflexibility of personality and outlook that undermined his ability to deal with the greatest economic collapse in the country's history. Yet at the time of his election in November 1928, Hoover's suitability for the presidency seemed unquestionable. At the start of his term in March 1929, the *New York Times* lauded his "versatile ability and sterling character" and noted his "Progressive leanings." He "has the feel of the people," the newspaper continued, and it labeled his presidency "the dawn of the Hoover era."

Hoover often said that he was happiest when fishing, which he once described as "discipline in the equality of men, for all men are equal before fish." The items shown here were among those he kept in his well-stocked tackle box.

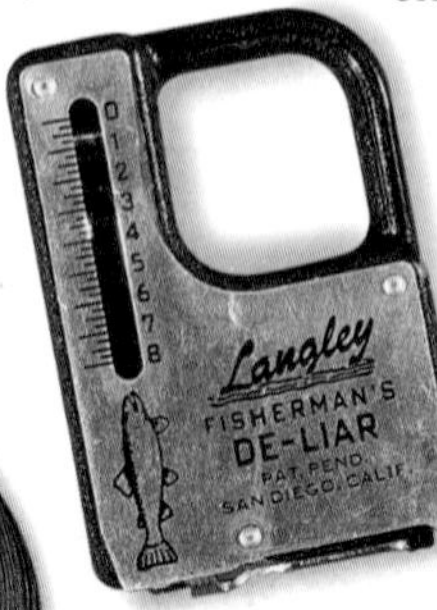

THE FIRST PRESIDENT BORN WEST of the Mississippi River, Hoover, an orphan at age nine, was raised by relatives in Iowa and later Oregon. In 1895, he earned a degree in mining engineering as a member of Stanford University's first graduating class, and during the next twenty years he enjoyed a brilliant career as an engineer and international businessman, traveling around the world five times. By age forty, he'd become a multimillionaire. He served as the director of eighteen mining and financial companies (valued at fifty-five million dollars) that were based in London but had interests around the globe. The three most productive companies in this conglomerate were the Zinc Corporation of Australia; Burma Mines, Ltd., which promised huge profits from silver, lead, and zinc deposits in a mine fifty miles from the Chinese border; and several Russian mines rich in copper, zinc, silver, and lead.

A Quaker motivated by humanitarian concerns, Hoover gained an international reputation during World War I when he masterminded

Belgian war relief, feeding and clothing hundreds of thousands of refugees. Once the United States entered the war in April 1917, President Wilson made Hoover his food administrator, with responsibility for food distribution at home and abroad. Hoover later advised Wilson on economic matters at the Versailles conference and became a central figure in organizing famine relief for Russia, where war and revolution had destroyed the country's capacity to feed itself.

In 1920, Hoover unsuccessfully sought the Republican nomination for president. Nevertheless, he became a prominent political figure as commerce secretary to both Harding and Coolidge. The New Era economics of the 1920s, in which the federal government played an unprecedented role in supporting American business, put Hoover at the center of the executive branch—where, as one journalist put it, he was "Secretary of Commerce and undersecretary of everything else." Hoover appropriated many of the functions claimed previously by other cabinet departments. He also expanded the reach of his department to include the standardization of parts in many American industries, the development of domestic and

> **"[HE'S] THE SMARTEST GEEK I KNOW."**
>
> —*Warren G. Harding*—

*The **regulation of radio** was one more aspect of U.S. economic life that Hoover made part of his brief as commerce secretary under Presidents Harding and Coolidge.*

BORN
August 10, 1874

BIRTHPLACE
West Branch, Iowa

DIED
October 20, 1964

PARTY AFFILIATION
Republican

CHILDREN
Herbert Jr., Allan

MAJOR EVENTS

JUNE 17, 1930

Although a thousand economists petition him to veto the bill, President Hoover signs the Smoot-Hawley Tariff, which imposes the highest tariff rates in U.S. history. The new duties, intended to protect struggling American businesses, will instead provoke an international trade war that worsens the Great Depression.

APRIL 6, 1931

Nine black youths accused of raping two white women go on trial in Scottsboro, Alabama. The all-white jury will quickly vote to convict the "Scottsboro boys" despite testimony from the doctor who examined the women that he found no evidence of rape. Eight will be sentenced to death, and the ninth, just twelve years old, will receive life imprisonment. The Supreme Court will eventually overturn the verdicts.

Herbert Hoover met Lou Henry at Stanford, where she was one of the few female geology majors. Being three years ahead, Bert was already working in Australia when Lou graduated in 1898, so he had to cable his marriage proposal. She accepted by return wire, and they were married the following year, sailing soon afterward for China, where he had landed a new job. Later, in the White House, the Hoovers often spoke to each other in Mandarin when they wanted to foil potential eavesdroppers.

When China's Boxer Rebellion erupted in June 1900, the Hoovers were living in Tientsin. He stood watch at night and built barricades under fire while she worked in a hospital with a Mauser tucked inside her belt. This photograph shows a relieved Lou Hoover posing later with one of the cannon used to defend the foreigners' compound.

foreign markets, and the dissemination of statistical information that might help industries avoid the over- and understocking of goods that had led to numerous past cycles of boom and bust.

His popularity and visibility easily won him the Republican nomination in 1928, and his campaign against New York governor Alfred E. Smith, the first Catholic to win a major party nomination, produced one of the greatest landslides in presidential history. Many voters were reluctant to cast ballots for an urban Catholic, and Hoover was viewed as a superb technocrat who could effectively manage the smoothly running economy and make the entire country as rich as he was himself.

His subsequent presidency is perhaps best described as a series of disasters that left the nation immobilized both at home and abroad. At the center of this history, of course, is the Great Depression, which began with the October 1929 stock market crash. Others have explained this crash as the product of unregulated speculation— whatever its cause, Hoover publicly underestimated its impact by counseling Americans to remain confident about their economic future. "The fundamental business of the country—that is, production and distribution—is on a sound and prosperous basis," he declared in the spring of 1930. His statement belied private concerns that things would get worse.

His hidden fears were borne out by a downward spiral that began during the winter of 1929. By December, a million Americans were out of work; over the next three years, that number ballooned to thirteen million, or about one-quarter of the nation's workforce. The jump in unemployment paralleled a severe downturn in business—by the winter of 1932, Hoover's last in office, the steel industry, widely considered the bellwether of American industry, was operating at just 13 percent of capacity. Meanwhile, bank failures and small-business bankruptcies rose dramatically, as foreclosures on home mortgages and family farms, homelessness, and hunger reached unprecedented levels.

Hoover responded to the crisis with innovative actions. His efforts to increase loans through federal reserve banks and to stimulate economic expansion with increased government spending—some nineteen million dollars on highways, hospitals, waterways, and military bases—were bold steps when compared to earlier presidential responses to economic downturns (if not when compared to the New Deal). Moreover, the Reconstruction Finance Corporation, which Hoover pushed through Congress in 1932, was a significant attempt to stimulate business by infusing two billion dollars into the economy. RFC bonds funded federal loans to banks, railroads, agricultural credit corporations, and land banks.

Y ET HOOVER'S INITIATIVES were insufficient to restore economic growth and end the suffering. In fact, Hoover was simply too rigid about what a president could and should do in the face of such a crisis. He was opposed to government handouts, which he feared would weaken traditional American individualism (and the nation's moral fiber) by making citizens dependent on an intrusive federal government. Hoping the depression was no more than a particularly ugly turn in the business cycle, he kept assuring Americans that prosperity was right around the corner, believing that a change in national psychology would bring about a dramatic alteration in the economy. If only someone could tell a joke, write a song, or coin a phrase that would break the mood of despair, he said, it would dispel the gloom and restore the country's confidence in its traditional ways of doing business.

However, when Hoover ordered U.S. Army troops under Gen. Douglas MacArthur to remove World War I veterans from Washington's Anacostia Flats (where they'd gathered to ask, not unreasonably, for early payment of bonuses due them), it deepened the antagonism of most Americans toward their president and made him seem heartless. Hoover's restrained approach to the crisis and his tough response to the 1932 Bonus March destroyed his hold on the public, so strong only three years before. Shantytowns became Hoovervilles, and vaudeville comedians captured the public mood when one told another that the depression was ending: "Has Herbert Hoover died?" the other responded. Hoover grew so morose over his dwindling public approval that, as one commentator put it, "A rose would wilt in his hand."

FEBRUARY 27, 1933

Using the mysterious Reichstag fire as an excuse, German chancellor Adolf Hitler seizes emergency powers. In elections held a week later, Hitler's Nazi party will win enough votes to pass the Enabling Act, creating the Third Reich dictatorship.

In March 1938, *while visiting Berlin, Hoover received an unexpected invitation from Adolf Hitler. Hoover wanted to decline, but the U.S. ambassador persuaded him otherwise. During the meeting, Hoover's mention of the word* Jew *sent Hitler into a prolonged, standing rant. After several minutes, the former president told Hitler to sit down. "That's enough,"* Hoover said. "I'm not interested in your views."

OPPOSITE:

Although the stigma of the Great Depression never left Hoover (shown here delivering a radio address during his presidency), his reputation rebounded somewhat after World War II, when his efforts to relieve postwar famine reminded many of his similar service during World War I. It also helped Hoover that he remained active well into his eighties—or as he put it, "I outlived the bastards."

Hoover's routine as president included tossing a medicine ball for thirty minutes each morning before breakfast. The rules for Hooverball were similar to those of volleyball, but the heavy, bounceless ball (shown here) made for a very different game. Matches were played all year on the South Lawn no matter the weather, and regulars included cabinet members, congressional leaders, journalists, and even a Supreme Court justice.

Hoover was no more successful in foreign affairs. Initiatives aimed at expanding the arms control agreements reached at the Washington Conference of 1921–22 went nowhere. Worse, the Japanese invasion of Manchuria, which broke pledges to avoid war and expansion in East Asia, left Hoover and Secretary of State Henry L. Stimson without an effective response to the first major prelude to World War II. The Hoover-Stimson Doctrine, which declared America's unwillingness to recognize Japan's creation of a protectorate in Manchuria, was seen as nothing more than a rhetorical response to an assault on U.S. national security interests in the Pacific. Hoover's agreement to a moratorium on payment of war debt owed the United States was considered another instance of his administration's inability to serve the national interest.

"DEMOCRACY IS A HARSH EMPLOYER."

—Comment to a former secretary, 1936—

IN 1932, HOOVER COULDN'T MATCH the appeal of Franklin D. Roosevelt, who offered few specifics but gave voters hope with his promise of a New Deal. Even if people had their doubts about Roosevelt, whom Hoover labeled "a chameleon on plaid," he embodied the virtue of simply not being Herbert Hoover.

Hoover's defeat in 1932 opened the way to a postpresidential career lasting thirty-one years, the longest in American history. During this time, he never regained the popularity he enjoyed during the 1920s. In time, however, he did win respect for his principled conservatism and for serving on bipartisan commissions that recommended ways to streamline government procedures. One example of his improved status, the Boulder Dam, begun during his administration, was renamed in his honor in 1947.

Still, Hoover will never be seen as a successful president. He will always be remembered as too rigid an ideologue to have come to grips with the Great Depression and too unfeeling a man, despite his earlier relief work, to respond compassionately to the suffering of millions of Americans.

★ ★ ★

Franklin D. Roosevelt

32ⁿᵈ President · 1933–1945

Susan Ware

Franklin D. Roosevelt's great charm concealed a certain arrogance. Like his cousin Theodore Roosevelt before him, FDR believed, without reservation, that he was the man best suited to run the country.

This telephone sat on FDR's desk in the Oval Office.

ENCOUNTERING FRANKLIN ROOSEVELT, Winston Churchill once observed, was like opening one's first bottle of champagne: a heady experience. FDR's ebullient personality charmed not only heads of state but American voters as well. During his twelve years as president (a record that will never be matched, thanks to the Twenty-second Amendment), he established an unusually close rapport with the American people. "Mr. Roosevelt is the only man we ever had in the White House who would understand that my boss is a son of a bitch," asserted one industrial worker. Ordinary citizens, traumatized by hard times, credited him personally with positive changes in their lives, saying "He saved my home" or "He gave me a job." When Roosevelt died suddenly on April 12, 1945, many Americans, especially those who'd reached adulthood in the 1930s and 1940s, simply couldn't imagine another president in the White House. FDR so dominated the political landscape of his era that every president since, in historian William Leuchtenburg's apt phrase, has lived in his shadow.

As president, Franklin Roosevelt led a country devastated by the gravest economic crisis it had ever faced and then a world threatened by totalitarian aggression. These twin crises of depression and war offered Roosevelt unprecedented possibilities to succeed—or fail— as a national leader. His New Deal may not have ended the Great Depression, but it nevertheless represented one of the most significant changes in modern political life: the commitment of the federal government to intervene in the economy when private initiatives failed and to guarantee the economic security of all Americans. Later, as commander in chief and a global strategist during World War II, Roosevelt grasped America's predominant role in world affairs and helped to

Joseph Stalin, Roosevelt, and Winston Churchill *were in a remarkably jovial mood when this photograph was taken on the porch of the Russian embassy in Teheran in late 1943.*

BORN
January 30, 1882

BIRTHPLACE
Hyde Park, New York

DIED
April 12, 1945

PARTY AFFILIATION
Democrat

CHILDREN
Anna, James, Franklin, Elliot, Franklin Delano Jr., John

MAJOR EVENTS

MAY 18, 1933

Congress establishes the Tennessee Valley Authority to bring electricity and other modern services to one of the nation's poorest areas. Among the TVA's accomplishments will be the construction of dams that control Tennessee River flooding and generate cheap hydroelectric power.

DECEMBER 5, 1933

Utah's ratification of the Twenty-first Amendment completes the repeal of Prohibition, which had been the poorly observed law of the land for fourteen years.

MAY 27, 1935

The Supreme Court rules in Schechter Poultry v. U.S. that Congress has gone too far in regulating interstate commerce. The decision strikes down the National Industrial Recovery Act and its wage and price controls.

educate the country to accept its new international responsibilities. As British philosopher Isaiah Berlin noted, "He was one of the few statesmen in the twentieth century, or any century, who seemed to have no fear of the future."

FRANKLIN DELANO ROOSEVELT'S upbringing seemed more destined to produce a country squire than a world leader. Born January 30, 1882, the only child of two doting parents, he had a remarkably sheltered childhood at Hyde Park, his family's Hudson River estate. His mother, Sara, a formidable presence in his life, wanted her son "to grow up to be like his father, straight and honorable, just and kind, an upstanding American." The death of James Roosevelt in 1900, when Franklin was eighteen, tightened Sara's determination to remain an important part of Franklin's life. She even moved to Boston to be near her son, then an indifferent student at Harvard College. When Franklin announced his intention to marry his distant cousin Eleanor, Sara tried to delay the marriage. In this test of wills, Franklin prevailed. "Nothing like keeping the name in the family," quipped Eleanor's uncle Theodore Roosevelt, who presided over the wedding ceremony.

Women never stopped playing prominent roles in Franklin Roosevelt's life. First, of course, had been the indomitable Sara, who shaped Franklin as a boy and continued to have an enormous influence on his family as a doting (and often manipulative) grandmother. Then there was Eleanor, who blossomed from a timid bride and insecure

During
the 1930s,
*Franklin and
Eleanor Roosevelt enjoyed
a productive political part-
nership as Eleanor became
even more impressed with
her husband's leadership
abilities. "I have never
known a man who gave one
a greater sense of security,"
she observed. "I have never
heard him say there was a
problem that he thought it
was impossible for human
beings to solve."*

mother into one of the twentieth century's greatest public figures, the conscience of the New Deal and a standard-bearer for postwar liberalism and human rights. Franklin's affair with Lucy Mercer (Eleanor's social secretary) during World War I almost ended the Roosevelt marriage, yet Lucy, too, surreptitiously remained part of Franklin's life, visiting the White House during the 1940s and even Warm Springs on the day that he died. Franklin's devoted secretary, Missy LeHand, lived at the White House, shared FDR's sense of humor, and generally performed (with Eleanor's blessing, it seems) many of the duties of a surrogate wife. Finally, his firstborn child and only daughter, Anna, enjoyed an especially close relationship with her father and often served as his White House hostess when Eleanor was away.

I N 1921, WHEN HE WAS thirty-nine, Franklin Roosevelt confronted a crisis that threatened to end his political career: He contracted polio, which left both his legs paralyzed for the rest of his life. Many believe that Roosevelt emerged from this ordeal a stronger, more resilient person—including FDR himself: "If you had spent two years in bed trying to wiggle your toe, after that anything would seem easy." As he contemplated his return to politics (a move supported by Eleanor and trusted confidant Louis Howe but opposed by Sara), FDR realized that people who felt sorry for him because of his immobility wouldn't

This family snapshot,
*taken in February 1941,
is one of the few
photographs that show
Roosevelt in a
wheelchair. He never
complained or indulged
in self-pity about his
situation; instead, he
always made it seem as
though he couldn't
be happier about where
he was or what he
was doing.*

take him seriously as a candidate. So with great effort, Roosevelt taught himself to walk with braces—or, rather, to create the illusion of walking by grasping tightly the person next to him and swiveling his lower body forward in a simulation of movement. So great was the effort involved that FDR always sweated while walking in public, no matter the weather. In an act of media self-restraint that seems remarkable today, members of the press never mentioned or photographed him being carried up stairs, being lifted in and out of automobiles, or using a wheelchair to get around. As a result, most Americans didn't realize the president was paralyzed.

"The presidency is not merely an administrative office," Roosevelt once declared. "It is preeminently a place of moral leadership." No event of his administration demonstrated this more forcefully than his first inaugural address, delivered on March 4, 1933. On that day, the country

"THE COUNTRY NEEDS AND, UNLESS I MISTAKE ITS TEMPER, THE COUNTRY DEMANDS BOLD, PERSISTENT EXPERIMENTATION."

—Speech, 1932—

was three years into the Great Depression, with more than one-quarter of the workforce unemployed and hunger haunting cities and rural areas alike; banks had been closed in thirty-eight states and were operating on a restricted basis in the rest. Yet on that gray March day, using such phrases as "the only thing we have to fear is fear itself" and "This Nation asks for action, and action now," Roosevelt rallied the country with a performance as much sermon as speech. His first fireside chat several days later, reaching a radio audience estimated at sixty million, further reassured Americans that the banks were sound—and they believed him. Roosevelt's restoration of hope and confidence was perhaps his greatest contribution to American life during the 1930s, and his masterful use of radio made him the first national leader whose voice became part of everyday life.

The New Deal over which Franklin Roosevelt presided was not a carefully thought out plan but rather a series of sometimes contradictory responses to the ongoing economic contraction. If the multiplicity of measures enacted by Congress during the first hundred days of FDR's administration had solved that crisis, the rest of the New Deal—including the Works Progress Administration, the National Labor Relations (Wagner) Act, and the Social Security Act—would probably never have been attempted. But in the experimental reform climate that the ongoing depression created, Roosevelt was able to continue the

JULY 17, 1936

Gen. Francisco Franco mutinies against Spain's recently elected Socialist government, beginning the Spanish Civil War. Although fellow fascists in Germany and Italy send Franco copious military aid, the Western democracies, because of isolationist pressures at home, do little to help Spanish Loyalists.

MAY 1, 1937

In order to stop the U.S. arms trade with Spain, Congress extends the Neutrality Act to include civil wars. The original Neutrality Act of 1935 made illegal only the sale of weaponry to warring nations.

Twenty-two-year-old FDR *courts nineteen-year-old Eleanor on the porch of his Campobello Island house in August 1904. It was on Campobello seventeen years later that a vacationing Roosevelt contracted polio.*

A haggard FDR consults with Winston Churchill at the Yalta conference in February 1945.

The **president makes** *his second fireside chat of 1934. These broadcasts were so popular that sometimes eight out of ten American households were listening.*

This RCA carbon microphone, *used by NBC to broadcast Roosevelt's early fireside chats, is particularly large because the housing also contains an amplifier to boost the signal.*

expansion of presidential power begun during the administrations of Theodore Roosevelt and Woodrow Wilson, centralizing decision making in the White House and dramatically expanding the role of the executive in initiating policy. As a result, for the first time, people began to experience the federal government as a concrete part of their daily lives. This activist approach to government contrasted FDR, in the minds of the public, to the Republicans who'd immediately preceded him.

FRANKLIN ROOSEVELT ADORED being president, once asking a friend naively, "Wouldn't you be President if you could? Wouldn't anybody?" His supremely self-confident personality dovetailed perfectly with a pragmatic political style that prioritized results over ideology: "I have no expectation of making a hit every time I come to bat. What I seek is the highest possible batting average." Roosevelt's revitalization of the Democratic party into a potent urban-based coalition of organized labor, northern blacks, white ethnic groups, liberals, intellectuals, and the middle-class families who benefited from New Deal programs dominated American politics for decades. One of his few political missteps, however, came in 1937, when he proposed increasing the number of justices on the Supreme Court, which had recently been frustrating many of his New Deal initiatives. This flagrant attempt to pack the Court in his favor was a costly blunder at a time when he seemed vulnerable to the lame-duck syndrome that often afflicts second-term administrations. No one yet suspected that he'd seek a third term.

At heart an internationalist, President Roosevelt chafed throughout the 1930s at the limits (such as the Neutrality Acts of 1935–37) placed by Congress on his ability to respond to the increasingly dark news coming from Europe and Japan. At the same time, ever the pragmatic politician, he realized he shouldn't allow himself to get too far ahead of public opinion. Taking a middle path, he deftly built support for the Lend-Lease Act of March 1941 that authorized the transfer of military supplies to Britain, China, and later the Soviet Union in exchange for payments deferred until the end of the war. FDR described the plan as lending a neighbor a garden hose to put out a fire. On December 7, 1941, of course, "a date which will live in infamy," the American people finally joined the world crusade for democracy and freedom and put Roosevelt at the helm.

FDR played a particularly active role as wartime commander in chief. His unswerving commitment to Britain's survival provided the basis for a strong, if not always smooth, relationship with Prime Minister Winston Churchill. (Roosevelt aide Harry Hopkins described his role as being "a catalytic agent between two prima donnas.") Soviet premier Joseph Stalin was more of a mystery. Churchill and Roosevelt agreed that

> # "THE QUALITY OF HIS BEING ONE WITH THE PEOPLE...MADE IT POSSIBLE FOR HIM TO BE A LEADER WITHOUT EVER BEING, OR THINKING OF BEING, A DICTATOR."
>
> *—Labor Secretary Frances Perkins—*

defeating Hitler should be the first military priority, but repeated delays in opening a second front on the European continent meant that for most of the war, the Soviet Union bore the brunt of the land battle against Germany. Stalin's mistrust and bitterness over American and British intentions, evident during the last Big Three summit held at Yalta on the Black Sea in February 1945, carried over into the Cold War that followed.

With the president's attention focused on military matters, "Dr. Win the War" replaced "Dr. New Deal," as FDR playfully told a 1943 press conference. Less playfully, he acquiesced in the internment of approximately 112,000 Japanese Americans despite the lack of any evidence of disloyalty or sedition on their part. An even graver tragedy involved the Roosevelt administration's response to the systematic near-annihilation of European Jewry. Yet Roosevelt's justification never wavered: Winning the war would be the

Roosevelt, shown here with Fala, *had several automobiles custom-made with hand controls so that he could drive himself around and reinforce the illusion of his mobility.*

SEPTEMBER 1, 1939

World War II begins as German tanks invade Poland. Honoring a mutual defense treaty, Britain and France declare war on Germany two days later.

JUNE 25, 1941

Roosevelt issues Executive Order 8802 banning racial and religious discrimination in defense industries in response to Philip Randolph's threat to organize a protest march on Washington, D.C.

DECEMBER 7, 1941

Japanese dive-bombers attack the Pacific Fleet at Pearl Harbor. A day later, President Roosevelt asks Congress for a declaration of war. Historians still dispute whether FDR knew about the attack in advance and withheld the information to hasten U.S. entry into the war.

JUNE 6, 1944

Allied forces begin the D-Day invasion of German-occupied France. During the night 5,000 troop ships ferry 175,000 U.S., British, and Canadian soldiers across the English Channel.

FEBRUARY 4–11, 1945

With the defeat of Nazi Germany close at hand, the Big Three meet at Yalta to debate the future of Europe. Critics will later charge that Roosevelt, obviously in poor health, ceded too much to Stalin.

OPPOSITE:

The outpouring of grief that accompanied Roosevelt's sudden death in April 1945 confirmed the depth of his bond with the American populace. "I felt as if I knew him," one soldier said as he tearfully watched FDR's funeral procession.

FDR liked to wear *this particular felt hat while campaigning.*

Roosevelt used this magnifier, called a Roto-Gage, to peruse his famous stamp collection. Mindful of this obsession, one historian observed that FDR had "a collector's mind— broad but shallow."

strongest contribution America could make to liberating Hitler's death camps. Citizens and historians continue to debate the wisdom of his course.

"HE WAS THE ONE PERSON I EVER KNEW, ANYWHERE, WHO WAS NEVER AFRAID."

—Lyndon B. Johnson—

The war took its toll on Franklin Roosevelt. Security concerns isolated him from the public, and he sustained several emotional blows, including his mother's death in 1941 and the loss of Missy LeHand's companionship that same year when a stroke felled her. He also became further estranged from Eleanor, not always as willing or able to meet her demands for social justice as he had been during the 1930s.

Those who spent time with Roosevelt increasingly noticed that his color was terrible, his hands trembled, and he sometimes had trouble concentrating. Yet no one dared confront the president, who had spent his whole life avoiding such unpleasant situations.

"All that is within me cries out to go back to my home on the Hudson River," the president admitted in 1944, and his declining health became an issue during that year's presidential campaign. Few voters, however, were inclined to change leaders while the war continued, as it did for another year. FDR's own end came more quickly, less than three months into his fourth term, when a massive cerebral hemorrhage struck him as he posed for a portrait at his beloved getaway cottage in Warm Springs, Georgia. His sudden death at the age of sixty-three robbed him of the chance to preside over the beginning (and the tensions) of the new world order emerging from the ashes of World War II. It also robbed future generations of his personal reflections on his momentous twelve years in office.

Yet he did get his wish to go home. On a sparkling April day, Franklin Delano Roosevelt was laid to rest at his Hyde Park estate in a ceremony rich with symbolism and emotion. His beloved dog, Fala, barked when the final military salute was sounded, and for months afterward, whenever a distinguished guest arrived in a motorcade with blaring sirens, Fala would perk up his ears and think that his master was coming down the drive.

★ ★ ★

Harry S. Truman

33ʳᵈ President · 1945–1953

Allen Weinstein

"To many it was not just that the greatest of men had fallen," historian David McCullough has written, "but that the least of men—or at any rate the least likely of men—had assumed his place."

HARRY S. TRUMAN WAS an accidental president of whom, initially, little was expected. Only at the last minute in July 1944 did President Franklin Roosevelt choose Truman as his running mate, replacing controversial vice president Henry Wallace. Truman, a Missouri farm boy who saw military service in World War I, was personally honest. But, after failing in postwar small-business efforts, he developed his Democratic political career as an associate of the corrupt Pendergast machine in Kansas City. Elected to the Senate in 1934 and reelected in 1940, Truman was, and remained, a loyal supporter of Roosevelt's New Deal programs. During World War II, he became nationally known as chairman of a special Senate committee investigating waste, fraud, and abuse in the defense industry.

In the months after he became vice president—and before the ailing FDR finally succumbed on April 12, 1945—Truman managed to meet personally with the president only twice. Understandably shaken at the news of Roosevelt's death, Truman told a crowd of reporters during a courtesy visit to Capitol Hill the following day that he felt "like the moon, the stars, and all the planets had fallen on me." Not until he became president was Truman briefed on the super-secret atomic bomb project then nearing completion.

Truman's immediate challenges could hardly have been more formidable. As the little-known successor to a legendary president, he uncomfortably confronted a host of urgent tasks: concluding the war against Germany and shaping Europe's future (a process FDR, Joseph Stalin, and Winston Churchill had already begun at Yalta in February 1945); completing final preparations for what military leaders believed would be a difficult two-year struggle to conquer the Japanese home

Truman kept this sign, a gift from a friend, on his desk only a short time, but its message remained with him permanently.

The BUCK STOPS here!

According to David McCullough, Truman "had never been a simple, ordinary man. The homely attributes, the Missouri wit, the warmth of his friendship, the genuineness…, however appealing, were outweighed by the larger qualities that made him a figure of world stature." Winston Churchill would have agreed.

islands; and, at the same time, satisfying a restless American electorate eager for rapid "reconversion" to civilian life.

At first, Truman saw himself largely implementing the foreign policies that FDR had developed during the war, the centerpiece of which was the Grand Alliance of the United States, Great Britain, and the Soviet Union. Even in his earliest days at the White House, however, Truman displayed his hallmark bluntness, so unlike FDR's more delicate style in diplomatic matters. During an April 23, 1945, courtesy call made by Soviet foreign minister Vyacheslav Molotov, for example, Truman berated his visitor for the Soviet failure to fulfill its Yalta commitments regarding free elections in Poland and non-Communist participation in the new Polish provisional government. "I have never been talked to like that in my life," Molotov complained; the president simply responded, "Carry out your agreements, and you won't get talked to like that." Roosevelt's famous wooing of Stalin with soft words and concessions was replaced virtually overnight by Truman's crisper and more instinctively anti-Communist viewpoint.

At the Potsdam Conference in July 1945, the new U.S. president made a determined effort to treat evenhandedly Stalin and his British counterpart, Clement Attlee, who replaced Churchill midconference after the Labour party won the British elections. But a series of Soviet

BORN
May 8, 1884

BIRTHPLACE
Lamar, Missouri

DIED
December 26, 1972

PARTY AFFILIATION
Democrat

CHILDREN
Margaret

MAJOR EVENTS

APRIL 25, 1945

Delegates from fifty nations meet in San Francisco to approve the United Nations charter. The UN will include both a general assembly, in which every country will have a vote, and an eleven-nation security council, with the United States, the Soviet Union, Britain, France, and China as permanent members.

MAY 14, 1948

With the British mandate ending, Jewish leaders in Palestine announce the creation of the state of Israel. Truman waits only minutes before recognizing the new Jewish state.

JULY 26, 1948

Truman's executive order ends racial discrimination in the military. During World War II, nearly one million African Americans served in segregated units that were typically given the worst duties, quarters, and supplies.

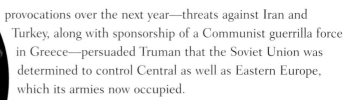

Bess Wallace's family lived only two blocks from the Trumans in Independence, Missouri, and she and Harry grew up together. "I only had one sweetheart from the time I was six," he recalled. Their long and methodical courtship lasted until 1917, when the thirty-three-year-old Truman volunteered for World War I. Knowing he might not come back finally gave him the courage to propose.

provocations over the next year—threats against Iran and Turkey, along with sponsorship of a Communist guerrilla force in Greece—persuaded Truman that the Soviet Union was determined to control Central as well as Eastern Europe, which its armies now occupied.

Yet on his return from Potsdam, Truman faced more immediate concerns relating to the war against Japan. Here, for the first time, emerged the decisiveness that would characterize Harry Truman's actions as president, especially in foreign affairs. As he once told a visiting British diplomat, "I am here to make decisions, and whether they prove right or wrong, I am going to make them."

No decision in Truman's White House years would be as closely (and controversially) identified with his presidency as his authorization to drop atomic bombs on the Japanese mainland. Supported in this decision by most of his military and civilian advisers, Truman wanted to compel Japan's unconditional surrender without undertaking a U.S.-led invasion projected to cost hundreds of thousands of casualties on both sides. The bombs dropped on Hiroshima and Nagasaki in early August 1945 accomplished that goal.

At home, the country once again prepared to reduce its global political and military involvements, as it had following World War I, believing that this time the United States was adequately defended by its dual monopolies of economic power and (for a time) nuclear weapons. Of overriding concern to the president was the desire of soldiers and sailors overseas to return home as quickly as possible. "No Boats, No Votes" was the gist of much mail from the troops. Congress and Truman responded

When Truman was called to the White House on April 12, 1945, he met Eleanor Roosevelt in her study. "Harry, the president is dead," she told him. "Is there anything I can do for you?" he asked. The first lady shook her head. "Is there anything I can do for you?" she replied. "You're the one in trouble now."

by rapidly demobilizing the great bulk of U.S. armed forces.

The transition to civilian life was cushioned for millions by the Servicemen's Readjustment Act of 1944, more commonly known as the GI Bill of Rights. Over the next decade, more than $13.5 billion was spent on veterans benefits, including college tuition, vocational training, special unemployment insurance, medical services, and low-interest home and business loans. By late 1946, Congress had also ended most wartime wage and price controls, cut taxes by billions of dollars, and agreed to Truman's proposal for a presidential Council of Economic Advisers.

Unhindered by wartime restraints, more strikes occurred during 1946 than in any year previous, deeply eroding Truman's popularity and causing many in business as well as labor to question his leadership capacity. After the 1946 midterm elections, Republicans controlled both houses of Congress for the first time since Herbert Hoover was president. Truman, meanwhile, alienated Republicans and southern Democrats by proposing a new package of FDR-style legislation that he called the Fair Deal. Truman's program called for expanding Social Security, increasing

"BOYS, IF YOU EVER PRAY, PRAY FOR ME NOW."

—Remark to the White House press corps, April 13, 1945—

the minimum wage, guaranteeing full employment, clearing slums, and building more public housing. (Later, he added federal aid to education and health insurance.) Most of these bills had no chance of passing Congress, yet, as Truman later wrote, they symbolized for him "my assumption of the office of President in my own right." More dramatic still, this border-state president, raised with deeply embedded racist attitudes, transcended his background by proposing a historic series of measures designed to strengthen the civil rights of African Americans and other minorities.

VIRTUALLY ALL THESE DOMESTIC initiatives were ignored, blocked, or rejected by the conservative Eightieth Congress, whose symbolic response to Roosevelt's legacy was the Twenty-second Amendment (limiting future presidents to two full terms). But if the body Truman enjoyed calling "the do-nothing Eightieth Congress" failed to act on his domestic proposals, neither did it roll back the New Deal, whose legislative legacy Truman consolidated.

Where Harry Truman's decisiveness proved more useful, even remarkable, was in his conduct of U.S. foreign policy. Soviet misbehavior and the urging of key advisers moved the president during his first term toward a more forceful assertion of U.S. goals abroad. Speaking

The extremely nearsighted *Truman, shown here in France during 1918, passed the army eye test only by memorizing the chart.*

MAY 31, 1949

Former State Department official Alger Hiss goes on trial for lying to a federal grand jury. The grand jury had been investigating charges that Hiss spied for the Soviet Union during the 1930s. Hiss's January 1950 perjury conviction will boost the political fortunes of his chief congressional accuser, Rep. Richard M. Nixon, who has brought the Hiss case to national attention.

FEBRUARY 9, 1950

At a speech in Wheeling, West Virginia, Wisconsin senator Joseph R. McCarthy claims to have "here in my hand" a list of 205 Communists working for the State Department. Although the senator never produces any evidence to support this inflammatory charge, the publicity that it generates wins him the chairmanship of a formal Senate investigation.

APRIL 11, 1951

An enraged President Truman relieves Gen. Douglas MacArthur of his command in Korea. Truman's action follows MacArthur's public criticism of Truman's conduct of the war. "I didn't fire him because he was a dumb sonofabitch, although he was," Truman said. "I fired him because he wouldn't respect the authority of the president."

With Lauren Bacall looking on, Vice President-elect Truman performs for servicemen in February 1945. "My choice early in life was either to be a piano player in a whorehouse or a politician," he once joked, "and to tell the truth, there's hardly a difference."

Truman brought to Washington the straight-arrow Victorian morality of his Missouri childhood. The senator, who made his own toast, valued fidelity in marriage, courage in battle, and honesty in business.

to a joint session of Congress on March 12, 1947, Truman offered what would become known as the Truman Doctrine, committing the country to assisting nations threatened by Soviet actions—assisting them economically, politically, and militarily, if necessary. "I believe that it must be the policy of the United States," Truman stated, "to support free peoples who are resisting attempted subjugation by armed minorities or by outside pressures....The free peoples of the world look to us for support in maintaining their freedoms. If we falter in our leadership, we may endanger the peace of the world—and we shall surely endanger the welfare of this Nation." With significant bipartisan support in Congress, four decades of Cold War had begun.

That same year, Truman and his advisers developed the administrative mechanisms that would carry out such open-ended and unprecedented peacetime involvement in world affairs. At the president's urging, Congress passed the National Security Act, which unified the armed forces into a single Department of Defense and established the Central Intelligence Agency as well as the National Security Council. Truman correctly believed that the National Security Act greatly strengthened his ability (and that of future presidents) to undertake America's apparently permanent new role of world leadership.

Also in 1947, within months of the Truman Doctrine speech, Secretary of State George Marshall signaled, in a Harvard commencement address, arguably the most creative and important initiative of America's emerging Cold War strategy: Marshall called for a massive multiyear aid program to revitalize the economies of Europe. In December, Truman submitted to Congress the European Recovery Program, popularly known as the Marshall Plan, which passed both houses by wide margins. In time, the Marshall Plan provided over thirteen billion dollars for the recovery of Western Europe. Within three years, the region's national economies had reached levels beyond their prewar highs.

Two events in 1948 further stiffened American resolve to resist the Soviet threat. In Czechoslovakia, Communists brutally consolidated their control over what had been nominally a coalition government with non-

Communist parties. Meanwhile, Stalin responded to the merger of the British, French, and U.S. occupation zones (which the following year would lead to creation of the new Federal Republic of Germany) with a blockage of West Berlin, which was surrounded by the Soviet zone. Truman rejected proposals that he use military force to break the blockade, instead ordering an immense allied airlift of supplies. These maintained the city's population at a minimal level until the Soviets lifted the blockade in May 1949.

APRIL 8, 1952

Truman orders a federal takeover of the nation's steel mills after a United Steelworkers strike threatens to shut down steel production all over the country. Truman claims the necessary authority because of steel's importance to the Korean War effort. On June 2, the Supreme Court rules against Truman and orders the mills returned to private control.

B
Y THAT TIME, HARRY TRUMAN, running as an underdog in the polls, had been reelected in the most stunning upset in U.S. presidential history. Less than three months into his second term, Truman hosted the signing ceremony for the recently negotiated treaty establishing an essential military and political component of the Truman Doctrine: the North Atlantic Treaty Organization (NATO). Through NATO, the United States became the dominant military defender of the Western world, a decisive break with American tradition.

Although war never came to Europe, its onset in Asia significantly affected Truman's policies. Despite political efforts to halt the 1947–49 advance of Mao's Communist army across mainland China, the United States had kept its military distance, permitting the exile of its Nationalist allies to the island of Formosa (now Taiwan). In June 1950, however, Truman felt no similar restraint when Communist North Korea attacked authoritarian but pro-American South Korea. Initially supported by public opinion, Truman immediately dispatched U.S. divisions stationed in Japan. Soviet diplomatic missteps then allowed Truman to turn his unilateral response into a United Nations mission, with

deployments from other countries joining the U.S. forces. Later, Chinese Communist troops entered the conflict in support of North Korea, forcing a stalemate close to the original North–South border.

As the war dragged on, Truman's popularity declined sharply, both from war weariness and from a range of domestic crises. At one point, the president felt compelled to relieve Gen. Douglas MacArthur of command in Korea, when strategic disagreements led to MacArthur's outright insubordination. For Truman (and for the Democratic party), the Korean War, which continued unabated for the duration of his presidency, proved

While at Potsdam
with Stalin and Churchill, Truman informed the Soviet leader that the United States had successfully tested "a new weapon of unusual destructive force." He didn't know that Soviet spies had already told Stalin about the bomb.

At times, Truman's obstinacy served him well, as when he fought back to defeat New York governor Thomas E. Dewey in the 1948 election (an election some impatient newspapers called wrong). At other times, though, his behavior could appear erratic and petty.

"I NEVER GIVE THEM HELL. I JUST TELL THE TRUTH, AND THEY THINK IT IS HELL."

—Saying, 1948—

OPPOSITE:

Although by 1948 most pundits had written off Truman as a caretaker president, "Give 'Em Hell" Harry refused to accept defeat passively. Instead, he undertook a prodigious thirty-thousand-mile whistle-stop train campaign.

to be extremely costly in political terms. An increasingly embattled president found himself waging both the Korean and Cold Wars while simultaneously defending his administration at home against aggressive Republican accusations of Democratic "softness" on Communism.

THROUGHOUT THE 1949–53 period, leading Republican spokesmen accused the Roosevelt and Truman administrations of somehow having "sold out" Eastern Europe and China to the Communists. None of Truman's efforts to strengthen Western Europe against Soviet expansionism silenced these adversaries, who even attacked Truman's loyalty-oath program, which civil libertarians criticized as *overly* aggressive. The reckless charges of Wisconsin senator Joseph R. McCarthy and the conviction of several Americans, notably Julius and Ethel Rosenberg, on charges of atomic espionage added significantly to the anti-Communist hysteria that permeated American politics from 1949 until the 1952 election campaign.

Truman could have sought reelection, but he chose not to run again. Instead, he watched as a fierce Republican campaign brought Dwight Eisenhower a landslide victory. Truman's popularity, by contrast, had sunk to its nadir. He left the White House with 56 percent of the American people disapproving of his leadership while only 31 percent endorsed it. Not until the 1970s did the Truman revival begin, initially in response to the collapse of Richard Nixon's presidency, as Americans found comfort in mythologizing Truman's candor, blunt speech, decisive judgments, and self-confidence. The passage of time also allowed scholars to recognize Truman's achievement in preparing postwar America for world leadership. The Truman Doctrine, the Marshall Plan, and NATO largely restored Western European stability, while Truman left the United States a safer, more secure, and far more prosperous country than the one he inherited from Franklin Roosevelt.

One of the first world figures to recognize this achievement was Winston Churchill. While dining with the president during a January 1950 visit to Washington, Churchill admitted his disappointment at first meeting Truman in Potsdam: "I must confess, sir, I held you in very low regard then. I loathed your taking the place of Franklin Roosevelt." But he continued, "I misjudged you badly. Since then, you, more than any other man, have saved Western civilization." In time, many of Truman's fellow citizens would reach the same conclusion.

★ ★ ★

Dwight D. Eisenhower

34th President · 1953–1961

Herbert S. Parmet

In March 1955, *Dwight D. Eisenhower's press secretary reminded him to be careful at an upcoming press conference answering questions about Communist Chinese intentions regarding Formosa. "Don't worry," Ike said. "If that question comes up, I'll just confuse them."*

Ike kept these sentimental *miniatures of his wife and mother on his desk in the Oval Office.*

IKE'S SINGLE GREATEST achievement, George Gallup's pollsters heard over and over again as the president prepared to leave office, was that he had "kept the peace." He had done this, through two terms in the White House, by using effective diplomacy and by resisting the Pentagon and the military buildup it wanted. As a hero for his service during World War II and a defense insider, Ike knew all the tricks that the Pentagon used to win money from Congress. He resisted them because he worried about the dangers of an arms race and the impact that continued high military spending would have on the domestic economy. Eisenhower feared that we might "spend ourselves to death" before the Russians even got at us. With this in mind, on the evening of January 17, 1961, three days before the inauguration of his successor, the president prepared to deliver his farewell address to the nation.

Although ever present, the Soviet threat had waxed and waned during Eisenhower's eight years as commander in chief. Joseph Stalin's death in March 1953, not long after Eisenhower's swearing-in, seemed to mellow the Soviets. Georgi Malenkov, Stalin's interim successor, denoted the change by expressing his openness to the possibility of peacefully settling "by mutual agreement" outstanding disputes with the West. Eisenhower responded with his own Atoms for Peace speech to the UN General Assembly, proposing that atomic materials be managed by a single international agency. Eisenhower biographer Stephen E. Ambrose has called the December 1953 speech "the most generous and the most serious offer on controlling the arms race ever made by an American president."

Meanwhile, when the fighting in Korea finally ended that summer, "Truman's war" became Ike's peace. Yet grumpy American nationalists had little cause to worry about another Yalta-type

"EVERY GUN THAT IS MADE, EVERY WARSHIP LAUNCHED, EVERY ROCKET FIRED SIGNIFIES...A THEFT FROM THOSE WHO HUNGER AND ARE NOT FED."

—Speech, 1953—

"sellout," because the United States soon assumed responsibility for what had been French Indochina. In deciding to sponsor Ngo Dinh Diem's presidency of South Vietnam, Ike ensured that America would inherit the opprobrium for French colonialism. The Southeast Asia Treaty Organization (SEATO), forged by Secretary of State John Foster Dulles, became both the cornerstone of the administration's response to the Communist challenge in Southeast Asia and the backbone of its commitment to South Vietnam. In April 1954, comparing the nations of Southeast Asia to a row of dominoes, Eisenhower said, "You knock over the first one, and what will happen to the last one is the certainty that it will go over very quickly."

During the summer of 1955, however, the prospects for détente brightened again. There was mutual acceptance of a peace treaty with Austria that not only ended tripartite occupation, which still existed in Germany, but also affirmed Austrian neutrality. In July, Soviet leaders Nikolai Bulganin and Nikita Khrushchev met Eisenhower and other Western leaders at the first superpower summit conference in Geneva. Not much substantive progress was made, but this lack was overshadowed by a new mood of cordiality dubbed the "spirit of Geneva" by the media.

At home in Eisenhower's America, there was peace and unprecedented prosperity, fueled by easy credit,

General Eisenhower *exhorts paratroopers of the 101st Airborne Division on the afternoon before D-Day. Ike's military achievements and wartime popularity as commander of the Allied forces were the main reasons for his political rise.*

BORN
October 14, 1890

BIRTHPLACE
Denison, Texas

DIED
March 28, 1969

PARTY AFFILIATION
Republican

CHILDREN
Doud, John

MAJOR EVENTS

JULY 27, 1953

At Panmunjom, United Nations and North Korean officials sign an armistice ending the Korean War. Korea remains divided close to the Thirty-eighth Parallel, near where the border was when the war began.

MAY 17, 1954

In Brown v. Board of Education, the Supreme Court outlaws segregation in public schools. The decision overturns Plessy v. Ferguson (1896), which had permitted "separate but equal" treatment.

JUNE 9, 1954

The Army-McCarthy hearings climax when lawyer Joseph Welch demands, "Have you no decency, sir, at long last?" (referring to McCarthy's attack on his young assistant). The hearings, called to air McCarthy's charge that the army has been harboring Communists, result instead in his censure.

Capt. Dwight Eisenhower poses in 1919 with one of World War I's most important technological innovations: the tank.

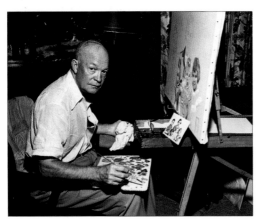

Unlike Winston Churchill, Eisenhower had no pretensions to being an artist, but he did tend to search the walls of friends' houses to see whether his paintings were being properly displayed.

Ike met Mamie Doud in San Antonio, where the army had sent him after his 1915 graduation from West Point and where Mamie's wealthy parents had a winter home. She found him attractive because he looked like a "bruiser"; he liked her saucy, flirtatious manner. Having grown up with a full complement of domestic servants, including a personal maid, Mamie had no household skills. Either Ike cooked (he was famous for his vegetable soup) or they ate at the officers' mess. When Mamie became pregnant, Ike let out her dresses.

rampant consumer spending, and brisk demand for houses, cars, and appliances. The president signed a balanced budget, thus achieving one of his major objectives, and he would do so twice more before his administration ended. He also proposed a network of interstate multilane highways to link major U.S. cities and make it easier for all those consumer goods to reach their intended markets. Little wonder, then, that Eisenhower left for a Colorado vacation in September 1955 with a Gallup poll approval rating of nearly 75 percent. He was reinforcing the GOP's fragile coalition and using his nonpartisan image to quiet divisive Truman-era Red Scare and Korean War bitterness. Ike skillfully allowed Dulles to romance the hard-liners and take the heat from liberals, while he avoided being identified with the Supreme Court's recent desegregation decisions. He also kept aloof from Joe McCarthy's crusading excesses, choosing instead to cut McCarthy down from offstage. This was the most comfortable place for Eisenhower, and he often used obfuscation to protect the opacity of his maneuvers.

When a reporter wanted to know where he stood on a controversial issue that separated Republican isolationists from the party's internationalists, Eisenhower made sure that he answered the question without answering the question: "I have to remember the old adage that a man has two ears and one tongue, and I therefore have tried to keep twice as still as I would in other places."

Eisenhower's reelection in 1956 was even more impressive than his original win, yet it came amid new crises. In July 1956, Egyptian president Gamal Abdel Nasser nationalized the Suez Canal. Determined to reduce the European presence in Egypt, he also coveted the canal tolls, most of which had been going to British and French stockholders. On October 29, having made secret arrangements with Britain and France, Israel invaded Egypt and advanced on the canal. A week later, using the Israeli invasion as an excuse, Britain and France landed their own troops.

About the same time, rebelliousness within the Soviet bloc seemed to raise the possibility of U.S. intervention in Eastern Europe. A Polish uprising in June was put down before serious questions could be raised about what action Washington should take. On October 23, however, a full-scale revolt in Budapest turned the Hungarian army against the Soviets and returned ousted premier Imre Nagy to power. On November 4, three days after Nagy announced Hungary's withdrawal from the Warsaw Pact, the Soviet Union invaded, sending in tanks to crush the revolt.

With regard to Hungary, a realistic Eisenhower never considered intervening in a matter so consequential to the Soviets and so deep within Eastern Europe. The Suez crisis was another matter. Erupting as it did just days before the presidential election, it took the Washington foreign policy establishment mostly by surprise. Without the help of Dulles, who had been hospitalized, the president worked through the United Nations to demand and receive a cease-fire in place, with the invaders just miles short of the canal. Khrushchev backed the American position, threatening to enter the war on Egypt's side, and this led to a speedy resolution that left control of the canal in Nasser's hands.

NEITHER CRISIS MUCH AFFECTED the wide margin of his 1956 victory, yet reelection left Eisenhower with some new problems. The Twenty-second Amendment ensured that sooner or later he would become a lame duck, and his age and health emphasized this point. Only two years after his much-publicized September 1955 heart attack, the president was hospitalized again, this time for a mild stroke in November 1957; he recovered quickly but was left with a slight speech impediment.

On the world front, things were also getting tough. The Soviet Union, in an effective bit of Cold War theater, upstaged the United States with the October 1957 launch of Sputnik, Earth's first artificial satellite. The success of Sputnik not only suggested a Soviet advantage in technology but also frightened Americans who feared the Russians might just as easily orbit a nuclear bomb.

On the domestic front, Eisenhower's tap dance around the *Brown* decision came to an end when Gov. Orval Faubus called out the Arkansas National Guard in September 1957 to prevent the enrollment of nine black students at Little Rock's Central High School. Faubus's open defiance of a federal court order forced the president to send in federal troops to enforce the will of the court. Meanwhile, a slowdown, combined with rising inflation, sent the economy into a recession that lasted for the rest of Ike's second term, and a 1958 influence-peddling scandal cost him the services of his valued chief of staff, Sherman Adams.

Eisenhower's determination to leave office as a peacemaker depended on the perception that both great powers considered World War III unthinkable. In order to avoid a Berlin crisis like that of 1948, East-West summitry was resumed. Vice President Richard Nixon visited the Soviet Union in July

FEBRUARY 25, 1956

At the Twentieth Communist Party Congress in Moscow, Nikita Khrushchev denounces the late Joseph Stalin. Khrushchev's description of Stalin's ruthlessness disillusions many American Communists, who abandon the Communist Party USA in large numbers.

AUGUST 23, 1958

Congress responds to Sputnik-related fears of a "missile gap" with the National Defense Education Act. The new law provides nearly a billion dollars in funding for science education so that Americans can better compete with the Soviets.

On September 24, 1955, *Eisenhower suffered a severe heart attack at his mother-in-law's Denver home. He spent the next six weeks at nearby Fitzsimmons Army Hospital (he's shown here at a press conference on the roof), but it was another two months before he resumed his normal schedule.*

OPPOSITE:

Security concerns *kept Nikita Khrushchev from visiting Disneyland during his September 1959 trip to the United States, but he did get to enjoy Camp David, named by Ike for his grandson.*

America embraced
Ike's middle-class hobbies, especially golf, and it suited a president who liked to work behind the scenes for the country to think he spent most of his time on the links.

1959, and Khrushchev put on an even better show when he toured the United States two months later. Plans were made at that time for another summit conference to be held in Paris the following May.

O N MAY 1, 1960, however, two weeks before the Paris summit, the Soviets shot down an American U-2 spy plane over the Russian heartland. Administration denials were quickly countered by Khrushchev, who gleefully produced the pilot, Francis Gary Powers. Not wanting to appear ignorant, Eisenhower abandoned his usual obfuscation and candidly admitted he had known of and approved the U-2 flights. Relishing the propaganda feast, Khrushchev insisted on an apology, which Eisenhower refused to make. The spirit of Geneva was dead.

Still, as Eisenhower closed his presidential years, he felt strongly that there was one more contribution he could make. The campaign of Democratic presidential candidate John F. Kennedy had worried him with its reckless charge that the Eisenhower administration had weakened national defenses, especially by tolerating a "missile gap."

"HIS SMILE AND SIMPLE FRONTIER APPROACH TO COMPLEX PROBLEMS MADE HIM AS AMERICAN AS APPLE PIE."

—*Justice William O. Douglas*—

Kennedy was merely playing politics, reversing (and thus inoculating himself against) earlier Republican charges that Democrats were "soft" on Communism. Yet Eisenhower feared the danger posed by uncontrolled defense spending and "unwarranted influence, whether sought or unsought, by the military-industrial complex."

In his farewell address, delivered the night of January 17, 1961, Eisenhower warned the nation pointedly, "Only an alert and knowledge-able citizenry can compel the proper meshing of the huge industrial and military machinery of defense with our peaceful methods and goals, so that security and liberty may prosper together." Ike lived on until March 28, 1969, when he died after a long series of heart attacks.

★ ★ ★

John F. Kennedy

35ᵗʰ President · 1961–1963

Richard Reeves

John F. Kennedy was *a cold warrior fascinated with covert action and the culture of assassination that enveloped the murders of Diem and Dominican dictator Rafael Trujillo, the repeated attempts on the life of Cuba's Fidel Castro, and ultimately his own death.*

JOHN F. KENNEDY WAS THE FIRST of the self-selected presidents. He didn't wait his turn because that turn might never have come. Old-fashioned national conventions, reflecting the judgment of the party's senior establishment, were likely to reject him because of his age, his religion (there had never been a Roman Catholic president), and his record in Congress (which was both casual and ordinary).

So Kennedy found a new route to the White House. He institutionalized his great charm, exaggerated his thin biography, and spent a good deal of his family's money winning over the Democratic primary voters of a few small states (and the gentlemen of the national press corps). Then he presented himself as the people's choice. By the time the 1960 Democratic national convention began in Los Angeles, young "Jack" Kennedy, the self-proclaimed war hero whose first slogan was "The New Generation Offers a Leader," had personal control of enough delegates—men and women committed not to party or to ideology but to him—to roll over the old leaders and old ways.

Then the forty-three-year-old nominee chose as his running mate one of the more traditionally deserving candidates, Senate Majority Leader Lyndon Johnson. The party, old and new, rallied around, and Kennedy defeated Vice President Richard Nixon in one of the closest elections in American history. Nixon was young too, only forty-seven, and a navy veteran as well, but he was an old man's idea of what a young man should be.

Perhaps because *of his fondness for sailing, Kennedy liked to collect scrimshaw. This is one of the pieces he acquired.*

Unfortunately, Kennedy knew more about becoming president than being president. He demonstrated a cavalier ignorance when he authorized the disastrous April 1961 invasion of Cuba at the Bay of Pigs and followed that with an amateurish performance at the June 1961 Vienna summit that convinced Soviet premier Nikita

Khrushchev this charming young American could be pushed around.

The Vienna summit came as a particular shock to Kennedy, a man convinced that he could always prevail one on one with men and with women. This time, he'd been outmaneuvered and out-thought by the Soviet leader—a fact cleaned up for American consumption by a protective staff misleading a patriotic press. But Kennedy was no fool, and he came away from Vienna with a valuable seed of experience: He realized that the rough-mouthed premier was just another politician. The Soviet rules were different, but the tricks and the scoring of the game were the same.

Kennedy inspects a checkpoint during his June 1963 visit to Berlin. In an emotional speech delivered in front of the city hall, Kennedy declared, "Ich bin ein Berliner."

I N THE EARLY SUMMER of that same year, as thousands of refugees fled Communist East Berlin, Kennedy told one aide, "This is unbearable for Khrushchev. East Germany is hemorrhaging to death. The entire East bloc is in danger. He has to do something to stop this. Perhaps a wall...." A year later, during the Cuban Missile Crisis, this same insight helped Kennedy understand why Khrushchev would risk so much to place a few nuclear missiles on Cuba. He told his brother Robert that he thought the Soviet leader was right to try to neutralize the hundreds of U.S. missiles ringing the Soviet Union—but that didn't necessarily mean Khrushchev intended to use the Cuban missiles. In the simplest terms, nuclear terms, Kennedy knew that he wasn't going to push the button first, and neither was Khrushchev. This was politics, not war—and Kennedy said privately that he might have tried the same trick.

In Berlin in 1961, both leaders had problems. The Soviet problem was that Communism was being mocked and drained by the flight of educated men and women, more than three thousand a day, escaping to

BORN
May 29, 1917

BIRTHPLACE
Brookline, Massachusetts

DIED
November 22, 1963

PARTY AFFILIATION
Democrat

CHILDREN
Caroline, John Jr., Patrick

MAJOR EVENTS

MARCH 1, 1961

President Kennedy creates the Peace Corps, which over the next five years will send more than ten thousand volunteers to developing countries to help improve their agricultural practices and public health.

APRIL 12, 1961

Cosmonaut Yuri Gagarin becomes the first human in space when his Vostok 1 capsule completes a single orbit of the earth. Alan Shepard will become the first American in space on May 5 aboard Freedom 7.

MAY 3, 1963

Birmingham's notorious police chief, Eugene "Bull" Connor, orders fire hoses and police dogs turned loose on peaceful civil rights marchers. Viewers around the nation are shocked by television news footage of black schoolchildren being attacked by dogs and knocked down by powerful jets of water.

Most Americans listening on radio believed that Vice President Nixon had won the first Kennedy-Nixon debate.

Jacqueline Bouvier
*attended Miss Porter's
School, Vassar College,
and the Sorbonne before
finding work as the
Washington Herald's
Inquiring Camera Girl.
She gave up her $42.50
weekly salary, though, to
marry America's most
eligible bachelor in
September 1953. As
first lady, she used her
beauty and grace to
enhance her husband's
public image. The chic
Jackie Look—skirted
suit, bouffant hairstyle,
pillbox hat—came to
dominate American
fashion, and Jackie
herself became
a consequential
arbiter of taste.*

the West through the divided city. The American problem was that the fifteen thousand U.S., British, and French troops in West Berlin were surrounded by hundreds of thousands of Red Army troops in East Germany. If Khrushchev opted for a military solution to his problem, the only practical Allied defense would be to use nuclear weapons— an unacceptable option for Kennedy.

More than once he signaled, openly and secretly, the American bottom line: continued and unhampered access to West Berlin on the autobahn from West Germany and checkpoint access into East Berlin for Allied occupation officers. What the Communists did on their own side of the border, Kennedy made clear, was their business.

In the early-morning hours of Sunday, August 13, 1961, breaking the dark of night with giant lights, East German troops rolled out a long barbed-wire fence on their side of the border between East and West Berlin. Access for Allied teams inspecting East Berlin was unaffected, but the exodus to the West was over. On Cape Cod, Kennedy went sailing, avoiding public comment.

A little more than a year later, in October 1962, U.S. spy planes discovered evidence that the Soviets were building missile sites in Cuba. For two extraordinarily tense weeks, in what seemed to be the first true nuclear confrontation, the words and moves of Kennedy and Khrushchev transfixed the world. However, with Kennedy pledging never to invade Cuba, the Soviets backed down and removed their missiles.

The missile crisis demonstrated an important fact about Kennedy's presidency: He was the first American chief executive since the War of 1812 to enter office facing the tangible possibility that an adversary could do grave damage to the United States. Sophisticated Soviet delivery systems developed late in the Eisenhower years meant that the great oceans could no longer guarantee continental security. In response to this threat, Kennedy set a pattern of disciplined Cold War leadership that

***The story of the 1960
election*** *can be told
with two campaign
photographs: In one,
Nixon poses stiffly in his
navy dress blues; in the
other, a bare-chested
Kennedy, wearing a
battered fatigue hat,
grins widely from the
cockpit of PT-109.*

> "KENNEDY HAD TWO PRINCIPAL POLITICAL LIABILITIES... ONE WAS ONLY APPARENT—HIS CATHOLICISM; THE OTHER WAS REAL—HIS LACK OF EXPERIENCE."
>
> —Richard M. Nixon—

included negotiating the Limited Nuclear Test Ban Treaty of 1963 and, more important, changing U.S. military strategy to rule out the general use of nuclear weapons in regional conflicts.

Kennedy's great foreign policy failure came in Southeast Asia, where he tried to impress Khrushchev with his resolve (and inoculate himself against the standard Republican charge that Democrats were "soft" on Communism). When he took office, there were a few hundred U.S. military advisers in South Vietnam—a number that he increased to more than seventeen thousand. By late 1963, however, he'd lost faith in the determination and competence of the South Vietnamese government, and he signed off on a generals' plot to overthrow President Ngo Dinh Diem. With Diem's November 1 assassination, South Vietnam became, in effect, an American protectorate, one to be held at high cost.

To America's Cold War leaders, including Kennedy, domestic policy was more often than not a function of foreign policy. Roads were built, engineers educated, and corporations supported for essentially military reasons in the all-encompassing fight against world Communism. Kennedy's initial concern about civil rights for "Negroes," the term of the time, had less to do with justice than with the fact that civil rights demonstrations were being used as effective Communist propaganda, especially in Africa. The president didn't learn of the May 1961 Freedom Rides, designed to test a recent Supreme Court desegregation decision, until he saw a newspaper photograph of the riders being beaten in Alabama.

Kennedy wanted to avoid federal involvement in the civil rights movement, but aggressive lawyers and television footage of police brutality in the South forced him to place the resources of the

AUGUST 28, 1963

Thirty special trains and more than two thousand chartered buses carry demonstrators to the March on Washington, the largest civil rights rally in U.S. history. Martin Luther King Jr. delivers his "I Have a Dream" speech before 250,000 people gathered at the Lincoln Memorial.

OCTOBER 7, 1963

Kennedy and Khrushchev sign the Limited Nuclear Test Ban Treaty, which bans atmospheric testing. The president calls it the most important achievement of his administration.

Kennedy meets with advisers *on October 29, 1962, one day after accepting Khrushchev's offer to remove the Cuban missiles in exchange for a U.S. pledge not to invade Cuba.*

Among JFK
assassination books,
Mark Lane's 1966
Rush to Judgment is
noteworthy for being
the first to raise public
doubt about the
Warren Commission's
findings. Of course,
many more books
have followed it.

OPPOSITE:

The Democratic
nominee and his wife
enjoy a ticker-tape parade
through lower Manhattan's
Canyon of Heroes. The
parade highlighted a
mid-October campaign
swing through New York.

government on the side of the black minority—no small thing in a democracy. In September 1962, he ordered federal troops onto the campus of the University of Mississippi to end anti-Negro rioting, and on June 11, 1963, in the middle of a legal battle to desegregate the University of Alabama, he went on national television to say: "This is not a sectional issue. This is not even a legal or legislative issue alone....We are confronted primarily with a moral issue. It is as old as the Scriptures and as clear as the American Constitution."

"I COULD NOT REALIZE, NOR COULD ANY MAN REALIZE WHO DOES NOT BEAR THE BURDENS OF THIS OFFICE, HOW HEAVY AND CONSTANT WOULD BE THOSE BURDENS."

—Speech, 1961—

WITHIN SIX MONTHS HE WAS DEAD, shot down in Dallas on November 22. The reasons for his death may never be clear, but his life and his short presidency have been celebrated more than most Americans could have imagined then. He touched the nation with youthful ideas and rhetoric: The Peace Corps. The space program. "Ask not what your country can do for you; ask what you can do for your country." He was an athlete dying young; a beautiful man who disguised his own fragile health and constant pain; a magical cultural figure with a cool, ironic style who changed the way Americans saw and projected themselves. He was also a man of secrets, some of which disguised a personal carelessness, a recklessness involving both drugs and women, kept secret by assistants and family retainers who were always there to clean up the messes he made.

In private, he was a rich prince, living life as a race against boredom—a fact that didn't really come out until a decade after his death, when investigations of the Central Intelligence Agency revealed White House–Mafia plots to assassinate foreign leaders and a pattern of irresponsible womanizing. By then, however, his status as a gifted public figure was already well established—with some merit. Of all the prerequisites for democratic greatness, he had this one in abundance: the ability to bring out the best in people, the American people.

★ ★ ★

Lyndon B. Johnson

36th President · 1963–1969

Robert Dallek

Lyndon B. Johnson was a master of vulgarity, *which he used both to intimidate and to entertain. According to George Reedy, the president's "lapses from civilized conduct were deliberate and usually intended to subordinate someone else to his will."*

NEW YORK TIMES COLUMNIST Russell Baker, who first met Lyndon Johnson during the 1950s when Johnson was Senate majority leader, described him as "a human puzzle so complicated that nobody could ever understand it....He was a character out of a Russian novel, one of those human complications that filled the imagination of Dostoyevsky, a storm of warring human instincts: sinner and saint, buffoon and statesman, cynic and sentimentalist, a man torn between hungers for immortality and self-destruction."

Evidencing a different taste in literature, George Reedy, Johnson's Senate aide and first press secretary, liked to compare his boss to a character in Luigi Pirandello's play *Six Characters in Search of an Author.* You never knew what was real and what was contrived by Johnson, Reedy said. It may have been that even Johnson didn't know at times. Far seeing and shortsighted, generous and mean spirited, wise and foolish, a great and a failed chief executive, Lyndon Baines Johnson was a walking contradiction and undoubtedly one of the most enigmatic personalities ever to serve in the White House.

A contemporary psychologist treating Johnson would likely have described him as having a narcissistic personality. Throughout his life, LBJ suffered from a painful sense of inadequacy and emptiness. As is common to people afflicted with such problems, he filled the holes in his ego with womanizing, overeating, excessive drinking, and work. He once said of his affinity for work, "I never think about politics more than eighteen hours a day." He had little choice; it was a need.

Likewise, Johnson always needed to be top dog—to be the best, eclipsing all those around him.

Johnson took these riding boots *with him everywhere he went from 1961 until his death in 1973. They even accompanied him on his surprise visit to South Vietnam in October 1966.*

When people mentioned John Kennedy's womanizing to him, he would bang the table and shout, "Why I had more women by accident than he ever had on purpose!" Even relatively minor triumphs were savored by him. For example, Johnson was the first U.S. senator to have a telephone installed in his limousine. Soon enough, Minority Leader Everett Dirksen, a principal Senate rival, got one and called Lyndon, limo to limo, to let Johnson know. "Can you hang on a second Ev?" LBJ told him. "My other phone is ringing."

Johnson and grandson Lyn *take a dip with Yuki, a stray that Lyn's mother, Luci, discovered at a Texas gas station. Johnson often allowed the dog into cabinet meetings and other high-level executive functions.*

A S KENNEDY'S VICE PRESIDENT, Johnson sulked. He resented playing second fiddle to JFK, a younger and much less accomplished political leader. Once he succeeded Kennedy in November 1963, however, Johnson drove himself and his staff to ensure that he became the greatest chief executive in the country's history. Most people as needy and troubled as Johnson lead dysfunctional lives. Yet not LBJ, who turned his difficulties into advantages that helped him become one of the two greatest domestic reform presidents in U.S. history (the other being Franklin Roosevelt).

Johnson's unrelenting efforts on behalf of the public programs for which he hoped to be remembered translated into extraordinary accomplishments. His War on Poverty and Great Society reforms included a litany of enduring major laws: the Civil Rights Act of 1964,

BORN
August 27, 1908

BIRTHPLACE
Stonewall, Texas

DIED
January 22, 1973

PARTY AFFILIATION
Democrat

CHILDREN
Lynda Bird, Luci Baines

MAJOR EVENTS

AUGUST 4, 1964

FBI agents locate the bodies of missing civil rights workers Andrew Goodman, Michael Schwerner, and James Chaney. Yet Mississippi governor Paul Johnson still refuses to let the state bring any murder charges against the white suspects, who include two policemen.

AUGUST 7, 1964

After North Vietnamese patrol boats engage a U.S. destroyer in the Gulf of Tonkin, Congress overwhelmingly approves a resolution granting President Johnson nearly unlimited power to use military force in Vietnam without a formal declaration of war.

SEPTEMBER 27, 1964

The Warren Commission, appointed by President Johnson to investigate the Kennedy assassination and chaired by Chief Justice Earl Warren, concludes that gunman Lee Harvey Oswald acted alone.

On November 22, 1963, with the president's widow looking on, Vice President Lyndon Johnson takes the oath of office aboard Air Force One.

barring discrimination in public places and employment; the Voting Rights Act of 1965, which outlawed poll taxes, literacy tests, and other barriers that white southerners had erected to keep blacks from voting; Medicaid and Medicare; federal aid to education; environmental protection laws; food stamps; Head Start; public radio and television; consumer protections; and much more.

Many of Johnson's legislative achievements rested on his brilliant deal making. An exchange he had with Sen. Frank Church of Idaho said it all: "I voted against you because I was following the lead of [columnist] Walter Lippmann," Church told Johnson about his opposition to a White House proposal. "Fine," LBJ replied. "Next time you need a dam, go ask Walter Lippmann."

Lyndon Johnson's courtship of Claudia Taylor, nicknamed Lady Bird, was excessively brief. On their first date, he proposed. "I thought it was some kind of joke," she remembered. As first lady, Mrs. Johnson was best known for her efforts to "beautify" American public spaces, particularly U.S. highways. ("Alas, we never did think of a better word," she has said.)

A GREAT IRONY OF JOHNSON'S presidency, however, is that its accomplishments touched off a powerful counterreaction that has since dominated American politics. Beginning with Richard Nixon's successful campaign for president in 1968, conservative politicians struck responsive chords with voters when they charged that Lyndon Johnson had oversold the idea that government bureaucracies could transform America into a modern-day Eden. During the 1980 presidential campaign, Ronald Reagan told a sympathetic public that America had indeed fought a war on poverty, and poverty had won. Reagan also gained popularity for championing the idea that government wasn't the solution but the problem. A decade later, when Bill Clinton presided over radical welfare reform, the policy shift was considered an implicit repudiation of LBJ's "failed" War on Poverty.

Although since his death in 1973 Johnson has received little credit for what he did as president, that may be changing. Much has transpired recently— the end of the Cold War, diminished recriminations over Vietnam—that suggests Americans may finally be ready to reconsider their opinion of Johnson.

The war that Lyndon Johnson fought in Vietnam embodies another of the great ironies that defined his

When this picture ran on the front pages of newspapers in April 1964, the ASPCA demanded to know why the president insisted on picking up his beagles, named Him and Her, by their ears. "To make them bark," Johnson replied contemptuously.

presidency. Specifically, Johnson saw himself as a domestic and not a foreign policy leader. He once said, not altogether jokingly, that "foreigners are not like the folks I'm used to." Presidential historian Eric Goldman has emphasized this point, explaining that Johnson considered foreign policy "something you had, like measles, and got over with as quickly as possible."

This photograph of Johnson with Abe Fortas *(whom he later elevated to the Supreme Court) graphically illustrates the physical intimidation widely known as the Johnson Treatment.*

Despite Johnson's reluctance to place overseas concerns at the center of his presidency, the Vietnam War consumed much of his administration. Tape recordings of Oval Office conversations that he made secretly during his presidency reveal a man deeply troubled by his substantial commitment of blood and treasure to the increasingly draining fighting in Vietnam. Yet the compulsion he felt to escalate U.S. involvement was too strong to resist. Johnson believed, correctly or not, that failure to meet the Communist challenge in Southeast Asia would lead to a "domino effect," as neighboring countries, one by one, fell under Communist control. He also worried that "losing" Vietnam, as Truman

"A PRESIDENT'S HARDEST TASK IS NOT TO DO WHAT IS RIGHT, BUT TO KNOW WHAT IS RIGHT."

—State of the Union address, 1965—

had "lost" China, would touch off another round of McCarthyism at home, resulting in the defeat of his administration by right-wing Republicans who would undo all his cherished domestic reforms.

His judgment clouded by his fears, Johnson made two great errors in dealing with Vietnam. He forgot the proposition that he otherwise diligently observed in all domestic matters—namely, that significant actions affecting millions of Americans needed to rest on a congressional and national consensus. No other president was more pragmatic about that need when it came to passing domestic legislation. Johnson's presidential library, in fact, has in its archive a congressional file entitled, "What Can We Do for You This Week?" Throughout his political life, Johnson demonstrated again and again how masterful he could be at

JUNE 13, 1966

The Supreme Court rules in Miranda v. Arizona *that police must inform suspects of their constitutional rights, including the right to remain silent, before questioning them.*

JANUARY 30–31, 1968

During Tet, the Vietnamese New Year, the Viet Cong launches a major surprise attack. Its size, if not its success, causes many Americans to question their government's claim that South Vietnam is winning the war.

APRIL 4, 1968

James Earl Ray shoots Martin Luther King Jr. in Memphis, where the civil rights leader has been helping organize a garbage collectors' strike. Two months later, Jordanian immigrant Sirhan Sirhan, angered by Robert F. Kennedy's support for Israel, will shoot and kill the New York senator on the night of his momentous victory in the California Democratic presidential primary.

OPPOSITE:

"When I left for Vietnam, the president gave me a small battery-operated tape recorder…so that I could send Lynda occasional recordings," LBJ son-in-law Charles Robb, then a marine captain, recalled. "I think [those tapes] gave him some of the texture of the war at company levels." In this photograph, taken in the Cabinet Room, the president listens to one of Captain Robb's tapes.

Johnson so enjoyed riding in helicopters that in 1965 he had a helicopter seat specially refitted for use as his Oval Office desk chair. The right armrest of the green vinyl chair (shown here) had a built-in ashtray, and its seat cushion could have functioned as a flotation device in the event of a White House flood.

reaching out to and accommodating congressional leaders. He once called a congressman at four o'clock in the morning to lobby him on a bill. "Sorry to be calling you so early in the morning," Johnson began. "Oh, that's all right," the congressman replied. "I was just lying here hoping you would call."

WITH REGARD TO VIETNAM, however, Johnson was unwisely high handed. When he escalated the war in July 1965, sending 100,000 more ground troops to join the fighting, he announced only half the deployment and even this not in a nationally televised speech but during a press conference at which he also announced his nomination of Abe Fortas to the Supreme Court. The following January, when he and his military advisers decided to send in another 120,000 troops, Johnson again attempted to conceal the move, this time by resorting to number games. Hoping to defuse worries about another costly escalation of the war, Johnson hid the full extent of the deployment by announcing it piecemeal, as individual ten-thousand-troop increases once a month for the next twelve months. Later, of course, when a stalemate in the fighting triggered strong opposition to the war, critics complained that Johnson had misled the country, and he lost political control. By March 1968, Johnson was so unpopular that he decided not to run for another term.

Johnson's historical reputation, like his presidency, will remain the focus of considerable debate, and his standing with the public will rise and fall with popular attitudes regarding the value of government

"HE WANTED EVERYONE WITH HIM ALL THE TIME, AND WHEN THEY WEREN'T, IT BROKE HIS HEART."

—Max Frankel—

activism, particularly in relation to the solving of domestic problems. Yet there are two certainties about Johnson: One is that his prestige will always suffer from his having been the only American president to lose a war. The other is that his larger-than-life personality, coupled with his significant record of both achievement and defeat, will ensure that, unlike so many other presidents, he will never be forgotten.

★ ★ ★

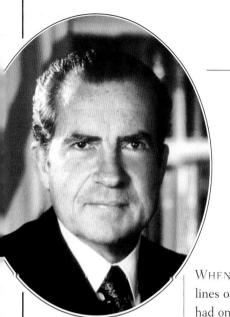

Richard M. Nixon

37ᵗʰ President · 1969–1974

Tom Wicker

Even after the trauma *of Watergate, many Americans honored Richard M. Nixon when he died at the ripe old age of eighty-one. After all, he'd been with them, almost one of them, for a very long time.*

Nixon was a repressed *intellectual who presented himself as an outgoing politician. Relating to ordinary voters was always difficult for him, but it probably helped that he genuinely liked bowling. He even owned his own ball (shown below).*

WHEN RICHARD NIXON WAS buried at San Clemente in 1994, long lines of mourners stood in a hot southern California sun outside what had once been the Western White House. The occasion was broadcast on national television, and many prominent Americans paid high tribute to the memory of the thirty-seventh president of the United States.

To quite a few others, such honors seemed paradoxical, misplaced. Hadn't Nixon been the first president forced to resign under the certainty of impeachment? Wasn't he the brooding loner who for years had lied to his family, his friends, and the nation about the Watergate scandal? Wasn't he the self-styled "gut fighter" who had never quite shed his early notoriety as an implacable Red hunter? The faintly menacing hawk who had prolonged the war in Vietnam and longed to punish the enemies he perceived at every side?

Richard Nixon was all those things. Even in his coffin, he still was Tricky Dick—the "chronic campaigner" (as Lyndon Johnson had called him), a threatening political figure for going on half a century, the Republican that Democrats and liberals most loved to hate. Enigmatic, opportunistic, resentful of the many who'd had easier lives than his, convinced that people—particularly those in the press—didn't like him and that myriad "Nixon haters" were out to "get" him, Richard Nixon bore the scars, real and imagined, of a single-minded thirty-year ambition to win the presidency.

Those long funeral lines were not so surprising, however; those mourners might well have thought they were honoring one of their own. The reverse side of Nixon's early and ruthless anti-Communism, after all, was an outspoken, sentimental patriotism shared by many of his countrymen. His quick rise and ultimate longevity in politics, his vocal belief in hard work and traditional values, his fabled pertinacity, exemplified the national will to "get ahead." Even his reputation for sharp practice in a political system widely considered "dirty" anyway earned him a certain understanding from the many Americans who had also thought it necessary to cut a few corners in their own lives.

Richard Nixon was chosen by a major party (the Republicans) to run on five national tickets, a distinction shared only by FDR.

In the 1960s, moreover, when longhaired young people "dropped out and turned on," Nixon stood steadfastly with the "squares." Earnestly pursuing both the Cold War and the conflict in Vietnam, he reflected what he called the "silent majority" in America, which respected tough guys and tough policies—even as he also recognized the prevalent dread of nuclear war and sought détente with the Soviet Union.

WHATEVER NIXON THOUGHT, and in spite of his known flaws, a lot of Americans obviously did like him—enough to make the 1960 presidential election about as close as an election can be in a continental democracy. In that national referendum, beard-shadowed, often-derided Dick Nixon received just about as many votes (49.5 percent of the total) as did the stylish, charismatic Democrat (49.7 percent) who in memory has become something of a young American emperor. John F. Kennedy defeated Nixon that year by only 119,000 votes out of nearly 70 million cast. A shift of fewer than 10,000 votes in Illinois, Missouri, and Hawaii would have elected Nixon, who even in defeat carried four more states than Kennedy did.

Supposedly left on the trash heap of politics after his razor-edge loss to Kennedy—which, in the most selfless act of his career, even Tricky

BORN
January 9, 1913

BIRTHPLACE
Yorba Linda, California

DIED
April 22, 1994

PARTY AFFILIATION
Republican

CHILDREN
Patricia, Julie

MAJOR EVENTS

APRIL 30, 1970

Nixon announces on television that he has ordered U.S. troops across the South Vietnamese border into Cambodia, where he believes North Vietnamese forces are hiding. Four days later, National Guardsmen fire into a crowd of students at Kent State University protesting the invasion. Four are killed.

MAY 26, 1972

In Moscow, President Nixon and Soviet premier Leonid Brezhnev sign the first strategic arms limitation treaty. The landmark SALT I accord limits nuclear defense systems and freezes the number of missiles on each side.

JANUARY 22, 1973

The Supreme Court rules in the case of Roe v. Wade that every woman has the constitutional right to obtain an abortion during the first three months of her pregnancy.

Although Nixon didn't pick up the nickname until his 1950 Senate campaign against Helen Gahagan Douglas (whom he dubbed the Pink Lady), his murky, repellent Tricky Dick persona was already in evidence during his first term in the House.

Nixon had only one serious relationship. In 1937, he met Pat Ryan, a former movie extra who had recently moved to Nixon's hometown of Whittier, California, to teach shorthand and typing at the local high school. Hearing that a pretty new teacher had joined the community theater, Nixon auditioned for a role. He proposed that night. "I thought he was nuts," Pat said later.

Dick didn't challenge—and another defeat in an ill-advised race for governor of California, Nixon staged a remarkable political comeback and was finally elected president in 1968. Perhaps even more remarkable, after his forced resignation from the White House in 1974, was the personal comeback in which he managed to reestablish himself by the time of his death in 1994 as an elder statesman, a sort of "wise old head," particularly in foreign affairs.

EVEN SO, NIXON REMAINED unable to escape the prominent legacies of Watergate and resignation that have tended to dominate his memory. These legacies, along with the derision and dislike heaped upon Tricky Dick to this day, have obscured a distinctly un-Republican aspect of his first term that few now remember. A few examples: school desegregation (more schools, particularly in the South, were desegregated in 1970 than in any year since 1954); the Family Assistance Plan, designed to replace welfare with a federally guaranteed minimum income (a revolutionary proposal ultimately rejected by a Democratic Congress); the creation of the Environmental Protection Agency; the first strong affirmative-action scheme (the Philadelphia Plan, requiring construction unions in that city to accept qualified black members); a comprehensive health insurance plan so radical in 1971 that it went nowhere; and, not least, the replacement of the draft with the volunteer army (a "market solution," Nixon's advisers called it).

The first Nixon administration may have been most remarkable, however, for "Nixonomics"—an economic policy that caused a supposedly conservative president to "jawbone" business to keep prices down and employment up; then to proclaim himself a "Keynesian" and propose a "full-employment budget" with a built-in deficit; and finally to become the first president in history to impose wage and price controls in peacetime. Perhaps even more shocking to economic orthodoxy, Nixon took the nation off the gold standard. Yet even this was less sensational than what appeared to be a remarkable personal turnaround, the so-called "opening to China" that he accomplished in 1971. For such a move, critics cried, the old Red-baiting Tricky Dick would have pilloried any other president. Its success, however, stifled all such complaints and enabled even as partisan a president as Nixon to call himself at last a "statesman."

Henry Kissinger (shown here with the president aboard Air Force One) once described his frequent sessions with Nixon as "excruciatingly long conversations" that went over the same material endlessly.

At home and abroad, however, there were setbacks. Nixon-imposed budget cuts began the long decline of a once-flourishing space program. The president also failed famously to persuade the Senate to approve two southern nominees, Clement Haynsworth and Harold Carswell, for the Supreme Court. An ambitious project to encourage black capitalism accomplished little. Meanwhile, the Organization of Petroleum Exporting Countries (OPEC) ran up oil prices, causing long lines of motorists outside service stations, while rising inflation and unemployment created an unprecedented "stagflation." By the end of 1973, despite Nixonomics, the economy was in its most severe recession since the Great Depression.

Worse was Nixon's inability to end the war in Vietnam, as he had promised and expected to do. His policy of Vietnamization, returning the burden of combat to ineffective South Vietnamese forces, eventually brought U.S. troops home but undermined the military position of the South. Nixon also proved wrong in his assumption that the Soviet Union could or would put pressure on Hanoi to make peace. Perhaps more important, Nixon with his celebrated persistence stuck to the geopolitical view that withdrawal would destroy U.S. credibility and reliability as an ally. Thus, stalemate continued on the battlefield, noisy opposition continued in the streets and on the campuses, and Johnson's war slowly but surely became Nixon's.

> **"THIS IS A MAN OF MANY MASKS. WHO CAN SAY THEY HAVE SEEN HIS REAL FACE?"**
>
> —Adlai E. Stevenson—

As 1972 neared, however, his China diplomacy and the signing of the first strategic arms limitation treaty with the Soviet Union put "the President," as he always tried to refer to himself, in a strong position for reelection. The Democrats cooperated with a ticket headed by George McGovern, a strong opponent of the war but a weak candidate. Nevertheless, Nixon's landslide reelection brought about his downfall and resignation in 1974.

OCTOBER 6, 1973

The Yom Kippur War begins when Egypt and Syria attack Israel on the most sacred of Jewish holidays. Although it suffers early losses, the Israeli army soon pushes into Syria and Egypt, redrawing the map of the Middle East.

OCTOBER 20, 1973

After Special Prosecutor Archibald Cox refuses to give up his fight for the White House tapes, Nixon orders Attorney General Elliot Richardson to fire him. Richardson and his deputy, William Ruckelshaus, both resign rather than carry out the president's order. Finally, Solicitor General Robert H. Bork dismisses Cox, concluding the Saturday Night Massacre.

Extensive television coverage of Nixon's trip to China in February 1972 provided Americans with their first glimpse of life inside a country largely hidden from Western view for more than twenty years.

Nixon and Chinese premier Zhou Enlai review troops at the Beijing airport shortly after Nixon's arrival in China.

In July 1973,
*Nixon told a staffer
that he wanted all the
subpoenaed White House
tapes (made with this tape
recorder) stored under his
bed. The order was never
carried out because it would
have required raising the
ceiling of his bedroom by
at least twenty feet.*

He had left the campaign largely to his Committee to Re-Elect the President, which had contracted with one G. Gordon Liddy to gather intelligence for use against the Democrats. When Liddy's team of former CIA operatives, including several Cubans, were caught breaking into the offices of the Democratic National Committee in Washington's Watergate building, items in their possession suggested a White House connection.

UNTIL THE SUMMER of 1974, Nixon stonewalled, denying all complicity in and knowledge of the break-ins. But during a June 23, 1972, conversation in the Oval Office, Tricky Dick had incautiously agreed to tell the FBI that the Watergate break-in had been a "national security" operation into which the FBI shouldn't inquire. This fabrication, a clear obstruction of justice, was recorded on Nixon's secret taping system. When the June 23 tape—the "smoking gun"—

> ## "I BROUGHT MYSELF DOWN. I GAVE THEM A SWORD. AND THEY STUCK IT IN. AND THEY TWISTED IT WITH RELISH."
>
> *—Interview with David Frost, 1977—*

finally became public in 1974, the president was left with only two choices: resign or be impeached. He chose resignation—and the sixty-three-thousand-dollar annual pension to which it entitled him.

So ended the contradictory presidency of a man both despised and admired, of outstanding ability but flawed character, secretly contemptuous of the Everyman he tried to appear. In his relentless pursuit of the White House, Nixon had accumulated hatreds and insecurities that seemed to grip him even more tightly when he at last achieved the long-sought power. In the apparent haven of the presidency, with bands playing "Hail to the Chief" and men standing up when he entered a room, Nixon had more than ever to lose and gathered a shell of isolation even more defiantly about himself.

Or perhaps, reveling in the success of his dreams, he simply forgot what he had said he had learned during his years of travail—that "the one sure thing about politics is that what goes up comes down, and what goes down often comes up."

OPPOSITE:

On August 9, 1974, *the
Fords escorted the Nixons
from the White House to a
helicopter parked on the
South Lawn. Nixon shook
his successor's hand while
Pat kissed Betty Ford good-
bye. Standing behind them
are Nixon's two daughters,
Tricia and Julie, with
their husbands.*

★ ★ ★

Gerald R. Ford

38th President · 1974–1977

Laura Kalman

"I STOOD ON MY BALCONY AND WATCHED that chopper taking Nixon away after he resigned," *Newsweek*'s Washington bureau chief recalled, "and it was like I was coming out of Buchenwald."

After escorting the Nixons to their helicopter on August 9, 1974, Gerald Ford walked back into the White House and took the oath of office. In his acceptance speech, which he characterized as "a little straight talk among friends," Ford confronted the Watergate scandal directly. "My fellow Americans," he said, "our long national nightmare is over." He'd worried about the sentence being too hard on Nixon, but speechwriter Robert Hartmann insisted it was "what everybody needs to hear…like FDR saying all we have to fear is fear itself."

HARTMANN WAS RIGHT. Ford's acclaimed speech—which underlined his honesty, humility, and desire to heal—enabled Americans to begin contemplating an end to their Watergate ordeal. "The sun is shining again," Senate Majority Leader Mike Mansfield exulted.

A sunny outlook, Mansfield knew, had fueled much of Ford's rise. Unlike Nixon, the new president thrived on camaraderie, conciliation, and compromise. His simple philosophy of life had stayed the same since junior high school: "Everyone, I decided, had more good qualities than bad. If I understood and tried to accentuate those good qualities in others, I could get along much better."

A football scholarship as well as dishwashing and other part-time jobs paid for his education at the University of Michigan, and Ford worked his way through Yale Law School as the university's head boxing and assistant football coach. Although he graduated in the top quarter of his class at both schools, his academic record

Gerald R. Ford once said that he was determined as president to *"replace a national frown with a national smile." Not coincidentally, the revival of another honest, genial Everyman president— Harry Truman—began around this time.*

Ford used this helmet *while playing football at Michigan. An All-America center, he was offered professional contracts by the Green Bay Packers and the Detroit Lions but chose law school instead.*

came as a surprise to most of his later acquaintances, who considered him neither articulate nor very bright. Lyndon Johnson once described him as "the only man I ever knew who can't chew gum and fart at the same time."

But everyone knew that Ford was dependable. After serving in the navy during World War II, he was elected to Congress from heavily Republican Grand Rapids in 1948. Eight terms later, he became House minority leader and dreamed of being speaker. Although Nixon scorned Ford's intelligence, only one member of Congress voted the president's way more often. When Vice President Spiro Agnew resigned in 1973, Ford was the obvious replacement: a Republican loyalist known for his integrity and therefore acceptable to the Democrats who controlled Congress. When Ford succeeded Nixon a year later, his ordinariness was welcome. As Hartmann later observed, few presidents have entered office "with a greater reservoir of public goodwill." And few have enjoyed a happier honeymoon with Congress and the media.

Ford meets with Nixon *in the Oval Office on August 8, 1974, the day that Nixon announced his resignation. According to House Speaker Carl Albert, he and Mike Mansfield, meeting with Nixon in October 1973, gave the president only one choice for Agnew's replacement: Ford.*

Or a shorter one. It ended after just one month with Ford's September 8 pardon of Richard Nixon. Asked about a possible pardon during his vice-presidential confirmation hearings, Ford had answered, "I do not think the public would stand for it." But a pardon, he now reasoned, would remove his administration from Watergate's shadow and save the country from a long, tumultuous trial. Although no evidence has ever surfaced that Ford made a secret deal for the presidency (as some

BORN
July 14, 1913

BIRTHPLACE
Omaha, Nebraska

PARTY AFFILIATION
Republican

CHILDREN
Michael, John, Steven, Susan

MAJOR EVENTS

SEPTEMBER 12, 1974

Violence erupts on the first day of school in Boston, where a federal judge has ordered busing to promote integration. Many white parents and students riot rather than accept black students into their schools.

SEPTEMBER 5, 1975

Lynette "Squeaky" Fromme, a disciple of Charles Manson, attempts to shoot President Ford in Sacramento. Although loaded, her gun doesn't fire. On September 22 in San Francisco, Sara Jane Moore will pull a revolver from her purse and get off a shot at Ford, missing him completely.

NOVEMBER 26, 1975

After the state passes a tax hike to finance New York City's mounting debt, Ford changes his mind and agrees to help. His earlier threat to veto a federal bailout had prompted the Daily News to run the headline: "Ford to City: Drop Dead."

This photograph was taken on September 5, 1975, only moments after Lynette "Squeaky" Fromme attempted to shoot President Ford.

Ford had stumbled *in public before, particularly while skiing, but his awkward fall down the steps of Air Force One on June 2, 1975, was treated differently by the press. Afterward, it was much more common to hear the line, attributed to LBJ, that Ford had played too much football with his helmet off.*

As first lady, *Betty Ford championed women's rights, including the right to an abortion. After September 1974, when doctors detected a lump in her breast, she waged a public campaign to increase awareness of breast cancer and encourage breast exams. In 1978, following her own treatment for alcohol and prescription drug abuse, she again went public so that others might benefit from her experience. The Betty Ford Center, opened in 1982, quickly became a national leader in treating drug and alcohol dependency.*

have charged), the Nixon pardon destroyed nearly as much trust in government as the Watergate scandal itself. Afterward, few still thought the sun was shining.

Ford's popularity was further eroded by the state of the economy. According to an August 1974 *New York Times* assessment, Ford inherited "the worst inflation in the country's peacetime history, the highest interest rates in a century, [and] a stagnant economy with large-scale unemployment in prospect." The upshot was stagflation, meaning persistent high inflation coupled with stagnant consumer demand and high unemployment. Downplaying the unemployment figures, Ford asked Congress to slash spending and raise taxes. Labeling inflation "public enemy number one," he announced "an all-out nationwide volunteer mobilization" to "whip inflation now." Meanwhile, the economy plunged into its worst slump since the 1930s.

Ford seemed to remain in denial: "I didn't think it would be wise for me as president to stand up and say, 'Yes, we're in a recession.'" So he refused to ease unemployment (through pump priming) and insisted that he wouldn't change his mind. He said specifically that he would make no "180-degree turn" from his fight against inflation. Yet that's exactly what he did in early 1975 when his administration announced its

> ## "I AM A FORD, NOT A LINCOLN."
>
> —
>
> *Vice-presidential acceptance speech, 1973*

support for a tax cut to jump-start the economy. (Press Secretary Ron Nessen wisecracked that Ford had turned only 179 degrees.)

The Democratic Congress, however, enacted a tax cut far higher than the president wanted and gutted his energy program, designed to promote domestic production by decontrolling crude oil and natural gas prices. As Ford recognized, Congress's energy plan ran "counter to my strategy of saving energy by raising prices," but he reluctantly went along despite the protests of conservative Republicans. Usually, Ford was more stubborn. In his half term as president, Mr. Veto rejected sixty-six bills (compared to forty-two vetoed by Nixon). The resulting legislative stalemate added a new phrase to the American political vocabulary: "gridlock."

In March 1975, after condemning congressional irresponsibility (but then signing the tax cut), Ford flew to Palm Desert for a vacation. It was a mistake. Television footage of Ford golfing while the nation suffered hard times would have been bad enough, but nightly broadcasts detailing the collapse of South Vietnam made his political problems worse.

Convinced that the United States must "stand up to aggression" or else "lose our credibility around the world," Ford (spurred by Secretary of State Henry Kissinger) asked Congress for emergency aid—even though his advisers warned him that Congress would surely turn him down. When Congress did refuse, Ford blamed legislative hamstringing for the debacle in Indochina. That led journals as diverse as the *Nation* and the *National Review* to accuse Ford of scapegoating—which, internal administration documents suggest, was indeed his intention.

JULY 4, 1976

The United States observes its bicentennial with celebrations all over the country. The two-hundredth anniversary of the signing of the Declaration of Independence is marked with the ringing of the Liberty Bell in Philadelphia, a jazz marathon in New Orleans, and a parade of "tall ships" up the Hudson River in New York City.

WHILE THE PRESIDENT and Congress bickered, the situation worsened. By mid-April, the Khmer Rouge had won control of Cambodia, and in Vietnam, the North Vietnamese were overrunning province after province. The evacuation of Americans had begun, but it was proceeding slowly. The North Vietnamese had privately promised Washington that they would delay occupying Saigon until the Americans left, so Ford kept Americans in Saigon to give the armed forces more time to evacuate South Vietnamese whom the Communists had marked for death. When North Vietnamese rockets hit Tan Son Nhut Airport, however, Ford knew there was little time left. He ordered the final pullout on April 29, but he'd waited too long to use fixed-wing aircraft. In order for the last helicopter to lift off the roof of the U.S. embassy, its marine gunners had to shoot at the bitter South Vietnamese being left behind.

Two weeks later, a Khmer Rouge gunboat captured the U.S. merchant ship *Mayaguez,* claiming she had invaded Cambodian waters. Embarrassed by what he called "our humiliating retreat from Cambodia and South Vietnam," Ford seized the opportunity to rescue American crew and credibility. The May 14 military operation coordinated naval attacks and aerial bombing with a marine invasion of the island on which the crew was being held. Forty-one servicemen died (and another fifty were wounded) in saving forty *Mayaguez* sailors. When the mission ended, Ford covered it with glory. "[T]he psychological boost the incident [gave] us as a people was significant," he insisted. "All of a sudden, the gloomy national mood began to fade."

Although prepared to battle Congress in domestic affairs, Ford (shown here with Soviet premier Leonid Brezhnev in December 1974) expected the same free hand in foreign policy enjoyed by his postwar predecessors. He was furious when Congress tried to tie his hands on matters ranging from Angola to Cyprus to Vietnam.

Hoping to reduce inflation, Ford wore a WIN button and promised one to every American who enlisted in his Whip Inflation Now campaign.

"CONGRESS MADE JERRY FORD PRESIDENT."

—

Speaker of the House Carl Albert

OPPOSITE:

During an October 1976 *debate with Carter, Ford declared, "There is no Soviet domination of Eastern Europe, and there never will be under a Ford administration"—a mistake he compounded by stonewalling for five days before acknowledging his error. The gaffe was significant not because it alienated Polish-American voters, but because it seemed to prove a point hinted at by the media: that Ford lacked the intelligence to govern.*

It didn't help Ford, who in early June fell down a flight of stairs while deplaning in Salzburg. The tumble made him look foolish, but he'd fallen down before, and he assured Ron Nessen that the media would soon lose interest in his missteps. "I was wrong," he later realized. "From that moment on, every time I stumbled or bumped my head or fell in the snow, reporters zeroed in on that to the exclusion of almost all else." As comedians lampooned him on television, the editor of his daily news summary mourned Ford's transformation from "good-hearted, not-very-bright jock" to "klutz."

FORD'S POLICIES also suffered. He had the misfortune of becoming president as the mood of his party shifted right. Détente was one casualty. With the July 1975 Helsinki Accords, the West formally recognized the postwar division of Europe and the Soviets promised to respect human rights. But the agreement, détente's high-water mark, had no enforcement mechanism. Already infuriated by Ford's nomination of liberal Republican Nelson Rockefeller as vice president, GOP conservatives compared the Helsinki Accords to FDR's Yalta "surrender."

And, as Ford recognized, conservative "grumbles swelled to a roar" when first lady Betty Ford, in a *60 Minutes* interview, condoned sex outside marriage, applauded the Equal Rights Amendment, called the Supreme Court's legalization of abortion "the best thing in the world," and speculated that her children had probably smoked marijuana. As Ford said, "I should have known that a primary challenge was inevitable—and prepared for it." But he didn't.

The challenge became official in November, when Ronald Reagan announced he would oppose Ford for the 1976 Republican nomination. Reagan arrived at the convention neck and neck with Ford, but the president's support among uncommitted delegates enabled him to eke out a 1,187–1,070 first-ballot victory. He was sufficiently bruised, though, to begin the general election campaign thirty points behind Democratic nominee Jimmy Carter, and he never recovered.

With the first words of his inaugural address, President Carter paid tribute to Ford: "For myself and for our Nation, I want to thank my predecessor for all he has done to heal our land." Whether or not Ford healed the United States remains debatable; in either case, most Americans now remember him comfortably as the person who restored integrity to the presidency.

★ ★ ★

Jimmy Carter

39th President · 1977–1981

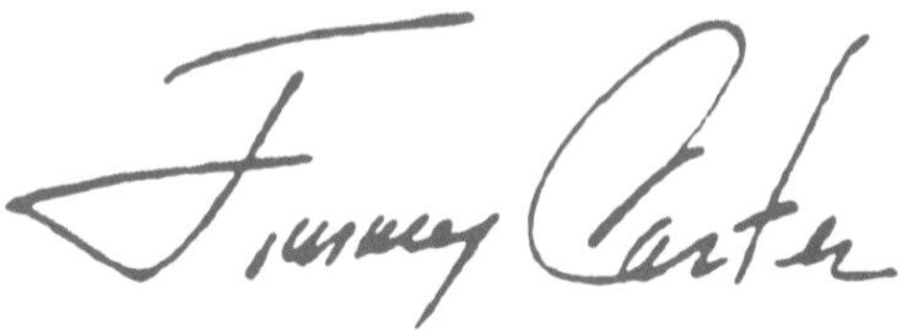

Douglas Brinkley

Jimmy Carter was elected by a public grown leery of political sophistication. Americans were eager for a leader whose wife, on asking the White House chef whether he could prepare certain Carter family favorites, was told, "Yes, ma'am. We've been fixing that kind of food for the servants for a long time."

AS ODD AS IT SEEMS that a presidential candidate could run on the slogan "Jimmy Who?," the wonder remains that he won. Yet in America's bicentennial year, Democrat James Earl Carter Jr. did indeed edge out incumbent Gerald R. Ford to become the first president ever born in the Deep South. Carter's platform pretty much came down to what he told a crowd in Sacramento on May 20, 1976: "All I want is the same thing you want: to have a nation with a government that is as good and honest and decent and competent and compassionate and as filled with love as are the American people."

THE PECULIAR TIMES inspired Americans to find their leader in a Bible-spouting peanut farmer from Plains, Georgia, whose only prior experience with the federal government came working under Hyman Rickover in the U.S. Navy's fledgling nuclear submarine program. When Carter's father died in 1953, the twenty-eight-year-old Annapolis graduate left the navy to take over the family peanut farm (and other businesses), which he ran until politics beckoned a decade later. He served in the Georgia state senate (1963–67) and as governor (1971–75) before launching his unlikely presidential campaign.

The soft-drawling, broad-grinning Carter took pride in his ignorance of Washington's ways. This was welcome two years after Richard Nixon's destruction by his own chicanery, especially coming from a seemingly sincere born-again Christian who emphasized his compassion for the poor. Watergate-weary Americans swooned when Carter told TV interviewer Bill Moyers, "If I'm elected, at the end of four years or eight years I hope people will say, 'You know, Jimmy Carter made a lot of mistakes, but he never told me a lie.'"

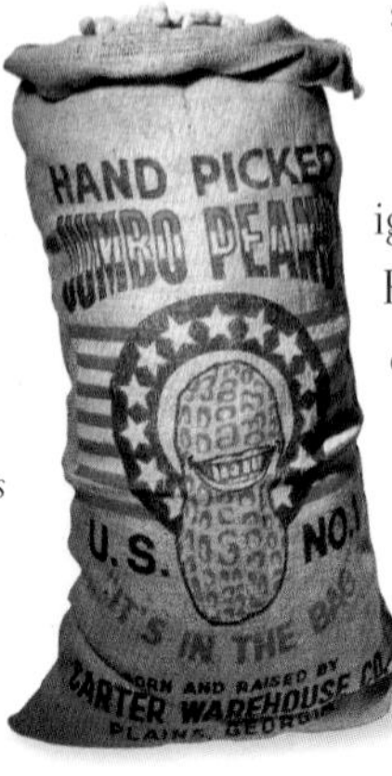

Using modern farming techniques he learned from the local agricultural station, Carter steadily improved yields on his family farm. The peanuts he grew were packed for sale in gunnysacks such as this one.

For twelve days in September 1978, Carter hosted Begin (left) and Sadat at Camp David. He called the summit to work out differences that had arisen since Sadat's groundbreaking visit to Israel in November 1977. Several times the talks nearly broke down, but Carter always found a way to keep them going.

BORN
October 1, 1924

BIRTHPLACE
Plains, Georgia

PARTY AFFILIATION
Democrat

CHILDREN
John, James Earl III, Jeffrey, Amy

MAJOR EVENTS

FEBRUARY 24, 1977

Just one month into the new administration, Secretary of State Cyrus Vance announces that the United States will be reducing foreign aid to three nations because of their poor human rights records. The action redeems Carter's campaign pledge to make human rights a central theme of his foreign policy.

JUNE 6, 1978

By a margin of nearly two to one, Californians approve Proposition 13, a ballot measure that dramatically reduces property taxes in the state.

JUNE 28, 1978

In a case brought by white medical school applicant Allan P. Bakke, the Supreme Court rules that racial quotas are an unconstitutional form of reverse discrimination. The Court's decision, however, does permit schools to give minorities special consideration, a practice known as affirmative action.

Given the sad state of the nation's affairs in 1976, it's hard to understand why anyone wanted the job. Indeed, even Carter's critics concede that perhaps no one could have done it any better. Humorist Art Buchwald spoke for many when he quipped at Carter's election, "I worship the very quicksand he walks on."

The refreshingly down-home Carter had some early success reorganizing the federal government, to which he added new cabinet posts for education and energy. But his welfare and tax reform plans went nowhere because Carter unwisely ignored his party's congressional leaders—notably Speaker of the House Thomas P. "Tip" O'Neill, without whose backing no executive initiative had a hope of passing Congress.

But Carter's problems extended well beyond political obtuseness. His plan for ending stagflation, the devastating 1970s combination of rising inflation and stagnant growth, was to cut spending and raise taxes, but it didn't work: Between 1973 and 1980, inflation climbed steadily, and the consumer price index almost doubled. This was not, of course, Carter's fault. In response to the October 1973 Yom Kippur War, Arab members of the Organization of Petroleum Exporting Countries (OPEC) had imposed a ban on oil exports to the United States and other countries that had supported Israel. The oil embargo sent the inflation rate into double digits throughout the industrialized world, and unemployment and interest rates soared also.

What Carter inherited was an economic mess, and ever-rising oil prices kept him from cleaning it up. By the spring of 1979, he had little choice but to decontrol domestic oil prices while OPEC continued to slash production, further jacking up prices at the pump and leaving Americans fuming in hours-long gas lines. Over the July 4 weekend in many states, half the gas stations shut down for lack of anything to sell. (In New York City, the figure was 90 percent.) Carter hadn't created the "energy crisis," but he'd certainly caught the blame for it.

*During the summer of
1945,* Carter was back
home in Plains, having
finished his sophomore year
at Annapolis, when he
surprised his younger sister
Ruth with a request.
He wanted her to fix him
up with Rosalynn Smith,
Ruth's best friend. The
night of their first date,
Carter returned home and
announced that he'd found
the girl he would marry.
Like Carter, Smith was
hardworking, independent,
and determined to explore
the possibilities of life
beyond Plains. Yet
biographers have pointed
out that, by marrying her,
Carter was able to take a
little of Plains with him
into the outside world.

The president retreated to Camp David for eight days to consider the recommendation of his trusted pollster, Pat Caddell, that he stop talking about the specifics of his energy policy and instead speak to Americans about their "crisis of confidence." He invited upward of 150 best-and-brightest thinkers to opine on the subject, and most agreed with Caddell.

On Sunday night, July 15, 1979, Carter delivered on national television a speech in which he averred: "Our people are losing [their] faith not only in government itself but in their ability as citizens to serve as the ultimate rulers and shapers of our democracy." He afterward pronounced the speech "one of my best," and the press and public seemed to agree—until the president almost immediately asked for the resignations of his cabinet and top staff, giving rise to the perception that a crisis existed in government and forever tainting his performance. Although he never used the word, the address came to be known as the "malaise speech," and it later rankled many who, with hindsight, considered it an attempt by Carter to blame the country for his own failures, particularly in managing the economy.

In fact, what Carter had in mind was as much foreign as domestic policy—specifically, America's reluctance to redefine its place in the world and in history. As he had explained in an October 1976 campaign speech, "A strong nation, like a strong person, can afford to be gentle, firm, thoughtful, and restrained. It can afford to extend a helping hand to others. It's a weak nation, like a weak person, that must behave with bluster and boasting and rashness and other signs of insecurity."

Carter stuck to his principles, even if most of his bold foreign policy initiatives met with considerable opposition. He persevered, and this determination enabled him to rescue more than a few victories from fiery congressional debate: He pushed through the Senate a treaty giving back

Ensign Carter
with the former
Rosalynn Smith
on their wedding
day, July 1946.
Carter had just
graduated 59th in
his naval academy
class of 820.

the Panama Canal, normalized relations with the People's Republic of China, and shepherded Egyptian president Anwar Sadat and Israeli prime minister Menachem Begin through the negotiations that produced the Camp David Accords.

Carter also threw himself into promoting international human rights and restructuring U.S. foreign policy around his belief that "we should live our lives as though Christ were coming this afternoon." When the Soviet Union invaded Afghanistan in December 1979, the president responded with a grain embargo and two even more unpopular steps: a boycott of the 1980 Moscow Olympics and suspension of the SALT II arms control talks. These difficulties he could have weathered, but his caring policy soon dragged him into the debacle that would ruin his presidency.

> "IF THE MISERY OF OTHERS LEAVES YOU INDIFFERENT AND WITH NO FEELING OF SORROW, THEN YOU CANNOT BE CALLED A HUMAN BEING."
>
> —*Memoirs, 1982*—

Carter's original policy regarding the ousted shah of Iran was geostrategically sound: Don't let him into the country. But when the exiled dictator needed cancer treatment, Carter granted his October 1979 request for a visa on humanitarian grounds. It was this act of compassion that inspired a mob of angry young Iranians in Teheran to storm the U.S. embassy on November 4 and take fifty-two Americans hostage, making their release contingent on the extradition of the shah. After months of fruitless negotiations, the president authorized a military rescue; however, the bungling of the April 1980 mission only deepened the nation's sense of humiliation. Carter was pilloried, and his popularity plummeted to record lows in polls taken just months before the 1980 election.

Whether they blamed him more for the Iranian hostage crisis or for the ailing U.S. economy, most Americans had decided they'd had enough of Jimmy Carter, and they resoundingly denied him a second term in favor of sunny-minded but tough-talking former actor. As if on cue, minutes after Ronald Reagan's inauguration, Iran freed the hostages (prompted largely by Carter's decision to release several billion dollars of Iranian assets frozen in U.S. banks). Nevertheless, the freeing of the hostages was seen as proof of the Ayatollah Ruhollah

MARCH 28, 1979

At 4:00 A.M., workers at the Three Mile Island nuclear power plant near Harrisburg, Pennsylvania, mistakenly shut down a cooling pump, causing a nuclear reactor core to overheat. When dangerous radioactive gases are released into the air, nearby residents are quickly evacuated. Had the core melted down (which it nearly did), the huge explosion would have killed thousands.

JUNE 18, 1979

Following a five-year negotiation, President Carter and Soviet premier Leonid Brezhnev sign the SALT II agreement. This arms limitation treaty, which faces difficult Senate ratification hearings, will be withdrawn by Carter in December when Soviet troops invade Afghanistan.

Since leaving office, *in addition to making peace, Carter has been notably supportive of the Christian housing ministry Habitat for Humanity. Each year, he spends a week helping volunteers build an affordable home for a needy family.*

Jimmy Carter's election naturally focused some attention on his three siblings— particularly his brother, Billy, who became a minor sensation. A former gas station owner and peanut broker who later sold mobile homes, Billy Carter seemed to embody the worst northern stereotypes of drinking, drawling southerners. His endorsement of Billy Beer made a great deal of marketing sense but, unfortunately, not a lot of money.

OPPOSITE:

Carter's public relations problems stemmed from the tin ear he had for public opinion, and he was just as maladroit when it came to forming political alliances. Early on, he alienated the Democratic establishment when he passed over Washington professionals and instead staffed his administration with a posse of eccentric young Georgians. In this way and many others, he made it clear that he trusted the good ol' boys even more than his own cabinet.

Khomeini's nervousness at the prospect of dealing with Reagan. This cleared the way for the new administration to abandon Carter's moral approach to foreign policy in favor of a much more realpolitik stance.

In the end, as former national security adviser Zbigniew Brzezinski wrote in his 1983 memoir *Power and Principle*, "Carter was not good at public relations. He did not fire enthusiasm in the public or inspire fear in his adversaries. He was trusted, but—very unfairly—that trust was in him as a person but not in him as a leader. He had ambitious goals for this nation, both at home and abroad, and yet he did not succeed in being seen as a visionary or in captivating the nation's imagination. His personal qualities—honesty, integrity, religious conviction, compassion— were not translated in the public mind into statesmanship with a historical sweep."

> ## "JIMMY CARTER WAS THE SMARTEST PUBLIC OFFICIAL I'VE EVER KNOWN. THE RANGE AND EXTENT OF HIS KNOWLEDGE WERE ASTONISHING."
>
> —*Speaker of the House Thomas P. "Tip" O'Neill*—

THAT CHANGED ONCE CARTER left office and dedicated his postpresidential career to active humanitarian service. In February 1989, for example, he helped mediate an end to the long Nicaraguan civil war between the Sandinistas and the contra rebels, and three months later he led the international team of observers that pronounced Panama's elections a fraud. Although his efforts to mediate civil disputes in Sudan and Ethiopia met with less success, in June 1994, with the blessing of the Clinton administration, he accepted an invitation from President Kim Il Sung to visit North Korea and returned from Pyongyang with an agreement outlining an end to North Korea's nuclear weapons program. He also carried a letter to South Korean president Kim Young Sam requesting a summit meeting to discuss reunification.

In addition, Carter has continued to work tirelessly for the health and human rights of poor and oppressed people everywhere. Twenty years after voters booted Jimmy Who? from office, Carter has become Jimmy Everywhere, renowned the world over as the epitome of the caring, compassionate, best sort of American statesman. His postpresidency has made him an exemplar of behavior for all national leaders in retirement.

★ ★ ★

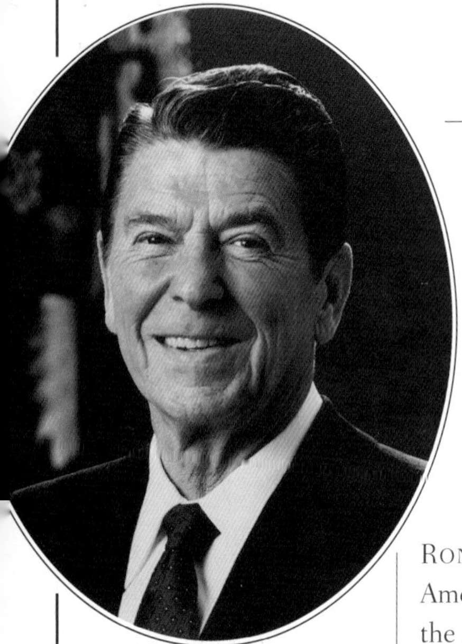

Ronald Reagan

40ᵗʰ President · 1981–1989

James T. Patterson

As Ted Kennedy once noted, Ronald Reagan might forget your name, but he always remembered his goals.

RONALD REAGAN IS AMONG the most complex and puzzling of America's chief executives. An admirer of Franklin D. Roosevelt and the New Deal, he nevertheless hung a portrait of Calvin Coolidge, another idol, in the Cabinet Room of the White House. Like Coolidge, Reagan stood for fiscal restraint, tax reduction, and small government, yet as president he ran up record budget deficits. He was ideological in his rhetoric yet often chose to act the pragmatist: He denounced the Soviet Union as an "evil empire," for example, then did more to moderate the Cold War than any other president.

Although famously charming and gregarious, Reagan was also extraordinarily passive and remote, even with his children. This passivity, and his at-times tenuous command of facts (he once asserted that acid rain was caused by an excess of trees), led many to question his intelligence. Democratic political insider Clark Clifford called him an "amiable dunce," and others wondered publicly whether he was merely a puppet of the right. If so, he was an extremely popular one. Twice elected by substantial margins, Ronald Reagan left office in 1989 with a compelling public approval rating of 70 percent.

Reagan was a compulsive doodler; his staff thought it helped him think. "If you gave him a pencil and said these are the options," one aide explained, "he would start doodling around…and the first thing you knew…you had a whole new option."

What the public liked was clear. Reagan took office when the nation faced stagflation at home and frustration abroad. In response, the serenely self-confident Republican repeatedly proclaimed the greatness of the American way of life, often invoking Lincoln's poignant description of the United States as "the last best hope of earth." By the time he left office, the country was prosperous and Communism was reeling. Thanks in part to Ronald Reagan, a tireless cheerleader for democratic values, the American people found renewed faith in their national institutions. This was his major accomplishment as president.

Reagan meets the press *on the first anniversary of John Hinckley's assassination attempt. The skills that he honed as an entertainer made him seem likable and appealing, but his gift went well beyond that: He made people want to believe him.*

Reagan's early life offers a few clues that might explain his later serenity. He was born in Tampico, Illinois, in 1911, the son of Jack Reagan, a shoe salesman and a great raconteur (a trait that his son inherited). Jack constantly moved his wife and two sons about in search of success, but he was an alcoholic and never struck it rich. Reagan said later, "We didn't live on the wrong side of the tracks, but we lived so close to them we could hear the whistle real loud."

Jack was a Catholic of Irish background, while Reagan's mother, Nelle, found consolation in the Disciples of Christ Church. Ronald was baptized in her faith and later embraced its optimistic belief that those who worked hard would get ahead. Peggy Noonan, a Republican speechwriter, later concluded that Reagan grew up in a "sad home." Still, she speculated, he drew strength from his childhood. He "thought it was his job to cheer everyone up."

As a boy Reagan was popular, playing sports, acting in plays, and winning election as student body president at both Dixon (Illinois) High and Eureka College, also in Illinois. After his graduation from Eureka in 1932, Reagan took a job as a sports announcer in Des Moines before moving in 1937 to Hollywood, where he embarked on a film career. Although he was not a star—he described himself as "the Errol Flynn of the B's"—he ultimately appeared in fifty-two movies.

During the Great Depression, Reagan became an avid Democrat, in part because his father found work with New Deal relief agencies. During the Truman years, he headed the liberal Screen Actors Guild and was an

BORN
February 6, 1911

BIRTHPLACE
Tampico, Illinois

PARTY AFFILIATION
Republican

CHILDREN
Maureen, Michael, Patricia, Ronald

MAJOR EVENTS

JUNE 30, 1982

The deadline set by Congress passes with the Equal Rights Amendment still three states short of ratification. Congress extended the deadline in 1978, but no additional states have ratified the ERA in that time.

OCTOBER 23, 1983

A truck loaded with dynamite explodes inside the U.S. compound in Beirut. The blast kills 241 sleeping marines, sent to Lebanon by President Reagan as part of an international peacekeeping force.

NOVEMBER 25, 1986

The White House admits that profits from secret sales of arms to Iran have been used to fund the Nicaraguan contras. The diversion clearly violates the Boland Amendment banning military aid to the contras. National Security Adviser John Poindexter resigns, and Poindexter aide Oliver North is fired.

Reagan was the first president to have been divorced. His first marriage, to actress Jane Wyman, ended in 1949. Three years later, he married Nancy Davis. Unlike Jane, Nancy never complained about her husband's political activities and the time that they consumed. Instead, she gave up her acting career to become his most loyal supporter and one of his toughest and shrewdest advocates.

active member of the California chapter of Americans for Democratic Action, a liberal anti-Communist organization that normally backed Democratic political candidates.

Several developments then conspired to shift his politics to the right. Among the most important was his 1952 marriage to Nancy Davis, whose father was a conservative physician. Another was his new job as corporate spokesman for the General Electric Company, which employed Reagan from 1954 until 1962, the year that he became a Republican. Reagan also became familiar to millions of Americans as the host for eight years of television's *General Electric Theater.*

DURING THE 1964 election campaign, Reagan attracted a great deal of attention when he delivered a nationally televised speech on behalf of GOP presidential candidate Barry Goldwater. Impressed by his effective delivery, conservative Republicans in California backed him for governor in 1966. Reagan won that year and again in 1970. Running for president in 1980 on a highly conservative platform, he easily outpolled incumbent Jimmy Carter, whose administration had become very unpopular. Unemployment that year topped 7 percent, inflation was at 13 percent, and the prime interest rate at 15 percent.

When Reagan's coattails in 1980 proved long enough to win Republicans control of the Senate for the first time since 1955, phrasemakers began speaking of a Reagan Revolution. Then, four years later, Reagan's decimation of Democrat Walter Mondale moved the center of American political discourse even farther to the right. Democrats, however, maintained control of the House throughout the 1980s and recaptured the Senate in 1986—thus ensuring that, while significant, Reagan's political legacy was far from revolutionary.

As president, Reagan spoke for many staunchly conservative positions. In his first inaugural address, he declared that "government is not the solution to our problem." When he tried to cut federal programs, however, organized constituencies prevented significant changes. Instead he concentrated on achieving tax reduction, which he promised would "expand our national prosperity, enlarge national incomes, and increase opportunities for all Americans." Working skillfully, he secured the largest tax cut, 25 percent over three years, in U.S. history.

On March 30, 1981, *President Reagan was shot by a man hoping to impress actress Jodie Foster. In the emergency room, a courageous and characteristically upbeat Reagan told his wife, "Honey, I forgot to duck." He even joked with his surgeons: "Please tell me you're all Republicans." The public levity helped conceal how very close he came to dying.*

Economic problems nonetheless threatened to damage Reagan's public standing. To curb inflation, the Federal Reserve Board was keeping interest rates high, and in 1982 unemployment topped 10 percent, its highest level since the Great Depression. The 1981 tax cut, moreover, combined with large increases in military spending to create huge budget deficits. During Reagan's term in office, the national debt rose from $900 million to nearly $2.7 trillion, and despite the president's stated desire for

"APPALLED BY WHAT SEEMS TO ME A LACK OF DEPTH, I STAND IN AWE NEVERTHELESS OF HIS POLITICAL SKILL."

—Speaker of the House Jim Wright—

small government, federal spending increased 11 percent per capita (measured in constant dollars). At the same time, careless deregulation of the savings-and-loan industry saddled the government with an enormous cleanup estimated by some economists at five hundred billion dollars, while hikes in Social Security, state, and local taxes contributed to greater inequalities of income.

Many of Reagan's critics identify his years in office with gross materialism. Yet an improving economy after 1983 helped more than the rich. By 1989, unemployment had fallen to 5.3 percent and inflation to 4.7 percent. Whether Reagan's policies initiated this recovery or merely basked in its glory remains hotly debated. There was no doubt, however, that prosperity had returned, and Reagan happily took credit for it.

Meanwhile, his foreign policies evolved. Early in his presidency he remained an outspoken cold warrior. In 1983 he proposed the Strategic Defense Initiative (SDI), an ambitious plan ("Star Wars," his opponents called it) to erect a space-based missile shield. He also took on left-wing elements in Central America and the Caribbean, sending troops to overthrow a Marxist regime in Grenada, transferring arms to the often brutal government of El Salvador, and maneuvering to aid a predominantly right-wing group of Nicaraguan rebels—contras, they were called.

Then in late 1986, it was revealed that members of Reagan's National Security Council had diverted to the contras profits from secret arms deals with Iran. As details of the subsequent Iran-contra scandal emerged, it became clear that Reagan had either deliberately defied a congressional resolution prohibiting such aid or—as he maintained—

OCTOBER 19, 1987

Two months after reaching a record high, the stock market collapses, with the Dow Jones Industrial Average plunging 508 points in a single day. The panic breaks records set in 1929 on Black Tuesday, but a similar depression will not follow.

DECEMBER 8, 1987

Reagan and Mikhail Gorbachev sign the Intermediate-Range Nuclear Forces Treaty. Unlike previous arms control agreements, which limited the number of specific weapons, the INF treaty actually orders the destruction of warheads.

The Reagans during the 1970s (*left to right*): *Patty, Nancy, the future president, Michael, Maureen, Ron. Reagan's relationships with his children were generally uncomfortable. Michael quarterbacked his high school football team, but Reagan, a lifelong football fan, never saw him play.*

President Reagan delivers a speech in February 1982, two days after his seventy-first birthday.

Political opponents often criticized President Reagan for acting as though he were still playing cowboys in B-grade westerns. He warned air traffic controllers in August 1981 not to strike, and when they did, he fired twelve thousand of them. His uncompromising action appalled labor leaders, but the public loved it.

OPPOSITE:

Reagan, shown here riding in April 1986, adored his Rancho del Cielo retreat in the mountains outside Santa Barbara. He spent nearly an eighth of his presidency (345 days altogether) riding and doing chores at the ranch.

not known what his top aides were doing. The televised congressional investigation that followed badly stained his presidential reputation.

Meanwhile, Reagan was developing a remarkable personal relationship with Soviet premier Mikhail Gorbachev. Between 1985 and 1988, the two world leaders met five times, and in 1987 they signed an agreement calling for the destruction of hundreds of intermediate-range nuclear missiles. Some scholars give Gorbachev the credit for this breakthrough, but others maintain that SDI, which the Soviets couldn't afford to emulate, forced Gorbachev's hand. In any case, Reagan's flexibility contributed to a stunningly unanticipated relaxation of tensions.

YET QUESTIONS LINGER as to which Reagan was the "real" one: the ideologue or the pragmatist? the great man or the dunce? Echoing the opinions of others, authorized biographer Edmund Morris has said that initially he considered the president "shatteringly banal...I couldn't conceive of writing more than a paragraph about him....After three or four meetings, I realized that culturally he was a yahoo and extremely unresponsive in conversation. When you asked him a question about himself, it was like dropping a stone into a well and not hearing a splash."

These characteristics also bothered many contemporaries. He seemed uninterested in policy discussions and, like his idol Coolidge, napped and vacationed a lot. Gaffes peppered his public statements, and he had an unfortunate tendency to make up "facts" spontaneously. (Once Reagan's Alzheimer's disease became public in 1994, many wondered whether the condition had begun to affect him during his second term.) Increasingly, detractors dismissed Reagan (perhaps somewhat enviously) as the Teflon President because, no matter what blunders he committed, dirt never seemed to stick. They argued that, stage-managed by his advisers, the telegenic yet empty-headed Great Communicator did little more than dispense feel-good bromides to the American people. Top aide Michael Deaver did confess later, "We kept apple pie and the flag going the whole time."

These critics miss three points: First, Reagan worked skillfully to accomplish his major goals of lower taxes, a stronger military, and the marginalization of Communism. Second, he had fixed convictions that distinguished him from many other politicians. Third, his infectious optimism made Americans feel better about themselves. He was more than a "communicator." As Reagan himself put it, "I never thought it was my style or the words that I used that made a difference; it was the content."

★ ★ ★

George Bush

41ˢᵗ President · 1989–1993

Herbert S. Parmet

When George Bush *became president, his immediate predecessors had been a peanut farmer and an actor. Bush, however, was unmistakably a member of the country's ruling class.*

For forty years, Bush carried in his wallet a shamrock, a photo of his wife from their engagement announcement, and a remembrance of their daughter Robin, who died of leukemia at age three.

THE NUMBERS "ARE ASTRONOMICAL," the forty-first president dictated for his diary. "The polls, by which we live and die, are up in astronomical heights, and the country is together." Gallup's figures showed 89 percent of Americans approving of Bush's leadership. Euphoria everywhere, he told his little tape recorder, yet the popular support neither satisfied him nor provided a sense of accomplishment. The "issue is how to find a clean end," he noted.

Bush knew that no resolution of the Persian Gulf War would have the finality of the Japanese surrender aboard the battleship *Missouri* that ended World War II. So far he had worked with the United Nations and complied with Security Council resolutions calling for the ejection of Iraqi forces from Kuwait. In full compliance, he had stopped at that point; yet he wished for something more, something definitive to show for the victory, and that would be the complete overthrow of Iraqi dictator Saddam Hussein.

Bush had carried out the UN mandate by building a coalition with contributions from twenty-nine nations. This triumph of American diplomacy over Middle Eastern political and cultural solidarity had been made possible by an Arab League vote, engineered by Secretary of Defense Dick Cheney, in which twelve of the twenty-one members—including, most vitally, Saudi Arabia—expressed their disapproval of the Iraqi invasion. Creating such a multinational response was as fine an example of presidential crisis management, given its scale, as can be found in the twentieth century. From the moment Bush heard that Saddam's troops had entered the Persian Gulf emirate of Kuwait on August 2, 1990, he used his energetic personality to conduct swift and effective diplomacy, much of it waged by telephone.

"President Bush," his special assistant for national security affairs, Brent Scowcroft, has written, "invested an enormous amount of time in personal diplomacy, and, in my opinion, it was indispensable to the success of our foreign policy. His direct relationship with his counterparts had a tremendous affect upon them—most were immensely flattered."

ALTHOUGH THE SON of a Wall Street banker from Greenwich, Connecticut, who later became a U.S. senator, George Bush always set his own goals. Fresh out of Andover and only months after Pearl Harbor, he enlisted in the naval air service and flew fifty-eight combat missions, surviving one by bailing out of his torpedo bomber over the South Pacific after the plane was hit by enemy fire. Following the end of the war and his graduation from Yale, Bush rejected more aristocratic comforts and instead used his ability to form strong personal bonds to succeed as a West Texas oilman and an early builder of the Republican party in Houston. The path for this young man, with a reputation for charm and efficiency, led him from two terms in Congress through a series of high-level appointments to eight years as Ronald Reagan's vice president. When Bush finally succeeded Reagan in 1989, he could hardly have known that Saddam's ambitions would pose the most direct challenge to his personal talents.

The five months of Operation Desert Shield were spent organizing the alliance, mobilizing and deploying the multinational force, demonstrating the inadequacy of economic sanctions, and building domestic political support in the United States for a military offensive. Only when the futility of lesser measures had been fully confirmed did Bush authorize the offensive. Designated Operation Desert Storm, it began on January 17,

Gen. Norman Schwarzkopf shows the president around Saudi Arabia during Bush's Thanksgiving 1990 inspection tour of Operation Desert Shield.

1991, with an aerial pounding of Iraqi military installations in and around Baghdad. Six weeks later, ground troops commenced the liberation of Kuwait—without, however, eradicating Saddam's elusive elite forces, the Republican Guard. So the Gulf War was an incomplete triumph, one that

BORN
June 12, 1924

BIRTHPLACE
Milton, Massachusetts

PARTY AFFILIATION
Republican

CHILDREN
George, Robin, John, Neil, Marvin, Dorothy

MAJOR EVENTS

AUGUST 9, 1989

President Bush commits $166 billion to bail out the nation's numerous failed savings-and-loan institutions. Most political observers blame lax federal regulation during the Reagan years for allowing these banks to risk depositors' money in reckless stock and real estate deals.

DECEMBER 10, 1989

More than forty years of Communist rule ends in Czechoslovakia with the establishment of a new Western-style democracy. The peaceful transfer of power under President Vaclav Havel will be known as the Velvet Revolution.

DECEMBER 20, 1989

President Bush orders the invasion of Panama to overthrow indicted drug trafficker Manuel Noriega. The Panamanian strongman initially takes refuge in the Vatican embassy, but he surrenders after two weeks.

*Bush met sixteen-
year-old* Barbara
Pierce at
a country-club
dance during the
1941 Christmas
holidays. With
Bush away, first
at Andover and
then in the navy,
their relationship
developed
primarily through
letters. Shortly
before he reported to
his navy squadron in
September 1943, they
became secretly engaged.
"I married the first man
I ever kissed," Barbara
recalled. "When I tell this
to my children, they just
about throw up."

President Nixon, shown
here with Bush in January
1970, asked the Texas
congressman to give up his
safe seat that year and run
for the Senate. When Bush
lost, Nixon rewarded him
with the post of UN ambassador. "Bush knows in his
bones what a President
Dukakis could learn only
by an arduous tutelage,"
William F. Buckley Jr.
boasted during the
1988 campaign.

achieved its original objective yet left Saddam Hussein with dangerous capabilities. Continuing the fight, however, would have split the alliance, particularly given the skittishness of Soviet support. In fact, Moscow had already begun reaching out to Baghdad on its own.

Yet, as Bush and the American command knew well, Soviet participation in the coalition was essential—both for Arab cooperation and, ultimately, for the winding down of the Cold War. In particular, Bush's personal relationship with the last Soviet leader, Mikhail Gorbachev, helped remove objections to Western intervention in the region. The Soviet Union was in its last days, and Gorbachev, whose reforms had done much to accelerate the implosion process, had become indispensable to the foreign policy goals of the United States. Bush and his national security people understood that, unless Gorbachev remained in power, it would be difficult to safeguard against the potentially calamitous effects of Moscow's economic collapse and the swift disintegration of the Soviet bloc.

WHEN THE BERLIN WALL was breached in November 1989 and some thought Bush should exult, he restrained himself. "I'm very pleased," he admitted, but he wouldn't "beat [his] chest and dance on the Wall." He later added, "I would have poured gasoline on the embers, an open provocation to the Soviet military to act." Meanwhile, he and Secretary of State James A. Baker III encouraged the process of German reunification, which became official on October 3, 1990.

Bush also resisted the urgings of hotter heads when Gorbachev sent Soviet troops into the Baltics. There was no need—indeed, it would have been counterproductive—for him to intervene or gloat over the plight of the USSR. Pursuing arms control initiatives already begun, Bush met with Gorbachev three times in 1991: in London, Moscow, and Madrid. During the summer, less than three weeks after Bush's July visit to Moscow, Red Army reactionaries within the Communist party staged a coup. Although Boris Yeltsin, then president of the Russian Republic, played the most vital role in putting down the conspirators, Bush never hesitated in backing Gorbachev, his friend in the Kremlin.

In contrast to the overt leadership he displayed during the Gulf War, Bush's relatively quiet diplomacy during the dismantling of the Soviet Union was just the right touch. Meanwhile, he withstood carping about his refusal to break with the Chinese Communists after their massacre of prodemocracy demonstrators at Tiananmen Square in June 1989. In dealing with both Communist superpowers, Bush maintained stability while incrementally improving each relationship.

"I'VE ALWAYS FELT IF THERE'S ONE THING YOU COULD COUNT ON GEORGE BUSH FOR, IT'S DECENCY AND FAIRNESS."

—Atlanta mayor Andrew Young—

Yet his foreign policy successes and the respect he had won from America's allies seemed to count for little during the months following the Gulf War. Among his fellow Republicans, those who had hoped for a "third" Reagan term were disappointed by Bush's drift in a less ideological direction. His vow to bring about a "kinder and gentler nation," made at the GOP's nominating convention in New Orleans, began their disenchantment, which deepened with the gradual disclosure of his lukewarm commitment to the social issues and low-tax orthodoxies of the Republican right.

His White House had too many "Bushies" and too few "Reaganauts" to allay suspicions about the Connecticut Yankee's true faith. Later, conservatives' worst fears were confirmed when Bush capitulated to the Democratic congressional majority and agreed to raise taxes as part of a balanced-budget deal. It's true that, in the face of the $2.7-trillion national debt left by Ronald Reagan, Bush did renege on his famous campaign promise, "Read my lips: No new taxes!" Yet little else about his

AUGUST 19, 1991

Hoping to reverse Gorbachev's reforms, a group of Communist hard-liners seize control of the Soviet government. The coup fails when President Boris Yeltsin of the Russian Republic organizes a general strike and workers take to the streets.

APRIL 29, 1992

A suburban jury acquits four white Los Angeles police officers of beating black motorist Rodney King, despite compelling videotape footage. The riots that follow last three days. Thirty-seven people are killed, and six hundred million dollars' worth of property is destroyed.

Bush and Gorbachev *get to know each other during a break in their June 1990 summit.*

As president, *Bush popularized the sport of horseshoe pitching. He had a horseshoe pit installed at the White House and sponsored annual tournaments. His stiffest competition invariably came from the permanent White House staff—the cooks, housemen, and groundskeepers.*

"I'M A CONSERVATIVE, BUT I'M NOT A NUT ABOUT IT."

—Interview, 1984—

OPPOSITE:

George Bush believed *devoutly in noblesse oblige—the duty of the privileged classes to return to society some of the benefits they enjoyed. He spent most of his adult life serving the American people, yet only rarely did he seem one of them.*

domestic record, which included the Americans with Disabilities Act as well as new clean air and civil rights legislation, sat well with conservatives. Nor did they give him much credit for using his veto power forty-four times to kill Democratic social, regulatory, taxation, and spending measures, not to mention ten abortion-related bills.

Everyone, it seemed, on both the left and the right, thought Bush lacked, as he called it, the "vision thing." One political scientist has even labeled the Bush administration "a custodial presidency." Reacting to this perception, a growing number of activists in the Republican party, led by House Minority Whip Newt Gingrich, eventually concluded that they would be better off without Bush, even if that meant abandoning the White House to the Democrats for a term while they rallied the true believers.

B USH'S APPROVAL RATING had indeed peaked with the end of the Gulf War. A domestic recession, which had become visible even before Saddam Hussein invaded Kuwait, persisted through most of the 1992 campaign. Although the economic numbers righted themselves just before the election, even some within his administration considered Bush's prior expressions of confidence somewhat lame. He did not, as he later acknowledged, persuade enough voters that he understood their problems and shared their dismay.

He was also hurt by a campaign that lacked the vigor of his 1988 effort, in both the acumen of its staff and the enthusiasm of the candidate. Furthermore, this time around he attracted two opponents, and together they proved insuperable. Maverick independent Ross Perot drew a crucial 19 percent of the vote, making crafty Democrat Bill Clinton the winner with 43 percent.

Now that the Cold War seemed over, voters apparently cared more about pocketbook issues than the "new world order" for which the president had been preparing the country and on which he had been focusing his leadership. Even so, immediately after the votes were in, opinion polls showed Bush's popularity headed right back up. By mid-December, for the first time since January, the Wall Street Journal/NBC News poll showed more Americans approving than disapproving of his job performance. Even as Bill Clinton was being sworn in as the forty-second president, a Gallup poll reported that George and Barbara Bush were America's "most admired" man and woman.

★ ★ ★

Bill Clinton

42ⁿᵈ President · 1993–2001

Evan Thomas

From high school on, the line between Bill Clinton the man and Bill Clinton the candidate became thinner and thinner. Certainly since college, he systematically collected people—Friends of Bill—who might one day be in a position to help him politically.

BILL CLINTON WAS A NATURAL-BORN politician—warm, physical, commanding, exuberant, soulful, tirelessly empathetic. Unlike many politicians, he was a master of substance, a policy wonk who could and did talk about the philosophy and minutiae of government for hours on end. "I've never seen anything like it," marveled David Osborne, author of *Re-inventing Government*. "He seems to be up on every social program in America." Canny as well as intellectual, Clinton was particularly clever about people and how to manipulate them. And he was lucky too: He had a knack for slipping out of tight spots at the last moment.

The first Democratic president to serve two full terms since Franklin Roosevelt, Clinton presided over an era of peace and prosperity highlighted by a booming economy, the lowest crime rates in years, dwindling welfare rolls, and America's undisputed position as the world's only superpower. Preoccupied with his place in history, Clinton consulted scholars, studied lists of great presidents, and wondered whether he'd be celebrated among them.

Having learned how to play the saxophone in high school, Clinton made clever use of his ability during the 1992 campaign. To court younger voters, he appeared on Arsenio Hall's late-night TV talk show and played Elvis Presley's "Heartbreak Hotel" on this saxophone. The next day, the spot made national headlines.

That seems doubtful. More likely, Clinton will be recalled as a president who *might* have been great, had he not squandered his talents. The first baby boomer to occupy the Oval Office, he seemed to embody the openness and ease of manner—but also the excesses and self-indulgence—of his generation. His impeachment in December 1998, for covering up a sexual relationship with a White House intern, was largely a self-inflicted wound. Prone to self-pity, he blamed an overzealous prosecutor and the late-twentieth-century scandal culture of Washington and the press. To be sure, Clinton was hounded, but his foolish dalliance was symptomatic of character weaknesses that undermined his effectiveness as a leader.

At times, as *Newsweek* columnist Jonathan Alter once observed, there seemed to be two Clintons: One was the inspirational "man from Hope" who could feel a nation's pain; the other, the reckless perpetual adolescent, characterized by political consultant Dick Morris as "Saturday Night Bill." Both were born in Hope, Arkansas, a tidy small town of heartland virtues, including racial tolerance. But William Jefferson Clinton also grew up in Hot Springs, where the Chicago mafia gambled and sin and sex were local industries. There he raised himself, fighting an abusive alcoholic stepfather. The young Clinton was dutiful and eager to please, and he believed in redemption, for himself as well as for others. He was also needy and mendacious. "When I was sixteen, I acted like I was forty," he once recalled; showing some self-awareness, he added, "and when I was forty I acted like I was sixteen."

Campaigning for office was the point at which Clinton's gregarious personality and boundless energy met his relentless political ambition.

A POLITICIAN WAS THE ONLY THING he ever wanted to be. He ran for Congress a year after his 1973 graduation from Yale Law School, lost, then ran successfully for attorney general of Arkansas in 1976. At thirty-two, he became the nation's youngest governor. However, he lost his first reelection campaign in 1980 and learned an important lesson: While in office, he explained to Dick Morris, he had tried to act as a governor, not as a politician. But a truly successful politician, Morris pointed out, never stops running. Thus was born a Clinton hallmark: the "permanent campaign." From that time on, Clinton would govern with a close eye on the public opinion polls and steer clear of politically risky public stands. Reelected governor in 1982, he shrewdly positioned himself as a "New Democrat" out to reinvigorate liberalism by stressing "opportunity and responsibility." As chairman of the National Governors Association (in 1986–87) and the Democratic Leadership Council (in 1990), he pushed moderation in the hope of winning middle-class votes.

BORN
August 19, 1946

BIRTHPLACE
Hope, Arkansas

PARTY AFFILIATION
Democrat

CHILDREN
Chelsea

MAJOR EVENTS

NOVEMBER 17, 1993

President Clinton wins a major victory when the House narrowly approves the North American Free Trade Agreement. NAFTA removes all trade barriers among Mexico, Canada, and the United States.

NOVEMBER 13, 1995

During a budget battle with congressional Republicans, Clinton vetoes a continuing resolution to fund government agencies. When Congress fails to override his veto, the government shuts down, sending home more than eight hundred thousand workers. The six-day shutdown will be followed in mid-December by an even more serious three-week work stoppage.

AUGUST 22, 1996

Clinton signs a welfare reform law that drastically alters the way benefits are delivered. Federally guaranteed payments to individuals are replaced by block grants to states, and most families are limited to five years of aid.

The courtship of Yale law students Bill Clinton and Hillary Rodham was, in the words of one Clinton biographer, "a fair fight." Both were smart, ambitious, and politically inclined. After Rodham's graduation, she worked for the Children's Defense Fund and then the House committee preparing to impeach Richard Nixon. After Nixon's resignation, Rodham moved to Fayetteville, where she joined Clinton on the faculty of the University of Arkansas Law School. They were married a year later, but not before some soul searching (according to friends) on Rodham's part. She was reportedly concerned about Clinton's flirtatiousness and her ability as his wife to pursue her own career goals.

Yet in his ten years as a popular governor with a growing national profile, Clinton did take heedless *personal* risks, earning a wide reputation as a philanderer. "This is fun," he told one of his alleged girlfriends, Susan McDougal. "Women are throwing themselves at me. All the while I was growing up I was the fat boy in the Big Boy jeans." Indeed, when Clinton contemplated running for president in 1992, his biggest concern was that the press might expose his womanizing. His fear seemed realized a couple of weeks before the February 1992 New Hampshire primary when Gennifer Flowers held a press conference and played tapes of her indiscreet conversations with Governor Clinton. Admitting, with lip-biting sincerity, "I have caused pain in my marriage," Clinton appeared on *60 Minutes* with his wife, Hillary, to ask for understanding. He got enough to squeak through the primaries. After that, his youth and vibrant charm carried him past a tired George Bush and into the White House.

ONCE IN OFFICE, Clinton was calculating, shrewd, and slovenly. He ignored his own campaign promise of a massive "reinvestment" program and instead attacked the federal deficit with cost cutting and a tax hike. The Clinton faithful, campaign manager James Carville among them, grumbled about their boss "selling out to the bond traders," but Wall Street responded with its greatest run-up ever. On questions of finance and trade, Clinton listened carefully to a pair of wise heads: economic adviser (and later Treasury Secretary) Robert Rubin and Federal Reserve chairman Alan Greenspan. At the same time, the president ran the White House like a college bull session, pulling all-nighters and exhausting his young, callow staff. Presumptuousness and overconfidence led him to allow his wife to send to Congress a Rube

The Clintons (shown here at an October 1999 White House conference) had a professional relationship unique among presidential couples. According to aide George Stephanopolous, "One thing was certain: Hillary was his most important adviser, and she wanted a senior post in the White House." First ladies traditionally had offices in the East Wing, but Mrs. Clinton made sure that her office was in the West Wing, the center of power.

E HOUSE CONFERENCE
N PHILANTHROPY

Goldberg–like scheme for reforming health care. The spectacular failure of this effort, together with a growing public perception that Clinton was "slick" and undisciplined, helped the Republicans seize control of the House of Representatives in 1994 for only the third time in fifty years.

Clinton seemed depressed, shattered. He complained to advisers about the unfairness of it all and blamed everyone but himself. Yet, at the same time, as he had in difficult moments throughout his life, he refused to give up. He secretly brought back his old adviser, Dick Morris, from whom he'd become estranged, and laid the groundwork for one of the great comebacks in the history of politics. Exploiting loopholes in the campaign finance laws, he raised large sums of money for an early blitz of TV ads that accused the Republicans of slashing entitlements for senior citizens. During a government shutdown in November 1995, he skillfully painted the Republicans as both heartless and inept. The demagoguery, combined with GOP bumbling, worked. Between August 1995 and January 1996,

> "HE CARED DEEPLY ABOUT WHERE HE CAME FROM, WHICH WAS UNUSUAL. HE WAS ROOTED, AND MOST OF US WERE DISCONNECTED."
>
> —*Hillary Rodham Clinton*—

Clinton went, in most public opinion polls, from ten to fifteen points behind Republican front-runner Bob Dole to ten to fifteen points ahead. He never looked back, defeating Dole easily in the November election.

This was about the time Clinton began cornering historians for their evaluation of his place in the pecking order of presidents. Though Clinton understood he couldn't aspire to the ranks of such war leaders as Lincoln and FDR, he did think he could reasonably hope for an above-average ranking. His reelection made him a model for European leaders, who saw in his example a "third way" between the bloated welfare state and the rawness of unfettered capitalism. Though not well grounded in foreign policy, Clinton had also become a surprisingly nimble peacemaker, intervening with some success— or at least without disaster—in Haiti, Bosnia, Northern Ireland,

MARCH 24, 1999

NATO begins a bombing campaign designed to force a Serbian pullback from the Yugoslavian province of Kosovo, where Serb militias have been massacring the mostly Albanian population. The air strikes will continue until Serbian president Slobodan Milosevic agrees on June 9 to withdraw his forces from Kosovo.

FEBRUARY 1, 2000

The U.S. economy enters its 107th consecutive month of growth, establishing a new record for peacetime expansion. Much of the credit is given to Alan Greenspan, who has served as chairman of the Federal Reserve since 1987.

In July 1963, *Clinton traveled to Washington as part of the Boys Nation mock government program sponsored by the American Legion. On July 24, Clinton and ninety-nine other teenage "senators" were invited to the White House to meet the president. Clinton made sure that he was in the front row when the handshaking began.*

Clinton's mother,
*Virginia Cassidy
Blythe, married Hot
Springs car dealer
Roger Clinton in 1950.
Four-year-old William
Jefferson Blythe III
subsequently took
his stepfather's name.
This photograph was
taken while young
Bill was still in
elementary school.*

OPPOSITE:

*In 1836, Vice President
Martin Van Buren
followed President
Andrew Jackson into the
White House. In 2000,
Al Gore campaigned to
become only the second
vice president since Van
Buren to be so elevated.
The other veep to have
succeeded his boss was
George Bush, who
coattailed Ronald
Reagan in 1988.*

and the Middle East. With Rubin's help, he'd even become an articulate spokesman for the global economy and the new Age of Information. In his second term, had he used his political capital and persuasive skills on one major domestic initiative—reforming benefit programs, for instance, so that they could serve the aging baby boom generation—Clinton would have guaranteed a sound legacy. Instead, he became enmeshed in a squalid scandal that threatened to become a constitutional crisis.

"I REFUSE TO BE PART OF A GENERATION THAT CELEBRATES THE DEATH OF COMMUNISM ABROAD WITH THE LOSS OF THE AMERICAN DREAM AT HOME."

—Speech, 1991—

CLINTON'S NEAR-DOWNFALL BEGAN at almost the precise moment of his political renaissance. During the November 1995 government shutdown, as he was outfoxing House Speaker Newt Gingrich, Clinton began a sexual relationship with a White House intern, Monica Lewinsky. The dalliance might have gone undiscovered, except that Clinton was being sued for sexual harassment by another woman, Paula Jones, whose lawyers subpoenaed Lewinsky to testify about Clinton's womanizing. Lewinsky and Clinton lied about their affair, causing independent counsel Kenneth Starr to open an obstruction-of-justice investigation. The ensuing media frenzy effectively ended any chance Clinton had of implementing a major domestic or international program. The scandal might have finished his presidency as well were it not for the common sense of voters, who disapproved of Clinton's character but didn't want him removed from office. Though impeached by the House, Clinton escaped conviction in the Senate in February 1999.

Even then, Bill Clinton's presidency was not over. With some Clintonian luck, he was able to avoid a messy ground war in the Balkans while helping trigger the downfall of Serbian strongman Slobodan Milosevic. His performance ratings, like the stock market, remained high during 1999–2000, and it seemed that he might be remembered as a kind of charming rogue with a deft political touch. But he left office amid a scandal over presidential pardons, a sour endnote that seemed to confirm doubts about his essential character.

★ ★ ★

George W. Bush

43ʳᵈ President · 2001–

William H. Chafe

*In 1999,
as George W. Bush
prepared to run for
president, he asked
a group of leading pastors
to come to the governor's
mansion in Austin, Texas,
for a "laying-on of hands."
During this gathering,
Bush explained that he
had been "called" to seek
higher office.*

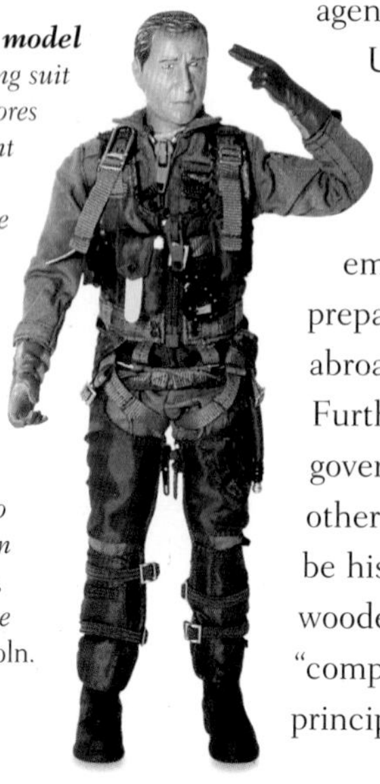

*This 1/6-scale model
of Bush in a flying suit
sold out of toy stores
after the president
reportedly flew
himself out to the
aircraft carrier
Abraham
Lincoln in a
navy jet. The
May 1, 2003
flight served as
an attention-
getting prelude to
Bush's declaration
of victory in Iraq,
delivered from the
deck of the* Lincoln.

RARELY HAS AN ELECTION as closely contested as the 2000 presidential race resulted in such a decisive shift in American politics. Al Gore, a master policy analyst with eight years of experience as Bill Clinton's vice president, was widely expected to defeat George W. Bush, a Texas governor with little experience in national or world affairs. Gore, in fact, received 500,000 more popular votes than Bush, but in the bitter postelection legal fight for Florida's 25 disputed electoral votes, Bush prevailed when the Supreme Court decided, by a vote of 5–4, to end the Florida recount with the Republicans leading by 537 votes.

Thus it was with something less than a mandate that Bush took charge of a sharply divided America. Yet by force of his personality, his ideological vision, and some stunning world events, he shortly found himself in a position to transform both the domestic and international agendas of the country. The result was a reversal of decades of U.S. foreign policy assumptions as well as the creation of a plan for change at home that made even Ronald Reagan's economic conservatism seem tepid by comparison.

Described as "intellectually juvenile" by foreign policy eminence George F. Kennan, Bush seemed utterly without preparation for world leadership. This son of a president had been abroad only twice in his life and seemed surprisingly incurious. Furthermore, he had little to show for his six years as Texas governor, except a reputation for likability and working well with others. During the 2000 campaign, this likability turned out to be his greatest asset, playing particularly well against Gore's woodenness. Bush took advantage of his image, advocating "compassionate conservatism" and asserting that his conservative principles in no way precluded government help for the needy.

Two particular events in his past apparently shaped Bush's approach to the world around him. The first was his decision shortly after his fortieth birthday, under pressure from his wife, to stop drinking and give up the playboy, fraternity lifestyle that had characterized his behavior to that point in his life. The second,

Supporters of Bush and Gore demonstrate in front of the Supreme Court on December 11, 2000. That day, the Court heard oral arguments in Bush v. Gore. The next day, it decided, 5–4, to halt the manual recount ordered by the Florida Supreme Court on December 8, thereby assuring Bush's election as president.

related to the first, was the emergence of his faith as a born-again Christian. From the time of his conversion during the mid-1980s, Bush began to pray regularly and take part in Bible study groups (a practice that would later become *de rigueur* in the Bush White House). Eventually, there emerged in Bush's mind a vision of the world in which people and causes tended to be defined either as "good" or "evil."

T HE NEW PRESIDENT BEGAN his administration by surrounding himself with distinguished advisors, many of whom (such as Secretary of State Colin Powell and National Security Advisor Condoleezza Rice) had served in his father's administration a decade earlier. He also launched a rhetorical initiative focusing on his commitment to inclusion and togetherness. In an inaugural address that one critic called "by far the best...in forty years," he spoke compassionately of the poor, using the language of religious charity to express his desire to help those who had been left out of society. Meanwhile, his pronouncements on foreign policy seemed predictably conservative and mainstream, reflecting the hint of isolationism that he had expressed during the campaign.

Bush's actions, on the other hand, signaled that he intended to pursue an extreme political agenda. Initiating a series of decisions that eventually caused the *New York Times* to editorialize that he was waging a war on women, Bush ended all U.S. aid to international family planning agencies and issued a series of executive orders solidly aligning his administration with the goals of the anti-abortion lobby. He also reversed

---

BORN
July 6, 1946

BIRTHPLACE
New Haven, Connecticut

PARTY AFFILIATION
Republican

CHILDREN
Barbara, Jenna

MAJOR EVENTS

OCTOBER 26, 2001

President Bush signs the USA PATRIOT Act, a controversial antiterrorism bill that makes it easier for federal authorities to initiate wiretaps, share information, and detain some suspects without specific charges.

NOVEMBER 13, 2001

Forces of the U.S.-supported Northern Alliance oust the fundamentalist Taliban regime from the Afghan capital of Kabul. The victory caps an offensive, begun in early October, designed to punish the Taliban for harboring Al Qaeda and its terrorist training camps.

DECEMBER 2, 2001

Houston-based Enron, the seventh largest U.S. corporation, becomes the largest company yet to seek bankruptcy protection. The leading executives of this energy-trading company will soon become, according to Time magazine, "poster boys for business-accounting scandals."

Laura Welch married "Dubya" in November 1977, just three months after meeting him for the first time at the home of mutual friends in Midland, Texas. The couple skipped their honeymoon, however, because at the time Bush was campaigning (unsuccessfully) for Congress.

Clinton administration policy on the environment—allowing, for example, logging in previously protected western forests and proposing an energy policy that appeared to many critics, Republicans and Democrats, as though it had been written by and for the oil industry.

This extremism was even more visible in Bush's economic policies, particularly his tax plan. During the years of the Clinton administration, Congress had increased the share of taxes paid by the nation's wealthiest citizens (the top 1 percent), while substantially reducing the taxes paid by the bottom 80 percent of the population. Now, Bush proposed a ten-year, $1.6 trillion tax cut (later reduced by Congress to $1.35 trillion), with 43 percent of the benefit accruing to the wealthiest 1 percent of the population.

THE SAME SORT OF REVERSAL also took place with regard to foreign policy. Turning his back on decades of multilateralism, the president withdrew American support for the Kyoto global warming accord, announced that he would reject a treaty banning land mines, abrogated the 1972 Anti-Ballistic Missile Treaty (so that the U.S. could resurrect Reagan's "Star Wars" missile-shield plan), and refused to participate in the new International Court of Justice being established at The Hague, even threatening to punish U.S. allies who chose to support the court. "Mr. Bush's America seems in danger of convincing itself that it can force everybody to make concessions, while itself remaining impervious to change," one usually pro-American British newspaper declared. Not surprisingly, the first major strategic document on foreign

Accompanied by Secretary of Defense Donald Rumsfeld, Bush inspects damage to the west side of the Pentagon on September 12, 2001, the day after the terrorist attacks that transfixed, tortured, and traumatized the country.

policy prepared by the Bush administration asserted the government's right to engage proactively in preventive war, regardless of international approval.

Nothing the Bush administration planned or anticipated, however, prepared the nation for the shock and upheaval caused by the terrorist attacks of September 11, 2001. That clear and brilliantly sunny morning, hijackers belonging to the Islamic terrorist group Al Qaeda seized four large passenger jets after their take-offs from east coast airports around 8:00 A.M. Beginning at 8:48 A.M. and continuing at approximately twenty-minute intervals, three of those planes plunged into first the North Tower of the World Trade Center, then the South Tower, and finally the Pentagon. The fourth jet was prevented from reaching a second target in the Washington area only by the heroism of some passengers, who learned of the World Trade Center attacks from cell-phone conversations and stormed the cockpit, forcing the plane to crash in rural western Pennsylvania.

Not since Franklin Roosevelt in the aftermath of the Pearl Harbor attack had an American president faced such a challenge of leadership. Bush responded, slowly and ineffectively at first, but then with growing confidence and strength. At first during a prayer service at the National Cathedral and later in a speech to Congress and the nation, he attempted to identify and describe the new world that had dawned. There had been precursors, to be sure: the February 1993 attack on the World Trade Center, the April 1995 destruction of the Murrah Federal Building in Oklahoma City (by an American extremist), the August 1998 bombings of U.S. embassies in Kenya and Tanzania, and the October 2000 attack on the USS *Cole*. But never had there been such a brazen attack on the American homeland against highly regarded symbols of the nation's military and economic might.

In interpreting this new political situation, George W. Bush naturally fell back on the deeply held ideological positions he had already set forth. Yet now he implemented those policies with a new and quite potent justification: the need for extreme measures to defeat the insidious and "evil" forces of Osama bin Laden's Al Qaeda network. The terrorists, Bush declared, were "evil-doers." Therefore, the United States was obligated to mount a "crusade" against them so that the evil they represented might be exterminated. There could be no equivocation. "Every nation in every region now has a decision to make," the president said. "Either you are with us, or you are with the terrorists."

Within such a Manichean moral construct, it became difficult to debate fully or weigh properly alternative courses of action. Framing each choice as "evil" versus "good" left little room for appreciating ambiguity or respecting differences of opinion. Instead, the Bush administration's ideological core—Vice President Dick Cheney, Secretary of Defense Donald Rumsfeld, and Rumsfeld deputy Paul Wolfowitz—determined within two weeks of 9/11 that not only would Afghanistan, the sanctuary of Al Qaeda, be invaded but also Iraq, where the "evil" Saddam Hussein still tenaciously held power despite Iraq's defeat

MARCH 19, 2003

After the UN Security Council refuses to endorse a U.S.-proposed invasion of Iraq, a small coalition of nations led by the United States and Great Britain invades Iraq on its own.

JANUARY 26, 2004

The Congressional Budget Office projects a record budget deficit of $477 billion for 2004. A major contributing factor is the new Medicare prescription drug benefit enacted in December 2003. Its cost was originally placed at $400 billion over ten years, but two months later the Bush administration revised that estimate upward by $135 billion.

After 9/11, Bush radically reorganized his administration to conduct the new "war on terrorism." Among the most important changes was the consolidation of 170,000 federal workers from twenty agencies into the new Department of Homeland Security. Here, Bush shakes hands with the first secretary of homeland security, Tom Ridge.

This family photograph, *perhaps a metaphor for Bush's rise to power, shows nine-month-old George W. sitting atop his father's shoulders in April 1947. At the time, the Bushes were living in New Haven, Connecticut. A year later, after the elder Bush's graduation from Yale, the family moved to oil-rich Midland, Texas.*

in the 1991 Persian Gulf War. (In a 2004 memoir, fired Bush treasury secretary Paul O'Neill went even farther, asserting that the administration's determination to oust Saddam preceded 9/11.)

Although United Nations weapons inspectors insisted that the Iraqis possessed no weapons of mass destruction and no evidence existed of any link between Saddam and Al Qaeda, President Bush waged an effective public relations campaign to persuade Americans that the threat posed by the Iraqis was both substantial and imminent. On the world stage, however, these arguments proved less than persuasive. With the notable exception of Great Britain, the same European allies who had supported the United States in Afghanistan vigorously opposed Bush's preemptive war in Iraq.

> "STATES LIKE [NORTH KOREA, IRAN, AND IRAQ, AND THEIR TERRORIST ALLIES, CONSTITUTE AN AXIS OF EVIL, ARMING TO THREATEN THE PEACE OF THE WORLD."
> —*State of the Union address, 2002*—

Historians will ultimately judge the Bush presidency on the effectiveness and validity of its domestic and foreign policy, which at this writing remain to be seen. One can already observe, however, that the Bush administration has been one of the most radical ever to hold office. It has pursued economic policies that have completely reversed the fiscal and monetary discipline of the past two administrations, creating record deficits of a magnitude sure to preclude for the foreseeable future any significant domestic reforms, such as the extension of health insurance to millions of the uninsured. Perhaps more important, however, the Bush administration has renounced the longstanding commitment to multilateralism that has defined American foreign policy since World War II.

The danger inherent in Bush's Manichean sensibility is that, with all complexity and nuance removed, the subtleties on which effective diplomacy depends become impossible. On the other hand, there exists the potential that the clarity of his moral vision may produce a new and effective brand of personal leadership. Historians of the next generation will have to judge.

★ ★ ★

OPPOSITE:

Bush hugs a soldier *during a surprise Thanksgiving Day 2003 visit to Iraq. In all, the president spent two hours and thirty-two minutes on the ground at the Baghdad International Airport.*

THE CAMPAIGNS
AND
INAUGURAL ADDRESSES

TEXT BY RICHARD M. PIOUS

IMAGES FROM THE MUSEUM OF AMERICAN POLITICAL LIFE
AT THE UNIVERSITY OF HARTFORD

1789 GEORGE WASHINGTON

THE FIRST PRESIDENTIAL ELECTION featured neither political parties nor hoopla. The nearest things to organized events were the demonstrations of support organized on July 4, 1788, by admirers of George Washington. Such was the extent of the campaign.

The outgoing Congress, convened under the expiring Articles of Confederation, passed a law establishing January 7, 1789, as the date for all states to name their presidential electors. Seventy-three electors were chosen by ten states (New York never got itself organized, and North Carolina and Rhode Island had not yet ratified the Constitution). Delaware, Maryland, Pennsylvania, and Virginia chose their electors by popular vote; in Connecticut, Georgia, New Jersey, and South Carolina, state legislatures made the choice; Massachusetts and New Hampshire used a combination of methods.

Every elector was to cast two ballots. The candidate with the most votes (if a majority) would be president; the runner-up, vice president. On February 4, 1789, the electors voted, and each who voted cast a ballot for George Washington, electing him unanimously.

Congress sent a messenger to notify Washington, who observed to Henry Knox, "My movements to the chair of government will be accompanied by feelings not unlike those of a culprit who is going to the place of his execution." Cheered along his route, the president-elect arrived in New York City, then the temporary capital, to a huge celebration. On April 30, he took the oath of office at Federal Hall. "Our Constitution is in actual operation," a jubilant Ben Franklin reported to friends abroad.

CANDIDATE	ELECTORAL VOTES
George Washington, Va.	69
John Adams, Mass.	34
John Jay, N.Y.	9
Robert H. Harrison, Md.	6
John Rutledge, S.C.	6
John Hancock, Mass.	4
George Clinton, N.Y.	3
Samuel Huntington, Ct.	2
John Milton, Ga.	2
James Armstrong, Pa.	1
Benjamin Lincoln, Mass.	1
Edward Telfair, Ga.	1
(not voted)	8

First Inaugural Address • New York City • Thursday, April 30, 1789

Fellow-Citizens of the Senate and of the House of Representatives:

Among the vicissitudes incident to life, no event could have filled me with greater anxieties than that of which the notification was transmitted by your order and received on the fourteenth day of the present month. On the one hand, I was summoned by my country, whose voice I can never hear but with veneration and love, from a retreat which I had chosen with the fondest predilection, and, in my flattering hopes, with an immutable decision, as the asylum of my declining years—a retreat which was rendered every day more necessary as well as more dear to me by the addition of habit to inclination, and of frequent interruptions in my health to the gradual waste committed on it by time. On the other hand, the magnitude and difficulty of the trust to which the voice of my country called me, being sufficient to awaken in the wisest and most experienced of her citizens a distrustful scrutiny into his qualifi-

cations, could not but overwhelm with despondence one who (inheriting inferior endowments from nature and unpracticed in the duties of civil administration) ought to be peculiarly conscious of his own deficiencies. In this conflict of emotions, all I dare aver is that it has been my faithful study to collect my duty from a just appreciation of every circumstance by which it might be affected. All I dare hope is that if, in executing this task, I have been too much swayed by a grateful remembrance of former instances, or by an affectionate sensibility to this transcendent proof of the confidence of my fellow-citizens, and have thence too little consulted my incapacity as well as disinclination for the weighty and untried cares before me, my error will be palliated by the motives which mislead me, and its consequences be judged by my country with some share of the partiality in which they originated.

Such being the impressions under which I have, in obedience to the public summons, repaired to the present station, it would be peculiarly improper to omit in this first official act my fervent supplications to that Almighty Being who rules over the universe, who presides in the councils of nations, and whose providential aids can supply every human defect, that His benediction may consecrate to the liberties and happiness of the people of the United States a Government instituted by themselves for these essential purposes, and may enable every instrument employed in its administration to execute with success the functions allotted to his charge. In tendering this homage to the Great Author of every public and private good, I assure myself that it expresses your sentiments not less than my own, nor those of my fellow-citizens at large less than either. No people can be bound to acknowledge and adore the Invisible Hand which conducts the affairs of men more than those of the United States. Every step by which they have advanced to the character of an independent nation seems to have been distinguished by some token of providential agency; and in the important revolution just accomplished in the system of their united government the tranquil deliberations and voluntary consent of so many distinct communities from which the event has resulted can not be compared with the means by which most governments have been established without some return of pious gratitude, along with an humble anticipation of the future blessings which the past seem to presage. These reflections, arising out of the present crisis, have forced themselves too strongly on my mind to be suppressed. You will join with me, I trust, in thinking that there are none under the influence of which the proceedings of a new and free government can more auspiciously commence.

BY THE ARTICLE establishing the executive department it is made the duty of the president "to recommend to your consideration such measures as he shall judge necessary and expedient." The circumstances under which I now meet you will acquit me from entering into that suject further than to refer to the great constitutional charter under which you are assembled, and which, in defining your powers, designates the objects to which your attention is to be given. It will be more consistent with those circumstances, and far more

> *I was summoned by my country whose voice I can never hear but with veneration....*

congenial with the feelings which actuate me, to substitute, in place of a recommendation of particular measures, the tribute that is due to the talents, the rectitude, and the patriotism which adorn the characters selected to devise and adopt them. In these honorable qualifications I behold the surest pledges that as on one side no local prejudices or attachments, no separate views nor party animosities, will misdirect the comprehensive and equal eye which ought to watch over this great assemblage of communities and interests, so, on another, that the foundation of our national policy will be laid in the pure and immutable principles of private morality, and the preeminence of free government be exemplified by all the attributes which can win the affections of its citizens and command the respect of the world. I dwell on this prospect with every satis-

faction which an ardent love for my country can inspire, since there is no truth more thoroughly established than that there exists in the economy and course of nature an indissoluble union between virtue and happiness; between duty and advantage; between the genuine maxims of an honest and magnanimous policy and the solid rewards of public prosperity and felicity; since we ought to be no less per-

suaded that the propitious smiles of Heaven can never be expected on a nation that disregards the eternal rules of order and right which Heaven itself has ordained; and since the preservation of the sacred fire of liberty and the destiny of the republican model of government are justly considered, perhaps, as deeply, as finally, staked on the experiment entrusted to the hands of the American people.

BESIDES THE ORDINARY objects submitted to your care, it will remain with your judgment to decide how far an exercise of the occasional power delegated by the fifth article of the Constitution is rendered expedient at the present juncture by the nature of objections which have been urged against the system, or by the degree of inquietude which has given birth to them. Instead of undertaking particular recom-

mendations on this subject, in which I could be guided by no lights derived from official opportunities, I shall again give way to my entire confidence in your discernment and pursuit of the public good; for I assure myself that whilst you carefully avoid every alteration which might endanger the benefits of an united and effective government, or which ought to await the future lessons of experience, a rever-

ence for the characteristic rights of freemen and a regard for the public harmony will sufficiently influence your deliberations on the question how far the former can be impregnably fortified or the latter be safely and advantageously promoted.

TO THE FOREGOING observations I have one to add, which will be most properly addressed to the House of Representatives. It concerns myself and will therefore be as brief as possible. When I was first honored with a call into the service of my country, then on the eve of an arduous struggle for its liberties, the light in which I contemplated my duty required that I should renounce every pecuniary compensation. From this resolution I have in no instance departed; and being still under the impressions which produced it, I must decline as inapplicable to myself any share in the personal emoluments which may be indispensably included in a permanent provision for the executive department and must accordingly pray that the pecuniary estimates for the station in which I am placed may during my continuance in it be limited to such actual expenditures as the public good may be thought to require.

Having thus imparted to you my sentiments as they have been awakened by the occasion which brings us together, I shall take my present leave; but not without resorting once more to the benign Parent of the Human Race in humble supplication that, since He has been pleased to favor the American people with opportunities for deliberating in perfect tranquillity and dispositions for deciding with unparalleled unanimity on a form of government for the security of their union and the advancement of their happiness, so His divine blessing may be equally conspicuous in the enlarged views, the temperate consultations, and the wise measures on which the success of this Government must depend.

* * *

1792 GEORGE WASHINGTON

EARLY IN HIS ADMINISTRATION, George Washington pledged to serve but a single term. However, the development of rival political factions led by Secretary of State Thomas Jefferson and Treasury Secretary Alexander Hamilton caused him to reconsider. Even Hamilton and Jefferson pleaded with him to serve another term in the interest of national unity. "North and South will hang together if they have you to hang on," Jefferson told the president.

When Washington failed to make a public statement one way or the other, the electors took his silence for consent. As in 1789, each elector cast one of his two ballots for Washington, whose reelection was unopposed.

The race for vice president, however, marked the beginning of America's two-party system. Despite being accused of pro-British, monarchical, and elitist sentiments. Vice President John Adams was reelected with seventy-seven votes. His Democratic-Republican challenger, George Clinton, finished with fifty votes (from Georgia, New York, North Carolina, Pennsylvania, and Virginia).

Washington was certainly the people's choice, but presidential politics had yet to engage the average voter. In states where at least some electors were chosen by popular vote (Kentucky, Maryland, Massachusetts, New Hampshire, Pennsylvania, and Virginia), only one-tenth as many people cast ballots in the presidential election as had voted in earlier congressional races.

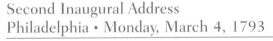

Second Inaugural Address
Philadelphia • Monday, March 4, 1793

Fellow Citizens: I am again called

upon by the voice of my country to execute the functions of its Chief Magistrate. When the occasion proper for it shall arrive, I shall endeavor to express the high sense I entertain of this distinguished honor, and of the confidence which has been reposed in me by the people of united America. Previous to the execution of any official act of the President the Constitution requires an oath of office. This oath I am now about to take, and in your presence: That if it shall be found during my administration of the Government I have in any instance violated willingly or knowingly the injunctions thereof, I may (besides incurring constitutional punishment) be subject to the upbraidings of all who are now witnesses of the present solemn ceremony.

CANDIDATE	PARTY	ELECTORAL VOTES
George Washington, Va.	Federalist	132
John Adams, Mass.	Federalist	77
George Clinton, N.Y.	Democratic-Republican	50
Thomas Jefferson, Va.	Democratic-Republican	4
Aaron Burr, N.Y.	Democratic-Republican	1
(not voted)		6

1796 John Adams

When George Washington decided not to serve a third term as president, the Federalist caucus in Congress endorsed Vice President John Adams to succeed him. Adams was opposed by Thomas Jefferson, leader of the Democratic-Republican party.

Jay's Treaty, negotiated in 1794, and U.S. neutrality in the Anglo-French wars were the principal campaign issues. The Democratic-Republicans charged that Jay's Treaty sold out American sovereignty to the British, while the Federalists responded by touting the agreement's favorable commerce clauses. The main domestic issue was the Whiskey Rebellion, which Washington had put down in 1794, much to the displeasure of western farmers.

Adams squeaked out a three-vote victory; however, because of the double-balloting system then in use by the electoral college, his rival, Jefferson, became vice president. While awkward, this arrangement did have its advantages for Adams, who was legitimately concerned that the Federalist party might turn against him. "If the Federalists go to playing pranks," Adams told his wife, "I will resign the office." In which case, Jefferson would become president. It was a substantial threat.

Candidate	Party	Electoral Votes
John Adams, Mass.	Federalist	71
Thomas Jefferson, Va.	Democratic-Republican	68
Thomas Pinckney, S.C.	Federalist	59
Aaron Burr, N.Y.	Democratic-Republican	30
Samuel Adams, Mass.	Federalist	15
Oliver Ellsworth, Ct.	Federalist	11
George Clinton, N.Y.	Democratic-Republican	7
John Jay, N.Y.	Federalist	5
James Iredell, N.C.	Federalist	3
John Henry, Md.	Democratic-Republican	2
Samuel Johnston, N.C.	Federalist	2
George Washington, Va.	Federalist	2
Charles C. Pinckney, S.C.	Federalist	1

Inaugural Address • Philadelphia • Saturday, March 4, 1797

When it was first perceived, in early times, that no middle course

for America remained between unlimited submission to a foreign legislature and a total independence of its claims, men of reflection were less apprehensive of danger from the formidable power of fleets and armies they must determine to resist than from those contests and dissensions which would certainly arise concerning the forms of government to be instituted over the whole and over the parts of this extensive country. Relying, however, on the purity of their intentions, the justice of their cause, and the integrity and intelligence of the people, under an overruling Providence which had so signally protected this country from the first, the representatives of this nation, then consisting of little more than half its present number, not only broke to pieces the chains which were forging and the rod of iron that was lifted up, but frankly cut asunder the ties which had bound them, and launched into an ocean of uncertainty.

The zeal and ardor of the people during the Revolutionary war, supplying the place of government, commanded a degree of order sufficient at least for the temporary preservation of society. The Confederation which was early felt to be necessary was prepared from the models of the Batavian and Helvetic confederacies, the only examples which remain with any detail and precision in history, and certainly the only ones which the people at large had ever considered. But reflecting on the striking difference in so many particulars between this country and those where a courier may go from the seat of government to the frontier in a single day, it was then certainly foreseen by some who assisted in Congress at the formation of it that it could not be durable.

Negligence of its regulations, inattention to its recommendations, if not disobedience to its authority, not only in individuals but in States, soon appeared with their melancholy consequences—universal languor, jealousies and rivalries of States, decline of navigation and commerce, discouragement of necessary manufactures, universal fall in the value of lands and their produce, contempt of public and private faith, loss of consideration and credit with  foreign nations, and at length in discontents, animosities, combinations, partial conventions, and insurrection, threatening some great national calamity.

In this dangerous crisis the people of America were not abandoned by their usual good sense, presence of mind, resolution, or integrity. Measures were pursued to concert a plan to form a more perfect union, establish justice, insure domestic tranquillity, provide for the common defense, promote the general welfare, and secure the blessings of liberty. The public disquisitions, discussions, and deliberations issued in the present happy Constitution of Government.

Employed in the service of my country abroad during the whole course of these transactions, I first saw the Constitution of the United States in a foreign country. Irritated by no literary altercation, animated by no public debate, heated by no party animosity, I read it with great satisfaction, as the result of good heads prompted by good hearts, as an experiment better adapted to the genius, character, situation, and relations of this nation and country than any which had ever been proposed or suggested. In its general principles and great outlines it was conformable to such a system of government as I had ever most esteemed, and in some States, my own native State in particular, had contributed to establish. Claiming a right of suffrage, in common with my fellow-citizens, in the adoption or rejection of a constitution which was to rule me and my posterity, as well as them and theirs, I did not hesitate to express my approbation of it on all occasions, in public and in private. It was not then, nor has been since, any objection to it in my mind that the Executive and Senate were not more permanent. Nor have I ever entertained a thought of promoting any alteration in it but such as the people themselves, in the course of their experience, should see and feel to be necessary or expedient, and by their representatives in Congress and the State legislatures, according to the Constitution itself, adopt and ordain.

Returning to the bosom of my country after a painful separation from it for ten years, I had the honor to be elected to a station under the new order of things, and I have repeatedly laid myself under the most serious obligations to support the Constitution. The operation of it has equaled the most sanguine expectations of its friends, and from an habitual attention to it, satisfaction in its administration, and delight in its effects upon the peace, order, prosperity, and happiness of the nation I have acquired an habitual attachment to it and veneration for it.

What other form of government, indeed, can so well deserve our esteem and love?

There may be little solidity in an ancient idea that congregations of men into cities and nations are the most pleasing objects in the sight of superior intelligences, but this is very certain, that to a benevolent human mind there can be no spectacle presented by any nation more pleasing, more noble, majestic, or august, than an assembly like that which has so often been seen in this and the other Chamber of Congress, of

a Government in which the Executive authority, as well as that of all the branches of the Legislature, are exercised by citizens selected at regular periods by their neighbors to make and execute laws for the general good. Can anything essential, anything more than mere ornament and decoration, be added to this by robes and diamonds? Can authority be more amiable and respectable when it descends from accidents or institutions established in remote antiquity

Can anything essential, anything more than mere ornament and decoration, be added to this by robes and diamonds?

than when it springs fresh from the hearts and judgments of an honest and enlightened people? For it is the people only that are represented. It is their power and majesty that is reflected, and only for their good, in every legitimate government, under whatever form it may appear. The existence of such a government as ours for any length of time is a full proof of a general dissemination of knowledge and virtue throughout the whole body of the people. And what object or consideration more pleasing than this can be presented to the human mind? If national pride is ever justifiable or excusable it is when it springs, not from power or riches, grandeur or glory, but from conviction of national innocence, information, and benevolence.

In the midst of these pleasing ideas we should be unfaithful to ourselves if we should ever lose sight of the danger to our liberties if anything partial or extraneous should infect the purity of our free, fair, virtuous, and independent elections. If an election is to be determined

by a majority of a single vote, and that can be procured by a party through artifice or corruption, the Government may be the choice of a party for its own ends, not of the nation for the national good. If that solitary suffrage can be obtained by foreign nations by flattery or menaces, by fraud or violence, by terror, intrigue, or venality, the Government may not be the choice of the American people, but of foreign nations. It may be foreign nations who govern us, and not we, the people, who govern ourselves; and candid men will acknowledge that in such cases choice would have little advantage to boast of over lot or chance.

Such is the amiable and interesting system of government (and such are some of the abuses to which it may be exposed) which the people of America have exhibited to the admiration and anxiety of the wise and virtuous of all nations for eight years under the administration of a citizen who, by a long course of great actions, regulated by prudence, justice, temperance, and fortitude, conducting a people inspired with the same virtues and animated with the same ardent patriotism and love of liberty to independence and peace, to increasing wealth and unexampled prosperity, has merited the gratitude of his fellow-citizens, commanded the highest praises of foreign nations, and secured immortal glory with posterity.

IN THAT RETIREMENT which is his voluntary choice may he long live to enjoy the delicious recollection of his services, the gratitude of mankind, the happy fruits of them to himself and the world, which are daily increasing, and that splendid prospect of the future fortunes of this country which is opening from year to year. His name may be still a rampart, and the knowledge that he lives a bulwark, against all open or secret enemies of his country's peace. This example has been recommended to the imitation of his successors by both Houses of Congress and by the voice of the legislatures and the people throughout the nation.

On this subject it might become me better to be silent or to speak with diffidence; but

as something may be expected, the occasion, I hope, will be admitted as an apology if I venture to say that if a preference, upon principle, of a free republican government, formed upon long and serious reflection, after a diligent and impartial inquiry after truth; if an attachment to the Constitution of the United States, and a conscientious determination to support it until it shall be altered by the judgments and wishes of the people, expressed in the mode prescribed in it; if a respectful attention to the constitutions of the individual States and a constant caution and delicacy toward the State governments; if an equal and impartial regard to the rights, interest, honor, and happiness of all the States in the Union, without preference or regard to a northern or southern, an eastern or western, position, their various political opinions on unessential points or their personal attachments; if a love of virtuous men of all parties and denominations; if a love of science and letters and a wish to patronize every rational effort to encourage schools, colleges, universities, academies, and every institution for propagating knowledge, virtue, and religion among all classes of the people, not only for their benign influence on the happiness of life in all its stages and classes, and of society in all its forms, but as the only means of preserving our Constitution from its natural enemies, the spirit of sophistry, the spirit of party, the spirit of intrigue, the profligacy of corruption, and the pestilence of foreign influence, which is the angel of destruction to elective governments; if a love of equal laws, of justice, and humanity in the interior administration; if an inclination to improve agriculture, commerce, and manufacturers for necessity, convenience, and defense; if a spirit of equity and humanity toward the aboriginal nations of America, and a disposition to meliorate their condition by inclining them to be more friendly to us, and our citizens to be more friendly to them; if an inflexible determination to maintain peace and inviolable faith with all nations, and that system of neutrality and impartiality among the belligerent powers of Europe which has

JOHN ADAMS.

President of the United States.

…my mind is prepared without hesitation to lay myself under the most solemn obligations.…

been adopted by this Government and so solemnly sanctioned by both Houses of Congress and applauded by the legislatures of the States and the public opinion, until it shall be otherwise ordained by Congress; if a personal esteem for the French nation, formed in a residence of seven years chiefly among them, and a sincere desire to preserve the friendship which has been so much for the honor and interest of both nations; if, while the conscious honor and integrity of the people of America and the internal sentiment of their own power and energies must be preserved, an earnest endeavor to investigate every just cause and remove every colorable pretense of complaint; if an intention to pursue by amicable negotiation

a reparation for the injuries that have been committed on the commerce of our fellow-citizens by whatever nation, and if success can not be obtained, to lay the facts before the Legislature, that they may consider what further measures the honor and interest of the Government and its constituents demand; if a resolution to do justice as far as may depend upon me, at all times and to all nations, and maintain peace, friendship, and benevolence with all the world; if an unshaken confidence in the honor, spirit, and resources of the American people, on which I have so often hazarded my all and never been deceived; if elevated ideas of the high destinies of this country and of my own duties toward it, founded on a knowledge of the moral

principles and intellectual improvements of the people deeply engraven on my mind in early life, and not obscured but exalted by experience and age; and, with humble reverence, I feel it to be my duty to add, if a veneration for the religion of a people who profess and call themselves Christians, and a fixed resolution to consider a decent respect for Christianity among the best recommendations for the public service, can enable me in any degree to comply with your wishes, it shall be my strenuous endeavor that this sagacious injunction of the two Houses shall not be without effect.

With this great example before me, with the sense and spirit, the faith and honor, the duty and interest, of the same

American people pledged to support the Constitution of the United States, I entertain no doubt of its continuance in all its energy, and my mind is prepared without hesitation to lay myself under the most solemn obligations to support it to the utmost of my power.

And may that Being who is supreme over all, the Patron of Order, the Fountain of Justice, and the Protector in all ages of the world of virtuous liberty, continue His blessing upon this nation and its Government and give it all possible success and duration consistent with the ends of His providence.

* * *

1800 Thomas Jefferson

DETERMINED TO OUST President Adams, the Democratic-Republicans organized their followers into the first state parties. These, in turn, carried out aggressive attacks on the Federalists for conducting a "reign of terror" exemplified by the Alien and Sedition Acts of 1798.

Party candidates were once again chosen by congressional caucus, with the Democratic-Republicans selecting Thomas Jefferson and Aaron Burr, while the Federalists endorsed Adams and Charles Cotesworth Pinckney. A resentful Alexander Hamilton wrote to all Federalist candidates for elector, urging them to back Pinckney for president (by withholding votes from Adams). The effort backfired when Burr obtained a copy of the letter and had it published. Meanwhile, Democratic-Republican newspapers spread the usual charges that Adams was a despot who longed for the return of monarchy, and Federalist organs countercharged that Jefferson was an atheist, a Jacobin, and a French agent.

In the end, the Democratic-Republicans won, but the electoral college produced an unintended result: a tie between Jefferson and Burr. When Burr declined to step aside, the election went to the House of Representatives, where the Federalists (and Hamilton in particular) held the balance of power. "I trust the Federalists will not be so mad as to vote for Burr," Hamilton wrote to Gouverneur Morris, adding that "the public good must be paramount to every private consideration." The House remained deadlocked for thirty-five ballots before Hamilton's maneuvering finally swung the election to Jefferson.

Later, when some Federalists threatened to block Jefferson's inauguration, the Virginia militia responded with its own threat to march on Washington. Had those Federalists not capitulated, civil war might have ensued. Instead, Jefferson's inauguration completed the first peaceful transition of power in U.S. history. Two years later, Congress passed the Twelfth Amendment ending double balloting in the electoral college.

CANDIDATE	PARTY	ELECTORAL VOTES
Thomas Jefferson, Va.	Democratic-Republican	73
Aaron Burr, N.Y.	Democratic-Republican	73
John Adams, Mass.	Federalist	65
Charles C. Pinckney, S.C.	Federalist	64
John Jay, N.Y.	Federalist	1

First Inaugural Address • Washington, D.C. • Wednesday, March 4, 1801

Friends and Fellow-Citizens: Called upon to undertake the duties of the

first executive office of our country, I avail myself of the presence of that portion of my fellow-citizens which is here assembled to express my grateful thanks for the favor with which they have been pleased to look toward me, to declare a sincere consciousness that the task is above my talents, and that I approach it with those anxious and awful presentiments which the greatness of the charge and the weakness of my powers so justly inspire. A rising nation, spread over a wide and fruitful land, traversing all the seas with the rich productions of their industry, engaged in commerce with nations who feel power and forget right, advancing rapidly to destinies beyond the reach of mortal eye—when I contemplate these transcendent objects, and see the honor, the happiness, and the hopes of this beloved country committed to the issue, and the auspices of this day, I shrink from the contemplation, and humble myself before the magnitude of the undertaking. Utterly, indeed, should I despair did not the presence of many whom I here see remind me that in

the other high authorities provided by our Constitution I shall find resources of wisdom, of virtue, and of zeal on which to rely under all difficulties. To you, then, gentlemen, who are charged with the sovereign functions of legislation, and to those associated with you, I look with encouragement for that guidance and support which may enable us to steer with safety the vessel in which we are all embarked amidst the conflicting elements of a troubled world.

During the contest of opinion through which we have passed the animation of discussions and of exertions has sometimes worn an aspect which might impose on strangers unused to think freely and to speak and to write what they think; but this being now decided by the voice of the nation, announced according to the rules of the Constitution, all will, of course, arrange themselves under the will of the law, and unite in common efforts for the common good. All, too, will bear in mind this sacred principle, that though the will of the majority

is in all cases to prevail, that will to be rightful must be reasonable; that the minority possess their equal rights, which equal law must protect, and to violate would be oppression. Let us, then, fellow-citizens, unite with one heart and one mind. Let us restore to social intercourse that harmony and affection without which liberty and even life itself are but dreary things. And let us reflect that, having banished from our land that religious intolerance under which mankind so long bled and suffered, we have yet gained little if we countenance a political intolerance as despotic, as wicked, and capable of as bitter and bloody persecutions. During the throes and convulsions of the ancient world, during the agonizing spasms of infuriated man, seeking through blood and slaughter his long-lost liberty, it was not wonderful that the agitation of the billows should reach even this distant and peaceful shore; that this should be more felt and feared by some and less by others, and should divide opinions as to measures of safety. But every difference of opinion is not a difference of principle. We have called by different names brethren of the same principle. We are all Republicans, we are all Federalists. If there be any among us who would wish to dissolve this Union or to change its republican form, let them stand undisturbed as monuments of the safety with which error of opinion may be tolerated where reason is left free to combat it. I know, indeed, that some honest men fear that a republican government can not be strong, that this Government is not strong enough; but would the honest patriot, in the full tide of successful experiment, abandon a government which has so far kept us free and firm on the theoretic and visionary fear that this Government, the world's best hope, may by possibility want energy to preserve itself? I trust not. I believe this, on the contrary, the strongest Government on earth. I believe it the only one where every man, at the call of the law, would fly to the standard of the law, and would meet invasions of the public order as his own personal concern. Sometimes it is said that man can not be trusted with the government of himself. Can he, then, be trusted with the government of others? Or have we found angels in the forms of kings to govern him? Let history answer this question.

Let us, then, with courage and confidence pursue our own Federal and Republican principles, our attachment to union and representative government. Kindly separated by nature and a wide ocean from the exterminating havoc of one quarter of the globe; too high-minded to endure the degradations of the others; possessing a chosen country, with room enough for our descendants to the thousandth and thousandth generation; entertaining a due sense of our equal right to the use of our own faculties, to the acquisitions of our own industry, to honor and confidence from our fellow-citizens, resulting not from birth, but from our actions and their sense of them; enlightened by a benign religion, professed, indeed, and practiced in various forms, yet all of them inculcating honesty, truth, temperance, gratitude, and the

love of man; acknowledging and adoring an overruling Providence, which by all its dispensations proves that it delights in the happiness of man here and his greater happiness hereafter—with all these blessings, what more is necessary to make us a happy and a prosperous

---

We are all Republicans, we are all Federalists.

---

people? Still one thing more, fellow-citizens—a wise and frugal Government, which shall restrain men from injuring one another, shall leave them otherwise free to regulate their own pursuits of industry and improvement, and shall not take from the mouth of labor the bread it has earned. This is the sum of good government, and this is necessary to close the circle of our felicities.

About to enter, fellow-citizens, on the exercise of duties which comprehend everything dear and valuable to you, it is proper you should understand what I deem the essential principles of our Government, and consequently those which ought to shape its Administration. I will compress them within the narrowest compass they will bear, stating the general principle, but not all its limitations. Equal and exact justice to all men, of whatever state or persuasion, religious or political; peace, commerce, and honest friendship with all nations, entangling alliances with none; the support of the State governments in all their rights, as the most competent administrations for our domestic concerns and the surest bulwarks against antirepublican tendencies; the preservation of the General Government in its whole constitutional vigor, as the sheet anchor of our peace at

home and safety abroad; a jealous care of the right of election by the people—a mild and safe corrective of abuses which are lopped by the sword of revolution where peaceable remedies are unprovided; absolute acquiescence in the decisions of the majority, the vital principle of republics, from which is no appeal but to force, the vital principle and immediate parent of despotism; a well disciplined militia, our best reliance in peace and for the first moments of war, till regulars may relieve them; the supremacy of the civil over the military authority; economy in the public expense, that labor may be lightly burthened; the honest payment of our debts and sacred preservation of the public faith; encouragement of agriculture, and of commerce as its handmaid; the diffusion of information and arraignment of all abuses at the bar of the public reason; freedom of religion; freedom of the press, and freedom of person under the protection of the habeas corpus, and trial by juries impartially selected. These principles form the bright constellation which has gone before us and guided

our steps through an age of revolution and reformation. The wisdom of our sages and blood of our heroes have been devoted to their attainment. They should be the creed of our political faith, the text of civic instruction, the touchstone by which to try the services of those we trust; and should we wander from them in moments of error

or of alarm, let us hasten to retrace our steps and to regain the road which alone leads to peace, liberty, and safety.

I REPAIR, THEN, FELLOW-CITIZENS, to the post you have assigned me. With experience enough in subordinate offices to have seen the difficulties of this the greatest of all, I have learnt to expect that it will rarely fall to the lot of imperfect man to retire from this station with the reputation and the favor which bring him into it. Without pretensions to that high confidence you reposed in our first and greatest revolutionary character, whose preeminent services had entitled him to the first place in his country's love and destined for him the fairest page in the volume of faithful history, I ask so much confidence only as may give firmness and effect to the legal administration of your affairs. I shall often go wrong through defect of judgment. When right, I shall often be thought wrong by those whose positions will not command a view of the whole ground. I ask your indulgence for my own errors, which will never be intentional, and your support against the errors of others, who may condemn what they would not if seen in all its parts. The approbation implied by your suffrage is a great consolation to me for the past, and my future solicitude will be to retain the good opinion of those who have bestowed it in advance, to conciliate that of others by doing them all the good in my power, and to be instrumental to the happiness and freedom of all.

Relying, then, on the patronage of your good will, I advance with obedience to the work, ready to retire from it whenever you become sensible how much better choice it is in your power to make. And may that Infinite Power which rules the destinies of the universe lead our councils to what is best, and give them a favorable issue for your peace and prosperity.

* * *

1804 THOMAS JEFFERSON

MEETING PUBLICLY FOR the first time, the Democratic-Republican congressional caucus predictably endorsed Thomas Jefferson for a second term. Also without much fuss, it dropped from the ticket Jefferson's unreliable vice president, Aaron Burr, in favor of George Clinton, Burr's main rival in New York politics.

The Federalists, who campaigned little outside New England, accused Jefferson of reducing taxes to appease the South, squandering public funds on the purchase of Louisiana, and slashing government, in particular the military. Meanwhile, Jefferson's followers boasted that he had lowered taxes, acquired Louisiana, and limited federal power. They also warned of uncertainty should the Federalists regain that power.

A certain wariness regarding the Federalists was reasonable. Burr, then running for governor of New York, had allied himself with the Essex Junto, a group of Federalist extremists planning to take New England (and New York) out of the Union. The plot fell apart, however, when Alexander Hamilton helped the Clinton forces defeat Burr in the April 1804 gubernatorial election. Three months later, Burr shot Hamilton in a duel; five months after that, Jefferson and Clinton carried nearly all of New England. The Federalists never recovered.

PARTY	ELECTORAL VOTES
DEMOCRATIC-REPUBLICAN Thomas Jefferson, Va. George Clinton, N.Y.	162
FEDERALIST Charles C. Pinckney, S.C. Rufus King, N.Y.	14

Second Inaugural Address • Washington, D.C. • Monday, March 4, 1805

Proceeding, fellow-citizens, to that qualification which the Constitution

requires before my entrance on the charge again conferred on me, it is my duty to express the deep sense I entertain of this new proof of confidence from my fellow-citizens at large, and the zeal with which it inspires me so to conduct myself as may best satisfy their just expectations.

On taking this station on a former occasion I declared the principles on which I believed it my duty to administer the affairs of our Commonwealth. My conscience tells me I have on every occasion acted up to that declaration according to its obvious import and to the understanding of every candid mind.

In the transaction of your foreign affairs we have endeavored to cultivate the friendship of all nations, and especially of those with which we have the most important relations. We have done them justice on all occasions, favored where favor was lawful, and cherished mutual interests and intercourse on fair and equal terms. We are firmly convinced, and we act on that conviction, that with nations as with individuals our interests soundly calculated will ever be found inseparable from our moral duties, and history bears witness to the fact that a just nation is trusted on its word when recourse is had to armaments and wars to bridle others.

At home, fellow-citizens, you best know whether we have done well or ill. The suppression of unnecessary offices, of useless establishments and expenses, enabled us to discontinue our internal taxes. These, covering our land with officers and opening our doors to their intrusions, had already begun that process of domiciliary vexation which

once entered is scarcely to be restrained from reaching successively every article of property and produce. If among these taxes some minor ones fell which had not been inconvenient, it was because their amount would not have paid the officers who collected them, and because, if they had any merit, the State authorities might adopt them instead of others less approved.

The remaining revenue on the consumption of foreign articles is paid chiefly by those who can afford to add foreign luxuries to domestic comforts, being collected on our seaboard and frontiers only, and incorporated with the transactions of our mercantile citizens, it may be the pleasure and the pride of an American to ask, What farmer, what mechanic, what laborer ever sees a taxgatherer of the United States? These contributions enable us to support the current expenses of the Government, to fulfill contracts with foreign nations, to extinguish the native right of soil within our limits, to extend those limits, and to apply such a surplus to our public debts as places at a short day their final redemption, and that redemption once effected the revenue thereby liberated may, by a just repartition of it among the States and a corresponding amendment of the Constitution, be applied in time of peace to rivers, canals, roads, arts, manufactures, education, and other great objects within each State. In time of war, if injustice by ourselves or others must sometimes produce war, increased as the same revenue will be by increased population and consumption, and aided by other resources reserved for

that crisis, it may meet within the year all the expenses of the year without encroaching on the rights of future generations by burthening them with the debts of the past. War will then be but a suspension of useful works, and a return to a state of peace, a return to the progress of improvement.

I have said, fellow-citizens, that the income reserved had enabled us to extend our limits, but that extension may possibly pay for itself before we are called on, and in the meantime may keep down the accruing interest; in all events, it will replace the advances we shall have made. I know that the acquisition of Louisiana had been disapproved by some from a candid apprehension that the enlargement of our territory would endanger its union. But who can limit the extent to which the federative principle may operate effectively? The larger our association the less will it be shaken by local passions; and in any view is it not better that the opposite bank of the Mississippi should be settled by our own brethren and children than by strangers of another family? With which should we be most likely to live in harmony and friendly intercourse?

In matters of religion I have considered that its free exercise is placed by the Constitution independent of the powers of the General Government. I have therefore undertaken on no occasion to prescribe the religious exercises suited to it, but have left them, as the Constitution found them, under the direction and discipline of the church or state authorities acknowledged by the several religious societies.

The aboriginal inhabitants of these countries I have regarded with the commiseration their history inspires. Endowed with the faculties and the rights of men, breathing an ardent love of liberty and independence, and occupying a country which left them no desire but to be undisturbed, the stream of overflowing population from other regions directed itself on these shores; without power to divert or habits to contend against it, they have been overwhelmed by the current or driven before it; now reduced within limits too narrow for the hunter's state, humanity enjoins us to teach them agriculture and the domestic arts; to encourage them to that industry which alone can enable them to maintain their place in existence and to prepare them in time for that state of society which to bodily comforts adds the improvement of the mind and morals. We have therefore liberally furnished them with the implements of husbandry and household use; we have placed among them instructors in the arts of first necessity, and they are covered with the aegis of the law against aggressors from among ourselves.

But the endeavors to enlighten them on the fate which awaits their present course of life, to induce them to exercise their reason, follow its dictates, and change their pursuits with the change of circumstances have powerful obstacles to encounter; they are combated by the habits of their bodies, prejudices of their minds, ignorance, pride, and the influence of interested and crafty individuals among them who feel themselves something in the present order of things and fear to become nothing in any other. These persons inculcate a sanctimonious reverence for the customs of their ancestors; that whatsoever they did must be done through all time; that reason is a false guide, and to advance under its counsel in their physical, moral, or political condition is perilous innovation; that their duty is to remain as their Creator made them, ignorance being safety and knowledge full of danger; in short, my friends, among them also is seen the action and counteraction of good sense and of bigotry; they too have their antiphilosophists who find an interest in keeping things in their present state, who dread reformation, and exert all their faculties to maintain the ascendancy of habit over the duty of improving our reason and obeying its mandates.

In giving these outlines I do not mean, fellow-citizens, to arrogate to myself the merit of the measures. That is due, in the first place, to the reflecting character of our citizens at large, who, by the weight of public opinion, influence and strengthen the public measures. It is due to the sound discretion with which they select from among themselves those to whom they confide the legislative duties. It is due to the zeal and wisdom of the characters thus selected, who lay the foundations of public happiness in wholesome laws, the execution of which alone remains for others, and it is due to the able and faithful auxiliaries, whose patriotism has associated them with me in the executive functions.

During this course of administration, and in order to disturb it, the artillery of the press has been leveled against us, charged with whatsoever its licentiousness could devise or

---

The larger our association the less will it be shaken by local passions....

---

dare. These abuses of an institution so important to freedom and science are deeply to be regretted, inasmuch as they tend to lessen its usefulness and to sap its safety. They might, indeed, have been corrected by the wholesome punishments reserved to and provided by the laws of the several States against falsehood and defamation, but public duties more urgent press on the time of public servants, and the offenders have therefore been left to find their punishment in the public indignation.

Nor was it uninteresting to the world that an experiment should be fairly and fully made, whether freedom of discussion, unaided by power, is not sufficient for the propagation and protection of truth—whether a government conducting itself in the true spirit of its constitution, with zeal and purity, and doing no act which it would be unwilling the whole world should witness, can be written down by falsehood and defamation. The experiment has been tried; you have witnessed the scene; our fellow-citizens looked on, cool and collected; they saw the latent source from which these outrages proceeded; they gathered around their public functionaries, and when the Constitution called them to the decision by suffrage, they pronounced their verdict, honorable to those who had served them and consolatory to the friend of man who believes that he may be trusted with the control of his own affairs.

No inference is here intended that the laws provided by the States against false and defamatory publications should not be enforced; he who has time renders a service to public morals and public tranquillity in reforming these abuses by the salutary coercions of the law; but the experiment is noted to prove that, since truth and reason have maintained their ground against false opinions in league with false facts, the press, confined to truth, needs no other legal restraint; the public judgment will correct false reasoning and opinions on a full hearing of all parties; and no other definite line can be drawn between the inestimable liberty of the press and its demoralizing licentiousness. If there be still improprieties which this rule would not restrain, its supplement must be sought in the censorship of public opinion.

Contemplating the union of sentiment now manifested so generally as auguring harmony and happiness to our future course, I offer to our country sincere congratulations. With those, too, not yet rallied to the same point the disposition to do so is gaining strength; facts are piercing through the veil drawn over them, and our doubting brethren will at length see that the mass of their fellow-citizens with whom they can not yet resolve to act as to principles and measures, think as they think and desire what they desire;

that our wish as well as theirs is that the public efforts may be directed honestly to the public good, that peace be cultivated, civil and religious liberty unassailed, law and order preserved, equality of rights maintained, and that state of property, equal or unequal, which results to every man from his own industry or that of his father's. When satisfied of these views it is not in human nature that they should not approve and support them. In the meantime let us cherish them with patient affection, let us do them justice, and more than justice, in all competitions of interest; and we need not doubt that truth, reason, and their own interests will at length prevail, will gather them into the fold of their country, and will complete that entire union of opinion which gives to a nation the blessing of harmony and the benefit of all its strength.

I shall now enter on the duties to which my fellow-citizens have again called me, and shall proceed in the spirit of those principles which they have approved. I fear not that any motives of interest may lead me astray; I am sensible of no passion which could seduce me knowingly from the path of justice, but the weaknesses of human nature and the limits of my own understanding will produce errors of judgment sometimes injurious to your interests. I shall need, therefore, all the indulgence which I have heretofore experienced from my constituents; the want of it will certainly not lessen with increasing years. I shall need, too, the favor of that Being in whose hands we are, who led our fathers, as Israel of old, from their native land and planted them in a country flowing with all the necessaries and comforts of life; who has covered our infancy with His providence and our riper years with His wisdom and power, and to whose goodness I ask you to join in supplications with me that He will so enlighten the minds of your servants, guide their councils, and prosper their measures that whatsoever they do shall result in your good, and shall secure to you the peace, friendship, and approbation of all nations.

* * *

1808 JAMES MADISON

JEFFERSON'S DECISION TO GIVE UP THE presidency—or "shake off the shackles of power," as he called it—reinforced Washington's two-term precedent. It also seemed to give the Federalists an electoral opportunity. Along with the failure of his foreign policy toward France and England (the Embargo Act in particular), Jefferson's retirement should have been enough to fuel a Federalist resurgence—had not the opposition to the Democratic-Republicans been so weak and divided.

The Democratic-Republican congressional caucus nominated Secretary of State James Madison for president and Vice President George Clinton to continue in that role. However, as a protest against the administration's embargo policy, the New York party endorsed Clinton for president, and in Virginia, a rump group of state legislators nominated James Monroe. The practice of selecting candidates by congressional caucus was also challenged for the first time as being undemocratic.

Federalist candidates Charles C. Pinckney and Rufus King—the same ticket that ran against Jefferson and Clinton in 1804—attacked

Madison as a tool of France and blamed him for the ruinous "Dambargo." Democratic-Republicans countered by singing "Jefferson to the shade retires, but Madison, like morn, appears." The Federalists carried most of New England but little else, while Madison easily parried the intraparty challenge: George Clinton received only six of New York's nineteen electoral votes, and Monroe (who had withdrawn) got none at all from Virginia.

PARTY	ELECTORAL VOTES
DEMOCRATIC-REPUBLICAN James Madison, Va. George Clinton, N.Y.	122
FEDERALIST Charles C. Pinckney, S.C. Rufus King, N.Y.	47
(INDEPENDENT) George Clinton, N.Y.	6
(NOT VOTED)	1

First Inaugural Address • Washington, D.C. • Saturday, March 4, 1809

Unwilling to depart from examples of the most revered authority,

I avail myself of the occasion now presented to express the profound impression made on me by the call of my country to the station to the duties of which I am about to pledge myself by the most solemn of sanctions. So distinguished a mark of confidence, proceeding from the deliberate and tranquil suffrage of a free and virtuous nation, would under any circumstances have commanded my gratitude and devotion, as well as filled me with an awful sense of the trust to be assumed. Under the various circumstances which give peculiar solemnity to the existing period, I feel that both the honor and the responsibility allotted to me are inexpressibly enhanced.

The present situation of the world is indeed without a parallel, and that of our own country full of difficulties. The pressure of these, too, is the more severely felt because they have fallen upon us at a moment when the national prosperity being at a height not before attained, the contrast resulting from the change has rendered the more striking. Under the benign influence of our republican institutions, and the maintenance of peace with all nations whilst so many of them were engaged in bloody and wasteful wars, the fruits of a just policy were enjoyed in an unrivaled growth of our facul-

ties and resources. Proofs of this were seen in the improvements of agriculture, in the successful enterprises of commerce, in the progress of manufacturers and useful arts, in the increase of the public revenue and the use made of it in reducing the public debt, and in the valuable works and establishments everywhere multiplying over the face of our land.

It is a precious reflection that the transition from this prosperous condition of our country to the scene which has for some time been distressing us is not chargeable on any unwarrantable views, nor, as I trust, on any involuntary errors in the public councils. Indulging no passions which trespass on the rights or the repose of other nations, it has been the true glory of the United States to cultivate peace by observing justice, and to entitle themselves to the respect of the nations at war by fulfilling their neutral obligations with the most scrupulous impartiality. If there be candor in the world, the truth of these assertions will not be questioned; posterity at least will do justice to them.

This unexceptionable course could not avail against the injustice and violence of the belligerent powers. In their rage against each other, or impelled by more direct mo-

tives, principles of retaliation have been introduced equally contrary to universal reason and acknowledged law. How long their arbitrary edicts will be continued in spite of the demonstrations that not even a pretext for them has been given by the United States, and of the fair and liberal attempt to induce a revocation of them, can not be anticipated. Assuring myself that under every vicissitude the determined spirit and united councils of the nation will be safeguards to its honor and its essential interests, I repair to the post assigned me with no other discouragement than what springs from my own inadequacy to its high duties. If I do not sink under the weight of this deep conviction it is because I find some support in a consciousness of the purposes and a confidence in the principles which I bring with me into this arduous service.

To cherish peace and friendly intercourse with all nations having correspondent dispositions; to maintain sincere neutrality toward belligerent nations; to prefer in all cases amicable discussion and reasonable accommodation of differences to a decision of them by an appeal to arms; to exclude foreign intrigues and foreign partialities, so degrading to all countries and so baneful to free ones; to foster a spirit of independence too just to invade the rights of others, too proud to surrender our own, too liberal to indulge unworthy prejudices ourselves and too elevated not to look down upon them in others; to hold the union of the States as the basis of their peace and happiness; to support the Constitution, which is the cement of the Union, as well in its limitations as in its authorities; to respect the rights and authorities reserved to the States and to the people as equally incorporated with and essential to the success of the general system; to avoid the slightest interference with the right of conscience or the functions of religion, so wisely exempted from civil jurisdiction; to preserve in their full energy the other salutary provisions in behalf of private and personal rights, and of the freedom of the press; to observe economy in public expenditures; to liberate the public resources by an honorable discharge of the public debts; to keep within the requisite limits a standing military force, always remembering that an armed and trained militia is the firmest bulwark of republics—that without standing armies their liberty can never be in danger, nor with large ones safe; to promote by authorized means improvements friendly to agriculture, to manufactures, and to external as well as internal commerce; to favor in like manner the advancement of science and the diffusion of information as the best aliment to true liberty; to carry on the benevolent plans which have been so meritoriously applied to the conversion of our aboriginal neighbors from the degradation and wretchedness of savage life to a participation of the improvements of which the human mind and manners are susceptible in a civilized state—as far as sentiments and intentions such as these can aid the fulfillment of my duty, they will be a resource which can not fail me.

It is my good fortune, moreover, to have the path in which I am to tread lighted by examples of illustrious services successfully rendered in the most trying difficulties by those who have marched before me. Of those of my immediate predecessor it might least become me here to speak. I may, however, be pardoned for not suppressing the sympathy with which my heart is full in the rich reward he enjoys in the benedictions of a beloved country, gratefully bestowed or exalted talents zealously devoted through a long career to the advancement of its highest interest and happiness.

But the source to which I look or the aids which alone can supply my deficiencies is in the well-tried intelligence and virtue of my fellow-citizens, and in the counsels of those representing them in the other de-

> ...it has been the true glory of the United States to cultivate peace by observing justice....

partments associated in the care of the national interests. In these my confidence will under every difficulty be best placed, next to that which we have all been encouraged to feel in the guardianship and guidance of that Almighty Being whose power regulates the destiny of nations, whose blessings have been so conspicuously dispensed to this rising Republic, and to whom we are bound to address our devout gratitude for the past, as well as our fervent supplications and best hopes for the future.

* * *

1812 JAMES MADISON

THE ELECTION OF 1812 WAS the first presidential contest conducted during wartime. Although a U.S. invasion of Canada had failed, early naval victories boosted support for the war, and the campaign took place before a British blockade turned the course of the fighting against the Americans.

Madison was renominated by the Democratic-Republican congressional caucus—his only rival being DeWitt Clinton, the vice president's nephew, who was endorsed by the New York state party. Clinton was also supported by the Federalists, who made no formal nomination of their own for president but did endorse party member Jared Ingersoll for vice president.

Madison's followers defended his conduct of the War of 1812 while chanting "On to Canada." The Clintonians, whose slogan was "Too much Virginia," once again attacked the legitimacy of nomination by congressional caucus and suggested, somewhat self-servingly, that presidents should be limited to a single term. Running as the candidate of "the Peace Party," Clinton carried most of New England and some mid-Atlantic states, but Madison won all of the South and the West, both of which regions enthusiastically supported "Mr. Madison's War."

PARTY	ELECTORAL VOTES
DEMOCRATIC-REPUBLICAN James Madison, Va. Elbridge Gerry, Mass.	128
FUSION DeWitt Clinton, N.Y. Jared Ingersoll, Pa.	89
(NOT VOTED)	1

Second Inaugural Address • Washington, D.C. • Thursday, March 4, 1813

About to add the solemnity of an oath to the obligations imposed

by a second call to the station in which my country heretofore placed me, I find in the presence of this respectable assembly an opportunity of publicly repeating my profound sense of so distinguished a confidence and of the responsibility united with it. The impressions on me are strengthened by such an evidence that my faithful endeavors to discharge my arduous duties have been favorably estimated, and by a consideration of the momentous period at which the trust has been renewed. From the weight and magnitude now belonging to it I should be compelled to shrink if I had less reliance on the support of an enlightened and generous people, and felt less deeply a conviction that the war with a powerful nation, which forms so prominent a feature in our situation, is

stamped with that justice which invites the smiles of Heaven on the means of conducting it to a successful termination.

May we not cherish this sentiment without presumption when we reflect on the characters by which this war is distinguished?

It was not declared on the part of the United States until it had been long made on them, in reality though not in name; until arguments and postulations had been exhausted; until a positive declaration had been received that the wrongs provoking it would not be discontinued; nor until this last appeal could no longer be delayed without breaking down the spirit of the nation, destroying all confidence in itself and in its political institutions, and either perpetuating a state of disgraceful suffering or regaining by more costly sacrifices and more severe struggles our lost rank and respect among independent powers.

On the issue of the war are staked our national sovereignty on the high seas and the security of an important class of citizens, whose occupations give the proper value to those of every other class. Not to contend for such a stake is to surrender our equality with other powers on the element common to all and to violate the sacred title which every member of the society has to its protection. I need not call into view the unlawfulness of the practice by which our mariners are forced at the will of every cruising officer from their own vessels into foreign ones, nor paint the outrages inseparable from it. The proofs are in the records of each successive Administration of our Government, and the cruel sufferings of that portion of the American people have found their way to every bosom not dead to the sympathies of human nature.

As the war was just in its origin and necessary and noble in its objects, we can reflect with a proud satisfaction that in carrying it on no principle of justice or honor, no usage of civilized nations, no precept of courtesy or humanity, have been infringed. The war has been waged on our part with scrupulous regard to all these obligations, and in a spirit of liberality which was never surpassed.

How little has been the effect of this example on the conduct of the enemy!

They have retained as prisoners of war citizens of the United States not liable to be so considered under the usages of war.

They have refused to consider as prisoners of war, and threatened to punish as traitors and deserters, persons emigrating without restraint to the United States, incorporated by naturalization into our political family, and fighting under the authority of their adopted country in open and honorable war for the maintenance of its rights and safety. Such is the avowed purpose of a Government which is in the practice of naturalizing by thousands citizens of other countries, and not only of permitting but

perity is visible in the public countenance. The means employed by the British cabinet to undermine it have recoiled on themselves; have given to our national faculties a more rapid development, and, draining or diverting the precious metals from British circulation and British vaults, have poured them into those of the United States. It is a propitious consideration that an unavoidable war should have found this seasonable facility for the contributions required to support it.

> *...the war was just in its origin and necessary and noble in its objects....*

When the public voice called for war, all knew, and still know, that without them it could not be carried on through the period which it might last, and the patriotism, the good sense, and the manly spirit of our fellow-citizens are pledges for the cheerfulness with which they will bear each his share of the common burden. To render the war short and its success sure, animated and systematic exertions alone are necessary, and the success of our arms now may long preserve our country from the necessity of another resort to them. Already have the gallant exploits of our naval heroes proved to the world our inherent capacity to maintain our rights on one element. If the reputation of our arms has been thrown under clouds on the other, presaging flashes of heroic enterprise assure us that nothing is wanting to correspondent triumphs there also but the discipline and habits which are in daily progress.

* * *

compelling them to fight its battles against their native country.

They have not, it is true, taken into their own hands the hatchet and the knife, devoted to indiscriminate massacre, but they have let loose the savages armed with these cruel instruments; have allured them into their service, and carried them to battle by their sides, eager to glut their savage thirst with the blood of the vanquished and to finish the work of torture and death on maimed and defenseless captives. And, what was never before seen, British commanders have extorted victory over the unconquerable valor of our troops by presenting to the sympathy of their chief captives awaiting massacre from their savage associates. And now we

find them, in further contempt of the modes of honorable warfare, supplying the place of a conquering force by attempts to disorganize our political society, to dismember our confederated Republic. Happily, like others, these will recoil on the authors; but they mark the degenerate counsels from which they emanate, and if they did not belong to a sense of unexampled inconsistencies might excite the greater wonder as proceeding from a Government which founded the very war in which it has been so long engaged on a charge against the disorganizing and insurrectional policy of its adversary.

To render the justice of the war on our part the more conspicuous, the reluctance to

commence it was followed by the earliest and strongest manifestations of a disposition to arrest its progress. The sword was scarcely out of the scabbard before the enemy was apprised of the reasonable terms on which it would be resheathed. Still more precise advances were repeated, and have been received in a spirit forbidding every reliance not placed on the military resources of the nation.

These resources are amply sufficient to bring the war to an honorable issue. Our nation is in number more than half that of the British Isles. It is composed of a brave, a free, a virtuous, and an intelligent people. Our country abounds in the necessaries, the arts, and the comforts of life. A general pros-

1816 James Monroe

By 1816, the Federalists had lost their political teeth. The Hartford Convention of late 1814, held during wartime, had substantially discredited the party with its calls for secession. Meanwhile, the Treaty of Ghent and Andrew Jackson's early 1815 victory at New Orleans obscured the ineffectiveness of James Madison's war policy and made the Federalists look even worse. As a result, for the next three presidential elections, the only contest that mattered was the one for the Democratic-Republican nomination.

The retiring president backed Secretary of State (and fellow Virginian) James Monroe over Secretary of War William H. Crawford. Although a Georgian, Crawford had the support of the New York party and that of other Democratic-Republicans opposed to a "Virginia dynasty."

At the party's congressional caucus, Henry Clay was sufficiently critical of the nomination process to move that it was "not expedient." Clay's motion reflected sharp complaints about the selection of candidates by congressional caucus; even so, his motion failed, and Monroe edged out Crawford in the balloting that followed.

In the general election, the Democratic-Republicans drowned out more rumblings about a Virginia dynasty with noisy parades that featured a new song, "The Star-Spangled Banner," intended to remind voters of the recent "victory" in the War of 1812. Monroe's supporters further preempted Federalist appeals to nationalism by proposing the chartering of a new national bank and the imposition of a protective tariff. Left with no issues of his own, Federalist Rufus King received such limited and scattered support that he referred to his candidacy as a "fruitless struggle." After the election, no longer even a regional force, the Federalists disappeared as a party.

Party	Electoral Votes
Democratic-Republican	183
James Monroe, Va.	
Daniel D. Tompkins, N.Y.	
Federalist	34
Rufus King, N.Y.	
John E. Howard, Md.	
(Not Voted)	4

First Inaugural Address • Washington, D.C. • Tuesday, March 4, 1817

I should be destitute of feeling if I was not deeply affected by the strong proof

which my fellow-citizens have given me of their confidence in calling me to the high office whose functions I am about to assume. As the expression of their good opinion of my conduct in the public service, I derive from it a gratification which those who are conscious of having done all that they could to merit it can alone feel. My sensibility is increased by a just estimate of the importance of the trust and of the nature and extent of its duties, with the proper discharge of which the highest interests of a great and free people are intimately connected. Conscious of my own deficiency, I cannot enter on these duties without great anxiety for the result. From a just responsibility I will never shrink, calculating with confidence that in my best efforts to promote the public welfare my motives will always be duly appreciated and my conduct be viewed with that candor and indulgence which I have experienced in other stations.

In commencing the duties of the chief executive office it has been the practice of the distinguished men who have gone before me to explain the principles which would govern them in their respective Administrations. In following their venerated example my attention is naturally drawn to the great causes which have contributed in a principal degree to produce the present happy condition of the United States. They will best explain the nature of our duties and shed much light on the policy which ought to be pursued in future.

From the commencement of our Revolution to the present day almost forty years have elapsed, and from the establishment of this Constitution twenty-eight. Through this whole term the Government has been what may emphatically be called self-government. And what has been the effect? To whatever object we turn our attention, whether it relates to our foreign or domestic concerns, we find abundant cause to felicitate ourselves in the excellence of our institutions. During a period fraught with difficulties and marked by very extraordinary events the United States have flourished beyond example. Their citizens individually have been happy and the nation prosperous.

Under this Constitution our commerce has been wisely regulated with foreign nations and between the States; new States have been admitted into our Union; our territory has been enlarged by fair and honor-able treaty, and with great advantage to the original States; the States, respectively protected by the National Government under a mild, parental system against foreign dangers, and enjoying within their separate spheres, by a wise partition of power, a just proportion of the sovereignty, have improved their police, extended their settlements, and attained a strength and maturity which are the best proofs of wholesome laws well administered. And if we look to the condition of individuals what a proud spectacle does it exhibit! On whom has oppression fallen in any quarter of our Union? Who has been deprived of any right of person or property? Who restrained from offering his vows in the mode which he prefers to the Divine Author of his being? It is well known that all these blessings have been enjoyed in their fullest extent; and I add with peculiar satisfaction that there has been no example of a capital punishment being inflicted on anyone for the crime of high treason.

Some who might admit the competency of our Government to these beneficent duties might doubt it in trials which put to the test its strength and efficiency as a member of the great community of nations. Here too experience has afforded us the most satisfactory proof in its favor. Just as this Constitution was put into action several of the principal States of Europe had become much agitated and some of them seriously convulsed. Destructive wars ensued, which have of late only been terminated. In the course of these conflicts the United States received great injury from several of the parties. It was their interest to stand aloof from the contest, to demand justice the party committing the injury, and to cultivate by a fair and honorable conduct the friendship of all. War became at length inevitable, and the result has shown that our Government is equal to that, the greatest of trials, under the most unfavorable circumstances. Of the virtue of the people and of the heroic exploits of the Army, the Navy, and the militia I need not speak.

Such, then, is the happy Government under which we live—a Government adequate to every purpose for which the social compact is formed; a Government elective in all its branches, under which every citizen may by his merit obtain the highest trust recognized by the Constitution; which contains within it no cause of discord, none to put at variance one portion of the community with another; a Government which protects every citizen in the full enjoyment of his rights, and is able to protect the nation against injustice from foreign powers.

OTHER CONSIDERATIONS OF THE highest importance admonish us to cherish our Union and to cling to the Government which supports it. Fortunate as we are in our political institutions, we have not been less so in other circumstances on which our prosperity and happiness essentially depend. Situated within the temperate zone, and extending through many degrees of latitude along the Atlantic, the United States enjoy all the varieties of climate, and every production incident to that portion of the globe. Penetrating internally to the Great Lakes and beyond the sources of the great rivers which communicate through our whole interior, no country was ever happier with respect to its domain. Blessed,

too, with a fertile soil, our produce has always been very abundant, leaving, even in years the least favorable, a surplus for the wants of our fellow-men in other countries. Such is our peculiar felicity that there is not a part of our Union that is not particularly interested in preserving it. The great agricultural interest of the nation prospers under its protection. Local interests are not less fostered by it. Our fellow-citizens of the North engaged in navigation find great encouragement in being made the favored carriers of the vast productions of the other portions of the United States, while the inhabitants of these are amply recompensed, in their turn, by the nursery for seamen and naval force thus formed and reared up for the support of our common rights. Our manufactures find a generous encouragement by the policy which patronizes domestic industry, and the surplus of our produce a steady and profitable market by local wants in less-favored parts at home.

Such, then, being the highly favored condition of our country, it is the interest of every citizen to maintain it. What are the dangers which menace us? If any exist they ought to be ascertained and guarded against.

In explaining my sentiments on this subject it may be asked, What raised us to the present happy state? How did we accomplish the Revolution? How remedy the defects of the first instrument of our Union, by infusing into the National Government sufficient power for national purposes, without impairing the just rights of the States or affecting those of individuals? How sustain and pass with glory through the late war? The Government has been in the hands of the people. To the people, therefore, and to the faithful and able depositaries of their trust is the credit due. Had the people of the United States been educated in different principles, had they been less intelligent, less independent, or less virtuous, can it be believed that we should have maintained the same steady and consistent career or been blessed with the same success? While, then, the constituent body retains its present sound and healthful state everything will be safe. They will choose competent and

faithful representatives for every department. It is only when the people become ignorant and corrupt, when they degenerate into a populace, that they are incapable of exercising the sovereignty. Usurpation is then an easy attainment, and an usurper soon found. The people themselves become the willing instruments of their own debasement and ruin. Let us, then, look to the great cause, and endeavor to preserve it in full force. Let us by all wise and constitutional measures promote intelligence among

…the heart of every citizen must expand with joy when he reflects how near our Government has approached to perfection….

the people as the best means of preserving our liberties.

Dangers from abroad are not less deserving of attention. Experiencing the fortune of other nations, the United States may be again involved in war, and it may in that event be the object of the adverse party to overset our Government, to break our Union, and demolish us as a nation. Our distance from Europe and the just, moderate, and pacific policy of our Government may form some security against these dangers, but they ought to be anticipated and guarded against. Many of our citizens are engaged in commerce and navigation, and all of them are in a certain degree dependent on their prosperous state. Many are engaged in the fisheries. These interests are exposed to invasion in the wars between other powers, and we should disregard the faithful admonition of experience if we did not expect it. We must support our rights or lose our character, and with it, perhaps, our liberties. A people who fail to do

it can scarcely be said to hold a place among independent nations. National honor is national property of the highest value. The sentiment in the mind of every citizen is national strength. It ought therefore to be cherished.

To secure us against these dangers our coast and inland frontiers should be fortified, our Army and Navy, regulated upon just principles as to the force of each, be kept in perfect order, and our militia be placed on the best practicable footing. To put our extensive coast in such a state of defense as to secure our cities and interior from invasion will be attended with expense, but the work when finished will be permanent, and it is fair to presume that a single campaign of invasion by a naval force superior to our own, aided by a few thousand land troops, would expose us to greater expense, without taking into the estimate the loss of property and distress of our citizens, than would be sufficient for this great work. Our land and naval forces should be moderate, but adequate to the necessary purposes—the former to garrison and preserve our fortifications and to meet the first invasions of a foreign foe, and, while constituting the elements of a greater force, to preserve the science as well as all the necessary implements of war in a state to be brought into activity in the event of war; the latter, retained within the limits proper in a state of peace, might aid in maintaining the neutrality of the United States with dignity in the wars of other powers and in saving the property of their citizens from spoliation. In time of war, with the enlargement of which the great naval resources of the country render it susceptible, and which should be duly fostered in time of peace, it would contribute essentially, both as an auxiliary of defense and as a powerful engine of annoyance, to diminish the calamities of war and to bring the war to a speedy and honorable termination.

But it ought always to be held prominently in view that the safety of these States and of everything dear to a free people must depend in an eminent degree on the militia. Invasions may be made too formidable to be resisted by any land and naval force which it would comport either with the principles of our Government or the circumstances of the United States to maintain. In such cases recourse must be had to the great body of the people, and in a manner to produce the best effect. It is of the highest importance, therefore, that they be so organized and trained as to be prepared for any emergency. The arrangement should be such as to put at the command of the Government the ardent patriotism and youthful vigor of the country. If formed on equal and just principles, it can not be oppressive. It is the crisis which makes the pressure, and not the laws which provide a remedy for it. This arrangement should be formed, too, in time of peace, to be the better prepared for war. With such an organization of such a people the United States have nothing to dread from foreign invasion. At its approach an overwhelming force of gallant men might always be put in motion.

Other interests of high importance will claim attention, among which the improvement of our country by roads and canals, proceeding always with a constitutional sanction, holds a distinguished place. By thus facilitating the intercourse between the States we shall add much to the convenience and comfort of our fellow-citizens, much to the ornament of the country, and, what is of greater importance, we shall shorten distances, and, by making each part more accessible to and dependent on the other, we shall bind the Union more closely together. Nature has done so much for us by intersecting the country with so many great rivers, bays, and lakes, approaching from distant points so near to each other, that the inducement to complete the work seems to be peculiarly strong. A more interesting spectacle was perhaps never seen than is exhibited within the limits of the United States—a territory so vast and advantageously situated, containing objects so grand, so useful, so happily connected in all their parts!

Our manufacturers will likewise require the systematic and fostering care of the Government. Possessing as we do all the raw materials, the fruit of our own soil and industry, we ought not to depend in the degree we have done on supplies from other countries. While we are thus dependent the sudden event of war, unsought and unexpected, can not fail to plunge us into the most serious difficulties. It is important, too, that the capital which nourishes our manufacturers should be domestic, as its influence in that case instead of exhausting, as it may do in foreign hands, would be felt advantageously on agriculture and every other branch of industry. Equally important is it to provide at home a market for our raw materials, as by extending the competition it will enhance the price and protect the cultivator against the casualties incident to foreign markets.

With the Indian tribes it is our duty to cultivate friendly relations and to act with kindness and liberality in all our transactions. Equally proper is it to persevere in our efforts to extend to them the advantages of civilization.

The great amount of our revenue and the flourishing state of the Treasury are a full proof of the competency of the national resources for any emergency, as they are of the willingness of our fellow-citizens to bear the burdens which the public necessities require. The vast amount of vacant lands, the value of which daily augments, forms an additional resource of great extent and duration. These resources, besides accomplishing every other necessary purpose, put it completely in the power of the United States to discharge the national debt at an early period. Peace is the best time for improvement and preparation of every kind; it is in peace that our commerce flourishes most, that taxes are most easily paid, and that the revenue is most productive.

The Executive is charged officially in the Departments under it with the disbursement of the public money, and is responsible for the faithful application of it to the purposes for which it is raised. The Legislature is the watchful guardian over the public purse. It is its duty to see that the disbursement has been honestly made. To meet the requisite responsibility every facility should be afforded to the Executive to enable it to bring the public agents intrusted with the public money strictly and promptly to account. Nothing should be presumed against them; but if, with the requisite facilities, the public money is suffered to lie long and uselessly in their hands, they will not be the only defaulters, nor will the demoralizing effect be confined to them. It will evince a relaxation and want of tone in the Administration which will be felt by the whole community. I shall do all I can to secure economy and fidelity in this important branch of the Administration, and I doubt not that the Legislature will perform its duty with equal zeal. A thorough examination should be regularly made, and I will promote it.

IT IS PARTICULARLY GRATIfying to me to enter on the discharge of these duties at a time when the United States are blessed with peace. It is a state most consistent with their prosperity and happiness. It will be my sincere desire to preserve it, so far as depends on the Executive, on just principles with all nations, claiming nothing unreasonable of any and rendering to each what is its due.

Equally gratifying is it to witness the increased harmony of opinion which pervades our Union. Discord does not belong to our system. Union is recommended as well by the free and benign principles of our Government, extending its blessings to every individual, as by the other eminent advantages attending it. The American people have encountered together great dangers and sustained severe trials with success. They constitute one great family with a common interest. Experience has enlightened us on some questions of essential importance to the country. The progress has been slow, dictated by a just reflection and a faithful regard to every interest connected with it. To promote this harmony in accord with the principles of our republican Government and in a manner to give them the most complete effect, and to advance in all other respects the best interests of our Union, will be the object of my constant and zealous exertions.

Never did a government commence under auspices so favorable, nor ever was success so complete. If we look to the history of other nations, ancient or modern, we find no example of a growth so rapid, so gigantic, of a people so prosperous and happy. In contemplating what we have still to perform, the heart of every citizen must expand with joy when he reflects how near our Government has approached to perfection; that in respect to it we have no essential improvement to make; that the great object is to preserve it in the essential principles and features which characterize it, and that is to be done by preserving the virtue and enlightening the minds of the people; and as a security against foreign dangers to adopt such arrangements as are indispensable to the support of our independence, our rights and liberties. If we persevere in the career in which we have advanced so far and in the path already traced, we can not fail, under the favor of a gracious Providence, to attain the high destiny which seems to await us.

In the Administrations of the illustrious men who have preceded me in this high station, with some of whom I have been connected by the closest ties from early life, examples are presented which will always be found highly instructive and useful to their successors. From these I shall endeavor to derive all the advantages which they may afford. Of my immediate predecessor, under whom so important a portion of this great and successful experiment has been made, I shall be pardoned for expressing my earnest wishes that he may long enjoy in his retirement the affections of a grateful country, the best reward of exalted talents and the most faithful and meritorious service. Relying on the aid to be derived from the other departments of the Government, I enter on the trust to which I have been called by the suffrages of my fellow-citizens with my fervent prayers to the Almighty that He will be graciously pleased to continue to us that protection which He has already so conspicuously displayed in our favor.

* * *

1820 JAMES MONROE

DESPITE THE "GOOD FEELINGS" AND consensus that supposedly defined this era in American politics, economic troubles and sectional tensions over slavery briefly threatened James Monroe's renomination. In fact, Democratic-Republicans in Monroe's native state of Virginia came close to opposing his candidacy until he was able to persuade them that the 1820 Missouri Compromise was essential to the survival of the Union.

Otherwise, Monroe kept his opinions about tariffs, internal improvements, and slavery to himself while deflecting most of the blame for the country's economic problems onto the Second Bank of the United States. These tactics worked well enough that the Democratic-Republican congressional caucus, only one-fourth of its members showing up, deemed it "not necessary" to make a formal nomination. With even ex–Federalists rallying behind Monroe, "the Last of the Fathers" ran unopposed.

He won every electoral vote cast save that of New Hampshire governor William Plumer, who voted for Secretary of State John Quincy Adams— in part because he wanted to deny Monroe the unanimous vote that only George Washington had received, and also because he didn't approve of Monroe's policies.

Their ascendancy complete, the Democratic-Republicans soon opened their party caucus to former Federalists, temporarily ending the two-party system in congressional as well as presidential elections.

PARTY	ELECTORAL VOTES
DEMOCRATIC-REPUBLICAN James Monroe, Va. Daniel D. Tompkins, N.Y.	231
(INDEPENDENT) John Quincy Adams, Mass.	1
(NOT VOTED)	3

Second Inaugural Address • Washington, D.C. • Monday, March 5, 1821

Fellow-Citizens:I shall not attempt to describe the grateful emotions which

the new and very distinguished proof of the confidence of my fellow-citizens, evinced by my reelection to this high trust, has excited in my bosom. The approbation which it announces of my conduct in the preceding term affords me a consolation which I shall profoundly feel through life. The general accord with which it has been expressed adds to the great and never-ceasing obligations which it imposes. To merit the continuance of this good opinion, and to carry it with me into my retirement as the solace of advancing years, will be the object of my most zealous and unceasing efforts.

Having no pretensions to the high and commanding claims of my predecessors, whose names are so much more conspicuously identified with our Revolution, and who contributed so preeminently to promote its success, I consider myself rather as the instrument than the cause of the union which has prevailed in the late election. In surmounting, in favor of my humble pretensions, the difficulties which so often produce division in like occurrences, it is obvious that other powerful causes, indicating the great strength and stability of our Union, have essentially contributed to draw you together. That these powerful causes exist, and that they may produce a like accord in all questions touching, however remotely, the liberty,

prosperity, and happiness of our country will always be the object of my most fervent prayers to the Supreme Author of All Good.

In a government which is founded by the people, who possess exclusively the sovereignty, it seems proper that the person who may be placed by their suffrages in this high trust should declare on commencing its duties the principles on which he intends to conduct the Administration. If the person thus elected has served the preceding term, an opportunity is afforded him to review its principal occurrences and to give such further explanation respecting them as in his judgment may be useful to his constituents. The events of one year have influence on those of another, and, in like manner, of a preceding on the succeeding Administration. The movements of a great nation are connected in all their parts. If errors have been committed they ought to be corrected; if the policy is sound it ought to be supported. It is by a thorough knowledge of the whole subject that our fellow-citizens are enabled to judge correctly of the past and to give a proper direction to the future.

Just before the commencement of the last term the United States had concluded a war with a very powerful nation on conditions equal and honorable to both parties. The events of that war are too recent and too deeply impressed on the memory of all to re-

quire a development from me. Our commerce had been in a great measure driven from the sea, our Atlantic and inland frontiers were invaded in almost every part; the waste of life along our coast and on some parts of our inland frontiers, to the defense of which our gallant and patriotic citizens were called, was immense, in addition to which not less than $120,000,000 were added at its end to the public debt.

As soon as the war had terminated, the nation, admonished by its events, resolved to place itself in a situation which should be better calculated to prevent the recurrence of a like evil, and, in case it should recur, to mitigate its calamities. With this view, after reducing our land force to the basis of a peace establishment, which has been further modified since, provision was made for the construction of fortifications at proper points through the whole extent of our coast and such an augmentation of our naval force as should be well adapted to both purposes. The laws making this provision were passed in 1815 and 1816, and it has been since the constant effort of the Executive to carry them into effect.

The advantage of these fortifications and of an augmented naval force in the extent contemplated, in a point of economy, has been fully illustrated by a report of the Board of Engineers and Naval Commissioners lately communicated to Congress, by which it appears that in an invasion by 20,000 men, with a correspondent naval force, in a campaign of six months only, the whole expense of the construction of the works would be defrayed by the difference in the sum necessary to maintain the force which would be adequate to our defense with the aid of those works and that which would be incurred without them. The reason of this difference is obvious. If fortifications are judiciously placed on our great inlets, as distant from our cities as circumstances will permit, they will form the only points of attack, and the enemy will be detained there by a small regular force a sufficient time to enable our militia to collect and repair to that on which the attack is made. A force adequate to the enemy, collected at that single point, with suitable preparation for such others as might be menaced, is all that would be requisite. But if there were no fortifications, then the enemy might go where he pleased, and, changing his position and sailing from place to place, our force must be called out and spread in vast numbers along the whole coast and on both sides of every bay and river as high up in each as it might be navigable for ships of war. By these fortifications, supported by our Navy, to which they would afford like support, we should present to other powers an armed front from St. Croix to the Sabine, which would protect in the event of war our whole coast and interior from invasion; and even in the wars of other powers, in which we were neutral, they would be found eminently useful, as, by keeping their public ships at a distance from our cities, peace and order in them would be preserved and the Government be protected from insult.

It need scarcely be remarked that these measures have not been resorted to in a spirit of hostility to other powers. Such a disposition does not exist toward any power. Peace and good will have been, and will hereafter be, cultivated with all, and by the most faithful regard to justice. They have been dictated by a love of peace, of economy, and an

earnest desire to save the lives of our fellow-citizens from that destruction and our country from that devastation which are inseparable from war when it finds us unprepared for it. It is believed, and experience has shown, that such a preparation is the best expedient that can be resorted to prevent war. I add with much pleasure that considerable progress has already been made in these measures of defense, and that they will be completed in a few years, considering the great extent and importance of the object, if the plan be zealously and steadily persevered in.

The conduct of the Government in what relates to foreign powers is always an object of the highest importance to the nation. Its agriculture, commerce, manufactures, fisheries, revenue, in short, its peace, may all be affected by it. Attention is therefore due to this subject.

At the period adverted to the powers of Europe, after having been engaged in long and destructive wars with each other, had concluded a peace, which happily still exists. Our peace with the power with whom we had been engaged had also been concluded. The war

between Spain and the colonies in South America, which had commenced many years before, was then the only conflict that remained unsettled. This being a contest between different parts of the same community, in which other powers had not interfered, was not affected by their accommodations.

This contest was considered at an early stage by my predecessor a civil war in which the parties were entitled to equal rights in our ports. This decision, the first made by any power, being formed on great consideration of the comparative strength and resources of the parties, the length of time, and successful opposition made by the colonies, and of all other circumstances on which it ought to depend, was in strict accord with the law of nations. Congress has invariably acted on this principle, having made no change in our relations with either party. Our attitude has therefore been that of neutrality between them, which has been maintained by the Government with the strictest impartiality. No aid has been afforded to either, nor has any privilege been enjoyed by the one which has not been equally

open to the other party, and every exertion has been made in its power to enforce the execution of the laws prohibiting illegal equipments with equal rigor against both.

By THIS EQUALITY BETWEEN the parties their public vessels have been received in our ports on the same footing; they have enjoyed an equal right to purchase and export arms, munitions of war, and every other supply, the exportation of all articles whatever being permitted under laws which were passed long before the commencement of the contest; our citizens have traded equally with both, and their commerce with each has been alike protected by the Government.

Respecting the attitude which it may be proper for the United States to maintain hereafter between the parties, I have no hesitation in stating it as my opinion that the neutrality heretofore observed should still be adhered to. From the change in the Government of Spain and the negotiation now depending, invited by the Cortes and accepted by the colonies, it may be presumed, that their differences will be settled on the terms proposed by the colonies. Should the war be continued, the United States, regarding its occurrences, will always have it in their power to adopt such measures respecting it as their honor and interest may require.

Shortly after the general peace a band of adventurers took advantage of this conflict and of the facility which it afforded to establish a system of buccaneering in the neighboring seas, to the great annoyance of the commerce of the United States, and, as was represented, of that of other powers. Of this spirit and of its injurious bearing on the United States strong proofs were afforded by the establishment at Amelia Island, and the purposes to which it was made instrumental by this band in 1817, and by the occurrences which took place in other parts of Florida in 1818, the details of which in both instances are too well known to require to be now recited. I am satisfied had a less decisive course been adopted that the worst consequences would have resulted from it. We have seen that these checks, decisive as they were, were not sufficient to crush that piratical spirit. Many culprits brought within our limits have been condemned to suffer death, the punishment due to that atrocious crime. The decisions of upright and enlightened tribunals fall equally on all whose crimes subject them, by a fair interpretation of the law, to its censure. It belongs to the Executive not to suffer the executions under these decisions to transcend the great purpose for which punishment is necessary. The full benefit of example being secured, policy as well as humanity equally forbids that they should be carried further. I have acted on this principle, pardoning those who appear to have been led astray by ignorance of the criminality of the acts they had committed, and suffering the law to take effect on those only in whose favor no extenuating circumstances could be urged.

GREAT CONFIDENCE IS entertained that the late treaty with Spain, which has been ratified by both the parties, and the ratifications whereof have been exchanged, has placed the relations of the two countries on a basis of permanent friendship. The provision made by it for such of our citizens as have claims on Spain of the character described will, it is presumed, be very satisfactory to them, and the boundary which is established between the territories of the parties westward of the Mississippi, heretofore in dispute, has, it is thought, been settled on conditions just and advantageous to both. But to the acquisition of Florida too much importance can not be attached. It secures to the United States a territory important in itself, and whose importance is much increased by its bearing on many of the highest interests of the Union. It opens to several of the neighboring States a free passage to the ocean, through the Province ceded, by several rivers, having their sources high up within their limits. It secures us against all future annoyance from powerful Indian tribes. It gives us several excellent harbors in the Gulf of Mexico for ships of war of the largest size. It covers by its position in the

Gulf the Mississippi and other great waters within our extended limits, and thereby enables the United States to afford complete protection to the vast and very valuable productions of our whole Western country, which find a market through those streams.

By a treaty with the British Government, bearing date on the 20th of October, 1818, the convention regulating the commerce between the United States and Great Britain, concluded on the 3d of July, 1815, which was about expiring, was revived and continued for the term of ten years from the time of its expiration. By that treaty, also, the differences which had arisen under the treaty of Ghent respecting the right claimed by the United States for their citizens to take and cure fish on the coast of His Britannic Majesty's dominions in America, with other differences on important interests, were adjusted to the satisfaction of both parties. No agreement has yet been entered into respecting the commerce between the United States and the British dominions in the West Indies and on this continent. The restraints imposed on that commerce by Great Britain, and reciprocated by the United States on a principle of defense, continue still in force.

The negotiation with France for the regulation of the commercial relations between the two countries, which in the course of the last summer had been commenced at Paris, has since been transferred to this city, and will be pursued on the part of the United States in the spirit of conciliation, and with an earnest desire that it may terminate in an arrangement satisfactory to both parties.

Our relations with the Barbary Powers are preserved in the same state and by the same means that were employed when I came into this office. As early as 1801 it was found necessary to send a squadron into the Mediterranean for the protection of our commerce, and no period has intervened, a short term excepted, when it was thought advisable to withdraw it. The great interests which the United States have in the Pacific, in commerce and in the fisheries, have also made it

necessary to maintain a naval force there. In disposing of this force in both instances the most effectual measures in our power have been taken, without interfering with its other duties, for the suppression of the slave trade and of piracy in the neighboring seas.

> *…we have shunned all the defects which unceasingly preyed on the vitals and destroyed the ancient Republics.*

The situation of the United States in regard to their resources, the extent of their revenue, and the facility with which it is raised affords a most gratifying spectacle. The payment of nearly $67,000,000 of the public debt, with the great progress made in measures of defense and in other improvements of various kinds since the late war, are conclusive proofs of this extraordinary prosperity, especially when it is recollected that these expenditures have been defrayed without a burthen on the people, the direct tax and excise having been repealed soon after the conclusion of the late war, and the revenue applied to these great objects having been raised in a manner not to be felt. Our great resources therefore remain untouched for any purpose which may affect the vital interests of the nation. For all such purposes they are inexhaustible. They are more especially to be found in the virtue, patriotism, and intelligence of our fellow-citizens, and in the devotion with which they would yield up by any just measure of taxation all their property in support of the rights and honor of their country.

Under the present depression of prices, affecting all the productions of the country and

every branch of industry, proceeding from causes explained on a former occasion, the revenue has considerably diminished, the effect of which has been to compel Congress either to abandon these great measures of defense or to resort to loans or internal taxes to supply the deficiency. On the presumption that this depression and the deficiency in the revenue arising from it would be temporary, loans were authorized for the demands of the last and present year. Anxious to relieve my fellow-citizens in 1817 from every burthen which could be dispensed with, and the state of the Treasury permitting it, I recommended the repeal of the internal taxes, knowing that such relief was then peculiarly necessary in consequence of the great exertions made in the late war. I made that recommendation under a pledge that should the public exigencies require a recurrence to them at any time while I remained in this trust, I would with equal promptitude perform the duty which would then be alike incumbent on me. By the experiment now making it will be seen by the next session of Congress whether the revenue shall have been so augmented as to be adequate to all these necessary purposes. Should the deficiency still continue, and especially should it be probable that it would be permanent, the course to be pursued appears to me to be obvious. I am satisfied that under certain circumstances loans may be resorted to with great advantage. I am equally well satisfied, as a general rule, that the demands of the current year, especially in time of peace, should be provided for by the revenue of that year.

I have never dreaded, nor have I ever shunned, in any situation in which I have been placed making appeals to the virtue and patriotism of my fellow-citizens, well knowing that they could never be made in vain, especially in times of great emergency or for purposes of high national importance. Independently of the exigency of the case, many considerations of great weight urge a policy having in view a provision of revenue to meet to a certain extent the demands of the nation, without relying altogether on the precarious resource of foreign commerce. I am satisfied that internal duties and excises, with corresponding imposts on foreign articles of the same kind, would, without imposing any serious burdens on the people, enhance the price of produce, promote our manufactures, and augment the revenue, at the same time that they made it more secure and permanent.

THE CARE OF THE INDIAN tribes within our limits has long been an essential part of our system, but, unfortunately, it has not been executed in a manner to accomplish all the objects intended by it. We have treated them as independent nations, without their having any substantial pretensions to that rank. The distinction has flattered their pride, retarded their improvement, and in many instances paved the way to their destruction. The progress of our settlements westward, supported as they are by a dense population, has constantly driven them back, with almost the total sacrifice of the lands which they have been compelled to abandon. They have claims on the magnanimity and, I may add, on the justice of this nation which we must all feel. We should become their real benefactors; we should perform the office of their Great Father, the endearing title which they emphatically give to the Chief Magistrate of our Union. Their sovereignty over vast territories should cease, in lieu of which the right of soil should be secured to each individual and his posterity in competent portions; and for the territory thus ceded by each tribe some reasonable equivalent should be granted, to be vested in permanent funds for the support of civil government over them and for the education of their children, for their instruction in the arts of husbandry, and to provide sustenance for them until they could provide it for themselves. My earnest hope is that Congress will digest some plan, founded on these principles, with such improvements as their wisdom may suggest, and carry it into effect as soon as it may be practicable.

Europe is again unsettled and the prospect of war increasing. Should the flame light up in any quarter, how far it may extend it is impossible to foresee. It is our peculiar felicity to be altogether unconnected with the causes which produce this menacing aspect elsewhere. With every power we are in perfect amity, and it is our interest to remain so if it be practicable on just conditions. I see no reasonable cause to apprehend variance with any power, unless it proceed from a violation of our maritime rights. In these contests, should they occur, and to whatever extent they may be carried, we shall be neutral; but as a neutral power we have rights which it is our duty to maintain. For like injuries it will be incumbent on us to seek redress in a spirit of amity, in full confidence that, injuring none, none would knowingly injure us. For more imminent dangers we should be prepared, and it should always be recollected that such preparation adapted to the circumstances and sanctioned by the judgment and wishes of our constituents can not fail to have a good effect in averting dangers of every kind. We should recollect also that the season of peace is best adapted to these preparations.

If we turn our attention, fellow-citizens, more immediately to the internal concerns of our country, and more especially to those on which its future welfare depends, we have every reason to anticipate the happiest results. It is now rather more than forty-four years since we declared our independence, and thirty-seven since it was acknowledged. The talents and virtues which were displayed in that great struggle were a sure presage of all that has since followed. A people who were able to surmount in their infant state such great perils would be more competent as they rose into manhood to repel any which they might meet in their progress. Their physical strength would be more adequate to foreign danger, and the practice of self-government, aided by the light of experience, could not fail to produce an effect equally salutary on all those questions connected with the internal organization. These favorable anticipations have been realized.

In our whole system, national and State, we have shunned all the defects which unceasingly preyed on the vitals and destroyed the ancient Republics. In them there were distinct orders, a nobility and a people, or the people governed in one assembly. Thus, in the one instance there was a perpetual conflict between the orders in society for the ascendency, in which the victory of either terminated in the overthrow of the government and the ruin of the state; in the other, in which the people governed in a body, and whose dominions seldom exceeded the dimensions of a county in one of our States, a tumultuous and disorderly movement permitted only a transitory existence. In this great nation there is but one order, that of the people, whose power, by a peculiarly happy improvement of the representative principle, is transferred from them, without impairing in the slightest degree their sovereignty, to bodies of their own creation, and to persons elected by themselves, in the full extent necessary for all the purposes of free, enlightened and efficient government. The whole system is elective, the complete sovereignty being in the people, and every officer in every department deriving his authority from and being responsible to them for his conduct.

Our career has corresponded with this great outline. Perfection in our organization could not have been expected in the outset either in the National or State Governments or in tracing the line between their respective powers. But no serious conflict has arisen, nor any contest but such as are managed by argument and by a fair appeal to the good sense of the people, and many of the defects which experience had clearly demonstrated in both Governments have been remedied. By steadily pursuing this course in this spirit there is every reason to believe that our system will soon attain the highest degree of perfection of which human institutions are capable, and that the movement in all its branches will exhibit such a degree of order and harmony as to command the admiration and respect of the civilized world.

Our physical attainments have not been less eminent.

Twenty-five years ago the river Mississippi was shut up and our Western brethren had no outlet for their commerce. What has been the progress since that time? The river has not only become the property of the United States from its source to the ocean, with all its tributary streams (with the exception of the upper part of the Red River only), but Louisiana, with a fair and liberal boundary on the western side and the Floridas on the eastern, have been ceded to us. The United States now enjoy the complete and uninterrupted sovereignty over the whole territory from St. Croix to the Sabine. New States, settled from among ourselves in this and in other parts, have been admitted into our Union in equal participation in the national sovereignty with the original States. Our population has augmented in an astonishing degree and extended in every direction. We now, fellow-citizens, comprise within our limits the dimensions and faculties of a great power under a Government possessing all the energies of any government ever known to the Old World, with an utter incapacity to oppress the people.

Entering with these views the office which I have just solemnly sworn to execute with fidelity and to the utmost of my ability, I derive great satisfaction from a knowledge that I shall be assisted in the several Departments by the very enlightened and upright citizens from whom I have received so much aid in the preceding term. With full confidence in the continuance of that candor and generous indulgence from my fellow-citizens at large which I have heretofore experienced, and with a firm reliance on the protection of Almighty God, I shall forthwith commence the duties of the high trust to which you have called me.

* * *

1824 John Quincy Adams

The election of 1820 may have produced a one-party system, but it didn't end factionalism. Certainly James Monroe's successor would be a Democratic-Republican, but which one? The ensuing contest was largely regional: Secretary of State John Quincy Adams of Massachusetts enjoyed the support of New England; Treasury Secretary William H. Crawford of Georgia was backed by most of the South; and the West had two native sons, Speaker of the House Henry Clay of Kentucky and Gen. Andrew Jackson of Tennessee.

Crawford won a rump congressional caucus, but its endorsement carried little weight because only one-third of the eligible congressmen voted (and most of those were Crawford partisans). The nomination meant so little, in fact, that congressional caucuses would never again nominate presidential candidates.

Because it focused on personalities rather than issues, the campaign of 1824 produced a number of interesting innovations. The Jackson camp, for example, published the first campaign biography. Called "a man of the people" by his supporters (and a "military chieftain" by his enemies), Jackson won a plurality of the popular and electoral votes but not the electoral majority specified by the Constitution.

As required under the Twelfth Amendment, the names of the top three vote-getters were submitted to the House of Representatives, where each state delegation had a single vote. With eleven states already committed to him, Jackson needed two more for a majority. Adams, backed by the six New England states and New York, needed six more.

Eliminated from contention, Clay threw his support behind Adams, helping him carry Illinois, Kentucky, Louisiana, Maryland, Missouri, and Ohio. Even before the votes were counted, though, Jackson's followers charged that Clay and Adams had made a "corrupt bargain," whereby Adams agreed to make Clay secretary of state in exchange for Clay's votes. Jackson called Clay "the Judas of the West" and prophesied that "his end will be the same."

Presidential Candidate	Popular Votes	Electoral Votes
Andrew Jackson, Tenn.	151,271	99
John Quincy Adams, Mass.	113,122	84
William H. Crawford, Ga.	40,856	41
Henry Clay, Ky.	47,531	37

Vice-Presidential Candidate	Electoral Votes
John C. Calhoun, S.C.	182
Nathan Sanford, N.Y.	30
Nathaniel Macon, N.C.	24
Andrew Jackson, Tenn.	13
Martin Van Buren, N.Y.	9
Henry Clay, Ky.	2

Inaugural Address • Washington, D.C. • Friday, March 4, 1825

In compliance with an usage coeval with the existence of our Federal

Constitution, and sanctioned by the example of my predecessors in the career upon which I am about to enter, I appear, my fellow-citizens, in your presence and in that of Heaven to bind myself by the solemnities of religious obligation to the faithful performance of the duties allotted to me in the station to which I have been called.

In unfolding to my countrymen the principles by which I shall be governed in the fulfillment of those duties my first resort will be to that Constitution which I shall swear to the best of my ability to preserve, protect, and defend. That revered instrument enumerates the powers and prescribes the duties of the Executive Magistrate, and in its first words declares the purposes to which these and the whole action of the

Government instituted by it should be invariably and sacredly devoted—to form a more perfect union, establish justice, insure domestic tranquillity, provide for the common defense, promote the general welfare, and secure the blessings of liberty to the people of this Union in their successive generations. Since the adoption of this social compact one of these generations has passed away. It is the work of our forefathers. Administered by some of the most eminent men who contributed to its formation, through a most eventful period in the annals of the world, and through all the vicissitudes of peace and war incidental to the condition of associated man, it has not disappointed the hopes and aspirations of those illustrious benefactors of their age and nation. It has

promoted the lasting welfare of that country so dear to us all; it has to an extent far beyond the ordinary lot of humanity secured the freedom and happiness of this people. We now receive it as a precious inheritance from those to whom we are indebted for its establishment, doubly bound by the examples which they have left us and by the blessings which we have enjoyed as the fruits of their labors to transmit the same unimpaired to the succeeding generation.

In the compass of thirty-six years since this great national covenant was instituted a body of laws enacted under its authority and in conformity with its provisions has unfolded its powers and carried into practical operation its effective energies. Subordinate departments have distributed the executive functions in their various relations to foreign affairs, to the revenue and expenditures, and to the military force of the Union by land and sea. A coordinate department of the judiciary has expounded the Constitution and the laws, settling in harmonious coincidence with the legislative will numerous weighty questions of construction which the imperfection of human language had rendered unavoidable. The year of jubilee since the first formation of our Union has just elapsed; that of the declaration of our independence is at hand. The consummation of both was effected by this Constitution.

Since that period a population of four millions has multiplied to twelve. A territory bounded by the Mississippi has been extended from sea to sea. New States have been admitted to the Union in numbers nearly equal to those of the first Confederation. Treaties of peace, amity, and commerce have been concluded with the principal dominions of the earth. The people of other nations, inhabitants of regions acquired not by conquest, but by compact, have been united with us in the participation of our rights and duties, of our burdens and blessings. The forest has fallen by the ax of our woodsmen; the soil has been made to teem by the tillage of our farmers; our commerce has whitened every ocean. The dominion of man over physical nature has been extended by the invention of our artists. Liberty and law have marched hand in hand. All the purposes of human association have been accomplished as effectively as under any other government on the globe, and at a cost little exceeding in a whole generation the expenditure of other nations in a single year.

Such is the unexaggerated picture of our condition under a Constitution founded upon the republican principle of equal rights. To admit that this picture has its shades is but to say that it is still the condition of men upon earth. From evil—physical, moral, and political—it is not our claim to be exempt. We have suffered sometimes by the visitation of Heaven through disease; often by the wrongs and injustice of other nations, even to the extremities

of war; and, lastly, by dissensions among ourselves—dissensions perhaps inseparable from the enjoyment of freedom, but which have more than once appeared to threaten the dissolution of the Union, and with it the overthrow of all the enjoyments of our present lot and all our earthly hopes of the future. The causes of these dissensions have been various, founded upon differences of speculation in the theory of republican government; upon conflicting views of policy in our relations with foreign nations; upon jealousies of partial and sectional interests, aggravated by prejudices and prepossessions which strangers to each other are ever apt to entertain.

It is a source of gratification and of encouragement to me to observe that the great result of this experiment upon the theory of human rights has at the close of that generation by which it was formed been crowned with success equal to the most sanguine expectations of its founders. Union, justice, tranquillity, the common defense, the general welfare, and

---

...I am deeply conscious of the prospect that I shall stand more and oftener in need of your indulgence.

---

the blessings of liberty—all have been promoted by the Government under which we have lived. Standing at this point of time, looking back to that generation which has gone by and forward to that which is advancing, we may at once indulge in grateful exultation and in cheering hope. From the experience of the past we derive instructive lessons for the future. Of the two great political parties which have divided the opinions and feelings of our country, the candid and the just will now admit that both have contributed splendid talents, spotless integrity, ardent patriotism, and disinterested sacrifices to the

formation and administration of this Government, and that both have required a liberal indulgence for a portion of human infirmity and error. The revolutionary wars of Europe, commencing precisely at the moment when the Government of the United States first went into operation under this Constitution, excited a collision of sentiments and of sympathies which kindled all the passions and imbittered the conflict of parties till the nation was involved in war and the Union was shaken to its center. This time of trial embraced a period of five and twenty years, during which the policy of the Union in its relations with Europe constituted the principal basis of our political divisions and the most arduous part of the action of our Federal Government. With the catastrophe in which the wars of the French Revolution terminated, and our own subsequent peace with Great Britain, this baneful weed of party strife was uprooted. From that time no difference of principle, connected either with the theory of government or with our intercourse with foreign nations, has existed or been called forth in force sufficient to sustain a continued combination of parties or to give more than wholesome animation to public sentiment or legislative debate. Our political creed is, without a dissenting voice that can be heard, that the will of the people is the source and the happiness of the people the end of all legitimate government upon earth; that the best security for the beneficence and the best guaranty against the abuse of power consists in the freedom, the purity, and the frequency of popular elections; that the General Government of the Union and the separate governments of the States are all sovereignties of limited powers, fellow-servants of the same masters, uncontrolled within their respective spheres, uncontrollable by encroachments upon each other; that the firmest security of peace is the preparation during peace of the defenses of war; that a rigorous economy and accountability of public expenditures should guard against the aggravation and alleviate when possible the burden of taxation; that the military should be kept in strict sub-

ordination to the civil power; that the freedom of the press and of religious opinion should be inviolate; that the policy of our country is peace and the ark of our salvation union are articles of faith upon which we are all now agreed. If there have been those who doubted whether a confederated representative democracy were a government competent to the wise and orderly management of the common concerns of a mighty nation, those doubts have been dispelled; if there have been projects of partial confederacies to be erected upon the ruins of the Union, they have been scattered to the winds; if there have been dangerous attachments to one foreign nation and antipathies against another, they have been extinguished. Ten years of peace, at home and abroad, have assuaged the animosities of political contention and blended into harmony the most discordant elements of public opinion. There still remains one effort of magnanimity, one sacrifice of prejudice and passion, to be made by the individuals throughout the nation who have heretofore followed the standards of political party. It is that of discarding every remnant of rancor against each other, of embracing as countrymen and friends, and of yielding to talents and virtue alone that confidence which in times of contention for principle was bestowed only upon those who bore the badge of party communion.

The collisions of party spirit which originate in speculative opinions or in different views of administrative policy are in their nature transitory. Those which are founded on geographical divisions, adverse interests of soil, climate, and modes of domestic life are more permanent, and therefore, perhaps, more dangerous. It is this which gives inestimable value to the character of our Government, at once federal and national. It holds out to us a perpetual admonition to preserve alike and with equal anxiety the rights of each individual State in its own government and the rights of the whole nation in that of the Union. Whatsoever is of domestic concernment, unconnected with the other members of the Union or with foreign lands, belongs exclusively to the administration of the State governments. Whatsoever directly involves the rights and interests of the federative fraternity or of foreign powers is of the resort of this General Government. The duties of both are obvious in the general principle, though sometimes perplexed with difficulties in the detail. To respect the rights of the State governments is the inviolable duty of that of the Union; the government of every State will feel its own obligation to respect and preserve the rights of the whole. The prejudices everywhere too commonly entertained against distant strangers are worn away, and the jealousies of jarring interests are allayed by the composition and functions of the great national councils annually assembled from all quarters of the Union at this place. Here the distinguished men from every section of our country, while meeting to deliberate upon the great interests of those by whom they are deputed, learn to estimate the talents and do justice to the virtues of each other. The harmony of the nation is promoted and the whole Union is knit together by the sentiments of mutual respect, the habits of social intercourse, and the ties of personal friendship formed between the representatives of its several parts in the performance of their service at this metropolis.

Passing from this general review of the purposes and injunctions of the Federal Constitution and their results as indicating the first traces of the path of duty in the discharge of my public trust, I turn to the Administration of my immediate predecessor as the second. It has passed away in a period of profound peace, how much to the satisfaction of our country and to the honor of our country's name is known to you all. The great features of its policy, in general concurrence with the will of the Legislature, have been to cherish peace while preparing for defensive war; to yield exact justice to other nations and maintain the rights of our own; to cherish the principles of freedom and of equal rights wherever they were proclaimed; to discharge with all possible promptitude the na-

tional debt; to reduce within the narrowest limits of efficiency the military force; to improve the organization and discipline of the Army; to provide and sustain a school of military science; to extend equal protection to all the great interests of the nation; to promote the civilization of the Indian tribes, and to proceed in the great system of internal improvements within the limits of the constitutional power of the Union. Under the pledge of these promises, made by that eminent citizen at the time of his first induction to this office, in his career of eight years the internal taxes have been repealed; sixty millions of the public debt have been discharged; provision has been made for the comfort and relief of the aged and indigent among the surviving warriors of the Revolution; the regular armed force has been reduced and its constitution revised and perfected; the accountability for the expenditure of public moneys has been made more effective; the Floridas have been peaceably acquired, and our boundary has been extended to the Pacific Ocean; the independence of the southern nations of this hemisphere has been recognized, and recommended by example and by counsel to the potentates of Europe; progress has been made in the defense of the country by fortifications and the increase of the Navy, toward the effectual suppression of the African traffic in slaves; in alluring the aboriginal hunters of our land to the cultivation of the soil and of the mind, in exploring the interior regions of the Union, and in preparing by scientific researches and surveys for the further application of our national resources to the internal improvement of our country.

In this brief outline of the promise and performance of my immediate predecessor the line of duty for his successor is clearly delineated. To pursue to their consummation those pur-

poses of improvement in our common condition instituted or recommended by him will embrace the whole sphere of my obligations. To the topic of internal improvement, emphatically urged by him at his inauguration, I recur with peculiar satisfaction. It is that from which I am convinced that the unborn millions of our posterity

who are in future ages to people this continent will derive their most fervent gratitude to the founders of the Union; that in which the beneficent action of its Government will be most deeply felt and acknowledged. The magnificence and splendor of their public works are among the imperishable glories of the ancient republics. The roads and aqueducts of Rome have been the admiration of all after ages, and have survived thousands of years after all her conquests have been swallowed up in despotism or become the spoil of barbarians. Some diversity of opinion has prevailed with regard to the powers of Congress for legislation upon objects of this nature. The most respectful deference is due to doubts originating in pure patriotism and sustained by venerated authority. But nearly twenty years have passed since the construction of the first national road was commenced. The authority for its construction was then unquestioned. To how many thousands of our countrymen has it proved a benefit? To what sin-

gle individual has it ever proved an injury? Repeated, liberal, and candid discussions in the Legislature have conciliated the sentiments and approximated the opinions of enlightened minds upon the question of constitutional power. I can not but hope that by the same process of friendly, patient, and persevering deliberation all constitutional objections will ultimately be removed. The extent and limitation of the powers of the General Government in relation to this transcendently important interest will be settled and acknowledged to the common satisfaction of all, and every speculative scruple will be solved by a practical public blessing.

Fellow-citizens, you are acquainted with the peculiar circumstances of the recent election, which have resulted in affording me the opportunity of addressing you at this time. You have heard the exposition of the principles which will direct me in the fulfillment of the high and solemn trust imposed upon me in this station. Less possessed of your confidence in advance than any of my predecessors, I am deeply conscious of the prospect that I shall stand more and oftener in need of your indulgence. Intentions upright and pure, a heart devoted to the welfare of our country, and the unceasing application of all the faculties allotted to me to her service are all the pledges that I can give for the faithful performance of the arduous duties I am to undertake. To the guidance of the legislative councils, to the assistance of the executive and subordinate departments, to the friendly cooperation of the respective State governments, to the candid and liberal support of the people so far as it may be deserved by honest industry and zeal, I shall look for whatever success may attend my public service; and knowing that "except the Lord keep the city the watchman waketh but in vain," with fervent supplications for His favor, to His overruling providence I commit with humble but fearless confidence my own fate and the future destinies of my country.

* * *

1828 ANDREW JACKSON

THE TWO-PARTY SYSTEM was back. Workers, farmers, states' rights activists, and other supporters of Andrew Jackson spent the four years of the John Quincy Adams administration organizing the new Democratic party. Meanwhile, former Federalists, nationalists, and other conservative backers of Adams came together as the National Republican party.

With congressional caucuses no longer selecting candidates, Adams was renominated by state party conventions and Jackson by the Tennessee legislature. The Jacksonians championed democratic causes, including an end to property qualifications for voting, lower prices for public land in the West, and a reduction in tariff rates. They also revived the "corrupt bargain" charge of 1825 and added to it charges of more recent corruption in office—which the National Republicans countered with their own scurrilous allegations, including one that Jackson had committed adultery with his wife while she was still married

to her first husband. It was the first campaign to emphasize gutter politics.

Growth in the population, a loosening of eligibility requirements, and high voter turnout produced a huge vote, more than triple that of 1824. The Democrats mobilized their supporters well, making particularly effective use of party newspapers and their "Hurrah Boys" campaign workers. The organization paid off. Jackson beat up Adams, winning 56 percent of the popular vote and more than doubling his opponent's electoral-vote total. Adams, like his father, chose not to attend the inauguration of his successor.

PARTY	POPULAR VOTES	ELECTORAL VOTES
DEMOCRATIC Andrew Jackson, Tenn. John C. Calhoun, S.C.	642,553	178
NATIONAL REPUBLICAN John Quincy Adams, Mass. Richard Rush, Pa.	500,897	83

First Inaugural Address • Washington, D.C. • Wednesday, March 4, 1829

Fellow-Citizens:About to undertake the arduous duties that I have been

appointed to perform by the choice of a free people, I avail myself of this customary and solemn occasion to express the gratitude which their confidence inspires and to acknowledge the accountability which my situation enjoins. While the magnitude of their interests convinces me that no thanks can be adequate to the honor they have conferred, it admonishes me that the best return I can make is the zealous dedication of my humble abilities to their service and their good.

As the instrument of the Federal Constitution it will devolve on me for a stated period to execute the laws of the United States, to superintend their foreign and their confederate relations, to manage their revenue, to command their forces, and, by communications to the Legislature, to watch over and to promote their interests generally. And the principles of action by which I shall endeavor to accomplish this circle of duties it is now proper for me briefly to explain.

In administering the laws of Congress I shall keep steadily in view the limitations as well as the extent of the Executive power, trusting thereby to discharge the functions of my office without transcending its authority. With foreign nations it will be my study to preserve peace and to cultivate friendship on fair and honorable terms, and in the adjustment of any differences that may exist or

arise to exhibit the forbearance becoming a powerful nation rather than the sensibility belonging to a gallant people.

In such measures as I may be called on to pursue in regard to the rights of the separate States I hope to be animated by a proper respect for those sovereign members of our Union, taking care not to confound the pow-

ers they have reserved to themselves with those they have granted to the Confederacy.

The management of the public revenue—that searching operation in all governments—is among the most delicate and important trusts in ours, and it will, of course, demand no inconsiderable share of my official solicitude. Under every aspect in which it can be considered it would appear that advantage must result from the observance of a strict and faithful economy. This I shall aim at the more anxiously both because it will facilitate the extinguishment of the national debt, the unnecessary duration of which is incompatible with real independence, and because it will counteract that tendency to public and private profligacy which a profuse expenditure of money by the Government is but too apt to engender. Powerful auxiliaries to the attainment of this desirable end are to be found in the regulations provided by the wisdom of Congress for the specific appropriation of public money and the prompt accountability of public officers.

With regard to a proper selection of the subjects of impost with a view to revenue, it would seem to me that the spirit of equity, caution, and compromise in which the Constitution was formed requires that the great interests of agriculture, commerce, and manufactures should be equally favored, and that

...a million of armed freemen, possessed of the means of war, can never be conquered by a foreign foe.

perhaps the only exception to this rule should consist in the peculiar encouragement of any products of either of them that may be found essential to our national independence.

Internal improvement and the diffusion of knowledge, so far as they can be promoted by the constitutional acts of the Federal Government, are of high importance.

Considering standing armies as dangerous to free governments in time of peace, I shall not seek to enlarge our present establishment, nor disregard that salutary lesson of political experience which teaches that the military should be held subordinate to the civil power. The gradual increase of our Navy, whose flag has displayed in distant climes our skill in navigation and our fame in arms, the preservation of our forts, arsenals, and dockyards, and the introduction of progressive improvements in the discipline and science of both branches of our military service are so plainly prescribed by prudence that I should be excused for omitting their mention

sooner than for enlarging on their importance. But the bulwark of our defense is the national militia, which in the present state of our intelligence and population must render us invincible. As long as our Government is administered for the good of the people, and is regulated by their will; as long as it secures to us the rights of person and of property, liberty of conscience and of the press, it will be worth defending; and so long as it is worth defending a patriotic militia will cover it with an impenetrable aegis. Partial injuries and occasional mortifications we may be subjected to, but a million of armed freemen, possessed of the means of war, can never be conquered by a foreign foe. To any just system, therefore, calculated to strengthen this natural safeguard of the country I shall cheerfully lend all the aid in my power.

It will be my sincere and constant desire to observe toward the Indian tribes within our limits a just and liberal policy, and to give that humane and considerate attention to their

rights and their wants which is consistent with the habits of our Government and the feelings of our people.

The recent demonstration of public sentiment inscribes on the list of Executive duties, in characters too legible to be overlooked, the task of reform, which will require particularly the correction of those abuses that have brought the patronage of the Federal Government into conflict with the freedom of elections, and the counteraction of those causes which have disturbed the rightful course of appointment and have placed or continued power in unfaithful or incompetent hands.

In the performance of a task thus generally delineated I shall endeavor to select men whose diligence and talents will insure in their respective stations able and faithful cooperation, depending for the advancement of the public service more on the integrity and zeal of the public officers than on their numbers.

A diffidence, perhaps too just, in my own qualifications will teach me to look with rever-

ence to the examples of public virtue left by my illustrious predecessors, and with veneration to the lights that flow from the mind that founded and the mind that reformed our system. The same diffidence induces me to hope for instruction and aid from the coordinate branches of the Government, and for the indulgence and support of my fellow-citizens generally. And a firm reliance on the goodness of that Power whose providence mercifully protected our national infancy, and has since upheld our liberties in various vicissitudes, encourages me to offer up my ardent supplications that He will continue to make our beloved country the object of His divine care and gracious benediction.

* * *

1832 Andrew Jackson

I N SEPTEMBER 1831, the Anti-Masons, an upstart third party, held the first national nominating convention, attended by delegates from the state parties. Three months later, the National Republicans staged their own gathering, nominating Henry Clay.

The Democrats, not wanting to be outdone, held a national convention, too; its delegates renominated Andrew Jackson by acclamation and went on to adopt two convention rules that would figure prominently in later campaigns: a "two-thirds rule" intended to ensure party unity by requiring a two-thirds vote for the nomination and a "unit rule" that forced each state to cast all its ballots as a bloc for the candidate favored by the majority of that state's delegates.

The principal campaign issues of 1832 were Jackson's contempt for the Second Bank of the United States and, less so, Clay's support for internal improvements. The incumbent president's charge that the Second Bank "made the rich richer and the potent more powerful" curiously positioned him as an outsider challenging entrenched economic interests. ("Let the people rule" was his campaign slogan.) A

Party	Popular Votes	Electoral Votes
Democratic Andrew Jackson, Tenn. Martin Van Buren, N.Y.	701,780	219
National Republican Henry Clay, Ky. John Sergeant, Pa.	484,205	49
(Independent) John Floyd, Va. Henry Lee, Mass.		11
Anti-Mason William Wirt, Md. Amos Ellmaker, Pa.	100,715	7
(Not Voted)		2

confident Jackson predicted that Clay would "not get one electoral vote west of the mountains or south of the Potomac," and—except for the votes Clay received from his home state of Kentucky—Jackson was right.

Second Inaugural Address · Washington, D.C. · Monday, March 4, 1833

Fellow-Citizens: *The will of the American people, expressed through their*

unsolicited suffrages, calls me before you to pass through the solemnities preparatory to taking upon myself the duties of President of the United States for another term. For their approbation of my public conduct through a period which has not been without its difficulties, and for this renewed expression of their confidence in my good intentions, I am at a loss for terms adequate to the expression of my gratitude. It shall be displayed to the extent of my humble abilities in continued efforts so to administer the Government as to preserve their liberty and promote their happiness.

So many events have occurred within the last four years which have necessarily called forth—sometimes under circumstances the most delicate and painful—my views of the principles and policy which ought to be pursued by the General Government that I need on this occasion but allude to a few leading considerations connected with some of them.

The foreign policy adopted by our Government soon after the formation of our present Constitution, and very generally pursued by successive Administrations, has been crowned with almost complete success, and has elevated our character among the nations of the earth. To do justice to all and to submit to wrong from none has been during my Administration its governing maxim, and so happy have been its results that we are not only at peace with all the world, but have few causes of controversy, and those of minor importance, remaining unadjusted.

In the domestic policy of this Government there are two objects which especially deserve the attention of the people and their representatives, and which have been and will continue to be the subjects of my increasing solicitude. They are the preservation of the rights of the several States and the integrity of the Union.

These great objects are necessarily connected, and can only be attained by an en-

lightened exercise of the powers of each within its appropriate sphere in conformity with the public will constitutionally expressed. To this end it becomes the duty of all to yield a ready and patriotic submission to the laws constitutionally enacted, and thereby promote and strengthen a proper confidence in those institutions of the several States and of the United States which the people themselves have ordained for their own government.

My experience in public concerns and the observation of a life somewhat advanced confirm the opinions long since imbibed by me, that the destruction of our State governments or the annihilation of their control over the local concerns of the people would lead directly to revolution and anarchy, and finally to despotism and military domination. In proportion, therefore, as the General Government encroaches upon the rights of the States, in the same proportion does it impair its own power and detract from its ability to fulfill the purposes of its creation. Solemnly impressed with these considerations, my countrymen will ever find me ready to exercise my constitutional powers in arresting measures which may directly or indirectly encroach upon the rights of the States or tend to consolidate all political power in the General Government. But of equal, and, indeed, of incalculable, importance is the union of these

rest or to enfeeble the sacred ties which now link together the various parts." Without union our independence and liberty would never have been achieved; without union they never can be maintained. Divided into twenty-four, or even a smaller number, of separate communities, we shall see our internal trade burdened with numberless restraints and exactions; communication between

The time at which I stand before you is full of interest. The eyes of all nations are fixed on our Republic. The event of the existing crisis will be decisive in the opinion of mankind of the practicability of our federal system of government. Great is the stake placed in our hands; great is the responsibility which must rest upon the people of the United States. Let us realize the importance of the

cate by my official acts the necessity of exercising by the General Government those powers only that are clearly delegated; to encourage simplicity and economy in the expenditures of the Government; to

The loss of liberty, of all good government, of peace, plenty, and happiness, must inevitably follow a dissolution of the Union.

raise no more money from the people than may be requisite for these objects, and in a manner that will best promote the interests of all classes of the community and of all portions of the Union. Constantly bearing in mind that in entering into society "individuals must give up a share of liberty to preserve the rest," it will be my desire so to discharge my duties as to foster with our brethren in all parts of the country a spirit of liberal concession and compromise, and, by reconciling our fellow-citizens to those partial sacrifices which they must unavoidably make for the preservation of a greater good, to recommend our invaluable Government and Union to the confidence and affections of the American people.

Finally, it is my most fervent prayer to that Almighty Being before whom I now stand, and who has kept us in His hands from the infancy of our Republic to the present day, that He will so overrule all my intentions and actions and inspire the hearts of my fellow-citizens that we may be preserved from dangers of all kinds and continue forever a united and happy people.

States, and the sacred duty of all to contribute to its preservation by a liberal support of the General Government in the exercise of its just powers. You have been wisely admonished to "accustom yourselves to think and speak of the Union as of the palladium of your political safety and prosperity, watching for its preservation with jealous anxiety, discountenancing whatever may suggest even a suspicion that it can in any event be abandoned, and indignantly frowning upon the first dawning of any attempt to alienate any portion of our country from the

distant points and sections obstructed or cut off; our sons made soldiers to deluge with blood the fields they now till in peace; the mass of our people borne down and impoverished by taxes to support armies and navies, and military leaders at the head of their victorious legions becoming our lawgivers and judges. The loss of liberty, of all good government, of peace, plenty, and happiness, must inevitably follow a dissolution of the Union. In supporting it, therefore, we support all that is dear to the freeman and the philanthropist.

attitude in which we stand before the world. Let us exercise forbearance and firmness. Let us extricate our country from the dangers which surround it and learn wisdom from the lessons they inculcate.

Deeply impressed with the truth of these observations, and under the obligation of that solemn oath which I am about to take, I shall continue to exert all my faculties to maintain the just powers of the Constitution and to transmit unimpaired to posterity the blessings of our Federal Union. At the same time, it will be my aim to incul-

* * *

1836 Martin Van Buren

DURING ANDREW JACKSON's second term, the political forces opposing him coalesced to form the Whig party. The nascent Whigs, however, had no national leader, so they decided to back three regional candidates: William Henry Harrison of Ohio, Daniel Webster of Massachusetts, and Hugh Lawson White of Tennessee. (Although not Whigs themselves, anti-Jackson Democrats in South Carolina put up a fourth regional candidate: Willie P. Mangum.) The Whigs hoped that their favorite sons could steal enough votes from the Democrats to throw the election into the House of Representatives, where anything could happen.

As for the Democrats, President Jackson made it clear that he wanted Vice President Martin Van Buren to succeed him and Richard M. Johnson to succeed Van Buren. Albeit with some grumbling, the party went along, but doubts about Johnson lingered. Jackson wanted to reward the former Kentucky congressman for his unswerving loyalty, yet Johnson had discreetly taken a slave as his common-law wife and was raising their children as free people—none of which pleased the party's southern wing.

After a campaign that featured much partisan bickering but no real issues, Van Buren won a comfortable electoral majority. But

Virginia's Democratic electors refused to vote for Johnson, denying him the same electoral majority. For the first and only time in history, the Senate met to decide the matter, choosing Johnson over Francis Granger by a vote of 33–16. On leaving office, Jackson confided to friends that he had only two regrets, never having shot Clay or hanged Calhoun.

PARTY	POPULAR VOTES	ELECTORAL VOTES
DEMOCRATIC Martin Van Buren, N.Y. Richard M. Johnson, Ky.	764,176	170
WHIG William H. Harrison, Ohio Francis Granger, N.Y.	550,816	73
WHIG Hugh L. White, Tenn. John Tyler, Va.	146,107	26
WHIG Daniel Webster, Mass. Francis Granger, N.Y.	41,201	14
(INDEPENDENT) Willie P. Mangum, N.C. John Tyler, Va.		11

Inaugural Address • Washington, D.C. • Monday, March 4, 1837

Fellow-Citizens: The practice of all my predecessors imposes on me

an obligation I cheerfully fulfill—to accompany the first and solemn act of my public trust with an avowal of the principles that will guide me in performing it and an expression of my feelings on assuming a charge so responsible and vast. In imitating their example I tread in the footsteps of illustrious men, whose superiors it is our happiness to believe are not found on the executive calendar of any country. Among them we recognize the earliest and firmest pillars of the Republic—those by whom our national independence was first declared, him who above all others contributed to establish it on the field of battle, and those whose expanded intellect and patriotism constructed, improved, and perfected the inestimable institutions under which we live. If such men in the position I now occupy felt themselves overwhelmed by a sense of gratitude for this highest of all marks of their country's confidence, and by a consciousness of their inability adequately to discharge the duties of an office so difficult and exalted, how much more

must these considerations affect one who can rely on no such claims for favor or forbearance! Unlike all who have preceded me, the Revolution that gave us existence as one people was achieved at the period of my birth; and whilst I contemplate with grateful reverence that memorable event, I feel that I belong to a later age and that I may not expect my countrymen to weigh my actions with the same kind and partial hand.

So sensibly, fellow-citizens, do these circumstances press themselves upon me that I should not dare to enter upon my path of duty did I not look for the generous aid of those who will be associated with me in the various and coordinate branches of the Government; did I not repose with unwavering reliance on the patriotism, the intelligence, and the kindness of a people who never yet deserted a public servant honestly laboring their cause; and, above all, did I not permit myself humbly to hope for the sustaining support of an everwatchful and beneficent Providence.

To the confidence and consolation derived from these sources it would be un-

grateful not to add those which spring from our present fortunate condition. Though not altogether exempt from embarrassments that disturb our tranquillity at home and threaten it abroad, yet in all the attributes of a great, happy, and flourishing people we stand without a parallel in the world. Abroad we enjoy the respect and, with scarcely an exception, the friendship of every nation; at home, while our Government quietly but efficiently performs the sole legitimate end of political institutions—in doing the greatest good to the greatest number—we present an aggregate of human prosperity surely not elsewhere to be found.

How imperious, then, is the obligation imposed upon every citizen, in his own sphere of action, whether limited or extended, to exert himself in perpetuating a condition of things so singularly happy! All the lessons of history and experience must be lost upon us if we are content to trust alone to the peculiar advantages we happen to possess. Position and climate and the bounteous resources that nature has scattered with so liberal a hand—even the diffused intelligence and elevated character of our people—will avail us nothing if we fail sacredly to uphold those political institutions that were wisely and deliberately formed with reference to every circumstance that could preserve or might endanger the blessings we enjoy. The thoughtful framers of our Constitution legislated for our country as they found it. Looking upon it with the eyes of statesmen and patriots, they saw all the sources of rapid and wonderful prosperity; but they saw also that various habits, opinions, and institutions peculiar to the various portions of so vast a region were deeply fixed. Distinct sovereignties were in actual existence, whose cordial union was essential to the welfare and happiness of all. Between many of them there was, at least to some extent, a real diversity of interests, liable to be exaggerated through sinister designs; they differed in size, in popula-

> *I must go into the Presidential chair…with a determination equally decided to resist the slightest interference with [slavery] in the States where it exists.*

tion, in wealth, and in actual and prospective resources and power; they varied in the character of their industry and staple productions, and [in some] existed domestic institutions which, unwisely disturbed, might endanger the harmony of the whole. Most carefully were all these circumstances weighed, and the foundations of the new Government laid upon principles of reciprocal concession and equitable com-

promise. The jealousies which the smaller States might entertain of the power of the rest were allayed by a rule of representation confessedly unequal at the time, and designed forever to remain so. A natural fear that the broad scope of general legislation might bear upon and unwisely control particular interests was counteracted by limits strictly drawn around the action of the Federal authority, and to the people and the States was left unimpaired their sovereign power over the innumerable subjects embraced in the internal government of a just republic, excepting such only as necessarily appertain to the concerns of the whole confederacy or its intercourse as a united community with the other nations of the world.

This provident forecast has been verified by time. Half a century, teeming with extraordinary events, and elsewhere producing astonishing results, has passed along, but on our institutions it has left no injurious mark. From a small community we have risen to a people powerful in numbers and in strength; but with our increase has gone hand in hand the progress of just principles. The privileges, civil and religious, of the humblest individual are still sacredly protected at home, and while the valor and fortitude of our people have removed far from us the slightest apprehension of foreign power, they have not yet induced us in a single instance to forget what is right. Our commerce has been extended to the remotest nations; the value and even nature of our productions have been greatly changed; a wide difference has arisen in the relative wealth and resources of every portion of our country; yet the spirit of mutual regard and of faithful adherence to existing compacts has continued to prevail in our councils and never long been absent from our conduct. We have learned by experience a fruitful lesson—that an implicit and undeviating adherence to the principles on which we set out can carry us prosperously onward through all the conflicts of circumstances and vicissitudes inseparable from the lapse of years.

The success that has thus attended our great experiment is in itself a sufficient cause for gratitude, on account of the happiness it has actually conferred and the example it has unanswerably given. But to me, my fellow-citizens, looking forward to the far-distant future with ardent prayers and confiding hopes, this retrospect presents a ground for still deeper delight. It impresses on my mind a firm belief that the perpetuity of our institutions depends upon ourselves; that if we maintain the principles on which they were established they are destined to confer their benefits on countless generations yet to come, and that America will present to every friend of mankind the cheering proof that a popular government, wisely formed, is wanting in no element of endurance or strength. Fifty years ago its rapid failure was boldly predicted. Latent and uncon-

trollable causes of dissolution were supposed to exist even by the wise and good, and not only did unfriendly or speculative theorists anticipate for us the fate of past republics, but the fears of many an honest patriot overbalanced his sanguine hopes. Look back on these forebodings, not hastily but reluctantly made, and see how in every instance they have completely failed.

An imperfect experience during the struggles of the Revolution was supposed to warrant the belief that the people would not bear the taxation requisite to discharge an immense public debt already incurred and to pay the necessary expenses of the Government. The cost of two wars has been paid, not only without a murmur, but with unequaled alacrity. No one is now left to doubt that every burden will be cheerfully borne that may be necessary to sustain our civil institutions or guard our honor or welfare. Indeed, all experience has shown that the willingness of the people to contribute to these ends in cases of emergency has uniformly outrun the confidence of their representatives.

In the early stages of the new Government, when all felt the imposing influence as they recognized the unequaled services of the first President, it was a common sentiment that the great weight of his character could alone bind the discordant materials of our Government together and save us from the violence of contending factions. Since his death nearly forty years are gone. Party exasperation has been often carried to its highest point; the virtue and fortitude of the people have sometimes been greatly tried; yet our system, purified and enhanced in value by all it has encountered, still preserves its spirit of free and fearless discussion, blended with unimpaired fraternal feeling.

The capacity of the people for self-government, and their willingness, from a high sense of duty and without those exhibitions of coercive power so generally employed in other countries, to submit to all needful restraints and exactions of municipal law, have also been favorably exemplified in the history of the American States. Occasionally, it is true, the ardor of public sentiment, outrunning the regular progress of the judicial tribunals or seeking to reach cases not denounced as criminal by the existing law, has displayed itself in a manner calculated to give pain to the friends of free government and to encourage the hopes of those who wish for its overthrow. These occurrences, however, have been far less frequent in our country than in any other of equal population on the globe, and with the diffusion of intelligence it may well be hoped that they will constantly diminish in frequency and violence. The generous patriotism and sound common sense of the great mass of our fellow-citizens will assuredly in time produce this result; for as every assumption of illegal power not only wounds the majesty of the law, but furnishes a pretext for abridging the liberties of the people, the latter have the most direct and permanent interest in preserving the landmarks of social order and maintaining on all occasions the inviolability of those constitutional and legal provisions which they themselves have made.

In a supposed unfitness of our institutions for those hostile emergencies which no country can always avoid their friends found a fruitful source of apprehension, their enemies of hope. While they foresaw less promptness of action than in governments differently formed, they overlooked the far more important consideration that with us war could never be the result of individual or irresponsible will, but must be a measure of redress for injuries sustained, voluntarily resorted to by those who were to bear the necessary sacrifice, who would consequently feel an individual interest in the contest, and whose energy would be commensurate with the difficulties to be encountered. Actual events have proved their error; the last war, far from impairing, gave new confidence to our Government, and amid recent apprehensions of a similar conflict we saw that the energies of our country would not be wanting in ample season to vindicate its rights. We may not possess, as we should not desire to possess, the extended and ever-ready military organization of other nations; we may occasionally suffer in the outset for the want of it; but among ourselves all doubt upon this great point has ceased, while a salutary experience will prevent a contrary opinion from inviting aggression from abroad.

Certain danger was foretold from the extension of our territory, the multiplication of States, and the increase of population. Our system was supposed to be adapted only to boundaries comparatively narrow. These have been widened beyond conjecture; the members of our Confederacy are already doubled, and the numbers of our people are incredibly augmented. The alleged causes of danger have long surpassed anticipation, but none of the consequences have followed. The power and influence of the Republic have arisen to a height obvious to all mankind; respect for its authority was not more apparent at its ancient than it is at its present limits; new and inexhaustible sources of general prosperity have been opened; the effects of distance have been averted by the inventive genius of our people, developed and fostered by the spirit of our institutions; and the enlarged variety and amount of interests, productions, and pursuits have strengthened the chain of mutual dependence and formed a circle of mutual benefits too apparent ever to be overlooked.

In justly balancing the powers of the Federal and State authorities difficulties nearly insurmountable arose at the outset and subsequent collisions were deemed inevitable. Amid these it was scarcely believed possible that a scheme of government so complex in construction could remain uninjured. From time to time embarrassments have certainly occurred; but how just is the confidence of future safety imparted by the knowledge that each in succession has been happily removed! Overlooking partial and temporary evils as inseparable from the practical operation of all human institutions, and looking only to the general result, every patriot has reason to be satisfied. While the Federal Government has successfully performed its appropriate functions in relation to foreign affairs and concerns evidently national, that of every State has remarkably improved in protecting and developing local interests and individual welfare; and if the vibrations of authority have occasionally tended too much toward one or the other, it is unquestionably certain that the ultimate operation of the entire system has been to strengthen all the existing institutions and to elevate our whole country in prosperity and renown.

The last, perhaps the greatest, of the prominent sources of discord and disaster supposed to lurk in our political condition was the institution of domestic slavery. Our forefathers were deeply impressed with the delicacy of this subject, and they treated it with a forbearance so evidently wise that in spite of every sinister foreboding it never until the present period disturbed the tranquillity of our common country. Such a result is sufficient evidence of the justice and the patriotism of their course; it is evidence not to be mistaken that an adherence to it can prevent all embarrass-

ment from this as well as from every other anticipated cause of difficulty or danger. Have not recent events made it obvious to the slightest reflection that the least deviation from this spirit of forbearance is injurious to every interest, that of humanity included? Amidst the violence of excited passions this generous and fraternal feeling has been sometimes disregarded; and standing as I now do before my countrymen, in this high place of honor and of trust, I can not refrain from anxiously invoking my fellow-citizens never to be deaf to its dictates. Perceiving before my election the deep interest this subject was beginning to excite, I believed it a solemn duty fully to make known my sentiments in regard to it, and now, when every motive for misrepresentation has passed away, I trust that they will be candidly weighed and understood. At least they will be my standard of conduct in the path before me. I then declared that if the desire of those of my countrymen who were favorable to my election was gratified "I must go into the Presidential chair the inflexible and uncompromising opponent of every attempt on the part of Congress to abolish slavery in the District of Columbia against the wishes of the slaveholding States, and also with a determination equally decided to resist the slightest interference with it in the States where it exists." I submitted also to my fellow-citizens, with fullness and frankness, the reasons which led me to this determination. The result authorizes me to believe that they have been approved and are confided in by a majority of the people of the United States, including those whom they most immediately affect. It now only remains to add that no bill conflicting with these views can ever receive my constitutional sanction. These opinions have been adopted in the firm belief that they are in accordance with the spirit that actuated the venerated fathers of the Republic, and that succeeding experience has proved them to be humane, patriotic, expedient, honorable, and just. If the agitation of this subject was intended to reach the stability of our institutions, enough has occurred to show that it has signally failed, and that in this as in every other instance the apprehensions of the timid and the hopes of the wicked for the destruction of our Government are again destined to be disappointed. Here and there, indeed, scenes of dangerous excitement have occurred, terrifying instances of local violence have been witnessed, and a reckless disregard of the consequences of their conduct has exposed individuals to popular indignation; but neither masses of the people nor sections of the country have been swerved from their devotion to the bond of union and the principles it has made sacred. It will be ever thus. Such attempts at dangerous agitation may periodically return, but with each the object will be better understood. That predominating affection for our political system which prevails throughout our territorial limits, that calm and enlightened

judgment which ultimately governs our people as one vast body, will always be at hand to resist and control every effort, foreign or domestic, which aims or would lead to overthrow our institutions.

What can be more gratifying than such a retrospect as this? We look back on obstacles avoided and dangers overcome, on expectations more than realized and prosperity perfectly secured. To the hopes of the hostile, the fears of the timid, and the doubts of the anxious actual experience has given the conclusive reply. We have seen time gradually dispel every unfavorable foreboding and our

---

I bring with me a settled purpose to maintain the institutions of my country....

Constitution surmount every adverse circumstance dreaded at the outset as beyond control. Present excitement will at all times magnify present dangers, but true philosophy must teach us that none more threatening than the past can remain to be overcome; and we ought (for we have just reason) to entertain an abiding confidence in the stability of our institutions and an entire conviction that if administered in the true form, character, and spirit in which they were established they are abundantly adequate to preserve to us and our children the rich blessings already derived from them, to make our beloved land for a thousand generations that chosen spot where happiness springs from a perfect equality of political rights.

For myself, therefore, I desire to declare that the principle that will govern me in the high duty to which my country calls me is a strict adherence to the letter and spirit of the Constitution as it was designed by those who framed it. Looking back to it as a sacred instrument carefully and not easily

framed; remembering that it was throughout a work of concession and compromise; viewing it as limited to national objects; regarding it as leaving to the people and the States all power not explicitly parted with, I shall endeavor to preserve, protect, and defend it by anxiously referring to its provision for direction in every action. To matters of domestic concernment which it has intrusted to the Federal Government and to such as relate to our intercourse with foreign nations I shall zealously devote myself; beyond those limits I shall never pass.

To enter on this occasion into a further or more minute exposition of my views on the various questions of domestic policy would be as obtrusive as it is probably unexpected. Before the suffrages of my countrymen were conferred upon me I submitted to them, with great precision, my opinions on all the most prominent of these subjects. Those opinions I shall endeavor to carry out with my utmost ability.

Our course of foreign policy has been so uniform and intelligible as to constitute a rule of Executive conduct which leaves little to my discretion, unless, indeed, I were willing to run counter to the lights of experience and the known opinions of my constituents. We sedulously cultivate the friendship of all nations as the conditions most compatible with our welfare and the principles of our Government. We decline alliances as adverse to our peace. We desire commercial relations on equal terms, being ever willing to give a fair equivalent for advantages received. We endeavor to conduct our intercourse with openness and sincerity, promptly avowing our objects and seeking to establish that mutual frankness which is as beneficial in the dealings of nations as of men. We have no disposition and we disclaim all right to meddle in disputes, whether internal or foreign, that may molest other countries, regarding them in their actual state as social communities, and preserving a strict neutrality in all their controversies. Well knowing the tried valor of our people and our exhaustless resources,

we neither anticipate nor fear any designed aggression; and in the consciousness of our own just conduct we feel a security that we shall never be called upon to exert our determination never to permit an invasion of our rights without punishment or redress.

In approaching, then, in the presence of my assembled countrymen, to make the solemn promise that yet remains, and to pledge myself that I will faithfully execute the office I am about to fill, I bring with me a settled purpose to maintain the institutions of my country, which I trust will atone for the errors I commit.

In receiving from the people the sacred trust twice confided to my illustrious predecessor, and which he has discharged so faithfully and so well, I know that I can not expect to perform the arduous task with equal ability and success. But united as I have been in his counsels, a daily witness of his exclusive and unsurpassed devotion to his country's welfare, agreeing with him in sentiments which his countrymen have warmly supported, and permitted to partake largely of his confidence, I may hope that somewhat of the same cheering approbation will be found to attend upon my path. For him I but express with my own the wishes of all, that he may yet long live to enjoy the brilliant evening of his well-spent life; and for myself, conscious of but one desire, faithfully to serve my country, I throw myself without fear on its justice and its kindness. Beyond that I only look to the gracious protection of the Divine Being whose strengthening support I humbly solicit, and whom I fervently pray to look down upon us all. May it be among the dispensations of His providence to bless our beloved country with honors and with length of days. May her ways be ways of pleasantness and all her paths be peace!

***

1840 William Henry Harrison

THE FINANCIAL PANIC OF 1837 and the subsequent depression gave the Whigs an unusually fecund political opportunity. They had both a galvanizing issue (the perilous economy) and an easy target in "Martin Van Ruin." Whig nominee William Henry Harrison had finished a strong second to Van Buren in 1836, and it was thought that, with John Tyler on the ticket, Harrison could win enough states' rights votes to put him over the top. To safeguard this plan, the Whig convention appointed a special "committee of correspondence" to make sure that Harrison never committed himself in writing on any issue of importance.

The Democrats, who renominated President Van Buren, hoped that party loyalty would make up for certain deficiencies in their candidate, such as his lack of popularity. However, fed up with Richard Johnson's sexual peccadilloes, the convention refused to renominate Van Buren's vice

president. (Johnson ran anyway and again received most of the Democratic electoral votes.)

The Whigs avoided discussions of public policy and instead sponsored a great many picnics, parades, and other popular entertainments. The Democrats, on the other hand, wrote the first national platform, though it did them little good.

One Democratic journalist sneered that a simpleminded Harrison would likely give up the campaign if offered a barrel of hard cider and a modest pension. Turning this jibe into a boast of

Party	Popular Votes	Electoral Votes
Whig William H. Harrison, Ohio John Tyler, Va.	1,275,390	234
Democratic Martin Van Buren, N.Y. Richard M. Johnson, Ky.	1,128,854	60

Harrison's commonness, the Whigs organized Log Cabin clubs, held Log Cabin parties, published Log Cabin newspapers, and wrote Log Cabin songs, while serving cider and more cider to one and all. An electorate thirsty for change drank it up. Van Buren didn't even carry his home state of New York. Meanwhile, the "Tippecanoe and Tyler, Too" campaign confirmed the emergence of the second American two-party system—and with it, modern electioneering.

Inaugural Address • Washington, D.C. • Thursday, March 4, 1841

Called from a retirement which I had supposed was to continue for the

residue of my life to fill the chief executive office of this great and free nation, I appear before you, fellow-citizens, to take the oaths which the Constitution prescribes as a necessary qualification for the performance of its duties; and in obedience to a custom coeval with our Government and what I believe to be your expectations I proceed to present to you a summary of the principles which will govern me in the discharge of the duties which I shall be called upon to perform.

It was the remark of a Roman consul in an early period of that celebrated Republic that a most striking contrast was observable in the conduct of candidates for offices of power and trust before and after obtaining them, they seldom carrying out in the latter case the pledges and promises made in the former. However much the world may have improved in many respects in the lapse of upward of two thousand years since the remark was made by the virtuous and indignant Roman, I fear that a strict examination of the annals of some of the modern elective governments would develop similar instances of violated confidence.

Although the fiat of the people has gone forth proclaiming me the Chief Magistrate of this glorious Union, nothing upon their part remaining to be done, it may be thought that a motive may exist to keep up the delusion under which they may be supposed to have acted in relation to my principles and opinions; and perhaps there may be some in this assembly who have come here either prepared to condemn those I shall now deliver, or, approving them, to doubt the sincerity with which they are now uttered. But the lapse of a few months will confirm or dispel their fears. The outline of principles to govern and measures to be adopted by an Administration not yet begun will soon be exchanged for immutable history, and I shall stand either exonerated by my countrymen or classed with the mass of those who promised that they might deceive and flattered

with the intention to betray. However strong may be my present purpose to realize the expectations of a magnanimous and confiding people, I too well understand the dangerous temptations to which I shall be exposed from the magnitude of the power which it has been the pleasure of the people to commit to my hands not to place my chief confidence upon the aid of that Almighty Power which has hitherto protected me and enabled me to bring to favorable issues other important but still greatly inferior trusts heretofore confided to me by my country.

The broad foundation upon which our Constitution rests being the people—a breath of theirs having made, as a breath can unmake, change, or modify it—it can be assigned to none of the great divisions of government but to that of democracy. If such is its theory, those who are called upon to administer it must recognize as its leading principle the duty of shaping their measures so as to produce the greatest good to the greatest number. But with these broad admissions, if we would compare the sovereignty acknowledged to exist in the mass of our people with the power claimed by other sovereignties, even by those which have been considered most purely democratic, we shall find a most essential difference. All others lay claim to power limited only by their own will. The majority of our citizens, on the contrary, possess a sovereignty with an amount of power precisely equal to that which has been granted to them by the parties to the national compact, and nothing beyond. We admit of no government by divine right, believing that so far as power is concerned the Beneficent Creator has made no distinction amongst men; that all are upon an equality, and that the only legitimate right to govern is an express grant of power from the governed. The Constitution of the United States is the instrument containing this grant of power to the several departments composing the Government. On an examination of that instrument it will be found to contain declarations of power granted and of power withheld. The latter is also susceptible of division into power which the majority had the right to grant, but which they do not think proper to intrust to their agents, and that which they could not have granted, not being possessed by themselves. In other words, there are certain rights possessed by each individual American citizen which in his compact with the others he has never surrendered. Some of them, indeed, he is unable to surrender, being, in the language of our system, unalienable. The boasted privilege of a Roman citizen was to him a shield only against a petty provincial ruler, whilst the proud democrat of Athens would console himself under a sentence of death for a supposed violation of the national faith—which no one understood and which at times was the subject of the mockery of all—or the banishment from his home, his family, and his country with or without an alleged cause, that it was the act not of a single tyrant or hated aristocracy, but of his assembled countrymen. Far different is the power of our sovereignty. It can interfere with no one's faith, prescribe forms of worship for no one's observance, inflict no punishment but after well-ascertained guilt, the result of investigation under rules prescribed by the Constitution itself. These precious privileges, and those scarcely less important of giving expression to his thoughts and opinions, either by writing or speaking, unrestrained but by the liability for injury to others, and that of a full participation in all the advantages which flow from the Government, the acknowledged property of all, the American citizen derives from no charter granted by his fellow-man. He claims them because he is himself a man, fashioned by the same Almighty hand as the rest of his species and entitled to a full share of the blessings with which He has endowed them. Notwithstanding the limited sovereignty possessed by the people of the United States and the restricted grant of power to the Government which they have adopted, enough has been given to accomplish all the objects for which it was created. It has been found powerful in war, and hitherto justice has been administered, and intimate union effected, domestic tranquillity preserved, and personal liberty secured to the citizen. As was to be expected, however, from the defect of language and the necessarily sententious manner in which the Constitution is written, disputes have arisen as to the amount of power which it has actually granted or was intended to grant.

This is more particularly the case in relation to that part of the instrument which treats of the legislative branch, and not only as regards the exercise of powers claimed under a general clause giving that body the authority to pass all laws necessary to carry into effect the specified powers, but in relation to the latter also. It is, however, consolatory to reflect that most of the instances of alleged departure from the letter or spirit of the Constitution have ultimately received the sanction of a majority of the people. And the fact that many of our statesmen most distinguished for talent and patriotism have been at one time or other of their political career on both sides of each of the most warmly disputed questions forces upon us the inference that the errors, if errors there were, are attributable to the intrinsic difficulty in many instances of ascertaining the intentions of the framers of the Constitution rather than the influence of any sinister or unpatriotic motive. But the great danger to our institutions does not appear to me to be in a usurpation by the Government of power not granted by the people, but by the accumulation in one of the departments of that which was assigned to others. Limited as are the powers which have been granted, still enough have been granted to constitute a despotism if concentrated in one of the departments. This danger is greatly heightened, as it has been always observable that men are less jealous of encroachments

William Henry Harrison of Ohio

of one department upon another than upon their own reserved rights. When the Constitution of the United States first came from the hands of the Convention which formed it, many of the sternest republicans of the day were alarmed at the extent of the power which had been granted to the Federal Government, and more particularly of that portion which had been assigned to the executive branch. There were in it features which appeared not to be in harmony with their ideas of a simple representative democracy or republic, and knowing the tendency of power to increase itself, particularly when exercised by a single individual, predictions were made that at no very remote period the Government would terminate in virtual monarchy. It would not become me to say that the fears of these patriots have been already realized; but as I sincerely believe that the tendency of measures and of men's opinions for some years past has been in that direction, it is, I conceive, strictly proper that I should take this occasion to repeat the assurances I have heretofore given of my determination to arrest the progress of that tendency if it really exists and restore the Government to its pristine health and vigor, as far as this can be effected by any legitimate exercise of the power placed in my hands.

I proceed to state in as summary a manner as I can my opinion of the sources of the evils which have been so extensively complained of and the correctives which may be applied. Some of the former are unquestionably to be found in the defects of the Constitution; others, in my judgment, are attributable to a misconstruction of some of its provisions. Of the former is the eligibility of the same individual to a second term of the Presidency. The sagacious mind of Mr. Jefferson early saw and lamented this error, and attempts have been made, hitherto without success, to apply the amendatory power of the States to its correction. As, however, one mode of correction is in the power of every President, and consequently in mine, it would be useless, and perhaps invidious, to enumerate the evils of which, in the opinion of many of our fellow-citizens, this error of the sages who framed the Constitution may have been the source and the bitter fruits which we are still to gather from it if it continues to disfigure our system. It may be observed, however, as a general remark, that republics can commit no greater error than to adopt or continue any feature in their systems of government which may be calculated to create or increase the lover of power in the bosoms of those to whom necessity obliges them to commit the management of their affairs; and surely nothing is more likely to produce such a state of mind than the long continuance of an office of high trust. Nothing can be more corrupting, nothing more destructive of all those noble feelings which belong to the character of a devoted republican patriot. When this corrupting passion once takes possession of the human mind, like the love of gold it becomes insatiable. It is the never-dying worm in his bosom, grows with his growth and strengthens with the declining years of its victim. If this is true, it is the part of wisdom for a republic to limit the service of that officer at least to whom she has intrusted the management of her foreign relations, the execution of her laws, and the command of her armies and navies to a period so short as to prevent his forgetting that he is the accountable agent, not the principal; the servant, not the master. Until an amendment of the Constitution can be effected public opinion may secure the desired object. I give my aid to it by renewing the pledge heretofore given that under no circumstances will I consent to serve a second term.

But if there is danger to public liberty from the acknowledged defects of the Constitution in the want of limit to the continuance of the Executive power in the same hands, there is, I apprehend, not much less from a misconstruction of that instrument as it regards the powers actually given. I can not conceive that by a fair construction any or either of its provisions would be found to constitute the President a part of the legislative power. It can not be claimed from the power to recommend, since, although enjoined as a duty upon him, it is a privilege which he holds in common with every other citizen; and although there may be something more of confidence in the propriety of the measures recommended in the one case than in the other, in the obligations of ultimate decision there can be no difference. In the language of the Constitution, "all the legislative powers" which it grants "are vested in the Congress of the United States." It

would be a solecism in language to say that any portion of these is not included in the whole.

It may be said, indeed, that the Constitution has given to the Executive the power to annul the acts of the legislative body by refusing to them his assent. So a similar power has necessarily resulted from that instrument to the judiciary, and yet the judiciary forms no part of the Legislature. There is, it is true, this difference between these grants of power: The Executive can put his negative upon the acts of the Legislature for other cause than that of want of conformity to the Constitution, whilst the judiciary can only declare void those which violate that instrument. But the decision of the judiciary is final in such a case, whereas in every instance where the veto of the Executive is applied it may be overcome by a vote of two-thirds of both Houses of Congress. The negative upon the acts of the legislative by the executive authority, and that in the hands of one individual, would seem to be an incongruity in our system. Like some others of a similar character, however, it appears to be highly expedient, and if used only with the forbearance and in the spirit which was intended by its authors it may be productive of great good and be found one of the best safeguards to the Union. At the period of the formation of the Constitution the principle does not appear to have enjoyed much favor in the State governments. It existed but in two, and in one of these there was a plural executive. If we would search for the motives which operated upon the purely patriotic and enlightened assembly which framed the Constitution for the adoption of a provision so apparently repugnant to the leading democratic principle that the majority should govern, we must reject the idea that they anticipated from it any benefit to the ordinary course of legislation. They knew too well the high degree of intelligence which existed among the people and the enlightened character of the State legislatures not to have the fullest confidence that the two bodies elected by them would be worthy representatives of such constituents, and,

of course, that they would require no aid in conceiving and maturing the measures which the circumstances of the country might require. And it is preposterous to suppose that a thought could for a moment have been entertained that the President, placed at the capital, in the center of the country, could better understand the wants and wishes of the people than their own immediate representatives, who spend a part of every year among them, living with them, often laboring with them, and bound to them by the triple tie of interest, duty, and affection. To assist or control Congress, then, in its ordinary legislation could not, I conceive, have been the motive for conferring the veto power on the President. This argument acquires additional force from the fact of its never having been thus used by the first six Presidents—and two of them were members of the Convention, one presiding over its deliberations and the other bearing a larger share in consummating the labors of that august body than any other person. But if bills were never returned to Congress by either of the Presidents above referred to upon the ground of their being inexpedient or not as well adapted as they might be to the wants of the people, the veto was applied upon that of want of conformity to the Constitution or because errors had been committed from a too hasty enactment.

There is another ground for the adoption of the veto principle, which had probably more influence in recommending it to the Convention than any other. I refer to the security which it gives to the just and equitable action of the Legislature upon all parts of the Union. It could not but have occurred to the Convention that in a country so extensive, embracing so great a variety of soil and climate, and consequently of products, and which from the same causes must ever exhibit a great difference in the amount of the population of its various sections, calling for a great diversity in the employments of the people, that the legislation of the majority might not always justly regard the rights and interests of the minority, and that acts of this character might be

passed under an express grant by the words of the Constitution, and therefore not within the competency of the judiciary to declare void; that however enlightened and patriotic they might suppose from past experience the members of Congress might be, and however largely partaking, in the general, of the liberal feelings of the people, it was impossible to expect that bodies so constituted should not sometimes be controlled by local interests and sectional feelings. It was proper, therefore, to provide some umpire from whose situation and mode of appointment more independence and freedom from such influences might be expected. Such a one was afforded by the executive department constituted by the Constitution. A person elected to that high office, having his constituents in every section, State, and subdivision of the Union, must consider himself bound by the most solemn sanctions to guard, protect, and defend the rights of all and of every portion, great or small, from the injustice and oppression of the rest. I consider the veto power, therefore, given by the Constitution to the Executive of the United States solely as a conservative power, to be used only first, to protect the Constitution from violation; secondly, the people from the effects of hasty legislation where their will has been probably disregarded or not well understood, and, thirdly, to prevent the effects of combinations violative of the rights of minorities. In reference to the second of these objects I may observe that I consider it the right and privilege of the people to decide disputed points of the Constitution arising from the general grant of power to Congress to carry into effect the powers expressly given; and I believe with Mr. Madison that "repeated recognitions under varied circumstances in acts of the legislative, executive, and judicial branches of the Government, accompanied by indications in different modes of the concurrence of the general will of the nation," as affording to the President sufficient authority for his considering such disputed points as settled.

Upward of half a century has elapsed since the adoption

of the present form of government. It would be an object more highly desirable than the gratification of the curiosity of speculative statesmen if its precise situation could be ascertained, a fair exhibit made of the operations of each of its departments, of the powers which they respectively claim and exercise, of the collisions which have occurred between them or between the whole Government and those of the States or either of them. We could then compare our actual condition after fifty years' trial of our system with what it was in the commencement of its operations and ascertain whether the predictions of the patriots who opposed its adoption or the confident hopes of its advocates have been best realized. The great dread of the former seems to have been that the reserved powers of the States would be absorbed by those of the Federal Government and a consolidated power established, leaving to the States the shadow only of that independent action for which they had so zealously contended and on the preservation of which they relied as the last hope of liberty. Without denying that the result to which they looked with so much apprehension is in the way of being realized, it is obvious that they did not clearly see the mode of its accomplishment. The General Government has seized upon none of the reserved rights of the States. As far as any open warfare may have gone, the State authorities have amply maintained their rights. To a casual observer our system presents no appearance of discord between the different members which compose it. Even the addition of many new ones has produced no jarring. They move in their respective orbits in perfect harmony with the central head and with each other. But there is still an undercurrent at work by which, if not seasonably checked, the worst apprehensions of our antifederal patriots will be realized, and not only will the State authorities be overshadowed by the great increase of power in the executive department of the General Government, but the character of that Government, if not its designation, be essentially and rad-

ically changed. This state of things has been in part effected by causes inherent in the Constitution and in part by the never-failing tendency of political power to increase itself. By making the President the sole distributer of all the patronage of the Government the framers of the Constitution do not appear to have anticipated at how short a period it would become a formidable instrument to control the free operations of the State governments. Of trifling importance at first, it had early in Mr. Jefferson's Administration become so powerful as to create great alarm in the mind of that patriot from the potent influence it might exert in controlling the freedom of the elective franchise. If such could have then been the effects of its influence, how much greater must be the danger at this time, quadrupled in amount as it certainly is and more completely under the control of the Executive will than their construction of their powers allowed or the forbearing characters of all the early Presidents permitted them to make. But it is not by the extent of its patronage alone that the executive department has become dangerous, but by the use which it appears may be made of the appointing power to bring under its control the whole revenues of the country. The Constitution has declared it to be the duty of the President to see that the laws are executed, and it makes him the Commander in Chief of the Armies and Navy of the United States. If the opinion of the most approved writers upon that species of mixed government which in modern Europe is termed monarchy In contradistinction to despotism is correct, there was wanting no other addition to the powers of our Chief Magistrate to stamp a monarchical character on our Government but the control of the public finances; and to me it appears strange indeed that anyone should doubt that the

A SKETCH OF THE LIFE AND PUBLIC SERVICES OF
GENERAL WILLIAM HENRY HARRISON,
CANDIDATE OF THE PEOPLE
FOR PRESIDENT OF THE UNITED STATES.
To which is annexed an Appendix.

PRINTED BY JACOB GIDEON, JR., WASHINGTON CITY—1840.

entire control which the President possesses over the officers who have the custody of the public money, by the power of removal with or without cause, does, for all mischievous purposes at least, virtually subject the treasure also to his disposal. The first Roman Emperor, in his attempt to seize the sacred treasure, silenced the opposition of the officer to whose charge it had been committed by a significant allusion to his sword. By a selection of political instruments for the care of the public money a reference to their commissions by a President would be quite as effectual an argument as that of Caesar to the Roman knight. I am not insensible of the great difficulty that exists in drawing a proper plan for the safe-keeping and disbursement of the public revenues, and I know the importance which has been attached by men of great abilities and patriotism to the divorce, as it is called, of the Treasury from the banking institutions. It is not the divorce which is complained of, but the unhallowed union of the Treasury with the executive department, which has created such extensive alarm. To this danger to our republican institutions and that created by the influence given to the Executive through the instrumentality of the Federal officers I propose to apply all the remedies which may be at my

command. It was certainly a great error in the framers of the Constitution not to have made the officer at the head of the Treasury Department entirely independent of the Executive. He should at least have been removable only upon the demand of the popular branch of the Legislature. I have determined never to remove a Secretary of the Treasury without communicating all the circumstances attending such removal to both Houses of Congress.

The influence of the Executive in controlling the freedom of the elective franchise through the medium of the public officers can be effectually checked by renewing the prohibition published by Mr. Jefferson forbidding their interference in elections further than giving their own votes, and their own independence secured by an assurance of perfect immunity in exercising this sacred privilege of freemen under the dictates of their own unbiased judgments. Never with my consent shall an officer of the people, compensated for his services out of their pockets, become the pliant instrument of Executive will.

There is no part of the means placed in the hands of the Executive which might be used with greater effect for unhallowed purposes than the control of the public press. The maxim which our ancestors derived from the mother country that "the freedom of the press is the great bulwark of civil and religious liberty" is one of the most precious legacies which they have left us. We have learned, too, from our own as well as the experience of other countries, that golden shackles, by whomsoever or by whatever pretense imposed, are as fatal to it as the iron bonds of despotism. The presses in the necessary employment of the Government should never be used "to clear the guilty or to varnish crime." A decent and manly examination of the acts of the Government should be not only tolerated, but encouraged.

Upon another occasion I have given my opinion at some length upon the impropriety of Executive interference in the legislation of Congress—that the article in the Constitution making it the duty of the President to communicate information and authorizing him to recommend measures was not intended to make him the source in legislation, and, in particular, that he should never be looked to for schemes of finance. It would be very strange, indeed, that the Constitution should have strictly forbidden one branch of the Legislature from interfering in the origination of such bills and that it should be considered proper that an altogether different department of the Government should be permitted to do so. Some of our best political maxims and opinions have been drawn from our parent isle. There are others, however, which can not be introduced in our system without singular incongruity and the production of much mischief, and this I conceive to be one. No matter in which of the houses of Parliament a bill may originate nor by whom introduced—a minister or a member of the opposition—by the fiction of law, or rather of constitutional principle, the sovereign is supposed to have prepared it agreeably to his will and then submitted it to Parliament for their advice and consent. Now the very reverse is the case here, not only with regard to the principle, but the forms prescribed by the Constitution. The principle certainly assigns to the only body constituted by the Constitution (the legislative body) the power to make laws, and the forms even direct that the enactment should be ascribed to them. The Senate, in relation to revenue bills, have the right to propose amendments, and so has the Executive by the power given him to return them to the House of Representatives with his objections. It is in his power also to propose amendments in the existing revenue laws, suggested by his observations upon their defective or injurious operation. But the delicate duty of devising schemes of revenue should be left where the Constitution has placed it—with the immediate representatives of the people. For similar reasons the mode of keeping the public treasure should be prescribed by them, and the further removed it may be from the control of the Executive the more wholesome the arrangement and the more in accor-

dance with republican principle.

Connected with this subject is the character of the currency. The idea of making it exclusively metallic, however well intended, appears to me to be fraught with more fatal consequences than any other scheme having no relation to the personal rights of the citizens that has ever been devised. If any single scheme could produce the effect of arresting at once that mutation of condition by which thousands of our most indigent fellow-citizens by their industry and enterprise are raised to the possession of wealth, that is the one. If there is one measure better calculated than another to produce that state of things so much deprecated by all true republicans, by which the rich are daily adding to their hoards and the poor sinking deeper into penury, it is an exclusive metallic currency. Or if there is a process by which the character of the country for generosity and nobleness of feeling may be destroyed by the great increase and neck toleration of usury, it is an exclusive metallic currency.

Amongst the other duties of a delicate character which the President is called upon to perform is the supervision of the government of the Territories of the United States. Those of them which are destined to become members of our great political family are compensated by their rapid progress from infancy to manhood for the partial and temporary deprivation of their political rights. It is in this District only where American citizens are to be found who under a settled policy are deprived of many important political privileges without any inspiring hope as to the future. Their only consolation under circumstances of such deprivation is that of the devoted exterior guards of a camp—that their sufferings secure tranquillity and safety within. Are there any of their countrymen, who would subject them to greater sacrifices, to any other humiliations than those essentially necessary to the security

of the object for which they were thus separated from their fellow-citizens? Are their rights alone not to be guaranteed by the application of those great principles upon which all our constitutions are founded? We are told by the greatest of British orators and statesmen that at the commencement of the War of the Revolution the most stupid men in England spoke of "their American subjects." Are there, indeed, citizens of any of our States who have dreamed of their subjects in the District of Columbia? Such dreams can never be realized by any agency of mine. The people of the District of Columbia are not the subjects of the people of the States, but free American citizens. Being in the latter condition when the Constitution was formed, no words used in that instrument could have been intended to deprive them of that character. If there is anything in the great principle of unalienable rights so emphatically insisted upon in our Declaration of Independence, they could neither make nor the United States accept a surrender of their liberties and become the subjects—in other words, the slaves—of their former fellow-citizens. If this be true—and it will scarcely be denied by anyone who has a correct idea of his own rights as an American citizen—the grant to Congress of exclusive jurisdiction in the District of Columbia can be interpreted, so far as respects the aggregate people of the United

States, as meaning nothing more than to allow to Congress the controlling power necessary to afford a free and safe exercise of the functions assigned to the General Government by the Constitution. In all other respects the legislation of Congress should be adapted to their peculiar position and wants and be conformable with their deliberate opinions of their own interests.

I have spoken of the necessity of keeping the respective departments of the Government, as well as all the other authorities of our country, within their appropriate orbits. This is a matter of difficulty in some cases, as the powers which they respectively claim are often not defined by any distinct lines. Mischievous, however, in their tendencies as collisions of this kind may be, those which arise between the respective communities which for certain purposes compose one nation are much more so, for no such nation can long exist without the careful culture of those feelings of confidence and affection which are the effective bonds to union between free and confederated states. Strong as is the tie of interest, it has been often found ineffectual. Men blinded by their passions have been known to adopt measures for their country in direct opposition to all the suggestions of policy. The alternative, then, is to destroy or keep down a bad passion by creating and fostering a good one, and this seems to be the corner

stone upon which our American political architects have reared the fabric of our Government. The cement which was to bind it and perpetuate its existence was the affectionate attachment between all its members. To insure the continuance of this feeling, produced at first by a community of dangers, of sufferings, and of interests, the advantages of each were made accessible to all. No participation in any good possessed by any member of our extensive Confederacy, except in domestic government, was withheld from the citizen of any other member. By a process attended with no difficulty, no delay, no expense but that of removal, the citizen of one might become the citizen of any other, and successively of the whole. The lines, too, separating powers to be exercised by the citizens of one State from those of another seem to be so distinctly drawn as to leave no room for misunderstanding. The citizens of each State unite in their persons all the privileges which that character confers and all that they may claim as citizens of the United States, but in no case can the same persons at the same time act as the citizen of two separate States, and he is therefore positively precluded from any interference with the reserved powers of any State but that of which he is for the time being a citizen. He may, indeed, offer to the citizens of other States his advice as to their management, and the form in which it is tendered is left to his own discretion and sense of propriety. It may be observed, however, that organized associations of citizens requiring compliance with their wishes too much resemble the recommendations of Athens to her allies, supported by an armed and powerful fleet. It was, indeed, to the ambition of the leading States of Greece to control the domestic concerns of the others that the destruction of that celebrated Confederacy, and subsequently of all its members, is mainly to be attributed, and it is owing to the absence of that spirit that the Helvetic Confederacy has for so many years been preserved. Never has there been seen in the institutions of the separate members of any confederacy

more elements of discord. In the principles and forms of government and religion, as well as in the circumstances of the several Cantons, so marked a discrepancy was observable as to promise anything but harmony in their intercourse or permanency in their alliance, and yet for ages neither has been interrupted. Content with the positive benefits which their union produced, with the independence and safety from foreign aggression which it secured, these sagacious people respected the institutions of each other, however repugnant to their own principles and prejudices.

Our Confederacy, fellow-citizens, can only be preserved by the same forbearance. Our citizens must be content with the exercise of the powers with which the Constitution clothes them. The attempt of those of one State to control the domestic institutions of another can only result in feelings of distrust and jealousy, the certain harbingers of disunion, violence, and civil war, and the ultimate destruction of our free institutions. Our Confederacy is perfectly illustrated by the terms and principles governing a common copartnership. There is a fund of power to be exercised under the direction of the joint councils of the allied members, but that which has been reserved by the individual members is intangible by the common Government or the individual members composing it. To attempt it finds no support in the principles of our Constitution.

It should be our constant and earnest endeavor mutually to cultivate a spirit of concord and harmony among the various parts of our Confederacy. Experience has abundantly taught us that the agitation by citizens of one part of the Union of a subject not confided to the General Government, but exclusively under the guardianship of the local authorities, is productive of no other consequences than bitterness, alienation, discord, and injury to the very cause which is intended to be advanced. Of all the great interests which appertain to our country, that of union—cordial, confiding, fraternal union—is by far the most important, since it is the only true and sure guaranty of all others.

In consequence of the embarrassed state of business and the currency, some of the States may meet with difficulty in their financial concerns. However deeply we may regret anything imprudent or excessive in the engagements into which States have entered for purposes of their own, it does not become us to disparage the States governments, nor to discourage them from making proper efforts for their own relief. On the contrary, it is our

> *The attempt of those of one State to control the domestic institutions of another can only result in feelings of distrust and jealousy…*

duty to encourage them to the extent of our constitutional authority to apply their best means and cheerfully to make all necessary sacrifices and submit to all necessary burdens to fulfill their engagements and maintain their credit, for the character and credit of the several States form a part of the character and credit of the whole country. The resources of the country are abundant, the enterprise and activity of our people proverbial, and we may well hope that wise legislation and prudent administration by the respective governments, each acting within its own sphere, will restore former prosperity.

Unpleasant and even dangerous as collisions may sometimes be between the constituted authorities of the citizens of our country in relation to the lines which separate their respective jurisdictions, the results can be of no vital injury to our institutions if that ardent patriotism, that devoted attachment to liberty, that spirit of moderation and forbearance for

which our countrymen were once distinguished, continue to be cherished. If this continues to be the ruling passion of our souls, the weaker feeling of the mistaken enthusiast will be corrected, the Utopian dreams of the scheming politician dissipated, and the complicated intrigues of the demagogue rendered harmless. The spirit of liberty is the sovereign balm for every injury which our institutions may receive. On the contrary, no care that can be used in the construction of our Government, no division of powers, no distribution of checks in its several departments, will prove effectual to keep us a free people if this spirit is suffered to decay; and decay it will without constant nurture. To the neglect of this duty the best historians agree in attributing the ruin of all the republics with whose existence and fall their writings have made us acquainted. The same causes will ever produce the same effects, and as long as the love of power is a dominant passion of the human bosom, and as long as the understandings of men can be warped and their affections changed by operations upon their passions and prejudices, so long will the liberties of a people depend on their own constant attention to its preservation. The danger to all well-established free governments arises from the unwillingness of the people to believe in its existence or from the influence of designing men diverting their attention from the quarter whence it approaches to a source from which it can never come. This is the old trick of those who would usurp the government of their country. In the name of democracy they speak, warning the people against the influence of wealth and the danger of aristocracy. History, ancient and modern, is full of such examples. Caesar became the master of the Roman people and the senate under the pretense of supporting the democratic claims of the former against the aristocracy of the latter; Cromwell, in the character of protector of the liberties of the people, became the dictator of England, and Bolivar possessed himself of unlimited power with the title of his country's liberator. There is, on the contrary, no instance on record of an extensive and well-established republic being changed into an aristocracy. The tendencies of all such governments in their decline is to monarchy, and the antagonist principle to liberty there is the spirit of faction—a spirit which assumes the character and in times of great excitement imposes itself upon the people as the genuine spirit of freedom, and, like the false Christs whose coming was foretold by the Savior, seeks to, and were it possible would, impose upon the true and most faithful disciples of liberty. It is in periods like this that it behooves the people to be most watchful of those to whom they have intrusted power. And although there is at times much difficulty in distinguishing the false from the true spirit, a calm and dispassionate investigation will detect the counterfeit, as well by the character of its operations as the results that are produced. The true spirit of liberty, although devoted, persevering, bold, and uncompromising in principle, that secured is mild and tolerant and scrupulous as to the means it employs, whilst the spirit of party, assuming to be that of liberty, is harsh, vindictive, and intolerant, and totally reckless as to the character of the allies which it brings to the aid of its cause. When the genuine spirit of liberty animates the body of a people to a thorough examination of their affairs, it leads to the excision of every excrescence which may have fastened itself upon any of the departments of the government, and restores the system to its pristine health and beauty. But the reign of an intolerant spirit of party amongst a free people seldom fails to result in a dangerous accession to the executive power introduced and established amidst unusual professions of devotion to democracy.

The foregoing remarks relate almost exclusively to matters connected with our domestic concerns. It may be proper, however, that I should give some indications to my fellow-citizens of my proposed course of conduct in the management of our foreign relations. I assure them, therefore, that it is my intention to use every means in my power to preserve the friendly inter-course which now so happily subsists with every foreign nation, and that although, of course, not well informed as to the state of pending negotiations with any of them, I see in the personal characters of the sovereigns, as well as in the mutual interests of our own and of the governments with which our relations are most intimate, a pleasing guaranty that the harmony so important to the interests of their subjects as well as of our citizens will not be interrupted by the advancement of any claim or pretension upon their part to which our honor would not permit us to yield. Long the defender of my country's rights in the field, I trust that my fellow-citizens will not see in my earnest desire to preserve peace with foreign powers any indication that their rights will ever be sacrificed or the honor of the nation tarnished by any admission on the part of their Chief Magistrate unworthy of their former glory. In our intercourse with our aboriginal neighbors the same liberality and justice which marked the course prescribed to me by two of my illustrious predecessors when acting under their direction in the discharge of the duties of superintendent and commissioner shall be strictly observed. I can conceive of no more sublime spectacle, none more likely to propitiate an impartial and common Creator, than a rigid adherence to the principles of justice on the part of a powerful nation in its transactions with a weaker and uncivilized people whom circumstances have placed at its disposal.

Before concluding, fellow-citizens, I must say something to you on the subject of the parties at this time existing in our country. To me it appears perfectly clear that the interest of that country requires that the violence of the spirit by which those parties are at this time governed must be greatly mitigated, if not entirely extinguished, or consequences will ensue which are appalling to be thought of.

If parties in a republic are necessary to secure a degree of vigilance sufficient to keep the public functionaries within the bounds of law and duty, at that point their usefulness ends. Beyond that they become destructive of public virtue, the parent of a spirit antagonist to that of liberty, and eventually its inevitable conqueror. We have examples of republics where the love of country and of liberty at one time were the dominant passions of the whole mass of citizens, and yet, with the continuance of the name and forms of free government, not a vestige of these qualities remaining in the bosoms of any one of its citizens. It was the beautiful remark of a distinguished English writer that "in the Roman senate Octavius had a party and Anthony a party, but the Commonwealth had none." Yet the senate continued to meet in the temple of liberty to talk of the sacredness and beauty of the Commonwealth and gaze at the statues of the elder Brutus and of the Curtii and Decii, and the people assembled in the forum, not, as in the days of Camillus and the Scipios, to cast their free votes for annual magistrates or pass upon the acts of the senate, but to receive from the hands of the leaders of the respective parties their share of the spoils and to shout for one or the other, as those collected in Gaul or Egypt and the lesser Asia would furnish the larger dividend. The spirit of liberty had fled, and, avoiding the abodes of civilized man, had sought protection in the wilds of Scythia or Scandinavia; and so under the operation of the same causes and influences it will fly from our Capitol and our forums. A calamity so awful, not only to our country, but to the world, must be deprecated by every patriot and every tendency to a state of things likely to produce it immediately checked. Such a tendency has existed—does exist. Always the friend of my countrymen, never their flatterer, it becomes my duty to say to them from this high place to which their partiality has exalted me that there exists in the land a spirit hostile to their best interests—hostile to liberty itself. It is a spirit contracted in its views, selfish in its objects. It looks to the aggrandizement of a few even to the destruction of the interests of the whole. The entire remedy is with the people. Something, however, may be effected by the means which they have placed in my hands. It is union that we want, not of a party for the sake of that party, but a union of the whole country for the sake of the whole country, for the defense of its interests and its honor against foreign aggression, for the defense of those principles for which our ancestors so gloriously contended. As far as it depends upon me it shall be accomplished. All the influence that I possess shall be exerted to prevent the formation at least of an Executive party in the halls of the legislative body. I wish for the support of no member of that body to any measure of mine that does not satisfy his judgment and his sense of duty to those from whom he holds his appointment, nor any confidence in advance from the people but that asked for by Mr. Jefferson, "to give firmness and effect to the legal administration of their affairs."

I deem the present occasion sufficiently important and solemn to justify me in expressing to my fellow-citizens a profound reverence for the Christian religion and a thorough conviction that sound morals, religious liberty, and a just sense of religious responsibility are essentially connected with all true and lasting happiness; and to that good Being who has blessed us by the gifts of civil and religious freedom, who watched over and prospered the labors of our fathers and has hitherto preserved to us institutions far exceeding in excellence those of any other people, let us unite in fervently commending every interest of our beloved country in all future time.

Fellow-citizens, being fully invested with that high office to which the partiality of my countrymen has called me, I now take an affectionate leave of you. You will bear with you to your homes the remembrance of the pledge I have this day given to discharge all the high duties of my exalted station according to the best of my ability, and I shall enter upon their performance with entire confidence in the support of a just and generous people.

* * *

1844 James Knox Polk

Although President John Tyler sought the Democratic nomination, his old party hadn't forgotten his willingness to cross party lines when it suited him. Former president Martin Van Buren also wanted the nomination, and he had a majority of the delegates behind him, but the two-thirds rule stymied his candidacy. Hoping to resolve the impasse, southern and western delegates began promoting Tennessean James Knox Polk, who became the first presidential "dark horse" candidate.

The Whig camp asked derisively, "Who Is James K. Polk?" But the voters learned quickly that "Fifty-Four Forty or Fight" Polk stood for expansion of the Union across the continent—a policy not yet called "manifest destiny" but one that was still widely popular.

Meanwhile, the Whigs nominated by acclamation their well-known but aging leader, Henry Clay. The party's brief platform (just a hundred words) and "Hooray for Clay" slogan indicate the lackluster nature of its campaign. Clay had no new ideas to fire up the voters, and he was on the wrong side (or no side, which was just as bad) when it came to Texas annexation, which Polk demanded. Clay also wanted to avoid war with Mexico, while an aggressive Polk coveted Mexican territory in the Southwest.

Although Polk's "Fifty-Four Forty or Fight" slogan (referring to the disputed northern boundary of the Oregon Territory) won him a great deal of support, not all of his votes were legitimate. Big-city Democrats fraudulently registered thousands of immigrant voters to stuff the ballot box for Polk; and on the Mississippi, a steamboat carried Polk voters along the river so they could cast ballots at several different landings.

Even so, Clay would still have won the election had antislavery Whigs in New York not bolted the party for James G. Birney, the abolitionist Liberty party candidate. If Clay had retained just one third of Birney's vote, he would have taken New York and with it, the election.

Party	Popular Votes	Electoral Votes
Democratic James K. Polk, Tenn. George M. Dallas, Pa.	1,339,494	170
Whig. Henry Clay, Ky Theodore Frelinghuysen, N.J.	1,300,004	105
Liberty James G. Birney, N.Y. Thomas Morris, Ohio	62,103	

Inaugural Address • Washington, D.C. • Tuesday, March 4, 1845

Fellow-Citizens: Without solicitation on my part, I have been chosen by the

free and voluntary suffrages of my countrymen to the most honorable and most responsible office on earth. I am deeply impressed with gratitude for the confidence reposed in me. Honored with this distinguished consideration at an earlier period of life than any of my predecessors, I can not disguise the diffidence with which I am about to enter on the discharge of my official duties.

If the more aged and experienced men who have filled the office of President of the United States even in the infancy of the Republic distrusted their ability to discharge the duties of that exalted station, what ought not to be the apprehensions of one so much younger and less endowed now that our domain extends from ocean to ocean, that our people have so greatly increased in numbers, and at a time when so great diversity of opinion prevails in regard to the principles and policy which should characterize the administration of our Government? Well may the boldest fear and the wisest tremble when incurring responsibilities on which may depend our country's peace and prosperity, and in some degree the hopes and happiness of the whole human family.

In assuming responsibilities so vast I fervently invoke the aid of that Almighty Ruler of the Universe in whose hands are the destinies of nations and of men to guard this Heaven-favored land against the mischiefs which without His guidance might arise from an unwise public policy. With a firm reliance upon the wisdom of Omnipotence to sustain and direct me in the path of duty which I am appointed to pursue, I stand in the presence of this assembled multitude of my countrymen to take upon myself the solemn obligation "to the best of my ability to preserve, protect, and defend the Constitution of the United States."

A concise enumeration of the principles which will guide me in the administrative policy of the Government is not only in accordance with the examples set me by all my predecessors, but is eminently befitting the occasion.

The Constitution itself, plainly written as it is, the safeguard of our federative compact, the offspring of concession and compromise, binding together in the bonds of peace and union this great and increasing family of free and independent States, will be the chart by which I shall be directed.

It will be my first care to administer the Government in the true spirit of that instrument, and to assume no powers not expressly granted or clearly implied in its terms. The Government of the United States is one of delegated and limited powers, and it is by a strict adherence to the clearly granted powers and by abstaining from the exercise of doubtful or unauthorized implied powers that we have the only sure guaranty against the recurrence of those unfortunate collisions between the Federal and State authorities which have occasionally so much disturbed the harmony of our system and even threatened the perpetuity of our glorious Union.

"To the States, respectively, or to the people" have been reserved "the powers not delegated to the United States by the Constitution nor prohibited by it to the States." Each State is a complete sovereignty within the sphere of its reserved powers. The Government of the Union, acting within the sphere of its delegated authority, is also a complete sovereignty. While the General Government should abstain from the exercise of authority not clearly delegated to it, the States should be equally careful that in the maintenance of their rights they do not overstep the limits of powers reserved to them. One of the most distinguished of my predecessors attached deserved importance to "the support of the State governments in all their rights, as the most competent administration for our domestic concerns and the surest bulwark against antirepublican tendencies," and to the "preservation of the General Government in its whole constitutional vigor, as the sheet anchor of our peace at home and safety abroad."

To the Government of the United States has been intrusted the exclusive management of our foreign affairs. Beyond that it wields a few general enumerated powers. It does not force reform on the States. It leaves individuals, over whom it casts its protecting influence, entirely free to improve their own condition by the legitimate exercise of all

their mental and physical powers. It is a common protector of each and all the States; of every man who lives upon our soil, whether of native or foreign birth; of every religious sect, in their worship of the Almighty according to the dictates of their own conscience; of every shade of opinion, and the most free inquiry; of every art, trade,

and occupation consistent with the laws of the States. And we rejoice in the general happiness, prosperity, and advancement of our country, which have been the offspring of freedom, and not of power.

This most admirable and

wisest system of well-regulated self-government among men ever devised by human minds has been tested by its successful operation for more than half a century, and if preserved from the usurpations of the Federal Government on the one hand and the exercise by the States of powers not reserved to them on the other, will, I fervently hope

and believe, endure for ages to come and dispense the blessings of civil and religious liberty to distant generations. To effect objects so dear to every patriot I shall devote myself with anxious solicitude. It will be my desire to guard against that most fruit-

ful source of danger to the harmonious action of our system which consists in substituting the mere discretion and caprice of the Executive or of majorities in the legislative department of the Government for powers which have been withheld from the Federal Government by the Constitution. By the theory of our Government majorities rule, but this right is not an arbitrary or unlimited one. It is a right to be exercised in subordination to the Constitution and in conformity to it. One great object of the Constitution was to restrain majorities from oppressing minorities or encroaching upon their just rights. Minorities have a right to appeal to the Constitution as a shield against such oppression.

That the blessings of liberty which our Constitution secures may be enjoyed alike by minorities and majorities, the Executive has been wisely invested with a qualified veto upon the acts of the Legislature. It is a negative power, and is conservative in its character. It arrests for the time hasty, inconsiderate, or unconstitutional legislation, invites reconsideration, and transfers questions at issue between the legislative and executive departments to the tribunal of the people. Like all other powers, it is subject to be abused. When judiciously and properly exercised, the Constitution itself may be saved from infraction and the rights of all preserved and protected.

The inestimable value of our Federal Union is felt and acknowledged by all. By this system of united and confederated States our people are permitted collectively and individually to seek their own happiness in their own way, and the consequences have been most auspicious. Since the Union was formed the number of the States has increased from thirteen to twenty-eight; two of these have taken their position as members of the Confederacy within the last week. Our population has increased from three to twenty millions. New communities and States are seeking protection under its aegis, and multitudes from the Old World are flocking to our shores to participate in its blessings. Beneath its benign sway peace and prosperity prevail. Freed from the burdens and miseries of war, our trade and intercourse have extended throughout the world. Mind, no longer tasked in devising means to accomplish or resist schemes of ambition, usurpation, or conquest, is devoting itself to man's true interests in developing his faculties and powers and the capacity of nature to minister to his enjoyments. Genius is free to announce its inventions and discoveries, and the hand is free to accomplish whatever the head conceives not incompatible with the rights of a fellow-being. All distinctions of birth or of rank have been abolished. All citizens, whether native or adopted, are placed upon terms of precise equality. All are entitled to equal rights and equal protection. No union exists between church and state, and perfect freedom of opinion is guaranteed to all sects and creeds.

These are some of the blessings secured to our happy land by our Federal Union. To perpetuate them it is our sacred duty to preserve it. Who shall assign limits to the achievements of free minds and free hands under the protection of this glorious Union? No treason to mankind since the organization of society would be equal in atrocity to that of him who would lift his hand to destroy it. He would overthrow the noblest structure of human wisdom, which protects himself and his fellow-man. He would stop the progress of free government and involve his country either in anarchy or despotism. He would extinguish the fire of liberty, which warms and animates the hearts of happy millions and invites all the nations of the earth to imitate our example. If he say that error and wrong are committed in the administration of the Government, let him remember that nothing human can be perfect, and that under no other system of government revealed by Heaven or devised by man has reason been allowed so free and broad a scope to combat error. Has the sword of despots proved to be a safer or surer instrument of reform in government than enlightened reason? Does he expect to find among the ruins of this Union a happier abode for our swarming

millions than they now have under it? Every lover of his country must shudder at the thought of the possibility of its dissolution, and will be ready to adopt the patriotic sentiment, "Our Federal Union—it must be preserved." To preserve it the compromises which alone enabled our fathers to form a common constitution for the government and protection of so many States and distinct communities, of such diversi-

> *It is confidently believed that our system may be safely extended to the utmost bounds of our territorial limits....*

fied habits, interests, and domestic institutions, must be sacredly and religiously observed. Any attempt to disturb or destroy these compromises, being terms of the compact of union, can lead to none other than the most ruinous and disastrous consequences.

It is a source of deep regret that in some sections of our country misguided persons have occasionally indulged in schemes and agitations whose object is the destruction of domestic institutions existing in other sections—institutions which existed at the adoption of the Constitution and were recognized and protected by it. All must see that if it were possible for them to be successful in attaining their object the dissolution of the Union and the consequent destruction of our happy form of government must speedily follow.

I am happy to believe that at every period of our existence as a nation there has existed, and continues to exist, among the great mass of our people a devotion to the Union of the States which will shield and protect it against the moral trea-

son of any who would seriously contemplate its destruction. To secure a continuance of that devotion the compromises of the Constitution must not only be preserved, but sectional jealousies and heartburnings must be discountenanced, and all should remember that they are members of the same political family, having a common destiny. To increase the attachment of our people to the Union, our laws should be just. Any policy which shall tend to favor monopolies or the peculiar interests of sections or classes must operate to the prejudice of the interest of their fellow-citizens, and should be avoided. If the compromises of the Constitution be preserved, if sectional jealousies and heartburnings be discountenanced, if our laws be just and the Government be practically administered strictly within the limits of power prescribed to it, we may discard all apprehensions for the safety of the Union.

With these views of the nature, character, and objects of the Government and the value of the Union, I shall steadily oppose the creation of those institutions and systems which in their nature tend to pervert it from its legitimate purposes and make it the instrument of sections, classes, and individuals. We need no national banks or other extraneous institutions planted around the Government to control or strengthen it in opposition to the will of its authors. Experience has taught us how unnecessary they are as auxiliaries of the public authorities—how impotent for good and how powerful for mischief.

Ours was intended to be a plain and frugal government, and I shall regard it to be my duty to recommend to Congress and, as far as the Executive is concerned, to enforce by all the means within my power the strictest economy in the expenditure of the public money which may be compatible with the public interests.

A national debt has become almost an institution of European monarchies. It is viewed in some of them as an essential prop to existing governments. Melancholy is the condition of that people whose government can be sustained only by a system which periodi-

cally transfers large amounts from the labor of the many to the coffers of the few. Such a system is incompatible with the ends for which our republican Government was instituted. Under a wise policy the debts contracted in our Revolution and during the War of 1812 have been happily extinguished. By a judicious application of the revenues not required for other necessary purposes, it is not doubted that the debt which has grown out of the circumstances of the last few years may be speedily paid off.

I congratulate my fellow-citizens on the entire restoration of the credit of the General Government of the Union and that of many of the States. Happy would it be for the indebted States if they were freed from their liabilities, many of which were incautiously contracted. Although the Government of the Union is neither in a legal nor a moral sense bound for the debts of the States, and it would be a violation of our compact of union to assume them, yet we can not but feel a deep interest in seeing all the States meet their public liabilities and pay off their just debts at the earliest practicable period. That they will do so as soon as it can be done without imposing too heavy burdens on their citizens there is no reason to doubt. The sound moral and honorable feeling of the people of the indebted States can not be questioned, and we are happy to perceive a settled disposition on their part, as their ability returns after a season of unexampled pecuniary embarrassment, to pay off all just demands and to acquiesce in any reasonable measures to accomplish that object.

One of the difficulties which we have had to encounter in the practical administration of the Government consists in the adjustment of our revenue laws and the levy of the taxes necessary for the support of Government. In the general proposition that no more money shall be collected than the necessities of an economical administration shall require all parties seem to acquiesce. Nor does there seem to be any material difference of opinion as to the absence of right in the Government to tax one section of country, or one class of citizens, or one occupation, for the mere profit of another. "Justice and sound policy forbid the Federal Government to foster one branch of industry to the detriment of another, or to cherish the interests of one portion to the injury of another portion of our common country." I have heretofore declared to my fellow-citizens that "in my judgment it is the duty of the Government to extend, as far as it may be practicable to do so, by its revenue laws and all other means within its power, fair and just protection to all of the great interests of the whole Union, embracing agriculture, manufactures, the mechanic arts, commerce, and navigation."

I have also declared my opinion to be "in favor of a tariff for revenue," and that "in adjusting the details of such a tariff I have sanctioned such moderate discriminating duties as would produce the amount of revenue needed and at the same time afford reasonable incidental protection to our home industry," and that I was "opposed to a tariff for protection merely, and not for revenue."

The power "to lay and collect taxes, duties, imposts, and excises" was an indispensable one to be conferred on the Federal Government, which without it would possess no means of providing for its own support. In executing this power by levying a tariff of duties for the support of Government, the raising of revenue should be the object and protection the incident. To reverse this principle and make protection the object and revenue the incident would be to inflict manifest injustice upon all other than the protected interests. In levying duties for revenue it is doubtless proper to make such discriminations within the revenue principle as will afford incidental protection to our home interests. Within the revenue limit there is a discretion to discriminate; beyond that limit the rightful exercise of the power is not conceded. The incidental protection af-

forded to our home interests by discriminations within the revenue range it is believed will be ample. In making discriminations all our home interests should as far as practicable be equally protected. The largest portion of our people are agriculturists. Others are employed in manufactures, commerce, navigation, and the mechanic arts. They are all engaged in their respective pursuits and their joint labors constitute the national or home industry. To tax one branch of this home industry for the benefit of another would be unjust. No one of these interests can rightfully claim an advantage over the others, or to be enriched by impoverishing the others. All are equally entitled to the fostering care and protection of the Government. In exercising a sound discretion in levying discriminating duties within the limit prescribed, care should be taken that it be done in a manner not to benefit the wealthy few at the expense of the toiling millions by taxing lowest the luxuries of life, or articles of superior quality and high price,

which can only be consumed by the wealthy, and highest the necessaries of life, or articles of coarse quality and low price, which the poor and great mass of our people must consume. The burdens of government should as far as practicable be distributed justly and equally among all classes of our population. These general views, long entertained on this subject, I have deemed it proper to reiterate. It is a subject upon which conflicting interests of sections and occupations are supposed to exist, and a spirit of mutual concession and compromise in adjusting its details should be cherished by every part of our widespread country as the only means of preserving harmony and a cheerful acquiescence of all in the operation of our revenue laws. Our patriotic citizens in every part of the Union will readily submit to the payment of such taxes as shall be needed for the support of their Government, whether in peace or in war, if they are so levied as to distribute the burdens as equally as possible among them.

The Republic of Texas has made known her desire to come into our Union, to form a part of our Confederacy and enjoy with us the blessings of liberty secured and guaranteed by our Constitution. Texas was once a part of our country—was unwisely ceded away to a foreign power—is now independent, and possesses an undoubted right to dispose of a part or the whole of her territory and to merge her sovereignty as a sepa-

rate and independent state in ours. I congratulate my country that by an act of the late Congress of the United States the assent of this Government has been given to the reunion, and it only remains for the two countries to agree upon the terms to consummate an object so important to both.

I regard the question of annexation as belonging exclusively to the United States and Texas. They are independent powers competent to contract, and foreign nations have no right to interfere with them or to take exceptions to their reunion. Foreign powers do not seem to appreciate the true character of our Government. Our Union is a confederation of independent States, whose policy is peace with each other and all the world. To enlarge its limits is to extend the dominions of peace over additional territories and increasing millions. The world has nothing to fear from military ambition in our Government. While the Chief Magistrate and the popular branch of Congress are elected for short terms by the suffrages of those millions who must in their own persons bear all the burdens and miseries of war, our Government can not be otherwise than pacific. Foreign powers should therefore look on the annexation of Texas to the United States not as the conquest of a nation seeking to extend her dominions by arms and violence, but as the peaceful acquisition of a territory once her own, by adding another member to our confederation, with the consent of that member, thereby diminishing the chances of war and opening to them new and ever-increasing markets for their products.

To Texas the reunion is important, because the strong protecting arm of our Government would be extended over her, and the vast resources of her fertile soil and genial climate would be speedily developed, while the safety of New Orleans and of our whole southwestern frontier against hostile aggression, as well as the interests of the whole Union, would be promoted by it.

In the earlier stages of our national existence the opinion prevailed with some that our system of confederated States could not operate successfully over an extended territory, and serious objections have at different times been made to the enlargement of our boundaries. These objections were earnestly urged when we acquired Louisiana. Experience has shown that they were not well founded. The title of numerous Indian tribes to vast tracts of country has been extinguished; new States have been admitted into the Union; new Territories have been created and our jurisdiction and laws extended over them. As our population has expanded, the Union has been cemented and strengthened. As our boundaries have been en-

larged and our agricultural population has been spread over a large surface, our federative system has acquired additional strength and security. It may well be doubted whether it would not be in greater danger of overthrow if our present population were confined to the comparatively narrow limits of the original thirteen States than it is now that they are sparsely settled over a more expanded territory. It is confidently believed that our system may be safely extended to the utmost bounds of our territorial limits, and that as it shall be extended the bonds of our Union, so far from being weakened, will become stronger.

None can fail to see the danger to our safety and future peace if Texas remains an independent state or becomes an ally or dependency of some foreign nation more powerful than herself. Is there one among our citizens who would not prefer perpetual peace with Texas to occasional wars, which so often occur between bordering independent nations? Is there one who would not prefer free intercourse with her to high duties on all our products and manufactures which enter her ports or cross her frontiers? Is there one who would not prefer an unrestricted communication with her citizens to the frontier obstructions which must occur if she remains out of the Union? Whatever is good or evil in the local institutions of Texas will remain her own whether annexed to the United States or not. None of the present States will be responsible for them any more than they are for the local institutions of each other. They have confederated together for certain specified objects. Upon the same principle that they would refuse to form a perpetual union with Texas because of her local institutions our forefathers would have been prevented from forming our present Union. Perceiving no valid objection to the measure and many reasons for its adoption vitally affecting the peace, the safety, and the prosperity of both countries, I shall on the broad principle which formed the basis and produced the adoption of our Constitution, and not in any narrow spirit of sectional policy, endeavor by all

constitutional, honorable, and appropriate means to consummate the expressed will of the people and Government of the United States by the reannexation of Texas to our Union at the earliest practicable period.

Nor will it become in a less degree my duty to assert and maintain by all constitutional means the right of the United States to that portion of our territory which lies beyond the Rocky Mountains. Our title to the country of the Oregon is "clear and unquestionable," and already are our people preparing to perfect that title by occupying it with their wives and children. But eighty years ago our population was confined on the west by the ridge of the Alleghanies. Within that period—within the lifetime, I might say, of some of my hearers—our people, increasing to many millions, have filled the eastern valley of the Mississippi, adventurously ascended the Missouri to its headsprings, and are already engaged in establishing the blessings of self-government in valleys of which the rivers flow to the Pacific. The world beholds the peaceful triumphs of the industry of our emigrants. To us belongs the duty of protecting them adequately wherever they may be upon our soil. The jurisdiction of our laws and the benefits of our republican institutions should be extended over them in the distant regions which they have selected for their homes. The increasing facilities of intercourse will easily bring the States, of which the formation in that part of our territory can not be long delayed, within the sphere of our federative Union. In the meantime every obligation imposed by treaty or conventional stipulations should be sacredly respected.

In the management of our foreign relations it will be my aim to observe a careful respect for the rights of other nations, while our own will be the subject of constant watchfulness. Equal and exact justice should characterize all our intercourse with foreign countries. All alliances having a tendency to jeopard the welfare and honor of our country or sacrifice any one of the national interests will be studiously avoided, and yet no opportunity will be lost to culti-

vate a favorable understanding with foreign governments by which our navigation and commerce may be extended and the ample products of our fertile soil, as well as the manufactures of our skillful artisans, find a ready market and remunerating prices in foreign countries.

In taking "care that the laws be faithfully executed," a strict performance of duty will be exacted from all public officers. From those officers, especially, who are charged with the collection and disbursement of the public revenue will prompt and rigid accountability be required. Any culpable failure or delay on their part to account for the moneys intrusted to them at the times and in the manner required by law will in every instance terminate the official connection of such defaulting officer with the Government.

Although in our country the Chief Magistrate must almost of necessity be chosen by a party and stand pledged to its principles and measures, yet in his official action he should not be the President of a part only, but of the whole people of the United States. While he executes the laws with an impartial hand, shrinks from no proper responsibility, and faithfully carries out in the executive department of the Government the principles and policy of those who have chosen him, he should not be unmindful that our fellow-citizens who have differed with him in opinion are entitled to the full and free exercise of their opinions and judgments, and that the rights of all are entitled to respect and regard.

Confidently relying upon the aid and assistance of the coordinate departments of the Government in conducting our public affairs, I enter upon the discharge of the high duties which have been assigned me by the people, again humbly supplicating that Divine Being who has watched over and protected our beloved country from its infancy to the present hour to continue His gracious benedictions upon us, that we may continue to be a prosperous and happy people.

* * *

1848 ZACHARY TAYLOR

HAVING WON WITH A WAR HERO and then lost with a politician, the Whigs nominated another war hero, Gen. Zachary Taylor, the hero of Buena Vista. Like William Henry Harrison, Taylor had no political experience and no record on the issues, but the southern "cotton" Whigs accepted him because he kept slaves at his plantation and they assumed he would go along with the extension of slavery to the territories.

Careful not to antagonize northern "conscience" Whigs whose defection had sunk Henry Clay in 1844, the party declined to write a platform and refrained from discussing national issues during the campaign. The Democrats, similarly divided between moderate Hunkers and abolitionist Barnburners, settled on Sen. Lewis Cass, an expansionist from Michigan, to succeed James K. Polk, the retiring incumbent. However, when the Hunkers passed a platform endorsing the expansion of slavery, the Barnburners bolted, held their own convention, and nominated former president Martin Van Buren, who eventually ran as the Free Soil candidate.

With both major parties avoiding the issue of slavery, the election came down to a beauty contest between the daring Taylor and the colorless Cass. Van Buren knew that he couldn't win, but he also knew he could make a difference. In fact, the Free Soilers won 10.1 percent of the popular vote nationally (a new high for third parties) and 26.4 percent of the vote in New York state, where it swung thirty-six crucial electoral votes from Cass to Taylor. Van Buren's antislavery candidacy thus undermined his former party and ironically elected the only slaveholder in the race.

PARTY	POPULAR VOTES	ELECTORAL VOTES
WHIG Zachary Taylor, La. Millard Fillmore, N.Y.	1,361,393	163
DEMOCRATIC Lewis Cass, Mich. William O. Butler, Ky.	1,223,460	127
FREE SOIL Martin Van Buren, N.Y. Charles F. Adams, Mass.	291,501	

Inaugural Address • Washington, D.C. • Monday, March 5, 1849

Elected by the American people to the highest office known to our laws,

I appear here to take the oath prescribed by the Constitution, and, in compliance with a time-honored custom, to address those who are now assembled.

The confidence and respect shown by my countrymen in calling me to be the Chief Magistrate of a Republic holding a high rank among the nations of the earth have inspired me with feelings of the most profound gratitude; but when I reflect that the acceptance of the office which their partiality has bestowed imposes the discharge of the most arduous duties and involves the weightiest obligations, I am conscious that the position which I have been called to fill, though sufficient to satisfy the loftiest ambition, is surrounded by fearful responsibilities. Happily, however, in the performance of my new duties I shall not be without able cooperation. The legislative and judicial branches of the Government present prominent examples of distinguished civil attainments and matured experience, and it shall be my endeavor to call to my assistance in the Executive Departments individuals whose talents, integrity, and purity of character will furnish ample guaranties for the faithful and honorable performance of the trusts to be committed to their charge. With such aids and an honest purpose to do whatever is right, I hope to execute diligently, impartially, and for the best interests of the country the manifold duties devolved upon me.

In the discharge of these duties my guide will be the Constitution, which I this day swear to "preserve, protect, and defend." For the interpretation of that instrument I shall look to the decisions of the judicial tribunals established by its authority and to the practice of the Government under the earlier Presidents, who had so large a share in its formation. To the example of those illustrious patriots I shall always defer with reverence, and especially to his example who was by so many titles "the Father of his Country."

To command the Army and Navy of the United States; with the advice and consent of the Senate, to make treaties and to appoint ambassadors and other officers; to give to Congress information of the state of the Union and recommend such measures as he shall judge to be necessary; and to take care that the laws shall be faithfully executed—these are the most important functions intrusted to the President by the Constitution, and it may be expected that I shall briefly indicate the principles which will control me in their execution.

Chosen by the body of the people under the assurance that my Administration would be devoted to the welfare of the whole country, and not to the support of any particular section or merely local interest, I this day

> *In the discharge of these duties my guide will be the Constitution....*

renew the declarations I have heretofore made and proclaim my fixed determination to maintain to the extent of my ability the Government in its original purity and to adopt as the basis of my public policy those great republican doctrines which constitute the strength of our national existence.

In reference to the Army and Navy, lately employed with so much distinction on active service, care shall be taken to insure the highest condition of efficiency, and in furtherance of that object the military and naval schools, sustained by the liberality of Congress, shall receive the special attention of the Executive.

As American freemen we can not but sympathize in all efforts to extend the blessings of civil and political liberty, but at the same time we are warned by the admonitions of history and the voice of our own beloved Washington to abstain from entangling alliances with foreign nations. In all disputes between conflicting governments it is our interest not less than our duty to remain strictly neutral, while our geographical position, the genius of our institutions and our people, the advancing spirit of civilization, and, above all, the dictates of religion direct us to the cultivation of peaceful and friendly re-

lations with all other powers. It is to be hoped that no international question can now arise which a government confident in its own strength and resolved to protect its own just rights may not settle by wise negotiation; and it eminently becomes a government like our own, founded on the morality and intelligence of its citizens and upheld by their affections, to exhaust every resort of honorable diplomacy before appealing to arms. In the conduct of our foreign relations I shall conform to these views, as I believe them essential to the best interests and the true honor of the country.

The appointing power vested in the President imposes delicate and onerous duties. So far as it is possible to be informed, I shall make honesty, capacity, and fidelity indispensable prerequisites to the bestowal of office, and the absence of either of these qualities shall be deemed sufficient cause for removal.

It shall be my study to recommend such constitutional measures to Congress as may be necessary and proper to secure encouragement and protection to the great interests of agriculture, commerce, and manufactures, to improve our rivers and harbors, to provide for the speedy extinguishment

of the public debt, to enforce a strict accountability on the part of all officers of the Government and the utmost economy in all public expenditures; but it is for the wisdom of Congress itself, in which all legislative powers are vested by the Constitution, to regulate these and other matters of domestic policy. I shall look with confidence to the enlightened patriotism of that body to adopt such measures of conciliation as may harmonize conflicting interests and tend to perpetuate that Union which should be the paramount object of our hopes and affections. In any action calculated to promote an object so near the heart of everyone who truly loves his country I will zealously unite with the coordinate branches of the Government.

In conclusion I congratulate you, my fellow-citizens, upon the high state of prosperity to which the goodness of Divine Providence has conducted our common country. Let us invoke a continuance of the same protecting care which has led us from small beginnings to the eminence we this day occupy, and let us seek to deserve that continuance by prudence and moderation in our councils, by well-directed attempts to assuage the bitterness which too often marks

unavoidable differences of opinion, by the promulgation and practice of just and liberal principles, and by an enlarged patriotism, which shall acknowledge no limits but those of our own widespread Republic.

* * *

1852 FRANKLIN PIERCE

As in 1844, when James K. Polk was nominated, the Democrats' two-thirds rule produced another dark horse. This time, there were four Democratic front-runners, each of whom failed to overcome a small but determined opposition. On the forty-ninth ballot, the nomination finally went to Franklin Pierce of New Hampshire, who hadn't receive any votes until the thirty-fifth ballot, when Virginia raised his name as a compromise choice. Pierce was noncommittal on most issues but sufficiently open to the extension of slavery to placate southern delegates.

The Whigs nominated another Mexican War hero, Gen. Winfield Scott. However, unlike Zachary Taylor, Scott was tired, politically naive, and out of his depth as a candidate. Repelled by Scott's fervent nationalism, many southern Whigs crossed over to the Democrats and even the New York Barnburners returned to the Democratic fold.

Both party platforms embraced the Compromise of 1850, which was considered (at least publicly) a final settlement of the slavery issue. This suited the Democrats but caused great consternation among the Whigs, whose northern wing liked the candidate but not the compromise. Southern Whigs felt exactly opposite. So when Scott endorsed the platform, southerners were happy, but many northern Whigs bolted the party to nominate their own abolitionist candidate, John P. Hale, on the Free Soil line.

Party	Popular Votes	Electoral Votes
Democratic Franklin Pierce, N.H. William R. King, Ala.	1,607,510	254
Whig Winfield Scott, N.J. William A. Graham, N.C.	1,386,942	42
Free Soil John P. Hale, N.H. George W. Julian, Ind.	155,210	

As part of the now-customary mudslinging, Pierce was called a drunkard and "the hero of many well-fought bottles," while Old Fuss and Feathers was tarred with charges of rampant senility. Scott campaigned and lost votes; Pierce stayed home and won easily.

Inaugural Address • Washington, D.C. • Friday, March 4, 1853

My Countrymen: It is a relief to feel that no heart but my own can know

the personal regret and bitter sorrow over which I have been borne to a position so suitable for others rather than desirable for myself.

The circumstances under which I have been called for a limited period to preside over the destinies of the Republic fill me with a profound sense of responsibility, but with nothing like shrinking apprehension. I repair to the post assigned me not as to one sought, but in obedience to the unsolicited expression of your will, answerable only for a fearless, faithful, and diligent exercise of my best powers. I ought to be, and am, truly grateful for the rare manifestation of the nation's confidence; but this, so far from lightening my obligations, only adds to their weight. You have summoned me in my weakness; you must sustain me by your strength. When looking for the fulfillment of reasonable requirements, you will not be unmindful of the great changes which have occurred, even within the last quarter of a century, and the consequent augmentation and complexity of duties imposed in the administration both of your home and foreign affairs.

Whether the elements of inherent force in the Republic have kept pace with its unparalleled progression in territory, population, and wealth has been the subject of earnest thought and discussion on both sides of the ocean. Less than sixty-four years ago the Father of his Country made "the" then "recent accession of the important State of North Carolina to the Constitution of the United States" one of the subjects of his special congratulation. At that moment, however, when the agitation consequent upon the Revolutionary struggle had hardly subsided, when we were just emerging from the weakness and embarrassments of the Confederation, there was an evident consciousness of vigor equal to the great mission so wisely and bravely fulfilled by our fathers. It was not a presumptuous assurance, but a calm faith, springing from a clear view of the sources of power in a government constituted like ours. It is no paradox to say that although comparatively weak the new-born nation was intrinsically strong. Inconsiderable in population and apparent resources, it was upheld by a broad and intelligent comprehension of rights and an all-pervading purpose to maintain them, stronger than armaments. It came from the furnace of the Revolution, tempered to the necessities of the times. The thoughts of the men of that day were as practical as their sentiments were patriotic. They wasted no portion of their energies upon idle and delusive speculations, but with a firm and fearless step advanced beyond the governmental landmarks which had hitherto circumscribed the limits of human freedom and planted their standard, where it has stood against dangers which have threatened from abroad, and internal agitation, which has at times fearfully menaced at home. They proved themselves equal to the solution of the great problem, to understand which their minds had been illuminated by the dawning lights of the Revolution. The object sought was not a thing dreamed of; it was a thing realized. They had exhibited only the power to achieve, but, what all history affirms to be so much more unusual, the capacity to maintain. The oppressed throughout the world from that day to the present have turned their eyes hitherward, not to find those lights extinguished or to fear lest they should wane, but to be constantly cheered by their steady and increasing radiance.

In this our country has, in my judgment, thus far fulfilled its highest duty to suffering humanity. It has spoken and will continue to speak, not only by its words, but by its acts, the language of sympathy, encouragement, and hope to those who earnestly listen to tones which pronounce for the largest rational liberty. But after all, the most animating encouragement and potent appeal for freedom will be its own history—its trials and its triumphs. Preeminently, the power of our advocacy reposes in our example; but no example, be it remembered, can be powerful for lasting good, whatever apparent advantages may be gained, which is not based upon eternal principles of right and justice. Our fathers decided for themselves, both upon the hour to declare and the hour to strike. They were their own judges of the circumstances under which it became them to pledge to each other "their lives, their fortunes, and their sacred honor" for the acquisition of the priceless inheritance transmitted to us. The energy with which that great conflict was opened and, under the guidance of a manifest and beneficent Providence the uncomplaining endurance with which it was prosecuted to its consummation were only surpassed by the wisdom and patriotic spirit of concession which characterized all the counsels of the early fathers.

One of the most impressive evidences of that wisdom is to be found in the fact that the actual working of our system has dispelled a degree of solicitude which at the outset disturbed bold hearts and far-reaching intellects. The apprehension of dangers from extended territory, multiplied States, accumulated wealth, and augmented population has proved to be unfounded. The stars upon your banner have become nearly threefold their original number; your densely populated possessions skirt the shores of the two great oceans; and yet this vast increase of people and territory has not only shown itself compatible with the harmonious action of the States and Federal Government in their respective constitutional spheres, but has afforded an additional guaranty of the strength and integrity of both.

With an experience thus suggestive and cheering, the policy of my Administration will not be controlled by any timid forebodings of evil from expansion. Indeed, it is not to be disguised that our attitude as a nation and our position on the globe render the acquisition of certain possessions not within our jurisdiction eminently important for our protection, if not in the future essential for the preservation of the rights of commerce and the peace of the world. Should they be obtained, it will be through no grasping spirit, but with a view to obvious national interest and security, and in a manner entirely consistent with the strictest observance of national faith. We have nothing in our history or position to invite aggression; we have everything to beckon us to the cultivation of relations of peace and amity with all nations. Purposes, therefore, at once just and pacific will be significantly marked in the conduct of our foreign affairs. I intend that my Administration shall leave no blot upon our fair record, and trust I may safely give the assurance that no act within the legitimate scope of my constitutional control will be tolerated on the part of any portion of our citizens which can not challenge a ready justification before the tribunal of the civilized world. An Administration would be unworthy of confidence at home and respect abroad should it cease to be influenced by the conviction that no apparent advantage can be purchased at a price so dear as that of national wrong or dishonor. It is not your privilege as a nation to speak of a distant past. The striking incidents of your history, replete with instruction and furnishing abundant grounds for hopeful confidence, are comprised in a period comparatively brief. But if your past is limited, your future is boundless. Its obligations throng the unexplored pathway of advancement, and will be limitless as duration. Hence a sound and comprehensive policy should embrace not less the distant future than the urgent present.

The great objects of our pursuit as a people are best to

I believe that involuntary servitude, as it exists in different States of this Confederacy, is recognized by the Constitution.

---

be attained by peace, and are entirely consistent with the tranquillity and interests of the rest of mankind. With the neighboring nations upon our continent we should cultivate kindly and fraternal relations. We can desire nothing in regard to them so much as to see them consolidate their strength and pursue the paths of prosperity and happiness. If in the course of their growth we should open new channels of trade and create additional facilities for friendly intercourse, the benefits realized will be equal and mutual. Of the complicated European systems of national polity we have heretofore been independent. From their wars, their tumults, and anxieties we have been, happily, almost entirely exempt. Whilst these are confined to the nations which gave them existence, and within their legitimate jurisdiction, they can not affect us except as they appeal to our sympathies in the cause of human freedom and universal advancement. But the vast interests of commerce are common to all mankind, and the advantages of trade and international intercourse must always present a noble field for the moral influence of a great people.

With these views firmly and honestly carried out, we have a right to expect, and shall under all circumstances require, prompt reciprocity. The rights which belong to us as a nation are not alone to be regarded, but those which pertain to every citizen in his individual capacity, at home and abroad, must be sacredly maintained. So long as he can discern every star in its place upon that ensign, with-

out wealth to purchase for him preferment or title to secure for him place, it will be his privilege, and must be his acknowledged right, to stand unabashed even in the presence of princes, with a proud consciousness that he is himself one of a nation of sovereigns and that he can not in legitimate pursuit wander so far from home that the agent whom he shall leave behind in the place which I now occupy will not see that no rude hand of power or tyrannical passion is laid upon him with impunity. He must realize that upon every sea and on every soil where our enterprise may rightfully seek the protection of our flag American citizenship is an inviolable panoply for the security of American rights. And in this connection it can hardly be necessary to reaffirm a principle which should now be regarded as fundamental. The rights, security, and repose of this Confederacy reject the idea of interference or colonization on this side of the ocean by any foreign power beyond present jurisdiction as utterly inadmissible.

The opportunities of observation furnished by my brief experience as a soldier confirmed in my own mind the opinion, entertained and acted upon by others from the formation of the Government, that the maintenance of large standing armies in our country would be not only dangerous, but unnecessary. They also illustrated

the importance—I might well say the absolute necessity—of the military science and practical skill furnished in such an eminent degree by the institution which has made your Army what it is, under the discipline and instruction of officers not more distinguished for their

solid attainments, gallantry, and devotion to the public service than for unobtrusive bearing and high moral tone. The Army as organized must be the nucleus around which in every time of need the strength of your military power, the sure bulwark of your defense—a national militia—may be readily formed into a well-disciplined and efficient organization. And the skill and self-devotion of the Navy assure you that you may take the performance of the past as a pledge for the future, and may confidently expect that the flag which has waved its untarnished folds over every sea will still float in undiminished honor. But these, like many other subjects, will be appropriately brought at a future time to the attention of the coordinate branches of the Government, to which I shall always look with profound respect and with trustful confidence that they will accord to me the aid and support which I shall so much need and which their experience and wisdom will readily suggest.

In the administration of domestic affairs you expect a devoted integrity in the public service and an observance of rigid economy in all departments, so marked as never justly to be questioned. If this reasonable expectation be not realized, I frankly confess that one of your leading hopes is

> *Let it be impressed upon all hearts that, beautiful as our fabric is, no earthly power or wisdom could ever reunite its broken fragments.*

doomed to disappointment, and that my efforts in a very important particular must result in a humiliating failure. Offices can be properly regarded only in the light of aids for the accomplishment of these objects, and as occupancy can confer no prerogative nor importunate desire for preferment any claim, the public interest imperatively demands that they be considered with sole reference to the duties to be performed. Good citizens may well claim the protection of good laws and the benign influence of good government, but a claim for office is what the people of a republic should never recognize. No reasonable man of any party will expect the Administration to be so regardless of its responsibility and of the obvious elements of success as to retain persons known to be under the influence of political hostility and partisan prejudice in positions which will require not only severe labor, but cordial cooperation. Having no implied engagements to ratify, no rewards to bestow, no resentments to remember, and no personal wishes to consult in selections for official station, I shall fulfill this difficult and

delicate trust, admitting no motive as worthy either of my character or position which does not contemplate an efficient discharge of duty and the best interests of my country. I acknowledge my obligations to the masses of my countrymen, and to them alone. Higher objects than personal aggrandizement gave direction and energy to their exertions in the late canvass, and they shall not be disappointed. They require at my hands diligence, integrity, and capacity wherever there are duties to be performed. Without these qualities in their public servants, more stringent laws for the prevention or punishment of fraud, negligence, and peculation will be vain. With them they will be unnecessary.

But these are not the only points to which you look for vigilant watchfulness. The dangers of a concentration of all power in the general government of a confederacy so vast as ours are too obvious to be disregarded. You have a right, therefore, to expect your agents in every department to regard strictly the limits imposed upon them by the Constitution of the United States. The great scheme of our constitutional liberty rests upon a proper distribution of power between the State and Federal authorities, and experience has shown that the harmony and happiness of our people must depend upon a just discrimination between the separate rights and responsibilities of the States and your common rights and obligations under the General Government; and here, in my opinion, are the considerations which should form the true basis of future concord in regard to the questions which have most seriously disturbed public tranquillity. If the Federal Government will confine itself to the exercise of powers clearly granted by the Constitution, it can hardly happen that its action upon any question should endanger the institutions of the States or interfere with their right to manage matters strictly domestic according to the will of their own people.

In expressing briefly my views upon an important subject rich has recently agitated the nation to almost a fearful degree, I am moved by no other impulse than a most earnest desire for the perpetuation of that Union which has made us what we are, showering upon us blessings and conferring a power and influence which our fathers could hardly have anticipated, even with their most sanguine hopes directed to a far-off future. The sentiments I now announce were not unknown before the expression of the voice which called me here. My own position upon this subject was clear and unequivocal, upon the record of my words and my acts, and it is only recurred to at this time because silence might perhaps be misconstrued. With the Union my best and dearest earthly hopes are entwined. Without it what are we individually or collectively? What becomes of the noblest field ever opened for the advancement of our race in religion, in government, in the arts, and in all that dignifies and adorns mankind? From that radiant constellation which both illumines our own way and points out to struggling nations their course, let but a single star be lost, and, if these be not utter darkness, the luster of the whole is dimmed. Do my countrymen need any assurance that such a catastrophe is not to overtake them while I possess the power to stay it? It is with me an earnest and vital belief that as the Union has been the source, under Providence, of our prosperity to this time, so it is the surest pledge of a continuance of the blessings we have enjoyed, and which we are sacredly bound to transmit undiminished to our children. The field of calm and free discussion in our country is open, and will always be so, but never has been and never can be traversed for good in a spirit of sectionalism and uncharitableness. The founders of the Republic dealt with things as they were presented to them, in a spirit of self-sacrificing patriotism, and, as time has proved, with a comprehensive wisdom which it will always be safe for us to consult. Every measure tending to strengthen the fraternal feelings of all the members of our Union has had my heartfelt approbation. To every theory of society or government, whether the offspring of feverish ambition or of morbid enthusiasm, calculated to dissolve the bonds of law and affection which unite us, I shall interpose a ready and stern resistance. I believe that involuntary servitude, as it exists in different States of this Confederacy, is recognized by the Constitution. I believe that it stands like any other admitted right, and that the States where it exists are entitled to efficient remedies to enforce the constitutional provisions. I hold that the laws of 1850, commonly called the "compromise measures," are strictly constitutional and to be unhesitatingly carried into effect. I believe that the constituted authorities of this Republic are bound to regard the rights of the South in this respect as they would view any other legal and constitutional right, and that the laws to enforce them should be respected and obeyed, not with a reluctance encouraged by abstract opinions as to their propriety in a different state of society, but cheerfully and according to the decisions of the tribunal to which their exposition belongs. Such have been, and are, my convictions, and upon them I shall act. I fervently hope that the question is at rest, and that no sectional or ambitious or fanatical excitement may again threaten the durability of our institutions or obscure the light of our prosperity.

But let not the foundation of our hope rest upon man's wisdom. It will not be sufficient that sectional prejudices find no place in the public deliberations. It will not be sufficient that the rash counsels of human passion are rejected. It must be felt that there is no national security but in the nation's humble, acknowledged dependence upon God and His overruling providence.

We have been carried in safety through a perilous crisis. Wise counsels, like those which gave us the Constitution, prevailed to uphold it. Let the period be remembered as an admonition, and not as an encouragement, in any section of the Union, to make experiments where experiments are fraught with such fearful hazard. Let it be impressed upon all hearts that, beautiful as our fabric is, no earthly power or wisdom could ever reunite its broken fragments. Standing, as I do, almost within view of the green

We honor the Citizen and Soldier.

GENERAL FRANKLIN PIERCE.

slopes of Monticello, and, as it were, within reach of the tomb of Washington, with all the cherished memories of the past gathering around me like so many eloquent voices of exhortation from heaven, I can express no better hope for my country than that the kind Providence which smiled upon our fathers may enable their children to preserve the blessings they have inherited.

* * *

1856 JAMES BUCHANAN

NEITHER THE COMPROMISE OF 1850 nor the Kansas-Nebraska Act of 1854 could relax the tensions over slavery that finally split the Whig party along sectional lines. By 1856, the Whigs were scattered, replaced by a new party, the Republicans, formed of northern Whigs, Free Soilers, and antislavery Democrats. The party's first nominating convention, a mass meeting held in Philadelphia, chose Gen. John C. Frémont as its presidential candidate. Frémont was known as the Pathfinder because of his success exploring and surveying transportation routes in the trans–Mississippi west.

The Democrat party, hoping to strengthen the increasingly uneasy relationship between its northern and southern wings, nominated another doughface, James Buchanan of Pennsylvania, to replace the unsuccessful Franklin Pierce. Meanwhile, members of the secretive American party, called the Know-Nothings because they claimed to "know nothing" of their party's motives or platform, nominated former president Millard Fillmore, who also received support from the few state parties that still called themselves Whig.

Slavery was the only campaign issue. The Republicans chanted "Free Soil, Free Speech, Frémont," to which the Democrats added "Free Love," a reminder of Frémont's illegitimate birth. Also, foreshadowing the election of 1860, some southerners threatened to secede should Frémont win. (In the South, Frémont's name didn't even appear on the ballot.)

Like Pierce, Buchanan kept quiet, carried nearly every slave state, and won enough electoral votes in the West to beat Frémont convincingly. The election showed that, with nearly all its support concentrated in the North and Midwest, the new Republican party was still just a regional force.

PARTY	POPULAR VOTES	ELECTORAL VOTES
DEMOCRATIC James Buchanan, Pa. John C. Breckinridge, Ky.	1,836,072	174
REPUBLICAN John C. Frémont, Calif. William L. Dayton, N.J.	1,342,345	114
AMERICAN Millard Fillmore, N.Y. Andrew J. Donelson, Tenn.	873,053	8

Inaugural Address • Washington, D.C. • Wednesday, March 4, 1857

Fellow-Citizens: I appear before you this day to take the solemn oath

"that I will faithfully execute the office of President of the United States and will to the best of my ability preserve, protect, and defend the Constitution of the United States."

In entering upon this great office I must humbly invoke the God of our fathers for wisdom and firmness to execute its high and responsible duties in such a manner as to restore harmony and ancient friendship among the people of the several States and to preserve our free institutions throughout many generations. Convinced that I owe my election to the inherent love for the Constitution and the Union which still animates the hearts of the American people, let me earnestly ask their powerful support in sustaining all just measures calculated to perpetuate these, the richest political blessings which Heaven has ever bestowed upon any nation. Having determined not to become a candidate for reelection, I shall have no motive to influence my conduct in administering the Government except the desire ably

and faithfully to serve my country and to live in grateful memory of my countrymen.

We have recently passed through a Presidential contest in which the passions of our fellow-citizens were excited to the highest degree by questions of deep and vital importance; but when the people proclaimed their will the tempest at once subsided and all was calm.

The voice of the majority, speaking in the manner prescribed by the Constitution, was heard, and instant submission followed. Our own country could alone have exhibited so grand and striking a spectacle of the capacity of man for self-government.

What a happy conception, then, was it for Congress to apply this simple rule, that the will of the majority shall govern, to the settlement of the question of domestic slavery in the Territories. Congress is neither "to legislate slavery into any Territory or State nor to exclude it therefrom, but to leave the people thereof perfectly free to form and regulate their domestic institutions in their own

way, subject only to the Constitution of the United States."

As a natural consequence, Congress has also prescribed that when the Territory of Kansas shall be admitted as a State it "shall be received into the Union with or without slavery, as their constitution may prescribe at the time of their admission."

A difference of opinion has arisen in regard to the point of time when the people of a Territory shall decide this question for themselves.

This is, happily, a matter of but little practical importance. Besides, it is a judicial question, which legitimately belongs to the Supreme Court of the United States, before whom it is now pending, and will, it is understood, be speedily and finally settled. To their decision, in common with all good citizens, I shall cheerfully submit, whatever this may be, though it has ever been my individual opinion that under the Nebraska-Kansas act the appropriate period will be when the number of actual residents in the Territory shall justify the formation of a constitution with a view to its admission as a State into the Union. But be this as it may, it is the imperative and indispensable duty of the Government of the United States to secure to every resident inhabitant the free and independent expression of his opinion by his vote. This sacred right of each individual must be preserved. That being accomplished, nothing can be fairer than to leave the people of a Territory free from all foreign interference to decide their own destiny for themselves, subject only to the Constitution of the United States.

The whole Territorial question being thus settled upon the principle of popular sovereignty—a principle as ancient as free government itself—everything of a practical nature has been decided. No other question remains for adjustment, because all agree that under the Constitution slavery in the States is beyond the reach of any human power except that of the respective States themselves wherein it exists. May we not, then, hope that the long agitation on this subject is approaching its end, and that the geographical parties to which it has given birth, so much dreaded by the Father of his Country, will speedily become extinct? Most happy will it be for the country when the public mind shall be diverted from this question to others of more pressing and practical importance. Throughout the whole progress of this agitation, which has scarcely known any intermission for more than twenty years, whilst it has been productive of no positive good to any human being it has been the prolific source of great evils to the master, to the slave, and to the whole country. It has alienated and estranged the people of the sister States from each other, and has even seriously endangered the very existence of the Union. Nor has the danger yet entirely ceased. Under our system there is a remedy for all mere political evils in the sound sense and sober judgment of the people. Time is a great corrective. Political subjects which but a few years ago excited and exasperated the public mind have passed away and are now nearly

forgotten. But this question of domestic slavery is of far graver importance than any mere political question, because should the agitation continue it may eventually endanger the personal safety of a large portion of our countrymen where the institution exists. In that event no form of government, however admirable in itself and however productive of material benefits, can compensate for the loss of peace and domestic security around the family altar. Let every Union-loving man, therefore, exert his best influence to suppress this agitation, which since the recent legislation of Congress is without any legitimate object.

It is an evil omen of the times that men have undertaken to calculate the mere material value of the Union. Reasoned estimates have been presented of the pecuniary profits and local advantages which would result to different States and sections from its dissolution and of the comparative injuries which such an event would inflict on other States and sections. Even descending to this low and narrow view of the mighty question, all such calculations are at fault. The bare reference to a single con-

> *Let every Union-loving man, therefore, exert his best influence to suppress this agitation....*

sideration will be conclusive on this point. We at present enjoy a free trade throughout our extensive and expanding country such as the world has never witnessed. This trade is conducted on railroads and canals, on noble rivers and arms of the sea, which bind together the North and the South, the East and the West, of our Confederacy. Annihilate this trade, arrest its free progress by the geographical lines of jealous and hostile States, and you destroy

4TH MARCH, 1857.

Grand Inauguration Ball,
In honor of the Inauguration of
JAMES BUCHANAN,
AND
JOHN C. BRECKINRIDGE,
As President and Vice President of the United States,
AT LANCASTER HALL.

the prosperity and onward march of the whole and every part and involve all in one common ruin. But such considerations, important as they are in themselves, sink into insignificance when we reflect on the terrific evils which would result from disunion to every portion of the Confederacy—to the North, not more than to the South, to the East not more than to the West. These I shall not attempt to portray, because I feel an humble confidence that the kind Providence which inspired our fathers with wisdom to frame the most perfect form of government and union ever devised by man will not suffer it to perish until it shall have been peacefully instrumental by its example in the extension of civil and religious liberty throughout the world.

Next in importance to the maintenance of the Constitution and the Union is the duty of preserving the Government free from the taint or even the suspicion of corruption. Public virtue is the vital spirit of republics, and history proves that when this has decayed and the love of money has usurped its place, although the forms of free government may remain for a season, the substance has departed forever.

Our present financial condition is without a parallel in history. No nation has ever before been embarrassed from too large a surplus in its treasury. This almost necessarily gives birth to extravagant legislation. It produces wild schemes of expenditure and begets a race of speculators and jobbers, whose ingenuity is exerted in contriving and promoting expedients to obtain public money. The purity of official agents, whether rightfully or wrongfully, is suspected, and the character of the government suffers in the estimation of the people. This is in itself a very great evil.

The natural mode of relief from this embarrassment is to appropriate the surplus in the Treasury to great national objects for which a clear warrant can be found in the Constitution. Among these I might mention the extinguishment of the public debt, a reasonable increase of the Navy, which is at present inadequate to the protection of our vast tonnage afloat, now greater than that of any other nation, as well as to the defense of our extended seacoast.

It is beyond all question the true principle that no more revenue ought to be collected from the people than the amount necessary to defray the expenses of a wise, economical, and efficient administration of the Government. To reach this point it was necessary to resort to a modification of the tariff, and this has, I trust, been accomplished in such a manner as to do as little injury as may have been practicable to our domestic manufactures, especially those necessary for the defense of the country. Any discrimination against a particular branch for the purpose of benefiting favored corporations, individuals, or interests would have been unjust to the rest of the community and inconsistent with that spirit of fairness and equality which ought to govern in the adjustment of a revenue tariff.

But the squandering of the public money sinks into comparative insignificance as a

temptation to corruption when compared with the squandering of the public lands.

No nation in the tide of time has ever been blessed with so rich and noble an inheritance as we enjoy in the public lands. In administering this important trust, whilst it may be wise to grant portions of them for the improvement of the remainder, yet we should never forget that it is our cardinal policy to reserve these lands, as much as may be, for actual settlers, and this at moderate prices. We shall thus not only best promote the prosperity of the new States and Territories, by furnishing them a hardy and independent race of honest and industrious citizens, but shall secure homes for our children and our children's children, as well as for those exiles from foreign shores who may seek in this country to improve their condition and to enjoy the blessings of civil and religious liberty. Such emigrants have done much to promote the

growth and prosperity of the country. They have proved faithful both in peace and in war. After becoming citizens they are entitled, under the Constitution and laws, to be placed on a perfect equality with native-born citizens, and in this character they should ever be kindly recognized.

The Federal Constitution is a grant from the States to Congress of certain specific powers, and the question whether this grant should be liberally or strictly construed has more or less divided political parties from the beginning. Without entering into the argument, I desire to state at the commencement of my Administration that long experience and observation have convinced me that a strict construction of the powers of the Government is the only true, as well as the only safe, theory of the Constitution. Whenever in our past history doubtful powers have been exercised by Congress, these have never failed to produce injurious and unhappy consequences. Many such instances might be adduced if this were the proper occasion. Neither is it necessary for the public service to strain the language of the Constitution, because all the great and useful powers required for a successful administration of the Government, both in peace and in war, have been granted, either in express terms or by the plainest implication.

Whilst deeply convinced of these truths, I consider it clear that under the war-making power Congress may appropriate money toward the construction of a military road when this is absolutely necessary for the defense of any State or Territory of the Union against foreign invasion. Under the Constitution Congress has power "to declare war," "to raise and support armies," "to provide and maintain a navy," and to call forth the militia to "repel invasions." Thus endowed, in an ample manner, with the war-making power, the corresponding duty is required that "the United States shall protect each of

them [the States] against invasion." Now, how is it possible to afford this protection to California and our Pacific possessions except by means of a military road through the Territories of the United States, over which men and munitions of war may be speedily transported from the Atlantic States to meet and to repel the invader? In the event of a war with a naval power much stronger than our own we should then have no other available access to the Pacific Coast, because such a power would instantly close the route across the isthmus of Central America. It is impossible to conceive that whilst the Constitution has expressly required Congress to defend all the States it should yet deny to them, by any fair construction, the only possible means by which one of these States can be defended. Besides, the Government, ever since its origin, has been in the constant practice of constructing military roads. It might also be wise to consider whether the love for the Union which now animates our fellow-citizens on the Pacific Coast may not be impaired by our neglect or refusal to provide for them, in their remote and isolated condition, the only means by which the power of the States on this side of the Rocky Mountains can reach them in sufficient time to "protect" them "against invasion." I forbear for the present from expressing an opinion as to the wisest and most economical mode in which the Government can lend its aid in accomplishing this great and necessary work. I believe that many of the difficulties in the way, which now appear formidable, will in a great degree vanish as soon as the nearest and best route shall have been satisfactorily ascertained.

It may be proper that on this occasion I should make some brief remarks in regard to our rights and duties as a member of the great family of nations. In our intercourse with them there are some plain principles, approved by our own experience, from which we should never depart. We ought to cultivate peace, commerce, and friendship with all nations, and this not merely as the best means of promoting

our own material interests, but in a spirit of Christian benevolence toward our fellow-men, wherever their lot may be cast. Our diplomacy should be direct and frank, neither seeking to obtain more nor accepting less than is our due. We ought to cherish a sacred regard for the independence of all nations, and never attempt to interfere in the domestic concerns of any unless this shall be imperatively required by the great law of self-preservation. To avoid entangling alliances has been a maxim of our policy ever since the days of Washington, and its wisdom's no one will attempt to dispute. In short, we ought to do justice in a kindly spirit to all nations and require justice from them in return.

It is our glory that whilst other nations have extended their dominions by the sword we have never acquired any territory except by fair purchase or, as in the case of Texas, by the voluntary determination of a brave, kindred, and independent people to blend their destinies with our own. Even our acquisitions from Mexico form no exception. Unwilling to take advantage of the fortune of war against a sister republic, we purchased these possessions under the treaty of peace for a sum which was considered at the time a fair equivalent. Our past history forbids that we shall in the future acquire territory unless this be sanctioned by the laws of justice and honor. Acting on this principle, no nation will have a right to interfere or to complain if in the progress of events we shall still further extend our possessions. Hitherto in all our acquisitions the people, under the protection of the American flag, have enjoyed civil and religious liberty, as well as equal and just laws, and have been contented, prosperous, and happy. Their trade with the rest of the world has rapidly increased, and thus every commercial nation has shared largely in their successful progress.

I shall now proceed to take the oath prescribed by the Constitution, whilst humbly invoking the blessing of Divine Providence on this great people.

* * *

1860 ABRAHAM LINCOLN

HAVING WON CONTROL OF THE HOUSE and made gains in the Senate during the 1858 midterm elections, the Republicans entered the 1860 presidential race as a unified northern party. Their platform advocated internal improvements, a high tariff, and an end to the further expansion of slavery, though it contained nothing about abolishing slavery where it already existed. The party convention in Chicago nominated "Honest Abe" Lincoln of Illinois on the third ballot after his managers shrewdly exchanged seats in a future Lincoln cabinet for immediate delegate support. "I authorize no bargains and will be bound by none," Lincoln declared (but he honored the deals anyway).

At the Democratic convention in Charleston, southern delegates walked out after northerners refused to endorse a proslavery platform. Adjourning to Baltimore, the rest of the party nominated Sen. Stephen A. Douglas, also of Illinois, on a platform that called for letting the residents of the territories decide the matter for themselves, a doctrine known as popular sovereignty. Meanwhile, the southern Democrats nominated Vice President John C. Breckinridge of Kentucky, believing that no candidate would receive an electoral majority and that the final decision would be left to the House—in which case the House would likely deadlock while the Senate chose a prosouthern vice president, who would serve as acting president for the next four years.

Taking advantage of the Democratic disarray, Lincoln and the Republicans ran a campaign based on the Whig model of 1840 featuring nighttime marches (lit by "Wide Awake" torches) and rail iconography that honored Lincoln "the rail-splitter." Lincoln himself remained in Springfield and kept quiet, while Douglas broke with the tradition that candidates ought not to campaign for themselves and barnstormed the nation, warning of secession should Lincoln win.

PARTY	POPULAR VOTES	ELECTORAL VOTES
REPUBLICAN Abraham Lincoln, Ill. Hannibal Hamlin, Me.	1,865,908	180
SOUTHERN DEMOCRATIC John C. Breckinridge, Ky. Joseph Lane, Ore.	848,019	72
CONSTITUTIONAL UNION John Bell, Tenn. Edward Everett, Mass.	590,901	39
DEMOCRATIC Stephen A. Douglas, Ill. Herschel V. Johnson, Ga.	1,380,202	12

A fourth candidate, John Bell of the Constitutional Union party (pledged to little more than maintaining the Union), carried Virginia, Kentucky, and his home state of Tennessee. Douglas, though finishing second in the popular vote, won only Missouri. Breckinridge took every other slave state, but the support of the populous North was itself enough to give Lincoln an electoral majority, even though he won less than 40 percent of the popular vote. The results persuaded southerners that they had become a powerless minority with no choice but to secede.

First Inaugural Address • Washington, D.C. • Monday, March 4, 1861

Fellow-Citizens of the United States: In compliance with a custom

as old as the Government itself, I appear before you to address you briefly and to take in your presence the oath prescribed by the Constitution of the United States to be taken by the President "before he enters on the execution of this office."

I do not consider it necessary at present for me to discuss those matters of administration about which there is no special anxiety or excitement.

Apprehension seems to exist among the people of the Southern States that by the accession of a Republican Administration their property and their peace and personal security are to be endangered. There has never been any reasonable cause for such apprehension. Indeed, the most ample evidence to the contrary has all the while existed and been open to their inspection. It is found in nearly all the published speeches of him who now addresses you. I do but quote from one of those speeches when I declare that— I have no purpose, directly or indirectly, to interfere with the institution of slavery in the States where it exists. I believe I have no lawful right to do so, and I have no inclination to do so.

Those who nominated and elected me did so with full knowledge that I had made this and many similar declarations and had never recanted them; and more than this, they placed in the platform for my acceptance, and as a law to themselves and to me, the clear and emphatic resolution which I now read: Resolved, That the maintenance inviolate of the rights of the States, and especially the right of each State to order and control its own domestic institutions according to its own judgment exclusively, is essential to that balance of power on which the perfection and endurance of our political fabric depend; and we denounce the lawless invasion by armed force of the soil of any State or Territory, no matter what pretext, as among the gravest of crimes.

I now reiterate these sentiments, and in doing so I only press upon the public attention the most conclusive evidence of which the case is susceptible that the property, peace, and security of no section are to be in any wise endangered by the now incoming Administration. I add, too, that all the protection which, consistently with the Constitution and the laws, can be given will be cheerfully given to all the States when lawfully demanded, for whatever cause—as cheerfully to one section as to another.

There is much controversy about the delivering up of fugitives from service or labor. The clause I now read is as plainly written in the Constitution as any other of its provisions: No person held to service or labor in one State, under the laws thereof, escaping into another, shall in consequence of any law or regulation therein be discharged from such service or labor, but shall be delivered up on claim of the party to whom such service or labor may be due.

It is scarcely questioned that this provision was intended by those who made it for the reclaiming of what we call fugitive slaves; and the intention of the lawgiver is the law. All members of Congress swear their support to the whole Constitution—to this provision as much as to any other. To the proposition, then, that slaves whose cases come within the terms of this clause "shall be delivered up" their oaths are unanimous. Now, if they would make the effort in good temper, could they not with nearly equal unanimity frame and pass a law by means of which to keep good that unanimous oath?

There is some difference of opinion whether this clause should be enforced by national or by State authority, but surely that difference is not a very material one. If the slave is to be surrendered, it can be of but little consequence to him or to others by which authority it is done. And should anyone in any case be content that his oath shall go unkept on a merely unsubstantial controversy as to how it shall be kept?

Again: In any law upon this subject ought not all the safeguards of liberty known in civilized and humane jurisprudence to be introduced, so that a free man be not in any case surrendered as a slave? And might it not be well at the same time to provide by law for the enforcement of that clause in the Constitution which guarantees that "the citizens of each State shall be entitled to all privileges and immunities of citizens in the several States"?

I take the official oath to-day with no mental reservations and with no purpose to construe the Constitution or laws by any hypercritical rules; and while I do not choose now to specify particular acts of Congress as proper to be enforced, I do suggest that it will be much safer for all, both in official and private stations, to conform to and abide by all those acts which stand unrepealed than to violate any of them trusting to find impunity in having them held to be unconstitutional.

It is seventy-two years since the first inauguration of a President under our National Constitution. During that period fifteen different and greatly distinguished citizens have in succession administered the executive branch of the Government. They have conducted it through many perils, and generally with great success. Yet, with all this scope of precedent, I now enter upon the same task for the brief constitutional term of four years under great and peculiar difficulty. A disruption of the Federal Union, heretofore only menaced, is now formidably attempted.

I hold that in contemplation of universal law and of the Constitution the Union of these States is perpetual. Perpetuity is implied, if not expressed, in the fundamental law of all national governments. It is safe to assert that no government proper ever had a provision in its organic law for its own termination. Continue to execute all the express provisions of our National Constitution, and the Union will endure forever, it being impossible to destroy it except by some action not provided for in the instrument itself.

Again: If the United States be not a government proper, but an association of States in the nature of contract merely, can it, as a contract, be peaceably unmade by less than all the parties who made it? One party to a contract may violate it—break it, so to speak—but does it not require all to lawfully rescind it?

Descending from these general principles, we find the proposition that in legal contemplation the Union is perpetual confirmed by the history of the Union itself. The Union is much older than the Constitution. It was formed, in fact, by the Articles of Association in 1774. It was matured and continued by the Declaration of Independence in 1776. It was further matured, and the faith of all the then thirteen States expressly plighted and engaged that it should be perpetual, by the Articles of Confederation in 1778. And finally, in 1787, one of the declared objects for ordaining and establishing the Constitution was "to form a more perfect Union."

But if destruction of the Union by one or by a part only of the States be lawfully possible, the Union is less perfect than before the Constitution, having lost the vital element of perpetuity.

It follows from these views that no State upon its own mere motion can lawfully get out of the Union; that resolves and ordinances to that effect are legally void, and that acts of violence within any State or States against the authority of the United States are insurrectionary or revolutionary, according to circumstances.

I therefore consider that in view of the Constitution and the laws the Union is unbroken, and to the extent of my ability, I shall take care, as the Constitution itself expressly enjoins upon me, that the laws of the Union be faithfully executed in all the States. Doing this I deem to be only a simple duty on my part, and I shall perform it so far as practicable unless my rightful masters, the American people, shall withhold the requisite means or in some authoritative manner direct the contrary. I trust this will not be regarded as a menace, but only as the declared purpose of the Union that it will constitutionally defend and maintain itself.

In doing this there needs to be no bloodshed or violence, and there shall be none unless it be forced upon the national authority. The power confided to me will be used to hold, occupy, and possess the property and places belonging to the Government and to collect the duties and imposts; but beyond what may be necessary for these objects, there will be no invasion, no using of force against or among the people anywhere. Where hostility to the United States in any interior locality shall be so great and universal as to prevent competent resident citizens from holding the Federal offices, there will be no attempt to force obnoxious strangers among the people for that object. While the strict legal right may exist in the Government to enforce the exercise of these offices, the attempt to do so would be so irritating and so nearly impracticable withal that I deem it better to forego for the time the uses of such offices.

The mails, unless repelled, will continue to be furnished in all parts of the Union. So far as possible the people everywhere shall have that sense of perfect security which is most favorable to calm thought and reflection. The course here indicated will be followed unless current events and experience shall show a modification or change to be proper, and in every case and exigency my best discretion will be exercised, according to circumstances actually existing and with a view and a hope of a peaceful solution of the national troubles and the restoration of fraternal sympathies and affections.

That there are persons in one section or another who seek to destroy the Union at all events and are glad of any pretext to do it I will neither affirm nor deny; but if there be such, I need address no word to them. To those, however, who really love the Union may I not speak?

Before entering upon so grave a matter as the destruction of our national fabric, with all its benefits, its memories, and its hopes, would it not be wise to ascertain precisely why we do it? Will you hazard so desperate a step while there is any possibility that any portion of the ills you fly from have no real existence? Will you, while the certain ills you fly to are greater than all the real ones you fly from, will you risk the commission of so fearful a mistake?

All profess to be content in the Union if all constitutional rights can be maintained. Is it true, then, that any right plainly written in the Constitution has been denied? I think not. Happily, the human mind is so constituted that no party can reach to the audacity of doing this. Think, if you can, of a single instance in which a plainly written provision of the Constitution has ever been denied. If by the mere force of numbers a majority should deprive a minority of any clearly written constitutional right, it might in a moral point of view justify revolution; certainly would if such right were a vital one. But such is not our case. All the vital rights of minorities and of individuals are so plainly assured to them by affirmations and negations, guaranties and prohibitions, in the Constitution that controversies never arise concerning them. But no organic law can ever be framed with a

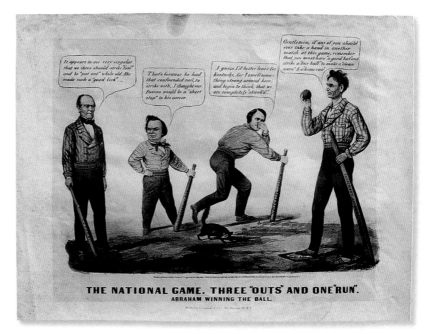

THE NATIONAL GAME. THREE "OUTS" AND ONE "RUN".
ABRAHAM WINNING THE BALL.

provision specifically applicable to every question which may occur in practical administration. No foresight can anticipate nor any document of reasonable length contain express provisions for all possible

In your hands, my dissatisfied fellow-countrymen, and not in mine, is the momentous issue of civil war.

questions. Shall fugitives from labor be surrendered by national or by State authority? The Constitution does not expressly say. May Congress prohibit slavery in the Territories? The Constitution does not expressly say. Must Congress protect slavery in the Territories? The Constitution does not expressly say. From questions of this class spring all our constitutional controversies, and we di-

vide upon them into majorities and minorities. If the minority will not acquiesce, the majority must, or the Government must cease. There is no other alternative, for continuing the Government is acquiescence on one side or the other. If a minority in such case will secede rather than acquiesce, they make a precedent which in turn will divide and ruin them, for a minority of their own will secede from them whenever a majority refuses to be controlled by such minority. For instance, why may not any portion of a new confederacy a year or two hence arbitrarily secede again, precisely as portions of the present Union now claim to secede from it? All who cherish disunion sentiments are now being educated to the exact temper of doing this.

Is there such perfect identity of interests among the States to compose a new union as to produce harmony only and prevent renewed secession?

Plainly the central idea of secession is the essence of anarchy. A majority held in restraint by constitutional checks and limitations, and always changing easily with deliberate changes of popular opinions and sentiments, is the only true sovereign of a free people. Whoever rejects it does of ne-

cessity fly to anarchy or to despotism. Unanimity is impossible. The rule of a minority, as a permanent arrangement, is wholly inadmissible; so that, rejecting the majority principle, anarchy or despotism in some form is all that is left.

I do not forget the position assumed by some that constitutional questions are to be decided by the Supreme Court, nor do I deny that such decisions must be binding in any case upon the parties to a suit as to the object of that suit, while they are also entitled to very high respect and consideration in all parallel cases by all other departments of the Government. And while it is obviously possible that such decision may be erroneous in any given case, still the evil effect following it, being limited to that particular case, with the chance that it may be overruled and never become a precedent for other cases, can better be borne than could the evils of a different practice. At the same time, the candid citizen must confess that if the policy of the Government upon vital questions affecting the whole people is to be irrevocably fixed by decisions of the Supreme Court, the instant they are made in ordinary litigation between parties in personal actions the people will have ceased to be their own rulers, having to that extent practically resigned their Government into the hands of that eminent tribunal. Nor is there in this view any assault upon the court or the judges. It is a duty from which they may not shrink to decide cases properly brought before them, and it is no fault of theirs if others seek to turn their decisions to political purposes.

One section of our country believes slavery is right and ought to be extended, while the other believes it is wrong and ought not to be extended. This is the only substantial dispute. The fugitive-slave clause of the Constitution and the law for the suppression of the foreign slave trade are each as well enforced, perhaps, as any law can ever be in a community where the moral sense of the people imperfectly supports the law itself. The great body of the people abide by the dry legal obligation in both cases, and a few break over in each. This, I think, can not be perfectly cured, and it would be worse in both cases after the separation of the sections than before. The foreign slave trade, now imperfectly suppressed, would be ultimately revived without restriction in one section, while fugitive slaves, now only partially surrendered, would not be surrendered at all by the other.

Physically speaking, we can not separate. We can not remove our respective sections from each other nor build an impassable wall between them. A husband and wife may be divorced and go out of the presence and beyond the reach of each other, but the different parts of our country can not do this. They can not but remain face to face, and intercourse, either amicable or hostile, must continue between them. Is it possible, then, to make that intercourse more advantageous or more satisfactory after separation than before? Can aliens make treaties easier than friends can make laws? Can treaties be more faithfully enforced between aliens than laws can among friends? Suppose you go to war, you can not fight always; and when, after much

loss on both sides and no gain on either, you cease fighting, the identical old questions, as to terms of intercourse, are again upon you.

This country, with its institutions, belongs to the people who inhabit it. Whenever they shall grow weary of the existing Government, they can exercise their constitutional right of amending it or their revolutionary right to dismember or overthrow it. I can not be ignorant of the fact that many worthy and patriotic citizens are desirous of having the National Constitution amended. While I make no recommendation of amendments, I fully recognize the rightful authority of the people over the whole subject, to be exercised in either of the modes prescribed in the instrument itself; and I should, under existing circumstances, favor rather than oppose a fair opportunity being afforded the people to act upon it. I will venture to add that to me the convention mode seems preferable, in that it allows amendments to originate with the people themselves, instead of only permitting them to take or reject propositions originated by others, not especially chosen for the purpose, and which might not be precisely such as they would wish to either accept or refuse. I understand a proposed amendment to the Constitution—which amendment, however, I have not seen—has passed Congress, to the effect that the Federal Government shall never interfere with the domestic institutions of the States, including that of persons held to service. To avoid misconstruction of what I have said, I depart from my purpose not to speak of particular amendments so far as to say that, holding such a provision to now be implied constitutional law, I have no objection to its being made express and irrevocable.

The Chief Magistrate derives all his authority from the people, and they have referred none upon him to fix terms for the separation of the States. The people themselves can do this if also they choose, but the Executive as such has nothing to do with it. His duty is to administer the present Govern-

ment as it came to his hands and to transmit it unimpaired by him to his successor.

Why should there not be a patient confidence in the ultimate justice of the people? Is there any better or equal hope in the world? In our present differences, is either party without faith of being in the right? If the Almighty Ruler of Nations, with His eternal truth and justice, be on your side of the North, or on yours of the South, that truth and that justice will surely prevail by the judgment of this great tribunal of the American people.

By the frame of the Government under which we live this same people have wisely given their public servants but little power for mischief, and have with equal wisdom provided for the return of that little to their own hands at very short intervals. While the people retain their virtue and vigilance no Administration by any extreme of wickedness or folly can very seriously injure the Government in the short space of four years.

My countrymen, one and all, think calmly and well upon this whole subject. Nothing valuable can be lost by taking time. If there be an object to hurry any of you in hot haste to a step which you would never take deliberately, that object will be frustrated by taking time; but no good object can be frustrated by it. Such of you as are now dissatisfied still have the old Constitution unimpaired, and, on the sensitive point, the laws of your own framing under it; while the new Administration will have no immediate power, if it would, to change either. If it were admitted that you who are dissatisfied hold the right side in the dispute, there still is no single good reason for precipitate action. Intelligence, patriotism, Christianity, and a firm reliance on Him who has never yet forsaken this favored land are still

competent to adjust in the best way all our present difficulty.

In your hands, my dissatisfied fellow-countrymen, and not in mine, is the momentous issue of civil war. The Government will not assail you. You can have no conflict without being yourselves the aggressors. You have no oath registered in heaven to destroy the Government, while I shall have the most solemn one to "preserve, protect, and defend it."

I am loath to close. We are not enemies, but friends. We must not be enemies. Though passion may have strained it must not break our bonds of affection. The mystic chords of memory, stretching from every battlefield and patriot grave to every living heart and hearthstone all over this broad land, will yet swell the chorus of the Union, when again touched, as surely they will be, by the better angels of our nature.

* * *

1864 ABRAHAM LINCOLN

DESPITE THE CIVIL WAR, American democracy continued to function. Midterm elections were held in 1862, and a presidential election in 1864. Having already made gains in the House, the Democrats were confident that, with casualties mounting, they could unseat Abraham Lincoln. To run against the president, they nominated Gen. George B. McClellan, the Union commander fired by Lincoln for failing to prosecute the war vigorously. The Republicans renominated Lincoln and, in a bid to expand their base, replaced Vice President Hannibal Hamlin with Unionist Democrat Andrew Johnson of Tennessee. Neither presidential candidate campaigned.

The Democratic platform charged that Lincoln's decision to wage war against the South was unconstitutional, as was his decision to suspend the writ of habeas corpus. Democrats also attacked Lincoln's emancipation of the slaves, while Republicans, marching to "The Battle Hymn of the Republic," praised the wisdom and compassion of "Father Abraham."

What made the most difference in the election, though, was the success of the Union army that summer and fall—particularly Gen. William T. Sherman's capture of Atlanta, which seemed to validate Lincoln's war strategy. (Just in case, Union soldiers were furloughed so they could return home and vote.) Although Lincoln had feared defeat, what he got was a resounding vote of confidence that ballooned his slim 1860 popular-vote plurality into a comfortable majority.

PARTY	POPULAR VOTES	ELECTORAL VOTES
REPUBLICAN Abraham Lincoln, Ill. Andrew Johnson, Tenn.	2,218,388	212
DEMOCRATIC George B. McClellan, N.Y. George H. Pendleton, Ohio	1,812,807	21
(NOT VOTED)		1

Second Inaugural Address • Washington, D.C. • Saturday, March 4, 1865

Fellow-Countrymen: At this second appearing to take the oath of the

Presidential office there is less occasion for an extended address than there was at the first. Then a statement somewhat in detail of a course to be pursued seemed fitting and proper. Now, at the expiration of four years, during which public declarations have been constantly called forth on every point and phase of the great contest which still absorbs the attention and engrosses the energies of the nation, little that is new could be presented. The progress of our arms, upon which all else chiefly depends, is as well known to the public as to myself, and it is, I trust, reasonably satisfactory and encouraging to all. With high hope for the future, no prediction in regard to it is ventured.

On the occasion corresponding to this four years ago all thoughts were anxiously directed to an impending civil war. All dreaded it, all sought to avert it. While the inaugural address was being delivered from this place, devoted altogether to saving the Union without war, urgent agents were in the city seeking to destroy it without war—seeking to dissolve the Union and divide effects by negotiation. Both parties deprecated war; but one of them would make war rather than let the nation survive; and the other would accept war rather than let it perish. And the war came.

One-eighth of the whole population were colored slaves, not distributed generally over the Union, but localized in the southern part of it. These slaves constituted a peculiar and powerful interest. All knew that this interest was somehow the cause of the war. To strengthen, perpetuate, and extend this interest was the object for which the insurgents would rend the Union even by war, while the Government claimed no right to do more than to restrict the territorial enlargement of it. Neither party expected for the war the magnitude or the duration which it has already attained. Neither anticipated that the cause of the conflict might cease with or even before the conflict itself should cease. Each looked for an easier triumph, and a result less fundamental and astounding. Both read the same Bible and pray to the same God, and each invokes His aid against the other. It may seem strange that any men should dare to ask a just God's assistance in wringing their bread from the sweat of other men's faces, but let us judge not, that we be not judged. The prayers of both could not be answered. That of neither has been answered fully. The Almighty has His own purposes. "Woe unto the world because of offenses; for it must needs be that offenses come, but woe to that man by whom the offense cometh." If we shall suppose that American slavery is one of those offenses which, in the providence of God, must needs come, but which, having continued through His appointed time, He now wills to remove, and that He gives to both North and South this terrible war as the woe due to those by whom the offense came, shall we discern therein any departure from those divine attributes which the believers in a living God always ascribe to Him? Fondly do we hope, fervently do we pray, that this mighty scourge of war may speedily pass away. Yet, if God wills that it continue until all the wealth piled by the bondsman's two hundred and fifty years of unrequited toil shall be sunk, and until every drop of blood drawn with the lash shall be paid by another drawn with the sword, as was said three thousand years ago, so still it must be said "the judgments of the Lord are true and righteous altogether."

With malice toward none, with charity for all, with firmness in the right as God gives us to see the right, let us strive on to finish the work we are in, to bind up the nation's wounds, to care for him who shall have borne the battle and for his widow and his orphan, to do all which may achieve and cherish a just and lasting peace among ourselves and with all nations.

***

1868 ULYSSES S. GRANT

ONE REASON THAT Gen. Ulysses S. Grant's friends in the Senate voted to acquit Andrew Johnson was that they didn't want Senate president pro tempore Benjamin F. Wade to run for president in 1868 as the incumbent. (Had Johnson been convicted, Wade would have succeeded him.) Instead, Grant's path to the nomination remained clear, and at the Republican convention in May he won a unanimous first-ballot victory. Meanwhile, northern and southern Democrats, uneasily reunited after the war, selected former New York governor Horatio Seymour from a crowded field, largely ignoring Johnson's candidacy.

During the campaign, Grant kept his thoughts to himself, while "Man of Peace" Seymour toured the country, pledging his party's eternal loyalty to the sacred Union. So soon after the war, however, Unionism was clearly a Republican issue. At every opportunity, the party of Lincoln applauded itself for saving the Union and, just as often, "waved the bloody shirt" of war to remind voters that the Democrats had been the party of secession. Democratic attacks on Republican currency and tax policies also fell on mostly deaf ears.

The race shouldn't have been close, but Democrats in the South combined with northern Copperheads to make the popular-vote totals closer than expected.

PARTY	POPULAR VOTES	ELECTORAL VOTES
REPUBLICAN Ulysses S. Grant, Ill. Schuyler Colfax, Ind.	3,013,650	214
DEMOCRATIC Horatio Seymour, N.Y. Francis P. Blair Jr. Mo.	2,708,744	80

First Inaugural Address • Washington, D.C. • Thursday, March 4, 1869

Citizens of the United States: Your suffrages having elected me to the office

of President of the United States, I have, in conformity to the Constitution of our country, taken the oath of office prescribed therein. I have taken this oath without mental reservation and with the determination to do to the best of my ability all that is required of me. The responsibilities of the position I feel, but accept them without fear. The office has come to me unsought; I commence its duties untrammeled. I bring to it a conscious desire and determination to fill it to the best of my ability to the satisfaction of the people.

On all leading questions agitating the public mind I will always express my views to Congress and urge them according to my judgment, and when I think it advisable will exercise the constitutional privilege of interposing a veto to defeat measures which I oppose; but all laws will be faithfully executed, whether they meet my approval or not.

I shall on all subjects have a policy to recommend, but none to enforce against the will of the people. Laws are to govern all alike—those opposed as well as those who favor them. I know no method to secure the repeal of bad or obnoxious laws so effective as their stringent execution.

The country having just emerged from a great rebellion, many questions will come before it for settlement in the next four years which preceding Administrations have never had to deal with. In meeting these it is desirable that they should be approached calmly, without prejudice, hate, or sectional pride, remembering that the greatest good to the greatest number is the object to be attained.

This requires security of person, property, and free religious and political opinion in every part of our common country, without regard to local prejudice. All laws to secure these ends will receive my best efforts for their enforcement.

A great debt has been contracted in securing to us and our posterity the Union. The payment of this, principal and interest, as well as the return to a specie basis as soon as it can be accomplished without material detriment to the debtor class or to the country at large, must be provided for. To protect the national honor, every dollar of Government indebtedness should be paid in gold, unless otherwise expressly stipulated in the contract. Let it be understood that no repudiator of one farthing of our public debt will be trusted in public place, and it will go far toward strengthening a credit which ought to be the best in the world, and will ultimately enable us to replace the debt with bonds bearing less interest than we now pay. To this should be added a faithful collection of the revenue, a strict accountability to the Treasury for every dollar collected, and the greatest practicable retrenchment in expenditure in every department of Government.

When we compare the paying capacity of the country now, with the ten States in poverty from the effects of war, but soon to emerge, I trust, into greater prosperity than

ever before, with its paying capacity twenty-five years ago, and calculate what it probably will be twenty-five years hence, who can doubt the feasibility of paying every dollar then with more ease than we now pay for useless luxuries? Why, it looks as though Providence had bestowed upon us a strong box in the precious metals locked up in the sterile mountains of the far West, and which we are now forging the key to unlock, to meet the very contingency that is now upon us.

Ultimately it may be necessary to insure the facilities to reach these riches and it may be necessary also that the General Government should give its aid to secure this access; but that should only be when a dollar of obligation to pay secures precisely the same sort of dollar to use now, and not before. Whilst the question of specie payments is in abeyance the prudent business man is careful about contracting debts payable in the distant future. The nation should follow the same rule. A prostrate commerce is to be rebuilt and all industries encouraged.

The responsibilities of the position I feel, but accept them without fear.

The young men of the country—those who from their age must be its rulers twenty-five years hence—have a peculiar interest in maintaining the national honor. A moment's reflection as to what will be our commanding influence among the nations of the earth in their day, if they are only true to themselves, should inspire them with national pride. All divisions—geographical, political, and religious—can join in this common sentiment. How the public debt is to be paid or specie payments resumed is not so important as that a plan should be adopted and acqui-

esced in. A united determination to do is worth more than divided counsels upon the method of doing. Legislation upon this subject may not be necessary now, or even advisable, but it will be when the civil law is more fully restored in all parts of the country and trade resumes its wonted channels.

It will be my endeavor to execute all laws in good faith, to collect all revenues assessed, and to have them properly accounted for and economically disbursed. I will to the best of my ability appoint to office those only who will carry out this design.

In regard to foreign policy, I would deal with nations as equitable law requires individuals to deal with each other, and I would protect the law-abiding citizen, whether of native or foreign birth, wherever his rights are jeopardized or the flag of our country floats. I would respect the rights of all nations, demanding equal respect for our own. If others depart from this rule in their dealings with us, we may be compelled to follow their precedent.

The proper treatment of the original occupants of this land—the Indians one deserving of careful study. I will favor any course toward them which tends to their civilization and ultimate citizenship.

The question of suffrage is one which is likely to agitate the public so long as a portion of the citizens of the nation are excluded from its privileges in any State. It seems to me very desirable that this question should be settled now, and I entertain the hope and express the desire that it may be by the ratification of the fifteenth article of amendment to the Constitution.

In conclusion I ask patient forbearance one toward another throughout the land, and a determined effort on the part of every citizen to do his share toward cementing a happy union; and I ask the prayers of the nation to Almighty God in behalf of this consummation.

* * *

1872 ULYSSES S. GRANT

ALTHOUGH NONE OF THE emerging reports of corruption threatened the renomination of President Ulysses. S. Grant, Vice President Schuyler Colfax was dropped from the Republican ticket (and subsequently implicated in the Crédit Mobilier railroad construction scandal). Colfax's departure, though, wasn't enough to satisfy liberal Republicans, who left the party in large numbers to support Democratic nominee Horace Greeley, the crusading New York newspaper editor who ironically had helped found the Republican party in 1854.

3d Ward

GRANT

BOYS

IN BLUE.

Greeley took to the stump, while Grant sent out surrogates from the White House to make speeches for him. Charging that the Grant administration was thoroughly incompetent and corrupt, the Democrats pledged to reform the civil service and end the rampant abuse of patronage. The Grant forces defended the president and warned that Greeley's ideas, ranging from free trade to free love, were too radical for the country. In a futile attempt to overtake the president, Greeley pandered to southern and border state racists, but the Republican state parties were simply too well organized, too well funded, and too enthusiastic to beat.

PARTY	POPULAR VOTES	ELECTORAL VOTES
REPUBLICAN Ulysses S. Grant, Ill. Henry Wilson, Mass.	3,598,235	286
DEMOCRATIC Horace Greeley, N.Y. Benjamin G. Brown, Mo.	2,834,761	66

On Election Day, Greeley carried six states with a total of sixty-six electoral votes. Before the electoral college met, however, he died. When the electoral college did meet, forty-two of the Democratic electors voted for Thomas A. Hendricks, the governor-elect of Indiana. The rest scattered their votes among other Democrats, except for three Georgia electors who insisted on casting ballots for Greeley, even though Congress refused to count them.

Second Inaugural Address • Washington, D.C. • Tuesday, March 4, 1873

Fellow-Citizens: Under Providence I have been called a second time

to act as Executive over this great nation. It has been my endeavor in the past to maintain all the laws, and, so far as lay in my power, to act for the best interests of the whole people. My best efforts will be given in the same direction in the future, aided, I trust, by my four years' experience in the office.

When my first term of the office of Chief Executive began, the country had not recovered from the effects of a great internal revolution, and three of the former States of the Union had not been restored to their Federal relations.

It seemed to me wise that no new questions should be raised so long as that condition of affairs existed. Therefore the past four years, so far as I could control events, have been consumed in the effort to restore harmony, public credit, commerce, and all the arts of peace and progress. It is my firm conviction that the civilized world is tending toward republicanism, or government by the people through their chosen representatives, and that our own great Republic is destined to be the guiding star to all others.

Under our Republic we support an army less than that of any European power of any standing and a navy less than that of either of at least five of them. There could be no extension of territory on the continent which would call for an increase of this force, but rather might such extension enable us to diminish it.

The theory of government changes with general progress. Now that the telegraph is made available for communicating thought, together with rapid transit by steam, all parts of a continent are made contiguous for all purposes of government, and communication between the extreme limits of the country made easier than it was throughout the old thirteen States at the beginning of our national existence.

The effects of the late civil strife have been to free the slave and make him a citizen. Yet he is not possessed of the civil rights which citizenship should carry with it. This is wrong, and should be corrected. To this correction I stand committed, so far as Executive influence can avail.

Social equality is not a subject to be legislated upon, nor shall I ask that anything be done to advance the social status of the colored man, except to give him a fair chance to develop what there is good in him, give him access to the schools, and when he travels let him feel assured that his conduct will regulate the treatment and fare he will receive.

The States lately at war with the General Government are now happily rehabilitated, and no Executive control is exercised in any one of them that would not be exercised in any other State under like circumstances.

In the first year of the past Administration the proposition came up for the admission of Santo Domingo as a Territory of the Union. It was not a question of my seeking, but was a proposition from the people of Santo Domingo, and which I entertained. I believe now, as I did then, that it was for the best interest of this country, for the people of Santo Domingo, and all concerned that the proposition should be received favorably. It was, however, rejected constitutionally, and therefore the

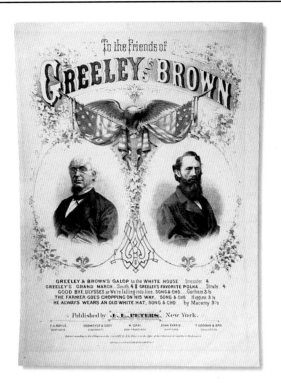

subject was never brought up again by me.

In future, while I hold my present office, the subject of acquisition of territory must have the support of the people before I will recommend any proposition looking to such acquisition. I say here, however, that I do not share in the apprehension held by many as to the danger of governments becoming weakened and destroyed by reason of their extension of territory. Commerce, education, and rapid transit of thought and matter by telegraph and steam have changed all this. Rather do I believe that our Great Maker is preparing the world, in His own good time, to become one nation, speaking one language, and when armies and navies will be no longer required.

My efforts in the future will be directed to the restoration of good feeling between the different sections of our common country; to the restoration of our currency to a fixed value as compared with the world's standard of values—gold—and, if possible, to a par with it; to the construction of cheap routes of transit throughout the land, to the end that the products of all may find a mar-

...nor shall I ask that anything be done to advance the social status of the colored man, except to give him a fair chance to develop what there is good in him....

ket and leave a living remuneration to the producer; to the maintenance of friendly relations with all our neighbors and with distant nations; to the reestablishment of our commerce and share in the carrying trade upon the ocean; to the encouragement of such manufacturing industries as can be economically pursued in this country, to the end that the exports of home products and

industries may pay for our imports—the only sure method of returning to and permanently maintaining a specie basis; to the elevation of labor; and, by a humane course, to bring the aborigines of the country under the benign influences of education and civilization. It is either this or war of extermination: Wars of extermination, engaged in by people pursuing commerce and all industrial pursuits, are expensive even against the weakest people, and are demoralizing and wicked. Our superiority of strength and advantages of civilization should make us lenient toward the Indian. The wrong inflicted upon him should be taken into account and the balance placed to his credit. The moral view of the question should be considered and the question asked, Can not the Indian be made a useful and productive member of society by proper teaching and treatment? If the effort is made in good faith, we will stand better before the civilized nations of the earth and in our own consciences for having made it.

All these things are not to be accomplished by one individual, but they will receive my support and such recommendations to Congress as will in my judgment best serve to carry them into effect. I beg your support and encouragement.

It has been, and is, my earnest desire to correct abuses that have grown up in the civil service of the country. To secure this reformation rules regulating methods of appointment and promotions were established and have been tried. My efforts for such reformation shall be continued to the best of my judgment. The spirit of the rules adopted will be maintained.

I acknowledge before this assemblage, representing, as it does, every section of our country, the obligation I am under to my countrymen for the great honor they have conferred on me by returning me to the highest office within their gift, and the further obligation resting on me to render to them the best services within

my power. This I promise, looking forward with the greatest anxiety to the day when I shall be released from responsibilities that at times are almost overwhelming, and from which I have scarcely had a respite since the eventful firing upon Fort Sumter, in April, 1861, to the present day. My services were then tendered and accepted under the first call for troops growing out of that event.

I did not ask for place or position, and was entirely without influence or the acquaintance of persons of influence, but was resolved to perform my part in a struggle threatening the very existence of the nation. I performed a conscientious duty, without asking promotion or command, and without a revengeful feeling toward any section or individual.

Notwithstanding this, throughout the war, and from my candidacy for my present office in 1868 to the close of the last Presidential campaign, I have been the subject of abuse and slander scarcely ever equaled in political history, which to-day I feel that I can afford to disregard in view of your verdict, which I gratefully accept as my vindication.

* * *

1876 Rutherford B. Hayes

The scandals of the Grant administration so stained the Republican party that at the close of his second term the president offered an apology to the nation. To capitalize on this issue, the Democrats nominated New York governor Samuel J. Tilden, the nationally famous reformer who'd broken up the Tweed Ring.

At the Republican convention, the delegates passed over a somewhat tainted James G. Blaine and nominated instead the most reform-minded candidate they could find: Rutherford B. Hayes, the governor of Ohio. Also, in an appeal to black voters, the convention invited Frederick Douglass to address the delegates.

Tilden campaigned effectively on the corruption in Grant's cabinet, while the Republicans praised Hayes's courageous war record (Tilden had none) and

"waved the bloody shirt" of secession. It was a close race that, at least in the popular vote, Tilden clearly won. Tilden also led in the electoral college, 184–165, but the returns from four states were in dispute, leaving twenty votes up for grabs.

Party	Popular Votes	Electoral Votes
Republican Rutherford B. Hayes, Ohio William A. Wheeler, N.Y.	4,034,311	185
Democratic Samuel J. Tilden, N.Y. Thomas A. Hendricks, Ind.	4,288,546	184

To sort out the controversy, Congress appointed a fifteen-member electoral commission with an 8–7 Republican majority. Meanwhile, the two parties made a deal, which became known as the Great Compromise. The Democrats agreed not to contest a commission finding that all twenty disputed votes belonged to Hayes; in return, the Republicans promised to remove all remaining federal troops from the South, ending Reconstruction. African-Americans called the deal the Great Betrayal.

Inaugural Address • Washington, D.C. • Monday, March 5, 1877

Fellow-Citizens: we have assembled to repeat the public ceremonial begun

by Washington, observed by all my predecessors, and now a time-honored custom, which marks the commencement of a new term of the Presidential office. Called to the duties of this great trust, I proceed, in compliance with usage, to announce some of the leading principles, on the subjects that now chiefly engage the public attention, by which it is my desire to be guided in the discharge of those duties. I shall not undertake to lay down irrevocably principles or measures of administration, but rather to speak of the motives which should animate us, and to suggest certain important ends to be attained in accordance with our institutions and essential to the welfare of our country.

At the outset of the discussions which preceded the recent Presidential election it seemed to me fitting that I should fully make known my sentiments in regard to several of the important questions which then appeared to demand the consideration of the country. Following the example, and in part adopting the language, of one of my prede-

cessors, I wish now, when every motive for misrepresentation has passed away, to repeat what was said before the election, trusting that my countrymen will candidly weigh and understand it, and that they will feel assured that the sentiments declared in accepting the nomination for the Presidency will be the standard of my conduct in the path before me, charged, as I now am, with the grave and difficult task of carrying them out in the practical administration of the Government so far as depends, under the Constitution and laws on the Chief Executive of the nation.

The permanent pacification of the country upon such principles and by such measures as will secure the complete protection of all its citizens in the free enjoyment of all their constitutional rights is now the one subject in our public affairs which all thoughtful and patriotic citizens regard as of supreme importance.

Many of the calamitous efforts of the tremendous revolution which has passed

over the Southern States still remain. The immeasurable benefits which will surely follow, sooner or later, the hearty and generous acceptance of the legitimate results of that revolution have not yet been realized. Difficult and embarrassing questions meet us at the threshold of this subject. The people of those States are still impoverished, and the inestimable blessing of wise, honest, and peaceful local self-government is not fully enjoyed. Whatever difference of opinion may exist as to the cause of this condition of things, the fact is clear that in the progress of events the time has come when such government is the imperative necessity required by all the varied interests, public and private, of those States. But it must not be forgotten that only a local government which recognizes and maintains inviolate the rights of all is a true self-government.

With respect to the two distinct races whose peculiar relations to each other have brought upon us the deplorable complications and perplexities which exist in those States, it must be a government which guards the interests of both races carefully and equally. It must be a government which submits loyally and heartily to the Constitution and the laws—the laws of the nation and the laws of the States themselves—accepting and obeying faithfully the whole Constitution as it is.

Resting upon this sure and substantial foundation, the superstructure of beneficent local governments can be built up, and not otherwise. In furtherance of such obedience to the letter and the spirit of the Constitution, and in behalf of all that its attainment implies, all so-called party interests lose their apparent importance, and party lines may well be permitted to fade into insignificance. The question we have to consider for the immediate welfare of those States of the Union is

> *The President… should strive to be always mindful of the fact that he serves his party best who serves the country best.*

the question of government or no government; of social order and all the peaceful industries and the happiness that belongs to it, or a return to barbarism. It is a question in which every citizen of the nation is deeply interested, and with respect to which we ought not to be, in a partisan sense, either Republicans or Democrats, but fellow-citizens and fellowmen, to whom the interests of a common country and a common humanity are dear.

The sweeping revolution of the entire labor system of a large portion of our country and the advance of 4,000,000 people from a condition of servitude to that of citizenship, upon an

equal footing with their former masters, could not occur without presenting problems of the gravest moment, to be dealt with by the emancipated race, by their former masters, and by the General Government, the author of the act of emancipation. That it was a wise, just, and providential act, fraught with good for all concerned, is not generally conceded throughout the country. That a moral obligation rests upon the National Government to employ its constitutional power and influence to establish the rights of the people it has emancipated, and to protect them in the enjoyment of those rights when they are infringed or assailed, is also generally admitted.

The evils which afflict the Southern States can only be removed or remedied by the united and harmonious efforts of both races, actuated by motives of mutual sympathy and regard; and while in duty bound and fully determined to protect the rights of all by every constitutional means at the disposal of my Administration, I am sincerely anxious to use every legitimate influence in favor of honest and efficient local self-government as the true resource of those States for the promotion of the contentment and prosperity of their citizens. In the effort I shall make to accomplish this purpose I ask the cordial cooperation of all who cherish an interest in the welfare of the country, trusting that party ties and the prejudice of race will be freely surrendered in behalf of the great purpose to be accomplished. In the important work of restoring the South it is not the political situation alone that merits attention. The material development of that section of the country has been arrested by the social and political revolution through which it has passed, and now needs and deserves the considerate care of the National Government within the just limits prescribed by the Constitution and wise public economy.

But at the basis of all prosperity, for that as well as for

every other part of the country, lies the improvement of the intellectual and moral condition of the people. Universal suffrage should rest upon universal education. To this end, liberal and permanent provision should be made for the support of free schools by the State governments, and, if need be, supplemented by legitimate aid from national authority.

Let me assure my countrymen of the Southern States that it is my earnest desire to regard and promote their truest interest—the interests of the white and of the colored people both and equally—and to put forth my best efforts in behalf of a civil policy which will forever wipe out in our political affairs the color line and the distinction between North and South, to the end that we may have not merely a united North or a united South, but a united country.

I ask the attention of the public to the paramount necessity of reform in our civil service—a reform not merely as to

certain abuses and practices of so-called official patronage which have come to have the sanction of usage in the several Departments of our Government, but a change in the system of appointment itself; a reform that shall be thorough, radical, and complete; a return to the principles and practices of the founders of the Government. They neither expected nor desired from public officers any partisan service. They meant that public officers should owe their whole service to the Government and to the people. They meant that the officer should be secure in his tenure as long as his personal character remained untarnished and the performance of his duties satisfactory. They held that appointments to office were not to be made nor expected merely as rewards for partisan services, nor merely on the nomination of members of Congress, as being entitled in any respect to the control of such appointments.

The fact that both the great political parties of the

country, in declaring their principles prior to the election, gave a prominent place to the subject of reform of our civil service, recognizing and strongly urging its necessity, in terms almost identical in their specific import with those I have here employed, must be accepted as a conclusive argument in behalf of these measures. It must be regarded as the expression of the united voice and will of the whole country upon this subject, and both political parties are virtually pledged to give it their unreserved support.

ues. It is very gratifying, however, to be able to say that there are indications all around us of a coming change to prosperous times.

Upon the currency question, intimately connected, as it is, with this topic, I may be permitted to repeat here the statement made in my letter of acceptance, that in my judgment the feeling of uncertainty inseparable from an irredeemable paper currency, with its fluctuation of values, is one of the greatest obstacles to a return to prosperous times. The

foreign powers points to a new, and incomparably the best, instrumentality for the preservation of peace, and will, as I believe, become a beneficent example of the course to be pursued in similar emergencies by other nations.

If, unhappily, questions of difference should at any time during the period of my Administration arise between the United States and any foreign government, it will certainly be my disposition and my hope to aid in their settlement in the same peaceful and honorable way, thus securing to our country the great blessings of peace and mutual good offices with all the nations of the world.

Fellow-citizens, we have reached the close of a political contest marked by the excitement which usually attends the contests between great political parties whose members espouse and advocate with earnest faith their respective creeds. The circumstances were, perhaps, in no respect extraordinary save in the closeness and the consequent uncertainty of the result.

For the first time in the history of the country it has been deemed best, in view of the peculiar circumstances of the case, that the objections and questions in dispute with reference to the counting of the electoral votes should be referred to the decision of a tribunal appointed for this purpose.

That tribunal—established by law for this sole purpose; its members, all of them, men of long-established reputation for integrity and intelligence, and, with the exception of those who are also members of the supreme judiciary, chosen equally from both political parties; its deliberations enlightened by the research and the arguments of able counsel—was entitled to the fullest confidence of the American people. Its decisions have been patiently waited for, and accepted as legally conclusive by the general judgment of the public. For the present, opinion will widely

vary as to the wisdom of the several conclusions announced by that tribunal. This is to be anticipated in every instance where matters of dispute are made the subject of arbitration under the forms of law. Human judgment is never unerring, and is rarely regarded as otherwise than wrong by the unsuccessful party in the contest.

The fact that two great political parties have in this way settled a dispute in regard to which good men differ as to the facts and the law no less than as to the proper course to be pursued in solving the question in controversy is an occasion for general rejoicing.

Upon one point there is entire unanimity in public sentiment—that conflicting claims to the Presidency must be amicably and peaceably adjusted, and that when so adjusted the general acquiescence of the nation ought surely to follow.

It has been reserved for a government of the people, where the right of suffrage is universal, to give to the world the first example in history of a great nation, in the midst of the struggle of opposing parties for power, hushing its party tumults to yield the issue of the contest to adjustment according to the forms of law.

Looking for the guidance of that Divine Hand by which the destinies of nations and individuals are shaped, I call upon you, Senators, Representatives, judges, fellow-citizens, here and everywhere, to unite with me in an earnest effort to secure to our country the blessings, not only of material prosperity, but of justice, peace, and union— a union depending not upon the constraint of force, but upon the loving devotion of a free people; "and that all things may be so ordered and settled upon the best and surest foundations that peace and happiness, truth and justice, religion and piety, may be established among us for all generations."

* * *

The President of the United States of necessity owes his election to office to the suffrage and zealous labors of a political party, the members of which cherish with ardor and regard as of essential importance the principles of their party organization; but he should strive to be always mindful of the fact that he serves his party best who serves the country best.

In furtherance of the reform we seek, and in other important respects a change of great importance, I recommend an amendment to the Constitution prescribing a term of six years for the Presidential office and forbidding a reelection.

With respect to the financial condition of the country, I shall not attempt an extended history of the embarrassment and prostration which we have suffered during the past three years. The depression in all our varied commercial and manufacturing interests throughout the country, which began in September, 1873, still contin-

only safe paper currency is one which rests upon a coin basis and is at all times and promptly convertible into coin.

I adhere to the views heretofore expressed by me in favor of Congressional legislation in behalf of an early resumption of specie payments, and I am satisfied not only that this is wise, but that the interests, as well as the public sentiment, of the country imperatively demand it.

Passing from these remarks upon the condition of our own country to consider our relations with other lands, we are reminded by the international complications abroad, threatening the peace of Europe, that our traditional rule of noninterference in the affairs of foreign nations has proved of great value in past times and ought to be strictly observed.

The policy inaugurated by my honored predecessor, President Grant, of submitting to arbitration grave questions in dispute between ourselves and

1880 James A. Garfield

DURING THE 1878 MIDTERM elections, Democrats took control of both houses of Congress for the first time since James Buchanan was president. Having lost popularity around the country (for crushing the 1877 railroad strike) and support within his own party (for limiting patronage), President Rutherford B. Hayes gladly retired. At the Republican convention, the conservative Stalwart wing of the party tried to bring back Ulysses S. Grant for a third term, but moderate Half-Breeds led by Maine senator James G. Blaine blocked the move. Finally, on the thirty-sixth ballot, the anti–Grant forces united behind Rep. James A. Garfield of Ohio, who became the dark horse nominee. New York City party operative Chester A. Arthur was later added to the ticket in the hope that his nomination might placate Stalwart boss Roscoe Conkling, also of New York. The Democrats ran a much more orderly convention, nominating Civil War general Winfield Scott Hancock on the second ballot after 1876 nominee Samuel J. Tilden withdrew his name from consideration.

Garfield ran a front-porch campaign in Ohio (meaning that he delivered speeches to visitors from his front steps); meanwhile, Hancock declined to campaign at all and was also reluctant to discuss his military exploits. Democratic surrogates called for lower tariff rates, but Republicans successfully persuaded northern laborers that lower tariffs would encourage foreign competition and put downward pressure on their wages. The Republicans also outspent the poorly funded Democrats three to one.

Although Garfield won the presidency with a comfortable electoral margin, he took the popular vote by less than two thousand votes, or 0.002 percent of the total. This was because his strength was essentially regional, concentrated in the Northeast and Midwest. Fortunately for the Republicans, these regions were more than populous enough to elect a president. Almost everywhere else, Garfield lost badly.

Party	Popular Votes	Electoral Votes
Republican James A. Garfield, Ohio Chester A. Arthur, N.Y.	4,446,158	214
Democratic Winfield S. Hancock, Pa. William H. English, Ind.	4,444,260	155
Greenback Labor James B. Weaver, Iowa Benjamin J. Chambers, Tex.	305,997	

Inaugural Address • Washington, D.C. • Friday, March 4, 1881

Fellow-Citizens: We stand to-day upon an eminence which overlooks

a hundred years of national life—a century crowded with perils, but crowned with the triumphs of liberty and law. Before continuing the onward march let us pause on this height for a moment to strengthen our faith and renew our hope by a glance at the pathway along which our people have traveled.

It is now three days more than a hundred years since the adoption of the first written constitution of the United States—the Articles of Confederation and Perpetual Union. The new Republic was then beset with danger on every hand. It had not conquered a place in the family of nations. The decisive battle of the war for independence, whose centennial anniversary will soon be gratefully celebrated at Yorktown, had not yet been fought. The colonists were struggling not only against the armies of a great nation, but against the settled opinions of mankind; for the world did not then believe that the supreme authority of government could be safely intrusted to the guardianship of the people themselves.

We can not overestimate the fervent love of liberty, the intelligent courage, and the sum of common sense with which our fathers made the great experiment of self-government. When they found, after a short trial, that the confederacy of States, was too weak to meet the necessities of a vigorous and expanding republic, they boldly set it aside, and in its stead established a National Union, founded directly upon the will of the people, endowed with full power of self-preservation and ample authority for the accomplishment of its great object.

Under this Constitution the boundaries of freedom have been enlarged, the foundations of order and peace have been strengthened, and the growth of our people in all the better elements of national life has indicated the wisdom of the founders and given new hope to their descendants. Under this Constitution our people long ago made themselves safe against danger from without and secured for their mariners and flag equality of rights on all the seas. Under this Constitution twenty-five States have been added to the Union, with constitutions and laws, framed and enforced by their own citizens, to secure the manifold blessings of local self-government.

The jurisdiction of this Constitution now covers an area fifty times greater than that of the original thirteen States and a population twenty times greater than that of 1780.

The supreme trial of the Constitution came at last under the tremendous pressure of civil war. We ourselves are witnesses that the Union emerged from the blood and fire of that conflict purified and made stronger for all the beneficent purposes of good government.

And now, at the close of this first century of growth, with the inspirations of its history in their hearts, our people have lately reviewed the condition of the nation, passed judgment upon the conduct and opinions of political parties, and have registered their will concerning the future administration of the Government. To interpret and to execute that will in accordance with the Constitution is the paramount duty of the Executive.

Even from this brief review it is manifest that the nation is resolutely facing to the front, resolved to employ its best energies in developing the great possibilities of the future. Sacredly preserving whatever has been gained to liberty and good government during the century, our people are determined to leave behind them all those bitter controversies concerning things which have been irrevocably settled, and the further discussion of which can only stir up strife and delay the onward march.

The supremacy of the nation and its laws should be no longer a subject of debate. That discussion, which for half a century threatened the existence of the Union, was closed at last in the high court of war by a decree from which there is no appeal—that the Constitution and the laws made in pursuance thereof are and shall continue to be the supreme law of the land, binding alike upon the States and the people. This decree does not disturb the autonomy of the States nor interfere with any of their necessary rights of local self-government, but it does fix and establish the permanent supremacy of the Union.

The will of the nation, speaking with the voice of battle and through the amended Constitution, has fulfilled the great promise of 1776 by proclaiming "liberty throughout the land to all the inhabitants thereof."

The elevation of the negro race from slavery to the full rights of citizenship is the most important political change we have known since the adoption of the Constitution of 1787. No thoughtful man can fail to appreciate its beneficent effect upon our institutions and people. It has freed us from the perpetual danger of war and

dissolution. It has added immensely to the moral and industrial forces of our people. It has liberated the master as well as the slave from a relation which wronged and enfeebled both. It has surrendered to their own guardianship the manhood of more than 5,000,000 people, and has opened to each one of them a career of freedom and usefulness. It has given new inspiration to the power of self-help in both races by making labor more honorable to the one and more necessary to the other. The influence of this force will grow greater and bear richer fruit with the coming years.

No doubt this great change has caused serious disturbance to our Southern communities. This is to be deplored, though it was perhaps unavoidable. But those who resisted the change should remember that under our institutions there was no middle ground for the negro race between slavery and equal citizenship. There can be no permanent disfranchised peasantry in the United States. Freedom can never yield its fullness of blessings so long as the law or its administration places the smallest obstacle in the pathway of any virtuous citizen.

The emancipated race has already made remarkable progress. With unquestioning devotion to the Union, with a patience and gentleness not born of fear, they have "followed the light as God gave them to see the light." They are rapidly laying the material foundations of self-support, widening their circle of intelligence, and beginning to enjoy the blessings that gather around the homes of the industrious poor. They deserve the generous encouragement of all good men. So far as my authority can lawfully extend they shall enjoy the full and equal protection of the Constitution and the laws.

The free enjoyment of equal suffrage is still in question, and a frank statement of the issue may aid its solution. It is alleged that in many communities negro citizens are practically denied the freedom of the ballot. In so far as the truth of

this allegation is admitted, it is answered that in many places honest local government is impossible if the mass of uneducated negroes are allowed to vote. These are grave allegations. So far as the latter is true, it is the only palliation that can be offered for opposing the freedom

---

The elevation of the negro race...has added immensely to the moral and industrial forces of our people.

---

of the ballot. Bad local government is certainly a great evil, which ought to be prevented; but to violate the freedom and sanctities of the suffrage is more than an evil. It is a crime which, if persisted in, will destroy the Government itself. Suicide is not a remedy. If in other lands it be high treason to compass the death of the king, it shall be counted no less a crime here to strangle our sovereign power and stifle its voice.

It has been said that unsettled questions have no pity for the repose of nations. It should be said with the utmost emphasis that this question of the suffrage will never give repose or safety to the States or to the nation until each, within its own jurisdiction, makes and keeps the ballot free and pure by the strong sanctions of the law.

But the danger which arises from ignorance in the voter can not be denied. It covers a field far wider than that of negro suffrage and the present condition of the race. It is a danger that lurks and hides in the sources and fountains of power in every state. We have no standard by which to measure the disaster that may be brought upon us by ignorance and vice in the citizens when joined to corruption and fraud in the suffrage.

The voters of the Union, who make and unmake constitutions, and upon whose will hang the destinies of our govern-

ments, can transmit their supreme authority to no successors save the coming generation of voters, who are the sole heirs of sovereign power. If that generation comes to its inheritance blinded by ignorance and corrupted by vice, the fall of the Republic will be certain and remediless.

The census has already sounded the alarm in the appalling figures which mark how dangerously high the tide of illiteracy has risen among our voters and their children.

To the South this question is of supreme importance. But the responsibility for the existence of slavery did not rest upon the South alone. The nation itself is responsible for the extension of the suffrage, and is under special obligations to aid in removing the illiteracy which it has added to the voting population. For the North and South alike there is but one remedy. All the constitutional power of the nation and of the States and all the volunteer forces of the people should be surrendered to meet this danger by the savory influence of universal education.

It is the high privilege and sacred duty of those now living to educate their successors and fit them, by intelligence and virtue, for the inheritance which awaits them.

In this beneficent work sections and races should be forgotten and partisanship should be unknown. Let our people find a new meaning in the divine oracle which declares that "a little child shall lead them," for our own little children will soon control the destinies of the Republic.

My countrymen, we do not now differ in our judgment concerning the controversies of past generations, and fifty years hence our children will not be divided in their opinions concerning our controversies. They will surely bless their fathers and their fathers' God that the Union was preserved, that slavery was overthrown, and that both races were made equal before the law. We may hasten or we may retard, but we can not prevent, the final reconciliation. Is it not possible for us now to make a truce with time by anticipating and accepting its inevitable verdict?

Enterprises of the highest importance to our moral and material well-being unite us and offer ample employment of our best powers. Let all our people, leaving behind them the battle-fields of dead issues, move forward and in their strength of liberty and the restored Union win the grander victories of peace.

The prosperity which now prevails is without parallel in our history. Fruitful seasons have done much to secure it, but they have not done all. The preservation of the public credit and the resumption of specie payments, so successfully attained by the Administration of my predecessors, have enabled our people to secure the blessings which the seasons brought.

By the experience of commercial nations in all ages it has been found that gold and silver afford the only safe foundation for a monetary system. Confusion has recently been created by variations in the relative value of the two metals, but I confidently believe that arrangements can be made between the leading commercial nations which will secure the general use of both metals. Congress should provide that the compulsory coinage of silver now required by law may not disturb our monetary system by driving either metal out of circulation. If possible, such an adjustment should be made that the purchasing power of every coined dollar will be exactly equal to its debt-paying power in all the markets of the world.

The chief duty of the National Government in connection with the currency of the country is to coin money and declare its value. Grave doubts have been entertained whether Congress is authorized by the Constitution to make any form of paper money legal tender. The present issue of United States notes has been sustained by the necessities of war; but such paper should depend for its value and currency upon its convenience in use and its prompt redemption in coin at the will of the holder, and not upon its compulsory circulation. These notes are not money, but promises to pay money. If the holders demand it, the promise should be kept.

The refunding of the national debt at a lower rate of interest should be accomplished without compelling the withdrawal of the national-bank notes, and thus disturbing the business of the country.

I venture to refer to the position I have occupied on financial questions during a long service in Congress, and to say that time and experience have strengthened the opinions I have so often expressed on these subjects.

The finances of the Government shall suffer no detriment which it may be possible for my Administration to prevent.

The interests of agriculture deserve more attention from the Government than they have yet received. The farms of the United States afford homes and employment for more than one-half our people, and furnish much the largest part of all our exports. As the Government lights our coasts for the protection of mariners and the benefit of commerce, so it should give to the tillers of the soil the best lights of practical science and experience.

Our manufacturers are rapidly making us industrially independent, and are opening to capital and labor new and profitable fields of employment. Their steady and healthy growth should still be matured. Our facilities for transportation should be promoted by the continued improvement of our harbors and great interior waterways and by the increase of our tonnage on the ocean.

The development of the world's commerce has led to an urgent demand for shortening the great sea voyage around Cape Horn by constructing ship canals or railways across the isthmus which unites the continents. Various plans to this end have been suggested and will need consideration, but none of them has been sufficiently matured to warrant the United States in extending pecuniary aid. The subject, however, is one which will immediately engage the attention of the Government with a view to a thorough protection to American interests. We will urge no narrow policy nor seek peculiar or exclusive privileges in any commercial route; but, in the language of my predecessor,

I believe it to be the right "and duty of the United States to assert and maintain such supervision and authority over any interoceanic canal across the isthmus that connects North and South America as will protect our national interest."

The Constitution guarantees absolute religious freedom. Congress is prohibited from making any law respecting an establishment of religion or prohibiting the free exercise thereof. The Territories of the United States are subject to the direct legislative authority of Congress, and hence the General Government is responsible for any violation of the Constitution in any of them. It is therefore a reproach to the Government that in the most populous of the Territories the constitutional guaranty is not enjoyed by the people and the authority of Congress is set at naught. The Mormon Church not only offends the moral sense of manhood by sanctioning polygamy, but prevents the administration of justice through ordinary instrumentalities of law.

In my judgment it is the duty of Congress, while respecting to the uttermost the conscientious convictions and religious scruples of every citizen, to prohibit within its jurisdiction all criminal practices, especially of that class which destroy the family relations and endanger social order. Nor can any ecclesiastical organization be safely permitted to usurp in the smallest degree the functions and powers of the National Government.

The civil service can never be placed on a satisfactory basis until it is regulated by law. For the good of the service itself, for the protection of those who are intrusted with the appointing power against the waste of time and obstruction to the public business caused by the inordinate pressure for place, and for the protection of incumbents against intrigue and wrong, I shall at the proper time ask Congress to fix the tenure of the minor offices of the several Executive Departments and prescribe the grounds upon which removals shall be made during the terms for which incumbents have been appointed.

Finally, acting always within the authority and limitations of the Constitution, invading neither the rights of the States nor the reserved rights of the people, it will be the purpose of my Administration to maintain the authority of the nation in all places within its jurisdiction; to enforce obedience to all the laws of the Union in the interests of the people; to demand rigid economy in all the expenditures of the Government, and to require the honest and faithful service of all executive officers, remembering that the offices were created, not for the benefit of incumbents or their supporters, but for the service of the Government.

And now, fellow-citizens, I am about to assume the great trust which you have committed to my hands. I appeal to you for that earnest and thoughtful support which makes this Government in fact, as it is in law, a government of the people.

I shall greatly rely upon the wisdom and patriotism of Congress and of those who may share with me the responsibilities and duties of administration, and, above all, upon our efforts to promote the welfare of this great people and their Government I reverently invoke the support and blessings of Almighty God.

* * *

383

1884 Grover Cleveland

Although Chester A. Arthur had performed better than expected following the assassination of his predecessor, the patronage-hungry Stalwarts, Arthur's natural base of support in the Republican party, had no intention of nominating him for another term. When Gen. William T. Sherman declined to run—famously telegraphing the convention, "I will not accept if nominated and will not serve if elected"— James G. Blaine finally received the endorsement that had eluded him in 1876 and again in 1880.

Dissatisfied with the choice of Blaine, a group of reformist Republicans, known as Mugwumps, left the party and invited the Democrats to nominate an honest, public-minded citizen whom they could support. The Democrats obliged, choosing New York governor Grover Cleveland on the second ballot.

The campaign was one of the dirtiest in U.S. history. Unlike "Slippery Jim" Blaine, whose public career was full of evasions, Cleveland had a spotless public record—so the Republicans went after his private life. Charging that Cleveland had fathered an illegitimate child, the Republicans sneered, "Ma, Ma, where's my pa?" Unwilling to lie or obfuscate, a defiant (and unmarried) Cleveland admitted paternity, explained the situation reasonably, and won praise for his forthrightness.

Party	Popular Votes	Electoral Votes
Democratic Grover Cleveland, N.Y. Thomas A. Hendricks, Ind.	4,874,621	219
Republican James G. Blaine, Me. John A. Logan, Ill.	4,848,936	182

The race remained close all summer and fall but turned in Cleveland's favor just days before the election when Blaine failed to condemn a supporter who had attacked the Democrats as the party of "rum, Romanism, and rebellion." The remark understandably upset New York's many Catholic voters, enough of whom swung to Cleveland to give him the state (by just one thousand votes) and the election.

First Inaugural Address • Washington, D.C. • Wednesday, March 4, 1885

Fellow-Citizens: In the presence of this vast assemblage of my countrymen

I am about to supplement and seal by the oath which I shall take the manifestation of the will of a great and free people. In the exercise of their power and right of self-government they have committed to one of their fellow-citizens a supreme and sacred trust, and he here consecrates himself to their service.

This impressive ceremony adds little to the solemn sense of responsibility with which I contemplate the duty I owe to all the people of the land. Nothing can relieve me from anxiety lest by any act of mine their interests may suffer, and nothing is needed to strengthen my resolution to engage every faculty and effort in the promotion of their welfare.

Amid the din of party strife the people's choice was made, but its attendant circumstances have demonstrated anew the strength and safety of a government by the people. In each succeeding year it more clearly appears that our democratic principle needs no apology, and that in its fearless and faithful application is to be found the surest guaranty of good government.

But the best results in the operation of a government wherein every citizen has a share largely depend upon a proper limitation of purely partisan zeal and effort and a correct appreciation of the time when the heat of the partisan should be merged in the patriotism of the citizen.

To-day the executive branch of the Government is transferred to new keeping. But this is still the Government of all the people, and it should be none the less an object of their affectionate solicitude. At this hour the animosities of political strife, the bitterness of partisan defeat, and the exultation of partisan triumph should be supplanted by an ungrudging acquiescence in the popular will and a sober, conscientious concern for the general weal. Moreover, if from this hour we cheerfully and honestly abandon all sectional prejudice and distrust, and determine, with manly confidence in one another, to work out harmoniously the achievements of our national destiny, we shall deserve to realize all the benefits which our happy form of government can bestow.

On this auspicious occasion we may well renew the pledge of our devotion to the Constitution, which, launched by the founders of the Republic and consecrated by their prayers and patriotic devotion, has for almost a century borne the hopes and the aspirations of a great people through prosperity and peace and through the shock of foreign conflicts and the perils of domestic strife and vicissitudes.

By the Father of his Country our Constitution was commended for adoption as "the result of a spirit of amity and mutual concession." In that same spirit it should be administered, in order to promote the lasting welfare of the country and to secure the full measure of its priceless benefits to us and to those who will succeed to the blessings of our national life. The large variety of diverse

and competing interests subject to Federal control, persistently seeking the recognition of their claims, need give us no fear that "the greatest good to the greatest number" will fail to be accomplished if in the halls of national legislation that spirit of amity and mutual concession shall prevail in which the Constitution had its birth. If this involves the surrender or postponement of private interests and the abandonment of local advantages, compensation will be found in the assurance that the common interest is subserved and the general welfare advanced.

In the discharge of my official duty I shall endeavor to be guided by a just and unstrained construction of the Constitution, a careful observance of the distinction between the powers granted to the Federal Government and those reserved to the States or to the people, and by a cautious appreciation of those functions which by the Constitution and laws have been especially assigned to the executive branch of the Government.

But he who takes the oath today to preserve, protect, and defend the Constitution of the United States only assumes the solemn obligation which every patriotic citizen—on the farm, in the workshop, in the busy marts of trade, and everywhere—should share with him. The Constitution which prescribes his oath, my countrymen, is yours; the Government you have chosen him to administer for a time is yours; the suffrage which executes the will of freemen is yours; the laws and the entire scheme of our civil rule, from the town meeting to the State capitals and the national capital, is yours. Your every voter, as surely as your Chief Magistrate, under the same high sanction, though in a different sphere, exercises a public trust. Nor is this all. Every citizen owes to the country a vigilant watch and close scrutiny of its public servants and a fair and reasonable estimate of their fidelity and usefulness. Thus is the people's will impressed upon the whole framework of our civil polity—municipal, State, and Federal; and this is the price of our liberty and the inspiration of our faith in the Republic.

It is the duty of those serving the people in public place to closely limit public expenditures to the actual needs of the Government economically administered, because this bounds the right of the Government to exact tribute from the earnings of labor or the property of the citizen, and because public extravagance begets extravagance among the people. We should never be ashamed of the simplicity and prudential economies which are best suited to the operation of a republican form of government and most compatible with the mission of the American people. Those who are selected for a limited time to manage public affairs are still of the people, and may do much by

Every citizen owes to the country a vigilant watch and close scrutiny of its public servants...

their example to encourage, consistently with the dignity of their official functions, that plain way of life which among their fellow-citizens aids integrity and promotes thrift and prosperity.

The genius of our institutions, the needs of our people in their home life, and the attention which is demanded for the settlement and development of the resources of our vast territory dictate the scrupulous avoidance of any departure from that foreign policy commended by the history, the traditions, and the prosperity of our Republic. It is the policy of independence, favored by our position and defended by our known love of justice and by our power. It is the policy of peace suitable to our interests. It is the policy of neutrality, rejecting any share in foreign broils and ambitions upon other continents and repelling their intrusion here. It is the policy of Monroe and of Washington and Jefferson—"Peace, com-

merce, and honest friendship with all nations; entangling alliance with none."

A due regard for the interests and prosperity of all the people demands that our finances shall be established upon such a sound and sensible basis as shall secure the safety and confidence of business interests and make the wage of labor sure and steady, and that our system of revenue shall be so adjusted as to relieve the people of unnecessary taxation, having a due regard to the interests of capital invested and workingmen employed in American industries, and preventing the accumulation of a surplus in the Treasury to tempt extravagance and waste.

Care for the property of the nation and for the needs of future settlers requires that the public domain should be protected from purloining schemes and unlawful occupation.

The conscience of the people demands that the Indians within our boundaries shall be fairly and honestly treated as wards of the Government and their education and civilization promoted with a view to their ultimate citizenship, and that polygamy in the Territories, destructive of the family relation and offensive to the moral sense of the civilized world, shall be repressed.

The laws should be rigidly enforced which prohibit the immigration of a servile class to compete with American labor, with no intention of acquiring citizenship, and bringing with them and retaining habits and customs repugnant to our civilization.

The people demand reform in the administration of the Government and the application of business principles to public affairs. As a means to this end, civil-service reform should be in good faith enforced. Our citizens have the right to protection from the incompetency of public employees who hold their places solely as the reward of partisan service, and from the corrupting influence of those

who promise and the vicious methods of those who expect such rewards; and those who worthily seek public employment have the right to insist that merit and competency shall be recognized instead of party subserviency or the surrender of honest political belief.

In the administration of a government pledged to do equal and exact justice to all men there should be no pretext for anxiety touching the protection of the freedmen in their rights or their security in the enjoyment of their privileges under the Constitution and its amendments. All discussion as to their fitness for the place accorded to them as American citizens is idle and unprofitable except as it suggests the necessity for their improvement. The fact that they are citizens entitles them to all the rights due to that relation and charges them with all its duties, obligations, and responsibilities.

These topics and the constant and ever-varying wants of an active and enterprising population may well receive the attention and the patriotic endeavor of all who make and execute the Federal law. Our duties are practical and call for industrious application, an intelligent perception of the claims of public office, and, above all, a firm determination, by united action, to secure to all the people of the land the full benefits of the best form of government ever vouchsafed to man. And let us not trust to human effort alone, but humbly acknowledging the power and goodness of Almighty God, who presides over the destiny of nations, and who has at all times been revealed in our country's history, let us invoke His aid and His blessings upon our labors.

***

1888 BENJAMIN HARRISON

ALTHOUGH GROVER CLEVELAND was renominated easily, his scrupulous honesty hadn't made him popular with everybody. He'd lost support among farmers with his opposition to drought relief and alienated Civil War veterans, a large and important constituency, with his vetoes of so many veterans' pension bills. The Republicans took advantage of this as best they could, nominating Benjamin Harrison of Indiana, Tippecanoe's grandson and a Civil War brigadier. Harrison's war record was somewhat inflated, but it easily outpaced that of Cleveland, who had hired a substitute.

Cleveland ran on a platform advocating lower tariff rates—which put most business leaders (and northern workers), scared of foreign competition, firmly in the Republican column. Also, to win back the Irish Catholics who'd bolted the party in 1884, a Republican trickster wrote to the British ambassador, pretended to be of English descent, and asked him which way to vote. Foolishly, Lord Sackville-West responded that the Crown preferred Cleveland.

Publication of this letter inflamed anti–British sentiment among the Irish and hurt Cleveland badly in New York. Also hurting Cleveland in New York was his refusal to channel patronage to Tammany Hall, which denied him use of the machine's numerous campaign workers.

In the general election, the first to use a secret ballot but also the most corrupt yet (featuring widespread vote buying), Harrison lost the popular vote but won in the electoral college anyway. Again, New York made the difference, this time going to the Republicans by fifteen thousand votes out of more than a million cast.

PARTY	POPULAR VOTES	ELECTORAL VOTES
REPUBLICAN Benjamin Harrison, Ind. Levi P. Morton, N.Y.	5,443,892	233
DEMOCRATIC Grover Cleveland, N.Y. Allen G. Thurman, Ohio	5,534,488	168
PROHIBITION Clinton B. Fisk, N.J. John A. Brooks, Mo.	249,819	

Inaugural Address • Washington, D.C. • Monday, March 4, 1889

Fellow-Citizens: There is no constitutional or legal requirement that

the President shall take the oath of office in the presence of the people, but there is so manifest an appropriateness in the public induction to office of the chief executive officer of the nation that from the beginning of the Government the people, to whose service the official oath consecrates the officer, have been called to witness the solemn ceremonial. The oath taken in the presence of the people becomes a mutual covenant. The officer covenants to serve the whole body of the people by a faithful execution of the laws, so that they may be the unfailing defense and security of those who respect and observe them, and that neither wealth, station, nor the power of combinations shall be able to evade their just penalties or to wrest them from a beneficent public purpose to serve the ends of cruelty or selfishness.

My promise is spoken; yours unspoken, but not the less real and solemn. The people of every State have here their representatives. Surely I do not misinterpret the spirit of the occasion when I assume that the whole body of the people covenant with me and with each other to-day to support and

defend the Constitution and the Union of the States, to yield willing obedience to all the laws and each to every other citizen his equal civil and political rights. Entering thus solemnly into covenant with each other, we may reverently invoke and confidently expect the favor and help of Almighty God—that He will give to me wisdom, strength, and fidelity, and to our people a spirit of fraternity and a love of righteousness and peace.

This occasion derives peculiar interest from the fact that the Presidential term which begins this day is the twenty-sixth under our Constitution. The first inauguration of President Washington took place in New York, where Congress was then sitting, on the 30th day of April, 1789, having been deferred by reason of delays attending the organization of the Congress and the canvass of the electoral vote. Our people have already worthily observed the centennials of the Declaration of Independence, of the battle of Yorktown, and of the adoption of the Constitution, and will shortly celebrate in New York the institution of the second

great department of our constitutional scheme of government. When the centennial of the institution of the judicial department, by the organization of the Supreme Court, shall have been suitably observed, as I trust it will be, our nation will have fully entered its second century.

I will not attempt to note the marvelous and in great part happy contrasts between our country as it steps over the threshold into its second century of organized existence under the Constitution and that weak but wisely ordered young nation that looked undauntedly down the first century, when all its years stretched out before it.

Our people will not fail at this time to recall the incidents which accompanied the institution of government under the Constitution, or to find inspiration and guidance in the teachings and example of Washington and his great associates, and hope and courage in the contrast which thirty-eight populous and prosperous States offer to the thirteen States, weak in everything except courage and the love of liberty, that then fringed our Atlantic seaboard.

The Territory of Dakota has now a population greater than any of the original States (except Virginia) and greater than the aggregate of five of the smaller States in 1790. The center of population when our national capital was located was east of Baltimore, and it was argued by many well-informed persons that it would move eastward rather than westward; yet in 1880 it was found to be near Cincinnati, and the new census about to be taken will show another stride to the westward. That which was the body has come to be only the rich fringe of the nation's robe. But our growth has not been limited to territory, population and aggregate wealth, marvelous as it has been in each of those directions. The masses of our people are better fed, clothed, and housed than their fathers were. The facilities for popular education have been vastly enlarged and more generally diffused.

The virtues of courage and patriotism have given recent proof of their continued presence and increasing power in the hearts and over the lives of our people. The influences of religion have been multiplied and strengthened. The sweet offices of charity have greatly increased. The virtue of temperance is held in higher estimation. We have not attained an ideal condition. Not all of our people are happy and prosperous; not all of them are virtuous and law-abiding. But on the whole the opportunities offered to the individual to secure the comforts of life are better than are found elsewhere and largely better than they were here one hundred years ago.

The surrender of a large measure of sovereignty to the General Government, effected by the adoption of the Constitution, was not accomplished until the suggestions of reason were strongly reenforced by the more imperative voice of experience. The divergent interests of peace speedily demanded a "more perfect union." The merchant, the shipmaster, and the manufacturer discovered and disclosed to our statesmen and to the people that commercial emancipation must be added to the political freedom which had been so bravely won. The commercial policy of the mother country had not relaxed any of its hard and oppressive features. To hold in check the development of our commercial marine, to prevent or retard the establishment and growth of manufactures in the States, and so to secure the American market for their shops and the carrying trade for their ships, was the policy of European statesmen, and was pursued with the most selfish vigor.

Petitions poured in upon Congress urging the imposition of discriminating duties that should encourage the production of needed things at home. The patriotism of the people, which no longer found afield of exercise in war, was energetically directed to the duty of equipping the young Republic for the defense of its independence by making its people self-dependent. Societies for the promotion of home manufactures and for encouraging the use of domestics in the dress of the people were organized in many of the States. The revival at the end of the century of the same patriotic interest in the preservation and development of domestic industries and the defense of our working people against injurious foreign competition is an incident worthy of attention. It is not a departure but a return that we have witnessed. The protective policy had then its opponents. The argument was made, as now, that its benefits inured to particular classes or sections.

If the question became in any sense or at any time sectional, it was only because slavery existed in some of the States. But for this there was no reason why the cotton-producing States should not have led or walked abreast with the New England States in the production of cotton fabrics. There was this reason only why the States that divide with Pennsylvania the mineral treasures of the great southeastern and central mountain ranges should have been so tardy in bringing to the smelting furnace and to the mill the coal and iron from their near opposing hillsides. Mill fires were lighted at the funeral pile of slavery. The emancipation proclamation was heard in the depths of the earth as well as in the sky; men were made free, and material things became our better servants.

The sectional element has happily been eliminated from the tariff discussion. We have no longer States that are necessarily only planting States. None are excluded from achieving that diversification of pursuits among the people which brings wealth and contentment. The cotton plantation will not be less valuable when the product is spun in the country town by operatives whose necessities call for diversified crops and create a home demand for garden and agricultural products. Every new mine, furnace, and factory is an extension of the productive capacity of the State more real and valuable than added territory.

Shall the prejudices and paralysis of slavery continue to hang upon the skirts of progress? How long will those who rejoice that slavery no longer exists cherish or tolerate the incapacities it put upon their communities? I look hopefully to the continuance of our protective system and to the consequent development of manufacturing and mining enterprises in the States hitherto wholly given to agriculture as a potent influence in the perfect unification of our people. The men who have invested their capital in these enterprises, the farmers who have felt the benefit of their neighborhood, and the men who work in shop or field will not fail to find and to defend a community of interest.

Is it not quite possible that the farmers and the promoters of the great mining and manufacturing enterprises which have recently been established in the South may yet find that the free ballot of the working-

---

I do not mistrust the future.

---

man, without distinction of race, is needed for their defense as well as for his own? I do not doubt that if those men in the South who now accept the tariff views of Clay and the constitutional expositions of Webster would courageously avow and defend their real convictions they would not find it difficult, by friendly instruction and cooperation, to make the black man their efficient and safe ally, not only in establishing correct principles in our national administration, but in preserving for their local communities the benefits of social order and economical and honest government. At least until the good offices of kindness and education have been fairly tried the contrary conclusion can not be plausibly urged.

I have altogether rejected the suggestion of a special Executive policy for any section of our country. It is the duty of the Executive to administer and enforce in the methods and by the instrumentalities pointed out and provided by the Constitution all the laws enacted by Congress. These laws are general and their administration should be uniform and equal. As a citizen may not elect what laws he will obey, neither may the Executive eject which he will enforce. The duty to obey and to execute embraces the Constitution in its entirety and the whole code of laws enacted under it. The evil example of permitting individuals, corporations, or communities to nullify the laws because they cross some selfish or local interest or prejudices is full of danger, not only to the nation at large, but much more to those who use this pernicious expedient to escape their just obligations or to obtain an unjust advantage over others. They will presently themselves be compelled to appeal to the law for protection, and those who would use the law as a defense must not deny that use of it to others.

If our great corporations would more scrupulously observe their legal limitations and duties, they would have less cause to complain of the unlawful limitations of their rights or of violent interference with their operations. The community that by concert, open or secret, among its citizens denies to a portion of its members their plain rights under the law has severed the only safe bond of social order and prosperity. The evil works from a bad center both ways. It demoralizes those who practice it and destroys the faith of those who suffer by it in the efficiency of the law as a safe protector. The man in whose breast that faith has been darkened is naturally the subject of dangerous and uncanny suggestions. Those who use unlawful methods, if moved by no higher motive than the selfishness that prompted them, may well stop and inquire what is to be the end of this.

An unlawful expedient can not become a permanent condition of government. If the educated and influential classes in a community either practice or connive at the systematic violation of laws that seem to them to cross their convenience, what can they expect when the lesson that convenience or a supposed class interest is a sufficient cause for lawlessness has been well learned by the ignorant classes? A community where law is the rule of conduct and where courts, not mobs, execute its penalties is the only attractive field for business investments and honest labor.

Our naturalization laws should be so amended as to make the inquiry into the character and good disposition of persons applying for citizenship

more careful and searching. Our existing laws have been in their administration an unimpressive and often an unintelligible form. We accept the man as a citizen without any knowledge of his fitness, and he assumes the duties of citizenship without any knowledge as to what they are. The privileges of American citizenship are so great and its duties so grave that we may well insist upon a good knowledge of every person applying for citizenship and a good knowledge by him of our institutions. We should not cease to be hospitable to immigration,

but we should cease to be careless as to the character of it. There are men of all races, even the best, whose coming is necessarily a burden upon our public revenues or a threat to social order. These should be identified and excluded.

We have happily maintained a policy of avoiding all interference with European affairs. We have been only interested spectators of their contentions in diplomacy and in war, ready to use our friendly offices to promote peace, but never obtruding our advice and never attempting unfairly to coin the distresses of other powers into commercial advantage to ourselves. We have a just right to expect that our European policy will be the American policy of European courts.

It is so manifestly incompatible with those precautions for our peace and safety which all the great powers habitually observe and enforce in matters affecting them that a shorter waterway between our eastern and western seaboards should

be dominated by any European Government that we may confidently expect that such a purpose will not be entertained by any friendly power.

We shall in the future, as in the past, use every endeavor to maintain and enlarge our friendly relations with all the great powers, but they will not expect us to look kindly upon any project that would leave us subject to the dangers of a hostile observation or environment. We have not sought to dominate or to absorb any of our weaker neighbors, but rather to aid and encourage them to establish free and stable governments resting upon the consent of their own people. We have a clear right to expect, therefore, that no European Government will seek to establish colonial dependencies upon the territory of these independent American States. That which a sense of justice restrains us from seeking they may be reasonably expected willingly to forego.

It must not be assumed, however, that our interests are so exclusively American that our entire inattention to any events that may transpire elsewhere can be taken for granted. Our citizens domiciled for purposes of trade in all countries and in many of the islands of the sea demand and will have our adequate care in their personal and commercial rights. The necessities of our Navy require convenient coaling stations and dock and harbor privileges. These and other trading privileges we will feel free to obtain only by means that do not in any degree partake of coercion, however feeble the government from which we ask such concessions. But having fairly obtained them by methods and for purposes entirely consistent with the most friendly disposition toward all other powers, our consent will be necessary to any modification

or impairment of the concession.

We shall neither fail to respect the flag of any friendly nation or the just rights of its citizens, nor to exact the like treatment for our own. Calmness, justice, and consideration should characterize our diplomacy. The offices of an intelligent diplomacy or of friendly arbitration in proper cases should be adequate to the peaceful adjustment of all international difficulties. By such methods we will make our contribution to the world's peace, which no nation values more highly, and avoid the opprobrium which must fall upon the nation that ruthlessly breaks it.

The duty devolved by law upon the President to nominate and, by and with the advice and consent of the Senate, to appoint all public officers whose appointment is not otherwise provided for in the Constitution or by act of Congress has become very burdensome and its wise and efficient discharge full of difficulty. The civil list is so large that a personal knowledge of any large number of the applicants is impossible. The President must rely upon the representations of others, and these are often made inconsiderately and without any just sense of responsibility. I have a right, I think, to insist that those who volunteer or are invited to give advice as to appointments shall exercise consideration and fidelity. A high sense of duty and an ambition to improve the service should characterize all public officers.

There are many ways in which the convenience and comfort of those who have business with our public offices may be promoted by a thoughtful and obliging officer, and I shall expect those whom I may appoint to justify their selection by a conspicuous efficiency in the discharge of their duties. Honorable party service will certainly not be esteemed by me a disqualification for public office, but it will in no case be allowed to serve as a shield of official negligence, incompetency, or delinquency. It is entirely creditable to seek public office by proper methods and with proper motives, and all applicants will be treated with consideration; but I shall need, and the heads of Departments will need, time for inquiry and deliberation. Persistent importunity will not, therefore, be the best support of an application for office. Heads of Departments, bureaus, and all other public officers having any duty connected therewith will be expected to enforce the civil-service law fully and without evasion. Beyond this obvious duty I hope to do something more to advance the reform of the civil service. The ideal, or even my own ideal, I shall probably not attain. Retrospect will be a safer basis of judgment than promises. We shall not, however, I am sure, be able to put our civil service upon a nonpartisan basis until we have secured an incumbency that fair-minded men of the opposition will approve for impartiality and integrity. As the number of such in the civil list is increased removals from office will diminish.

While a Treasury surplus is not the greatest evil, it is a serious evil. Our revenue should be ample to meet the ordinary annual demands upon our Treasury, with a sufficient margin for those extraordinary but scarcely less imperative demands which arise now and then. Expenditure should always be made with economy and only upon public necessity. Wastefulness, profligacy, or favoritism in public expenditures is criminal. But there is nothing in the condition of our country or of our people to suggest that anything presently necessary to the public prosperity, security, or honor should be unduly postponed.

It will be the duty of Congress wisely to forecast and estimate these extraordinary demands, and, having added them to our ordinary expenditures, to so adjust our revenue laws that no considerable annual surplus will remain. We will fortunately be able to apply to the redemption of the public debt any small and unforeseen excess of revenue. This is better than to reduce our income below our necessary expenditures, with the resulting choice between another change of our revenue laws and an increase of the public debt. It is quite possible, I am sure, to effect the necessary reduction in our revenues without breaking down our protective tariff or seriously injuring any domestic industry.

The construction of a sufficient number of modern war ships and of their necessary armament should progress as rapidly as is consistent with care and perfection in plans and workmanship. The spirit, courage, and skill of our naval officers and seamen have many times in our history given to weak ships and inefficient guns a rating greatly beyond that of the naval list. That they will again do so upon occasion I do not doubt; but they ought not, by premeditation or neglect, to be left to the risks and exigencies of an unequal combat. We should encourage the establishment of American steamship lines. The exchanges of commerce demand stated, reliable, and rapid means of communication, and until these are provided the development of our trade with the States lying south of us is impossible.

Our pension laws should give more adequate and discriminating relief to the Union soldiers and sailors and to their widows and orphans. Such occasions as this should remind us that we owe everything to their valor and sacrifice.

It is a subject of congratulation that there is a near prospect of the admission into the Union of the Dakotas and Montana and Washington Territories. This act of justice has been unreasonably delayed in the case of some of them. The people who have settled these Territories are intelligent, enterprising, and patriotic, and the accession these new States will add strength to the nation. It is due to the settlers in the Territories who have availed themselves of the invitations of our land laws to make homes upon the public domain that their titles should be speedily adjusted and their honest entries confirmed by patent.

It is very gratifying to observe the general interest now being manifested in the reform of our election laws. Those who have been for years calling attention to the pressing necessity of throwing about the ballot box and about the elector further safeguards, in order that our elections might not only be free and pure, but might clearly appear to be so, will welcome the accession of any who did not so soon discover the need of reform. The National Congress has not as yet taken control of elections in that case over which the Constitution gives it jurisdiction, but has accepted and adopted the election laws of the several States, provided penalties for their violation and a method of supervision. Only the inefficiency of the State laws or an unfair partisan administration of them could suggest a departure from this policy.

It was clearly, however, in the contemplation of the framers of the Constitution that such an exigency might arise, and provision was wisely made for it. The freedom of the ballot is a condition of our national life, and no power vested in Congress or in the Executive to secure or perpetuate it should remain unused upon occasion. The people of all the Congressional districts have an equal interest that the election in each shall truly express the views and wishes of a majority of the qualified electors residing within it. The results of such elections are not local, and the insistence of electors residing in other districts that they shall be pure and free does not savor at all of impertinence.

If in any of the States the public security is thought to be threatened by ignorance among the electors, the obvious remedy is education. The sympathy and help of our people will not be withheld from any community struggling with special embarrassments or difficulties connected with the suffrage if the remedies proposed proceed upon lawful lines and are promoted by just and honorable methods. How shall those who practice election frauds recover that respect for the sanctity of the ballot which is the first condition and obligation of good citizenship? The man who has come to regard the ballot box as a juggler's hat has renounced his allegiance.

Let us exalt patriotism and moderate our party contentions. Let those who would die for the flag on the field of battle give a better proof of their patriotism and a higher glory to their country by promoting fraternity and justice. A party success that is achieved by unfair methods or by practices that partake of revolution is hurtful and evanescent even from a party standpoint. We should hold our differing opinions in mutual respect, and, having submitted them to the arbitrament of the ballot, should accept an adverse judgment with the same respect that we would have demanded of our opponents if the decision had been in our favor.

No other people have a government more worthy of their respect and love or a land so magnificent in extent, so pleasant to look upon, and so full of generous suggestion to enterprise and labor. God has placed upon our head a diadem and has laid at our feet power and wealth beyond definition or calculation. But we must not forget that we take these gifts upon the condition that justice and mercy shall hold the reins of power and that the upward avenues of hope shall be free to all the people.

I do not mistrust the future. Dangers have been in frequent ambush along our path, but we have uncovered and vanquished them all. Passion has swept some of our communities, but only to give us a new demonstration that the great body of our people are stable, patriotic, and law-abiding. No political party can long pursue advantage at the expense of public honor or by rude and indecent methods without protest and fatal disaffection in its own body. The peaceful agencies of commerce are more fully revealing the necessary unity of all our communities, and the increasing intercourse of our people is promoting mutual respect. We shall find unalloyed pleasure in the revelation which our next census will make of the swift development of the great resources of some of the States. Each State will bring its generous contribution to the great aggregate of the nation's increase. And when the harvests from the fields, the cattle from the hills, and the ores of the earth shall have been weighed, counted, and valued, we will turn from them all to crown with the highest honor the State that has most promoted education, virtue, justice, and patriotism among its people.

* * *

1892 GROVER CLEVELAND

BENJAMIN HARRISON'S WEAK performance in office had led to sweeping gains for the Democrats in the 1890 midterm elections, yet Harrison was renominated in 1892 without much opposition. Once again, he faced Grover Cleveland, who chose a silverite as his running mate in the hope of unifying the Democrats. The People's party, organized in 1891, chose James B. Weaver of Iowa as its first presidential candidate.

While Cleveland vehemently attacked the McKinley Tariff of 1890, the Republicans defended its exorbitantly high rates and warned voters of the danger posed by Cleveland's "free-trade tendencies." Meanwhile, the People's party, also known as the Populists, attacked both candidates as tools of Wall Street. Cleveland spent more money, had more enthusiastic campaign workers, and won the labor vote by condemning government interference with legitimate union organizing. The Populists pulled farm votes away from both candidates, but more from Harrison than from Cleveland, who won the election

PARTY	POPULAR VOTES	ELECTORAL VOTES
DEMOCRATIC Grover Cleveland, N.Y. Adlai E. Stevenson, Ill.	5,551,883	277
REPUBLICAN Benjamin Harrison, Ind. Whitelaw Reid, N.Y.	5,179,244	145
PEOPLE'S James B. Weaver, Iowa James G. Field, Va.	1,024,280	22
PROHIBITION John Bidwell, Calif. James B. Cranfill, Tex.	270,770	

with merely a plurality of the popular vote but a sizable electoral majority. For a new party, the Populists did remarkably well, carrying four western states and demonstrating that voters' concerns about the currency and the tariff reflected much deeper fears of corporate influence in American politics.

Second Inaugural Address • Washington, D.C. • Saturday, March 4, 1893

My Fellow-Citizens: In obedience of the mandate of my countrymen I am

am about to dedicate myself to their service under the sanction of a solemn oath. Deeply moved by the expression of confidence and personal attachment which has called me to this service, I am sure my gratitude can make no better return than the pledge I now give before God and these witnesses of unreserved and complete devotion to the interests and welfare of those who have honored me.

I deem it fitting on this occasion, while indicating the opinion I hold concerning public questions of present importance, to also briefly refer to the existence of certain conditions and tendencies among our people which seem to menace the integrity and usefulness of their Government.

While every American citizen must contemplate with the utmost pride and enthusiasm the growth and expansion of our country, the sufficiency of our institutions to stand against the rudest shocks of violence, the wonderful thrift and enterprise of our people,

and the demonstrated superiority of our free government, it behooves us to constantly watch for every symptom of insidious infirmity that threatens our national vigor.

The strong man who in the confidence of sturdy health courts the sternest activities of life and rejoices in the hardihood of constant labor may still have lurking near his vitals the unheeded disease that dooms him to sudden collapse.

It can not be doubted that our stupendous achievements as a people and our country's robust strength have given rise to heedlessness of those laws governing our national health which we can no more evade than human life can escape the laws of God and nature.

Manifestly nothing is more vital to our supremacy as a nation and to the beneficent purposes of our Government than a sound and stable currency. Its exposure to degradation should at once arouse to activity the

most enlightened statesmanship, and the danger of depreciation in the purchasing power of the wages paid to toil should furnish the strongest incentive to prompt and conservative precaution.

In dealing with our present embarrassing situation as related to this subject we will be wise if we temper our confidence and faith in our national strength and resources with the frank concession that even these will not permit us to defy with impunity the inexorable laws of finance and trade. At the same time, in our efforts to adjust differences of opinion we should be free from intolerance or passion, and our judgments should be unmoved by alluring phrases and unvexed by selfish interests.

I am confident that such an approach to the subject will result in prudent and effective remedial legislation. In the meantime, so far as the executive branch of the Government can intervene, none of the powers with which it is invested will be withheld when their exercise is deemed necessary to maintain our national credit or avert financial disaster.

Closely related to the exaggerated confidence in our country's greatness which tends to a disregard of the rules of national safety, another danger confronts us not less serious. I refer to the prevalence of a popular disposition to expect from the operation of the Government especial and direct individual advantages.

The verdict of our voters which condemned the injustice of maintaining protection for protection's sake enjoins upon the people's servants the duty of exposing and destroying the

> *Manifestly nothing is more vital to our supremacy as a nation...than a sound and stable currency.*

brood of kindred evils which are the unwholesome progeny of paternalism. This is the bane of republican institutions and the constant peril of our government by the people. It degrades to the purposes of wily craft the plan of rule our fathers established and bequeathed to us as an object of our love and veneration. It perverts the patriotic sentiments of our countrymen and tempts them to pitiful calculation of the sordid gain to be derived from their Government's maintenance. It undermines the self-reliance of our people and substitutes in its place dependence upon governmental favoritism. It stifles the spirit of true Americanism and stupefies every ennobling trait of American citizenship.

The lessons of paternalism ought to be unlearned and the better lesson taught that while the people should patriotically and cheerfully support their Government its functions do not include the support of the people.

The acceptance of this principle leads to a refusal of bounties and subsidies, which burden the labor and thrift of a portion of our citizens to aid ill-advised or languishing enterprises in which they have no concern. It leads also to a challenge of wild and reckless pension expenditure, which overleaps the bounds of grateful recognition of patriotic service and prostitutes to vicious uses the people's prompt and generous impulse to aid those disabled in their country's defense.

Every thoughtful American must realize the importance of checking at its beginning any tendency in public or private station to regard frugality and economy as virtues which we may safely outgrow. The toleration of this idea results in the waste of the people's money by their chosen servants and encourages prodigality and extravagance in the home life of our countrymen.

Under our scheme of government the waste of public money is a crime against the citizen, and the contempt of our people for economy and frugality in their personal affairs deplorably saps the strength and sturdiness of our national character.

It is a plain dictate of honesty and good government that public expenditures should be limited by public necessity, and that this should be measured by the rules of strict economy; and it is equally clear that frugality among the people is the best guaranty of a contented and strong support of free institutions.

One mode of the misappropriation of public funds is avoided when appointments to office, instead of being the rewards of partisan activity, are awarded to those whose efficiency promises a fair return of work for the compensation paid to them. To secure the fitness and competency of appointees to office and remove from political action the demoralizing madness for spoils, civil-service reform has found a place in our public policy and laws. The benefits already gained through this instrumentality and the further usefulness it promises entitle it to the hearty support and encouragement of all who desire to see our public service

well performed or who hope for the elevation of political sentiment and the purification of political methods.

The existence of immense aggregations of kindred enterprises and combinations of business interests formed for the purpose of limiting production and fixing prices is inconsistent with the fair field which ought to be open to every independent activity. Legitimate strife in business should not be superseded by an enforced concession to the demands of combinations that have the power to destroy, nor should the people to be served lose the benefit of cheapness which usually results from wholesome competition. These aggregations and combinations frequently constitute conspiracies against the interests of the people, and in all their phases they are unnatural and opposed to our American sense of fairness. To the extent that they can be reached and restrained by Federal power the General Government should relieve our citizens from their interference and exactions.

Loyalty to the principles upon which our Government rests positively demands that the equality before the law which it guarantees to every citizen should be justly and in good faith conceded in all parts of the land. The enjoyment of this right follows the badge of citizenship wherever found, and, unimpaired by race or color, it appeals for recognition to American manliness and fairness.

Our relations with the Indians located within our border impose upon us responsibilities we can not escape. Humanity and consistency require us to treat them with forbearance and in our dealings with them to honestly and considerately regard their rights and interests. Every effort should be made to lead them, through the paths of civilization and education, to self-supporting and independent citizenship. In the meantime, as the nation's wards, they should be promptly defended against the cupidity of designing men and shielded from every influence or temptation that retards their advancement.

The people of the United States have decreed that on this day the control of their Government in its legislative and executive branches shall be given to a political party pledged in the most positive terms to the accomplishment of tariff reform. They have thus determined in favor of a more just and equitable system of Federal taxation. The agents they have chosen to carry out their purposes are

bound by their promises not less than by the command of their masters to devote themselves unremittingly to this service.

While there should be no surrender of principle, our task must be undertaken wisely and without heedless vindictiveness. Our mission is not punishment, but the rectification of wrong. If in lifting burdens from the daily life of our people we reduce inordinate and unequal advantages too long enjoyed, this is but a necessary incident of our return to right and justice. If we exact from unwilling minds ac-

quiescence in the theory of an honest distribution of the fund of the governmental beneficence treasured up for all, we but insist upon a principle which underlies our free institutions. When we tear aside the delusions and misconceptions which have blinded our countrymen to their condition under vicious tariff laws, we but show them how far they have been led away from the paths of contentment and prosperity. When we proclaim that the necessity for revenue to support the Government furnishes the only justification for taxing the people, we announce a truth so plain that its denial would seem to indicate the extent to which judgment may be influenced by familiarity with perversions of the taxing power. And when we seek to reinstate the self-confidence and business enterprise of our citizens by discrediting an abject dependence upon governmental favor, we strive to stimulate those elements of American character which support the hope of American achievement.

Anxiety for the redemption of the pledges which my party has made and solicitude for the complete justification of the trust the people have reposed in us constrain me to remind those with whom I am to cooperate that we can succeed in doing the work which has been especially set before us only by the most sincere, harmonious, and disinterested effort. Even if insuperable obstacles and opposition prevent the consummation of our task, we shall hardly be excused; and if failure can be traced to our fault or neglect we may be sure the people will hold us to a swift and exacting accountability.

The oath I now take to preserve, protect, and defend the Constitution of the United States not only impressively defines the great responsibility I assume, but suggests obedi-

ence to constitutional commands as the rule by which my official conduct must be guided. I shall to the best of my ability and within my sphere of duty preserve the Constitution by loyally protecting every grant of Federal power it contains, by defending all its restraints when attacked by impatience and restlessness, and by enforcing its limitations and reservations in favor of the States and the people.

Fully impressed with the gravity of the duties that confront me and mindful of my weakness, I should be appalled if it were my lot to bear unaided the responsibilities which await me. I am, however, saved from discouragement when I remember that I shall have the support and the counsel and cooperation of wise and patriotic men who will stand at my side in Cabinet places or will represent the people in their legislative halls.

I find also much comfort in remembering that my countrymen are just and generous and in the assurance that they will not condemn those who by sincere devotion to their service deserve their forbearance and approval.

Above all, I know there is a Supreme Being who rules the affairs of men and whose goodness and mercy have always followed the American people, and I know He will not turn from us now if we humbly and reverently seek His powerful aid.

* * *

1896 WILLIAM MCKINLEY

GROVER CLEVELAND'S USE OF the army to break up the 1894 railroad strike and his insistence on the gold standard made him terrifically unpopular. This became clear during the 1894 midterm elections, when the Republicans picked up more than a hundred seats in the House and won control of the Senate as well. By the time the Democrats convened in 1896, Cleveland's goldbugs were in retreat, and the populist silverites had seized control of the party. Once thirty-six-year-old William Jennings Bryan of Nebraska delivered his thrilling "Cross of Gold" speech to the delegates, it became impossible to deny him the nomination.

Opposing Bryan was Ohio governor William McKinley, who ran on a platform endorsing the gold standard and advocating high tariffs. McKinley's stance against bimetallism led to the defection of some western Republicans, but campaign manager Mark Hanna clearly understood that McKinley's core constituencies would be business and labor. The Republicans promised workers in particular that protective tariffs would ensure domestic prosperity and a "full dinner pail."

Bryan stumped the country, making dozens of speeches a day, while McKinley sat on his front porch in Canton, Ohio, and received delegations of party workers, encouraging them in their efforts to distribute campaign buttons and get out the vote. Mark Hanna paid for all of this with the first systematic campaign fundraising, extracting millions of dollars from corporations scared by the populist surge.

With such a huge financial advantage, McKinley was able to hold the entire industrial North and Midwest, where enough Americans lived to give him a sizable electoral majority.

PARTY	POPULAR VOTES	ELECTORAL VOTES
REPUBLICAN William McKinley, Ohio Garret A. Hobart, N.J.	7,108,480	271
DEMOCRATIC William Jennings Bryan, Neb. Arthur Sewall, Me.	6,511,495	149
PEOPLE'S William Jennings Bryan, Neb. Thomas E. Watson, Ga.		27

First Inaugural Address · Washington, D.C. · Thursday, March 4, 1897

Fellow-Citizens: In obedience to the will of the people, and in their presence,

by the authority vested in me by this oath, I assume the arduous and responsible duties of President of the United States, relying upon the support of my countrymen and invoking the guidance of Almighty God. Our faith teaches that there is no safer reliance than upon the God of our fathers, who has so singularly favored the American people in every national trial, and who will not forsake us so long as we obey His commandments and walk humbly in His footsteps.

The responsibilities of the high trust to which I have been called—always of grave importance—are augmented by the prevailing business conditions entailing idleness upon willing labor and loss to useful enterprises. The country is suffering from industrial disturbances from which speedy relief must be had. Our financial system needs some revision; our money is all good now, but its value must not further be threatened. It should all be put upon an enduring basis, not subject to easy attack, nor its stability to

doubt or dispute. Our currency should continue under the supervision of the Government. The several forms of our paper money offer, in my judgment, a constant embarrassment to the Government and a safe balance in the Treasury. Therefore I believe it necessary to devise a system which, without diminishing the circulating medium or offering a premium for its contraction, will present a remedy for those arrangements which, temporary in their nature, might well in the years of our prosperity have been displaced by wiser provisions. With adequate revenue secured, but not until then, we can enter upon such changes in our fiscal laws as will, while insuring safety and volume to our money, no longer impose upon the Government the necessity of maintaining so large a gold reserve, with its attendant and inevitable temptations to speculation. Most of our financial laws are the outgrowth of experience and trial, and should not be amended without investigation and demonstration of

the wisdom of the proposed changes. We must be both "sure we are right" and "make haste slowly." If, therefore, Congress, in its wisdom, shall deem it expedient to create a commission to take under early consideration the revision of our coinage, banking and currency laws, and give them that exhaustive, careful and dispassionate examination that their importance demands, I shall cordially concur in such action. If such power be vested in the President, it is my purpose to appoint a commission of prominent, well-informed citizens of different parties, who will command public confidence, both on account of their ability and special fitness for the work. Business experience and public training may thus be combined, and the patriotic zeal of the friends of the country be so directed that such a report will be made as to receive the support of all parties, and our finances cease to be the subject of mere partisan contention. The experiment is, at all events, worth a trial, and, in my opinion, it

every form of direct taxation, except in time of war. The country is clearly opposed to any needless additions to the subject of internal taxation, and is committed by its latest popular utterance to the system of tariff taxation. There can be no misunderstanding, either, about the principle upon which this tariff taxation shall be levied. Nothing has ever been made plainer at a general election than that the controlling principle in the raising of revenue from duties on imports is zealous care for American interests and American labor. The

can but prove beneficial to the entire country.

The question of international bimetallism will have early and earnest attention. It will be my constant endeavor to secure it by co-operation with the other great commercial powers of the world. Until that condition is realized when the parity between our gold and silver money springs from and is supported by the relative value of the two metals, the value of the silver already coined and of that which may hereafter be coined, must be kept constantly at par with gold by every resource at our command. The credit of the Government, the integrity of its currency, and the inviolability of its obligations must be preserved. This was the commanding verdict of the people, and it will not be unheeded.

Economy is demanded in every branch of the Government at all times, but especially in periods, like the present, of depression in business and distress among the people. The severest economy must be observed in all public expenditures, and extravagance stopped wherever it is found, and prevented wherever in the future it may be developed. If the revenues are to remain as now, the only relief that can come must be from decreased expenditures. But the present must not become the permanent condition of the Government. It has been our uniform practice to retire, not increase our outstanding obligations, and this policy must again

be resumed and vigorously enforced. Our revenues should always be large enough to meet with ease and promptness not only our current needs and the principal and interest of the public debt, but to make proper and liberal provision for that most deserving body of public creditors, the soldiers and sailors

War should never be entered upon until every agency of peace has failed....

and the widows and orphans who are the pensioners of the United States.

The Government should not be permitted to run behind or increase its debt in times like the present. Suitably to provide against this is the mandate of duty—the certain and easy remedy for most of our financial difficulties. A deficiency is inevitable so long as the expenditures of the Government exceed its receipts. It can only be met by loans or an increased revenue. While a large annual surplus of revenue may invite waste and extravagance, inadequate revenue creates distrust and undermines public and private credit. Neither

should be encouraged. Between more loans and more revenue there ought to be but one opinion. We should have more revenue, and that without delay, hindrance, or postponement. A surplus in the Treasury created by loans is not a permanent or safe reliance. It will suffice while it lasts, but it can not last long while the outlays of the Government are greater than its receipts, as has been the case during the past two years. Nor must it be forgotten that however much such loans may temporarily relieve the situation, the Government is still indebted for the amount of the surplus thus accrued, which it must ultimately pay, while its ability to pay is not strengthened, but weakened by a continued deficit. Loans are imperative in great emergencies to preserve the Government or its credit, but a failure to supply needed revenue in time of peace for the maintenance of either has no justification.

The best way for the Government to maintain its credit is to pay as it goes—not by resorting to loans, but by keeping out of debt—through an adequate income secured by a system of taxation, external or internal, or both. It is the settled policy of the Government, pursued from the beginning and practiced by all parties and Administrations, to raise the bulk of our revenue from taxes upon foreign productions entering the United States for sale and consumption, and avoiding, for the most part,

people have declared that such legislation should be had as will give ample protection and encouragement to the industries and the development of our country. It is, therefore, earnestly hoped and expected that Congress will, at the earliest practicable moment, enact revenue legislation that shall be fair, reasonable, conservative, and just, and which, while supplying sufficient revenue for public purposes, will still be signally beneficial and helpful to every section and every enterprise of the people. To this policy we are all, of whatever party, firmly bound by the voice of the people—a power vastly more potential than the expression of any political platform. The paramount duty of Congress is to stop deficiencies by the restoration of that protective legislation which has always been the firmest prop of the Treasury. The passage of such a law or laws would strengthen the credit of the Government both at home and abroad, and go far toward stopping the drain upon the gold reserve held for the redemption of our currency, which has been heavy and well-nigh constant for several years.

In the revision of the tariff especial attention should be given to the re-enactment and extension of the reciprocity principle of the law of 1890, under which so great a stimulus was given to our foreign trade in new and advantageous markets for our surplus agricultural and manufactured products. The brief trial given this legislation amply justifies a further experiment and additional discretionary power in the making of commercial treaties, the end in view always to be the opening up of new markets for the products of our country, by granting concessions to the products of other lands that we need and cannot produce ourselves, and which do not involve any loss of labor to our own people, but tend to increase their employment.

The depression of the past four years has fallen with especial severity upon the great body of toilers of the country, and upon none more than the holders of small farms. Agriculture has languished and labor suffered. The revival of manufacturing will be a relief to both. No portion of our population is more devoted to the institution of free government nor more loyal in their support, while none bears more cheerfully or fully its proper share in the maintenance of the Government or is better entitled to its wise and liberal care and protection. Legislation helpful to producers is beneficial to all. The depressed condition of industry on the farm and in the mine and factory has lessened the ability of the people to meet the demands upon them, and they rightfully expect that not only a system of revenue shall be established that will secure the largest income with the least burden, but that every means will be taken to decrease, rather than increase, our public expenditures. Business conditions are not the most promising. It will take time to restore the prosperity of former years. If we cannot promptly attain it, we can resolutely turn our faces in that direction and aid its return by friendly legislation. However troublesome the situation may appear, Congress will not, I am sure, be found lacking in disposition or ability to relieve it as far as legislation can do so. The restoration of confidence and the revival of business, which

men of all parties so much desire, depend more largely upon the prompt, energetic, and intelligent action of Congress than upon any other single agency affecting the situation.

It is inspiring, too, to remember that no great emergency in the one hundred and eight years of our eventful national life has ever arisen that has not been met with wisdom and courage by the American people, with fidelity to their best interests and highest destiny, and to the honor of the American name. These years of glorious history have exalted mankind and advanced the cause of freedom throughout the world, and immeasurably strengthened the precious free institutions which we enjoy. The people love and will sustain these institutions. The great essential to our happiness and prosperity is that we adhere to the principles upon which the Government was established and insist upon their faithful observance. Equality of rights must prevail, and our laws be always and everywhere respected and obeyed. We may

have failed in the discharge of our full duty as citizens of the great Republic, but it is consoling and encouraging to realize that free speech, a free press, free thought, free schools, the free and unmolested right of religious liberty and worship, and free and fair elections are dearer and more universally enjoyed to-day than ever before. These guaranties must be sacredly preserved and wisely strengthened. The constituted authorities must be cheerfully and vigorously upheld. Lynch-

ings must not be tolerated in a great and civilized country like the United States; courts, not mobs, must execute the penalties of the law. The preservation of public order, the right of discussion, the integrity of courts, and the orderly administration of justice must continue forever the rock of safety upon which our Government securely rests.

One of the lessons taught by the late election, which all can rejoice in, is that the citizens of the United States are both law-respecting and law-abiding people, not easily swerved from the path of patriotism and honor. This is in entire accord with the genius of our institutions, and but emphasizes the advantages of inculcating even a greater love for law and order in the future. Immunity should be granted to none who violate the laws, whether individuals, corporations, or communities; and as the Constitution imposes upon the President the duty of both its own execution, and of the statutes enacted in pursuance of its provisions, I shall endeavor carefully to carry them into effect. The declaration of the party now restored to power has been in the past that of "opposition to all combinations of capital organized in trusts, or otherwise, to control arbitrarily the condition of trade among our citizens," and it has supported "such legislation as will prevent the execution of all schemes to oppress the people by undue charges on their supplies, or by unjust rates for the transportation of their products to the market." This purpose will be steadily pursued, both by the enforcement of the laws now in existence and the recommendation and support of such new statutes as may be necessary to carry it into effect.

Our naturalization and immigration laws should be further improved to the constant promotion of a safer, a better, and a higher citizenship. A grave peril to the Republic would be a citizenship too ignorant to understand or too vicious to appreciate the great value and beneficence of our in-

stitutions and laws, and against all who come here to make war upon them our gates must be promptly and tightly closed. Nor must we be unmindful of the need of improvement among our own citizens, but with the zeal of our forefathers encourage the spread of knowledge and free education. Illiteracy must be banished from the land if we shall attain that high destiny as the foremost of the enlightened nations of the world which, under Providence, we ought to achieve.

Reforms in the civil service must go on; but the changes should be real and genuine, not perfunctory, or prompted by a zeal in behalf of any party simply because it happens to be in power. As a member of Congress I voted and spoke in favor of the present law, and I shall attempt its enforcement in the spirit in which it was enacted. The purpose in view was to secure the most efficient service of the best men who would accept appointment under the Government, retaining faithful and devoted public servants in office, but shielding none, under the authority of any rule or custom, who are inefficient, incompetent, or unworthy. The best interests of the country demand this, and the people heartily approve the law wherever and whenever it has been thus administrated.

Congress should give prompt attention to the restoration of our American merchant marine, once the pride of the seas in all the great ocean highways of commerce. To my mind, few more important subjects so imperatively demand its intelligent consideration. The United States has progressed with marvelous rapidity in every field of enterprise and endeavor until we have become foremost in nearly all the great lines of inland trade, commerce, and industry. Yet, while this is true, our American merchant marine has been steadily declining until it is now lower, both in the percentage of tonnage and the number of vessels employed, than it was prior to the Civil War. Commendable progress has been made of late years in the upbuilding of the American Navy, but we must supplement these efforts by providing as a proper consort for it a merchant marine amply sufficient for our own carrying trade to foreign countries. The question is one that appeals both to our business necessities and the patriotic aspirations of a great people.

It has been the policy of the United States since the foundation of the Government to cultivate relations of peace and amity with all the nations of the world, and this accords with my conception of our duty now. We have cherished the policy of non-interference with affairs of foreign governments wisely inaugurated by Washington, keeping ourselves free from entanglement, either as allies or foes, content to leave undisturbed with them the settlement of their own domestic concerns. It will be our aim to pursue a firm and dignified foreign policy, which shall be just, impartial, ever watchful of our national honor, and always insisting upon the enforcement of the lawful rights of American citizens everywhere. Our diplomacy should seek nothing more and accept nothing less than is due us. We want no wars of conquest; we must avoid the temptation of territorial aggression. War should never be entered upon until every agency of peace has failed; peace is preferable to war in almost every contingency. Arbitration is the true method of settlement of international as well as local or individual differences. It was recognized as the best means of adjustment of differences between employers and employees by the Forty-ninth Congress, in 1886, and its application was extended to our diplomatic relations by the unanimous concurrence of the Senate and House of the Fifty-first Congress in 1890. The latter resolution was accepted as the basis of negotiations with us by the British House of Commons in 1893, and upon our invitation a treaty of arbitration between the United States and Great Britain was signed at Washington and transmitted to the Senate for its ratification in January last. Since this treaty is clearly the result of our own initiative; since it has been recognized as the leading feature of our foreign policy throughout our entire national history—the adjustment of difficulties by judicial methods rather than force

of arms—and since it presents to the world the glorious example of reason and peace, not passion and war, controlling the relations between two of the greatest nations in the world, an example certain to be followed by others, I respectfully urge the early action of the Senate thereon, not merely as a matter of policy, but as a duty to mankind. The importance and moral influence of the ratification of such a treaty can hardly be overestimated in the cause of advancing civilization. It may well engage the best thought of the statesmen and people of every country, and I cannot but consider it fortunate that it was reserved to the United States to have the leadership in so grand a work.

It has been the uniform practice of each President to avoid, as far as possible, the convening of Congress in extraordinary session. It is an example which, under ordinary circumstances and in the absence of a public necessity, is to be commended. But a failure to convene the representatives of the people in Congress in extra session when it involves neglect of a public duty places the responsibility of such neglect upon the Executive himself. The condition of the public Treasury, as has been indicated, demands

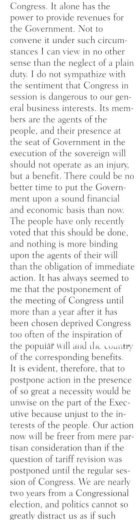

the immediate consideration of Congress. It alone has the power to provide revenues for the Government. Not to convene it under such circumstances I can view in no other sense than the neglect of a plain duty. I do not sympathize with the sentiment that Congress in session is dangerous to our general business interests. Its members are the agents of the people, and their presence at the seat of Government in the execution of the sovereign will should not operate as an injury, but a benefit. There could be no better time to put the Government upon a sound financial and economic basis than now. The people have only recently voted that this should be done, and nothing is more binding upon the agents of their will than the obligation of immediate action. It has always seemed to me that the postponement of the meeting of Congress until more than a year after it has been chosen deprived Congress too often of the inspiration of the popular will and the country of the corresponding benefits. It is evident, therefore, that to postpone action in the presence of so great a necessity would be unwise on the part of the Executive because unjust to the interests of the people. Our action now will be freer from mere partisan consideration than if the question of tariff revision was postponed until the regular session of Congress. We are nearly two years from a Congressional election, and politics cannot so greatly distract us as if such contest was immediately pending. We can approach the problem calmly and patriotically, without fearing its effect upon an early election.

Our fellow-citizens who may disagree with us upon the character of this legislation prefer to have the question settled now, even against their preconceived views, and perhaps settled so reasonably, as I trust and believe it will be, as to insure great permanence, than to have further uncertainty menacing the vast and varied business interests of the United States. Again, whatever action Congress may take will be given a fair opportunity for trial before the people are called to pass judgment

upon it, and this I consider a great essential to the rightful and lasting settlement of the question. In view of these considerations, I shall deem it my duty as President to convene Congress in extraordinary session on Monday, the 15th day of March, 1897.

In conclusion, I congratulate the country upon the fraternal spirit of the people and the manifestations of good will everywhere so apparent. The recent election not only most fortunately demonstrated the obliteration of sectional or geographical lines, but to some extent also the prejudices which for years have distracted our councils and marred our true greatness as a nation. The triumph of the people, whose verdict is carried into effect today, is not the triumph of one section, nor wholly of one party, but of all sections and all the people. The North and the South no longer divide on the old lines, but upon principles and policies; and in this fact surely every lover of the country can find cause for true felicitation. Let us rejoice in and cultivate this spirit; it is ennobling and will be both a gain and a blessing to our beloved country. It will be my constant aim to do nothing, and permit nothing to be done, that will arrest or disturb this growing sentiment of unity and cooperation, this revival of esteem and affiliation which now animates so many thousands in both the old antagonistic sections, but I shall cheerfully do everything possible to promote and increase it.

Let me again repeat the words of the oath administered by the Chief Justice which, in their respective spheres, so far as applicable, I would have all my countrymen observe: "I will faithfully execute the office of President of the United States, and will, to the best of my ability, preserve, protect, and defend the Constitution of the United States." This is the obligation I have reverently taken before the Lord Most High. To keep it will be my single purpose, my constant prayer; and I shall confidently rely upon the forbearance and assistance of all the people in the discharge of my solemn responsibilities.

* * *

1900 WILLIAM McKINLEY

T HOUGH A RELUCTANT CONVERT to the cause of the Spanish-American War, President William McKinley still benefited from its popularity and won renomination without opposition. However, he needed a new running mate. (Vice President Garret A. Hobart had died in office not long after casting the tie-breaking Senate vote in favor of retaining the Philippines.) At the request of New York Republicans who wanted Gov. Theodore Roosevelt out of their state—but against the advice of Mark Hanna—the president agreed to put the Hero of San Juan Hill on the ticket. "That cowboy is just a heartbeat from the presidency," a disgusted Hanna warned.

William Jennings Bryan, once again the Democratic nominee, attacked McKinley even more fiercely this time for colluding with the moneyed interests financing his campaign. Calling pointedly for prosecution of trusts, Bryan also condemned the new American imperialism and demanded independence for the Philippines. "Four more years of a full dinner pail," the Republican promised.

PARTY	POPULAR VOTES	ELECTORAL VOTES
REPUBLICAN William McKinley, Ohio Theodore Roosevelt, N.Y.	7,218,039	292
DEMOCRATIC William Jennings Bryan, Neb. Adlai E. Stevenson, Ill.	6,358,345	155

As usual, peace and prosperity delivered victory to McKinley, who won by an even larger—though again not overwhelming—margin. Celebrating with friends, Vice President-elect Theodore Roosevelt remarked that for the next four years he expected to remain "a dignified nonentity" with plenty of time available for hunting and other outdoor pursuits.

Second Inaugural Address • Washington, D.C. • Monday, March 4, 1901

My Fellow-Citizens: When we assembled here on the 4th of March, 1897,

there was great anxiety with regard to our currency and credit. None exists now. Then our Treasury receipts were inadequate to meet the current obligations of the Government. Now they are sufficient for all public needs, and we have a surplus instead of a deficit. Then I felt constrained to convene the Congress in extraordinary session to devise revenues to pay the ordinary expenses of the Government. Now I have the satisfaction to announce that the Congress just closed has reduced taxation in the sum of $41,000,000. Then there was deep solicitude because of the long depression in our manufacturing, mining, agricultural, and mercantile industries and the consequent distress of our laboring population. Now every avenue of production is crowded with activity, labor is well employed, and American products find good markets at home and abroad.

Our diversified productions, however, are increasing in such unprecedented volume as to admonish us of the necessity of still further enlarging our foreign markets by broader commercial relations. For this purpose reciprocal trade arrangements with other nations should in liberal spirit be carefully cultivated and promoted.

The national verdict of 1896 has for the most part been executed. 3 Whatever remains unfulfilled is a continuing obligation resting with undiminished force upon the Executive and the Congress. But fortunate as our condition is, its permanence can only be assured by sound business methods and strict economy in national administration and legislation. We should not permit our great prosperity to lead us to reckless ventures in business or profligacy in public expenditures. While the Congress determines the objects and the sum of appropriations, the officials of the executive departments are responsible for honest and faithful disbursement, and it should be their constant care to avoid waste and extravagance.

Honesty, capacity, and industry are nowhere more indispensable than in public employment. These should be fundamental requisites to original appointment and the surest guaranties against removal.

Four years ago we stood on the brink of war without the people knowing it and without any preparation or effort at preparation for the impending peril. I did all that in honor could be done to avert the war, but without avail. It be-

came inevitable; and the Congress at its first regular session, without party division, provided money in anticipation of the crisis and in preparation to meet it. It came. The result was signally favorable to American arms and in the highest degree honorable to the Government. It imposed upon us obligations from which we cannot escape and from which it would be dishonorable to seek escape. We are now at peace with the world, and it is my fervent prayer that if differences arise between us and other powers they may be settled by peaceful arbitration and that hereafter we may be spared the horrors of war.

Intrusted by the people for a second time with the office of President, I enter upon its administration appreciating the great responsibilities which attach to this renewed honor and commission, promising unreserved devotion on my part to their faithful discharge and reverently invoking for my guidance the direction and favor of Almighty God. I should shrink from the duties this day assumed if I did not feel that in their performance I should have the co-operation of the wise and patriotic men of all parties. It encourages me for the great task which I now undertake to believe that those who voluntarily committed to me the trust imposed upon the Chief Executive of the Republic will give to me generous support in my duties to "preserve, protect, and defend, the Constitution of the United States" and to "care that the laws be faithfully executed." The national purpose is indicated through a national election. It is the constitutional method of ascertaining the public will. When once it is registered it is a law to us all, and faithful observance should follow its decrees.

Strong hearts and helpful hands are needed, and, fortunately, we have them in every part of our beloved country. We are reunited. Sectionalism has disappeared. Division on public questions can no longer be traced by the war maps of 1861. These old differences less and less disturb the judgment. Existing problems demand the thought and quicken the conscience of the country, and the responsibility for their presence, as well as for their righteous settlement, rests upon us all—no more upon me than upon you. There are some national questions in the solution of which patriotism should exclude partisanship. Magnifying their difficulties will not take them off our hands nor facilitate their adjustment. Distrust of the capacity, integrity, and high purposes of the American people will not

be an inspiring theme for future political contests. Dark pictures and gloomy forebodings are worse than useless. These only becloud, they do not help to point the way of safety and honor. "Hope maketh not ashamed." The prophets of evil were not the builders of the Republic, nor in its crises since have they saved or served it. The faith of the fathers was a mighty force in its creation, and the faith of their descendants has wrought its progress and furnished its defenders. They are obstructionists who despair, and who would destroy confidence in the ability of our people to solve wisely and for civilization the mighty problems resting upon them. The American people, intrenched in freedom at home, take their love for it with them wherever they go, and they reject as mistaken and unworthy the doctrine that we lose our own liberties by securing the enduring foundations of liberty to others. Our institutions will not deteriorate by extension, and our sense of justice will not abate under tropic suns in distant seas. As heretofore, so hereafter will the nation demonstrate its fitness to administer any new estate which events devolve upon it, and in the fear of God will

"take occasion by the hand and make the bounds of freedom wider yet." If there are those among us who would make our way more difficult, we must not be disheartened, but the more earnestly dedicate ourselves to the task upon which we have rightly entered. The path of progress is seldom smooth. New things are often found hard to do. Our fathers found them so. We find them so. They are inconvenient. They cost us something. But are we not made better for the effort and sacrifice, and are not those

> *...the necessity of still further enlarging our foreign markets....*

we serve lifted up and blessed?

We will be consoled, too, with the fact that opposition has confronted every onward movement of the Republic from its opening hour until now, but without success. The Republic has marched on and on, and its step has exalted freedom and humanity. We are undergoing the same ordeal as did our predecessors nearly a century ago. We are following the course they blazed. They triumphed. Will their successors falter and plead organic impotency in the nation? Surely after 125 years of achievement for mankind we will not now surrender our equality with other powers on matters fundamental and essential to nationality. With no such purpose was the nation created. In no such spirit has it developed its full and independent sovereignty. We adhere to the principle of equality among ourselves, and by no act of ours will we assign to ourselves a subordinate rank in the family of nations.

My fellow-citizens, the public events of the past four years have gone into history.

They are too near to justify recital. Some of them were unforeseen; many of them momentous and far-reaching in their consequences to ourselves and our relations with the rest of the world. The part which the United States bore so honorably in the thrilling scenes in China, while new to American life, has been in harmony with its true spirit and best traditions, and in dealing with the results its policy will be that of moderation and fairness.

We face at this moment a most important question that of the future relations of the United States and Cuba. With our near neighbors we must remain close friends. The declaration of the purposes of this Government in the resolution of April 20, 1898, must be made good. Ever since the evacuation of the island by the army of Spain, the Executive, with all practicable speed, has been assisting its people in the successive steps necessary to the establishment of a free and independent government prepared to assume and perform the obligations of international law which now rest upon the United States under the treaty of Paris. The convention elected by the people to frame a constitution is approaching the completion of its labors. The transfer of American control to the new government is of such great importance, involving an obligation resulting from our intervention and the treaty of peace, that I am glad to be advised by the recent act of Congress of the policy which the legislative branch of the Government deems essential to the best interests of Cuba and the United States. The principles which led to our intervention require that the fundamental law upon which the new government rests should be adapted to secure a government capable of performing the duties and discharging the functions of a separate nation, of observing its international obligations of protecting life and property, insuring order, safety, and liberty, and conforming to the established and historical policy of the United States in its relation to Cuba.

The peace which we are pledged to leave to the Cuban people must carry with it the

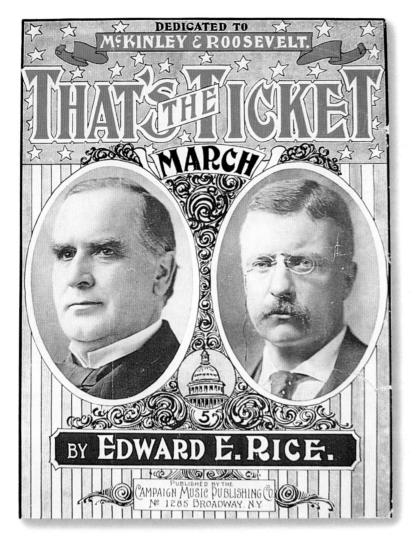

DEDICATED TO
McKINLEY & ROOSEVELT.
THAT'S THE TICKET MARCH
BY EDWARD E. RICE.
PUBLISHED BY THE
CAMPAIGN MUSIC PUBLISHING CO.
No 1285 BROADWAY. N.Y.

tions permit will establish local governments, in the formation of which the full co-operation of the people has been already invited, and when established will encourage the people to administer them. The settled purpose, long ago proclaimed, to afford the inhabitants of the islands self-government as fast as they were ready for it will be pursued with earnestness and fidelity. Already something has been accomplished in this direction. The Government's representatives, civil and military, are doing faithful and noble work in their mission of emancipation and merit the approval and support of their countrymen. The most liberal terms of amnesty have already been communicated to the insurgents, and the way is still open for those who have raised their arms against the Government for honorable submission to its authority. Our countrymen should not be deceived. We are not waging war against the inhabitants of the Philippine Islands. A portion of them are making war against the United States. By far the greater part of the inhabitants recognize American sovereignty and welcome it as a guaranty of order and of security for life, property, liberty, freedom of conscience, and the pursuit of happiness. To them full protection will be given. They shall not be abandoned. We will not leave the destiny of the loyal millions the islands to the disloyal thousands who are in rebellion against the United States. Order under civil institutions will come as soon as those who now break the peace shall keep it. Force will not be needed or used when those who make war against us shall make it no more. May it end without further bloodshed, and there be ushered in the reign of peace to be made permanent by a government of liberty under law!

* * *

guaranties of permanence. We became sponsors for the pacification of the island, and we remain accountable to the Cubans, no less than to our own country and people, for the reconstruction of Cuba as a free commonwealth on abiding foundations of right, justice, liberty, and assured order. Our enfranchisement of the people will not be completed until free Cuba shall "be a reality, not a name; a perfect entity, not a hasty experiment bearing within itself the elements of failure."

While the treaty of peace with Spain was ratified on the 6th of February, 1899, and ratifications were exchanged nearly two years ago, the Congress has indicated no form of government for the Philippine Islands. It has, however, provided an army to enable the Executive to suppress insurrection, restore peace, give security to the inhabitants, and establish the authority of the United States throughout the archipelago. It has authorized the organization of native troops as auxiliary to the regular force. It has been advised from time to time of the acts of the military and naval officers in the islands, of my action in appointing civil commissions, of the instructions with which they were charged, of their duties and powers, of their recommendations, and of their several acts under executive commission, together with the very complete general information they have submitted. These reports fully set forth the conditions, past and present, in the islands, and the instructions clearly show the principles which will guide the Executive until the Congress shall, as it is required to do by the treaty, determine "the civil rights and political status of the native inhabitants." The Congress having added the sanction of its authority to the powers already possessed and exercised by the Executive under the Constitution, thereby leaving with the Executive the responsibility for the government of the Philippines, I shall continue the efforts already begun until order shall be restored throughout the islands, and as fast as condi-

1904 THEODORE ROOSEVELT

DESPITE SOME MISGIVINGS about Theodore Roosevelt's Progressive leanings, the Republicans weren't eager to dump an incumbent president, so they nominated him unanimously for another term. The Democrats, having lost the last two elections with William Jennings Bryan (who declined to run in 1904), decided to play it "safe and sane" themselves with Alton B. Parker, chief justice of the New York Court of Appeals.

Parker railed against "Rooseveltism," calling it "volcanic, eruptive, and reckless." But voters *liked* Roosevelt's Square Deal for the common man, and Parker never understood the depth of affection that most Americans had for the president.

Roosevelt was apparently oblivious as well. Cooped up in his Sagamore Hill retreat on Long Island and frustrated by the custom that barred incumbents from campaigning for themselves, the president wrote letters exhorting his cabinet secretaries to "Attack Parker!!" whom TR called "the most formidable man the Democrats could have

PARTY	POPULAR VOTES	ELECTORAL VOTES
REPUBLICAN Theodore Roosevelt, N.Y. Charles W. Fairbanks, Ind.	7,626,593	336
DEMOCRATIC Alton B. Parker, N.Y. Henry G. Davis, W.Va.	5,082,898	140
SOCIALIST Eugene V. Debs, Ind. Benjamin Hanford, N.Y.	402,489	

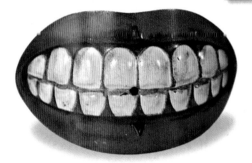

nominated." Why Roosevelt feared Parker is more a matter of psychology than politics, but it mattered not. The candidates argued about Panama, protectionism, and labor relations, but the election turned on personality. TR won by a landslide, the largest since the government began counting the popular vote in 1824. "Tomorrow I shall come into my office in my own right," Roosevelt told friends on the eve of his inauguration, "then watch out for me!"

Inaugural Address • Washington, D.C. • Saturday, March 4, 1905

My fellow-citizens, no people on earth have more cause to be thankful than

ours, and this is said reverently, in no spirit of boastfulness in our own strength, but with gratitude to the Giver of Good who has blessed us with the conditions which have enabled us to achieve so large a measure of well-being and of happiness. To us as a people it has been granted to lay the foundations of our national life in a new continent. We are the heirs of the ages, and yet we have had to pay few of the penalties which in old countries are exacted by the dead hand of a bygone civilization. We have not been obliged to fight for our existence against any alien race; and yet our life has called for the vigor and effort without which the manlier and hardier virtues wither away. Under such conditions it would be our own fault if we failed; and the success which we have had in the past, the success which we confidently believe the future will bring, should cause in us no feeling of vainglory, but rather a deep and abiding realization of all which life has

offered us; a full acknowledgment of the responsibility which is ours; and a fixed determination to show that under a free government a mighty people can thrive best, alike as regards the things of the body and the things of the soul.

Much has been given us, and much will rightfully be expected from us. We have duties to others and duties to ourselves; and we can shirk neither. We have become a great nation, forced by the fact of its greatness into relations with the other nations of the earth, and we must behave as beseems a people with such responsibilities. Toward all other nations, large and small, our attitude must be one of cordial and sincere friendship. We must show not only in our words, but in our deeds, that we are earnestly desirous of securing their good will by acting toward them in a spirit of just and generous recognition of all their rights. But justice and generosity in a nation, as in an individual, count most when

shown not by the weak but by the strong. While ever careful to refrain from wrongdoing others, we must be no less insistent that we are not wronged ourselves. We wish peace, but we wish the peace of justice, the peace of righteousness. We wish it because we think it is right and not because we are afraid. No weak nation that acts manfully and justly should ever have cause to fear us, and no strong power should ever be able to single us out as a subject for insolent aggression.

Our relations with the other powers of the world are important; but still more important are our relations among ourselves. Such growth in wealth, in population, and in power as this nation has seen during the century and a quarter of its national life is inevitably accompanied by a like growth in the problems which are ever before every nation that rises to greatness. Power invariably means both responsibility and danger. Our forefathers faced certain perils which we

But justice and generosity in a nation, as in an individual, count most when shown not by the weak but by the strong.

have outgrown. We now face other perils, the very existence of which it was impossible that they should foresee. Modern life is both complex and intense, and the tremendous changes wrought by the extraordinary industrial development of the last half century are felt in every fiber of our social and political being. Never before have men tried so vast and formidable an experiment as that of administering the affairs of a continent under the forms of a Democratic republic. The conditions which have told for our marvelous material well-being, which have developed to a very high degree our energy, self-reliance, and individual initiative, have also brought the care and anxiety inseparable from the accumulation of great wealth in industrial centers. Upon the success of our experiment much depends, not only as regards our own welfare, but as regards the welfare of mankind. If we fail,

the cause of free self-government throughout the world will rock to its foundations, and therefore our responsibility is heavy, to ourselves, to the world as it is to-day, and to the generations yet unborn. There is no good reason why we should fear the future, but there is every reason why we should face it seriously, neither hiding from ourselves the gravity of the problems before us nor fearing to approach these problems with the unbending, unflinching purpose to solve them aright.

Yet, after all, though the problems are new, though the tasks set before us differ from the tasks set before our fathers who founded and preserved this Republic, the spirit in which these tasks must be undertaken and these problems faced, if our duty is to be well done, remains essentially unchanged. We know that self-government is difficult. We know that no people needs such high traits of

character as that people which seeks to govern its affairs aright through the freely expressed will of the freemen who compose it. But we have faith that we shall not prove false to the memories of the men of the mighty past. They did their work, they left us the splendid heritage we now enjoy. We in our turn have an assured confidence that we shall be able to leave this heritage unwasted and enlarged to our children and our children's children. To do so we must show, not merely in great crises, but in the everyday affairs of life, the qualities of practical intelligence, of courage, of hardihood, and endurance, and above all the power of devotion to a lofty ideal, which

made great the men who founded this Republic in the days of Washington, which made great the men who preserved this Republic in the days of Abraham Lincoln.

* * *

1908 WILLIAM HOWARD TAFT

SECRETARY OF STATE WILLIAM HOWARD Taft was a reluctant nominee. Nevertheless, he acceded to the wishes of his wife (and those of President Theodore Roosevelt) when she pointed out to him that he would never get his cherished seat on the Supreme Court unless he did his duty to his party. The Democrats, somewhat desperately, brought back William Jennings Bryan, who had lost to William McKinley in 1896 and again in 1900. Bryan's selection made him the first candidate ever to win three major-party nominations.

The portly Taft, who gained even more weight during the campaign, promised administrative reforms, high tariff rates to protect U.S. industries, and a sound currency—all traditional Republican programs. Bryan campaigned on the claim that he was the candidate best suited to carry on Theodore Roosevelt's popular policies, especially trustbusting and environmental protection.

Even though Taft was a lackluster candidate, the fact that Roosevelt supported him strongly throughout the campaign made Bryan's argument a difficult one for voters to accept. In the end, they didn't.

PARTY	POPULAR VOTES	ELECTORAL VOTES
REPUBLICAN William Howard Taft, Ohio James S. Sherman, N.Y.	7,676,258	321
DEMOCRATIC William Jennings Bryan, Neb. John W. Kern, Ind.	6,406,801	162
SOCIALIST Eugene V. Debs, Ind. Benjamin Hanford, N.Y.	420,380	

Inaugural Address • Washington, D.C. • Thursday, March 4, 1909

My Fellow-Citizens: Anyone who has taken the oath I have just taken must

feel a heavy weight of responsibility. If not, he has no conception of the powers and duties of the office upon which he is about to enter, or he is lacking in a proper sense of the obligation which the oath imposes.

The office of an inaugural address is to give a summary outline of the main policies of the new administration, so far as they can be anticipated. I have had the honor to be one of the advisers of my distinguished predecessor, and, as such, to hold up his hands in the reforms he has initiated.

I should be untrue to myself, to my promises, and to the declarations of the party platform upon which I was elected to office, if I did not make the maintenance and enforcement of those reforms a most important feature of my administration. They were directed to the suppression of the lawlessness and abuses of power of the great combinations of capital invested in railroads and in industrial enterprises carrying on interstate commerce. The steps which my predecessor took and the legislation passed on his recommendation have accomplished much, have caused a general halt in the vicious policies which created popular alarm, and have brought about in the business affected a much higher regard for existing law.

To render the reforms lasting, however, and to secure at the same time freedom from alarm on the part of those pursuing proper and progressive business methods, further legislative and executive action are needed. Relief of the railroads from certain restrictions of the antitrust law have been urged by my predecessor and will be urged by me. On the other hand, the administration is pledged to legislation looking to a proper federal supervision and restriction to prevent excessive issues of bonds and stock by companies owning and operating interstate commerce railroads.

Then, too, a reorganization of the Department of Justice, of the Bureau of Corporations in the Department of Commerce and Labor, and of the Interstate Commerce Commission, looking to effective cooperation of these agencies, is needed to secure a more rapid and certain enforcement of the laws affecting interstate railroads and industrial combinations.

I hope to be able to submit at the first regular session of the incoming Congress, in December next, definite suggestions in respect to the needed amendments to the antitrust and the interstate commerce law and the changes required in the executive departments concerned in their enforcement.

It is believed that with the changes to be recommended American business can be assured of that measure of stability and certainty in respect to those things that may be done and those that are prohibited which is essential to the life and growth of all business. Such a plan must include the right of the people to avail themselves of those methods of combining capital and effort deemed necessary to reach the highest degree of economic efficiency, at the same time differentiating between combinations based upon legitimate economic reasons and those formed with the intent of creating monopolies and artificially controlling prices.

The work of formulating into practical shape such changes is creative word of the highest order, and requires all the deliberation possible in the interval. I believe that the amendments to be proposed are just as necessary in the protection of legitimate business as in the clinching of the reforms which properly bear the name of my predecessor.

A matter of most pressing importance is the revision of the tariff. In accordance with the promises of the platform upon which I was elected, I shall call Congress into extra session to meet on the 15th day of March, in order that consideration may be at once given to a bill revising the Dingley Act. This should secure an adequate revenue and adjust the duties in such a manner as to afford to labor and to all industries in this country, whether of the farm, mine or factory, protection by tariff equal to the difference between the cost of production abroad and the cost of production here, and have a provision which shall put into force, upon executive determination of certain facts, a higher or maximum tariff against those countries whose trade policy toward us equitably requires such discrimination. It is thought that there has been such a change in conditions since the enactment of the Dingley Act, drafted on a similarly protective principle, that the measure of the tariff above stated will permit the reduction of rates in certain schedules and will require the advancement of few, if any.

The proposal to revise the tariff made in such an authoritative way as to lead the business community to count upon it necessarily halts all those branches of business directly affected; and as these are most important, it disturbs the whole business of the country. It is imperatively necessary, therefore, that a tariff bill be drawn in good faith in accordance with promises made before the election by the party in power, and as promptly passed as due consideration will permit. It is not that the tariff is more important in the long run than the perfecting of the reforms in respect to antitrust legislation and interstate commerce regulation, but the need for action when the revision of the tariff has been determined upon is more immediate to avoid embarrassment of business. To secure the needed speed in the passage of the tariff bill, it

would seem wise to attempt no other legislation at the extra session. I venture this as a suggestion only, for the course to be taken by Congress, upon the call of the Executive, is wholly within its discretion.

In the mailing of a tariff bill the prime motive is taxation and the securing thereby of a revenue. Due largely to the business depression which followed

---

I should be untrue to myself [and] to my promises…if I did not make the maintenance and enforcement of [my predecessor's] reforms a most important feature of my administration.

---

the financial panic of 1907, the revenue from customs and other sources has decreased to such an extent that the expenditures for the current fiscal year will exceed the receipts by $100,000,000. It is imperative that such a deficit shall not continue, and the framers of the tariff bill must, of course, have in mind the total revenues likely to be produced by it and so arrange the duties as to secure an adequate income. Should it be impossible to do so by import duties, new kinds of taxation must be adopted, and among these I recommend a graduated inheritance tax as correct in principle and as certain and easy of collection.

The obligation on the part of those responsible for the expenditures made to carry on the Government, to be as economical as possible, and to make the burden of taxation as light as possible, is plain, and should be affirmed in every declaration of government policy. This is espe-

cially true when we are face to face with a heavy deficit. But when the desire to win the popular approval leads to the cutting off of expenditures really needed to make the Government effective and to enable it to accomplish its proper objects, the result is as much to be condemned as the waste of government funds in unnecessary expenditure. The scope of a modern government in what it can and ought to accomplish for its people has been widened far beyond the principles laid down by the old "laissez faire" school of political writers, and this widening has met popular approval.

In the Department of Agriculture the use of scientific experiments on a large scale and the spread of information derived from them for the improvement of general agriculture must go on.

The importance of supervising business of great railways and industrial combinations and the necessary investigation and prosecution of unlawful business methods are another necessary tax upon Government which did not exist half a century ago.

The putting into force of laws which shall secure the conservation of our resources, so far as they may be within the jurisdiction of the Federal Government, including the most important work of saving and restoring our forests and the great improvement of waterways, are all proper government functions which must involve large expenditure if properly performed. While some of them, like the reclamation of arid lands, are made to pay for themselves, others are of such an indirect benefit that this cannot be expected of them. A permanent improvement, like the Panama Canal, should be treated as a distinct enterprise, and should be paid for by the proceeds of bonds, the

issue of which will distribute its cost between the present and future generations in accordance with the benefits derived. It may well be submitted to the serious consideration of Congress whether the deepening and control of the channel of a great river system, like that of the Ohio or of the Mississippi, when definite and practical plans for the enterprise have been approved and determined upon, should not be provided for in the same way.

Then, too, there are expenditures of Government absolutely necessary if our country is to maintain its proper place among the nations of the world, and is to exercise its proper influence in defense of its own trade interests in the maintenance of traditional

STAND BY THE
REPUBLICAN PARTY

FOR PRESIDENT   FOR VICE PRESIDENT
W. H. TAFT   JAS. S. SHERMAN

SUPERIOR COURT
W. D. PORTER
JUDGES OF ORPHANS COURT
CLEMENT B. PENROSE
WILLIAM N. ASHMAN
SHERIFF
JOSEPH GILFILLAN
CORONER
JOHN W. FORD
COUNTY COMMISSIONERS
HARRY D. BEASTON
ROBERT J. MOORE

ELECTION DAY, NOV. 3RD 1908.

American policy against the colonization of European monarchies in this hemisphere, and in the promotion of peace and international morality. I refer to the cost of maintaining a proper army, a proper navy, and suitable fortifications upon the mainland of the United States and in its dependencies.

We should have an army so organized and so officered as to be capable in time of emergency, in cooperation with the national militia and under the provisions of a proper national volunteer law, rapidly to expand into a force sufficient to resist all probable invasion from abroad and to furnish a respectable expeditionary force if necessary in the maintenance of our traditional American policy which bears the name of President Monroe.

Our fortifications are yet in a state of only partial completeness, and the number of men to man them is insufficient. In a few years however, the usual annual appropriations for our coast defenses, both on the mainland and in the dependencies, will make them

sufficient to resist all direct attack, and by that time we may hope that the men to man them will be provided as a necessary adjunct. The distance of our shores from Europe and Asia of course reduces the necessity for maintaining under arms a great army, but it does not take away the requirement of mere prudence—that we should have an army sufficiently large and so constituted as to form a nucleus out of which a suitable force can quickly grow.

What has been said of the army may be affirmed in even a more emphatic way of the navy. A modern navy can not be improvised. It must be built and in existence when the emergency arises which calls for its use and operation. My distinguished

predecessor has in many speeches and messages set out with great force and striking language the necessity for maintaining a strong navy commensurate with the coast line, the governmental resources, and the foreign trade of our Nation; and I wish to reiterate all the reasons which he has presented in favor of the policy of maintaining a strong navy as the best conservator of our peace with other nations, and the best means of securing respect for the assertion of our rights, the defense of our interests, and the exercise of our influence in international matters.

Our international policy is always to promote peace. We shall enter into any war with a full consciousness of the awful consequences that it always entails, whether successful or not, and we, of course, shall make every effort consistent with national honor and the highest national interest to avoid a resort to arms. We favor every instrumentality like that of the Hague Tribunal and arbitration treaties made with a view to its use in all international controversies, in order to maintain peace and to avoid war. But we should be blind to existing conditions and should allow ourselves to become foolish idealists if we did not realize that, with all the nations of the world armed and prepared for war, we must be ourselves in a similar condition, in order to prevent other nations from taking advantage of us and of our inability to defend our interests and assert our rights with a strong hand.

In the international controversies that are likely to arise in the Orient growing out of the question of the open door and other issues the United States can maintain her interests intact and can secure respect for her just demands. She will not be able to do so, however, if it is understood that she never intends to back up her assertion of right and her defense of her interest by anything but mere verbal protest and diplomatic note. For these reasons the expenses of the army and navy and of coast defenses should

always be considered as something which the Government must pay for, and they should not be cut off through mere consideration of economy. Our Government is able to afford a suitable army and a suitable navy. It may maintain them without the slightest danger to the Republic or the cause of free institutions, and fear of additional taxation ought not to change a proper policy in this regard.

The policy of the United States in the Spanish war and since has given it a position of influence among the nations that it never had before, and should be constantly exerted to securing to its bona fide citizens, whether native or naturalized, respect for them as such in foreign countries. We should make every effort to prevent humiliating and degrading prohibition against any of our citizens wishing temporarily to sojourn in foreign countries because of race or religion.

The admission of Asiatic immigrants who cannot be amalgamated with our population has been made the subject either of prohibitory clauses in our treaties and statutes or of strict administrative regulation secured by diplomatic negotiation. I sincerely hope that we may continue to minimize the evils likely to arise from such immigration without unnecessary friction and by mutual concessions between self-respecting governments. Meantime we must take every precaution to prevent, or failing that, to punish outbursts of race feeling among our people against foreigners of whatever nationality who have by our grant a treaty right to pursue lawful business here and to be protected against lawless assault or injury.

This leads me to point out a serious defect in the present federal jurisdiction, which ought to be remedied at once. Having assured to other countries by treaty the protection of our laws for such of their subjects or citizens as we permit to come within our jurisdiction, we now leave to a state or a city, not under the control of the Federal Government, the duty of performing our international obligations in this respect. By proper legislation we may, and

ought to, place in the hands of the Federal Executive the means of enforcing the treaty rights of such aliens in the courts of the Federal Government. It puts our Government in a pusillanimous position to make definite engagements to protect aliens and then to excuse the failure to perform those engagements by an explanation that the duty to keep them is in States or cities, not within our control. If we would promise we must put ourselves in a position to perform our promise. We cannot permit the possible failure of justice, due to local prejudice in any State or municipal government, to expose us to the risk of a war which might be avoided if federal jurisdiction was asserted by suitable legislation by Congress and carried out by proper proceedings instituted by the Executive in the courts of the National Government.

One of the reforms to be carried out during the incoming administration is a change of our monetary and banking laws, so as to secure greater elasticity in the forms of currency available for trade and to prevent the limitations of law from operating to increase the embarrassment of a financial panic. The monetary commission, lately appointed, is giving full consideration to existing conditions and to all proposed remedies, and will doubtless suggest one that will meet the requirements of business and of public interest.

We may hope that the report will embody neither the narrow dew of those who believe that the sole purpose of the new system should be to secure a large return on banking capital or of those who would have greater expansion of currency with little regard to provisions for its immediate redemption or ultimate security. There is no subject of economic discussion so intricate and so likely to evoke differing views and dogmatic statements as this one. The commission, in studying the general influence of currency on business and of business on currency, have wisely extended their investigations in European banking and monetary methods. The information that they have derived from such experts as they have found abroad will undoubtedly be found helpful in the solution of the difficult problem they have in hand.

The incoming Congress should promptly fulfill the promise of the Republican platform and pass a proper postal savings bank bill. It will not be unwise or excessive paternalism. The promise to repay by the Government will furnish an inducement to savings deposits which private enterprise can not supply and at such a low rate of interest as not to withdraw custom from existing banks. It will substantially increase the funds available for investment as capital in useful enterprises. It will furnish absolute security which makes the proposed scheme of government guaranty of deposits so alluring, without its pernicious results.

I sincerely hope that the incoming Congress will be alive, as it should be, to the importance of our foreign trade and of encouraging it in every way feasible. The possibility of increasing this trade in the Orient, in the Philippines, and in South America are known to everyone who has given the matter attention. The direct effect of free trade between this country and the Philippines will be marked upon our sales of cottons, agricultural machinery, and other manufactures. The necessity of the establishment of direct lines of steamers between North and South America has been brought to the attention of Congress by my predecessor and by Mr. Root before and after his noteworthy visit to that continent, and I sincerely hope that Congress may be induced to see the wisdom of a tentative effort to establish such lines by the use of mail subsidies.

The importance of the part which the Departments of Agriculture and of Commerce and Labor may play in ridding the markets of Europe of prohibitions and discriminations against the importation of our products is fully understood, and it is hoped that the use of the maximum and minimum feature of our tariff law to be soon passed will be effective to remove many of those restrictions.

The Panama Canal will have a most important bearing upon the trade between the eastern and far western sections of our country, and will greatly increase the facilities for transportation between the eastern and the western seaboard, and may possibly revolutionize the transcontinental rates with respect to bulky merchandise. It will also have a most beneficial effect to increase the trade between the eastern seaboard of the United States and the western coast of South America, and, indeed, with some of the important ports on the east coast of South America reached by rail from the west coast.

The work on the canal is making most satisfactory progress. The type of the canal as a lock canal was fixed by Congress after a full consideration of the conflicting reports of the majority and minority of the consulting board, and after the recommendation of the War Department and the Executive upon those reports. Recent suggestion that something had occurred on the Isthmus to make the lock type of the canal less feasible than it was supposed to be when the reports were made and the policy determined on led to a visit to the Isthmus of a board of competent engineers to examine the Gatun dam and locks, which are the key of the lock type. The report of that board shows nothing has occurred in the nature of newly revealed evidence which should change the views once formed in the original discussion. The construction will go on under a most effective organization controlled by Colonel Goethals and his fellow army engineers associated with him, and will certainly be completed early in the next administration.

Some type of canal must be constructed. The lock type has been selected. We are all in favor of having it built as promptly as possible. We must not now, therefore, keep up a fire in the rear of the agents whom we have authorized to do our work on the Isthmus. We must hold up their hands, and speaking for the incoming administration I wish to say that I propose to devote all the energy possible and under my control to pushing of this work on the plans which have been adopted, and to stand behind the men who are doing faithful, hard work to bring about the early completion of this, the greatest constructive enterprise of modern times.

The governments of our dependencies in Porto Rico and the Philippines are progressing as favorably as could be desired. The prosperity of Porto Rico continues unabated. The business conditions in the Philippines are not all that we could wish them to be, but with the passage of the new tariff bill permitting free trade between the United States and the archipelago, with such limitations on sugar and tobacco as shall prevent injury to domestic interests in those products, we can count on an improvement in business conditions in the Philippines and the development of a mutually profitable trade between this country and the islands. Meantime our Government in each dependency is upholding the traditions of civil liberty and increasing popular control which might be expected under American auspices. The work which we are doing there redounds to our credit as a nation.

I look forward with hope to increasing the already good feeling between the South and the other sections of the country. My chief purpose is not to effect a change in the electoral vote of the Southern States. That is a secondary consideration. What I look forward to is an increase in the tolerance of political views of all kinds and their advocacy throughout the South, and the existence of a respectable political opposition in every State; even more than this, to an increased feeling on the part of all the people in the South that this Government is their Government, and that its officers in their states are their officers.

The consideration of this question can not, however, be complete and full without reference to the negro race, its progress and its present condition. The thirteenth amendment secured them freedom; the fourteenth amendment due process of law, protection of property, and the pursuit of happiness; and the fifteenth amendment attempted to secure the negro against any deprivation of the privilege to vote because he was a negro. The thirteenth and fourteenth amendments have been generally enforced and have secured the objects for which they are intended. While the fifteenth amendment has not been generally observed in the past, it ought to be observed, and the tendency of Southern legislation today is toward the enactment of electoral qualifications which shall square with that amendment. Of course, the mere adoption of a constitutional law is only one step in the right direction. It must be fairly and justly enforced as well. In time both will come. Hence it is clear to all that the domination of an ignorant, irresponsible element can be prevented by constitutional laws which shall exclude from voting both negroes and whites not having education or other qualifications thought to be necessary for a proper electorate. The danger of the control of an ignorant electorate has therefore passed. With this change, the interest which many of the Southern white citizens take in the welfare of the negroes has increased. The colored men must base their hope on the results of their own industry, self-restraint, thrift, and business success, as well as upon the aid and comfort and sympathy which they may receive from their white neighbors of the South.

There was a time when Northerners who sympathized with the negro in his necessary struggle for better conditions sought to give him the suffrage as a protection to enforce its exercise against the prevailing sentiment of the South. The movement proved to be a failure. What remains is the fifteenth amendment to the Constitution and the right to have statutes of States specifying qualifications for electors subjected to the test of compliance with that amendment. This is a great protection to the negro. It never will be repealed, and it never ought to be repealed. If it had not passed, it might be difficult now to adopt it; but with it in our fundamental law, the policy of Southern legislation must and will tend to obey it, and so long as the statutes of the States meet the test of this amendment and are not otherwise in conflict with the Constitution and laws of the United States,

it is not the disposition or within the province of the Federal Government to interfere with the regulation by Southern States of their domestic affairs. There is in the South a stronger feeling than ever among the intelligent well-to-do, and influential element in favor of the industrial education of the negro and the encouragement of the race to make themselves useful members of the community. The progress which the negro has made in the last fifty years, from slavery, when its statistics are reviewed, is marvelous, and it furnishes every reason to hope that in the next twenty-five years a still greater improvement in his condition as a productive member of society, on the farm, and in the shop, and in other occupations may come.

The negroes are now Americans. Their ancestors came here years ago against their will, and this is their only country and their only flag. They have shown themselves anxious to live for it and to die for it. Encountering the race feeling against them, subjected at times to cruel injustice growing out of it, they may well have our profound sympathy and aid in the struggle they are making. We are charged with the sacred duty of making their path as smooth and easy as we can. Any recognition of their distinguished men, any appointment to office from among their number, is properly taken as an encouragement and an appreciation of their progress, and this just policy should be pursued when suitable occasion offers.

But it may well admit of doubt whether, in the case of any race, an appointment of one of their number to a local office in a community in which the race feeling is so widespread and acute as to interfere with the ease and facility with which the local government business can be done by the appointee is of sufficient benefit by way of encouragement to the race to outweigh the recurrence and increase of race feeling which such an appointment is likely to engender. Therefore the Executive, in recognizing the negro race by appointments, must exercise a careful discretion not thereby to do it more harm than good. On the other hand, we must be careful not to encourage the mere pretense of race feeling manufactured in the interest of individual political ambition.

Personally, I have not the slightest race prejudice or feeling, and recognition of its existence only awakens in my heart a deeper sympathy for those who have to bear it or suffer from it, and I question the wisdom of a policy which is likely to increase it. Meantime, if nothing is done to prevent it, a better feeling between the negroes and the whites in the South will continue to grow, and more and more of the white people will come to realize that the future of the South is to be much benefited by the industrial and intellectual progress of the negro. The exercise of political franchises by those of this race who are intelligent and well to do will be acquiesced in, and the right to vote will be withheld only from the ignorant and irresponsible of both races.

There is one other matter to which I shall refer. It was made the subject of great controversy during the election and calls for at least a passing reference now. My distinguished predecessor has given much attention to the cause of labor, with whose struggle for better things he has shown the sincerest sympathy. At his instance Congress has passed the bill fixing the liability of interstate carriers to their employees for injury sustained in the course of employment, abolishing the rule of fellow-servant and the common-law rule as to contributory negligence, and substituting therefor the so-called rule of "comparative negligence." It has also passed a law fixing the compensation of government employees for injuries sustained in the employ of the Government through the negligence of the superior. It has also passed a model child-labor law for the District of Columbia. In previous administrations an arbitration law for interstate commerce railroads and their employees, and laws for the application of safety devices to save the lives and limbs of employees of interstate railroads had been passed. Additional legislation of this kind was passed by the outgoing Congress.

I wish to say that insofar as I can I hope to promote the enactment of further legislation of this character. I am strongly convinced that the Government should make itself as responsible to employees injured in its employ as an interstate-railway corporation is made responsible by federal law to its employees; and I shall be glad, whenever any additional reasonable safety device can be invented to reduce the loss of life and limb among railway employees, to urge Congress to require its adoption by interstate railways.

Another labor question has arisen which has awakened the most excited discussion. That is in respect to the power of the federal courts to issue injunctions in industrial disputes. As to that, my convictions are fixed. Take away from the courts, if it could be taken away, the power to issue injunctions in labor disputes, and it would create a privileged class among the laborers and save the lawless among their number from a most needful remedy available to all men for the protection of their business against lawless invasion. The proposition that business is not a property or pecuniary right which can be protected by equitable injunction is utterly without foundation in precedent or reason. The proposition is usually linked with one to make the secondary boycott lawful. Such a proposition is at variance with the American instinct, and will find no support, in my judgment, when submitted to the American people. The secondary boycott is an instrument of tyranny, and ought not to be made legitimate.

The issue of a temporary restraining order without notice has in several instances been abused by its inconsiderate exercise, and to remedy this the platform upon which I was elected recommends the formulation in a statute of the conditions under which such a temporary restraining order ought to issue. A statute can and ought to be framed to embody the best modern practice, and can bring the subject so closely to the attention of the court as to make abuses of the process unlikely in the future. The American people, if I understand them, insist that the authority of the courts shall be sustained, and are opposed to any change in the procedure by which the powers of a court may be weakened and the fearless and effective administration of justice be interfered with.

Having thus reviewed the questions likely to recur during my administration, and having expressed in a summary way the position which I expect to take in recommendations to Congress and in my conduct as an Executive, I invoke the considerate sympathy and support of my fellow-citizens and the aid of the Almighty God in the discharge of my responsible duties

* * *

1912 Woodrow Wilson

No Democrat could have wished for a messier Republican convention. Incredibly, former president Theodore Roosevelt was opposing incumbent William Howard Taft for the nomination. After breaking with Taft over the filing of an antitrust suit, Roosevelt had beaten him in ten of the twelve Republican state primaries and was clearly the choice of the party's rank and file. However, party regulars still controlled the nominating process, and they backed Taft, putting him over the top on the first ballot. The next day, a defiant Roosevelt announced that he would be forming a new party, the Progressives, also known as the Bull Moose party for its candidate and raison d'être.

At the Democratic convention, a determined Woodrow Wilson struggled ballot after ballot to gain an edge over Speaker of the House Champ Clark. The New Jersey governor kept maneuvering, obtaining the support of William Jennings Bryan and making deals with various state bosses, until he finally bested Clark on the forty-sixth ballot. From that point on, with Taft and Roosevelt savaging one another, Wilson merely had to remain composed. Making a few rather dull appearances, Taft became the first incumbent president to hit the campaign trail, but more energy wouldn't have helped—

he had no chance of winning. The only possible threat to Wilson came from Roosevelt, who campaigned vigorously around the country (as did Wilson). TR called for a New Nationalism featuring increased regulation of the trusts and a continuation of his Square Deal for workers. Wilson promoted his New Freedom program, which called for the dissolution of the trusts and the creation of new regulatory agencies along with banking reform.

Party	Popular Votes	Electoral Votes
Democratic Woodrow Wilson, N.J. Thomas R. Marshall, Ind.	6,293,152	435
Progressive Theodore Roosevelt, N.Y. Hiram W. Johnson, Calif.	4,119,207	88
Republican William Howard Taft, Ohio Nicholas M. Butler, N.Y.	3,486,333	8
Socialist Eugene V. Debs, Ind. Emil Seidel, Wis.	900,369	

Roosevelt and Taft combined to win more than 50 percent of the popular vote, but they weren't running together, so Wilson swept to a huge electoral college victory with just a 41.8 percent plurality. Eugene V. Debs, running for the fourth consecutive time as the Socialist party candidate, improved to 6.0 percent, receiving nearly a million votes.

First Inaugural Address • Washington, D.C. • Tuesday, March 4, 1913

There has been a change of government. It began two years ago, when the

House of Representatives became Democratic by a decisive majority. It has now been completed. The Senate about to assemble will also be Democratic. The offices of President and Vice-President have been put into the hands of Democrats. What does the change mean? That is the question that is uppermost in our minds to-day. That is the question I am going to try to answer, in order, if I may, to interpret the occasion. It means much more than the mere success of a party. The success of a party means little except when the Nation is using that party for a large and definite purpose. No one can mistake the purpose for which the Nation now seeks to use the Democratic Party. It seeks to use it to interpret a change in its own plans and point of view. Some old things with which we had grown familiar, and which had begun to creep into the very habit of our thought and of our lives, have altered their aspect as we have latterly looked critically upon them, with fresh, awakened eyes; have dropped their disguises and shown themselves alien and sinister. Some new things, as we look frankly upon them, willing to comprehend their real character, have come to assume the aspect of things long believed in and familiar, stuff of our own convictions. We have been refreshed by a new insight into our own life.

We see that in many things that life is very great. It is incomparably great in its material aspects, in its body of wealth, in the diversity and sweep of its energy, in the industries which have been conceived and built up by the genius of individual men and the limitless enterprise of groups of men. It is great, also, very great, in its moral force. Nowhere else in the world have noble men and women exhibited in more striking forms the beauty and the energy of sympathy and helpfulness and counsel in their efforts to rectify wrong, alleviate suffering, and set the weak in the way of strength and hope. We have built up, moreover, a great system of government, which has stood through a long age as in many respects a model for those who seek to set liberty upon foundations that will endure against fortuitous change, against storm and accident. Our life contains every great thing, and contains it in rich abundance.

But the evil has come with the good, and much fine gold has been corroded. With riches has come inexcusable waste. We have squandered a great part of what we might have used, and have not stopped to conserve the exceeding bounty of nature, without which our genius for enterprise would have been worthless and impotent, scorning to be careful, shamefully prodigal as well as admirably efficient. We have been proud of our industrial achievements, but we have not hitherto stopped thoughtfully enough to count the human cost, the cost of lives snuffed out, of energies overtaxed and broken, the fearful physical and spiritual cost to the men and women and children upon whom the dead weight and burden of it all has fallen pitilessly the years through. The groans and agony of it all had not yet reached our ears, the solemn, moving undertone of our life, coming up out of the mines and factories, and out of every home where the struggle had its intimate and familiar seat. With the great Government went many deep secret things which we too long delayed to look into and scrutinize with candid, fearless eyes. The great Government we loved has too often been made use of for private and selfish purposes, and those who used it had forgotten the people.

At last a vision has been vouchsafed us of our life as a whole. We see the bad with the good, the debased and decadent with the sound and vital. With this vision we approach new affairs. Our duty is to cleanse, to reconsider, to restore, to correct the evil without impairing the good, to purify and humanize every process of our common life without weakening or sentimentalizing it. There has been something crude and heartless and unfeeling in our haste to succeed and be great. Our thought has been "Let every man look out for himself, let every generation look out for itself," while we reared giant machinery which made it impossible that any but those who stood at the levers of control should have a chance to look out for themselves. We had not forgotten our morals. We re-

membered well enough that we had set up a policy which was meant to serve the humblest as well as the most powerful, with an eye single to the standards of justice and fair play, and remembered it with pride. But we were very heedless and in a hurry to be great.

We have come now to the sober second thought. The scales of heedlessness have fallen from our eyes. We have made up our minds to square every process of our national life again with the standards we so proudly set up at the beginning and have always carried at our hearts. Our work is a work of restoration.

We have itemized with some degree of particularity the things that ought to be altered and here are some of the chief items: A tariff which cuts us off from our proper part in the commerce of the world, violates the just principles of taxation, and makes the Government a facile instrument in the hand of private interests; a banking and currency system based upon the necessity of the Government to sell its bonds fifty years ago and perfectly adapted to concentrating cash and restricting credits; an industrial system which, take it on all its sides, financial as well as administrative, holds capital in leading strings, restricts the liberties and limits the opportunities of labor, and exploits without renewing or conserving the natural resources of the country; a body of agricultural activities never yet given the efficiency of great business undertakings or served as it should be through the instrumentality of science taken directly to the farm, or afforded the facilities of credit best suited to its practical needs; watercourses undeveloped, waste places unreclaimed, forests untended, fast disappearing without plan or prospect of renewal, unregarded waste heaps at every mine. We have studied as perhaps no other nation has the most effective means of production, but we have not studied cost or economy as we should either as organizers of industry, as statesmen, or as individuals.

Nor have we studied and perfected the means by which government may be put at the service of humanity, in safe-

guarding the health of the Nation, the health of its men and its women and its children, as well as their rights in the struggle for existence. This is no sentimental duty. The firm basis of government is justice, not pity. These are matters of justice. There can be no equality or opportunity, the first essential of justice in the body politic, if men and women and children be not shielded in their lives, their very vitality, from the consequences of great industrial and social processes which they can not alter, control, or singly cope with. Society must see to it that it does not itself crush or weaken or damage its own constituent parts. The first duty of law is to

Men's hearts wait upon us; men's lives hang in the balance; men's hopes call upon us to say what we will do.

keep sound the society it serves. Sanitary laws, pure food laws, and laws determining conditions of labor which individuals are powerless to determine for themselves are intimate parts of the very business of justice and legal efficiency.

These are some of the things we ought to do, and not leave the others undone, the old-fashioned, never-to-be-neglected, fundamental safeguarding of property and of individual right. This is the high enterprise of the new day: To lift everything that concerns our life as a Nation to the light that shines from the hearthfire of every man's conscience and vision of the right. It is inconceivable that we should do this as partisans; it

is inconceivable we should do it in ignorance of the facts as they are or in blind haste. We shall restore, not destroy. We shall deal with our economic system as it is and as it may be modified, not as it might be if we had a clean sheet of paper to write upon; and step by step we shall make it what it should be, in the spirit of those who question their own wisdom and seek counsel and knowledge, not shallow self-satisfaction or the excitement of excursions whither they can not tell. Justice, and only justice, shall always be our motto.

And yet it will be no cool process of mere science. The Nation has been deeply stirred, stirred by a solemn passion, stirred by the knowledge of wrong, of ideals lost, of government too often debauched and made an instrument of evil. The feelings with which we face this new age of right and opportunity sweep across our heartstrings like some air out of God's own presence, where justice and mercy are reconciled and the judge and the brother are one. We know our task to be no mere task of politics but a task which shall search us through and through, whether we be able to understand our time and the need of our people, whether we be indeed their spokesmen and interpreters, whether we have the pure heart to comprehend and the rectified will to choose our high course of action.

This is not a day of triumph; it is a day of dedication. Here muster, not the forces of party, but the forces of humanity. Men's hearts wait upon us; men's lives hang in the balance; men's hopes call upon us to say what we will do. Who shall live up to the great trust? Who dares fail to try? I summon all honest men, all patriotic, all forward-looking men, to my side. God helping me, I will not fail them, if they will but counsel and sustain me!

★ ★ ★

1916 WOODROW WILSON

ALTHOUGH WOODROW WILSON successfully navigated many of his New Freedom programs through Congress during his first two years in office, Democratic losses in the 1914 midterm elections left him with sixty-one fewer House votes and considerably less influence within his party. Even so, the president had kept the nation prosperous and largely at peace despite the outbreak of war in Europe; his renomination was assured.

To oppose Wilson, the Republicans nominated Supreme Court Justice Charles Evans Hughes, who abandoned his Court seat and judicial demeanor to wage a grassroots campaign that made use of billboards, magazine ads, newsreels, and other new media. Refusing the nomination of the Progressive party, which he had helped found in 1912, Theodore Roosevelt backed Hughes, but Roosevelt's endorsement apparently wasn't enough to lure most Progressives back into the Republican camp, and Hughes trailed from the start.

Wilson didn't campaign personally, but his surrogates made sure that voters knew "He Kept Us Out of War." The Republicans, still chasing the Progressive vote, countered with "He Kept Us Out of Suffrage," a reference to Wilson's refusal to back the proposed Nineteenth Amendment.

The Socialist party's 3.2 percent made the race closer than it otherwise would have been, with Wilson just managing a narrow electoral majority. One thing the confused election did make clear, however, was that, as both American and European commentators noted, the voters had no intention of going to war.

PARTY	POPULAR VOTES	ELECTORAL VOTES
DEMOCRATIC Woodrow Wilson, N.J. Thomas R. Marshall, Ind.	9,126,300	277
REPUBLICAN Charles Evans Hughes, N.Y. Charles W. Fairbanks, Ind.	8,546,789	254
SOCIALIST Allan L. Benson, N.Y. George R. Kirkpatrick, N.J.	589,924	

Second Inaugural Address • Washington, D.C. • Monday, March 5, 1917

My Fellow Citizens: The four years which have elapsed since last I stood

in this place have been crowded with counsel and action of the most vital interest and consequence. Perhaps no equal period in our history has been so fruitful of important reforms in our economic and industrial life or so full of significant changes in the spirit and purpose of our political action. We have sought very thoughtfully to set our house in order, correct the grosser errors and abuses of our industrial life, liberate and quicken the processes of our national genius and energy, and lift our politics to a broader view of the people's essential interests.

It is a record of singular variety and singular distinction. But I shall not attempt to review it. It speaks for itself and will be of increasing influence as the years go by. This is not the time for retrospect. It is time rather to speak our thoughts and purposes concerning the present and the immediate future.

Although we have centered counsel and action with such unusual concentration and success upon the great problems of domestic legislation to which we addressed ourselves four years ago, other matters have more and more forced themselves upon our attention—matters lying outside our own life as a nation and over which we had no control, but which, despite our wish to keep free of them, have drawn us more and more irresistibly into their own current and influence.

It has been impossible to avoid them. They have affected the life of the whole world. They have shaken men everywhere with a passion and an apprehension they never knew before. It has been hard to preserve calm counsel while the thought of our own people swayed this way and that under their influence. We are a composite and cosmopolitan people. We are of the blood of all the nations that are at war. The currents of our thoughts as well as the currents of our trade run quick at all seasons back and forth between us and them. The war inevitably set its mark from the first alike upon our minds, our industries, our commerce, our politics and our social action. To be indifferent to it, or independent of it, was out of the question.

And yet all the while we have been conscious that we were not part of it. In that consciousness, despite many divisions, we have drawn closer together. We have been deeply wronged upon the seas, but we have not wished to wrong or injure in return; have retained throughout the consciousness of standing in some sort apart, intent upon an interest that transcended the immediate issues of the war itself.

As some of the injuries done us have become intolerable we have still been clear that we wished nothing for ourselves that we were not ready to demand for all mankind—fair dealing, justice, the freedom to live and to be at ease against organized wrong.

It is in this spirit and with this thought that we have grown more and more aware, more and more certain that the part we wished to play was the part of those who mean to vindicate and fortify peace. We have been obliged to arm ourselves to make good our claim to a certain minimum of right and

FOR PRESIDENT

CHARLES E. HUGHES

of freedom of action. We stand firm in armed neutrality since it seems that in no other way we can demonstrate what it is we insist upon and cannot forget. We may even be drawn on, by circumstances, not by our own purpose or desire, to a more active assertion of our rights as we see them and a more immediate association with the great struggle itself. But nothing will alter our thought or our purpose. They are too clear to be obscured. They are too deeply rooted in the principles of our national life to be altered. We desire neither conquest nor advantage. We wish nothing that can be had only at the cost of another people. We always professed unselfish purpose and we covet the opportunity to prove our professions are sincere.

There are many things still to be done at home, to clarify our own politics and add new vitality to the industrial processes of our own life, and we shall do them as time and opportunity serve, but we realize that the greatest things that remain to be done must be done with the whole world for stage and in cooperation with the wide and universal forces of mankind, and we are making our spirits ready

for those things.

We are provincials no longer. The tragic events of the thirty months of vital turmoil through which we have just passed have made us citizens of the world. There can be no turning back. Our own fortunes as a nation are involved whether we would have it so or not.

And yet we are not the less Americans on that account. We shall be the more American if we but remain true to the principles in which we have been bred. They are not the principles of a province or of a single continent. We have known and boasted all along that they were the principles of a liberated mankind. These, therefore, are the things we shall stand for, whether in war or in peace:

That all nations are equally interested in the peace of the world and in the political stability of free peoples, and equally responsible for their maintenance; that the essential principle of peace is the actual equality of nations in all matters of right or privilege; that peace cannot securely or justly rest upon an armed balance of power; that governments derive all their just powers from the consent of the governed and

that no other powers should be supported by the common thought, purpose or power of the family of nations; that the seas should be equally free and safe for the use of all peoples, under rules set up by common agreement and consent, and that, so far as practicable, they should be accessible to all upon equal terms; that national armaments shall be limited to the necessities of national order and domestic safety; that the community of interest and of power upon which peace must henceforth depend imposes upon

---

We are provincials no longer.... There can be no turning back. Our own fortunes as a nation are involved whether we would have it so or not.

---

each nation the duty of seeing to it that all influences proceeding from its own citizens meant to encourage or assist revolution in other states should be sternly and effectually suppressed and prevented.

I need not argue these principles to you, my fellow countrymen; they are your own part and parcel of your own thinking and your own motives in affairs. They spring up native amongst us. Upon this as a platform of purpose and of action we can stand together. And it is imperative that we should stand together. We are being forged into a new unity amidst the fires that now blaze throughout the world. In their ardent heat we shall, in God's Providence, let us hope, be purged of faction and division, purified of the errant humors of party and of private interest, and shall stand forth in the days to come with a new dignity of national pride and spirit. Let each man see to

it that the dedication is in his own heart, the high purpose of the nation in his own mind, ruler of his own will and desire.

I stand here and have taken the high and solemn oath to which you have been audience because the people of the United States have chosen me for this august delegation of power and have by their gracious judgment named me their leader in affairs.

I know now what the task means. I realize to the full the responsibility which it involves. I pray God I may be given the wisdom and the prudence to do my duty in the true spirit of this great people. I am their servant and can succeed only as they sustain and guide me by their confidence and their counsel. The thing I shall count upon, the thing without which neither counsel nor action will avail, is the unity of America—an America united in feeling, in purpose and in its vision of duty, of opportunity and of service. We are to beware of all men who would turn the tasks and the necessities of the nation to their own private profit or use them for the building up of private power.

United alike in the conception of our duty and in the high resolve to perform it in the face of all men, let us dedicate ourselves to the great task to which we must now set our hand. For myself I beg your tolerance, your countenance and your united aid.

The shadows that now lie dark upon our path will soon be dispelled, and we shall walk with the light all about us if we be but true to ourselves—toourselves as we have wished to be known in the counsels of the world and in the thought of all those who love liberty and justice and the right exalted.

* * *

IT FITS HUGHES

1920 WARREN G. HARDING

WOODROW WILSON, DEFEATED in foreign policy and bedridden by a stroke, was in no condition to influence the choice of his successor. At the wide-open Democratic convention, forty-four ballots were necessary before the delegates settled on Governor James M. Cox of Ohio. The Republicans also nominated an Ohioan, Sen. Warren G. Harding, who emerged as a compromise choice after the convention deadlocked among Sen. Hiram Johnson of California, Gen. Leonard Wood, and Gov. Frank Lowden of Illinois.

Cox toured the nation, paying particular attention to the western states, while Harding ran another Ohio front-porch campaign of the sort that had elected Benjamin Harrison and William McKinley. Known for his unpredictable use of language, Harding famously called for a return to "normalcy." More specifically, he supported Prohibition (which Cox opposed), and Republicans accordingly targeted rural conservatives and women voters, newly enfranchised courtesy of the Nineteenth Amendment.

In a contest pitting one nonentity against another, Harding won a huge victory, mostly because after eight years of Wilson the country wanted a change. Harding's 60.3 percent of the popular vote set a new record, substantially improving on the 56.4 percent Theodore Roosevelt received in 1904.

PARTY	POPULAR VOTES	ELECTORAL VOTES
REPUBLICAN Warren G. Harding, Ohio Calvin Coolidge, Mass.	16,153,115	404
DEMOCRATIC James M. Cox, Ohio Franklin D. Roosevelt, N.Y.	9,133,092	127
SOCIALIST Eugene V. Debs, Ind. Seymour Stedman, Ill.	915,490	

Inaugural Address • Washington, D.C. • Friday, March 4, 1921

My Countrymen: When on surveys the world about him after the great

storm, noting the marks of destruction and yet rejoicing in the ruggedness of the things which withstood it, if he is an American he breathes the clarified atmosphere with a strange mingling of regret and new hope. We have seen a world passion spend its fury, but we contemplate our Republic unshaken, and hold our civilization secure. Liberty—liberty within the law—and civilization are inseparable, and though both were threatened we find them now secure; and there comes to Americans the profound assurance that our representative government is the highest expression and surest guaranty of both.

Standing in this presence, mindful of the solemnity of this occasion, feeling the emotions which no one may know until he senses the great weight of responsibility for himself, I must utter my belief in the divine inspiration of the founding fathers. Surely there must have been God's intent in the making of this new-world Republic. Ours is an organic law which had but one ambiguity, and we saw that effaced in a baptism of sacrifice and blood, with union maintained, the Nation supreme, and its concord inspiring. We have seen the world rivet its hopeful gaze on the great truths on which the founders wrought. We have seen civil, human, and religious liberty verified and glorified. In the

beginning the Old World scoffed at our experiment; today our foundations of political and social belief stand unshaken, a precious inheritance to ourselves, an inspiring example of freedom and civilization to all mankind. Let us express renewed and strengthened devotion, in grateful reverence for the immortal beginning, and utter our confidence in the supreme fulfillment.

The recorded progress of our Republic, materially and spiritually, in itself proves the wisdom of the inherited policy of noninvolvement in Old World affairs. Confident of our ability to work out our own destiny, and jealously guarding our right to do so, we seek no part in directing the destinies of the Old World. We do not mean to be entangled. We will accept no responsibility except as our own conscience and judgment, in each instance, may determine.

Our eyes never will be blind to a developing menace, our ears never deaf to the call of civilization. We recognize the new order in the world, with the closer contacts which progress has wrought. We sense the call of the human heart for fellowship, fraternity, and cooperation. We crave friendship and harbor no hate. But America, our America, the America builded on the foundation laid by the inspired fathers, can be a party to no

permanent military alliance. It can enter into no political commitments, nor assume any economic obligations which will subject our decisions to any other than our own authority.

I am sure our own people will not misunderstand, nor will the world misconstrue. We have no thought to impede the paths to closer relationship. We wish to promote understanding. We want to do our part in making offensive warfare so hateful that Governments and peoples who resort to it must prove the righteousness of their cause or stand as outlaws before the bar of civilization.

We are ready to associate ourselves with the nations of the world, great and small, for conference, for counsel; to seek the expressed views of world opinion; to recommend a way to approximate disarmament and relieve the crushing burdens of military and naval establishments. We elect to participate in suggesting plans for mediation, conciliation, and arbitration, and would gladly join in that expressed conscience of progress, which seeks to clarify and write the laws of international relationship, and establish a world court for the disposition of such justiciable questions as nations are agreed to submit thereto. In expressing aspirations, in seeking practical plans, in translating humanity's new concept of righteousness and justice and its hatred of war into recommended action we are ready most heartily to unite, but every commitment must be made in the exercise of our national sovereignty. Since freedom impelled, and independence inspired, and nationality exalted, a world supergovernment is contrary to everything we cherish and can have no sanction by our Republic. This is not selfishness, it is sanctity. It is not aloofness, it is security. It is not suspicion of others, it is patriotic adherence to the things which made us what we are.

Today, better than ever before, we know the aspirations of humankind, and share them. We have come to a new realization of our place in the world and a new appraisal of our Nation by the world. The unselfishness of these United States is a thing proven; our devotion to peace for ourselves and for the world is well established; our concern for preserved civilization has had its impassioned and heroic expression. There was no American failure to resist the attempted reversion of civilization; there will be no failure today or tomorrow.

The success of our popular government rests wholly upon the correct interpretation of the deliberate, intelligent, dependable popular will of America. In a deliberate questioning of a suggested change of national policy, where internationality was to supersede nationality, we turned to a referendum, to the American people. There was ample discussion, and there is a public mandate in manifest understanding.

America is ready to encourage, eager to initiate, anxious to participate in any seemly program likely to lessen the probability of war, and promote that brotherhood of mankind which must be God's highest conception of human relationship. Because we cherish ideals of justice and peace, because we appraise international comity and helpful relationship no less highly than any people of the world, we aspire to a high place in the moral leadership of civilization, and we hold a maintained America, the proven Republic, the unshaken temple of representative democracy, to be not only an inspiration and example, but the highest agency of strengthening good will and promoting accord on both continents.

Mankind needs a worldwide benediction of understanding. It is needed among individuals, among peoples, among governments, and it will inaugurate an era of good feeling to make the birth of a new order. In such understanding men will strive confidently for the promotion of their better relationships and nations will promote the comities so essential to peace.

We must understand that ties of trade bind nations in closest intimacy, and none may receive except as he gives. We have not strengthened ours in accordance with our resources or our genius, notably on our own continent, where a galaxy of Republics reflects the glory of new-world democracy, but in the new order of finance and trade we mean to promote enlarged activities and seek expanded confidence.

Perhaps we can make no more helpful contribution by example than prove a Republic's capacity to emerge from the wreckage of war. While the world's embittered travail did not leave us devastated lands nor desolated cities, left no gaping wounds, no breast with hate, it did involve us in the delirium of expenditure, in expanded currency and credits, in unbalanced industry, in unspeakable waste, and disturbed relationships. While it uncovered our portion of hateful selfishness at home, it also revealed the heart of America as sound and fearless, and beating in confidence unfailing. Amid it all we have riveted the gaze of all civilization to the unselfishness and the righteousness of representative democracy, where our freedom never has made offensive warfare, never has sought territorial aggrandizement through force, never has turned to the arbitrament of arms until reason has been exhausted. When the Governments of the earth shall have established a freedom like our own and shall have sanctioned the pursuit of peace as we have practiced it, I believe the last sorrow and the final sacrifice of international warfare will have been written.

Let me speak to the maimed and wounded soldiers who are present today, and through them convey to their comrades the gratitude of the Republic for their sacrifices in its defense. A generous country will never forget the services you rendered, and you may hope for a policy under Government that will relieve any maimed successors from taking your places on another such occasion as this.

Our supreme task is the resumption of our onward, normal way. Reconstruction, readjustment, restoration all these must follow. I would like to hasten them. If it will lighten the spirit and add to the resolution with which we take up the task, let me repeat for our Nation, we shall give no people just cause to make war upon us; we hold no national prejudices; we entertain no spirit of revenge; we do not hate; we do not covet; we dream of no conquest, nor boast of armed prowess.

If, despite this attitude, war is again forced upon us, I earnestly hope a way may be found which will unify our individual and collective strength and consecrate all America, materially and spiritually, body and soul, to national defense. I can vision the ideal republic, where every man and woman is called under the flag for assignment to duty for whatever service, military or civic, the individual is best fitted; where we may call to universal service every plant, agency, or facility, all in the sublime sacrifice for country, and not one penny of war profit shall inure to the benefit of private individual, corporation, or combination, but all above the normal shall flow into the defense chest of the Nation. There is something inherently wrong, something out of accord with the ideals of representative democracy, when one portion of our citizenship turns its activities to private gain amid defensive war while another is fighting, sacrificing, or dying for national preservation.

Out of such universal service will come a new unity of spirit and purpose, a new confidence and consecration, which would make our defense impregnable, our triumph assured. Then we should have little or no disorganization of our economic, industrial, and commercial systems at home, no staggering war debts, no swollen fortunes to flout the sacrifices of our soldiers, no excuse for sedition, no pitiable slackerism, no outrage of treason. Envy and jealousy would have no soil for their menacing development, and revolution would be without the passion which engenders it.

A regret for the mistakes of yesterday must not, however, blind us to the tasks of today. War never left such an aftermath. There has been staggering loss of life and measureless wastage of materials. Nations are still groping for return to stable ways. Discouraging indebtedness confronts us like all the war-torn nations, and these obligations must be provided for. No civilization can survive repudiation.

We can reduce the abnormal expenditures, and we will. We can strike at war taxation, and we must. We must face the grim necessity, with full knowledge that the task is to be solved, and we must proceed with a full realization that no statute enacted by man can repeal the inexorable laws of nature. Our most dangerous tendency is to expect too much of government, and at the same time do for it too little. We contemplate the immediate task of putting our public household in order. We need a rigid and yet sane economy, combined with fiscal justice, and it must be attended by individual prudence and thrift, which are so essential to this trying hour and reassuring for the future.

The business world reflects the disturbance of war's reaction. Herein flows the lifeblood of material existence. The economic mechanism is intricate and its parts interdependent, and has suffered the shocks and jars incident to abnormal demands, credit inflations, and price upheavals. The normal balances have been impaired, the channels of distribution have been clogged, the relations of labor and management have been strained. We must seek the readjustment with care and courage. Our people must give and take. Prices must reflect the receding fever of war activities. Perhaps we never shall know the old levels of wages again, because war invariably readjusts compensations, and the necessaries of life will show their inseparable relationship, but we must strive for normalcy to reach stability. All the penalties will not be light, nor evenly distributed. There is no way of making them so. There is no instant step from disorder to order. We must face a condition of grim reality, charge off our losses and start afresh. It is the oldest lesson of civilization. I would like government to do all it can to mitigate; then, in understanding, in mutuality of interest, in concern for the common good, our tasks will be solved. No altered system will work a miracle. Any wild experiment will only add to the confusion. Our best assurance lies in efficient administration of our proven system.

The forward course of the business cycle is unmistakable. Peoples are turning from destruction to production. Industry has sensed the changed order and our own people are turning to resume their normal, onward way. The call is for productive America to go on. I know that Congress and the Administration will favor every wise Government policy to aid the resumption and encourage continued progress.

I speak for administrative efficiency, for lightened tax burdens, for sound commercial practices, for adequate credit facilities, for sympathetic concern for all agricultural problems, for the omission of unnecessary interference of Government with business, for an end to Government's experiment in business, and for more efficient business in Government administration. With all of this must attend a mindfulness of the human side of all activities, so that social, industrial, and economic justice will be squared with the purposes of a righteous people.

With the nation-wide induction of womanhood into our political life, we may count upon her intuitions, her refinements, her intelligence, and her influence to exalt the social order. We count upon her exercise of the full privileges and the performance of the duties of citizenship to speed the attainment of the highest state.

I wish for an America no less alert in guarding against dangers from within than it is watchful against enemies from without. Our fundamental law recognizes no class, no group, no section; there must be none in legislation or administration. The supreme inspiration is the common weal. Humanity hungers

for international peace, and we crave it with all mankind. My most reverent prayer for America is for industrial peace, with its rewards, widely and generally distributed, amid the inspirations of equal opportunity. No one justly may deny the equality of opportunity which made us what we are. We have mistaken unpreparedness to embrace it to be a challenge of the reality, and due concern for making all citizens fit for participation will give added strength of citizenship and magnify our achievement.

If revolution insists upon overturning established order, let other peoples make the tragic experiment. There is no place for it in America. When World War threatened civilization we pledged our resources and our lives to its preservation, and when revolution threatens we unfurl the flag of law and order and renew our consecration. Ours is a constitutional freedom where the popular will is the law supreme and minorities are sacredly protected. Our revisions, reformations, and evolutions reflect a deliberate judgment and an orderly progress, and we mean to cure our ills, but never destroy or permit destruction by force.

I had rather submit our industrial controversies to the conference table in advance than to a settlement table after conflict and suffering. The earth is thirsting for the cup of good will, understanding is its fountain source. I would like to acclaim an era of good feeling amid dependable prosperity and all the blessings which attend.

It has been proved again and again that we cannot, while throwing our markets open to the world, maintain American standards of living

and opportunity, and hold our industrial eminence in such unequal competition. There is a luring fallacy in the theory of banished barriers of trade, but preserved American standards require our higher production costs to be reflected in our tariffs on imports. Today, as never before, when peoples are seeking trade restoration and expansion, we must adjust our tariffs to the new order. We seek participation in the world's exchanges, because therein lies our way to widened influence and the triumphs of peace. We know full well we cannot sell where we do not buy, and we cannot sell successfully where we do not carry. Opportunity is calling not alone for the restoration, but for a new era in production, transportation and trade. We shall answer it best by meeting the demand of a surpassing home market, by promoting self-reliance in production, and by bidding enterprise, genius, and efficiency to carry our cargoes in American bottoms to the marts of the world.

We would not have an America living within and for herself alone, but we would have her self-reliant, independent, and ever nobler, stronger, and richer. Believing in our higher standards, reared through constitutional liberty and maintained opportunity, we invite the world to the same heights. But pride in things wrought is no reflex of a completed task. Common welfare is the goal of our national endeavor. Wealth is not inimical to welfare; it ought to be its friendliest agency. There never can be equality of rewards or possessions so long as the human plan contains varied talents and differing degrees of industry and thrift, but ours ought to be a country free from the great blotches of distressed poverty. We ought to find a way to guard against the perils and penalties of unemployment. We want an America of homes, illumined with hope and happiness, where mothers, freed from the necessity for long hours of toil beyond their own doors, may preside as befits the hearthstone of American citizenship. We want the cradle of American childhood rocked under conditions so wholesome and so hopeful that no blight may touch it in its de-

velopment, and we want to provide that no selfish interest, no material necessity, no lack of opportunity shall prevent the gaining of that education so essential to best citizenship.

There is no short cut to the making of these ideals into glad realities. The world has witnessed again and again the futility and the mischief of ill-considered remedies for social and economic disorders. But we are mindful today as never before of the friction of modern industrialism, and we must learn its causes and reduce its evil consequences by sober and tested methods. Where genius has made for great possibilities, justice and happiness must be reflected in a greater common welfare.

Service is the supreme commitment of life. I would rejoice to acclaim the era of the Golden Rule and crown it with the autocracy of service. I pledge an administration wherein all the agencies of Government are called to serve, and ever promote an understanding of Government purely as an expression of the popular will.

One cannot stand in this presence and be unmindful of the tremendous responsibility. The world upheaval has added heavily to our tasks. But with the realization comes the surge of high resolve, and there is reassurance in belief in the God-given destiny of our Republic. If I felt that there is to be sole responsibility in the Executive for the America of tomorrow I should shrink from the burden. But here are a hundred millions, with common concern and shared responsibility, answerable to God and country. The Republic summons them to their duty, and I invite co-operation.

I accept my part with single-mindedness of purpose and humility of spirit, and implore the favor and guidance of God in His Heaven. With these I am unafraid, and confidently face the future.

I have taken the solemn oath of office on that passage of Holy Writ wherein it is asked: "What doth the Lord require of thee but to do justly, and to love mercy, and to walk humbly with thy God?" This I plight to God and country.

* * *

1924 CALVIN COOLIDGE

S ILENT CAL" COOLIDGE, who had done so much to help the Republicans recover from the scandals of the Harding administration, was rewarded for his efforts with a first-ballot nomination at the first national party convention ever broadcast on radio. The Democrats, meanwhile, took 103 ballots to decide between Governor Alfred E. Smith of New York and former treasury secretary William G. McAdoo, finally choosing neither. Instead, the party nominated John W. Davis, an obscure West Virginian who had served as U.S. ambassador to Great Britain during World War I and helped Wilson negotiate the ill-fated Treaty of Versailles. Nebraska governor Charles W. Bryan, younger brother of three-time loser William Jennings Bryan, completed the weak ticket. Disgruntled liberal Republicans with no interest in supporting Davis and Bryan joined agrarian populists and urban socialists in forming a new Progressive party and nominating Wisconsin senator Robert M. La Follette.

Coolidge didn't campaign—and didn't have to: The apparent prosperity of the Roaring Twenties spoke for itself and drowned out all the Harding scandals. Davis traveled widely and made several radio addresses, but most voters ignored him, having already heard more than they wanted to about Teapot Dome. In fact, after the chaos of the Democratic convention, even loyal party members came to appreciate Will Rogers' celebrated gibe: "I'm not a member of an organized party. I'm a Democrat." The Republicans mostly ignored Davis and instead concentrated their efforts on halting defections to the Progressives, whom they attacked for favoring socialism.

Coolidge would have won in any case, but his election became a landslide when urban Catholics abandoned the Democratic party, believing that Al Smith had been denied the nomination because of his Catholic religion. Davis (with 28.8 percent of the popular vote) and La Follette (with 16.6 percent) lagged far behind the president in an election marked by one of the lowest turnouts in American history.

PARTY	POPULAR VOTES	ELECTORAL VOTES
REPUBLICAN Calvin Coolidge, Mass. Charles G. Dawes, Ill.	15,719,921	382
DEMOCRATIC John W. Davis, W.Va. Charles W. Bryan, Neb.	8,386,704	136
PROGRESSIVE Robert M. La Follette, Wis. Burton K. Wheeler, Mont.	4,832,532	13

Inaugural Address • Washington, D.C. • Wednesday, March 4, 1925

My Countrymen: No one can contemplate current conditions whithout

finding much that is satisfying and still more that is encouraging. Our own country is leading the world in the general readjustment to the results of the great conflict. Many of its burdens will bear heavily upon us for years, and the secondary and indirect effects we must expect to experience for some time. But we are beginning to comprehend more definitely what course should be pursued, what remedies ought to be applied, what actions should be taken for our deliverance, and are clearly manifesting a determined will faithfully and conscientiously to adopt these methods of relief. Already we have sufficiently rearranged our domestic affairs so that confidence has returned, business has revived, and we appear to be entering an era of prosperity which is gradually reaching into every part of the Nation. Realizing that we can not live unto ourselves alone, we have contributed of our resources and our counsel to the relief of the suffering and the settlement of the disputes among the European nations. Because of what America is and what America has done, a firmer courage, a higher hope, inspires the heart of all humanity.

These results have not occurred by mere chance. They have been secured by a constant and enlightened effort marked by many sacrifices and extending over many generations. We can not continue these brilliant successes in the future, unless we continue to learn from the past. It is necessary to keep the former experiences of our country both at home and abroad continually before us, if we are to have any science of government. If we wish to erect new structures, we must have a definite knowledge of the old foundations. We must realize that human nature is about the most constant thing in the universe and that the essentials of human relationship do not change. We must frequently take our bearings from these fixed stars of our political firmament if we expect to hold a true course. If we examine carefully what we have done, we can determine the more accurately what we can do.

We stand at the opening of the one hundred and fiftieth year since our national consciousness first asserted itself by unmistakable action with an array of force. The old sentiment of detached and dependent colonies disappeared in the new sentiment of a united and independent Nation. Men began to discard the narrow confines of a local charter for the broader opportunities of a national constitution. Under the eternal urge of freedom we became an independent Nation. A little less than 50 years later that freedom and independence were reasserted in the face of all the world, and guarded, supported, and secured by the Monroe doctrine. The narrow fringe of States along the Atlantic seaboard advanced its frontiers across the hills and plains of an intervening continent until it passed down the golden slope to the Pacific. We made freedom a birthright. We extended our domain over distant islands in order to safeguard our own interests and accepted the consequent obligation to bestow justice and liberty upon less favored peoples. In the defense of our own ideals and in the general cause of liberty we entered the Great War. When victory had been fully secured, we withdrew to our own shores unrecompensed save in the consciousness of duty done.

Throughout all these experiences we have enlarged our freedom, we have strengthened our independence. We have been, and propose to be, more and more American. We believe that we can best serve our own country and most successfully discharge our obligations to humanity by continuing to be openly and candidly, intensely and scrupulously, American. If we have any heritage, it has been that. If we have any destiny, we have found it in that direction.

But if we wish to continue to be distinctively American, we must continue to make that term comprehensive enough to embrace the legitimate desires of a civilized and enlightened people determined in all their relations to pursue a conscientious and religious life. We can not permit ourselves to be narrowed and dwarfed by slogans and phrases. It is not the adjective, but the substantive, which is of real importance. It is not the name of the action, but the result of the action, which is the chief concern. It will be well not to be too much disturbed by the thought of either isolation or entanglement of pacifists and militarists. The physical configuration of the earth has separated us from all of the Old World, but the common brotherhood of man, the highest law of all our being, has united us by inseparable bonds with all humanity. Our country represents nothing but peaceful

---

This country believes in prosperity. It is absurd to suppose that it is envious of those who are already prosperous.

---

intentions toward all the earth, but it ought not to fail to maintain such a military force as comports with the dignity and security of a great people. It ought to be a balanced force, intensely modern, capable of defense by sea and land, beneath the surface and in the air. But it should be so conducted that all the world may see in it, not a menace, but an instrument of security and peace.

This Nation believes thoroughly in an honorable peace under which the rights of its citizens are to be everywhere protected. It has never found that the necessary enjoyment of such a peace could be maintained only by a great and threatening array of arms. In common with other nations, it is now more determined than ever to promote peace through friendliness and good will, through mutual understandings and mutual forbearance. We have never practiced the policy of competitive armaments. We have recently committed ourselves by covenants with the other great nations to a limitation of our sea power. As one result of this, our Navy ranks larger, in comparison, than it ever did before. Removing the burden of expense and jealousy, which must always accrue from a keen rivalry, is one of the most effective methods of diminishing that unreasonable hysteria and misunderstanding which are the most potent means of fomenting war. This policy represents a new departure in the world. It is a thought, an ideal, which has led to an entirely new line of action. It will not be easy to maintain. Some never moved from their old positions, some are constantly slipping back to the old ways of thought and the old action of seizing a musket and relying on force. America has taken the lead in this new direction, and that lead America must continue to hold. If we expect others to rely on our fairness and justice we must show that we rely on their fairness and justice.

If we are to judge by past experience, there is much to be hoped for in international relations from frequent conferences and consultations. We have before us the beneficial results of the Washington conference and the various consultations recently held upon European affairs, some of which were in response to our suggestions and in some of which we were active participants. Even the failures can not but be accounted useful and an immeasurable advance over threatened or actual warfare. I am strongly in favor of continuation of this policy, whenever conditions are such that there is even a promise that practical and favorable results might be secured.

In conformity with the principle that a display of reason rather than a threat of force should be the determining factor in the intercourse among nations, we have long advocated the peaceful settlement of disputes by methods of arbitration and have negotiated many treaties to secure that result. The same considerations should lead to our adherence to the Permanent Court of International Justice. Where great principles are involved, where great

movements are under way which promise much for the welfare of humanity by reason of the very fact that many other nations have given such movements their actual support, we ought not to withhold our own sanction because of any small and inessential difference, but only upon the ground of the most important and compelling fundamental reasons. We can not barter away our independence or our sovereignty, but we ought to engage in no refinements of logic, no sophistries, and no subterfuges, to argue away the undoubted duty of this country by reason of the might of its numbers, the power of its resources, and its position of leadership in the world, actively and comprehensively to signify its approval and to bear its full share of the responsibility of a candid and disinterested attempt at the establishment of a tribunal for the administration of even-handed justice between nation and nation. The weight of our enormous influence must be cast upon the side of a reign not of force but of law and trial, not by battle but by reason.

We have never any wish to interfere in the political conditions of any other countries. Especially are we determined not to become implicated in the political controversies of the Old World. With a great deal of hesitation, we have responded to appeals for help to maintain order, protect life and property, and establish responsible government in some of the small countries of the Western Hemisphere. Our private citizens have advanced large sums of money to assist in the necessary financing and relief of the Old World. We have not failed, nor shall we fail to respond, whenever necessary to mitigate human suffering and assist in the rehabilitation of distressed nations. These, too, are requirements which must be met by reason of our vast powers and the place we hold in the world.

Some of the best thought of mankind has long been seeking for a formula for permanent peace. Undoubtedly the clarification of the principles of international law would be helpful, and the efforts of scholars to prepare such a work for adoption by the various nations should have our sympathy and

support. Much may be hoped for from the earnest studies of those who advocate the outlawing of aggressive war. But all these plans and preparations, these treaties and covenants, will not of themselves be adequate. One of the greatest dangers to peace lies in the economic pressure to which people find themselves subjected. One of the most practical things to be done in the world is to seek arrangements under which such pressure may be removed, so that opportunity may be renewed and hope may be revived. There must be some assurance that effort and endeavor will be followed by success and prosperity. In the making and financing of such adjustments there is not only an opportunity, but a real duty, for America to respond with her counsel and her resources. Conditions must be provided under which people can make a living and work out of their difficulties. But there is another element, more important than all, without which there can not be the slightest hope of a permanent peace. That element lies in the heart of humanity. Unless the desire for peace be cherished there, unless this fundamental and only natural source of brotherly love be cultivated to its highest degree, all artificial efforts will be in vain. Peace will come when there is realization that only under a reign of law, based on righteousness and supported by the religious conviction of the brotherhood of man, can there be any hope of a complete and satisfying life. Parchment will

fail, the sword will fail, it is only the spiritual nature of man that can be triumphant.

It seems altogether probable that we can contribute most to these important objects by maintaining our position of political detachment and independence. We are not identified with any Old World interests. This position should be made more and more clear in our relations with all foreign countries. We are at peace with all of them. Our program is never to oppress, but always to assist. But while we do justice to others, we must require that justice be done to us. With us a treaty of peace means peace, and a treaty of amity means amity. We have made great contributions to the settlement of contentious differences in both Europe and Asia. But there is a very definite point beyond which we can not go. We can only help those who help themselves. Mindful of these limitations, the one great duty that stands out requires us to use our enormous powers to trim the balance of the world.

While we can look with a great deal of pleasure upon what we have done abroad, we must remember that our continued success in that direction depends upon what we do at home. Since its very outset, it has been found necessary to conduct our Government by means of political parties. That system would not have survived from generation to generation if it had not been fundamentally sound and provided the best instrumentalities for the most complete expression of the popular will. It is not necessary to

claim that it has always worked perfectly. It is enough to know that nothing better has been devised. No one would deny that there should be full and free expression and an opportunity for independence of action within the party. There is no salvation in a narrow and bigoted partisanship. But if there is to be responsible party government, the party label must be something more than a mere device for securing office. Unless those who are elected under the same party designation are willing to assume sufficient responsibility and exhibit sufficient loyalty and coherence, so that they can cooperate with each other in the support of the broad general principles, of the party platform, the election is merely a mockery, no decision is made at the polls, and there is no representation of the popular will. Common honesty and good faith with the people who support a party at the polls require that party, when it enters office, to assume the control of that portion of the Government to which it has been elected. Any other course is bad faith and a violation of the party pledges.

When the country has bestowed its confidence upon a party by making it a majority in the Congress, it has a right to expect such unity of action as will make the party majority an effective instrument of government. This Administration has come into power with a very clear and definite mandate from the people. The expression of the popular will in favor of maintaining our constitutional guarantees was overwhelming and decisive. There was a manifestation of such faith in the integrity of the courts that we can consider that issue rejected for some time to come. Likewise, the policy of public ownership of railroads and certain electric utilities met with unmistakable defeat. The people declared that they wanted their rights to have not a political but a judicial determination, and their independence and freedom continued and supported by having the ownership and control of their property, not in the Government, but in their own hands. As they always do when they have a fair chance, the people demonstrated that they are sound and are determined

to have a sound government.

When we turn from what was rejected to inquire what was accepted, the policy that stands out with the greatest clearness is that of economy in public expenditure with reduction and reform of taxation. The principle involved in this effort is that of conservation. The resources of this country are almost beyond computation. No mind can comprehend them. But the cost of our combined governments is likewise almost beyond definition. Not only those who are now making their tax returns, but those who meet the enhanced cost of existence in their monthly bills, know by hard experience what this great burden is and what it does. No matter what others may want, these people want a drastic economy. They are opposed to waste. They know that extravagance lengthens the hours and diminishes the rewards of their labor. I favor the policy of economy, not because I wish to save money, but because I wish to save people. The men and women of this country who toil are the ones who bear the cost of the Government. Every dollar that we carelessly waste means that their life will be so much the more meager. Every dollar that we prudently save means that their life will be so much the more abundant. Economy is idealism in its most practical form.

If extravagance were not reflected in taxation, and through taxation both directly and indirectly injuriously affecting the people, it would not be of so much consequence. The wisest and soundest method of solving our tax problem is through economy. Fortunately, of all the great nations this country is best in a position to adopt that simple remedy. We do not any longer need wartime revenues. The collection of any taxes which are not absolutely required, which do not beyond reasonable doubt contribute to the public welfare, is only a species of legalized larceny. Under this republic the rewards of industry belong to those who earn them. The only constitutional tax is the tax which ministers to public necessity. The property of the country belongs to the people of the country. Their title is absolute. They do not support any privileged class; they do not need to maintain great military forces; they ought not to be burdened with a great array of public employees. They are not required to make any contribution to Government expenditures except that which they voluntarily assess upon themselves through the action of their own representatives. Whenever taxes become burdensome a remedy can be applied by the people; but if they do not act for themselves, no one can be very successful in acting for them.

The time is arriving when we can have further tax reduction, when, unless we wish to hamper the people in their right to earn a living, we must have tax reform. The method of raising revenue ought not to impede the transaction of business; it ought to encourage it. I am opposed to extremely high rates, because they produce little or no revenue, because they are bad for the country, and, finally, because they are wrong. We can not finance the country, we can not improve social conditions, through any system of injustice, even if we attempt to inflict it upon the rich. Those who suffer the most harm will be the poor. This country believes in prosperity. It is absurd to suppose that it is envious of those who are already prosperous. The wise and correct course to follow in taxation and all other economic legislation is not to destroy those who have already secured success but to create conditions under which every one will have a better chance to be successful. The verdict of the country has been given on this question. That verdict stands. We shall do well to heed it.

These questions involve moral issues. We need not concern ourselves much about the rights of property if we will faithfully observe the rights of persons. Under our institutions their rights are supreme. It is not property but the right to hold property, both great and small, which our Constitution guarantees. All owners of property are charged with a service. These rights and duties have been revealed, through the conscience of society, to have a divine sanction. The very stability of our society rests upon production and conservation. For individuals or for governments to waste and squander their resources is to deny these rights and disregard these obligations. The result of economic dissipation to a nation is always moral decay.

These policies of better international understandings, greater economy, and lower taxes have contributed largely to peaceful and prosperous industrial relations. Under the helpful influences of restrictive immigration and a protective tariff, employment is plentiful, the rate of pay is high, and wage earners are in a state of contentment seldom before seen. Our transportation systems have been gradually recovering and have been able to meet all the requirements of the service. Agriculture has been very slow in reviving, but the price of cereals at last indicates that the day of its deliverance is at hand.

We are not without our problems, but our most important problem is not to secure new advantages but to maintain those which we already possess. Our system of government made up of three separate and independent departments, our divided sovereignty composed of Nation and State, the matchless wisdom that is enshrined in our Constitution, all these need constant effort and tireless vigilance for their protection and support.

In a republic the first rule for the guidance of the citizen is obedience to law. Under a despotism the law may be imposed upon the subject. He has no voice in its making, no influence in its administration, it does not represent him. Under a free government the citizen makes his own laws, chooses his own administrators, which do represent him. Those who want their rights respected under the Constitution and the law ought to set the example themselves of observing the Constitution and the law. While there may be those of high intelligence who violate the law at times, the barbarian and the defective always violate it. Those who disregard the rules of society are not exhibiting a superior intelligence, are not promoting freedom and independence, are not following the path of civilization, but are displaying the traits of ignorance, of servitude, of savagery, and treading the way that leads back to the jungle.

The essence of a republic is representative government. Our Congress represents the people and the States. In all legislative affairs it is the natural collaborator with the President. In spite of all the criticism which often falls to its lot, I do not hesitate to say that there is no more independent and effective legislative body in the world. It is, and should be, jealous of its prerogative. I welcome its cooperation, and expect to share with it not only the responsibility, but the credit, for our common effort to secure beneficial legislation.

These are some of the principles which America represents. We have not by any means put them fully into practice, but we have strongly signified our belief in them. The encouraging feature of our country is not that it has reached its destination, but that it has overwhelmingly expressed its determination to proceed in the right direction. It is true that we could, with profit, be less sectional and more national in our thought. It would be well if we could replace much that is only a false and ignorant prejudice with a true and enlightened pride of race. But the last election showed that appeals to class and nationality had little effect. We were all found loyal to a common citizenship. The fundamental precept of liberty is toleration. We can not permit any inquisition either within or without the law or apply any religious test to the holding of office. The mind of America must be forever free.

It is in such contemplations, my fellow countrymen, which are not exhaustive but only representative, that I find ample warrant for satisfaction and encouragement. We should not let the much that is to do obscure the much which has been done. The past and present show faith and hope and courage fully justified. Here stands our country, an example of tranquillity at home, a patron of tranquillity abroad. Here stands its Government, aware of its might but obedient to its conscience. Here it will continue to stand, seeking peace and prosperity, solicitous for the welfare of the wage earner, promoting enterprise, developing waterways and natural resources, attentive to the intuitive counsel of womanhood, encouraging education, desiring the advancement of religion, supporting the cause of justice and honor among the nations. America seeks no earthly empire built on blood and force. No ambition, no temptation, lures her to thought of foreign dominions. The legions which she sends forth are armed, not with the sword, but with the cross. The higher state to which she seeks the allegiance of all mankind is not of human, but of divine origin. She cherishes no purpose save to merit the favor of Almighty God.

* * *

KEEP COOL WITH **COOLIDGE** FOR PRESIDENT

CAMPAIGN HEADQUARTERS - THE RED GARTER

1928 Herbert Hoover

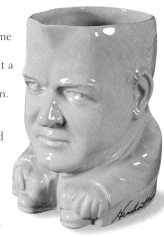

WHEN CALVIN Coolidge decided not to seek another term, his energetic commerce secretary, Herbert Hoover, coasted easily to the Republican nomination. On the Democratic side, New York governor Alfred E. Smith, known as the Happy Warrior, received the nomination denied him four years earlier. Aware that Smith's Catholicism and support for the repeal of Prohibition made him a problematic candidate, the Democrats balanced their ticket with Senate Minority Leader Joseph T. Robinson of Arkansas, a running mate they believed could hold the fundamentalist South.

Republicans emphasized the peace and prosperity of the Coolidge years with the slogan, "A Car in Every Garage and a Chicken in Every Pot," to which Smith had no real comeback. His New York accent played poorly on the new medium of radio, and the Democratic campaign song "Better Times with Al" wasn't very persuasive no matter how loudly it was sung. Discreet charges of "Romanism" hurt him most of all.

Hoover won in a rout, but Smith's campaign laid some of the groundwork for what would become in the hands of Franklin Roosevelt a multifaceted governing coalition. Smith and the Democrats particularly gained ground among Catholic and other urban workers who previously had voted Republican.

Party	Popular Votes	Electoral Votes
Republican Herbert C. Hoover, Calif. Charles Curtis, Kan.	21,437,277	444
Democratic Alfred E. Smith, N.Y. Joseph T. Robinson, Ark.	15,007,698	87

Inaugural Address • Washington, D.C. • Monday, March 4, 1929

My Countrymen: This occasion is not alone the administration of the most

sacred oath which can be assumed by an American citizen. It is a dedication and consecration under God to the highest office in service of our people. I assume this trust in the humility of knowledge that only through the guidance of Almighty Providence can I hope to discharge its ever-increasing burdens.

It is in keeping with tradition throughout our history that I should express simply and directly the opinions which I hold concerning some of the matters of present importance.

If we survey the situation of our Nation both at home and abroad, we find many satisfactions; we find some causes for concern. We have emerged from the losses of the Great War and the reconstruction following it with increased virility and strength. From this strength we have contributed to the recovery and progress of the world. What America has done has given renewed hope and courage to all who have faith in government by the people. In the large view, we have reached a higher degree of comfort and security than ever existed before in the history of the world. Through liberation from widespread poverty we have reached a higher

degree of individual freedom than ever before. The devotion to and concern for our institutions are deep and sincere. We are steadily building a new race—a new civilization great in its own attainments. The influence and high purposes of our Nation are respected among the peoples of the world. We aspire to distinction in the world, but to a distinction based upon confidence in our sense of justice as well as our accomplishments within our own borders and in our own lives. For wise guidance in this great period of recovery the Nation is deeply indebted to Calvin Coolidge.

But all this majestic advance should not obscure the constant dangers from which self-government must be safeguarded. The strong man must at all times be alert to the attack of insidious disease.

The most malign of all these dangers today is disregard and disobedience of law. Crime is increasing. Confidence in rigid and speedy justice is decreasing. I am not prepared to believe that this indicates any decay in the moral fiber of the American people. I am not prepared to believe that it indicates an impotence of the Federal Government to enforce its laws.

It is only in part due to the additional burdens imposed upon our judicial system by the eighteenth amendment. The problem is much wider than that. Many influences had increasingly complicated and weakened our law enforcement organization long before the adoption of the eighteenth amendment.

To reestablish the vigor and effectiveness of law enforcement we must critically consider the entire Federal machinery of justice, the redistribution of its functions, the simplification of its procedure, the provision of additional special tribunals, the better selection of juries, and the more effective organization of our agencies of investigation and prosecution that justice may be sure and that it may be swift. While the authority of the Federal Government extends to but part of our vast system of national, State, and local justice, yet the standards which the Federal Government establishes have the most profound influence upon the whole structure.

We are fortunate in the ability and integrity of our Federal judges and attorneys. But the system which these officers are called upon to administer is in many respects ill adapted to present-day conditions.

Its intricate and involved rules of procedure have become the refuge of both big and little criminals. There is a belief abroad that by invoking technicalities, subterfuge, and delay, the ends of justice may be thwarted by those who can pay the cost.

Reform, reorganization and strengthening of our whole judicial and enforcement system, both in civil and criminal sides, have been advocated for years by statesmen, judges, and bar associations. First steps toward that end should not longer be delayed. Rigid and expeditious justice is the first safeguard of freedom, the basis of all ordered liberty, the vital force of progress. It must not come to be in our Republic that it can be defeated by the indifference of the citizen, by exploitation of the delays and entanglements of the law, or by combinations of criminals. Justice must not fail because the agencies of enforcement are either delinquent or inefficiently organized. To consider these evils, to find their remedy, is the most sore necessity of our times.

Of the undoubted abuses which have grown up under the eighteenth amendment, part are due to the causes I have just mentioned; but part are due to the failure of some States to accept their share of responsibility for concurrent enforcement and to the failure of many State and local officials to accept the obligation under their oath of office zealously to enforce the laws. With the failures from these many causes has come a dangerous expansion in the criminal elements who have found enlarged opportunities in dealing in illegal liquor.

But a large responsibility rests directly upon our citizens. There would be little traffic in illegal liquor if only criminals patronized it. We must awake to the fact that this patronage from large numbers of law-abiding citizens is supplying the rewards and stimulating crime.

I have been selected by you to execute and enforce the laws of the country. I propose to do so to the extent of my own abilities, but the measure of

success that the Government shall attain will depend upon the moral support which you, as citizens, extend. The duty of citizens to support the laws of the land is coequal with the duty of their Government to enforce the laws which exist. No greater national service can be given by men and women of good will—who, I know, are not unmindful of the responsibilities of citizenship—than that they should, by their example, assist in stamping out crime and outlawry by refusing participation in and condemning all transactions with illegal liquor. Our whole system of self-government will crumble either if officials elect what laws they will enforce or citizens elect what laws they will support. The worst evil of disregard for some law is that it destroys respect for all law. For our citizens to patronize the violation of a particular law on the ground that they are opposed to it is destructive of the very basis of all that protection of life, of

homes and property which they rightly claim under other laws. If citizens do not like a law, their duty as honest men and women is to discourage its violation; their right is openly to work for its repeal.

To those of criminal mind there can be no appeal but vigorous enforcement of the law. Fortunately they are but a small percentage of our people. Their activities must be stopped.

I propose to appoint a national commission for a searching investigation of the whole structure of our Federal system of jurisprudence, to include the method of enforcement of the

eighteenth amendment and the causes of abuse under it. Its purpose will be to make such recommendations for reorganization of the administration of Federal laws and court procedure as may be found desirable. In the meantime it is essential that a large part of the enforcement activities be transferred from the Treasury Department to the Department of Justice as a beginning of more effective organization.

> *The worst evil of disregard for some law is that it destroys respect for all law.*

The election has again confirmed the determination of the American people that regulation of private enterprise and not Government ownership or operation is the course rightly to be pursued in our relation to business. In recent years we have established a differentiation in the whole method of business regulation between the industries which produce and distribute commodities on the one hand and public utilities on the other. In the former, our laws insist upon effective competition; in the latter, because we substantially confer a monopoly by limiting competition, we must regulate their services and rates. The rigid enforcement of the laws applicable to both groups is the very base of equal opportunity and freedom from domination for all our people, and it is just as essential for the stability and prosperity of business itself as for the protection of the public at large. Such regulation should be extended by the Federal Government within the limitations of the Constitution and only when the individual States are without power to protect their citizens through their own authority. On the other hand, we should be fearless when the authority rests only in the Federal Government.

The larger purpose of our economic thought should be to establish more firmly stability and security of business and employment and thereby remove poverty still further from our borders. Our people have in recent years developed a new-found capacity for cooperation among themselves to effect high purposes in public welfare. It is an advance toward the highest conception of self-government. Self-government does not and should not imply the use of political agencies alone. Progress is born of cooperation in the community—not from governmental restraints. The Government should assist and encourage these movements of collective self-help by itself cooperating with them. Business has by cooperation made great progress in the advancement of service, in stability, in regularity of employment and in the correction of its own abuses. Such progress, however, can continue only so long as business manifests its respect for law.

There is an equally important field of cooperation by the Federal Government with the multitude of agencies, State, municipal and private, in the systematic development of those processes which directly affect public health, recreation, education, and the home. We have need further to perfect the means by which Government can be adapted to human service.

Although education is primarily a responsibility of the States and local communities, and rightly so, yet the Nation as a whole is vitally concerned in its development everywhere to the highest standards and to complete universality. Self-government can succeed only through an instructed electorate. Our objective is not simply to overcome illiteracy. The Nation has marched far beyond that. The more complex the problems of the Nation become, the greater is the need for more and more advanced instruction. Moreover, as our numbers increase and as our life expands with science and invention, we must discover more and more leaders for every walk of life. We can not hope to succeed in directing this increasingly complex civilization unless we can draw all the talent of leadership from the whole people. One civilization after another has been wrecked upon the attempt to secure sufficient leadership from a single group or class. If we would prevent the growth of class distinctions and would constantly refresh our leadership with the ideals of our people, we must draw constantly from the general mass. The full opportunity for every boy and girl to rise through the selective processes of education can alone secure to us this leadership.

In public health the discoveries of science have opened a new era. Many sections of our country and many groups of our citizens suffer from diseases the eradication of which are mere matters of administration and moderate expenditure. Public health service should be as fully organized and as universally incorporated into our governmental system as is public education. The returns are a thousand fold in economic benefits, and infinitely more in reduction of suffering and promotion of human happiness. World Peace

The United States fully accepts the profound truth that our own progress, prosperity, and peace are interlocked with the progress, prosperity, and peace of all humanity. The whole world is at peace. The dangers to a continuation of this peace to-day are largely the fear and suspicion which still haunt the world. No suspicion or fear can be rightly directed toward our country.

Those who have a true understanding of America know that we have no desire for territorial expansion, for economic or other domination of other peoples. Such purposes are repugnant to our ideals of human freedom. Our form of government is ill adapted to the responsibilities which inevitably follow permanent limitation of the independence of other peoples. Superficial observers seem to find no destiny for our abounding increase in population, in wealth and power except that of imperialism. They fail to see that the American people are engrossed in the building for themselves of a new economic system, a new social system, a new political system all of which are charac-

terized by aspirations of freedom of opportunity and thereby are the negation of imperialism. They fail to realize that because of our abounding prosperity our youth are pressing more and more into our institutions of learning; that our people are seeking a larger vision through art, literature, science, and travel; that they are moving toward stronger moral and spiritual life—that from these things our sympathies are broadening beyond the bounds of our Nation and race toward their true expression in a real brotherhood of man. They fail to see that the idealism of America will lead it to no narrow or selfish channel, but inspire it to do its full share as a nation toward the advancement of civilization. It will do that not by mere declaration but by taking a practical part in supporting all useful international undertakings. We not only desire peace with the world, but to see peace maintained throughout the world. We wish to advance the reign of justice and reason toward the extinction of force.

The recent treaty for the renunciation of war as an instrument of national policy sets an advanced standard in our conception of the relations of nations. Its acceptance should pave the way to greater limitation of armament, the offer of which we sincerely extend to the world. But its full realization also implies a greater and greater perfection in the instrumentalities for pacific settlement of controversies between nations. In the creation and use of these instrumentalities we should support every sound method of conciliation, arbitration, and judicial settlement. American statesmen were among the first to propose and they have constantly urged upon the world, the establishment of a tribunal for the settlement of controversies of a justiciable character. The Permanent Court of International Justice in its major purpose is thus peculiarly identified with American ideals and with American statesmanship. No more potent instrumentality for this purpose has ever been conceived and no other is practicable of establishment. The reservations placed upon our adherence should not be misinterpreted. The United

States seeks by these reservations no special privilege or advantage but only to clarify our relation to advisory opinions and other matters which are subsidiary to the major purpose of the court. The way should, and I believe will, be found by which we may take our proper place in a movement so fundamental to the progress of peace.

Our people have determined that we should make no political engagements such as membership in the League of Nations, which may commit us in advance as a nation to become involved in the settlements of controversies between other countries. They adhere to the belief that the independence of America from such obligations increases its ability and availability for service in all fields of human progress.

> *I have no fears for the future of our country. It is bright with hope.*

I have lately returned from a journey among our sister Republics of the Western Hemisphere. I have received unbounded hospitality and courtesy as their expression of friendliness to our country. We are held by particular bonds of sympathy and common interest with them. They are each of them building a racial character and a culture which is an impressive contribution to human progress. We wish only for the maintenance of their independence, the growth of their stability, and their prosperity. While we have had wars in the Western Hemisphere, yet on the whole the record is in encouraging contrast with that of other parts of the world. Fortunately the New World is largely free from the inheritances of fear and distrust which have so troubled the Old World. We should keep it so.

It is impossible, my countrymen, to speak of peace without profound emotion. In thousands of homes in America,

in millions of homes around the world, there are vacant chairs. It would be a shameful confession of our unworthiness if it should develop that we have abandoned the hope for which all these men died. Surely civilization is old enough, surely mankind is mature enough so that we ought in our own lifetime to find a way to permanent peace. Abroad, to west and east, are nations whose sons mingled their blood with the blood of our sons on the battlefields. Most of these nations have contributed to our race, to our culture, our knowledge, and our progress. From one of them we derive our very language and from many of them much of the genius of our institutions. Their desire for peace is as deep and sincere as our own.

Peace can be contributed to by respect for our ability in defense. Peace can be promoted by the limitation of arms and by the creation of the instrumentalities for peaceful settlement of controversies. But it will become a reality only through self-restraint and active effort in friendliness and helpfulness. I covet for this administration a record of having further contributed to advance the cause of peace.

In our form of democracy the expression of the popular will can be effected only through the instrumentality of political parties. We maintain party government not to promote intolerant partisanship but because opportunity must be given for expression of the popular will, and organization provided for the execution of its mandates and for accountability of government to the people. It follows that the government both in the executive and the legislative branches must carry out in good faith the platforms upon which the party was entrusted with power. But the government is that of the whole people; the party is the instrument through which policies are determined and men chosen to bring them into being. The animosities of elections should have no place in our Government, for government must concern itself alone with the common weal.

Action upon some of the proposals upon which the Republican Party was returned to power, particularly further

★ For President ★

ALFRED E. SMITH

Wm. T. Wager 500 Willis Ave. Bronx N.Y. Tel. Melrose 7592-5021

ening of poverty; the freedom of public opinion; the sustaining of education and of the advancement of knowledge; the growth of religious spirit and the tolerance of all faiths; the strengthening of the home; the advancement of peace.

There is no short road to the realization of these aspirations. Ours is a progressive people, but with a determination that progress must be based upon the foundation of experience. Ill-considered remedies for our faults bring only penalties after them. But if we hold the faith of the men in our mighty past who created these ideals, we shall leave them heightened and strengthened for our children.

This is not the time and place for extended discussion. The questions before our country are problems of progress to higher standards; they are not the problems of degeneration. They demand thought and they serve to quicken the conscience and enlist our sense of responsibility for their settlement. And that responsibility rests upon you, my countrymen, as much as upon those of us who have been selected for office.

Ours is a land rich in resources; stimulating in its glorious beauty; filled with millions of happy homes; blessed with comfort and opportunity. In no nation are the institutions of progress more advanced. In no nation are the fruits of accomplishment more secure. In no nation is the government more worthy of respect. No country is more loved by its people. I have an abiding faith in their capacity, integrity and high purpose. I have no fears for the future of our country. It is bright with hope.

In the presence of my countrymen, mindful of the solemnity of this occasion, knowing what the task means and the responsibility which it involves, I beg your tolerance, your aid, and your cooperation. I ask the help of Almighty God in this service to my country to which you have called me.

* * *

agricultural relief and limited changes in the tariff, cannot in justice to our farmers, our labor, and our manufacturers be postponed. I shall therefore request a special session of Congress for the consideration of these two questions. I shall deal with each of them upon the assembly of the Congress.

It appears to me that the more important further mandates from the recent election were the maintenance of the integrity of the Constitution; the vigorous enforcement of the laws; the continuance of economy in public expenditure; the continued regulation of business to prevent domination in the community; the denial of ownership or operation of business by the Government in competition with its citizens;

the avoidance of policies which would involve us in the controversies of foreign nations; the more effective reorganization of the departments of the Federal Government; the expansion of public works; and the promotion of welfare activities affecting education and the home.

These were the more tangible determinations of the election, but beyond them was the confidence and belief of the people that we would not neglect the support of the embedded ideals and aspirations of America. These ideals and aspirations are the touchstones upon which the day-to-day administration and legislative acts of government must be tested. More than this, the Government must, so far as lies within its proper powers, give leader-

ship to the realization of these ideals and to the fruition of these aspirations. No one can adequately reduce these things of the spirit to phrases or to a catalogue of definitions. We do know what the attainments of these ideals should be: The preservation of self-government and its full foundations in local government; the perfection of justice whether in economic or in social fields; the maintenance of ordered liberty; the denial of domination by any group or class; the building up and preservation of equality of opportunity; the stimulation of initiative and individuality; absolute integrity in public affairs; the choice of officials for fitness to office; the direction of economic progress toward prosperity for the further less-

1932 Franklin D. Roosevelt

After retaking the House in 1930 thanks to the stock market crash, the Democrats gathered in Chicago in June 1932 with some optimism. The front-runners for the party's presidential nomination were New York governor Franklin D. Roosevelt and Speaker of the House "Cactus Jack" Garner of Texas. Joseph Kennedy, a strong backer of FDR, pulled wires with William Randolph Hearst to move the California delegation from Garner's column into Roosevelt's. Party unity was then secured by adding Garner to the ticket.

More remarkable was FDR's unprecedented decision to fly to Chicago, appear in the convention hall, and accept the nomination personally. His acceptance speech was the first ever delivered by a presidential candidate.

In columnist Walter Lippmann's words, Roosevelt was "a pleasant man who, without any important qualifications for the office, would very much like to be president." Yet FDR surprised Lippmann and other pundits with an aggressive old-fashioned stumping tour of the nation. The New Deal program that he espoused called for the repeal of Prohibition, lower tariffs, aid to farmers, and help for the unemployed. "We are going to make a country where no one is left out," he told voters. "Play It Safe with Hoover," the Republicans countered, but Roosevelt's activism proved irresistible. "This is the greatest night of my life," FDR told his mother as he embraced her on hearing news of his victory.

Party	Popular Votes	Electoral Votes
Democratic Franklin D. Roosevelt, N.Y. John Nance Garner, Tex.	22,829,501	472
Republican Herbert C. Hoover, Calif. Charles Curtis, Kan.	15,760,684	59
Socialist Norman M. Thomas, N.Y. James H. Maurer, Pa.	884,649	

First Inaugural Address • Washington, D.C. • Sunday, March 4, 1933

I am certain that my fellow Americans expect that on my induction

into the Presidency I will address them with a candor and a decision which the present situation of our Nation impels. This is preeminently the time to speak the truth, the whole truth, frankly and boldly. Nor need we shrink from honestly facing conditions in our country today. This great Nation will endure as it has endured, will revive and will prosper. So, first of all, let me assert my firm belief that the only thing we have to fear is fear itself—nameless, unreasoning, unjustified terror which paralyzes needed efforts to convert retreat into advance. In every dark hour of our national life a leadership of frankness and vigor has met with that understanding and support of the people themselves which is essential to victory. I am convinced that you will again give that support to leadership in these critical days.

In such a spirit on my part and on yours we face our common difficulties. They concern, thank God, only material things. Values have shrunken to fantastic levels; taxes have risen; our ability to pay has fallen; government of all kinds is faced by serious curtailment of income; the means of exchange are frozen in the currents of trade; the withered leaves of industrial enterprise

lie on every side; farmers find no markets for their produce; the savings of many years in thousands of families are gone.

More important, a host of unemployed citizens face the grim problem of existence, and an equally great number toil with little return. Only a foolish optimist can deny the dark realities of the moment.

Yet our distress comes from no failure of substance. We are stricken by no plague of locusts. Compared with the perils which our forefathers conquered because they believed and were not afraid, we have still much to be thankful for. Nature still offers her bounty and human efforts have multiplied it. Plenty is at our doorstep, but a generous use of it languishes in the very sight of the supply. Primarily this is because the rulers of the exchange of mankind's goods have failed, through their own stubbornness and their own incompetence, have admitted their failure, and abdicated. Practices of the unscrupulous money changers stand indicted in the court of public opinion, rejected by the hearts and minds of men.

True they have tried, but their efforts have been cast in the pattern of an outworn tradition. Faced by failure of credit they have

proposed only the lending of more money. Stripped of the lure of profit by which to induce our people to follow their false leadership, they have resorted to exhortations, pleading tearfully for restored confidence. They know only the rules of a generation of self-seekers. They have no vision, and when there is no vision the people perish.

The money changers have fled from their high seats in the temple of our civilization. We may now restore that temple to the ancient truths. The measure of the restoration lies in the extent to which we apply social values more noble than mere monetary profit.

Happiness lies not in the mere possession of money; it lies in the joy of achievement, in the thrill of creative effort. The joy and moral stimulation of work no longer must be forgotten in the mad chase of evanescent profits. These dark days will be worth all they cost us if they teach us that our true destiny is not to be ministered unto but to minister to ourselves and to our fellow men.

Recognition of the falsity of material wealth as the standard of success goes hand in hand with the abandonment of the false belief that public office and high political position are to be valued only by the standards of pride of place and personal profit; and there must be an end to a conduct in banking and in business which too often has given to a sacred trust the likeness of callous and selfish wrongdoing. Small wonder that confidence languishes, for it thrives only on honesty, on honor, on the sacredness of obligations, on faithful protection, on unselfish performance; without them it cannot live.

Restoration calls, however, not for changes in ethics alone. This Nation asks for action, and action now.

Our greatest primary task is to put people to work. This is no unsolvable problem if we face it wisely and courageously. It can be accomplished in part by direct recruiting by the Government itself, treating the task as we would treat the emergency of a war, but at the same time, through this employment, accomplishing greatly needed projects to stimulate and reorganize the use of our natural resources.

Hand in hand with this we must frankly recognize the overbalance of population in our industrial centers and, by engaging on a national scale in a redistribution, endeavor to provide a better use of the land for those best fitted for the land. The task can be helped by definite efforts to raise the values of agricultural products and with this the power to purchase the output of our cities. It can be helped by preventing realistically the tragedy of the growing loss through foreclosure of our small homes and our farms. It can be helped by insistence that the Federal, State, and local governments act forthwith on the demand that their cost be drastically reduced. It can be helped by the unifying of relief activities which today are often scattered, uneconomical, and unequal. It can be helped by national planning for and supervision of all forms of transportation and of communications and other utilities which have a definitely public character. There are many ways in which it can be helped, but it can never be helped merely by talking about it. We must act and act quickly.

Finally, in our progress toward a resumption of work we require two safeguards against a return of the evils of the old order; there must be a strict supervision of all banking and credits and investments; there must be an end to speculation with other people's money, and there must be provision for an adequate but sound currency.

There are the lines of attack. I shall presently urge upon a new Congress in special session detailed measures for their fulfillment, and I shall seek the immediate assistance of the several States.

Through this program of action we address ourselves to

...the only thing we have to fear is fear itself.

---

putting our own national house in order and making income balance outgo. Our international trade relations, though vastly important, are in point of time and necessity secondary to the establishment of a sound national economy. I favor as a practical policy the putting of first things first. I shall spare no effort to restore world trade by international economic readjustment, but the emergency at home cannot wait on that accomplishment.

The basic thought that guides these specific means of national recovery is not narrowly nationalistic. It is the insistence, as a first consideration, upon the interdependence of the various elements in all parts of the United States—a recognition of the old and permanently important manifestation of the American spirit of the pioneer. It is the way to recovery. It is the immediate way. It is the strongest assurance that the recovery will endure.

In the field of world policy I would dedicate this Nation to the policy of the good neighbor—the neighbor who resolutely respects himself and, because he does so, respects the rights of others—the neighbor who respects his obligations and respects the sanctity of his agreements in and with a world of neighbors.

If I read the temper of our people correctly, we now realize as we have never realized before our interdependence on each other; that we can not merely take but we must give as well; that if we are to go forward, we must move as a trained and loyal army willing to sacrifice for the good of a common discipline, because without such discipline no progress is made, no leadership becomes effective. We are, I know, ready and willing to submit our lives and property to such discipline, because it makes possible a leadership which aims at a larger good. This I propose to offer, pledging that the larger purposes will bind upon us all as a sacred obligation with a unity of duty hitherto evoked only in time of armed strife.

With this pledge taken, I assume unhesitatingly the leadership of this great army of our people dedicated to a disciplined attack upon our common problems.

Action in this image and to this end is feasible under the form of government which we have inherited from our ancestors. Our Constitution is so simple and practical that it is possible always to meet extraordinary needs by changes in emphasis and arrangement without loss of essential form. That is why our constitutional system has proved itself the most superbly enduring political mechanism the modern world has produced. It has met every stress of vast expansion of territory, of foreign wars, of bitter internal strife, of world relations.

It is to be hoped that the normal balance of executive and legislative authority may be wholly adequate to meet the unprecedented task before us. But it may be that an unprecedented demand and need for undelayed action may call for temporary departure from that normal balance of public procedure.

I am prepared under my constitutional duty to recommend the measures that a stricken nation in the midst of a stricken world may require. These measures, or such other measures as the Congress may build out of its experience and wisdom, I shall seek, within my constitutional authority, to bring to speedy adoption.

But in the event that the Congress shall fail to take one of these two courses, and in the event that the national emergency is still critical, I shall not evade the clear course of duty that will then confront me. I shall ask the Congress for the one remaining instrument to meet the crisis—broad Executive power to wage a war against the emergency, as great as the power that would be given to me if we were in fact invaded by a foreign foe.

For the trust reposed in me I will return the courage and the devotion that befit the time. I can do no less.

We face the arduous days that lie before us in the warm courage of the national unity; with the clear consciousness of seeking old and precious moral values; with the clean satisfaction that comes from the stern performance of duty by old and young alike. We aim at the assurance of a rounded and permanent national life.

We do not distrust the future of essential democracy. The people of the United States have not failed. In their need they have registered a mandate that they want direct, vigorous action. They have asked for discipline and direction under leadership. They have made me the present instrument of their wishes. In the spirit of the gift I take it.

In this dedication of a Nation we humbly ask the blessing of God. May He protect each and every one of us. May He guide me in the days to come.

* * *

1936 Franklin D. Roosevelt

THE BIGGEST NEWS TO COME OUT of the 1936 Democratic convention was the repeal of the two-thirds rule that had plagued so many front-runners during the nineteenth century. Less noteworthy was New York judge John E. Mack's renominating speech, which was followed by fifty-six seconding speeches, after which the president and vice president were renominated by acclamation. The Republicans rallied behind Alfred M. Landon, the moderately progressive governor of Kansas.

The campaigning was polite, with each presidential candidate declining to make negative comments about the other. The Democratic campaign song, "Happy Days Are Here Again," was somewhat premature, given the continuing depression, but voters were eager to believe that the country was moving forward. The Republican slogan, "Save America from Socialism," appealed to a disgruntled, rather small constituency that despised Franklin Roosevelt and his invasive social policies.

Had Landon been as comfortable as FDR with the new science of public opinion polling, he would have known that Roosevelt was on his way to the largest landslide yet. The president received a record 60.8 percent of the popular vote and every electoral vote except those few cast by Maine and Vermont. The wealthy voted Republican, but FDR won the labor, Catholic, Jewish,

Party	Popular Votes	Electoral Votes
Democratic Franklin D. Roosevelt, N.Y. John Nance Garner, Tex.	27,757,333	523
Republican Alfred M. Landon, Kan. Frank Knox, Ill.	16,684,231	8
Union William Lemke, N.D. Thomas C. O'Brien, Mass.	892,267	

and African-American votes handily, with his largest margins coming in the cities. Two months later, he became the first president inaugurated on January 20, the new date set for the end of the president's term by the Twentieth Amendment.

Second Inaugural Address • Washington, D.C. • Wednesday, January 20, 1937

When four years ago we met to inaugurate a President, the Republic,

single-minded in anxiety, stood in spirit here. We dedicated ourselves to the fulfillment of a vision—to speed the time when there would be for all the people that security and peace essential to the pursuit of happiness. We of the Republic pledged ourselves to drive from the temple of our ancient faith those who had profaned it; to end by action, tireless and unafraid, the stagnation and despair of that day. We did those first things first.

Our covenant with ourselves did not stop there. Instinctively we recognized a deeper need—the need to find through government the instrument of our united purpose to solve for the individual the ever-rising problems of a complex civilization. Repeated attempts at their solution without the aid of government had left us baffled and bewildered. For, without that aid, we had been unable to create those moral controls over the services of science which are necessary to make science a useful servant instead of a ruthless master of mankind. To do this we knew that we must find practical controls over blind economic forces and blindly selfish men.

We of the Republic sensed the truth that democratic government has innate capacity to protect its people against disasters once considered inevitable, to solve problems once considered unsolvable. We would not admit that we could not find a way to master economic epidemics just as, after centuries of fatalistic suffering, we had found a way to master epidemics of disease. We refused to leave the problems of our common welfare to be solved by the winds of chance and the hurricanes of disaster.

In this we Americans were discovering no wholly new truth; we were writing a new chapter in our book of self-government.

This year marks the one hundred and fiftieth anniversary of the Constitutional Convention which made us a nation. At that Convention our forefathers found the way out of the chaos which followed the Revolutionary War; they created a strong government with powers of united action sufficient then and now to solve problems utterly beyond individual or local solution. A century and a half ago they established the Federal Government in order to pro-

mote the general welfare and secure the blessings of liberty to the American people. Today we invoke those same powers of government to achieve the same objectives.

Four years of new experience have not belied our historic instinct. They hold out the clear hope that government within communities, government within the separate States, and government of the United States can do the things the times require, without yielding its democracy. Our tasks in the last four years did not force democracy to take a holiday.

Nearly all of us recognize that as intricacies of human relationships increase, so power to govern them also must increase—power to stop evil; power to do good. The essential democracy of our Nation and the safety of our people depend not upon the absence of power, but upon lodging it with those whom the people can change or continue at stated intervals through an honest and free system of elections. The Constitution of 1787 did not make our democracy impotent.

In fact, in these last four years, we have made the exercise of all power more democratic; for we have begun to bring private autocratic powers into their proper subordination to the public's government. The legend that they were invincible—above and beyond the processes of a democracy—has been shattered. They have been challenged and beaten.

Our progress out of the depression is obvious. But that is not all that you and I mean by the new order of things. Our pledge was not merely to do a patchwork job with secondhand materials. By using the new materials of social justice we have undertaken to erect on the old foundations a more enduring structure for the better use of future generations.

In that purpose we have been helped by achievements of mind and spirit. Old truths have been relearned; untruths have been unlearned. We have always known that heedless self-interest was bad morals; we know now that it is bad economics. Out of the collapse of a prosperity whose builders boasted their practicality has come the conviction that in the long run economic morality pays. We are beginning to wipe out the line that divides the practical from the ideal; and in so doing we are fashioning an instrument of unimagined power for the establishment of a morally better world.

This new understanding undermines the old admiration of worldly success as such. We are beginning to abandon our tolerance of the abuse of power by those who betray for profit the elementary decencies of life.

In this process evil things formerly accepted will not be so easily condoned. Hard-headedness will not so easily excuse hardheartedness. We are moving toward an era of good feeling. But we realize that there can be no era of good feeling save among men of good will.

For these reasons I am justified in believing that the greatest change we have witnessed has been the change in the moral climate of America.

Among men of good will, science and democracy together offer an ever-richer life and ever-larger satisfaction to the individual. With this change in our moral climate and our rediscovered ability to improve our economic order,

we have set our feet upon the road of enduring progress.

Shall we pause now and turn our back upon the road that lies ahead? Shall we call this the promised land? Or, shall we continue on our way? For "each age is a dream that is dying, or one that is coming to birth."

Many voices are heard as we face a great decision. Comfort says, "Tarry a while." Opportunism says, "This is a good spot." Timidity asks, "How difficult is the road ahead?"

True, we have come far from the days of stagnation and despair. Vitality has been preserved. Courage and confidence have been restored. Mental and moral horizons have been extended.

But our present gains were won under the pressure of more than ordinary circumstances. Advance became imperative under the goad of fear and suffering. The times were on the side of progress.

To hold to progress today, however, is more difficult. Dulled conscience, irresponsibility, and ruthless self-interest already reappear. Such symptoms of prosperity may become portents of disaster! Prosperity already tests the persistence of our progressive purpose.

Let us ask again: Have we reached the goal of our vision of that fourth day of March 1933? Have we found our happy valley?

I see a great nation, upon a great continent, blessed with a great wealth of natural resources. Its hundred and thirty million people are at peace among themselves; they are making their country a good neighbor among the nations. I see a United States which can demonstrate that, under democratic methods of government, national wealth can be translated into a spreading volume of human comforts hitherto unknown, and the lowest standard of living can be raised far above the level of mere subsistence.

But here is the challenge to our democracy. In this nation I see tens of millions of its citizens—a substantial part of its whole population—who at this very moment are denied the

greater part of what the very lowest standards of today call the necessities of life.

I see millions of families trying to live on incomes so meager that the pall of family disaster hangs over them day by day.

I see millions whose daily lives in city and on farm continue under conditions labeled indecent by a so-called polite society half a century ago.

I see millions denied education, recreation, and the opportunity to better their lot and the lot of their children.

I see millions lacking the means to buy the products of farm and factory and by their poverty denying work and productiveness to many other millions.

I see one-third of a nation ill-housed, ill-clad, ill-nourished.

It is not in despair that I paint you that picture. I paint it for you in hope—because the Nation, seeing and understanding the injustice in it, proposes to paint it out. We are determined to make every American citizen the subject of his country's interest and concern; and we will never regard any faithful law-abiding group within our

DRIVE AHEAD WITH ROOSEVELT

borders as superfluous. The test of our progress is not whether we add more to the abundance of those who have much; it is whether we provide enough for those who have too little.

If I know aught of the spirit and purpose of our Nation, we will not listen to Comfort, Opportunism, and Timidity. We will carry on.

Overwhelmingly, we of the Republic are men and women of good will; men and women who have more than warm hearts of dedication; men and women who have cool heads and willing

hands of practical purpose as well. They will insist that every agency of popular government use effective instruments to carry out their will.

Government is competent when all who compose it work as trustees for the whole people. It can make constant progress when it keeps abreast of all the facts. It can obtain justified support and legitimate criticism when the people receive true information of all that government does.

If I know aught of the will of our people, they will demand that these conditions of effective government shall be created and maintained. They will demand a nation uncorrupted by cancers of injustice and, therefore, strong among the nations in its example of the will to peace.

Today we reconsecrate our country to long-cherished ideals in a suddenly changed civilization. In every land there are always at work forces that drive men apart and forces that draw men together. In our personal ambitions we are individualists. But in our seeking for economic and political progress as a nation, we all go up, or else we all go down, as one people.

To maintain a democracy of effort requires a vast amount of patience in dealing with differing methods, a vast amount of humility. But out of the confusion of many voices rises an understanding of dominant public need. Then political leadership can voice common ideals, and aid in their realization.

In taking again the oath of office as President of the United States, I assume the solemn obligation of leading the American people forward along the road over which they have chosen to advance.

While this duty rests upon me I shall do my utmost to speak their purpose and to do their will, seeking Divine guidance to help us each and every one to give light to them that sit in darkness and to guide our feet into the way of peace.

* * *

1940 Franklin D. Roosevelt

THE UNITED STATES WAS STILL recovering from the Great Depression when two events rocked the country: World War II broke out in Europe, and Franklin Roosevelt decided to run for a third term. His choice upset many Democrats, notably Postmaster General James A. Farley, who resigned in protest of Roosevelt's arrogance. Nevertheless, the president won renomination easily, then dropped his estranged vice president, John Nance Garner, in favor of Secretary of Agriculture Henry A. Wallace.

When the Republicans couldn't settle on either New York district attorney Thomas E. Dewey or Ohio senator Robert A. Taft (the former president's son), dark horse Wendell Willkie emerged as the compromise choice. A former Democrat, Willkie had broken with Roosevelt over the creation of the Tennessee Valley Authority, which Willkie believed competed unfairly with the utility company he ran.

Willkie conducted a spirited national campaign, attacking not only Roosevelt's public policies but also his indifference to the two-term precedent set by George Washington. Emphasizing Willkie's lack of political experience, the Democrats countered, "Better a Third-Termer Than a Third-Rater." Willkie charged that FDR had made secret deals that would lead the nation into war. Meanwhile, Roosevelt disingenuously promised American mothers, "Your boys are not going to be sent to foreign wars." He also savaged Republican isolationists in Congress for blocking his preparedness program. Though the president never campaigned formally, he did tour defense plants to highlight the preparedness issue and keep his face in the news.

It was a nasty election. Willkie did better than Alf Landon had in 1936, carrying ten states, but he was never competitive.

Party	Popular Votes	Electoral Votes
Democratic Franklin D. Roosevelt, N.Y. Henry A. Wallace, Iowa	27,313,041	449
Republican Wendell L. Willkie, N.Y. Charles L. McNary, Ore.	22,348,480	82

Third Inaugural Address • Washington, D.C. • Monday, January 20, 1941

On each national day of inauguration since 1789, the people have renewed

their sense of dedication to the United States.

In Washington's day the task of the people was to create and weld together a nation.

In Lincoln's day the task of the people was to preserve that Nation from disruption from within.

In this day the task of the people is to save that Nation and its institutions from disruption from without.

To us there has come a time, in the midst of swift happenings, to pause for a moment and take stock—to recall what our place in history has been, and to rediscover what we are and what we may be. If we do not, we risk the real peril of inaction.

Lives of nations are determined not by the count of years, but by the lifetime of the human spirit. The life of a man is three-score years and ten: a little more, a little less. The life of a nation is the fullness of the measure of its will to live.

There are men who doubt this. There are men who believe that democracy, as a form of Government and a frame of life, is limited or measured by a kind of mystical and artificial fate that, for some unexplained reason, tyranny and slavery have become the surging wave of the future—and that freedom is an ebbing tide.

But we Americans know that this is not true. Eight years ago, when the life of this Republic seemed frozen by a fatalistic terror, we proved that this is not true. We were in the midst of shock—but we acted. We acted quickly, boldly, decisively.

These later years have been living years—fruitful years for the people of this democracy. For they have brought to us greater security and, I hope, a better understanding that life's ideals are to be measured in other than material things.

Most vital to our present and our future is this experience of a democracy which successfully survived crisis at home; put away many evil things; built new structures on enduring lines; and, through it all, maintained the fact of its democracy.

For action has been taken within the three-way framework of the Constitution of the United States. The coordinate branches of the Government continue freely to function. The Bill of Rights remains inviolate. The freedom of elections is wholly maintained. Prophets of the downfall of American democracy have seen their dire predictions come to naught.

Democracy is not dying.

We know it because we have seen it revive—and grow.

We know it cannot die—because it is built on the unhampered initiative of individual men and women joined together in a common enterprise—an enterprise undertaken and carried through by the free expression of a free majority.

We know it because democracy alone, of all forms of government, enlists the full force of men's enlightened will.

We know it because democracy alone has constructed an unlimited civilization capable of infinite progress in the improvement of human life.

We know it because, if we look below the surface, we sense it still spreading on every continent—for it is the most humane, the most advanced, and in the end the most unconquerable of all forms of human society.

A nation, like a person, has a body—a body that must be fed and clothed and housed, invigorated and rested, in a manner that measures up to the objectives of our time.

A nation, like a person, has a mind—a mind that must be kept informed and alert, that must know itself, that understands the hopes and the needs of its neighbors—all the other nations that live within the narrowing circle of the world.

And a nation, like a person, has something deeper, something more permanent, something larger than the sum of all its parts. It is that something which matters most to its future—which calls forth the most sacred guarding of its present.

It is a thing for which we find it difficult—even impossible—to hit upon a single, simple word.

And yet we all understand what it is—the spirit—the faith of America. It is the product of centuries. It was born in the multitudes of those who came from many lands—some of high degree, but mostly plain people, who sought here, early and late, to find freedom more freely.

The democratic aspiration is no mere recent phase in human history. It is human history. It permeated the ancient life of early peoples. It blazed anew in the middle ages. It was written in Magna Charta.

In the Americas its impact has been irresistible. America

> *The life of a man is three-score years and ten: a little more, a little less. The life of a nation is the fullness of the measure of its will to live.*

has been the New World in all tongues, to all peoples, not because this continent was a new-found land, but because all those who came here believed they could create upon this continent a new life—a life that should be new in freedom.

Its vitality was written into our own Mayflower Compact, into the Declaration of Independence, into the Constitution of the United States, into the Gettysburg Address.

Those who first came here to carry out the longings of their spirit, and the millions who followed, and the stock that sprang from them—all have moved forward constantly and consistently toward an ideal which in itself has gained stature and clarity with each generation.

The hopes of the Republic cannot forever tolerate either undeserved poverty or self-serving wealth.

We know that we still have far to go; that we must more greatly build the security and the opportunity and the knowledge of every citizen, in the measure justified by the resources and the capacity of the land.

But it is not enough to achieve these purposes alone. It is not enough to clothe and feed the body of this Nation, and instruct and inform its mind. For there is also the spirit. And of the three, the greatest is the spirit.

Without the body and the mind, as all men know, the Nation could not live.

But if the spirit of America were killed, even though the Nation's body and mind, constricted in an alien world, lived on, the America we know would have perished.

That spirit—that faith—speaks to us in our daily lives in ways often unnoticed, because they seem so obvious. It speaks to us here in the Capital of the Nation. It speaks to us through the processes of governing in the sovereignties of 48 States. It speaks to us in our counties, in our cities, in our towns, and in our villages. It speaks to us from the other nations of the hemisphere, and from those across the seas—the enslaved, as well as the free. Sometimes we fail to hear or heed these voices of freedom because to us the privilege of our freedom is such an old, old story.

The destiny of America was proclaimed in words of prophecy spoken by our first President in his first inaugural in 1789—words almost directed, it would seem, to this year of 1941: "The preservation of the sacred fire of liberty and the destiny of the republican model of government are justly considered ... deeply,... finally, staked on the experiment intrusted to the hands of the American people."

If we lose that sacred fire—if we let it be smothered with doubt and fear—then we shall reject the destiny which Washington strove so valiantly and so triumphantly to establish. The preservation of the spirit and faith of the Nation does, and will, furnish the highest justification for every sacrifice that we may make in the cause of national defense.

In the face of great perils never before encountered, our strong purpose is to protect and to perpetuate the integrity of democracy.

For this we muster the spirit of America, and the faith of America.

We do not retreat. We are not content to stand still. As Americans, we go forward, in the service of our country, by the will of God.

* * *

1944 FRANKLIN D. ROOSEVELT

BY 1944, FRANKLIN ROOSEVELT had forged a bipartisan coalition behind his defense policies; and, as commander in chief, he was successful prosecuting the war against Germany and Japan. With his failing health kept well hidden, there was no serious opposition to his fourth nomination. Again, Roosevelt dumped an incumbent vice president, this time replacing the ultraliberal Henry A. Wallace with Missouri senator Harry S. Truman. (By selecting Truman, the president hoped to repair his frayed relations with the big-city Democratic machines.) On the Republican side, Thomas E. Dewey, now the governor of New York, coasted to a first-ballot nomination.

In the radio speeches that made up the bulk of his campaign, Dewey insisted that he could do a better job than Roosevelt as commander in chief (though he offered few specifics). Meanwhile, Dewey surrogates warned ominously that FDR was becoming a dictator and wanted to be president for life. A placid Roosevelt remained above the fray. When

Republicans charged that he'd used a navy destroyer as a transport for his dog Fala, FDR breezily replied that he could tolerate attacks against himself but not against his pet. The country laughed along with the president, and the Republicans looked foolish.

Dewey won twelve states, two more than Willkie had carried in 1940, but he failed to hold New York and never challenged the strength of the Roosevelt coalition in the North, the South, or even the West. Voters apparently agreed with the old saw that had become a Democratic mantra: "Never swap horses in the middle of a stream."

PARTY	POPULAR VOTES	ELECTORAL VOTES
DEMOCRATIC Franklin D. Roosevelt, N.Y. Harry S. Truman, Mo.	25,612,610	432
REPUBLICAN Thomas E. Dewey, N.Y. John W. Bricker, Ohio	22,017,617	99

Fourth Inaugural Address • Washington, D.C. • Saturday, January 20, 1945

Mr. Chief Justice, Mr. Vice President, my friends,

you will understand and, I believe, agree with my wish that the form of this inauguration be simple and its words brief.

We Americans of today, together with our allies, are passing through a period of supreme test. It is a test of our courage—of our resolve—of our wisdom—our essential democracy.

If we meet that test—successfully and honorably—we shall perform a service of historic importance which men and women and children will honor throughout all time.

As I stand here today, having taken the solemn oath of office in the presence of my fellow countrymen—in the presence of our God—I know that it is America's purpose that we shall not fail.

In the days and in the years that are to come we shall work for a just and honorable peace, a durable peace, as today we work and fight for total victory in war.

We can and we will achieve such a peace.

We shall strive for perfection. We shall not achieve it immediately—but we still shall strive. We may make mistakes—but

they must never be mistakes which result from faintness of heart or abandonment of moral principle.

I remember that my old schoolmaster, Dr. Peabody, said, in days that seemed to us then to be secure and untroubled: "Things in life will not always run smoothly. Sometimes we will be rising toward the heights—then all will seem to reverse itself and start downward. The great fact to remember is that the trend of civilization itself is forever upward; that a line drawn through the middle of the peaks and the valleys of the centuries always has an upward trend."

Our Constitution of 1787 was not a perfect instrument; it is not perfect yet. But it provided a firm base upon which all manner of men, of all races and colors and creeds, could build our solid structure of democracy.

And so today, in this year of war, 1945, we have learned lessons—at a fearful cost— and we shall profit by them.

We have learned that we cannot live alone, at peace; that our own well-being is dependent on the well-being of other na-

tions far away. We have learned that we must live as men, not as ostriches, nor as dogs in the manger.

We have learned to be citizens of the world, members of the human community.

We have learned the simple truth, as Emerson said, that "The only way to have a friend is to be one."

We can gain no lasting peace if we approach it with suspicion and mistrust or with fear. We can gain it only if we proceed with the understanding, the confidence, and the courage which flow from conviction.

The Almighty God has blessed our land in many ways. He has given our people stout hearts and strong arms with which to strike mighty blows for freedom and truth. He has given to our country a faith which has become the hope of all peoples in an anguished world.

So we pray to Him now for the vision to see our way clearly—to see the way that leads to a better life for ourselves and for all our fellow men—to the achievement of His will to peace on earth.

★ ★ ★

1948 HARRY S. TRUMAN

THE PUNDITS AND POLLSTERS made it clear that Harry S. Truman had no chance of beating Republican nominee Thomas E. Dewey. With Democratic governor Strom Thurmond of South Carolina running as a Dixiecrat favorite son in the South (to protest the Democrats' strong civil rights plank) and the Progressive party cndidacy of Henry A. Wallace pulling away liberal Democratic votes in the North, how could Truman win?

The president campaigned fiercely, boarding the *Ferdinand Magellan* for a thirty-thousand-mile whistle-stop tour, during which he delivered 271 speeches striking hard at "the do-nothing Eightieth Congress." Dewey, aboard the *Victory Special,* traveled sixteen thousand miles but made just thirteen speeches. During one of those rare addresses, the train's motorman accidentally put the engine into reverse, causing th candidateto lurch. Dewey's subsequent beration of the motorman was widely reported, hurting his efforts to appear a friend of the "common man." While Truman spoke to the issues, an overconfident Dewey mouthed platitudes such as "Our future lies before us."

PARTY	POPULAR VOTES	ELECTORAL VOTES
DEMOCRATIC Harry S. Truman, Mo. Alben W. Barkley, Ky.	24,179,345	303
REPUBLICAN Thomas E. Dewey, N.Y. Earl Warren, Calif.	21,991,291	189
STATES' RIGHTS J. Strom Thurmond, S.C. Fielding L. Wright, Miss.	1,176,125	39
PROGRESSIVE Henry A. Wallace, Iowa Glen H. Taylor, Idaho	1,157,326	

At midnight on Election Day, a serene Truman told his aides that he would win. Then went to bed. On his return to Washington, the winner of the greatest upset in presidential history was greeted by a sign on the Washington Post building that read: "Mr. President, we are ready to eat crow whenever you are ready to serve it."

Inaugural Address • Washington, D.C. • Thursday, January 20, 1949

Mr. Vice President, Mr. Chief Justice, and fellow citizens, I accept with

humility the honor which the American people have conferred upon me. I accept it with a deep resolve to do all that I can for the welfare of this Nation and for the peace of the world.

In performing the duties of my office, I need the help and prayers of every one of you. I ask for your encouragement and your support. The tasks we face are difficult, and we can accomplish them only if we work together.

Each period of our national history has had its special challenges. Those that con front us now are as momentous as any in the past. Today marks the beginning not only of a new administration, but of a period that will be eventful, perhaps decisive, for us and for the world.

It may be our lot to experience, and in large measure to bring about, a major turning point in the long history of the human race. The first half of this century has been marked by unprecedented and brutal attacks on the rights of man, and by the two most frightful wars in history. The supreme need of our time is for men to learn to live together in peace and harmony.

The peoples of the earth face the future with grave uncertainty, composed almost equally of great hopes and great fears. In this time of doubt, they look to the United States as never before for good will, strength, and wise leadership.

It is fitting, therefore, that we take this occasion to proclaim to the world the essential principles of the faith by which we live,

and to declare our aims to all peoples.

The American people stand firm in the faith which has inspired this Nation from the beginning. We believe that all men have a right to equal justice under law and equal opportunity to share in the common good. We believe that all men have the right to freedom of thought and expression. We believe that all men are created equal because they are created in the image of God.

From this faith we will not be moved.

The American people desire, and are determined to work for, a world in which all nations and all peoples are free to govern themselves as they see fit, and to achieve a decent and satisfying life. Above all else, our people desire, and are determined to work for, peace on earth—a just and lasting peace—based on genuine agreement freely arrived at by equals.

In the pursuit of these aims, the United States and other like-minded nations find themselves directly opposed by a regime with contrary aims and a totally different concept of life.

That regime adheres to a false philosophy which purports to offer freedom, security, and greater opportunity to mankind. Misled by this philosophy, many peoples have sacrificed their liberties only to learn to their sorrow that deceit and mockery, poverty and tyranny, are their reward.

That false philosophy is communism.

Communism is based on the belief that man is so weak and inadequate that he is unable to govern himself, and therefore requires the rule of strong masters.

Democracy is based on the conviction that man has the moral and intellectual capacity, as well as the inalienable right, to govern himself with reason and justice.

Communism subjects the individual to arrest without lawful cause, punishment without trial, and forced labor as the chattel of the state. It decrees what information he shall receive, what art he shall produce, what leaders he shall follow, and what thoughts he shall think.

Democracy maintains that government is established for the benefit of the individual, and is charged with the responsibility of protecting the rights of the individual and his freedom in the exercise of his abilities.

Communism maintains that social wrongs can be corrected only by violence.

Democracy has proved that social justice can be achieved through peaceful change.

Communism holds that the world is so deeply divided into opposing classes that war is inevitable.

Democracy holds that free nations can settle differences justly and maintain lasting peace.

These differences between communism and democracy do not concern the United States alone. People everywhere are coming to realize that what is involved is material well-being, human dignity, and the right to believe in and worship God.

I state these differences, not to draw issues of belief as such, but because the actions resulting from the Communist philosophy are a threat to the efforts of free nations to bring about world recovery and lasting peace.

Since the end of hostilities, the United States has invested its substance and its energy in a great constructive effort to restore peace, stability, and freedom to the world.

We have sought no territory and we have imposed our will on none. We have asked for no privileges we would not extend to others.

We have constantly and vigorously supported the United Nations and related agencies as a means of applying democratic principles to international relations. We have consistently advocated and relied upon peaceful settlement of disputes among nations.

We have made every effort to secure agreement on effective international control of our most powerful weapon, and we have worked steadily for the limitation and control of all armaments.

We have encouraged, by precept and example, the expansion of world trade on a sound and fair basis.

Almost a year ago, in company with 16 free nations of Europe, we launched the greatest cooperative economic program in history. The purpose of that unprecedented effort is to invigorate and strengthen democracy in Europe, so that the free people of that continent can resume their rightful place in the forefront of civilization and can contribute once more to the security and welfare of the world.

Our efforts have brought new hope to all mankind. We have beaten back despair and defeatism. We have saved a number of countries from losing their liberty. Hundreds of millions of people all over the world now agree with us, that we need not have war—that we can have peace.

The initiative is ours.

We are moving on with other nations to build an even stronger structure of international order and justice. We shall have as our partners countries which, no longer solely concerned with the problem of national survival, are now working to improve the standards of living of all their people. We are ready to undertake new projects to strengthen the free world.

In the coming years, our program for peace and freedom will emphasize four major courses of action.

First, we will continue to give unfaltering support to the United Nations and related agencies, and we will continue to search for ways to strengthen their authority and increase their effectiveness. We believe that the United Nations will be strengthened by the new nations which are being formed in lands now advancing toward self-government under democratic principles.

Second, we will continue our programs for world economic recovery.

This means, first of all, that we must keep our full weight behind the European recovery program. We are confident of the success of this major venture in world recovery. We believe that our partners in this effort will achieve the status of self-supporting nations once again.

In addition, we must carry out our plans for reducing the barriers to world trade and increasing its volume. Economic recovery and peace itself depend on increased world trade.

Third, we will strengthen freedom-loving nations against the dangers of aggression.

We are now working out with a number of countries a joint agreement designed to strengthen the security of the North Atlantic area. Such an agreement would take the form of a collective defense arrangement within the terms of the United Nations Charter.

We have already established such a defense pact for the Western Hemisphere by the treaty of Rio de Janeiro.

The primary purpose of these agreements is to provide unmistakable proof of the joint determination of the free countries to resist armed attack from any quarter. Each country participating in these arrangements

must contribute all it can to the common defense.

If we can make it sufficiently clear, in advance, that any armed attack affecting our national security would be met with overwhelming force, the armed attack might never occur.

I hope soon to send to the Senate a treaty respecting the North Atlantic security plan.

In addition, we will provide military advice and equipment to free nations which will cooperate with us in the maintenance of peace and security.

Fourth, we must embark on a bold new program for making the benefits of our scientific advances and industrial progress available for the improvement and growth of underdeveloped areas.

More than half the people of the world are living in conditions approaching misery. Their food is inadequate. They are victims of disease. Their economic life is primitive and stagnant. Their poverty is a handicap and

a threat both to them and to more prosperous areas.

For the first time in history, humanity possesses the knowledge and the skill to relieve the suffering of these people.

The United States is preeminent among nations in the development of industrial and scientific techniques. The material resources which we can afford to use for the assistance of other peoples are limited. But our imponderable resources in technical knowledge are constantly growing and are inexhaustible.

I believe that we should make available to peace-loving peoples the benefits of our store of technical knowledge in order to help them realize their aspirations for a better life. And, in cooperation with other nations, we should foster capital investment in areas needing development.

Our aim should be to help the free peoples of the world, through their own efforts, to produce more food, more clothing, more materials for housing, and more mechanical power to lighten their burdens.

We invite other countries to pool their technological resources in this undertaking. Their contributions will be warmly welcomed. This should be a cooperative enterprise in which all nations work together through the United Nations and its specialized agencies wherever practicable. It must be a worldwide effort for the achievement of peace, plenty, and freedom.

With the cooperation of business, private capital, agriculture, and labor in this coun-

try, this program can greatly increase the industrial activity in other nations and can raise substantially their standards of living.

Such new economic developments must be devised and controlled to benefit the peoples of the areas in which they

> *Communism is based on the belief that man is so weak and inadequate that he is unable to govern himself, and therefore requires the rule of strong masters.*

are established. Guarantees to the investor must be balanced by guarantees in the interest of the people whose resources and whose labor go into these developments.

The old imperialism—exploitation for foreign profit—has no place in our plans. What we envisage is a program of development based on the concepts of democratic fair-dealing.

All countries, including our own, will greatly benefit from a constructive program for the better use of the world's human and natural resources. Experi-

ence shows that our commerce with other countries expands as they progress industrially and economically.

Greater production is the key to prosperity and peace. And the key to greater production is a wider and more vigorous application of modern scientific and technical knowledge.

Only by helping the least fortunate of its members to help themselves can the human family achieve the decent, satisfying life that is the right of all people.

Democracy alone can supply the vitalizing force to stir the peoples of the world into triumphant action, not only against their human oppressors, but also against their ancient enemies—hunger, misery, and despair.

On the basis of these four major courses of action we hope to help create the conditions that will lead eventually to personal freedom and happiness for all mankind.

If we are to be successful in carrying out these policies, it is clear that we must have continued prosperity in this country and we must keep ourselves strong.

Slowly but surely we are weaving a world fabric of international security and growing prosperity.

We are aided by all who wish to live in freedom from fear—even by those who live today in fear under their own governments.

We are aided by all who want relief from the lies of propaganda—who desire truth and sincerity.

We are aided by all who desire self-government and a voice

in deciding their own affairs.

We are aided by all who long for economic security—for the security and abundance that men in free societies can enjoy.

We are aided by all who desire freedom of speech, freedom of religion, and freedom to live their own lives for useful ends.

Our allies are the millions who hunger and thirst after righteousness.

In due time, as our stability becomes manifest, as more and more nations come to know the benefits of democracy and to participate in growing abundance, I believe that those countries which now oppose us will abandon their delusions and join with the free nations of the world in a just settlement of international differences.

Events have brought our American democracy to new influence and new responsibilities. They will test our courage, our devotion to duty, and our concept of liberty.

But I say to all men, what we have achieved in liberty, we will surpass in greater liberty.

Steadfast in our faith in the Almighty, we will advance toward a world where man's freedom is secure.

To that end we will devote our strength, our resources, and our firmness of resolve. With God's help, the future of mankind will be assured in a world of justice, harmony, and peace.

* * *

1952 DWIGHT D. EISENHOWER

ALTHOUGH THE TWENTY-SECOND Amendment didn't prevent Harry S. Truman from running again, his unpopularity (due to the Korean War and the poor economy) made another term impractical. Instead, he supported Gov. Adlai E. Stevenson of Illinois, who edged out Tennessee senator Estes Kefauver for the Democratic nomination.

After declining to run as a Democrat, World War II commander Dwight D. Eisenhower accepted the Republican nomination. Without campaigning, Ike had won the New Hampshire Republican primary and nearly beaten Harold Stassen with 108,000 write-in votes in Stassen's home state of Minnesota. The convention was already turning in his direction (and away from front-runner Robert A. Taft, the Ohio senator known as as Mr. Republican) when Sen. Richard M. Nixon of California persuaded his state's delegation to switch to Eisenhower. At Thomas E. Dewey's suggestion, Eisenhower rewarded Nixon with the second spot on the ticket.

The Eisenhower campaign was the first to make television commercials and the first to hire marketing experts to "sell" its candidate. The most memorable moment of the campaign, however, was Nixon's "Checkers" speech. Accused of keeping a secret political slush fund, Nixon went on television to defend himself. He concluded by saying that he'd accepted only one gift, a cocker spaniel named Checkers, and that his family was going to keep it. The next day, after positive responses flooded the Republican National Committee, Eisenhower told Nixon, "You're my boy."

Stevenson, who was considered something of an egghead, made an intellectual appeal to voters. Much more effective, however, was the Republicans' "Communism, corruption, and Korea" campaign, which carried into office a Republican Congress as well. The South remained solid for Stevenson, but nearly everywhere else more Americans liked Ike.

PARTY	POPULAR VOTES	ELECTORAL VOTES
REPUBLICAN Dwight D. Eisenhower, N.Y. Richard M. Nixon, Calif.	33,936,234	442
DEMOCRATIC Adlai E. Stevenson, Ill. John J. Sparkman, Ala.	27,314,992	89

First Inaugural Address • Washington, D.C. • Tuesday, January 20, 1953

My friends, before I begin the expression of those thoughts

that I deem appropriate to this moment, would you permit me the privilege of uttering a little private prayer of my own? And I ask that you bow your heads:

Almighty God, as we stand here at this moment my future associates in the executive branch of government join me in beseeching that Thou will make full and complete our dedication to the service of the people in this throng, and their fellow citizens everywhere.

Give us, we pray, the power to discern clearly right from wrong, and allow all our words and actions to be governed thereby, and by the laws of this land. Especially we pray that our concern shall be for all the people regardless of station, race, or calling.

May cooperation be permitted and be the mutual aim of those who, under the concepts of our Constitution, hold to differing political faiths; so that all may work for the good of our beloved country and Thy glory. Amen.

My fellow citizens:

The world and we have passed the midway point of a century of continuing challenge. We sense with all our faculties that forces of good and evil are massed and armed and opposed as rarely before in history.

This fact defines the meaning of this day. We are summoned by this honored and historic ceremony to witness more than the act of one citizen swearing his oath of service, in the presence of God. We are called as a people to give testimony in the sight of the world to our faith that the future shall belong to the free.

Since this century's beginning, a time of tempest has seemed to come upon the continents of the earth. Masses of Asia have awakened to strike off shackles of the past.

Great nations of Europe have fought their bloodiest wars. Thrones have toppled and their vast empires have disappeared. New nations have been born.

For our own country, it has been a time of recurring trial. We have grown in power and in responsibility. We have passed through the anxieties of depression and of war to a summit unmatched in man's history. Seeking to secure peace in the world, we have had to fight through the forests of the Argonne, to the shores of Iwo Jima, and to the cold mountains of Korea.

In the swift rush of great events, we find ourselves groping to know the full sense and meaning of these times in which we live. In our quest of understanding, we beseech God's guidance. We summon all our knowledge of the past and we scan all signs of the future. We bring all our wit and all our will to meet the question:

How far have we come in man's long pilgrimage from darkness toward light? Are we nearing the light—a day of freedom and of peace for all mankind? Or are the shadows of another night closing in upon us?

Great as are the preoccupations absorbing us at home, concerned as we are with matters that deeply affect our livelihood today and our vision of the future, each of these domestic problems is dwarfed by, and often even created by, this question that involves all humankind.

This trial comes at a moment when man's power to achieve good or to inflict evil surpasses the brightest hopes and the sharpest fears of all ages. We can turn rivers in their courses, level mountains to the plains. Oceans and land and sky are avenues for our colossal commerce. Disease diminishes and life lengthens.

Yet the promise of this life is imperiled by the very genius that has made it possible. Nations amass wealth. Labor sweats to create—and turns out devices to level not only mountains but also cities. Science seems ready to confer upon us, as its final gift, the power to erase human life from this planet.

At such a time in history, we who are free must proclaim anew our faith. This faith is the abiding creed of our fathers. It is our faith in the deathless dignity of man, governed by eternal moral and natural laws.

This faith defines our full view of life. It establishes, beyond debate, those gifts of the Creator that are man's inalienable rights, and that make all men equal in His sight.

In the light of this equality, we know that the virtues most cherished by free people—love of truth, pride of work, devotion to country—all are treasures equally precious in the lives of the most humble and of the most exalted. The men who mine coal and fire furnaces and balance ledgers and turn lathes and pick cotton and plant corn—all serve as proudly, and as profitably, for America as the statesmen who

In the swift rush of great events, we find ourselves groping to know the full sense and meaning of these times in which we live.

draft treaties and the legislators who enact laws.

This faith rules our whole way of life. It decrees that we, the people, elect leaders not to rule but to serve. It asserts that we have the right to choice of our own work and to the reward of our own toil. It inspires the initiative that makes our productivity the wonder of the world. And it warns that any man who seeks to deny equality

among all his brothers betrays the spirit of the free and invites the mockery of the tyrant.

It is because we, all of us, hold to these principles that the political changes accomplished this day do not imply turbu-

lence, upheaval or disorder. Rather this change expresses a purpose of strengthening our dedication and devotion to the precepts of our founding documents, a conscious renewal of faith in our country and in the watchfulness of a Divine Providence.

The enemies of this faith know no god but force, no devotion but its use. They tutor men in treason. They feed upon the hunger of others. Whatever defies them, they torture, especially the truth.

Here, then, is joined no argument between slightly differing philosophies. This conflict strikes directly at the faith of our fathers and the lives of our sons. No principle or treasure that we hold, from the spiritual knowledge of our free schools and churches to the creative magic of free labor and capital, nothing lies safely beyond the reach of this struggle.

Freedom is pitted against slavery; lightness against the dark.

The faith we hold belongs not to us alone but to the free

of all the world. This common bond binds the grower of rice in Burma and the planter of wheat in Iowa, the shepherd in southern Italy and the mountaineer in the Andes. It confers a common dignity upon the French

soldier who dies in Indo-China, the British soldier killed in Malaya, the American life given in Korea.

We know, beyond this, that we are linked to all free peoples not merely by a noble idea but by a simple need. No free people can for long cling to any privilege or enjoy any safety in economic solitude. For all our own material might, even we need markets in the world for the surpluses of our farms and our factories. Equally, we need for these same farms and factories vital materials and products of distant lands. This basic law of interdependence, so manifest in the commerce of peace, applies with thousand-fold intensity in the event of war.

So we are persuaded by necessity and by belief that the strength of all free peoples lies in unity; their danger, in discord.

To produce this unity, to meet the challenge of our time, destiny has laid upon our country the responsibility of the free world's leadership.

So it is proper that we assure our friends once again that, in the discharge of this responsibility, we Americans know and we observe the difference between world leadership and imperialism; between firmness and truculence; between a thoughtfully calculated goal and spasmodic reaction to the stimulus of emergencies.

We wish our friends the world over to know this above all: we face the threat—not with dread and confusion—but with confidence and conviction.

We feel this moral strength because we know that we are not helpless prisoners of history. We are free men. We shall remain free, never to be proven guilty of the one capital offense against freedom, a lack of stanch faith.

In pleading our just cause before the bar of history and in pressing our labor for world peace, we shall be guided by certain fixed principles.

These principles are:

(1) Abhorring war as a chosen way to balk the purposes of those who threaten us, we hold it to be the first task of statesmanship to develop the strength that will deter the forces of ag-

gression and promote the conditions of peace. For, as it must be the supreme purpose of all free men, so it must be the dedication of their leaders, to save humanity from preying upon itself.

In the light of this principle, we stand ready to engage with any and all others in joint effort to remove the causes of mutual fear and distrust among nations, so as to make possible drastic reduction of armaments. The sole requisites for undertaking such effort are that—in their purpose—they be aimed logically and honestly toward secure peace for all; and that—in their result—they provide methods by which every participating nation will prove good faith in carrying out its pledge.

(2) Realizing that common sense and common decency alike dictate the futility of appeasement, we shall never try to placate an aggressor by the false and wicked bargain of trading honor for security. Americans, indeed all free men, remember that in the final choice a soldier's pack is not so heavy a burden as a prisoner's chains.

(3) Knowing that only a United States that is strong and immensely productive can help defend freedom in our world, we view our Nation's strength and security as a trust upon which rests the hope of free men everywhere. It is the firm duty of each of our free citizens and of every free citizen everywhere to place the cause of his country before the comfort, the convenience of himself.

(4) Honoring the identity and the special heritage of each nation in the world, we shall never use our strength to try to impress upon another people our own cherished political and economic institutions.

(5) Assessing realistically the needs and capacities of proven friends of freedom, we shall strive to help them to achieve their own security and well-being. Likewise, we shall count upon them to assume, within the limits of their resources, their full and just burdens in the common defense of freedom.

(6) Recognizing economic health as an indispensable basis of military strength and the free world's peace, we shall strive to foster everywhere, and to practice ourselves, policies that encourage productivity and profitable trade. For the impoverishment of any single people in the world means danger to the well-being of all other peoples.

(7) Appreciating that economic need, military security and political wisdom combine

to suggest regional groupings of free peoples, we hope, within the framework of the United Nations, to help strengthen such special bonds the world over. The nature of these ties must vary with the different problems of different areas.

In the Western Hemisphere, we enthusiastically join with all our neighbors in the work of perfecting a community of fraternal trust and common purpose.

In Europe, we ask that enlightened and inspired leaders of the Western nations strive with renewed vigor to make the unity of their peoples a reality. Only as free Europe unitedly marshals its strength can it effectively safeguard, even with our help, its spiritual and cultural heritage.

(8) Conceiving the defense of freedom, like freedom itself, to be one and indivisible, we hold all continents and peoples in equal regard and honor. We reject any insinuation that one race or another, one people or another, is in any sense inferior or expendable.

(9) Respecting the United Nations as the living sign of all people's hope for peace, we shall strive to make it not merely an eloquent symbol but an effective force. And in our quest for an honorable peace, we shall neither compromise, nor tire, nor ever cease.

By these rules of conduct, we hope to be known to all peoples.

By their observance, an earth of peace may become not a vision but a fact.

This hope—this supreme aspiration—must rule the way we live.

We must be ready to dare all for our country. For history does not long entrust the care of freedom to the weak or the timid. We must acquire proficiency in defense and display stamina in purpose. We must be willing, individually and as a Nation, to accept whatever sacrifices may be required of us. A people that values its privileges above its principles soon loses both.

These basic precepts are not lofty abstractions, far removed from matters of daily living. They are laws of spiritual strength that generate and define our material strength. Patriotism means equipped forces and a prepared citizenry. Moral stamina means more energy and more productivity, on the farm and in the factory. Love of liberty means the guarding of every resource that makes freedom possible—from the sanctity of our families and the wealth of our soil to the genius of our scientists.

And so each citizen plays an indispensable role. The productivity of our heads, our hands, and our hearts is the source of all the strength we can command, for both the enrichment of our lives and the winning of the peace.

No person, no home, no community can be beyond the reach of this call. We are summoned to act in wisdom and in conscience, to work with industry, to teach with persuasion, to preach with conviction, to weigh our every deed with care and with compassion. For this truth must be clear before us: whatever America hopes to bring to pass in the world must first come to pass in the heart of America.

The peace we seek, then, is nothing less than the practice and fulfillment of our whole faith among ourselves and in our dealings with others. This signifies more than the stilling of guns, easing the sorrow of war. More than escape from death, it is a way of life. More than a haven for the weary, it is a hope for the brave.

This is the hope that beckons us onward in this century of trial. This is the work that awaits us all, to be done with bravery, with charity, and with prayer to Almighty God.

* * *

1956 DWIGHT D. EISENHOWER

HAVING SATISFACTORILY CONCLUDED the Korean War, Dwight D. Eisenhower was able to run for reelection in 1956 on the best platform a sitting president could have: peace and prosperity. At the Democratic convention, Adlai E. Stevenson again beat out Estes Kefauver in a ho-hum race. After his renomination, though, Stevenson created some genuine excitement by offering to let the delegates choose his running mate. Kefauver prevailed this time over Massachusetts senator John F. Kennedy.

Kennedy was initially disappointed but later said he had been lucky to lose at the convention rather than in the fall.

Eisenhower ran on his record, but the five-minute television commercials developed by his campaign sold him like soap. Stevenson warned that nuclear weapons testing was producing dangerous radioactive fallout. He called for limits on aboveground tests. The voters preferred Ike's commercials.

On a more personal level, the Democrats questioned Eisenhower's health in the wake of his heart attack, while the Republicans faulted Stevenson for his divorce. On Election Day, Stevenson received even fewer votes than in 1952, as Eisenhower made gains among such traditional Democratic constituencies as union members, Catholics, Jews, and blacks.

PARTY	POPULAR VOTES	ELECTORAL VOTES
REPUBLICAN Dwight D. Eisenhower, N.Y. Richard M. Nixon, Calif.	35,590,472	457
DEMOCRATIC Adlai E. Stevenson, Ill. Estes Kefauver, Tenn.	26,022,752	73
(INDEPENDENT) Walter B. Jones, Ala. Herman E. Talmadge, Ga.		1

Second Inaugural Address • Washington, D.C. • Monday, January 21, 1957

Mr. Chairman, Mr. Vice President, Mr. Chief Justice, Mr. Speaker,

members of my family and friends, my countrymen, and the friends of my country, wherever they may be, we meet again, as upon a like moment four years ago, and again you have witnessed my solemn oath of service to you.

I, too, am a witness, today testifying in your name to the principles and purposes to which we, as a people, are pledged.

Before all else, we seek, upon our common labor as a nation, the blessings of Almighty God. And the hopes in our hearts fashion the deepest prayers of our whole people.

May we pursue the right—without self-righteousness.

May we know unity—without conformity.

May we grow in strength—without pride in self.

May we, in our dealings with all peoples of the earth, ever speak truth and serve justice.

And so shall America—in the sight of all men of good will—prove true to the honorable purposes that bind and rule us as a people in all this time of trial through which we pass.

We live in a land of plenty, but rarely has this earth known such peril as today.

In our nation work and wealth abound. Our population grows. Commerce crowds our rivers and rails, our skies, harbors, and highways. Our soil is fertile, our agriculture productive. The air rings with the song of our industry—rolling mills and blast furnaces, dynamos, dams, and assembly lines—the chorus of America the bountiful.

This is our home—yet this is not the whole of our world. For our world is where our full destiny lies—with men, of all people, and all nations, who are or would be free. And for them—and so for us—this is no time of ease or of rest.

In too much of the earth there is want, discord, danger. New forces and new nations stir and strive across the earth, with power to bring, by their fate, great good or great evil to the free world's future. From the deserts of North Africa to the islands of the South Pacific one third of all mankind has entered upon an historic struggle for a new freedom; freedom from grinding poverty. Across all continents, nearly a billion people seek, sometimes almost in desperation, for the skills and knowledge and assistance by which

they may satisfy from their own resources, the material wants common to all mankind.

No nation, however old or great, escapes this tempest of change and turmoil. Some, impoverished by the recent World War, seek to restore their means of livelihood. In the heart of Europe, Germany still stands tragically divided. So is the whole continent divided. And so, too, is all the world.

The divisive force is International Communism and the power that it controls.

The designs of that power, dark in purpose, are clear in practice. It strives to seal forever the fate of those it has enslaved. It strives to break the ties that unite the free. And it strives to capture—to exploit for its own greater power—all forces of change in the world, especially the needs of the hungry and the hopes of the oppressed.

Yet the world of International Communism has itself been shaken by a fierce and mighty force: the readiness of men who love freedom to pledge their lives to that love. Through the night of their bondage, the unconquerable will of heroes has struck with the swift, sharp thrust of lightning. Budapest is no longer merely the name of a city; henceforth

it is a new and shining symbol of man's yearning to be free.

Thus across all the globe there harshly blow the winds of change. And, we—though fortunate be our lot—know that we can never turn our backs to them.

We look upon this shaken earth, and we declare our firm and fixed purpose—the building of a peace with justice in a world where moral law prevails.

The building of such a peace is a bold and solemn purpose. To proclaim it is easy. To serve it will be hard. And to attain it, we must be aware of its full meaning—and ready to pay its full price.

We know clearly what we seek, and why.

We seek peace, knowing that peace is the climate of freedom. And now, as in no other age, we seek it because we have been warned, by the power of modern weapons, that peace may be the only climate possible for human life itself.

Yet this peace we seek cannot be born of fear alone: it must be rooted in the lives of nations. There must be justice, sensed and shared by all peoples, for, without justice the world can know only a tense and unstable truce. There must be law, steadily invoked and respected by all nations, for without law, the world promises only such meager justice as the pity of the strong upon the weak. But the law of which we speak, comprehending the values of freedom, affirms the equality of all nations, great and small.

Splendid as can be the blessings of such a peace, high will be its cost: in toil patiently sustained, in help honorably given, in sacrifice calmly borne.

We are called to meet the price of this peace.

To counter the threat of those who seek to rule by force, we must pay the costs of our own needed military strength, and help to build the security of others.

We must use our skills and knowledge and, at times, our substance, to help others rise from misery, however far the scene of suffering may be from our shores. For wherever in the world a people knows desperate want, there must appear at least the spark of hope, the hope of progress—or there will surely rise at last the flames of conflict.

We recognize and accept our own deep involvement in the destiny of men everywhere. We are accordingly pledged to honor, and to strive to fortify, the authority of the United Nations. For in that body rests the best hope of our age for the assertion of that law by which all nations may live in dignity.

And, beyond this general resolve, we are called to act a responsible role in the world's great concerns or conflicts—whether they touch upon the affairs of a vast region, the fate of an island in the Pacific, or the use of a canal in the Middle East. Only in respecting the hopes and cultures of others will we practice the equality of all nations. Only as we show willingness and wisdom in giving counsel—in receiving counsel—and in sharing burdens, will we wisely perform the work of peace.

For one truth must rule all we think and all we do. No peo-

ple can live to itself alone. The unity of all who dwell in freedom is their only sure defense. The economic need of all nations—in mutual dependence—makes isolation an impossibility; not even America's prosperity could long survive if other nations did not also prosper. No nation can longer be a fortress, lone and strong and safe. And any people, seeking such shelter for themselves, can now build only their own prison.

Our pledge to these principles is constant, because we believe in their rightness.

We do not fear this world of change. America is no stranger to much of its spirit. Everywhere we see the seeds of the same growth that America itself has known. The American

---

No nation can longer be a fortress, lone and strong and safe. And any people, seeking such shelter for themselves, can now build only their own prison.

---

experiment has, for generations, fired the passion and the courage of millions elsewhere seeking freedom, equality, and opportunity. And the American story of material progress has helped excite the longing of all needy peoples for some satisfaction of their human wants. These hopes that we have helped to inspire, we can help to fulfill.

In this confidence, we speak plainly to all peoples.

We cherish our friendship with all nations that are or would be free. We respect, no less, their independence. And when, in time of want or peril, they ask our help, they may honorably receive it; for we no

more seek to buy their sovereignty than we would sell our own. Sovereignty is never bartered among freemen.

We honor the aspirations of those nations which, now captive, long for freedom. We seek neither their military alliance nor any artificial imitation of our society. And they can know the warmth of the welcome that awaits them when, as must be, they join again the ranks of freedom.

We honor, no less in this divided world than in a less tormented time, the people of Russia. We do not dread, rather do we welcome, their progress in education and industry. We wish them success in their demands for more intellectual freedom, greater security before their own laws, fuller enjoyment of the rewards of their own toil. For as such things come to pass, the more certain will be the coming of that day when our peoples may freely meet in friendship.

So we voice our hope and our belief that we can help to heal this divided world. Thus may the nations cease to live in trembling before the menace of force. Thus may the weight of fear and the weight of arms be taken from the burdened shoulders of mankind.

This, nothing less, is the labor to which we are called and our strength dedicated.

And so the prayer of our people carries far beyond our own frontiers, to the wide world of our duty and our destiny.

May the light of freedom, coming to all darkened lands, flame brightly—until at last the darkness is no more.

May the turbulence of our age yield to a true time of peace, when men and nations shall share a life that honors the dignity of each, the brotherhood of all.

* * *

1960 John F. Kennedy

Although Dwight Eisenhower would have retired in any case, the Twenty-second Amendment forced the Republicans to find another candidate. The most likely choice, Vice President Richard M. Nixon, faced some early opposition from New York's liberal governor, Nelson A. Rockefeller, but Nixon made a platform deal with Rockefeller on the eve of the convention that included Rockefeller's endorsement.

As for the Democrats, Massachusetts senator John F. Kennedy knocked Minnesota senator Hubert H. Humphrey out of the race with a lopsided primary victory in West Virginia, where the Catholic Kennedy demonstrated he could win Protestant votes. Then, with the help of big-city machines (especially Richard J. Daley's in Chicago), Kennedy ran over Senate Majority Leader Lyndon B. Johnson at the convention for a first-ballot victory. Despite hard feelings on both sides, Johnson subsequently agreed to join the ticket as Kennedy's running mate.

Kennedy was the underdog, but his telegenic good looks attracted voters. More than one hundred million tuned in to watch the first televised presidential debates. A carefully prepared Kennedy used makeup and clothing to project an image of vitality that belied his chronically poor health. On the other hand, Nixon, confident that he was the better debater, gave little thought to his appearance, made worse by a recent hospitalization. Television viewers thought Kennedy had won; radio listeners generally believed Nixon had made the better showing. In general, Kennedy warned darkly of a "missile gap" and called for the overthrow of Fidel Castro's regime in Cuba, while the Nixon campaign cautioned Americans that "Experience Counts."

Party	Popular Votes	Electoral Votes
Democratic John F. Kennedy, Mass. Lyndon B. Johnson, Tex.	34,226,731	303
Republican Richard M. Nixon, Calif. Henry Cabot Lodge, Mass.	34,108,157	219
(Independent) Harry F. Byrd, Va. J. Strom Thurmond, S.C.		15

The return of Catholic voters to the Democratic party helped Kennedy, as did substantial vote fraud in Texas and Illinois. With Lyndon Johnson as his running mate, Kennedy barely squeaked out a victory; without Johnson, he surely would have lost. Choosing not to contest the fraudulent returns, an uncharacteristically magnanimous Nixon allowed Kennedy to become the first Catholic president and the youngest ever elected to the office.

Inaugural Address • Washington, D.C. • Friday, January 20, 1961

Vice President Johnson, Mr. Speaker, Mr. Chief Justice, President Eisenhower,

Vice President Nixon, President Truman, reverend clergy, fellow citizens, we observe today not a victory of party, but a celebration of freedom—symbolizing an end, as well as a beginning—signifying renewal, as well as change. For I have sworn before you and Almighty God the same solemn oath our forebears prescribed nearly a century and three quarters ago.

The world is very different now. For man holds in his mortal hands the power to abolish all forms of human poverty and all forms of human life. And yet the same revolutionary beliefs for which our forebears fought are still at issue around the globe—the belief that the rights of man come not from the generosity of the state, but from the hand of God.

We dare not forget today that we are the heirs of that first revolution. Let the word go forth from this time and place, to friend and foe alike, that the torch has been passed to a new generation of Americans—born in this century, tempered by war, disciplined by a hard and bitter peace, proud of our ancient heritage—and unwilling to witness or permit the slow undoing of those human rights to which this Nation has always been committed, and to which we are committed today at home and around the world.

Let every nation know, whether it wishes us well or ill, that we shall pay any price, bear any burden, meet any hardship, support any friend, oppose any foe, in order to assure the survival and the success of liberty.

This much we pledge—and more.

To those old allies whose cultural and spiritual origins we share, we pledge the loyalty of faithful friends. United, there is little we cannot do in a host of cooperative ventures. Divided, there is little we can do—for we dare not meet a powerful challenge at odds and split asunder.

To those new States whom we welcome to the ranks of the free, we pledge our word that one form of colonial control shall not have passed away merely to be replaced by a far more iron tyranny. We shall not always expect to find them supporting our view. But we shall always hope to find them strongly supporting their own freedom—and to remember that, in the past, those who foolishly sought power by riding the back of the tiger ended up inside.

And so, my fellow Americans: ask not what your country can do for you—ask what you can do for your country.

To those peoples in the huts and villages across the globe struggling to break the bonds of mass misery, we pledge our best efforts to help them help themselves, for whatever period is required—not because the Communists may be doing it, not because we seek their votes, but because it is right. If a free society cannot help the many who are poor, it cannot save the few who are rich.

To our sister republics south of our border, we offer a special pledge—to convert our good words into good deeds—in a new alliance for progress—to assist free men and free governments in casting off the chains of poverty. But this peaceful revolution of hope cannot become the prey of hostile powers. Let all our neighbors know that we shall join with them to oppose aggression or subversion anywhere in the Americas. And let every other power know that this Hemisphere intends to remain the master of its own house.

To that world assembly of sovereign states, the United Nations, our last best hope in an age where the instruments of war have far outpaced the instruments of peace, we renew our pledge of support—to prevent it from becoming merely a forum for invective—

to strengthen its shield of the new and the weak—and to enlarge the area in which its writ may run.

Finally, to those nations who would make themselves our adversary, we offer not a pledge but a request: that both sides begin anew the quest for peace, before the dark powers of destruction unleashed by science engulf all humanity in planned or accidental self-destruction.

We dare not tempt them with weakness. For only when our arms are sufficient beyond doubt can we be certain beyond doubt that they will never be employed.

But neither can two great and powerful groups of nations take comfort from our present course—both sides overburdened by the cost of modern weapons, both rightly alarmed by the steady spread of the deadly atom, yet both racing to alter that uncertain balance of terror that stays the hand of mankind's final war.

So let us begin anew—remembering on both sides that civility is not a sign of weakness, and sincerity is always subject to proof. Let us never negotiate out of fear. But let us never fear to negotiate.

Let both sides explore what problems unite us instead

of belaboring those problems which divide us.

Let both sides, for the first time, formulate serious and precise proposals for the inspection and control of arms—and bring the absolute power to destroy other nations under the absolute control of all nations.

Let both sides seek to invoke the wonders of science instead of its terrors. Together let us explore the stars, conquer the deserts, eradicate disease, tap the ocean depths, and encourage the arts and commerce.

Let both sides unite to heed in all corners of the earth the command of Isaiah—to "undo the heavy burdens ... and to let the oppressed go free."

And if a beachhead of cooperation may push back the jungle of suspicion, let both sides join in creating a new endeavor, not a new balance of power, but a new world of law, where the strong are just and the weak secure and the peace preserved.

All this will not be finished in the first 100 days. Nor will it be finished in the first 1,000 days, nor in the life of this Administration, nor even perhaps in our lifetime on this planet. But let us begin.

In your hands, my fellow citizens, more than in mine, will rest the final success or failure of our course. Since this country was founded, each generation of Americans has been summoned to give testimony to its national loyalty. The graves of young Americans who answered the call to service surround the globe.

Now the trumpet summons us again—not as a call to bear arms, though arms we need; not as a call to battle, though embattled we are—but a call to bear the burden of a long twilight struggle, year in and year out, "rejoicing in hope, patient in tribulation"—a struggle against the common enemies of man: tyranny, poverty, disease, and war itself.

Can we forge against these enemies a grand and

global alliance, North and South, East and West, that can assure a more fruitful life for all mankind? Will you join in that historic effort?

In the long history of the world, only a few generations

have been granted the role of defending freedom in its hour of maximum danger. I do not shrink from this responsibility, I welcome it. I do not believe that any of us would exchange places with any other people or any other generation. The energy, the faith, the devotion which we bring to this endeavor will light our country and all who serve it—and the glow from that fire can truly light the world.

And so, my fellow Americans: ask not what your country can do for you—ask what you can do for your country.

My fellow citizens of the world: ask not what America will do for you, but what together we can do for the freedom of man.

Finally, whether you are citizens of America or citizens of the world, ask of us the same high standards of strength and sacrifice which we ask of you. With a good conscience our only sure reward, with history the final judge of our deeds, let us go forth to lead the land we love, asking His blessing and His help, but knowing that here on earth God's work must truly be our own.

* * *

1964 LYNDON BAINES JOHNSON

LYNDON B. JOHNSON'S FLAWLESS handling of his transition to the presidency enabled him to consolidate his support within the Democratic party and win its nomination by acclamation. In order to avoid choosing Robert F. Kennedy as his running mate, LBJ announced he would not select any member of his cabinet, thus ruling out the attorney general. Instead, he chose Minnesota senator Hubert H. Humphrey, a favorite of party liberals, especially those in the Midwest.

The Republicans were badly divided, with conservatives supporting Arizona senator Barry M. Goldwater and liberals backing New York governor Nelson A. Rockefeller. After winning the nomination, Goldwater declared to the convention, "Extremism in the defense of liberty is no vice." Liberal Republicans were appalled.

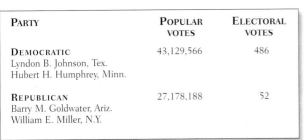

Goldwater hoped to attract conservative Democrats, independents, and even people who usually didn't vote by offering "a choice, not an echo." His campaign commercials emphasized the rising urban crime rate and other forms of civil unrest. Unfortunately for Goldwater, his vituperative style allowed Johnson to run as a moderate who could plausibly warn that Goldwater, if elected, might escalate the Vietnam War into a nuclear conflict. A famous Democratic campaign commercial showed a little girl pulling petals from a daisy, her count seguing abruptly into the countdown for a nuclear explosion.

The scare tactics worked. Though an amiable man, Goldwater proved to be a frightening candidate, and voters flocked like sheep to Johnson. The Republicans outspent the Democrats, but for nothing as Johnson won 61.1 percent of the popular vote, the greatest landslide yet in presidential election history.

PARTY	POPULAR VOTES	ELECTORAL VOTES
DEMOCRATIC Lyndon B. Johnson, Tex. Hubert H. Humphrey, Minn.	43,129,566	486
REPUBLICAN Barry M. Goldwater, Ariz. William E. Miller, N.Y.	27,178,188	52

Inaugural Address • Washington, D.C. • Wednesday, January 20, 1965

My fellow countrymen, on this occasion, the oath I have taken before you

and before God is not mine alone, but ours together. We are one nation and one people. Our fate as a nation and our future as a people rest not upon one citizen, but upon all citizens.

This is the majesty and the meaning of this moment.

For every generation, there is a destiny. For some, history decides. For this generation, the choice must be our own.

Even now, a rocket moves toward Mars. It reminds us that the world will not be the same for our children, or even for ourselves in a short span of years. The next man to stand here will look out on a scene different from our own, because ours is a time of change—rapid and fantastic change bearing the secrets of nature, multiplying the nations, placing in uncertain hands new weapons for mastery and destruction, shaking old values, and uprooting old ways.

Our destiny in the midst of change will rest on the unchanged character of our people, and on their faith.

They came here—the exile and the stranger, brave but frightened—to find a place where a man could be his own man. They made a covenant with this land. Conceived in justice, written in liberty, bound in union, it was meant one day to inspire the hopes of all mankind; and it binds us still. If we keep its terms, we shall flourish.

First, justice was the promise that all who made the journey would share in the fruits of the land.

In a land of great wealth, families must not live in hopeless poverty. In a land rich in harvest, children just must not go hungry. In a land of healing miracles, neighbors must not suffer and die unattended. In a great land of learning and scholars, young people must be taught to read and write.

For the more than 30 years that I have served this Nation, I have believed that this injustice to our people, this waste of our resources, was our real enemy. For 30 years or more, with the resources I have had, I have vigilantly fought against it. I have learned, and I know, that it will not surrender easily.

But change has given us new weapons. Before this generation of Americans is finished, this enemy will not only retreat—it will be conquered.

Justice requires us to remember that when any citizen denies his fellow, saying, "His color is not mine," or "His beliefs are strange and different," in that moment he betrays America, though his forebears created this Nation.

Liberty was the second article of our covenant. It was self-government. It was our Bill of Rights. But it was more. America would be a place where each man could be proud to be himself: stretching his

time, has really only a moment among our companions.

How incredible it is that in this fragile existence, we should hate and destroy one another. There are possibilities enough for all who will abandon mastery over others to pursue mastery over nature. There is world enough for all to seek their happiness in their own way.

Our Nation's course is abundantly clear. We aspire to nothing that belongs to others. We seek no dominion over our fellow man, but man's dominion over tyranny and misery.

But more is required. Men want to be a part of a common enterprise—a cause greater than themselves. Each of us must find a way to advance the purpose of the Nation, thus finding new purpose for ourselves. Without this, we shall become a nation of strangers.

The third article was union. To those who were small and few against the wilderness, the success of liberty demanded the strength of union. Two centuries of change have made this true again.

[The Great Society] is…is the excitement of becoming—— always becoming, trying, probing, falling, resting, and trying again——but always trying and always gaining.

No longer need capitalist and worker, farmer and clerk, city and countryside, struggle to divide our bounty. By working shoulder to shoulder, together we can increase the bounty of all. We have discovered that every child who learns, every man who finds work, every sick body that is

made whole—like a candle added to an altar—brightens the hope of all the faithful.

So let us reject any among us who seek to reopen old wounds and to rekindle old hatreds. They stand in the way of a seeking nation.

Let us now join reason to faith and action to experience, to transform our unity of interest into a unity of purpose. For the hour and the day and the time are here to achieve progress without strife, to achieve change without hatred—not without difference of opinion, but without the deep and abiding divisions which scar the union for generations.

Under this covenant of justice, liberty, and union we have become a nation—prosperous, great, and mighty. And we have kept our freedom. But we have no promise from God that our greatness will endure. We have been allowed by Him to seek greatness with the sweat of our hands and the strength of our spirit.

I do not believe that the Great Society is the ordered, changeless, and sterile battalion of the ants. It is the excitement of becoming—always becoming, trying, probing, falling, resting, and trying again—but always trying and always gaining.

In each generation, with toil and tears, we have had to earn our heritage again.

If we fail now, we shall have forgotten in abundance what we learned in hardship: that democracy rests on faith, that freedom asks more than it gives, and that the judgment of God is harshest on those who are most favored.

If we succeed, it will not be because of what we have, but it will be because of what we are; not because of what we own, but, rather because of what we believe.

For we are a nation of believers. Underneath the clamor of building and the rush of our day's pursuits, we are believers in justice and liberty and union, and in our own Union. We believe that every man must someday be free. And we believe in ourselves.

Our enemies have always made the same mistake. In my lifetime—in depression and in war—they have awaited our defeat. Each time, from the secret

places of the American heart, came forth the faith they could not see or that they could not even imagine. It brought us victory. And it will again.

For this is what America is all about. It is the uncrossed desert and the unclimbed ridge. It is the star that is not reached and the harvest sleeping in the unplowed ground. Is our world gone? We say "Farewell." Is a new world coming? We welcome it—and we will bend it to the hopes of man.

To these trusted public servants and to my family and those close friends of mine who have followed me down a long, winding road, and to all the people of this Union and the world, I will repeat today what I said on that sorrowful day in November 1963: "I will lead and I will do the best I can."

But you must look within your own hearts to the old promises and to the old dream. They will lead you best of all.

For myself, I ask only, in the words of an ancient leader: "Give me now wisdom and knowledge, that I may go out and come in before this people: for who can judge this thy people, that is so great?"

* * *

talents, rejoicing in his work, important in the life of his neighbors and his nation.

This has become more difficult in a world where change and growth seem to tower beyond the control and even the judgment of men. We must work to provide the knowledge and the surroundings which can enlarge the possibilities of every citizen.

The American covenant called on us to help show the way for the liberation of man. And that is today our goal. Thus, if as a nation there is much outside our control, as a people no stranger is outside our hope.

Change has brought new meaning to that old mission. We can never again stand aside, prideful in isolation. Terrific dangers and troubles that we once called "foreign" now constantly live among us. If American lives must end, and American treasure be spilled, in countries we barely know, that is the price that change has demanded of conviction and of our enduring covenant.

Think of our world as it looks from the rocket that is heading toward Mars. It is like a child's globe, hanging in space, the continents stuck to its side like colored maps. We are all fellow passengers on a dot of earth. And each of us, in the span of

1968 RICHARD MILHOUS NIXON

AFTER PEACE CANDIDATE EUGENE McCARTHY nearly beat him in the New Hampshire primary, President Lyndon Johnson withdrew from the race and supported Vice President Hubert H. Humphrey for the Democratic nomination. Senator Robert F. Kennedy of New York and McCarthy, a senator from Minnesota, split the overall primary vote. But on the night of Kennedy's victory in the June 4 California primary, he was assassinated, leaving the unlikely McCarthy as Humphrey's main opposition. At the unruly Chicago convention, where police gassed and brutalized young peace activists, the party leaders made sure that Humphrey was nominated. (In a somewhat more democratic fashion, the convention repealed the unit rule, which had prevented state delegations from splitting their votes for more than a century.)

The Republicans, meeting in Miami, had a much easier time. Former vice president Richard M. Nixon had emerged during the primaries as the clear favorite, and he won the nomination on the first ballot. Also competing against Humphrey was Democratic governor George C. Wallace of Alabama, who ran as the candidate of the American Independent party, an alliance of latter-day Dixiecrats opposed to integration and northern conservatives attracted by Wallace's calls for victory in Vietnam and order at home.

PARTY	POPULAR VOTES	ELECTORAL VOTES
REPUBLICAN Richard M. Nixon, Calif. Spiro T. Agnew, Md.	31,785,480	301
DEMOCRATIC Hubert H. Humphrey, Minn. Edmund S. Muskie, Me.	31,275,166	191
AMERICAN INDEPENDENT George C. Wallace, Ala. Curtis E. LeMay, Ohio	9,906,473	46

The chaos and violence at the Democratic convention, televised nationally, set back Humphrey's campaign, but the vice president steadily made up ground against Nixon until, by Election Day, the race was too close to call. Wallace carried five states in the Deep South, but these losses didn't hurt Humphrey as much as the votes Wallace took from him in California, Illinois, and Ohio, where Nixon won with modest pluralities. In general, Nixon's "Sunbelt strategy"—relying on states in the South and the West—signaled a transition in traditional Republican electoral politics.

First Inaugural Address • Washington, D.C. • Monday, January 20, 1969

Senator Dirksen, Mr. Chief Justice, Mr. Vice President, President Johnson,

Vice President Humphrey, my fellow Americans—and my fellow citizens of the world community:

I ask you to share with me today the majesty of this moment. In the orderly transfer of power, we celebrate the unity that keeps us free.

Each moment in history is a fleeting time, precious and unique. But some stand out as moments of beginning, in which courses are set that shape decades or centuries.

This can be such a moment.

Forces now are converging that make possible, for the first time, the hope that many of man's deepest aspirations can at last be realized. The spiraling pace of change allows us to contemplate, within our own lifetime, advances that once would have taken centuries.

In throwing wide the horizons of space, we have discovered new horizons on earth.

For the first time, because the people of the world want peace, and the leaders of the world are afraid of war, the times are on the side of peace.

Eight years from now America will celebrate its 200th anniversary as a nation. Within the lifetime of most people now living, mankind will celebrate that great new year which comes only once in a thousand years—the beginning of the third millennium.

What kind of nation we will be, what kind of world we will live in, whether we shape the future in the image of our hopes, is ours to determine by our actions and our choices.

The greatest honor history can bestow is the title of peacemaker. This honor now beckons America—the chance to help lead the world at last out of the valley of turmoil, and onto that high ground of peace that man has dreamed of since the dawn of civilization.

If we succeed, generations to come will say of us now living that we mastered our moment, that we helped make the world safe for mankind.

This is our summons to greatness.

I believe the American people are ready to answer this call.

The second third of this century has been a time of proud achievement. We have made enormous strides in science and industry and agriculture. We have shared our wealth more broadly than ever. We have learned at last to manage a modern economy to assure its continued growth.

We have given freedom new reach, and we have begun to make its promise real for

black as well as for white.

We see the hope of tomorrow in the youth of today. I know America's youth. I believe in them. We can be proud that they are better educated, more committed, more passionately driven by conscience than any generation in our history.

No people has ever been so close to the achievement of a just and abundant society, or so possessed of the will to achieve it. Because our strengths are so great, we can afford to appraise our weaknesses with candor and to approach them with hope.

Standing in this same place a third of a century ago, Franklin Delano Roosevelt addressed a Nation ravaged by depression and gripped in fear. He could say in surveying the Nation's troubles: "They concern, thank God, only material things."

Our crisis today is the reverse.

We have found ourselves rich in goods, but ragged in spirit; reaching with magnificent precision for the moon, but falling into raucous discord on earth.

We are caught in war, wanting peace. We are torn by division, wanting unity. We see around us empty lives, wanting fulfillment. We see tasks that need doing, waiting for hands to do them.

To a crisis of the spirit, we need an answer of the spirit.

To find that answer, we need only look within ourselves.

When we listen to "the better angels of our nature," we find that they celebrate the simple things, the basic things—such as goodness, decency, love, kindness.

Greatness comes in simple trappings.

The simple things are the ones most needed today if we are to surmount what divides us, and cement what unites us.

To lower our voices would be a simple thing.

In these difficult years, America has suffered from a fever of words; from inflated rhetoric that promises more than it can deliver; from angry rhetoric that fans discontents into hatreds; from bombastic rhetoric that postures instead of persuading.

We cannot learn from one another until we stop shouting at one another—until we speak quietly enough so that our words can be heard as well as our voices.

For its part, government will listen. We will strive to listen in new ways—to the voices of quiet anguish, the voices that speak without words, the voices of the heart—to the injured voices, the anxious voices, the voices that have despaired of being heard.

Those who have been left out, we will try to bring in.

Those left behind, we will help to catch up.

For all of our people, we will set as our goal the decent order that makes progress possible and our lives secure.

As we reach toward our hopes, our task is to build on what has gone before—not turning away from the old, but turning toward the new.

In this past third of a century, government has

and more, we will and must press urgently forward.

We shall plan now for the day when our wealth can be transferred from the destruction of war abroad to the urgent needs of our people at home.

The American dream does not come to those who fall asleep.

We cannot learn from one another until we stop shouting at one another—until we speak quietly enough so that our words can be heard as well as our voices.

But we are approaching the limits of what government alone can do.

Our greatest need now is to reach beyond government, and to enlist the legions of the concerned and the committed.

in grand enterprises, but more importantly in those small, splendid efforts that make headlines in the neighborhood newspaper instead of the national journal.

With these, we can build a great cathedral of the spirit—each of us raising it one stone at a time, as he reaches out to his neighbor, helping, caring, doing.

I do not offer a life of uninspiring ease. I do not call for a life of grim sacrifice. I ask you to join in a high adventure—one as rich as humanity itself, and as exciting as the times we live in.

The essence of freedom is that each of us shares in the shaping of his own destiny.

Until he has been part of a cause larger than himself, no man is truly whole.

The way to fulfillment is in the use of our talents; we achieve nobility in the spirit that inspires that use.

As we measure what can be done, we shall promise only what we know we can produce, but as we chart our goals we shall be lifted by our dreams.

No man can be fully free while his neighbor is not. To go forward at all is to go forward together.

This means black and white together, as one nation, not two. The laws have caught up with our conscience. What remains is to give life to what is

passed more laws, spent more money, initiated more programs, than in all our previous history.

In pursuing our goals of full employment, better housing, excellence in education; in rebuilding our cities and improving our rural areas; in protecting our environment and enhancing the quality of life—in all these

What has to be done, has to be done by government and people together or it will not be done at all. The lesson of past agony is that without the people we can do nothing; with the people we can do everything.

To match the magnitude of our tasks, we need the energies of our people—enlisted not only

in the law: to ensure at last that as all are born equal in dignity before God, all are born equal in dignity before man.

As we learn to go forward together at home, let us also seek to go forward together with all mankind.

Let us take as our goal: where peace is unknown, make it welcome; where peace is fragile, make it strong; where peace is temporary, make it permanent.

After a period of confrontation, we are entering an era of negotiation.

Let all nations know that during this administration our

lines of communication will be open.

We seek an open world—open to ideas, open to the exchange of goods and people—a world in which no people, great or small, will live in angry isolation.

We cannot expect to make everyone our friend, but we can try to make no one our enemy.

Those who would be our adversaries, we invite to a peaceful competition—not in conquering territory or extending dominion, but in enriching the life of man.

As we explore the reaches of space, let us go to the new worlds together—not as new worlds to be conquered, but as a new adventure to be shared.

With those who are willing to join, let us cooperate to reduce the burden of arms, to strengthen the structure of peace, to lift up the poor and the hungry.

But to all those who would be tempted by weakness, let us leave no doubt that we will be as strong as we need to be for as long as we need to be.

Over the past twenty years, since I first came to this Capital as a freshman Congressman, I have visited most of the nations of the world.

I have come to know the leaders of the world, and the great forces, the hatreds, the fears that divide the world.

I know that peace does not come through wishing for it—that there is no substitute for days and even years of patient and prolonged diplomacy.

I also know the people of the world.

I have seen the hunger of a homeless child, the pain of a man wounded in battle, the grief of a mother who has lost her son. I know these have no ideology, no race.

I know America. I know the heart of America is good.

I speak from my own heart, and the heart of my country, the deep concern we have for those who suffer, and those who sorrow.

I have taken an oath today in the presence of God and my countrymen to uphold and defend the Constitution of the United States. To that oath I now add this sacred commitment: I shall consecrate my office, my energies, and all the

wisdom I can summon, to the cause of peace among nations.

Let this message be heard by strong and weak alike:

The peace we seek to win is not victory over any other people, but the peace that comes "with healing in its wings"; with compassion for those who have suffered; with understanding for those who have opposed us; with the opportunity for all the peoples of this earth to choose their own destiny.

Only a few short weeks ago, we shared the glory of man's first sight of the world as God sees it, as a single sphere reflecting light in the darkness.

As the Apollo astronauts flew over the moon's gray surface on Christmas Eve, they spoke to us of the beauty of

earth—and in that voice so clear across the lunar distance, we heard them invoke God's blessing on its goodness.

In that moment, their view from the moon moved poet Archibald MacLeish to write:

"To see the earth as it truly is, small and blue and beautiful in that eternal silence where it floats, is to see ourselves as riders on the earth together, brothers on that bright loveliness in the eternal cold—brothers who know now they are truly brothers."

In that moment of surpassing technological triumph, men turned their thoughts toward home and humanity—seeing in that far perspective that man's destiny on earth is not divisible; telling us that however far we

reach into the cosmos, our destiny lies not in the stars but on Earth itself, in our own hands, in our own hearts.

We have endured a long night of the American spirit. But as our eyes catch the dimness of the first rays of dawn, let us not curse the remaining dark. Let us gather the light.

Our destiny offers, not the cup of despair, but the chalice of opportunity. So let us seize it, not in fear, but in gladness—and, "riders on the earth together," let us go forward, firm in our faith, steadfast in our purpose, cautious of the dangers; but sustained by our confidence in the will of God and the promise of man.

* * *

1972 RICHARD MILHOUS NIXON

AS THE 1972 ELECTION NEARED, Richard Nixon seemed vulnerable. With the peace talks in Paris stalled and the president's economic stabilization program unable to halt inflation, Democrats thought they might unseat him. However, new rules opened up the Democratic nominating process, allowing candidates to compete without any support from state party organizations. South Dakota senator George S. McGovern, chairman of the rules commission, took the greatest advantage, electing large numbers of young, women, and minority delegates committed to his candidacy. These delegates gave McGovern the nomination—but they also alienated party regulars, without whose support McGovern had no chance against Nixon.

The 1972 campaign shaped up much as 1964's had, except that this time it was the Democrat who was perceived as the extremist and the Republican who ran as the moderate. Representing the left-liberal wing of his party, McGovern opposed the war in Vietnam and promoted a plan to end poverty by guaranteeing a minimum income to all Americans. Nixon appealed to the working class by successfully characterizing the Democrats as the party of student radicals, draft dodgers, and militant minorities.

With George Wallace out of the race (following an assassination attempt that left him paralyzed), Nixon consolidated his conservative support in the South and West—outthinking, outfoxing, and outspending his opponent. McGovern couldn't even win his home state and managed to carry only liberal Massachusetts and the District of Columbia. Nixon won 60.7 percent of the popular vote, which makes one wonder why he felt it necessary to risk everything on an ill-conceived plan to bug the Watergate offices of the Democratic National Committee.

PARTY	POPULAR VOTES	ELECTORAL VOTES
REPUBLICAN Richard M. Nixon, Calif. Spiro T. Agnew, Md.	47,169,911	520
DEMOCRATIC George S. McGovern, S.D. R. Sargent Shriver, Md.	29,170,383	17
LIBERTARIAN John Hospers, Calif. Theodora N. Nathan, Ore.	3,673	1

Second Inaugural Address • Washington, D.C. • Saturday, January 20, 1973

Mr. Vice President, Mr. Speaker, Mr. Chief Justice, Senator Cook,

Mrs. Eisenhower, and my fellow citizens of this great and good country we share together:

When we met here four years ago, America was bleak in spirit, depressed by the prospect of seemingly endless war abroad and of destructive conflict at home.

As we meet here today, we stand on the threshold of a new era of peace in the world.

The central question before us is: How shall we use that peace? Let us resolve that this era we are about to enter will not be what other postwar periods have so often been: a time of retreat and isolation that leads to stagnation at home and invites new danger abroad.

Let us resolve that this will be what it can become: a time of great responsibilities greatly borne, in which we renew the spirit and the promise of America as we enter our third century as a nation.

This past year saw far-reaching results from our new policies for peace. By continu-ing to revitalize our traditional friendships, and by our missions to Peking and to Moscow, we were able to establish the base for a new and more durable pattern of relationships among the nations of the world. Because of America's bold initiatives, 1972 will be long remembered as the year of the greatest progress since the end of World War II toward a lasting peace in the world.

The peace we seek in the world is not the flimsy peace which is merely an interlude between wars, but a peace which can endure for generations to come.

It is important that we understand both the necessity and the limitations of America's role in maintaining that peace.

Unless we in America work to preserve the peace, there will be no peace.

Unless we in America work to preserve freedom, there will be no freedom.

But let us clearly understand the new nature of America's role, as a result of the new policies we have adopted over these past four years.

We shall respect our treaty commitments.

We shall support vigorously the principle that no country has the right to impose its will or rule on another by force.

We shall continue, in this era of negoti-ation, to work for the limitation of nuclear arms, and to reduce the danger of con-frontation between the great powers.

We shall do our share in defending peace and freedom in the world. But we shall expect others to do their share.

The time has passed when America will make every other nation's conflict our own, or make every other nation's future our responsibility, or presume to tell the people of other nations how to manage their own affairs.

Just as we respect the right of each nation to determine its own future, we also recognize the responsibility of each nation to secure its own future.

Just as America's role is indispensable in preserving the world's peace, so is each nation's role indispensable in preserving its own peace.

Together with the rest of the world, let us resolve to move forward from the beginnings we have made. Let us continue to bring down the walls of hostility which have divided the world for too long, and to build in their place bridges of understanding—so that despite profound differences between systems of government, the people of the world can be friends.

Let us build a structure of peace in the world in which the weak are as safe as the strong—in which each respects the right of the other to live by a different system—in which those who would influence others will do so by the strength of their ideas, and not by the force of their arms.

Let us accept that high responsibility not as a burden, but gladly—gladly because the chance to build such a peace is the noblest endeavor in which a nation can engage; gladly, also, because only if we act greatly in meeting our responsibilities abroad will we remain a great Nation, and only if we remain a great Nation will we act greatly in meeting our challenges at home.

We have the chance today to do more than ever before in our history to make life better in America—to ensure better education, better health, better housing, better transportation, a cleaner environment—to restore respect for law, to make our communities more livable—and to insure the God-given right of every American to full and equal opportunity.

Because the range of our needs is so great—because the reach of our opportunities is so great—let us be bold in our determination to meet those needs in new ways.

Just as building a structure of peace abroad has required turning away from old policies that failed, so building a new era of progress at home requires turning away from old policies that have failed.

Abroad, the shift from old policies to new has not been a retreat from our responsibilities, but a better way to peace.

And at home, the shift from old policies to new will not be a retreat from our responsibilities, but a better way to progress.

Abroad and at home, the key to those new responsibilities lies in the placing and the division of responsibility. We have lived too long with the consequences of attempting to gather all power and responsibility in Washington.

Abroad and at home, the time has come to turn away from the condescending policies of paternalism—of "Washington knows best."

A person can be expected to act responsibly only if he has responsibility. This is human nature. So let us encourage in-

At every turn, we have been beset by those who find everything wrong with America and little that is right.

dividuals at home and nations abroad to do more for themselves, to decide more for themselves. Let us locate responsibility in more places. Let us measure what we will do for others by what they will do for themselves.

That is why today I offer no promise of a purely governmental solution for every problem. We have lived too long with that false promise. In trusting too much in government, we have asked of it more than it can deliver. This leads only to inflated expectations, to reduced individual effort, and to a disappointment and frustration that erode confidence both in what government can do and in what people can do.

Government must learn to take less from people so that people can do more for themselves.

Let us remember that America was built not by government, but by people—not by welfare, but by work—not by shirking responsibility, but by seeking responsibility.

In our own lives, let each of us ask—not just what will

government do for me, but what can I do for myself?

In the challenges we face together, let each of us ask—not just how can government help, but how can I help?

Your National Government has a great and vital role to play. And I pledge to you that where this Government should act, we will act boldly and we will lead boldly. But just as important is the role that each and every one of us must play, as an individual and as a member of his own community.

From this day forward, let each of us make a solemn commitment in his own heart: to bear his responsibility, to do his part, to live his ideals—so that together, we can see the dawn of a new age of progress for America, and together, as we celebrate our 200th anniversary as a nation, we can do so proud in the fulfillment of our promise to ourselves and to the world.

As America's longest and most difficult war comes to an end, let us again learn to debate our differences with civility and decency. And let each of us reach out for that one precious quality government cannot provide—a new level of respect for the rights and feelings of one another, a new level of respect for the individual human dignity which is the cherished birthright of every American.

Above all else, the time has come for us to renew our faith in ourselves and in America.

In recent years, that faith has been challenged.

Our children have been taught to be ashamed of their country, ashamed of their parents, ashamed of America's record at home and of its role in the world.

At every turn, we have been beset by those who find everything wrong with America and little that is right. But I am confident that this will not be the judgment of history on these remarkable times in which we are privileged to live.

America's record in this century has been unparalleled in the world's history for its responsibility, for its generosity, for its creativity and for its progress.

Let us be proud that our system has produced and provided more freedom and more abundance, more widely shared, than any other system in the history of the world.

Let us be proud that in each of the four wars in which we have been engaged in this century, including the one we are now bringing to an end, we have fought not for our selfish advantage, but to help others resist aggression.

Let us be proud that by our bold, new initiatives, and by our steadfastness for peace with honor, we have made a breakthrough toward creating in the world what the world has not known before—a structure of peace that can last, not merely for our time, but for generations to come.

We are embarking here today on an era that presents challenges great as those any nation, or any generation, has ever faced.

We shall answer to God, to history, and to our conscience for the way in which we use these years.

As I stand in this place, so hallowed by history, I think of others who have stood here before me. I think of the dreams they had for America, and I think of how each recognized that he needed help far beyond himself in order to make those dreams come true.

Today, I ask your prayers that in the years ahead I may have God's help in making decisions that are right for America, and I pray for your help so that together we may be worthy of our challenge.

Let us pledge together to make these next four years the best four years in America's history, so that on its 200th birthday America will be as young and as vital as when it began, and as bright a beacon of hope for all the world.

Let us go forward from here confident in hope, strong in our faith in one another, sustained by our faith in God who created us, and striving always to serve His purpose.

* * *

1976 JIMMY CARTER

THE WATERGATE SCANDAL had so tarnished the Republicans that, most people believed, nearly any Democrat could beat Gerald R. Ford, the man who had pardoned Richard Nixon. Ford, however, showed surprising resilience in beating back a primary challenge from former California governor Ronald Reagan. On the Democratic side, a large field of candidates was gradually winnowed down by the primary process until a long shot, former governor Jimmy Carter of Georgia, finally emerged as the nominee.

While many conservative Republicans, disappointed by Reagan's defeat, sat out the election, Carter worked hard to unify his party, building up a substantial lead in postconvention polls. Ford concentrated on the Rust Belt and the Sun Belt; Carter secured his southern base, then pressed his campaign in the Midwest and the mid-Atlantic states. As the presidential debates began, Ford closed the gap between himself and Carter, but a major foreign policy gaffe (misstating his position on Poland) cost Ford momentum and reinforced the impression that he wasn't really up to the job.

The volunteers in Carter's "Peanut Brigade" helped Democratic state party organizations get out the vote, especially among minorities in the larger northern cities. This effort made a difference in an unexpectedly close race, enabling Carter to carry New York, Ohio, and Pennsylvania by narrow margins.

PARTY	POPULAR VOTES	ELECTORAL VOTES
DEMOCRATIC James Earl Carter Jr., Ga. Walter F. Mondale, Minn.	40,830,763	297
REPUBLICAN Gerald R. Ford, Mich. Robert J. Dole, Kan.	39,147,793	240
(INDEPENDENT) Ronald W. Reagan, Calif. Robert J. Dole, Kan.		1

Inaugural Address • Washington, D.C. • Thursday, January 20, 1977

For myself and for our Nation, I want to thank my predecessor

for all he has done to heal our land.

In this outward and physical ceremony we attest once again to the inner and spiritual strength of our Nation. As my high school teacher, Miss Julia Coleman, used to say: "We must adjust to changing times and still hold to unchanging principles."

Here before me is the Bible used in the inauguration of our first President, in 1789, and I have just taken the oath of office on the Bible my mother gave me a few years ago, opened to a timeless admonition from the ancient prophet Micah:

"He hath showed thee, O man, what is good; and what doth the Lord require of thee, but to do justly, and to love mercy, and to walk humbly with thy God." (Micah 6:8)

This inauguration ceremony marks a new beginning, a new dedication within our Government, and a new spirit among us all. A President may sense and proclaim that new spirit, but only a people can provide it.

Two centuries ago our Nation's birth was a milestone in the long quest for freedom, but the bold and brilliant dream which excited the founders of this Nation still awaits its consummation. I have no new dream to set forth today, but rather urge a fresh faith in the old dream.

Ours was the first society openly to define itself in terms of both spirituality and of human liberty. It is that unique self-definition which has given us an exceptional appeal, but it also imposes on us a special obligation, to take on those moral duties which, when assumed, seem invariably to be in our own best interests.

You have given me a great responsibility—to stay close to you, to be worthy of you, and to exemplify what you are. Let us create together a new national spirit of unity and trust. Your strength can compensate for my weakness, and your wisdom can help to minimize my mistakes.

Let us learn together and laugh together and work together and pray together, confident that in the end we will triumph together in the right.

The American dream endures. We must once again have full faith in our country—and in one another. I believe America can be better. We can be even stronger than before.

Let our recent mistakes bring a resurgent commitment to the basic principles of our Nation, for we know that if we despise our own government we have no future. We recall in special times when we have stood briefly, but magnificently, united. In those times no prize was beyond our grasp.

But we cannot dwell upon remembered glory. We cannot afford to drift. We reject the prospect of failure or mediocrity or an inferior quality of life for any person. Our Government must at the same time be both competent and compassionate.

We have already found a high degree of personal liberty, and we are now struggling to enhance equality of opportunity. Our commitment to human rights must be absolute, our laws fair, our natural beauty preserved; the powerful must not persecute the weak, and human dignity must be enhanced.

We have learned that "more" is not necessarily "better," that even our great Nation has its recognized limits, and

> *Let us create together a new national spirit of unity and trust. Your strength can compensate for my weakness, and your wisdom can help to minimize my mistakes.*

that we can neither answer all questions nor solve all problems. We cannot afford to do everything, nor can we afford to lack boldness as we meet the future. So, together, in a spirit of individual sacrifice for the common good, we must simply do our best.

Our Nation can be strong abroad only if it is strong at home. And we know that the best way to enhance freedom in other lands is to demonstrate here that our democratic system is worthy of emulation.

To be true to ourselves, we must be true to others. We will not behave in foreign places so as to violate our rules and standards here at home, for we know that the trust which our Nation earns is essential to our strength.

The world itself is now dominated by a new spirit. Peoples more numerous and

more politically aware are craving and now demanding their place in the sun—not just for the benefit of their own physical condition, but for basic human rights.

The passion for freedom is on the rise. Tapping this new spirit, there can be no nobler nor more ambitious task for America to undertake on this day of a new beginning than to help shape a just and peaceful world that is truly humane.

We are a strong nation, and we will maintain strength so sufficient that it need not be proven in combat—a quiet strength based not merely on the size of an arsenal, but on the nobility of ideas.

We will be ever vigilant and never vulnerable, and we will fight our wars against poverty, ignorance, and injustice—for those are the enemies against which our forces can be honorably marshaled.

We are a purely idealistic Nation, but let no one confuse our idealism with weakness.

Because we are free we can never be indifferent to the fate of freedom elsewhere. Our moral sense dictates a clearcut preference for these societies which share with us an abiding respect for individual human rights. We do not seek to intimidate, but it is clear that a world which others can dominate with impunity would be inhospitable to decency and a threat to the well-being of all people.

The world is still engaged in a massive armaments race designed to ensure continuing

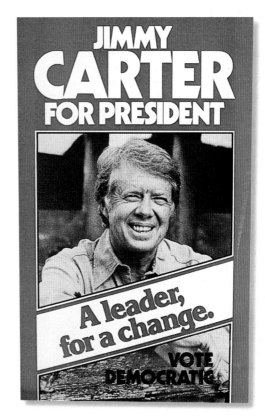

equivalent strength among potential adversaries. We pledge perseverance and wisdom in our efforts to limit the world's armaments to those necessary for each nation's own domestic safety. And we will move this year a step toward ultimate goal—the elimination of all nuclear weapons from this Earth. We urge all other people to join us, for success can mean life instead of death.

Within us, the people of the United States, there is evident a serious and purposeful rekindling of confidence. And I join in the hope that when my time as your President has ended, people might say this about our Nation:

—that we had remembered the words of Micah and renewed our search for humility, mercy, and justice;

—that we had torn down the barriers that separated those of different race and region and religion, and where there had been mistrust, built unity, with a respect for diversity;

—that we had found productive work for those able to perform it;

—that we had strengthened the American family, which is the basis of 28 our society;

—that we had ensured respect for the law, and equal treatment under the law, for the weak and the powerful, for the rich and the poor;

—and that we had enabled our people to be proud of their own Government once again.

I would hope that the nations of the world might say that we had built a lasting peace, built not on weapons of war but on international policies which reflect our own most precious values.

These are not just my goals, and they will not be my accomplishments, but the affirmation of our Nation's continuing moral strength and our belief in an undiminished, everexpanding American dream.

* * *

1980 RONALD REAGAN

AFTER THREE-PLUS YEARS OF JIMMY CARTER in the White House, the U.S. economy was still suffering from a record "misery index" of high inflation, high unemployment, and high interest rates. The ongoing Iranian hostage crisis also left many voters skeptical of the president's foreign policy skills. Although Carter was renominated, his primary battle with Massachusetts senator Edward M. Kennedy weakened him and alienated liberal Democrats, whose active support he badly needed.

When the Republicans nominated former California governor Ronald Reagan over the more moderate George Bush, some delegates (and not just the Bush supporters) worried that the ultraconservative Reagan might repeat the Goldwater debacle of 1964. An unusual arrangement was suggested under which former president Gerald Ford would join the ticket as a "co-president." But negotiations quickly broke down, and Bush was tapped instead. Meanwhile, Rep. John B. Anderson of Illinois, another Republican contender, chose to continue his campaign as an independent, offering Republican voters a moderate alternative to Reagan but actually drawing as many votes from Carter.

The choice in November was clear: Carter was centrist on domestic matters and liberal on foreign policy; Reagan was conservative on everything and particularly hawkish regarding the Soviets. During the presidential debates, Carter's attacks on the easygoing Reagan came off as shrill and unwarranted, while the former host of *General Electric Theater* disarmed his critics with such avuncular, seemingly offhand remarks as "There you go again" (in reference to Carter's alleged distortion of his record).

PARTY	POPULAR VOTES	ELECTORAL VOTES
REPUBLICAN Ronald W. Reagan, Calif. George H. W. Bush, Tex.	43,904,153	489
DEMOCRATIC James Earl Carter Jr., Ga. Walter F. Mondale, Minn.	35,483,883	49
(INDEPENDENT) John B. Anderson, Ill. Patrick J. Lucey, Wis.	5,720,060	

Reagan's question to voters at the close of one debate—"Are you better off than you were four years ago?"—appealed strongly to independents and working-class Democrats whose paychecks were shrinking. Although his victory was less a conservative mandate (he won just 50.7 percent of the vote) than a "throw the bums out" protest, the new Republican majority in the Senate allowed Reagan to pass huge tax cuts and enact other aspects of his economic and military programs.

First Inaugural Address • Washington, D.C. • Tuesday, January 20, 1981

Senator Hatfield, Mr. Chief Justice, Mr. President, Vice President Bush,

Vice President Mondale, Senator Baker, Speaker O'Neill, Reverend Moomaw, and my fellow citizens: To a few of us here today, this is a solemn and most momentous occasion; and yet, in the history of our Nation, it is a commonplace occurrence. The orderly transfer of authority as called for in the Constitution routinely takes place as it has for almost two centuries and few of us stop to think how unique we really are. In the eyes of many in the world, this every-4-year ceremony we accept as normal is nothing less than a miracle.

Mr. President, I want our fellow citizens to know how much you did to carry on this tradition. By your gracious cooperation in the transition process, you have shown a watching world that we are a united people pledged to maintaining a political system which guarantees individual liberty to a greater degree than any other, and I thank you and your people for all your help in maintaining the continuity which is the bulwark of our Republic.

The business of our nation goes forward. These United States are confronted with an economic affliction of great proportions. We suffer from the longest and one of the worst sustained inflations in our national history. It distorts our economic decisions, penalizes thrift, and crushes the struggling young and the fixed-income elderly alike. It threatens to shatter the lives of millions of our people.

Idle industries have cast workers into unemployment, causing human misery and personal indignity. Those who do work are denied a fair return for their labor by a tax system which penalizes successful achievement and keeps us from maintaining full productivity.

But great as our tax burden is, it has not kept pace with public spending. For decades, we have piled deficit upon deficit, mortgaging our future and our children's future for the temporary convenience of the present. To continue this long trend is to guarantee tremendous social, cultural, political, and economic upheavals.

You and I, as individuals, can, by borrowing, live beyond our means, but for only a limited period of time. Why, then, should we think that collectively, as a nation, we are not bound by that same limitation?

We must act today in order to preserve tomorrow. And let there be no misunderstanding—we are going to begin to act, beginning today.

The economic ills we suffer have come upon us over several decades. They will not go away in days, weeks, or months, but they will go away. They will go away because we, as Americans, have the capacity now, as we have had in the past, to do whatever needs to be done to preserve this last and greatest bastion of freedom.

In this present crisis, government is not the solution to our problem.

From time to time, we have been tempted to believe that society has become too complex to be managed by self-rule, that government by an elite group is superior to government for, by, and of the people. But if no one among us is capable of governing himself, then who among us has the capacity to govern someone else? All of us together, in and out of government, must bear the burden. The solutions we seek must be equitable, with no one group singled out to pay a higher price.

We hear much of special interest groups. Our concern must be for a special interest group that has been too long neglected. It knows no sectional boundaries or ethnic and racial divisions, and it crosses political party lines. It is made up of men and women who raise our food, patrol our streets, man our mines and our factories, teach our children, keep our homes, and heal us when we are sick—professionals, industrialists, shopkeepers, clerks, cabbies, and truckdrivers. They are, in short, "We the people," this breed called Americans.

Well, this administration's objective will be a healthy, vigorous, growing economy that provides equal opportunity for all Americans, with no barriers born of bigotry or discrimination. Putting America back to work means putting all Americans back to work. Ending inflation means freeing all Americans from the terror of runaway living costs. All must share in the productive work of this "new beginning" and all must share in the bounty of a revived economy. With the idealism and fair play which are the core of our system and our strength, we can have a strong and prosperous America at peace with itself and the world.

Now, so there will be no misunderstanding, it is not my intention to do away with government. It is, rather, to make it work....

So, as we begin, let us take inventory. We are a nation that has a government—not the other way around. And this makes us special among the nations of the Earth. Our Government has no power except that granted it by the people. It is time to check and reverse the growth of government which shows signs of having grown beyond the consent of the governed.

It is my intention to curb the size and influence of the Federal establishment and to demand recognition of the distinction between the powers granted to the Federal Government and those reserved to the States or to the people. All of us need to be reminded that the Federal Government did not create the States; the States created the Federal Government.

Now, so there will be no misunderstanding, it is not my intention to do away with government. It is, rather, to make it work—work with us, not over us; to stand by our side, not ride on our back. Government can and must provide opportunity, not smother it; foster productivity, not stifle it.

If we look to the answer as to why, for so many years, we achieved so much, prospered as no other people on Earth, it was because here, in this land, we unleashed the energy and individual genius of man to a greater extent than has ever been done before. Freedom and the dignity of the individual have been more available and assured here than in any other place on Earth. The price for this freedom at times has been high, but we have never been unwilling to pay that price.

It is no coincidence that our present troubles parallel and are proportionate to the intervention and intrusion in our lives that result from unnecessary and excessive growth of government. It is time for us to realize that we are too great a nation to limit ourselves to small dreams. We are not, as some would have us believe, doomed to an inevitable decline. I do not believe in a fate that will fall on us no matter what we do. I do believe in a fate that will fall on us if we do nothing. So, with all the creative energy at our command, let us begin an era of national renewal. Let us renew our determination, our courage, and our strength. And let us renew our faith and our hope.

We have every right to dream heroic dreams. Those who say that we are in a time when there are no heroes just don't know where to look. You can see heroes every day going in and out of factory gates. Others, a handful in number, produce enough food to feed all of us and then the world beyond. You meet heroes across a counter—and they are on both sides of that counter. There are entrepreneurs with faith in themselves and faith in an idea who create new jobs, new wealth and opportunity. They are individuals and families whose taxes support the Government and whose voluntary gifts support church, charity, culture, art, and education. Their patriotism is quiet but deep. Their values sustain our national life.

I have used the words "they" and "their" in speaking

A VOTE FOR **Anderson** FOR PRESIDENT
IS A VOTE FOR ANDERSON.

of these heroes. I could say "you" and "your" because I am addressing the heroes of whom I speak—you, the citizens of this blessed land. Your dreams, your hopes, your goals are going to be the dreams, the hopes, and the goals of this administration, so help me God.

We shall reflect the compassion that is so much a part of your makeup. How can we love our country and not love our countrymen, and loving them, reach out a hand when they fall, heal them when they are sick, and provide opportunities to make them self-sufficient so they will be equal in fact and not just in theory?

Can we solve the problems confronting us? Well, the answer is an unequivocal and emphatic "yes." To paraphrase Winston Churchill, I did not take the oath I have just taken with the intention of presiding over the dissolution of the world's strongest economy.

In the days ahead I will propose removing the roadblocks that have slowed our economy and reduced productivity. Steps will be taken aimed at restoring the balance between the various levels of government. Progress may be slow—measured in inches and feet, not miles—but we will progress. Is it time to reawaken this industrial giant, to get government back within its means, and to lighten our punitive tax burden. And these will be our first priorities, and on these principles, there will be no compromise.

On the eve of our struggle for independence a man who might have been one of the greatest among the Founding Fathers, Dr. Joseph Warren, President of the Massachusetts Congress, said to his fellow Americans, "Our country is in danger, but not to be despaired of.... On you depend the fortunes of America. You are to

decide the important questions upon which rests the happiness and the liberty of millions yet unborn. Act worthy of yourselves."

Well, I believe we, the Americans of today, are ready to act worthy of ourselves, ready to do what must be done to ensure happiness and liberty for ourselves, our children and our children's children.

And as we renew ourselves here in our own land, we will be seen as having greater strength throughout the world. We will again be the exemplar of freedom and a beacon of hope for those who do not now have freedom.

REAGAN '80

To those neighbors and allies who share our freedom, we will strengthen our historic ties and assure them of our support and firm commitment. We will match loyalty with loyalty. We will strive for mutually beneficial relations. We will not use our friendship to impose on their sovereignty, for our own sovereignty is not for sale.

As for the enemies of freedom, those who are potential adversaries, they will be reminded that peace is the highest aspiration of the American people. We will negotiate for it, sacrifice for it; we will not surrender for it—now or ever.

Our forbearance should never be misunderstood. Our reluctance for conflict should not be misjudged as a failure of will. When action is required to preserve our national security, we will act. We will maintain sufficient strength to prevail if need be, knowing that if we do so we have the best chance of never having to use that strength.

Above all, we must realize that no arsenal, or no weapon in the arsenals of the world, is so formidable as the will and moral courage of free men and women. It is a weapon our adversaries in today's world do not have. It is a weapon that we as Americans do have. Let that be understood by those who practice terrorism and prey upon their neighbors.

I am told that tens of thousands of prayer meetings are being held on this day, and for that I am deeply grateful. We are a nation under God, and I believe God intended for us to be free. It would be fitting and good, I think, if on each Inauguration Day in future years it should be declared a day of prayer.

This is the first time in history that this ceremony has been held, as you have been told, on this West Front of the Capitol. Standing here, one faces a magnificent vista, opening up on this city's special beauty and history. At the end of this open mall are those shrines to the giants on whose shoulders we stand.

Directly in front of me, the monument to a monumental man: George Washington, Father of our country. A man of humility who came to greatness reluctantly. He led America out of revolutionary victory into infant nationhood. Off to one side, the stately memorial to Thomas Jefferson. The Declaration of Independence flames with his eloquence.

And then beyond the Reflecting Pool the dignified columns of the Lincoln Memorial. Whoever would understand in his heart the meaning of America will find it in the life of Abraham Lincoln.

Beyond those monuments to heroism is the Potomac River, and on the far shore the sloping hills of Arlington National Cemetery with its row on row of simple white markers bearing crosses or Stars of David. They add up to only a tiny fraction of the price that has been paid for our freedom.

Each one of those markers is a monument to the kinds of hero I spoke of earlier. Their lives ended in places called Belleau Wood, The Argonne, Omaha Beach, Salerno and halfway around the world on Guadalcanal, Tarawa, Pork Chop Hill, the Chosin Reservoir, and in a hundred rice paddies and jungles of a place called Vietnam.

Under one such marker lies a young man—Martin Treptow—who left his job in a small town barber shop in 1917 to go to France with the famed Rainbow Division. There, on the western front, he was killed trying to carry a message between battalions under heavy artillery fire.

We are told that on his body was found a diary. On the flyleaf under the heading, "My Pledge," he had written these words: "America must win this war. Therefore, I will work, I will save, I will sacrifice, I will endure, I will fight cheerfully and do my utmost, as if the issue of the whole struggle depended on me alone."

The crisis we are facing today does not require of us the kind of sacrifice that Martin Treptow and so many thousands of others were called upon to make. It does require, however, our best effort, and our willingness to believe in ourselves and to believe in our capacity to perform great deeds; to believe that together, with God's help, we can and will resolve the problems which now confront us.

And, after all, why shouldn't we believe that? We are Americans. God bless you, and thank you.

* * *

1984 RONALD REAGAN

After suffering a deep recession during Ronald Reagan's first term, the country had sufficiently recovered by 1984 that Reagan could successfully run a "Morning in America" media campaign laced with idyllic images of rural tranquility and prosperity. At the Democratic convention that summer, former vice president Walter F. Mondale outpaced Colorado senator Gary Hart and the Reverend Jesse Jackson (the first African-American to win a significant number of delegates) for the unenviable task of taking on such a popular incumbent. To generate some much-needed excitement, Mondale chose as his running mate Rep. Geraldine Ferraro of New York, who became the first woman to run on a major-party ticket.

Mondale ran a traditional Democratic campaign that attracted the votes of liberal northerners, Minnesotans, blacks, and almost nobody else. He attacked Reagan for being too old, too conservative, and too out of touch. Reagan simply ignored him, responding in one debate, "I'm not going to exploit for political purposes my opponent's youth and inexperience." Mondale assailed the president for approving massive budget deficits, but Reagan scored many more points by emphasizing Mondale's refusal to rule out a tax increase. Years later, Mondale admitted that within days of the convention, he knew that he had no chance of upsetting Reagan.

PARTY	POPULAR VOTES	ELECTORAL VOTES
REPUBLICAN Ronald W. Reagan, Calif. George H. W. Bush, Tex.	54,455,075	525
DEMOCRATIC Walter F. Mondale, Minn. Geraldine A. Ferraro, N.Y.	37,577,185	13

Second Inaugural Address • Washington, D.C. • Monday, January 21, 1985

Senator Mathias, Chief Justice Burger, Vice President Bush,

Speaker O'Neill, Senator Dole, Reverend Clergy, members of my family and friends, and my fellow citizens:

This day has been made brighter with the presence here of one who, for a time, has been absent—Senator John Stennis.

God bless you and welcome back.

There is, however, one who is not with us today: Representative Gillis Long of Louisiana left us last night. I wonder if we could all join in a moment of silent prayer. (Moment of silent prayer.) Amen.

There are no words adequate to express my thanks for the great honor that you have bestowed on me. I will do my utmost to be deserving of your trust.

This is, as Senator Mathias told us, the 50th time that we the people have celebrated this historic occasion. When the first President, George Washington, placed his hand upon the Bible, he stood less than a single day's journey by horseback from raw, untamed wilderness. There were 4 million Americans in a union of 13 States. Today we are 60 times as many in a union of 50 States. We have lighted the world with our inventions, gone to the aid of mankind wherever in the world there was a cry for help, journeyed to the Moon and safely returned. So much has changed. And yet we stand together as we did two centuries ago.

When I took this oath four years ago, I did so in a time of economic stress. Voices were raised saying we had to look to our past for the greatness and glory. But we, the present-day Americans, are not given to looking backward. In this blessed land, there is always a better tomorrow.

Four years ago, I spoke to you of a new beginning and we have accomplished that. But in another sense, our new beginning is a continuation of that beginning created two centuries ago when, for the first time in history, government, the people said, was not our master, it is our servant; its only power that which we the people allow it to have.

That system has never failed us, but, for a time, we failed the system. We asked things of government that government was not equipped to give. We yielded authority to the National Government that properly belonged to States or to local governments or to the people themselves. We allowed taxes and inflation to rob us of our earnings and savings and watched the great industrial machine that had made us the most productive people on Earth slow down and the number of unemployed increase.

By 1980, we knew it was time to renew our faith, to strive with all our strength toward the ultimate in individual freedom consistent with an orderly society.

We believed then and now there are no limits to growth and human progress when men and women are free to follow their dreams.

And we were right to believe that. Tax rates have been reduced, inflation cut dramatically, and more people are employed than ever before in our history.

We are creating a nation once again vibrant, robust, and alive. But there are many mountains yet to climb. We will not rest until every American enjoys the fullness of freedom, dignity, and opportunity as our birthright. It is our birthright as citizens of this great Republic, and we'll meet this challenge.

These will be years when Americans have restored their confidence and tradition of progress; when our values of faith, family, work, and neighborhood were restated for a modern age; when our economy was finally freed from government's grip; when we made sincere efforts at meaningful arms reduction, rebuilding our defenses, our economy, and developing new technologies, and helped preserve peace in a troubled world; when Americans courageously supported the struggle for liberty, self-government, and free enterprise throughout the world, and turned the tide of history away from totalitarian darkness and into the warm sunlight of human freedom.

My fellow citizens, our Nation is poised for greatness. We must do what we know is right and do it with all our might. Let history say of us, "These were golden years— when the American Revolution was reborn, when freedom gained new life, when America reached for her best."

Our two-party system has served us well over the years, but never better than in those times of great challenge when we came together not as Democrats or Republicans, but as Americans united in a common cause.

Two of our Founding Fathers, a Boston lawyer named Adams and a Virginia planter named Jefferson, members of that remarkable group who met in Independence Hall and dared to think they could start the world over again, left us an important lesson. They had be-

come political rivals in the Presidential election of 1800. Then years later, when both were retired, and age had softened their anger, they began to speak to each other again through letters. A bond was reestablished between those two who had helped create this government of ours.

In 1826, the 50th anniversary of the Declaration of Independence, they both died. They died on the same day, within a few hours of each other, and that day was the Fourth of July.

In one of those letters exchanged in the sunset of their lives, Jefferson wrote: "It carries me back to the times when, beset with difficulties and dangers, we were fellow laborers in the same cause, struggling for what is most valuable to man, his right to self-government. Laboring always at the same oar, with some wave ever ahead threatening to overwhelm us, and yet passing harmless...we rode through the storm with heart and hand."

Well, with heart and hand, let us stand as one today: One people under God determined that our future shall be worthy of our past. As we do, we must not repeat the well-intentioned errors of our past. We must never again abuse the trust of working men and women, by

sending their earnings on a futile chase after the spiraling demands of a bloated Federal Establishment. You elected us in 1980 to end this prescription for disaster, and I don't believe you reelected us in 1984 to reverse course.

At the heart of our efforts is one idea vindicated by 25 straight months of economic growth: Freedom and incentives unleash the drive and entrepreneurial genius that are the core of human progress. We have begun to increase the rewards for work, savings, and investment; reduce the increase in the cost and size of government and its interference in people's lives.

We must simplify our tax system, make it more fair, and bring the rates down for all who work and earn. We must think anew and move with a new boldness, so every American who seeks work can find work; so the least among us shall have an equal chance to achieve the greatest things—to be heroes who heal our sick, feed the hungry, protect peace among nations, and leave this world a better place.

The time has come for a new American emancipation— a great national drive to tear down economic barriers and liberate the spirit of enterprise in the most distressed areas of our country. My friends, together we can do this, and do it we must, so help me God.

From new freedom will spring new opportunities for growth, a more productive, fulfilled and united people, and a stronger America—an America that will lead the technological revolution, and also open its mind and heart and soul to the treasures of literature, music, and poetry, and the values of faith, courage, and love.

A dynamic economy, with more citizens working and pay-

ing taxes, will be our strongest tool to bring down budget deficits. But an almost unbroken 50 years of deficit spending has finally brought us to a time of reckoning. We have come to a turning point, a moment for hard decisions. I have asked the Cabinet and my staff a question, and now I put the same question to all of you: If not us, who? And if not now, when? It must be done by all of us going forward with a program aimed at reaching a balanced budget. We can then begin reducing the national debt.

I will shortly submit a budget to the Congress aimed at freezing government program spending for the next year. Beyond that, we must take further steps to permanently control Government's power to tax and spend. We must act now to protect future generations from Government's desire to spend its citizens' money and tax them into servitude when the bills come due. Let us make it unconstitutional for the Federal Government to spend more than the Federal Government takes in.

We have already started returning to the people and to State and local governments responsibilities better handled by them. Now, there is a place for the Federal Government in matters of social compassion. But our fundamental goals must be to reduce dependency and upgrade the dignity of those who are infirm or disadvantaged. And here a growing economy and support from family and community offer our best chance for a society where compassion is a way of life, where the old and infirm are cared for, the young and, yes, the unborn protected, and the unfortunate looked after and made self-sufficient.

And there is another area where the Federal Government can play a part. As an older American, I remember a time when people of different race, creed, or ethnic origin in our land found hatred and prejudice installed in social custom and, yes, in law. There is no story more heartening in our history than the progress that we have made toward the "brotherhood of man" that God intended for us. Let us resolve there will be no turning back or hesitation on the road to an America rich in dignity and abundant with opportunity for all our citizens.

Let us resolve that we the people will build an American opportunity society in which all of us—white and black, rich and poor, young and old—will go forward together arm in arm. Again, let us remember that though our heritage is one of blood lines from every corner of the Earth, we are all Americans pledged to carry on this last, best hope of man on Earth.

I have spoken of our domestic goals and the limitations which we should put on our National Government. Now let me turn to a task which is the primary responsibility of National Government—the safety and security of our people.

Today, we utter no prayer more fervently than the ancient prayer for peace on Earth. Yet history has shown that peace will not come, nor will our freedom be preserved, by good will

These will be years when Americans have restored their confidence and tradition of progress; when…[they] turned the tide of history away from totalitarian darkness and into the warm sunlight of human freedom.

alone. There are those in the world who scorn our vision of human dignity and freedom. One nation, the Soviet Union, has conducted the greatest military buildup in the history of man, building arsenals of awesome offensive weapons.

We have made progress in restoring our defense capability. But much remains to be done. There must be no wavering by us, nor any doubts by others, that America will meet her responsibilities to remain free, secure, and at peace.

There is only one way safely and legitimately to reduce the cost of national security, and that is to reduce the need for it. And this we are trying to do in negotiations with the Soviet Union. We are not just discussing limits on a further increase of nuclear weapons. We seek, instead, to reduce their number. We seek the total elimination one day of nuclear weapons from the face of the Earth.

Now, for decades, we and the Soviets have lived under

the threat of mutual assured destruction; if either resorted to the use of nuclear weapons, the other could retaliate and destroy the one who had started it. Is there either logic or morality in believing that if one side threatens to kill tens of millions of our people, our only recourse is to threaten killing tens of millions of theirs?

I have approved a research program to find, if we can, a security shield that would destroy nuclear missiles before they reach their target. It wouldn't kill people, it would destroy weapons. It wouldn't militarize space, it would help demilitarize the arsenals of Earth. It would render nuclear weapons obsolete. We will meet with the Soviets, hoping that we can agree on a way to rid the world of the threat of nuclear destruction.

We strive for peace and security, heartened by the changes all around us. Since the turn of the century, the number of democracies in the world has grown fourfold. Human freedom is on the march, and nowhere more so than our own hemisphere. Freedom is one of the deepest and noblest aspirations of the human spirit. People, worldwide, hunger for the right of self-determination, for those inalienable rights that make for human dignity and progress.

America must remain freedom's staunchest friend, for freedom is our best ally.

And it is the world's only hope, to conquer poverty and preserve peace. Every blow we inflict against poverty will be a blow against its dark allies of oppression and war. Every victory for human freedom will be a victory for world peace.

So we go forward today, a nation still mighty in its youth and powerful in its purpose. With our alliances strengthened, with our economy leading the world to a new age of economic expansion, we look forward to a world rich in possibilities. And all this because we have worked and acted together, not as members of political parties, but as Americans.

My friends, we live in a world that is lit by lightning.

So much is changing and will change, but so much endures, and transcends time.

History is a ribbon, always unfurling; history is a journey. And as we continue our journey, we think of those who traveled before us. We stand together again at the steps of this symbol of our democracy—or we would have been standing at the steps if it hadn't gotten so cold. Now we are standing inside this symbol of our democracy. Now we hear again the echoes of our past: a general falls to his knees

in the hard snow of Valley Forge; a lonely President paces the darkened halls, and ponders his struggle to preserve the Union; the men of the Alamo call out encouragement to each other; a settler pushes west and sings a song, and the song echoes out forever and fills the unknowing air.

It is the American sound. It is hopeful, big-hearted, idealistic, daring, decent, and fair. That's our heritage; that is our song. We sing it still. For all our problems, our differences, we are together as of old, as we raise our voices to the God who is the Author of this most tender music. And may He continue to hold us close as we fill the world with our sound— sound in unity, affection, and love—one people under God, dedicated to the dream of freedom that He has placed in the human heart; called upon now to pass that dream on to a waiting and hopeful world.

God bless you and may God bless America.

* * *

1988 GEORGE BUSH

WITH RONALD REAGAN'S ENDORSEMENT, Vice President George Bush won the Republican nomination after a bitter primary fight marked by numerous attack ads, particularly those run by the Bush campaign against Kansas senator Bob Dole. Among the Democrats, Massachusetts governor Michael Dukakis emerged out of a primary field so weak that it was nicknamed "the seven dwarfs." At the convention, Dukakis attempted to placate the party's left-liberal wing by allowing Jesse Jackson, the winner of five primaries, a conspicuous role. This secured the black vote but also alienated many conservative Democrats and some independent voters watching at home. During the general election, Bush wrapped himself in the flag, denounced Dukakis for his membership in the "radical" American Civil Liberties Union, and ran another effective negative media campaign—this one focusing on Willie Horton, a convicted murderer who had raped a woman while furloughed from prison on a controversial Massachusetts program supported by the governor. With this and other attacks, the Republicans quickly turned "liberal" into a dirty word; meanwhile, the Dukakis campaign floundered. Responding to additional Republican charges that he was soft on defense, Dukakis decided to take a ride in a tank, but the oversize helmet he wore made him look too much like the *Peanuts* character Snoopy. Even pervasive voter concerns about the competence of Bush's running mate, Indiana senator Dan Quayle, weren't enough to help the Democrats. In November, Bush became the first sitting vice president since Martin Van Buren to win the White House.

PARTY	POPULAR VOTES	ELECTORAL VOTES
REPUBLICAN George H. W. Bush, Tex. J. Danforth Quayle, Ind.	48,886,097	426
DEMOCRATIC Michael S. Dukakis, Mass. Lloyd M. Bentsen Jr., Tex.	41,809,074	111
(INDEPENDENT) Lloyd M. Bentsen Jr., Tex. Michael S. Dukakis, Mass.		1

Inaugural Address • Washington, D.C. • Friday, January 20, 1989

Mr. Chief Justice, Mr. President, Vice President Quayle, Senator Mitchell,

Speaker Wright, Senator Dole, Congressman Michel, and fellow citizens, neighbors, and friends:

There is a man here who has earned a lasting place in our hearts and in our history. President Reagan, on behalf of our Nation, I thank you for the wonderful things that you have done for America.

I have just repeated word for word the oath taken by George Washington 200 years ago, and the Bible on which I placed my hand is the Bible on which he placed his. It is right that the memory of Washington be with us today, not only because this is our Bicentennial Inauguration, but because Washington remains the Father of our Country. And he would, I think, be gladdened by this day; for today is the concrete expression of a stunning fact: our continuity these 200 years since our government began.

We meet on democracy's front porch, a good place to talk as neighbors and as friends. For this is a day when our nation is made whole, when our differences, for a moment, are suspended.

And my first act as President is a prayer. I ask you to bow your heads:

Heavenly Father, we bow our heads and thank You for Your love. Accept our thanks for the peace that yields this day and the shared faith that makes its continuance likely. Make us strong to do Your work, willing to heed and hear Your will, and write on our hearts these words: "Use power to help people." For we are given power not to advance our own purposes, nor to make a great show in the world, nor a name. There is but one just use of power, and it is to serve people. Help us to remember it, Lord. Amen.

I come before you and assume the Presidency at a moment rich with promise.

We live in a peaceful, prosperous time, but we can make it better. For a new breeze is blowing, and a world refreshed by freedom seems reborn; for in man's heart, if not in fact, the day of the dictator is over. The totalitarian era is passing, its old ideas blown away like leaves from an ancient, lifeless tree. A new breeze is blowing, and a nation refreshed by freedom stands ready to push on. There is new ground to be broken, and new action to be taken. There are times when the future seems thick as a fog; you sit and wait, hoping the mists will lift and reveal the right path. But this is a time when the future seems a door you can walk right through into a room called tomorrow.

Great nations of the world are moving toward democracy through the door to freedom. Men and women of the world move toward free markets through the door to prosperity. The people of the world agitate for free expression and free thought through the door to the moral and intellectual satisfactions that only liberty allows.

We know what works: Freedom works. We know what's right: Freedom is right. We know how to secure a more just and prosperous life for man on Earth: through free markets, free speech, free elections, and the exercise of free will unhampered by the state.

For the first time in this century, for the first time in perhaps all history, man does not have to invent a system by which to live. We don't have to talk late into the night about which form of government is better. We don't have to wrest justice from the kings. We only have to summon it from within ourselves. We must act on what we know. I take as my guide the hope of a saint: In crucial things, unity; in important things, diversity; in all things, generosity.

America today is a proud, free nation, decent and civil, a place we cannot help but love. We know in our hearts, not loudly and proudly, but as a simple fact, that this country has meaning beyond what we see, and that our strength is a force for good. But have we changed as a nation even in our time? Are we enthralled with material things, less appreciative of the nobility of work and sacrifice?

My friends, we are not the sum of our possessions. They are not the measure of our lives. In our hearts we know what matters. We cannot hope only to leave our children a bigger car, a bigger bank account. We must hope to

give them a sense of what it means to be a loyal friend, a loving parent, a citizen who leaves his home, his neighborhood and town better than he found it. What do we want the men and women who work with us to say when we are no longer there? That we were

The totalitarian era is passing, its old ideas blown away like leaves from an ancient, lifeless tree.

more driven to succeed than anyone around us? Or that we stopped to ask if a sick child had gotten better, and stayed a moment there to trade a word of friendship?

No President, no government, can teach us to remember what is best in what we are. But if the man you have chosen to lead this government can help make a difference; if he can celebrate the quieter, deeper successes that are made not of gold and silk, but of better hearts and finer souls; if he can do these things, then he must.

America is never wholly herself unless she is engaged in high moral principle. We as a people have such a purpose today. It is to make kinder the face of the Nation and gentler the face of the world. My friends, we have work to do. There are the homeless, lost and roaming. There are the children who have nothing, no love, no normalcy. There are those who cannot free themselves of enslavement to whatever addiction—drugs, welfare, the demoralization that rules the slums. There is crime to be conquered, the rough crime of the streets. There are young women to be helped who are about to become mothers of children

they can't care for and might not love. They need our care, our guidance, and our education, though we bless them for choosing life.

The old solution, the old way, was to think that public money alone could end these problems. But we have learned that is not so. And in any case, our funds are low. We have a deficit to bring down. We have

more will than wallet; but will is what we need. We will make the hard choices, looking at what we have and perhaps allocating it differently, making our decisions based on honest need and prudent safety. And then we will do the wisest thing of all: We will turn to the only resource we have that in times of need always grows—the goodness and the courage of the American people.

I am speaking of a new engagement in the lives of others, a new activism, hands-on and involved, that gets the job done. We must bring in the generations, harnessing the unused talent of the elderly and

the unfocused energy of the young. For not only leadership is passed from generation to generation, but so is stewardship. And the generation born after the Second World War has come of age.

I have spoken of a thousand points of light, of all the community organizations that are spread like stars throughout the Nation, doing good. We will

work hand in hand, encouraging, sometimes leading, sometimes being led, rewarding. We will work on this in the White House, in the Cabinet agencies. I will go to the people and the programs that are the brighter points of light, and I will ask every member of my government to become involved. The old ideas are new again because they are not old, they are timeless: duty, sacrifice, commitment, and a patriotism that finds its expression in taking part and pitching in.

We need a new engagement, too, between the Executive and the Congress. The challenges before us will be thrashed out with the House and the Senate. We must bring the Federal budget into balance. And we must ensure that America stands before the world united, strong, at peace, and fiscally sound. But, of course, things may be difficult. We need compromise; we have had dissension. We need harmony; we have had a chorus of discordant voices.

For Congress, too, has changed in our time. There has

grown a certain divisiveness. We have seen the hard looks and heard the statements in which not each other's ideas are challenged, but each other's motives. And our great parties have too often been far apart and untrusting of each other. It has been this way since Vietnam. That war cleaves us still. But, friends, that war began in earnest a quarter of a century ago; and surely the statute of limitations has been reached. This is a fact: The final lesson of Vietnam is that no great nation can long afford to be sundered by a memory. A new breeze is

blowing, and the old bipartisanship must be made new again.

To my friends—and yes, I do mean friends—in the loyal opposition—and yes, I mean loyal: I put out my hand. I am putting out my hand to you, Mr. Speaker. I am putting out my hand to you, Mr. Majority Leader. For this is the thing: This is the age of the offered hand. We can't turn back clocks, and I don't want to. But when our fathers were

young, Mr. Speaker, our differences ended at the water's edge. And we don't wish to turn back time, but when our mothers were young, Mr. Majority Leader, the Congress and the Executive were capable of working together to produce a budget on which this nation could live. Let us negotiate soon and hard. But in the end, let us produce. The American people await action. They didn't send us here to bicker. They ask us to rise above the merely partisan. "In crucial things, unity"—and this, my friends, is crucial.

To the world, too, we offer new engagement and a renewed vow: We will stay strong to protect the peace. The "offered hand" is a reluctant fist; but once made, strong, and can be

> *We as a people have such a purpose today. It is to make kinder the face of the Nation and gentler the face of the world.*

used with great effect. There are today Americans who are held against their will in foreign lands, and Americans who are unaccounted for. Assistance can be shown here, and will be long remembered. Good will begets good will. Good faith can be a spiral that endlessly moves on.

Great nations like great men must keep their word. When America says something, America means it, whether a treaty or an agreement or a vow made on marble steps. We will always try to speak clearly, for candor is a compliment, but subtlety, too, is good and has its place. While keeping our alliances and friendships around the world strong, ever strong, we will continue the new closeness with the Soviet Union, consistent both with our security and with progress. One might say that our new relationship in part reflects the triumph of hope and strength over experience. But hope is good, and so are strength and vigilance.

Here today are tens of thousands of our citizens who feel the understandable satisfaction of those who have taken part in democracy and seen their hopes fulfilled. But my thoughts have been turning the past few days to those who would be watching at home, to an older fellow who will throw a salute by himself when the flag goes by, and the women

who will tell her sons the words of the battle hymns. I don't mean this to be sentimental. I mean that on days like this, we remember that we are all part of a continuum, inescapably connected by the ties that bind.

Our children are watching in schools throughout our great land. And to them I say, thank you for watching democracy's big day. For democracy belongs to us all, and freedom is like a beautiful kite that can go higher and higher with the breeze. And to all I say: No matter what your circumstances or where you are, you are part of this day, you are part of the life of our great nation.

A President is neither prince nor pope, and I don't seek a window on men's souls. In fact, I yearn for a greater tolerance, an easy-goingness about each other's attitudes and way of life.

There are few clear areas in which we as a society must rise up united and express our intolerance. The most obvious now is drugs. And when that first cocaine was smuggled in on a ship, it may as well have been a deadly bacteria, so much has it hurt the body, the soul of our country. And there is much to be done and to be said, but take my word for it: This scourge will stop.

And so, there is much to do; and tomorrow the work begins. I do not mistrust the future; I do not fear what is ahead. For our problems are large, but our heart is larger. Our challenges are great, but our will is greater. And if our flaws are endless, God's love is truly boundless.

Some see leadership as high drama, and the sound of trumpets calling, and sometimes it is that. But I see history as a book with many pages, and each day we fill a page with acts of hopefulness and meaning. The new breeze blows, a page turns, the story unfolds. And so today a chapter begins, a small and stately story of unity, diversity, and generosity—shared, and written, together.

Thank you. God bless you and God bless the United States of America.

* * *

1992 BILL CLINTON

As THE CAMPAIGN BEGAN, George Bush, still riding the crest of his Gulf War popularity, seemed invincible. But in the Republican primaries, he faced stiff opposition from conservative columnist Patrick Buchanan, who battered the president for abandoning his pledge not to raise taxes. Buchanan's attacks revealed a shallowness to Bush's support that gave the Democrats hope.

As in 1988, the Democratic nominee emerged from a crowded but weak field. Arkansas governor Bill Clinton had to weather stories about his alleged extramarital affairs, but his centrist policies and focus on the economy separated him from the rest of the pack as the primary season moved along.

Clinton proved to be a savvy campaigner whose health care proposals attracted liberals while his accomplished wife helped him secure the women's vote. Even though Republicans attacked him for evading the Vietnam draft, Clinton benefited from his status as a baby boomer, making the World War II veteran Bush seem tired and out of touch. And while Clinton attacked Bush's mounting

budget deficits from the center-left, billionaire Ross Perot piled on from the right, launching his own well-funded independent bid for the presidency.

PARTY	POPULAR VOTES	ELECTORAL VOTES
DEMOCRATIC William J. Clinton, Ark. Albert Gore Jr., Tenn.	44,909,326	370
REPUBLICAN George H. W. Bush, Tex. J. Danforth Quayle, Ind.	39,103,882	168
(INDEPENDENT) H. Ross Perot, Tex. James Stockdale, Calif.	19,741,657	

On Election Day, although statistics had already begun to show improvement in the economy, voters still felt the recent recession in their pocketbooks, and they weren't especially inclined to vote for Bush. In the three-way race, Clinton won with a substantial electoral majority, but that majority belied the closeness of the popular vote. Without Perot (18.9 percent) in the race, it's unclear whether Clinton (43.0 percent) would have beaten Bush (37.4 percent) at all. The low turnout was so well divided that only one state produced al popular-vote majority—Arkansas, which went for Clinton with 53.2 percent of the vote.

First Inaugural Address • Washington, D.C. • Wednesday, January 21, 1993

My fellow citizens: Today we celebrate the mystery of American renewal.

This ceremony is held in the depth of winter. But, by the words we speak and the faces we show the world, we force the spring.

A spring reborn in the world's oldest democracy, that brings forth the vision and courage to reinvent America.

When our founders boldly declared America's independence to the world and our purposes to the Almighty, they knew that America, to endure, would have to change.

Not change for change's sake, but change to preserve America's ideals—life, liberty, the pursuit of happiness. Though we march to the music of our time, our mission is timeless.

Each generation of Americans must define what it means to be an American.

On behalf of our nation, I salute my predecessor, President Bush, for his half-century of service to America.

And I thank the millions of men and women whose steadfastness and sacrifice triumphed over Depression, fascism and Communism.

Today, a generation raised in the shadows of the Cold War assumes new responsibilities in a world warmed by the sunshine of freedom but threatened still by ancient hatreds and new plagues.

Raised in unrivaled prosperity, we inherit an economy that is still the world's strongest, but is weakened by business failures, stagnant wages, increasing inequality, and deep divisions among our people.

When George Washington first took the oath I have just sworn to uphold, news traveled slowly across the land by horseback and across the ocean by boat. Now, the sights and sounds of this ceremony are broadcast instantaneously to billions around the world.

Communications and commerce are global; investment is mobile; technology is almost magical; and ambition for a better life is now universal. We earn our livelihood in peaceful competition with people all across the earth.

Profound and powerful forces are shaking and remaking our world, and the urgent question of our time is whether we can make change our friend and not our enemy.

This new world has already enriched the lives of millions of Americans who are able to compete and win in it. But when most people are working harder for less; when others cannot work at all; when the cost of health care devastates families and threatens to bankrupt many of our enterprises, great and small; when fear of crime robs law-abiding citizens of their freedom; and when millions

of poor children cannot even imagine the lives we are calling them to lead—we have not made change our friend.

We know we have to face hard truths and take strong steps. But we have not done so. Instead, we have drifted, and that drifting has eroded our resources, fractured our economy, and shaken our confidence.

Though our challenges are fearsome, so are our strengths. And Americans have ever been a restless, questing, hopeful people. We must bring to our task today the vision and will of those who came before us.

From our revolution, the Civil War, to the Great Depression to the civil rights movement, our people have always mustered the determination to construct from these crises the pillars of our history.

Thomas Jefferson believed that to preserve the very foundations of our nation, we would need dramatic change from time to time. Well, my fellow citizens, this is our time. Let us embrace it.

Our democracy must be not only the envy of the world but the engine of our own renewal. There is nothing wrong with America that cannot be cured by what is right with America.

And so today, we pledge an end to the era of deadlock and drift—a new season of American renewal has begun.

To renew America, we must be bold.

We must do what no generation has had to do before. We must invest more in our own people, in their jobs, in their future, and at the same time cut our massive debt. And we must do so in a world in which we must compete for every opportunity.

It will not be easy; it will require sacrifice. But it can be done, and done fairly, not choosing sacrifice for its own sake,

but for our own sake. We must provide for our nation the way a family provides for its children.

Our Founders saw themselves in the light of posterity. We can do no less. Anyone who has ever watched a child's eyes wander into sleep knows what posterity is. Posterity is the world to come—the world for whom we hold our ideals, from whom we have borrowed our planet, and to whom we bear sacred responsibility.

We must do what America does best: offer more opportunity to all and demand responsibility from all.

It is time to break the bad habit of expecting something for nothing, from our government or from each other. Let us all take more responsibility, not only for ourselves and our families but for our communities and our country.

To renew America, we must revitalize our democracy.

This beautiful capital, like every capital since the dawn of civilization, is often a place of intrigue and calculation. Powerful people maneuver for position and worry endlessly about who is in and who is out, who is up and who is down, forgetting those people whose toil and sweat sends us here and pays our way.

Americans deserve better, and in this city today, there are people who want to do better. And so I say to all of us here, let us resolve to reform our politics, so that power and privilege no longer shout down the voice of the people. Let us put aside personal advantage so that we can feel the pain and see the promise of America.

Let us resolve to make our government a place for what Franklin Roosevelt called "bold, persistent experimentation," a government for our tomorrows, not our yesterdays.

Let us give this capital back to the people to whom it belongs.

To renew America, we must meet challenges abroad as well at home. There is no longer division between what is foreign and what is domestic—the world economy, the world environment, the world AIDS crisis, the world arms race—they affect us all.

Today, as an old order passes, the new world is more

free but less stable. Communism's collapse has called forth old animosities and new dangers. Clearly America must continue to lead the world we did so much to make.

While America rebuilds at home, we will not shrink from the challenges, nor fail to seize the opportunities, of this new world. Together with our friends and allies, we will work to shape change, lest it engulf us.

There is nothing wrong with America that cannot be cured by what is right with America.

When our vital interests are challenged, or the will and conscience of the international community is defied, we will act—with peaceful diplomacy when ever possible, with force when necessary. The brave Americans serving our nation today in the Persian Gulf, in Somalia, and wherever else they stand are testament to our resolve.

But our greatest strength is the power of our ideas, which are still new in many lands. Across the world, we see them embraced—and we rejoice. Our hopes, our hearts, our hands, are with those on every continent who are building democracy and freedom. Their cause is America's cause.

The American people have summoned the change we celebrate today. You have raised your voices in an unmistakable chorus. You have cast your votes in historic numbers. And you have changed the face of Congress, the presidency and the political process itself. Yes, you, my fellow Americans have forced the spring. Now, we must do the work the season demands.

To that work I now turn, with all the authority of my office. I ask the Congress to join with me. But no president, no Congress, no government, can undertake this mission alone.

My fellow Americans, you, too, must play your part in our renewal. I challenge a new generation of young Americans to a season of service—to act on your idealism by helping troubled children, keeping company with those in need, reconnecting our torn communities. There is so much to be done—enough indeed for millions of others who are still young in spirit to give of themselves in service, too.

In serving, we recognize a simple but powerful truth—we need each other. And we must care for one another. Today, we do more than celebrate America; we rededicate ourselves to the very idea of America.

An idea born in revolution and renewed through 2 centuries of challenge. An idea tempered by the knowledge that, but for fate, we—the fortunate and the unfortunate—might have been each other. An idea ennobled by the faith that our nation can summon from its myriad diversity the deepest measure of unity. An idea infused with the conviction that America's long heroic journey must go forever upward.

And so, my fellow Americans, at the edge of the 21st century, let us begin with energy and hope, with faith and discipline, and let us work until our work is done. The scripture says, "And let us not be weary in well-doing, for in due season, we shall reap, if we faint not."

From this joyful mountaintop of celebration, we hear a call to service in the valley. We have heard the trumpets. We have changed the guard. And now, each in our way, and with God's help, we must answer the call.

Thank you and God bless you all.

* * *

1996 BILL CLINTON

AFTER THE DEMOCRATS LOST control of the House in the 1994 midterm elections (for the first time in forty years), Bill Clinton appeared to have lost his political way. Despite making progress on economic issues and cutting the government's budget deficits significantly, he proposed an overreaching health care program that had made him vulnerable to charges that he was actually a liberal posing as a moderate. To highlight this issue, the Republicans nominated Senate Majority Leader Bob Dole, whose reputation as a fierce campaigner (earned during his 1976 vice-presidential run) often overshadowed his wit and intelligence.

Again, Clinton ran a brilliant campaign. With the help of media adviser Dick Morris, he used a strategy of "triangulation" to distance himself from both conservative Republicans and liberal Democrats in Congress. This allowed him to run from the center as a pragmatist who cared deeply about the needs of "real people," particularly young families concerned

PARTY	POPULAR VOTES	ELECTORAL VOTES
DEMOCRATIC William J. Clinton, Ark. Albert Gore Jr., Tenn.	47,402,357	379
REPUBLICAN Robert J. Dole, Kan. Jack F. Kemp, N.Y.	39,198,755	159
REFORM H. Ross Perot, Tex. Pat Choate, D.C.	8,085,402	

about education, drugs, crime, and health care. Dole never developed a coherent strategy of his own, nor did he offer much more than diatribes against the Clintons and reminiscences about "how things used to be" a generation ago. Choosing the positive over the negative, voters reelected Clinton, although Ross Perot's second run for the presidency (this time as the leader of his own Reform party) again denied the president the popular majority and mandate he craved.

Second Inaugural Address • Washington, D.C. • Monday, January 20, 1997

My fellow citizens: At this last presidential inauguration of the

twentieth century, let us lift our eyes toward the challenges that await us in the next century. It is our great good fortune that time and chance have put us not only at the edge of a new century, in a new millennium, but on the edge of a bright new prospect in human affairs — a moment that will define our course, and our character, for decades to come. We must keep our old democracy forever young. Guided by the ancient vision of a promised land, let us set our sights upon a land of new promise.

The promise of America was born in the 18th century out of the bold conviction that we are all created equal. It was extended and preserved in the 19th century, when our nation spread across the continent, saved the union, and abolished the awful scourge of slavery.

Then, in turmoil and triumph, that promise exploded onto the world stage to make this the American Century.

And what a century it has been. America became the world's mightiest industrial power; saved the world from tyranny in two world wars and a long cold war; and time and again, reached out across the globe to millions who, like us, longed for the blessings of liberty.

Along the way, Americans produced a great middle class and security in old age; built unrivaled centers of learning and opened public schools to all; split the atom and explored the heavens; invented the computer and the microchip; and deepened the wellspring of justice by making a revolution in civil rights for African Americans and all minorities, and extending the circle of citizenship, opportunity and dignity to women.

Now, for the third time, a new century is upon us, and another time to choose. We began the 19th century with a choice, to spread our nation from coast to coast. We began the 20th century with a choice, to

harness the Industrial Revolution to our values of free enterprise, conservation, and human decency. Those choices made all the difference. At the dawn of the 21st century a free people must now choose to shape the forces of the Information Age and the global society, to unleash the limitless potential of all our people, and, yes, to form a more perfect union.

When last we gathered, our march to this new future seemed less certain than it does today. We vowed then to set a clear course to renew our nation.

In these four years, we have been touched by tragedy, exhilarated by challenge, strengthened by achievement. America stands alone as the world's indispensable nation. Once again, our economy is the strongest on Earth. Once again, we are building stronger families, thriving communities, better educational opportunities, a cleaner environment. Problems that once seemed destined to deepen now bend to our efforts: our streets are safer and record numbers of our fellow citizens have moved from welfare to work.

And once again, we have resolved for our time a great debate over the role of government. Today we can declare: Government is not the problem, and government is not the solution. We — the American people — we are the solution. Our founders understood that well and gave us a democracy strong enough to endure for centuries, flexible enough to face our common challenges and advance our common dreams in each new day.

As times change, so government must change. We need a new government for a new century — humble enough not to try to solve all our problems for us, but strong enough to give us the tools to solve our problems for ourselves; a government that is smaller, lives within its means, and does more with less. Yet where it can stand up for our values and interests in the world, and where it can give Americans the power to make a real difference in their everyday lives, government should do more, not less. The preeminent mission of our new government is to give all Americans an opportunity — not a guarantee, but a real opportunity — to build better lives.

Beyond that, my fellow citizens, the future is up to us. Our founders taught us that the preservation of our liberty and our union depends upon responsible citizenship. And we need a new sense of responsibility for a new century. There is work to do, work that government alone cannot do: teaching children to read; hiring people off welfare rolls; coming out from behind locked doors and shuttered windows to help reclaim our streets from drugs and gangs and crime; taking time out of our own lives to serve others.

Each and every one of us, in our own way, must assume personal responsibility — not only for ourselves and our families, but for our neighbors and

our nation. Our greatest responsibility is to embrace a new spirit of community for a new century. For any one of us to succeed, we must succeed as one America.

These obsessions cripple both those who hate and, of course, those who are hated, robbing both of what they might become. We cannot, we will not, succumb to the dark

The challenge of our past remains the challenge of our future — will we be one nation, one people, with one common destiny, or not? Will we all come together, or come apart?

The divide of race has been America's constant curse. And each new wave of immigrants gives new targets to old prejudices. Prejudice and contempt, cloaked in the pretense of religious or political conviction are no different. These forces have nearly destroyed our nation in the past. They plague us still. They fuel the fanaticism of terror. And they torment the lives of millions in fractured nations all around the world.

impulses that lurk in the far regions of the soul everywhere. We shall overcome them. And we shall replace them with the generous spirit of a people who feel at home with one another.

Our rich texture of racial, religious and political diversity will be a Godsend in the 21st century. Great rewards will come to those who can live together, learn together, work together, forge new ties that bind together.

As this new era approaches we can already see its broad outlines. Ten years ago, the Internet was the mystical province of physicists; today, it is a commonplace encyclopedia for millions of schoolchildren. Scientists now are decoding the blueprint of human life. Cures for our most feared illnesses seem close at hand.

The world is no longer divided into two hostile camps. Instead, now we are building bonds with nations that once were our adversaries. Growing connections of commerce and culture give us a chance to lift the fortunes and spirits of people the world over. And for the very first time in all of history, more people on this planet live under democracy than dictatorship.

My fellow Americans, as we look back at this remarkable century, we may ask, can we hope not just to follow, but even to surpass the achievements of the 20th century in America and to avoid the awful bloodshed that stained its legacy? To that question, every American here and every American in our land today must answer a resounding "Yes."

This is the heart of our task. With a new vision of government, a new sense of responsibility, a new spirit of community, we will sustain America's journey. The promise we sought in a new land we will find again in a land of new promise.

In this new land, education will be every citizen's most prized possession. Our schools will have the highest standards in the world, igniting the spark of possibility in the eyes of every girl and every boy. And the doors of higher education will be open to all. The knowledge and power of the Information Age will be within reach not just of the few, but of every classroom, every library, every child. Parents and children will

DOLE ★ KEMP

have time not only to work, but to read and play together. And the plans they make at their kitchen table will be those of a better home, a better job, the certain chance to go to college.

Our streets will echo again with the laughter of our children, because no one will try to shoot them or sell them drugs anymore. Everyone who can work, will work, with today's permanent under class part of tomorrow's growing middle class. New miracles of medicine at last will reach not only those who can claim care now, but the children and hardworking families too long denied.

We will stand mighty for peace and freedom, and maintain a strong defense against terror and destruction. Our children will sleep free from the threat of nuclear, chemical or biological weapons. Ports and airports, farms and factories will thrive with trade and innovation and ideas. And the world's greatest democracy will lead a whole world of democracies.

Our land of new promise will be a nation that meets its obligations — a nation that balances its budget, but never loses the balance of its values. A nation where our grandparents have secure retirement and health care, and their grandchildren know we have made the reforms necessary to sustain those benefits for their time. A nation that fortifies the world's most productive economy even as it protects the great natural bounty of our water, air, and majestic land.

And in this land of new promise, we will have reformed our politics so that the voice of the people will always speak

louder than the din of narrow interests — regaining the participation and deserving the trust of all Americans.

Fellow citizens, let us build that America, a nation ever moving forward toward re-

> *With a new vision of government, a new sense of responsibility, a new spirit of community, we will sustain America's journey. The promise we sought in a new land we will find again in a land of new promise.*

alizing the full potential of all its citizens. Prosperity and power — yes, they are important, and we must maintain them. But let us never forget: The greatest progress we have made, and the greatest progress we have yet to make, is in the human heart. In the end, all the world's wealth and a thou-

sand armies are no match for the strength and decency of the human spirit.

Thirty-four years ago, the man whose life we celebrate today spoke to us down there, at the other end of this Mall, in words that moved the conscience of a nation. Like a prophet of old, he told of his dream that one day America would rise up and treat all its citizens as equals before the law and in the heart. Martin Luther King's dream was the American Dream. His quest is our quest: the ceaseless striving to live out our true creed. Our history has been built on such dreams and labors. And by our dreams and labors we will redeem the promise of America in the 21st century.

To that effort I pledge all my strength and every power of my office. I ask the members of Congress here to join in that pledge. The American people returned to office a President of one party and a Congress of another. Surely, they did not do this to advance the politics of petty bickering and extreme partisanship they plainly deplore. No, they call on us instead to be repairers of the breach, and to move on with America's mission.

America demands and deserves big things from us — and nothing big ever came from being small. Let us remember the timeless wisdom of Cardinal Bernardin, when facing the end of his own life. He said: "It is wrong to waste the precious gift of time, on acrimony and division."

Fellow citizens, we must not waste the precious gift of this time. For all of us are on that same journey of our lives,

and our journey, too, will come to an end. But the journey of our America must go on.

And so, my fellow Americans, we must be strong, for there is much to dare. The demands of our time are great and they are different. Let us meet them with faith and courage, with patience and a grateful and happy heart. Let us shape the hope of this day into the noblest chapter in our history. Yes, let us build our bridge. A bridge wide enough and strong enough for every American to cross over to a blessed land of new promise.

May those generations whose faces we cannot yet see, whose names we may never know, say of us here that we led our beloved land into a new century with the American Dream alive for all her children; with the American promise of a more perfect union a reality for all her people; with America's bright flame of freedom spreading throughout all the world.

From the height of this place and the summit of this century, let us go forth. May God strengthen our hands for the good work ahead — and always, always bless our America.

* * *

2000 GEORGE W. BUSH

THERE HADN'T BEEN AN ELECTION like it since 1888, when Grover Cleveland won the popular vote but lost in the electoral college. Or 1876, when a special electoral commission gave Rutherford Hayes the presidency just days before his inauguration. This one was decided at 10 P.M. on December 12, when the Supreme Court halted hand recounting in several disputed Florida counties. The Court's 5–4 ruling, handed down just two hours before the deadline for state certification of presidential electors, effectively gave Florida and the presidency to Texas governor George W. Bush.

Vice President Al Gore had begun the 2000 campaign with a significant advantage—peace abroad and prosperity at home—but his inclination to distance himself from Bill Clinton's personal failings made it difficult for him to capitalize on Clinton's policy successes. Meanwhile, Bush, the oldest son of the forty-first president, overcame an unexpectedly robust challenge from Arizona senator John McCain, who turned Bush's record-setting fundraising against him by focusing attention on campaign finance reform. Strong grassroots support brought McCain victory in New Hampshire, but Bush's strength in money and party support

became clear two weeks later in South Carolina, where McCain's momentum faltered.

Throughout the general election campaign, the race between Bush and Gore stayed tight. Even after election day, the race remained too close to call. The results from several states were in doubt, but it soon became clear that whichever candidate took Florida's twenty-five electoral votes would become the next president.

In the end, after weeks filled with charges of irregularities and corruption, Bush won Florida (a state that happened to be governed by his brother Jeb) by 537 votes out of nearly six million cast.

PARTY	POPULAR VOTES	ELECTORAL VOTES
REPUBLICAN George W. Bush, Tex. Richard B. Cheney, Wyo.	50,456,141	271
DEMOCRATIC Albert A. Gore Jr., Tenn. Joseph Lieberman, Ct.	50,996,039	266
GREEN Ralph Nader, D.C. Winona LaDuke, Minn.	2,882,807	
(NOT VOTED)		1

Inaugural Address • Washington, D.C. • Saturday, January 20, 2001

President Clinton, distinguished guests, and my fellow citizens,

the peaceful transfer of authority is rare in history yet common in our country. With a simple oath, we affirm old traditions and make new beginnings. As I begin, I thank President Clinton for his service to our nation. And I thank Vice President Gore for a contest conducted with spirit and ended with grace. I am honored and humbled to stand here, where so many of America's leaders have come before me and so many will follow.

We have a place, all of us, in a long story—a story we continue, but whose end we will not see. It is the story of a new world that became a friend and liberator of the old, a story of a slave-holding society that became a servant of freedom, the story of a power that went into the world to protect but not possess, to defend but not to conquer. It is the American story—a story of flawed and fallible people, united across the generations by grand and enduring ideals. The grandest of these ideals is an unfolding American promise that everyone belongs, that everyone deserves a chance, that no insignificant person was ever born.

Americans are called to enact this promise in our lives and in our laws. And though our nation has sometimes halted, and sometimes delayed, we must follow no other course. Through much of the last century, America's faith in freedom and

democracy was a rock in a raging sea. Now it is a seed upon the wind, taking root in many nations.

Our democratic faith is more than the creed of our country; it is the inborn hope of our humanity, an ideal we carry but do not own, a trust we bear and pass along. And even after nearly 225 years, we have a long way yet to travel.

While many of our citizens prosper, others doubt the promise, even the justice, of our own country. The ambitions of some Americans are limited by failing schools and hidden prejudice and the circumstances of their birth. And sometimes our differences run so deep, it seems we share a continent but not a country.

We do not accept this, and we will not allow it. Our unity, our union, is the serious work of leaders and citizens in every generation. And this is my solemn pledge: I will work to build a single nation of justice and opportunity.

I know this is in our reach because we are guided by a power larger than ourselves who creates us equal in His image. And we are confident in principles that unite and lead us onward.

America has never been united by blood or birth or soil. We are bound by ideals that move us beyond our backgrounds, lift us above our interests, and teach us what it means to be citizens. Every child must be taught these principles. Every citizen must uphold them. And every immigrant, by embracing these ideals, makes our country more, not less, American.

Today, we affirm a new commitment to live out our nation's promise through civility, courage, compassion, and character. America, at its best, matches a commitment to principle with a concern for civility. A civil society demands from each of us good will and respect, fair dealing and forgiveness.

Some seem to believe that our politics can afford to be petty because, in a time of peace, the stakes of our debates appear small. But the stakes for America are never small. If our country does not lead the cause of freedom, it will not be led. If we do not turn the hearts of children toward knowledge and character, we will lose their gifts and undermine their idealism. If we permit our economy to drift and decline, the vulnerable will suffer most.

We must live up to the calling we share. Civility is not a tactic or a sentiment. It is the determined choice of trust over cynicism, of community over chaos. And this commitment, if we keep it, is a way to shared accomplishment.

America, at its best, is also courageous. Our national courage has been clear in times of depression and war, when defending common dangers defined our common good. Now we must choose if the example of our fathers and mothers will inspire us or condemn us. We must show courage in a time of blessing by confronting problems instead of passing them on to future generations.

Together, we will reclaim America's schools, before igno-

rance and apathy claim more young lives. We will reform Social Security and Medicare, sparing our children from struggles we have the power to prevent. And we will reduce taxes to recover the momentum of our economy and reward the effort and enterprise of working Americans.

We will build our defenses beyond challenge, lest weakness invite challenge. We will

---

What you do is as important as anything government does.

---

confront weapons of mass destruction, so that a new century is spared new horrors. The enemies of liberty and our country should make no mistake: America remains engaged in the world by history and by choice, shaping a balance of power that favors freedom. We will defend our allies and our interests. We

will show purpose without arrogance. We will meet aggression and bad faith with resolve and strength. And to all nations, we will speak for the values that gave our nation birth.

America, at its best, is compassionate. In the quiet of American conscience, we know that deep, persistent poverty is unworthy of our nation's promise. And whatever our views of its cause, we can agree that children at risk are not at fault. Abandonment and abuse are not acts of God, they are failures of love. And the proliferation of prisons, however necessary, is no substitute for hope and order in our souls.

Where there is suffering, there is duty. Americans in need are not strangers, they are citizens; not problems, but priorities. And all of us are diminished when any are hopeless. Government has great responsibilities for public safety and public health, for civil rights and common schools. Yet compassion is the work of a nation, not just a government. And some needs and hurts are so deep they will only respond to a mentor's touch or a pastor's prayer. Church and charity, synagogue and mosque lend our communities their humanity, and they will have an honored place in our plans and in our laws. Many in our country do not know the pain of poverty, but we can listen to those who do. And I can pledge our nation to a goal: When we see that wounded traveler on the road to Jericho, we will not pass to the other side.

America, at its best, is a place where personal responsibility is valued and expected. Encouraging responsibility is not a search for scapegoats, it is a call to conscience. And though it requires sacrifice, it brings a deeper fulfillment.

We find the fullness of life not only in options, but in commitments. And we find that children and community are the commitments that set us free.

Our public interest depends on private character, on civic duty and family bonds and basic fairness, on uncounted, unhonored acts of decency which give direction to our freedom. Sometimes in life we are called to do great things. But as a saint of our times has said, every day we are called to do small things with great love. The most important tasks of a democracy are done by everyone.

I will live and lead by these principles: to advance my con-

victions with civility, to pursue the public interest with courage, to speak for greater justice and compassion, to call for responsibility and try to live it as well. In all these ways, I will bring the values of our history to the care of our times.

What you do is as important as anything government does. I ask you to seek a common good beyond your comfort; to defend needed reforms against easy attacks; to serve your nation, beginning with your neighbor. I ask you to be citizens: citizens, not spectators; citizens, not subjects; responsible citizens, building communities of service and a nation of character.

Americans are generous and strong and decent, not because we believe in ourselves, but because we hold beliefs beyond ourselves. When this spirit of citizenship is missing, no government program can replace it. When this spirit is present, no wrong can stand against it. After the Declaration of Independence was signed, Virginia statesman John Page wrote to Thomas Jefferson: "We know the race is not to the swift nor the battle to the strong. Do you not think an angel rides in the whirlwind and directs this storm?"

Much time has passed since Jefferson arrived for his inauguration. The years and changes accumulate. But the themes of this day he would know: our nation's grand story of courage and its simple dream of dignity. We are not this story's author, who fills time and eternity with his purpose. Yet his purpose is achieved in our duty, and our duty is fulfilled in service to one another.

Never tiring, never yielding, never finishing, we renew that purpose today, to make our country more just and generous, to affirm the dignity of our lives and every life. This work continues. This story goes on. And an angel still rides in the whirlwind and directs this storm.

God bless you all, and God bless America.

* * *

ABOUT THE CONTRIBUTORS

JEAN HARVEY BAKER is Professor of History at Goucher College. Among her publications are *Affairs of Party: The Political Culture of Northern Democrats in the Nineteenth Century* (1983), *Mary Todd Lincoln: A Biography* (1987), and *The Stevensons: Biography of an American Family* (1996). She is currently writing a book on the American suffragists.

JAMES M. BANNER, JR., is an independent historian in Washington, D.C. He is the author most recently of "The Capital and the State: Washington, D.C., and the Nature of American Government" in Donald R. Kennon, ed., *A Republic for the Ages* (1999). Banner is now at work on a history of the origins of the American national state.

MICHAEL LES BENEDICT is Professor of History at The Ohio State University. He is the author of *A Compromise of Principle: Congressional Republicans and Reconstruction* (1975) and many articles and essays on legal and political issues of the Reconstruction era.

DOUGLAS BRINKLEY is director of the Eisenhower Center for American Studies and Professor of History at the University of New Orleans. He is the author of *The Unfinished Presidency: Jimmy Carter's Journey Beyond the White House* (1998).

MARK C. CARNES is Professor of History at Barnard College, Columbia University. He is the author of *Secret Ritual and Manhood in Victorian America* (1989), *Mapping America's Past* (1996), and (with John A. Garraty) *The American Nation* (1999). Carnes has also edited *Past Imperfect: History According to the Movies* (1995) and (with Garraty) the twenty-four-volume *American National Biography* (1999).

JAMES CHACE is Paul W. Williams Professor of Government and Public Law at Bard College. He is the editor of *World Policy Journal* and author of *Acheson: The Secretary of State Who Created the American World* (1998), among other books.

WILLIAM H. CHAFE is Alice Mary Baldwin Distinguished Professor of History at Duke University. His books include *Civilities and Civil Rights: Greensboro, North Carolina, and the Black Struggle for Freedom* (1980), which won the Robert F. Kennedy Book Award, and *Never Stop Running: Allard Lowenstein and the Struggle to Save American Liberalism* (1993), which won the Sidney Hillman Foundation Book Award. He has received fellowships from the National Endowment for the Humanities, the Rockefeller Foundation, and the Guggenheim Foundation.

CATHERINE CLINTON is Weissman Visiting Professor of History at Baruch College, City University of New York. Among her works on American history are *The Other Civil War: American Women in the Nineteenth Century* (1984), *Tara Revisited: Women, War, and the Plantation Legend* (1995), and *Fanny Kemble's Civil Wars* (2000).

ROBERT COWLEY is the founding editor of *MHQ: The Quarterly Journal of Military History*. He is (with Malcolm Cowley) the editor of *Fitzgerald and the Jazz Age* (1966) and an authority on the 1920s.

ROBERT DALLEK is currently Professor of History at Boston University, having taught for thirty years at UCLA. In 1994–95, he was Harmsworth Professor of American History at Oxford. An elected fellow of the American Academy of Arts and Sciences, Dallek is the author of numerous books on American diplomatic and presidential history, including a two-volume life of Lyndon B. Johnson.

VINCENT P. DE SANTIS is Professor Emeritus of History at the University of Notre Dame, where he has taught for many years. He is the author (or coauthor) of numerous books, including *The Republicans Face the Southern Question* (1959) and *The Shaping of Modern America, 1877–1920* (1973). He has been a Guggenheim Fellow and a Fulbright Professor to Italy, Australia, and India.

JOHN PATRICK DIGGINS is Distinguished Professor of History at the Graduate Center of the City University of New York. His latest books include *Foundations of American History* (2000), a Lincolnesque reinterpretation of America, and a forthcoming study of Eugene O'Neill, in whose play *More Stately Mansions* the antagonism between Jackson and John Quincy Adams reverberates.

JOSEPH J. ELLIS is Ford Foundation Professor of History at Mount Holyoke College. He is the author of six books on American history, including *American Sphinx: The Character of Thomas Jefferson*, which won the National Book Award in 1998. His forthcoming book *Founding Brothers: Stories from the Early Republic* focuses on the clash of personalities and ideologies within the political leadership of the revolutionary generation.

THOMAS FLEMING writes both history and historical novels. His most recent work of history is *Duel: Alexander Hamilton, Aaron Burr, and the Future of America* (1999). His recent novel *The Wages of Fame* (1998) deals with the intricacies of James Polk's war with Mexico.

ARI HOOGENBOOM is Professor Emeritus of History at Brooklyn College and the Graduate Center of the City University of New York. He is the author of *Outlawing the Spoils: A History of the Civil Service Reform Movement, 1865–1883* (1961), *The Presidency of Rutherford B. Hayes* (1988), and *Rutherford B. Hayes: Warrior and President* (1995). Hoogenboom has been a Guggenheim Fellow and a Fulbright Professor (while serving as George Bancroft Professor of American History at the University of Göttingen).

DANIEL WALKER HOWE is Rhodes Professor of American History at Oxford University; he has also taught at UCLA and Yale. The author of *The Political Culture of the American Whigs* (1979), among other books, he is currently writing a narrative history of the United States between 1815 and 1848.

LAURA KALMAN, Professor of History at the University of California—Santa Barbara, is the author of *Legal Realism at Yale, 1927–1960* (1986), *Abe Fortas: A Biography* (1990), and *The Strange Career of Legal Liberalism* (1996). She is presently at work on *Years of Transformation: The United States, 1974–1981*.

MORTON KELLER is Spector Professor of History at Brandeis University. Among his books are *Affairs of State: Public Life in Late Nineteenth Century America* (1977). He has also recently completed a history of modern Harvard.

JAMES M. McPHERSON is George Henry Davis '86 Professor of American History at Princeton University, where he has taught since 1962. He is the author of a dozen books, mostly on the era of the American Civil War. His *Battle Cry of Freedom: The Civil War Era* won the Pulitzer Prize in History in 1989, and his *For Cause and Comrades: Why Men Fought in the Civil War* won the Lincoln Prize in 1998.

HERBERT S. PARMET is Professor Emeritus of History at the City University of New York. He is the author of *Eisenhower and the American Crusades* (1972) and, most recently, *George Bush: The Life of a Lone Star Yankee* (1997), among other books.

JAMES T. PATTERSON is Ford Foundation Professor of History at Brown University, where he has taught modern U.S. history since 1972. He has also held visiting appointments as Harmsworth Professor of History at Oxford University, John Adams Professor of American Civilization at the University of Amsterdam, and Pitt Professor of American Institutions at Cambridge University. His publications include *Mr. Republican: A Biography of Robert A. Taft* (1972), *America's Struggle Against Poverty: 1900–1994* (1995), and *Grand Expectations: The United States, 1945–1974* (1996), which won the Bancroft Prize.

RICHARD M. PIOUS, Adolph and Effie Ochs Professor of American Studies, is chair of the Department of Political Science at Barnard College, Columbia University. He is the author of *The American Presidency* (1979), *The President, Congress, and the Constitution* (1984), and *The Young Oxford Companion to the*

Presidency (1996). He is a member of the editorial boards of *Political Science Quarterly* and *Presidential Studies Quarterly* and has served on panels to rate presidential performance organized by the *New York Times*.

JACK N. RAKOVE is Coe Professor of History and American Studies (and Professor of Political Science) at Stanford University, where he has taught since 1980. Among the books he has authored are *James Madison and the Creation of the American Republic* (1990) and *Original Meanings: Politics and Ideas in the Making of the Constitution* (1996), which received the Pulitzer Prize in History. His edition of *James Madison: Writings* was published by the Library of America in 1999.

JAMES A. RAWLEY is Carl Adolph Happold Distinguished Professor Emeritus of History at the University of Nebraska—Lincoln. His books include *Turning Points of the Civil War* (1966), *Race and Politics: "Bleeding Kansas" and the Coming of the Civil War* (1969), and *The Transatlantic Slave Trade: A History* (1981). He is a fellow of the Royal Historical Society and a recipient of the University of Nebraska's Outstanding Research and Creativity Award, as well as its Pound-Howard Award for his distinguished contributions to the university.

RICHARD REEVES, the author of *President Kennedy: Profile of Power* (1993), writes a syndicated newspaper column and teaches at the Annenberg School for Communications at the University of Southern California.

ROBERT V. REMINI is Professor Emeritus of History at the University of Illinois at Chicago. His three-volume biography of Andrew Jackson won the 1984 National Book Award. He has also written biographies of Henry Clay and Daniel Webster, and his latest book is *The Battle of New Orleans* (1999).

EVAN THOMAS is assistant managing editor of *Newsweek*. In addition to coauthoring (with Walter Isaacson) *The Wise Men: Six Friends and the World They Made* (1986), Thomas has written *The Man to See: Edward Bennett Williams* (1991) and *The Very Best Men: The Early Years of the CIA* (1995). His current project is a biography of Robert F. Kennedy.

HANS L. TREFOUSSE is Professor Emeritus of History at the Graduate Center of the City University of New York, where he taught from 1961 until 1998. His special areas of expertise are the Civil War and Reconstruction, and his publications include biographies of Andrew Johnson, Carl Schurz, Benjamin Butler, Benjamin Wade, and Thaddeus Stevens, as well as books on the Radical Republicans, Lincoln's decision to emancipate, and diplomatic history.

SUSAN WARE has written extensively on the New Deal and 1930s America. She is currently affiliated with the Radcliffe Institute for Advanced Study, where she is editing Volume Five of the biographical dictionary *Notable American Women*.

ALLEN WEINSTEIN chaired the American Studies Program at

Smith College from 1966 until 1981 and later taught as a University Professor at both Georgetown (1981–84) and Boston University (1985–89). In 1986, he won the United Nations Peace Medal for "efforts to promote peace, dialogue, and free elections in several critical parts of the world." His books include *Perjury: The Hiss Chambers Case* (1978), which was nominated for an American Book Award, and *The Haunted Wood: Soviet Espionage in America— The Stalin Era* (1999).

BERNARD A. WEISBERGER taught American history at Wayne State University, the University of Chicago, and the University of Rochester before undertaking a full-time writing career in 1968. He has written extensively for *American Heritage*, has been a historical consultant and scriptwriter for Ken Burns and Bill Moyers, and is the author of numerous books, including *The Age of Steam and Steel* (1964) and *The New Industrial Society* (1969). He has just completed a book on the election of 1800.

TOM WICKER was a political columnist for the *New York Times* from 1966 until 1991. He is the author of fourteen books, including *One of Us: Richard Nixon and the American Dream* (1991).

GORDON S. WOOD is Alva O. Way University Professor and Professor of History at Brown University. He is the author of *The Creation of the American Republic, 1776–1787* (1969) and *The Radicalism of the American Revolution* (1992), among other books.

INDEX

A

abortion, 267, 278, 280, 309
Acheson, Dean, 166
Adams, Abigail, 24
Adams, Charles Francis, 53
Adams, Henry, 152, 181
Adams, John, 19, **22-27,** 29, 32, 33, 45, 50, 52, 54, 73, 312, 313, 316, 334
    1797 inaugural address (complete), 313-315
Adams, John Quincy, 33, 46, 47, 48, **50-55,** 59, 66, 69, 73, 74, 75, 79, 80, 81, 140, 327, 331, 334
    1825 inaugural address (complete), 331-333
Adams, Louisa, 46, 52
Adams, Samuel Hopkins, 210
Adams, Sherman, 247
Adams-Onís Treaty (1819), 47, 59
affirmative action, 283
Afghanistan,
    1979 Soviet invasion of, 285
    2003 international invasion of, 309, 311-312
Agnew, Spiro T., 275
Aguinaldo, Emilio, 192
air traffic controllers strike (1981), 294
Alamo, siege of (1836), 63
Alaska, purchase of (1867), 129
Albany Regency, 66
Albert, Carl, 275, 280
Aldrich, Nelson W., 192
Algeciras Conference (1906), 185
Alien and Sedition Acts (1798), 24, 26, 40, 42, 316
Allen, Frederick Lewis, 210, 212
Al Qaeda, 309-312
Altgeld, John P., 165
American Civil Liberties Union, 448
American Federation of Labor, 213-214
American Gothic (Wood), 202
American Independence party, 435
American party, 102, 111, 114, 360
American Railway Union, 165
American Red Cross, 147
American System, 75, 119
American Tobacco Company, 169, 183, 193
Americans with Disabilities Act (1990), 300
Amistad mutiny (1839), 50, 67-68, 73

Anderson, John B., 442
Anthony, Susan B., 141
anthracite coal strike (1902), 183
Anti-Ballistic Missile Treaty (1972), 310
anti-Communist hysteria, 237, 240, 243, 246, 255, 263
Anti-Mason party, 336
Arab League, 296
Arab oil embargo (1973), 269, 283
Arlington National Cemetery, 191
arms limitation treaties, 209, 222, 254-255, 267, 269, 285, 291, 294, 429
Armstrong, John, 45
Army-McCarthy hearings (1954), 243
Aroostook War (1839), 70
Arrowsmith, Aaron, 33
Arthur, Chester A., 143, 144, **154-159,** 166, 375, 378
Arthur, Ellen, 156, 158
Atlee, Clement, 235
atom bomb, 234, 236, 239; see also *nuclear weapons*
atomic spies, 239, 240
Atoms for Peace, 242

B

Babcock, Orville E., 135
Bacall, Lauren, 238
Baker, James A., III, 298
Baker, Russell, 258
Bakke, Allan P., 283
Bakke case (1978), 283
Ballinger, Richard, 192
Baltimore & Ohio Railroad, 53
Bank of the United States,
    First, 15, 47
    Second, 63-64, 68, 84, 327, 336
    Whig banking bill, 80
Barbary pirates, 23, 31
Barnburners, 354, 356
Barnum, Phineas Taylor, 89, 138
Barton, Clara, 147
Bay of Pigs invasion (1961), 250
Bear Flag Revolt (1846), 85
Beard, Charles, 7
Begin, Menachem, 283, 284

Bell, John, 363
Ben Hur (Wallace), 168
Benton, Jesse, 58
Benton, Thomas Hart, 58, 86
Berlin airlift (1948-49), 239
Berlin Wall, 251-254, 298
Berryman, Clifford, 186
Betty Ford Center, 278
Billy Beer, 286
Billy the Kid, 143
bimetallism, see *currency policy*
Bingham, George Caleb, 115
bin Laden, Osama, 311
Birmingham civil rights protests (1963), 251
Birney, James G., 349
Birth of a Nation (Griffith), 199
Bismarck, Otto von, 134
Black Hawk, 59
Black Hawk War (1832), 59, 93
Black Warrior, 106
Blaine, James G., 146, 151, 152, 156, 161, 372, 375, 378
Bland-Allison Act (1878), 142-143
Bleeding Kansas, 100, 107-108
"bloody shirt" campaigns, 175, 368, 372
Blount, William, 58
Bolívar, Simon, 74
Bonney, William H., 143
Bonus March (1932), 215, 221
Booth, John Wilkes, 123, 178
Border Ruffians, 107-108
Bork, Robert H., 269
Boston Massacre (1770), 23
Boston police strike (1919), 213-214
Boston school busing violence (1974), 275
Boutwell, George, 134
Bowie, Jim, 63
Boxer Rebellion (1900), 177, 220
Boyle, Caleb, 34
Brady, Mathew, 54, 64, 69, 130, 138, 144
Breckinridge, John C., 115, 126, 363
Brezhnev, Leonid, 267, 279, 286
Britton, Nan, 210
Brook Farm, 73
Brooklyn Bridge, 157
Brooks, Preston, 108
Brown, John, 108, 111
Brown v. Board of Education (1954), 165, 243, 246, 247
Bryan, Charles W., 408

Bryan, William Jennings, 75, 165, 174, 176, 178, 192, 387, 391, 394, 396, 401, 408
Brzezinski, Zbigniew, 286
Buchanan, James, 10, 98, 100, 102, 105, 106, 108, **110-117,** 206, 360
    1857 inaugural address (complete), 360-362
Buchanan, Patrick, 451
Buchwald, Art, 283
Buckley, William F., Jr., 298
Bulganin, Nikolai, 243
Bull Moose party, see *Progressive party (1912)*
"bully pulpit," 180
Burlingame Treaty (1868), 144
Burr, Aaron, 29, 316, 318
Bush, Barbara, 296, 298, 300
Bush, George, **296-301,** 304, 306, 309, 312, 442, 448, 451, 456
    1989 inaugural address (complete), 448-451
Bush, George W., **308-313,** 456
    2001 inaugural address (complete), 456-457
Bush, John "Jeb," 456
Bush, Laura, 310
Bush, Robin, 296

C

Caddell, Pat, 284
Calhoun, John C., 37, 47, 48, 53, 69, 96, 100, 338
California,
    discovery of gold (1848), 87, 95-96
    independence from Mexico, 85, 87, 88
    Proposition 13 (1978), 283
Cambodia,
    Communist takeover of, 279
    invasion of (1970), 267
Camp David, 248, 284
Camp David Accords (1979), 283, 284
Canada,
    Aroostook War (1839), 70
    burning of the *Caroline* (1837), 67
    failed invasion during War of 1812, 41, 322
    North American Free Trade Agreement (1993), 303
    Webster-Ashburton Treaty (1842), 81
Carnegie, Andrew, 189
Carnegie Corporation, 189
Caroline, 67
carpetbag governments, 135, 137, 141
carpetbags, 108
Carroll, Charles, 53
Carswell, Harold, 269

Carter, Billy, 286
Carter, Jimmy, 280, **282-287,** 290, 440, 442
    1977 inaugural address (complete), 440-441
Carter, Rosalynn, 282, 284
Carville, James, 304
Cass, Lewis, 95, 105, 112-113, 354
Castro, Fidel, 250, 431
Catholics, 102, 175, 220, 250, 412, 431
Central Intelligence Agency (CIA), 238, 256
Chandler, William, 157
Chaney, James, 259
"Checkers" speech (Nixon), 426
Cheney, Dick, 296, 311
Cherokees, 62, 68
Chesapeake & Ohio Canal, 53
Cheyennes, 135
Chicago, Burlington & Quincy Railroad, 182
China,
    anti-Chinese sentiment, 133, 144
    Boxer Rebellion (1900), 177, 220
    Burlingame Treaty (1868), 144
    Communist takeover of, 239, 263
    immigration restrictions, 144, 154, 155,
        158, 213
    Lend-Lease Act (1941), 230
    Nixon's opening to, 268, 269, 270-271
    open door policy, 177
    Tiananmen Square massacre (1989), 299
    Treaty of 1880, 144
Chinese Exclusion Act (1882), 144, 158
Church, Frank, 262
Churchill, Winston, 224, 225, 228-229, 231,
    234, 235, 239, 240, 246
Civil Rights Act (1964), 259
civil rights legislation, 129, 165, 259
civil rights movement, 183, 231, 235, 237, 243,
    246, 247, 251, 255-256, 259-262, 263,
    275, 283, 423, 435
civil service reform, 134, 135, 143, 146, 150-152,
    154, 158, 370
Civil War (1861-65), 100-101, 110, 121-124,
    156, 367
    amnesty, general, 129
    amnesty, limited, 128
    battle of Antietam (1862), 119, 123, 144,
        174
    battle of Gettysburg (1863), 121
    battle of South Mountain (1862), 140, 144
    Battle of the Wilderness (1864), 135
    battlefield medicine, 147
    capture of Atlanta (1864), 121, 367

    Conscription Act (1863), 161
    draft riots (1863), 121
    fall of Richmond (1865), 121
    firing on Fort Sumter (1861), 111, 115,
        121-122
    Johnson-Crittenden Resolutions (1861), 126
    secession, 115, 120, 360, 363
    Sherman's March to the Sea (1864), 121
    siege of Petersburg (1864-65), 138
    siege of Vicksburg (1863), 121
    surrender of Lee (1865), 121, 123
    surrender of Smith (1865), 127
Clark, Champ, 401
Clark, William, 31, 32, 33
Clay, Henry, 37, 48, 53, 59, 64, 72, 74, 75, 76,
    79, 80, 85, 86, 96, 100, 119, 324, 331,
    336, 338, 349, 354
Clayton Anti-Trust Act (1914), 198
Clayton-Bulwer Treaty (1850), 93
Clemenceau, Georges, 202
Cleveland, Frances, 164, 166
Cleveland, Grover, 157, **160-167,** 170-171, 378,
    380, 384, 387, 456
    1885 inaugural address (complete), 378-379
    1893 inaugural address (complete), 384-386
Clifford, Clark, 288
Clinton, Bill, 262, 300, **302-307,** 308, 310, 451,
    453, 456
    1993 inaugural address (complete), 451-452
    1997 inaugural address (complete), 453-455
Clinton, DeWitt, 45, 322
Clinton, George, 312, 318, 320, 322
Clinton, Hillary Rodham, 304, 305, 451, 453
Clinton, Roger, 306
Clinton, Virginia, 306
Cockburn, George, 38
Cold War, 231, 238-240, 242-243, 246-248,
    250-255, 288, 291, 294, 297, 298-299
Cole, October 12, 2000, attack against, 311
Colfax, Schuyler, 370
Communist Party USA, 247
Compromise of 1850, 96, 99-100, 101, 105,
    356, 360
Confederate States of America, formation of,
    115, 120-121
Congress,
    first black member, 133
    First, 13, 45
    Thirty-ninth, 128-129
    Fortieth, 129
    Eightieth, 237, 423

congressional elections,
elections of 1810, 37
elections of 1838, 67
elections of 1840, 76
elections of 1854, 107
elections of 1858, 363
elections of 1862, 367
elections of 1866, 129
elections of 1878, 143, 375
elections of 1890, 384
elections of 1894, 387
elections of 1910, 192
elections of 1914, 403
elections of 1930, 416
elections of 1946, 237
elections of 1952, 426
elections of 1980, 290, 442
elections of 1986, 290
elections of 1994, 304, 453
Conkling, Roscoe, 143, 151-152, 154, 155-156,
157, 375
Connor, Eugene "Bull," 251
Constitution, 12, 18, 31, 32, 36, 37, 42, 45, 47,
80, 102, 105, 126, 128
implied powers, Hamilton's doctrine of, 15
Bill of Rights, 13
Eleventh Amendment, 23
Twelfth Amendment, 29, 316, 331
Thirteenth Amendment, 124, 128
Fourteenth Amendment, 129, 132
Fifteenth Amendment, 132, 133
Sixteenth Amendment, 193, 198
Seventeenth Amendment, 197
Eighteenth Amendment, 199
Nineteenth Amendment, 141, 199, 403, 405
Twentieth Amendment, 418
Twenty-first Amendment, 225
Twenty-second Amendment, 224, 237, 247,
426, 431
Equal Rights Amendment, 280, 289
Constitutional Union party, 120, 363
consumer protection, 184, 262
contras, 286, 289, 291-294
Convention of 1800, 25
Coolidge, Calvin, 10, 209, 210, **212-217**, 219,
288, 294, 408, 412
1925 inaugural address (complete), 408-411
Coolidge, Grace, 213, 214, 216
Coolidge, John, 213, 214, 216
Copley, John Singleton, 26, 52
Copperheads, 121, 368

Cortelyou, George B., 177
Cox, Archibald, 269
Cox, James M., 405
Coxey's Army (1894), 165
Crawford, William H., 48, 53, 324, 331
Crazy Horse, 141
Creeks, 15, 58
Crédit Mobilier scandal, 137, 151, 370
Crockett, Davy, 63, 70, 85
"Cross of Gold" speech (Bryan), 176, 387
Cuba,
Bay of Pigs invasion (1961), 250
policy toward, 106, 111, 175, 177-178, 250,
251, 254, 255, 431
Spanish-American War (1898), 175,
177-178, 183, 184, 391
Cuban Missile Crisis (1962), 251, 254, 255
Cumberland Road, 31
currency policy, 64, 132-133, 134, 138, 142-143,
165, 171-172, 176-177, 178, 384, 387
Currier, Nathaniel, 18, 93, 94, 105
Curtis, George William, 151
Custer, George A., 135
Cypress Grove, 94
Czechoslovakia,
Communist control of, 238-239
Velvet Revolution (1989), 297
Czolgosz, Leon, 178

D

Daley, Richard J., 431
Dallas, George M., 88
dark-horse candidates, 70, 349, 356, 375,
420
Dartmouth College v. Woodward (1819), 45
Daugherty, Harry M., 208, 209, 215
Davis, Jefferson, 95, 96, 100, 115, 120, 122
Davis, John W., 408
Dawes, Charles G., 216
Dawes, Henry L., 146, 151-152
Dawes Plan (1924), 216
Deaver, Michael, 294
Debs, Eugene V., 165, 199, 209, 401
Declaration of Independence (1776), 29
Democratic party,
Barnburner wing, 354, 356
formation of, 53, 66, 334
Franklin Roosevelt coalition, 230, 412,
418, 422
Hunker wing, 354
"softness" on Communism, 240, 248, 255

Democratic-Republican party, relationship to Federalists, 19
Dewey, Thomas E., 240, 420, 422, 423, 426
détente, 243, 267, 280
Dickens, Charles, 80
Dickinson, Charles, 58
Diem, Ngo Dinh, 243, 250, 255
Dingley Tariff (1897), 175, 177
Dirksen, Everett, 259
Dix, John A., 115
Dixiecrats, 423, 435
Díaz, Porfirio, 199
Dodd, Samuel C. T., 155
Dole, Robert, 305, 448, 453
Dole, Sanford B., 166
Dollar Diplomacy, 192, 193
domino theory, 243, 263
doughfaces, 68, 114, 360
Douglas, Helen Gahagan, 268
Douglas, Stephen A., 75, 99, 100, 105, 106, 111, 114, 115, 119-120, 363
Douglas, William O., 248
Douglass, Frederick, 87, 372
Dred Scott case (1857), 114
Du Bois, W. E. B., 183
Du Pont, 183
Duane, William, 63
Dukakis, Michael, 298, 448
Duke, James "Buck," 169
Dulles, John Foster, 243, 246, 247

E

Earl, Ralph E. W., 62
Eaton, John, 69
Eaton, Peggy Timberlake, 69
Edison, Thomas A., 155, 207, 213
Egypt,
    Camp David Accords (1979), 283, 284
    Suez crisis (1956), 246-247
    Yom Kippur War (1973), 269, 283
Eichholtz, Jacob, 114
Eisenhower, Dwight D., 20, 240, **242-249,** 426, 429, 431
    1953 inaugural address (complete), 426-428
    1957 inaugural address (complete), 429-430
Eisenhower, Mamie, 242, 246
elections, congressional, see congressional elections
elections, presidential, see presidential elections
electricity, introduction, 155, 172

Emancipation Proclamation (1863), 108, 124, 126
Embargo Act (1807), 34, 40, 52, 320
Emergency Quota Act (1921), 207, 213
Emerson, Ralph Waldo, 76
energy crisis (1970s), 283
environmental protection, 185, 262, 268, 310, 396
Equal Rights Amendment, 280, 289
Era of Good Feelings, 44, 48, 53, 327
Erie Canal, 45, 51
Espionage Act (1917), 199, 209
Essex Junto, 318
European Recovery Program, see Marshall Plan
Evarts, William M., 144
Ex Parte Milligan (1866), 169-170
Expansion of England (Seeley), 7

F

Fair Deal, 237
Fala, 231, 232, 422
Fall, Albert B., 208, 209-210, 215
Fallen Timbers, Battle of (1794), 15, 73
Family Assistance Plan, 268
Farley, James A., 420
Farnam, Henry, 105
Faubus, Orval, 247
federal budget, 30, 215, 246
    budget-making process, 209
    deficits, 288, 291, 304, 311, 312, 445, 451, 453
Federal Bureau of Investigation (FBI), 213
federal government,
    capital, 13, 14, 25, 28, 310
    Commerce and Labor Department established (1903), 181
    Council of Economic Advisers established (1946), 236
    Defense Department established (1947), 238
    Energy Department established (1977), 283
    Education Department established (1979), 283
    Environmental Protection Agency established (1970), 268
    Federal Trade Commission established (1914), 198
    Homeland Security Department established (2003), 311
    Interstate Commerce Commission established (1887), 161
    national debt, 30, 59, 134, 291, 299

federal government (*continued*)
    National Security Council established
        (1947), 238
    shutdown (1995), 303, 305, 306
Federal Reserve Act (1913), 198-199, 401
Federalist party,
    demise of, 48, 324
    High Federalists, 24, 25
    relationship to Democratic-
        Republicans, 19
Ferraro, Geraldine, 445
Ferdinand Magellan, 423
Fillmore, Abigail, 100
Fillmore, Millard, 10, 96, **98-103,** 111, 156,
    210, 360
fireside chats, 227, 230
Firestone, Harvey, 213
Firestone, Russell, 213
Fisk, James, 134
Fletcher v. Peck (1810), 37
Flowers, Gennifer, 304
Floyd, John B., 112-113, 115
Folsom, Oscar, 164
food stamps, 262
Ford, Betty, 272-273, 278, 280
Ford, Gerald R., 172, 272-273, **274-281,**
    440, 442
Ford, Henry, 207, 213
Forest Reserve Act (1891), 185
Fortas, Abe, 263, 264
Foster, Jodie, 290
Fourteen Points (1918), 203
France,
    Anglo-French wars, 18, 23, 31, 34,
        37-41, 313
    Convention of 1800, 25
    Louisiana Purchase (1803), 30-34, 318
    Quasi-War (1798-1800), 24-25
    Suez crisis (1956), 246-247
    XYZ Affair (1797), 24
Franco, Francisco, 227
Frankel, Max, 264
Franklin, Benjamin, 25, 85, 310
Free Soil party, 70, 90, 95, 104, 106-107, 354,
    356, 360
free trade, 133, 135, 150, 155, 303, 384
Freedmen's Bureau, 129
Freedom Rides (1961), 255
Frémont, John C., 111, 360
Fromme, Lynette "Squeaky," 275, 276-277
Frost, David, 272

Fugitive Slave Law (1850), 96, 99-100,
    101-102, 114

G

Gadsden Purchase (1853), 105
Gagarin, Yuri, 251
Gallatin, Albert, 30, 31
Gallup, George, 242
Garfield, James A., **146-153,** 154, 157, 158,
    166, 178, 375
    1881 inaugural address (complete), 375-377
Garfield, James R., 185
Garfield, Lucretia, 150
Garfield, Mary "Molly," 152-153
Garner, John Nance "Cactus Jack,"
    416, 420
Garrison, William Lloyd, 67
George III, king of England, 22, 28, 33
Gettysburg Address (1863), 121, 122
GI Bill of Rights (1944), 236
Gillett, Frederick, 215
Gingrich, Newt, 300, 306
Gladstone, William, 196
global warming 310
Godkin, Edward L., 154
gold standard, 150, 176-177, 178, 268, 387;
        see also *currency policy, hard money*
goldbugs, 165, 178, 387
Goldwater, Barry M., 290, 433, 442
golf, 189, 194, 248, 279
Gompers, Samuel, 214
Goodman, Andrew, 259
Gorbachev, Mikhail, 291, 294, 298-299
Gore, Albert, Jr., 306-307, 308-309, 456
Gould, Jay, 134
Graham, Mentor, 118
Granger, Francis, 338
Grant, Ellen "Nellie," 134
Grant, Julia, 134
Grant, Ulysses S., 9, 10, 121, 123, 129-130,
    132-139, 141, 143, 146, 158, 166,
    169, 176, 206, 368, 370, 372, 375
    1869 inaugural address (complete), 368-369
    1873 inaugural address (complete), 370-371
Great Britain,
    Anglo-French wars, 18, 23, 31, 34,
        37-41, 313
    Clayton-Bulwer Treaty (1850), 93
    impressment, 18, 34, 37
    Jay's Treaty (1794), 18, 313
    Lend-Lease Act (1941), 230

Oregon border dispute, 86, 349
Suez crisis (1956), 246-247
Treaty of Ghent (1814), 42, 53, 324
Treaty of Paris (1783), 26
Venezuelan border dispute (1895), 166
War of 1812 (1812-15), 36, 37, 38-39,
  41-42, 45, 46, 53, 56, 58-59, 73, 88,
  254, 322, 324
Great Depression, 210, 212, 219, 220-222, 224,
  227-230
Great Northern Railroad, 182
Great Society, 259
Great Uprising (1877), 142, 375
Great White Fleet, 185, 186-187
Greeley, Horace, 101, 136, 370
greenbacks, 132-133, 138, 142-143
Greenspan, Alan, 304, 305
Grenada, invasion of (1983), 291
Grier, Robert, 114
Griffith, D. W., 199
Guiteau, Charles J., 150, 178
Gulf War, see *Persian Gulf War*

H

Habitat for Humanity, 285
Hale, John P., 104, 356
Half-Breeds, 156, 375
Hall, Arsenio, 302
Helsinki Accords (1975), 280
Hamilton, Alexander, 7-8, 13, 14-15, 19, 23-24,
  25, 28, 30, 37-40, 312, 316, 318
Hamlin, Hannibal, 367
Hancock, Winfield S., 151, 375
Hanna, Marcus A., 175, 176, 177, 178, 184,
  387, 391
hard money, 64, 132-133, 134, 138, 142-143, 150;
  see also *currency policy, gold standard*
Harding, Florence, 208, 210
Harding, Warren G., 10, 194, 199, **206-211,**
  213, 214, 219, 405, 408
  1921 inaugural address (complete), 405-407
Harpers Ferry raid (1859), 111
Harrison, Anna, 74
Harrison, Benjamin, 10, 166, **168-173,** 380,
  384, 405
  1889 inaugural address (complete), 380-383
Harrison, Benjamin (father of William Henry),
  72-73
Harrison, Caroline, 168, 170, 172
Harrison, Elizabeth, 168
Harrison, John Scott, 168

Harrison, John Scott, Jr., 169
Harrison, Mary, 172
Harrison, William Henry, 10, 41, 52, 67, **72-77,**
  79-80, 81, 168, 170, 172, 338, 342,
  354, 380
  1841 inaugural address (complete), 342-348
Hart, Gary, 445
Hartford Convention (1814), 41, 324
Hartmann, Robert, 274
Havel, Vaclav, 297
Hawaii, annexation of, 166
Hawthorne, Nathaniel, 106
Hay, John, 146, 174, 175, 177
Hayes, Lucy, 140, 141, 142, 143
Hayes, Rutherford B., 138, **140-145,** 146,
  150, 151, 154, 166, 174, 372, 375,
  456
  1877 inaugural address (complete), 372-374
Hayes, Rutherford Platt, 141
Haymarket riot (1886), 161
Hayne, Robert Y., 57
Haynsworth, Clement, 269
Hays, Alexander, 135
Haywood, William "Big Bill," 183
Head Start, 262
health insurance, 237, 268, 304, 312, 451, 453
Healy, George P. A., 82, 88
Hearst, William Randolph, 416
Hendricks, Thomas A., 370
Hermitage, 64, 86
High Federalists, 24, 25
Hinckley, John, 289, 290
Hiss, Alger, 237
Hitler, Adolf, 221, 231
Hoar, Ebenezer R., 135
Hobart, Garret A., 391
Holden, W. W., 128
Holocaust, 231-232
homesteading, 105, 130
Hoover, Herbert, 10, 66, 206, 208, 215, 216,
  218-223, 237, 412
  1929 inaugural address (complete), 412-415
Hoover, J. Edgar, 213
Hoover, Lou, 220
Hoover-Stimson Doctrine, 222
Hopkins, Harry, 231
Hopkins, Mark, 147
Horton, Willie, 448
Houston, Sam, 85
Howe, Louis, 226
Hughes, Charles Evans, 208, 209, 403

human rights, as foreign-policy theme, 283, 284-285, 286
Humphrey, Hubert H., 431, 433, 435
Hungary, Communist control of, 246-247
Hunkers, 354
Hurrah Boys, 334
Hussein, Saddam, 296, 297-298, 311-312
Hyde Park, 225, 232

I

"I Have a Dream" speech (King), 255
Illinois Central Railroad, 99
immigration restrictions, 144, 154, 155, 158, 207, 209, 213
imperialism, 174, 177-178, 199, 391
Incredible Era (Adams), 210
Independent Treasury Act (1840), 68-69, 80, 87
Indian Removal Act (1830), 62
Indian Wars, 140
    battle of the Little Bighorn (1876), 135, 140, 141
    surrender of Crazy Horse (1877), 141
    Treaty of Fort Laramie (1868), 129
inflation, 278, 283, 290, 291, 438, 442
Ingersoll, Jared, 322
Intermediate Nuclear Forces Treaty (1987), 291, 294
internal improvements, 46, 50-51, 64, 69, 75, 81, 119, 327, 336, 363
International Court of Justice, 310
International Workers of the World, 183
Interstate Commerce Act (1887), 161
Iranian hostage crisis (1979-81), 285-286, 442
Iran-contra scandal, 289, 291-294
Iraq War (2003), 308, 311-313
Israel,
    Camp David Accords (1979), 283, 284
    creation of (1948), 235
    Suez crisis (1956), 246-247
    Yom Kippur War (1973), 269, 283

J

Jackie Look, 254
Jackson, Andrew, 8, 9, 42, 45, 48, 51, 52, 53, 54, **56-65,** 66, 67, 68, 69, 74, 78, 79, 81, 84, 85, 86, 88, 89, 90, 102, 110, 128, 306, 324, 331, 334, 336, 338
    1829 inaugural address (complete), 334-335
    1833 inaugural address (complete), 336-337

Jackson, Andrew, Jr., 57
Jackson, Jesse, 445, 448
Jackson, Rachel, 57, 58, 334
Japan,
    delegation to Washington (1860), 110
    invasion of Manchuria (1931), 222
    opening of, 99, 105
    Russo-Japanese War (1904-05), 185
    Treaty of Kanagawa (1854), 105
Japanese-American internments, 231
Jay, John, 18
Jay's Treaty (1794), 18, 313
Jefferson, Martha, 30
Jefferson, Martha "Patsy," 30
Jefferson, Thomas, 7-8, 9, 12, 13, 14, 15, 19-20, 22, 23, 24, 25, 26, **28-35,** 37, 40, 44-45, 46, 52, 72, 73, 78, 180, 312, 313, 316, 318, 320
    1801 inaugural address (complete), 316-317
    1805 inaugural address (complete), 318-319
Johnson, Andrew, 10, **126-131,** 141, 143, 156, 158, 166, 206, 367, 368
Johnson, Claudia "Lady Bird," 262
Johnson, Eliza, 128
Johnson, Hiram, 207, 405
Johnson, Lyndon B., 232, 250, **258-265,** 266, 275, 431, 433, 435
    1965 inaugural address (complete), 433-434
Johnson, Paul, 259
Johnson, Richard M., 338, 342
Johnson-Crittenden Resolutions (1861), 126
Johnson-Reed Act (1924), 213
Jones, Paula, 306
Jones, Slim Jimmy, 85
Judiciary Act of 1801, 25
Jungle (Sinclair), 184

K

Kansas,
    Bleeding Kansas, 100, 107-108
    Border Ruffians, 107-108
    Kansas Question, 106-108, 114
Kansas-Nebraska Act (1854), 106, 111, 114, 119, 360
Kefauver, Estes, 426, 429
Kellogg, Frank B., 216
Kellogg-Briand Pact (1928), 216
Kennan, George F., 308
Kennedy, Edward M., 288, 442
Kennedy, Jacqueline, 254, 256-257, 260-261

Kennedy, John F., 34, 248, **250-257,** 259, 260-261, 267, 305, 429, 431
    1961 inaugural address (complete), 431-432
Kennedy, Joseph, 416
Kennedy, Robert F., 263, 433, 435
Kennedy-Nixon debates (1960), 252-253, 431
Kent State killings (1970), 267
Kentucky Resolutions (1798), 24
Khmer Rouge, 279
Khomeini, Ayatollah Ruhollah, 285-286
Khrushchev, Nikita, 243, 247-249, 250-255
King, Martin Luther, Jr., 255, 263
King, Rodney, 299
King, Rufus, 45, 320, 324
Kissinger, Henry, 269, 279
Know-Nothings, see *American party*
Knox, Henry, 310
Knox, Philander C., 182
Korean War (1950-53), 237, 239-240, 242-243, 246, 426, 429
Kosovo crisis (1999), 305, 306
Ku Klux Klan, 127, 136, 197, 199
Kyoto accord on global warming, 310

L

La Follette, Robert M., 408
labor movement, 164-165, 183, 384
    Great Uprising (1877), 142, 375
    1886 general strike, 164
    Haymarket riot and trial (1886), 161
    Pullman strike (1894), 164-165, 387
    anthracite coal strike (1902), 183
    Boston police strike (1919), 213-214
    1946 strikes, 236
    1952 steel strike, 239
    air traffic controllers strike (1981), 294
    ten-hour workday, 67
    worker safety, 189
Land Act (1800), 73
Landon, Alfred M., 418, 420
Lane, Harriet, 114, 116
Lane, Mark, 256
Lawrence, Richard, 57
League of Nations, 203-204, 208, 209
Lebanon, attack on U.S. marines (1983), 289
Lee, Robert E., 111, 121
LeHand, Missy, 226, 232
Lend Lease Act (1941), 230
L'Enfant, Pierre, 14
Lewinsky, Monica, 206
Lewis, Meriwether, 31, 32, 33

Lewis and Clark expedition (1804-06), 31, 32, 33
Liberty party, 349
Library of Congress, 23, 123
Liddy, G. Gordon, 272
Liliuokalani, queen of Hawaii, 166
Limited Nuclear Test Ban Treaty (1963), 254-255
Lincoln, Abraham, 8, 9, 34, 75, 96, 101, 108, 111, 115, 116, **118-125,** 127, 140, 150, 156, 160, 178, 180, 212, 288, 363, 367
    1861 inaugural address (complete), 363-366
    1865 inaugural address (complete), 367
Lincoln, Mary, 120
Lincoln, Thomas "Tad," 122
Lincoln, William "Willie," 122
Lincoln County War (1878), 143
Lincoln-Douglas debates (1858), 111, 120
Lindenwald, 70
Lippmann, Walter, 216, 262, 416
Little Rock school integration (1957), 247
Lodge, Henry Cabot, 203-204
Los Angeles race riots (1992), 299
Louisiana Purchase (1803), 25, 30-34, 45, 47, 106, 318
Lowden, Frank, 207, 405
Lusitania, 197

M

MacArthur, Douglas, 221, 237, 239
Machiavelli, Niccoló, 174
Mack, John E., 418
Macon's Bill No. 2 (1810), 41
Madison, Dolley, 36, 40, 78, 142
Madison, James, 24, 29, 31, **36-43,** 45, 46, 53, 72, 80, 92, 320, 322, 324
    1809 inaugural address (complete), 320-321
    1813 inaugural address (complete), 322-323
Mafia, 256
Maine, 177
Malenkov, Georgi, 242
Manchuria, Japanese invasion of (1931), 222
Mangum, Willie P., 338
Manifest Destiny, 111, 349
Mansfield, Mike, 274, 275
Manson, Charles, 275
Mao Zedong, 239
Marbury, William, 29
Marbury v. Madison (1803), 29
March on Washington (1963), 255
Marion Star, 206, 208

Marshall, George, 238
Marshall, James, 87
Marshall, John, 26, 37
Marshall Plan, 238, 240
Masks in a Pageant (White), 210
Masons, 209
Mayaguez incident (1975), 279
McAdoo, William G., 210, 408
McCain, John, 456
McCarthy, Eugene, 435
McCarthy, Joseph R., 237, 240, 243,
        246, 263
McClellan, George B., 123, 367
McClernand, John A., 119
McCulloch v. Maryland (1819), 47
McDougal, Susan, 304
McGovern, George S., 269, 438
McKinley, Ida, 175, 176
McKinley, William, 171, **174-179,** 180, 181,
        188, 387, 391, 396, 405
    1897 inaugural address (complete), 387-390
    1901 inaugural address (complete), 391-393
McKinley Tariff (1890), 171, 175, 384
McNary-Haugen bill, 215
Means, Gaston, 210
Meat Inspection Act (1906), 184
Medicaid, 262
Medicare, 262
        prescription drug benefit, 311
Mellon, Andrew, 208, 209, 215-216
Mencken, H. L., 212
Mercer, Lucy, 226
Mexican War (1846-48), 85, 86, 87-88, 92,
        93-94, 95, 100, 104, 105, 202, 349
    battle of Buena Vista (1847), 93, 94, 95
    battle of Contreras (1847), 105
    battle of Monterrey (1846), 85, 93-94
    battle of Palo Alto (1846), 93
    battle of Resaca de la Palma (1846), 93
    Bear Flag Revolt (1846), 85
    Whig opposition, 94, 119
Mexico,
    Gadsden Purchase (1853), 105
    interventions under Wilson, 199-202
    North American Free Trade Agreement
        (1993), 303
Michtom, Morris, 186
Midnight Judges, 25, 29
"military-industrial complex" speech
        (Eisenhower), 242, 248
Milligan, Lambdin P., 169-170

Milosevic, Slobodan, 305, 306
Miranda v. Arizona (1966), 263
"missile gap," 248, 431
Missouri, 296
Missouri Compromise (1820), 47-48, 78, 106,
        111, 119, 327
Molotov, Vyacheslav, 235
Mondale, Walter F., 290, 445
Mongrel Tariff (1883), 158
Monroe, Elizabeth, 46
Monroe, James, 12, 31, **44-49,** 53, 59, 80, 320,
        324, 327, 331
    1817 inaugural address (complete), 324-326
    1821 inaugural address (complete), 327-330
Monroe Doctrine (1823), 25, 46, 50, 181,
        185, 192
Monticello, 30
Montpelier, 42
Moore, Sara Jane, 275
Morehead, John M., 95
Morgan, J. P., 165, 182
Morris, Dick, 303, 305, 453
Morris, Gouverneur, 316
Morse, Samuel F. B., 78
Mott, Lucretia, 67, 87
Mount Vernon, 13, 14, 18, 20
Moyers, Bill, 282
Mugwumps, 378
Muir, John, 183
Murrah Federal Building, April 19, 1995, attack
        against, 311

N

Nagy, Imre, 246-247
Napoleon (Bonaparte), 30-31, 40, 41, 56, 59
Nasser, Gamal Abdel, 246-247
Nast, Thomas, 135
National Industrial Recovery Act (1933), 225
National Labor Relations Act (1935), 227
National Republican party, formation of, 59, 334
National Road, 31
National Security Act (1947), 238
Nessen, Ron, 278, 280
Neutrality Acts (1935-37), 227, 230
New Deal, 221, 222, 224, 225, 227-230,
        237, 416
New Era economics, 219
New Freedom, 198, 401, 403
New Nationalism, 401
New Orleans race riot (1866), 129
New York City bailout (1975), 275

Niagara Movement, 183

Nicaragua, 199, 286
    Iran-contra scandal, 289, 291-294
    marines sent (1912), 193
    marines sent (1927), 215
    and William Walker, 106

Nicholas II, tsar of Russia, 181

Nixon, Pat, 268, 272-273

Nixon, Richard M., 10, 237, 240, 247, 250,
    252-253, 254, 255, 262, **266-273,**
    274-278, 298, 304, 426, 431, 435,
    438, 440
    1969 inaugural address (complete), 435-437
    1973 inaugural address (complete), 438-439

Nixonomics, 268, 269

Nobel Peace Prize, 185, 204, 216

Non-Intercourse Act (1809), 41

Noonan, Peggy, 289

Noriega, Manuel, 297

North, Oliver, 289

North American Free Trade Agreement
    (1993), 303

North Atlantic Treaty Organization (NATO), 239,
    240, 305, 306

North Dakota, statehood (1889), 169

Northern Alliance, 309

Northern Pacific Railroad, 182

Northern Securities case (1904), 182-183

nuclear weapons, 234, 236, 239, 247, 248,
    254-255, 267, 291, 294, 429, 433

nullification, 24, 57, 102
    nullification crisis (1832), 42, 63, 78

O

oil embargo, Arab, see *Arab oil embargo*

Oklahoma, white settlement (1889), 169

Oklahoma City terrorist attack (1995), 311

O'Neill, Paul, 312

O'Neill, Thomas P. "Tip," 283, 286

Only Yesterday (Allen), 210

open door policy toward China, 177

Oregon, border dispute with Great Britain, 86,
    87, 349

Organization of Petroleum Exporting Countries
    (OPEC), 269, 283

Ostend Manifesto (1854), 106, 108, 111

Oswald, Lee Harvey, 259

P

Palmer, A. Mitchell, 199

Palmer Raids (1920), 199, 208

Panama,
    invasion of (1989), 286, 297
    Panama Canal, 93, 177, 184,
        284, 394

Panic of 1837, 64, 68-69, 75, 85, 342

Panic of 1857, 111

Panic of 1873, 138, 142

Panic of 1893, 165, 171-172, 175

Parker, Alton B., 394

Parker, Dorothy, 212

Peace Corps, 251, 256

Peale, Charles Willson, 15, 31, 41

Peale, Rembrandt, 28, 44

Peanut Brigade, 440

Pemberton, John C., 121

Pendleton Civil Service Reform Act (1883),
    152, 154, 158

Pentagon, September 11, 2001, attack against,
    310-311

People's party, 384

Perkins, Frances, 231

Perot, H. Ross, 300, 451, 453

Perry, Mathew C., 99, 105

Perry, Oliver Hazard, 41

Pershing, John J. "Black Jack," 202

Persian Gulf War (1990-91), 296-298, 312, 451

"pet banks," 63, 68, 81

Philadelphia Plan, 268

Philippines,
    acquisition of (1898), 175, 391
    insurrection (1899-1902), 188-189, 192

Pickens, F. W., 111

Pierce, Benjamin "Bennie," 107

Pierce, Franklin, 10, 98, 100, 102, **104-109,**
    111, 115, 356, 360
    1853 inaugural address (complete), 356-359

Pierce, Jane, 104, 106, 107

Pinchot, Gifford, 185, 192

Pinckney, Charles C., 316, 320

Pinkerton, Allan, 119

Plessy v. Ferguson (1896), 165, 243

Plumer, William, 48, 327

Poindexter, John, 289

Poland, Communist control of, 235, 246,
    280, 440

Polk, James K., 70, **84-91,** 108, 110, 119, 349,
    354, 356
    1845 inaugural address (complete), 349-353

Polk, Sarah, 84-85, 86, 87, 89, 90

popular sovereignty, 106, 111, 114, 363

populism, 176, 177, 384, 387, 408

Populist party, see *People's party*
postage stamps, 85, 95
Potsdam conference (1945), 235-236, 239, 240
Powell, Colin, 309
Powers, Francis Gary, 248
presidential assassinations,
    Ford (attempt), 275, 276-277
    Garfield, 146, 148-149, 150, 151, 152, 157,
      158, 178
    Jackson (attempt), 57
    Kennedy, 250, 256, 259, 260-261
    Lincoln, 123, 127, 178
    McKinley, 176, 178, 180
    Reagan (attempt), 289, 290
presidential campaigning,
    active, 75, 176, 363, 394, 401
    campaign biographies, 106, 168, 331
    front-porch campaigns, 176, 375, 387, 405
presidential deaths in office, 76, 79-80, 94, 98,
        155-156; see also *presidential*
        assassinations
    Harding, 209-210, 214
    Harrison, William Henry, 76, 79-80
    Roosevelt, Franklin, 224, 226, 232,
      234, 236
    Taylor, 94, 98
presidential elections,
    election of 1789, 310
    election of 1792, 312
    election of 1796, 313
    election of 1800, 25, 29, 30, 45, 316
    election of 1804, 318
    election of 1808, 320
    election of 1812, 322
    election of 1816, 45, 324
    election of 1820, 48, 327, 331
    election of 1824, 48, 53, 59, 74, 331, 334
    election of 1828, 53-54, 58, 66, 334
    election of 1832, 63, 336
    election of 1836, 67, 74, 79, 306, 338,
      342
    election of 1840, 66, 70, 72, 74-76, 79,
      170, 342, 363
    election of 1844, 70, 79, 86, 88, 349,
      354, 356
    election of 1848, 70, 90, 95, 99, 354
    election of 1852, 104, 105, 110-111, 356
    election of 1856, 102, 111, 120, 360
    election of 1860, 115, 120, 126, 360,
      363, 367
    election of 1864, 127, 367

    election of 1868, 368
    election of 1872, 136, 176, 370
    election of 1876, 130, 141-142, 372,
      378, 456
    election of 1880, 130, 144, 146, 147, 151,
      154, 155-156, 375, 378
    election of 1884, 161, 164, 378, 380
    election of 1888, 168, 169, 170-171,
      380, 456
    election of 1892, 170, 171, 172, 384
    election of 1896, 165, 176, 178, 387,
      396
    election of 1900, 174, 178, 391, 396
    election of 1904, 183, 394
    election of 1908, 185-186, 189-192,
      194, 396
    election of 1912, 186, 193-194, 198,
      207, 401
    election of 1916, 403
    election of 1920, 199, 207-208, 214,
      219, 405
    election of 1924, 209, 210, 214, 215,
      216, 408, 412
    election of 1928, 216, 220, 412
    election of 1932, 222, 416
    election of 1936, 418, 420
    election of 1940, 420, 422
    election of 1944, 232, 234, 422
    election of 1948, 239, 240, 423
    election of 1952, 240, 426
    election of 1956, 246-247, 429
    election of 1960, 248, 250, 252-253,
      254, 256-257, 267, 431
    election of 1964, 290, 433, 438, 442
    election of 1968, 262, 263, 264, 268,
      435
    election of 1972, 269-270, 438
    election of 1976, 280, 440, 453
    election of 1980, 262, 285, 290, 442
    election of 1984, 290, 445
    election of 1988, 298, 299, 300, 306,
      448, 451
    election of 1992, 300, 302, 304, 451
    election of 1996, 305, 453
    election of 2000, 306, 308-309, 456
    national election day, 79
presidential impeachments,
    Clinton, 306
    Johnson, Andrew, 130, 141, 368
presidential resignations,
    Nixon, 268, 272-273, 274-278

presidential veto power, 64, 79, 166
Proclamation of Neutrality (1793), 15, 18, 40
Progressive party (1912), 186, 194, 198, 401, 403
Progressive party (1924), 408
Progressive party (1948), 423
Progressivism, 174, 184, 193, 198, 207, 394
Prohibition, 184, 199, 209, 225, 405, 412, 416
Pullman strike (1894), 164-165, 387
Pure Food and Drug Act (1906), 184

Q

Quayle, Dan, 448
Quasi-War (1798-1800), 24-25
    Convention of 1800, 25
Quay, Matt, 171
Quincy, Josiah, 23

R

Radical Republicans, 122, 123, 128-130,
        141, 150
radio,
    fireside chats, 227, 230
    first live remote broadcast (1923), 202
    first national party convention broadcast
        (1924), 408
railroads, 53, 165, 182
    first to cross Mississippi River (1856), 105
    introduction of time zones (1883), 157
    land grants, 99
    transcontinental, 105-106
Ramsey, Alexander, 141
Rancho del Cielo, 294
Randolph, A. Philip, 231
Randolph, Edmund, 78
Randolph, John, 69
Randolph, Thomas Mann, 30
Ray, James Earl, 263
Reagan, Jack, 289
Reagan, Maureen, 291
Reagan, Michael, 291
Reagan, Nancy, 290, 291
Reagan, Nelle, 289
Reagan, Patty, 291
Reagan, Ron (son), 291
Reagan, Ronald, 212, 262, 280, 285-286,
        288-295, 297, 299, 306, 308, 310,
        440, 442, 445, 448
    1981 inaugural address (complete), 442-444
    1985 inaugural address (complete), 445-447
Reconstruction, 127-138
    Andrew Johnson's policy, 128

carpetbag governments, 135, 137, 141
    end of (1877), 141-142, 372
    Joint Committee of Fifteen, 128
    Lincoln's policy, 123, 150
    Reconstruction Acts, 129-130, 143-144
Reconstruction Finance Corporation, 221
Red Cloud, 129
Red Scares, see *anti-Communist hysteria*
Reeder, Andrew, 107
Reedy, George, 258
Reform party, 453
Republican party,
    formation of, 106-107, 360, 370
    Half-Breed wing, 156, 375
    Mugwump wing, 378
    Stalwart wing, 143, 151, 155-156, 375, 378
Revels, Hiram R., 133
Revere, Paul, 23
Revolution of 1800, 26, 28, 30
Revolutionary War (1775-1783), 13, 15, 26, 37,
        44, 56-57, 104
    Treaty of Paris (1783), 26
Rice, Condoleezza, 309
Richardson, Elliot, 269
Richardson, William A., 133
Rickover, Hyman, 282
Ridge, Tom, 311
Ripley, George, 73
Rivers and Harbors Act (1882), 155
Robb, Charles, 264-265
Robinson, James Harvey, 7
Robinson, Joseph T., 412
Rockefeller, John D., 155, 189
Rockefeller, Nelson, 280, 431, 433
Roe v. Wade (1973), 267, 280
Rogers, Will, 408
Roosevelt, Alice (daughter), 182, 210
Roosevelt, Alice (wife), 182
Roosevelt, Anna, 226
Roosevelt, Edith, 182
Roosevelt, Eleanor, 225-226, 227, 232, 236
Roosevelt, Franklin D., 8, 9, 174, 222, **224-233,**
        234-235, 237, 240, 259, 267, 274, 280,
        311, 416, 418, 420, 422
    1933 inaugural address (complete), 416-417
    1937 inaugural address (complete), 418-419
    1941 inaugural address (complete), 420-421
    1945 inaugural address (complete), 422
Roosevelt, James, 225
Roosevelt, Quentin, 185, 186
Roosevelt, Sara, 225, 226, 232, 416

Roosevelt, Theodore, 8, 9, 75, 157, 160, 172, 176, **180-187,** 188, 189-194, 198, 207, 224, 225, 230, 391, 394, 396, 401, 403, 405
　　1905 inaugural address (complete), 394-395
Roosevelt Corollary to the Monroe Doctrine, 181, 185, 192
Root, Elihu, 188
Rosenberg, Ethel, 240
Rosenberg, Julius, 240
Ross, Robert, 38
Rough Riders, 184
Rubin, Robert, 304, 306
Ruckelshaus, William, 269
"rum, Romanism, and rebellion," 378
Rumsfeld, Donald, 310, 311
Rush, Benjamin, 25
Rush to Judgment (Lane), 256
Russia, see also *Soviet Union*
　　Bloody Sunday (1905), 181
　　Russo-Japanese War (1904-05), 185

S

Sacajawea, 31
Sacco, Nicola, 207
Sackville-West, Lord, 171, 380
Sadat, Anwar, 283, 284
Sagamore Hill, 180, 394
Salary Grab (1873), 137
SALT I accord (1972), 267, 269
SALT II accord, 285
San Francisco earthquake (1906), 183
Sanborn, John D., 133
Sandino, Augusto César, 215
Santa Anna, Antonio López de, 63, 94
Sargent, A. A., 141
Saturday Night Massacre (1973), 269
Sauks, 59
Savage, Edward, 19
savings-and-loan bailout (1989), 291, 297
Schechter Poultry v. U.S. (1935), 225
Schofield, John M., 130
Schwarzkopf, Norman, 297
Schwerner, Michael, 259
Scopes, John T., 213
Scott, Winfield, 88, 93, 94, 101, 104, 115, 356
Scottsboro boys, 219
Scowcroft, Brent, 297
Seeley, John Robert, 7
segregation, racial, 165, 199, 231, 235, 243, 246, 247, 255-256, 268, 275, 435

Selby, James J., 129
Seminoles,
　　First Seminole War (1817-18), 45, 59
　　Second Seminole War (1835-42), 62, 68, 93
Seneca Falls convention (1848), 87
Sené, Jean François, 47
"separate but equal" doctrine, 165, 243
September 11, 2001, terrorist attacks, 310-311
Servicemen's Readjustment Act, see *GI Bill of Rights*
Seward, William H., 96, 98, 120, 129
Seward's Folly, 129
Seymour, Horatio, 368
Shannon, Wilson, 107
Shawnees, 37, 73
Shepard, Alan, 251
Shepherd, Alexander R. "Boss," 136
Sheridan, Philip, 123
Sherman, John, 143, 146, 152
Sherman, William T., 121, 123, 378
Sherman Anti Trust Act (1890), 165, 172, 182-183, 194, 198
Sherman Silver Purchase Act (1890), 165, 171-172
Sherwood Forest, 81
Shriners, 209
silver, unlimited coinage of, 142-143, 171-172, 176, 178
silverites, 165, 176, 384, 387
Simmons, William J., 197
Sinclair, Upton, 184
Sioux, 135, 141
Sirhan, Sirhan, 263
60 Minutes, 280, 304
slavery, 34, 42, 86, 111, 119-121, 123-124, 126, 338, 360, 363
　　abolition in the District of Columbia, 96, 100
　　antislavery politics, 23, 67, 70, 79, 106-107, 349, 354, 356
　　ban in Mexico, 57
　　Compromise of 1850, 96, 99-100, 101, 105, 356, 360
　　Democratic support for, 67-68, 90, 105, 106-107, 108, 111, 114-115
　　Dred Scott case (1857), 114
　　Emancipation Proclamation (1863), 108, 124
　　expansion to Cuba, 111
　　extension to the western territories, 34, 46, 47, 88, 92, 95-96, 106-108, 114, 119-120, 354, 356, 363

Fugitive Slave Law (1850), 96, 99-100, 101-102, 114

Harpers Ferry raid (1859), 111

importation ban (1808), 31

Kansas Question, 106-108, 114

Missouri Compromise (1820), 44, 47-48, 78, 320

slave rebellions, 57

Underground Railroad, 93

Smith, Alfred E., 220, 408, 412

Smith, Kirby, 127

Smoot-Hawley Tariff (1930), 219

Social Security Act (1935), 227, 237

Socialist party, 184, 198, 199, 209, 401, 403

Solid South, 137, 426

South Dakota, statehood (1889), 169

Southeast Asia Treaty Organization (SEATO), 243

Soviet Union, see also *Russia*

as "evil empire," 288

attempted coup (1991), 298-299

Berlin airlift (1948), 239

Berlin Wall, 251-254, 298

Cuban Missile Crisis (1962), 251, 254, 255

Geneva summit (1955), 243

Hungarian uprising (1956), 247

Intermediate Nuclear Forces Treaty (1987), 291, 294

invasion of Afghanistan (1979), 285

Lend-Lease Act (1941), 230

Limited Nuclear Test Ban Treaty (1963), 254-255

Paris summit (1960), 248

SALT accords, 267, 269, 285

Twentieth Communist Party Congress (1956), 247

U-2 crisis (1960), 248

Vienna summit (1961), 250-251

space program, 247, 251, 256, 269

Spain,

Adams-Onís Treaty (1819), 47, 59

First Seminole War (1817-18), 45, 59

Florida cession (1819), 47

Spanish Civil War (1936-39), 227

Spanish-American War (1898), 175, 177-178, 183, 391

effect on the presidency, 177

Rough Riders, 184

sinking of the *Maine* (1898), 177

Treaty of Paris (1898), 175

specie, see *hard money*

Specie Circular (1836), 64

Specie Resumption Act (1875), 138, 142-143

spoils system, 52, 62, 151-152, 154

Sputnik, 247

Square Deal, 394, 401

stagflation, 278, 283, 288

Stalin, Joseph, 225, 231, 234-235, 239, 242, 247

Stalwarts, 143, 151-152, 155-156, 375, 378

Standard Oil trust, 155, 183, 189, 193

Standing Bear, Henry, 214

Stanford, Leland, 172

Stanley-Brown, Joseph, 152

Stanton, Edwin M., 87, 115, 129-130

Stanton, Elizabeth Cady, 67

Star of the West, 115

"Star-Spangled Banner" (Key), 324

Starr, Kenneth, 306

"Star Wars" missile shield, see *Strategic Defense Initiative*

Stassen, Harold, 426

Steel Navy, 154, 155

Stephanopoulos, George, 304

Stephens, Alexander H., 121, 128

Stevens, Thaddeus, 128

Stevenson, Adlai E., 269, 426, 429

Stimson, Henry L., 222

stock market crash (1929), 212, 216, 220, 291, 416

stock market crash (1987), 291

Strategic Defense Initiative, 291, 294, 310

Strong, George Templeton, 124

Stuart, Gilbert, 12, 13, 40, 48

Suez crisis (1956), 246-247

Sullivan, John L., 183

Sullivan, Mark, 188

Sully, Thomas, 42

Sumner, Charles, 108

Sun Belt strategy, 435

Supreme Court,

Bakke case (1978), 283

Brown v. Board of Education (1954), 165, 243, 246, 247

Bush v. Gore (2000), 308, 309, 456

Dartmouth College v. Woodward (1819), 45

Dred Scott case (1857), 114

Ex Parte Milligan (1866), 169-170

Fletcher v. Peck (1810), 37

Franklin Roosevelt's attempt to pack, 230

Marbury v. Madison (1803), 29

McCulloch v. Maryland (1819), 47

Miranda v. Arizona (1966), 263

Supreme Court (*continued*)
Northern Securities case (1904), 182-183
Plessy v. Ferguson (1896), 165, 243
Roe v. Wade (1973), 267, 280
Schechter Poultry v. U.S. (1935), 225
U.S. v. E. C. Knight (1895), 165
Sutter, John, 87

T

Taft, Nellie, 189, 192, 194, 396
Taft, Robert A., 420, 426
Taft, William Howard, 185-186, **188-195,** 198,
203, 207, 396, 401, 420
1909 inaugural address (complete), 396-400
Taliban, 309
Talleyrand, 32
Tammany Hall, 380
Taney, Roger B., 63-64, 66-67
tariffs,
Dingley Tariff (1897), 175
McKinley Tariff (1890), 171, 175, 384
Mongrel Tariff (1883), 158
Smoot-Hawley Tariff (1930), 219
Tariff of Abominations (1828), 51, 57
Underwood-Simmons Tariff (1913),
193, 198
taxes,
income, 193, 198, 209
income tax cuts, 278, 288, 290-291, 310,
442
Taylor, Margaret "Peggy," 94, 95
Taylor, Sarah Knox, 95
Taylor, Zachary, 70, 90, **92-97,** 98, 99, 354, 356
1849 inaugural address (complete), 354-355
Teapot Dome scandal, 209-210, 215, 408
Tecumseh, 37, 73
teddy bears, 186
temperance, 101, 135, 142, 143, 175; see also
Prohibition
Tennessee Valley Authority, 225, 420
Tenskwatawa, 73
Tenure of Office Act (1867), 129-130, 166
terrorism,
April 19, 1995, Oklahoma City bombing,
311
August 7, 1998, embassy bombings in
Kenya and Tanzania, 311
October 12, 2000, attack on the
USS *Cole,* 311
September 11, 2001, attacks, 310-311
George W. Bush's war on, 309, 311

Texas, annexation of, 69-70, 81-82, 84-85, 86,
87, 349
Thomas, George, 123
Three Mile Island nuclear accident (1979), 285
Thurmond, Strom, 423
Tiffany, Louis C., 156, 158
Tilden, Samuel J., 141, 372, 375
time zones, introduction of (1883), 157
Tippecanoe Creek, battle of (1811), 73, 75
Tocqueville, Alexis de, 54
trade policy, see *free trade*
Trail of Tears, 62, 68
Transcendentalism, 73
Travis, William Barret, 63
Treaty of 1880, 144
Treaty of Fort Laramie (1868), 129
Treaty of Ghent (1814), 42, 53, 324
Treaty of Greenville (1795), 15, 73
Treaty of Kanagawa (1854), 105
Treaty of Paris (1783), 26
Treaty of Paris (1898), 175
Treaty of Versailles (1919), 196, 203-204,
219, 408
Triangle Shirtwaist Company fire (1911), 189
Tripolitan War (1801-05), 31
Trujillo, Rafael, 250
Truman, Bess, 236
Truman, Harry S., 8, 9, 89, **234-241,** 263, 274,
422, 423, 426
1949 inaugural address (complete), 423-425
Truman Doctrine, 237-238, 239, 240
Trumbull, John, 29
trusts, 155, 165, 169, 181-183, 189, 192-193
trustbusting, 172, 181-183, 189, 192-193,
391, 396, 401
Truth, Sojourner, 99
Tubman, Harriet, 93
Tunstall, John 143
Turner, Nat, 57
Tuskegee Normal and Industrial Institute, 147
Twain, Mark, 140
Tweed, William M., 135
Tweed Ring, 135, 141, 372
two-thirds rule, 336, 349, 356, 418
Tyler, John, 10, 74, 75, 76, **78-83,** 156, 342, 349
Tyler, Julia, 79, 80, 82
Tyler, Letitia, 80

U

U-2 crisis (1960), 248
Underground Railroad, 93

Underwood-Simmons Tariff (1913), 193, 198
unit rule, 74, 336, 435
United Nations, 235, 239, 242, 243, 247, 296, 298, 311, 312
U.S. bicentennial (1976), 279
U.S. Military Academy, 88, 138, 246
U.S. Navy,
    Great White Fleet, 185, 186-187
    Steel Navy, 154, 155
U.S. Steel, 183, 192-193
U.S. v. E. C. Knight (1895), 165
United Steelworkers, 239
USA PATRIOT Act (2001), 309

V

Van Buren, Hannah, 68
Van Buren, Martin, 63, **66-71,** 74-75, 76, 79, 80, 85, 86, 90, 95, 306, 338, 342, 349, 354, 448
    1837 inaugural address (complete), 338-341
Vance, Cyrus, 283
Vanzetti, Bartolomeo, 207
Venezuelan border dispute (1895), 166
veto power, presidential, see *presidential veto power*
vice president, role of, 155-156, 214
Victory Special, 423
Vietnam War, 242-243, 255, 262-265, 266, 267, 269, 279, 433, 435, 438
    antiwar protests, 267, 269
    Gulf of Tonkin resolution (1964), 259
    invasion of Cambodia (1970), 267
    Tet Offensive (1968), 263
    troop escalation, 264
    Vietnamization, 269
Villa, Francisco "Pancho," 202
Virginia Resolutions (1798), 24, 42
Volstead Act (1919), 199
Voting Rights Act (1965), 262

W

Wade, Benjamin F., 130, 368
Wagner Act, see *National Labor Relations Act*
Walker, William, 106
Wallace, George C., 435, 437
Wallace, Henry A., 208, 234, 420, 422, 423
Wallace, Henry C., 208
Wallace, Lew, 168
Wallace, William, 168, 169
War Hawks, 37, 41

War of 1812 (1812-15), 36, 37, 41-42, 45, 46, 58, 88, 254, 322, 324
    battle of Bladensburg (1814), 42
    battle of Horseshoe Bend (1814), 58
    battle of Lake Erie (1813), 41
    battle of New Orleans (1815), 42, 56, 58-59, 324
    battle of the Thames River (1813), 73
    burning of White House (1814), 37, 42
    capture of Washington, D.C. (1814), 38-39, 42
    failed invasion of Canada (1812), 41, 322
    Treaty of Ghent (1814), 42, 53, 324
War on Poverty, 259, 262
Ward, Ferdinand, 136
Warren, Earl, 259
Warren Commission, 259
Warsaw Pact (1955), 247
Washington, Booker T., 147, 181
Washington, George, **12-21,** 22, 23, 24, 25, 28, 29, 31, 33, 40, 44, 45, 48, 52, 72, 85, 118, 212, 310, 312, 313, 320, 327, 420
    1789 inaugural address (complete), 310-311
    1793 inaugural address (complete), 312
Washington, Martha, 14, 19-20
Washington Conference (1921-22), 209, 222
Watergate scandal, 266, 269-272, 274-278, 282, 438, 440
    Saturday Night Massacre (1973), 269
    White House tapes, 269, 272
Wayne, "Mad" Anthony, 15, 73
Weaver, James B., 384
Webster, Daniel, 57, 72, 76, 79, 80, 81, 96, 100, 338
Webster-Ashburton Treaty (1842), 81
Webster-Hayne debate (1830), 57
Weed, Thurlow, 66
Welch, Joseph, 243
welfare reform, 262, 303
West Point, see *U.S. Military Academy*
Wheatland, 110
Whig party,
    demise of, 360
    formation of, 59, 338
Whip Inflation Now campaign, 278, 280
Whiskey Rebellion (1794), 19, 313
Whiskey Ring, 135, 137
White, William Allen, 207, 210, 218
White, Hugh Lawson, 338

White House,
  burning of (1814), 37, 42
  china, 42, 158
  installation of electricity, 172
  installation of gaslights, 86
  proposed additions (1891), 172
  redecoration, 69, 156, 158, 172
  Rose Garden, 198
  weddings, 134, 160, 164
White Leagues, 137
Whitfield, John W., 107
Wickersham, George R., 192-193
Williams, "Blue Jeans," 170
Willkie, Wendell, 420, 422
Wilmot, David, 88
Wilmot Proviso (1846), 88
Wilson, Edith, 198, 204
Wilson, Ellen, 197, 198
Wilson, Woodrow, 8, 9, 90, 142, 157, 166, 181,
    186, 193, 194, **196-205,** 208, 209, 210,
    219, 230, 401, 403, 405, 408
  1913 inaugural address (complete), 401-402
  1917 inaugural address (complete), 403-404
Winstanley, William, 25
Wobblies, see *International Workers of the World*
Wolfowitz, Paul, 311
Woman's Christian Temperance Union, 135
women's rights, 67, 99, 278, 280, 289
  Seneca Falls convention (1848), 87
  women's suffrage, 76, 87, 141, 199,
    403, 405
Wood, Grant, 202
Wood, Leonard, 207, 405
Woodrow, Thomas, 196
Works Progress Administration, 227
World Anti-Slavery Convention (1840), 67
World Court, 209
World Trade Center,
  February 26, 1993, attack against, 311
  September 11, 2001, attack against,
    310-311
World War I, 186, 199, 202-204, 209, 236,
    244-245, 403
  draft lottery, 197
  Fourteen Points (1918), 203
  League of Nations, 203-204, 208, 209
  relief efforts, 218-219, 222
  sinking of the *Lusitania* (1915), 197
  submarine warfare, 197, 202
  Treaty of Versailles (1919), 196, 203-204,
    219, 408

  U.S. entry (1917), 202-203
  U.S. neutrality, 202
World War II, 224-225, 231, 234-236
  atomic bombing of Hiroshima and Nagasaki
    (1945), 236
  D-Day (1944), 231, 243
  Holocaust, 231-232
  Japanese surrender (1945), 296
World War II (*continued*)
  Japanese-American internments, 231
  Lend-Lease Act (1941), 230
  Pearl Harbor attack (1941), 230, 231
  postwar relief efforts, 222
  Potsdam conference (1945), 235-236,
    239, 240
  prelude, 222, 230, 420
  Teheran conference (1943), 225
  Yalta conference (1945), 228-229, 231,
    234-235, 280
Wright, Jim, 291
Wyman, Jane, 290

X
XYZ Affair (1797), 24

Y
Yalta conference (1945), 228-229, 231,
    234-235, 280
Yeltsin, Boris, 298-299
Yom Kippur War (1973), 269, 283
Young, Andrew, 299
Young America movement, 105

Z
Zhou Enlai, 270-271
Zimmermann, Arthur, 202
Zimmermann Telegram (1917), 202

***

PHOTO CREDITS

We offer special thanks to Harmony Haskins of the White House Historical Association, as well as to Zina Davis and the staff of the Museum of American Political Life.

All images from the collections of Agincourt Press, the National Archives, or the Library of Congress, except:

Brooklyn Museum of Art: 13
Mount Vernon Ladies' Association: 14 (top)
Adams National Historical Park: 19 (both)
Harvard University Portrait Collection: 27
Monticello/Thomas Jefferson Memorial Foundation: 28 (bottom), 40 (bottom)
U.S. Department of State/Diplomatic Reception Rooms: 30 (top)
Richmond Times-Dispatch/Stuart T. Wagner: 32
Lafayette College/Kirby Collection of Historical Paintings: 35
Independence National Historical Park: 36 (top)
White House Historical Association: 40 (top), 42, 83, 158
Pennsylvania Academy of Fine Arts: 49
Hermitage: 56 (bottom), 58 (bottom), 64
New York State Capitol Governors Portrait Collection: 66 (top)
Sherwood Forest Plantation: 81 (bottom)
James K. Polk Memorial Association: 87, 88 (top), 89 (bottom)
Susan Ross: 95 (all)
Chicago Historical Society: 109
Bank of America Art Collection: 115
Harry N. Abrams: 123 (bottom)
Swann Galleries: 129
U.S. Military Academy/West Point Museum: 138
Rutherford B. Hayes Presidential Center: 140 (bottom), 141
Brown Brothers: 161, 175
President Benjamin Harrison Home: 168 (bottom)
Museum of American Political Life/University of Hartford: 178
Harvard College Library/Theodore Roosevelt Collection: 187
William Howard Taft National Historic Site: 188 (bottom)
U.S. Army Military History Institute: 192 (bottom)
Ohio Historical Society: 208 (bottom), 211
Herbert Hoover Presidential Library: 220 (bottom)
Corbis: 221, 238 (top), 257, 303, 309, 310 (both), 311, 313
Franklin D. Roosevelt Library: 227

John F. Kennedy Library: 251, 255
Richard Nixon Library & Birthplace: 254 (bottom right)
Lyndon B. Johnson Library: 264
Gerald R. Ford Library: 274 (top), 276–277, 278 (top)
Jimmy Carter Presidential Library: 282 (top), 283, 287
Habitat for Humanity International: 285
Ronald Reagan Library: 289
George Bush Presidential Library: 298 (bottom), 301, 312
Consolidated News Photos: 305

All objects reproduced in the Campaigns section are from the collections
of the Museum of American Political Life at the University of Hartford, except:
327, 328, 329, 334, 339, 375, 379, 394, 401 (top), 417, 419, 422, 423,
424, 425, 426, 427, 428, 430 (top), 433, 434 (top), 435, 436 (bottom),
438 (top), 444, 446 (bottom), 448, 450 (both), 451, 453, 455 (bottom),
457, 458 (both), 460 (bottom), 461, 462 (both), 463.

★ ★ ★

ABOUT THE SOCIETY OF AMERICAN HISTORIANS

The Society of American Historians was founded in 1939 by Allan Nevins and several fellow authors for the purpose of promoting literary distinction in historical writing. From its inception, the Society has sought ways to bring good historical writing to the largest possible audience. Membership in the Society is by invitation only and is limited to 250 authors. The Society administers four awards: the annual Francis Parkman Prize for the best-written nonfiction book on American history, the annual Allan Nevins Prize for the best-written dissertation on an important theme in American history, the biannual Bruce Catton Prize for lifetime achievement in historical writing, and the biannual James Fenimore Cooper Prize for the best historical novel.